FROMMER'S
DOLLARWISE GUIDE TO NEW ENGLAND

by Tom Brosnahan

1984-85 Edition

Published by Frommer/Pasmantier Publishers
A Division of Simon & Schuster, Inc.
1230 Avenue of the Americas
New York, New York 10020

ISBN 0–671–46794–8

Manufactured in the United States of America

CONTENTS

MAPS

SPECIAL SKI INDEX

For Jane Marie

A DOLLARWISE GUIDE TO NEW ENGLAND

The Reason Why

WHEN IT COMES TO American history and culture, New England is where it all began.

Certainly history is not the only thing to attract you to the six states which make up the region: Connecticut, Rhode Island, Massachusetts, Maine, New Hampshire, and Vermont. Each state has natural beauties worth bragging about, like the beaches of Rhode Island, the windswept dunes of Cape Cod, the rugged coasts of Maine, or the Green Mountains of Vermont. And there's the local cuisine, particularly the seafood: lobster, the freshest you can get; clam chowder easily the best in the world; Vermont cheddar cheese; hotcakes with New Hampshire's maple syrup.

New England is not all cities and civilization, either—despite all the talk about the Eastern megalopolis. The Appalachian Trail has its beginnings here; the sandy shores of Cape Cod are over 100 miles long; Vermont alone has over two dozen challenging ski areas; and if even these places are too busy for you, head for the untracked wilderness forests of northern Maine. In fact, it's not really the big cities such as Hartford, Providence, and Boston that set the tone of New England community life, but rather the small New England villages— Litchfield, Conn.; Newfane, Vt.; Kennebunkport, Me.—each with its village green surrounded by the church, school, library, and town hall, each village separated from its neighbor by rolling pastureland, lush woodland, and glacial lakes.

Although New England is not *just* history, one soon discovers that New Englanders love the region *because of* its history, because it is unique. Only here can you see Plymouth Rock, climb Bunker Hill, visit the site of the very first Thanksgiving feast. At Connecticut's Mystic Seaport you can see a New England maritime town out of the past, recreated and in full operation; and at Sturbridge Village and Plimoth Plantation the crafts of the colonial period are performed as they were centuries ago.

Even in modern Boston, the history of New England is everywhere, for you'll come across charming colonial buildings nestled between sleek skyscrapers; cobblestone streets lit by gas on Beacon Hill; and you can even trace America's ethnic history by exploring the neighborhoods which tenaciously hold to their native culture: Italian, Irish, Chinese, Afro-American.

You might say that the lifeblood of New England is tradition. And out of this very tradition spring so many new ideas and ways of doing things. Harvard is an excellent example of the particular relationship of old to new in New England. Harvard, the oldest college in the United States and so tradition-bound, is one of the great institutions to which we look for innovation in research and progress in education.

THE DOLLARWISE WAY: This is a complete guidebook, containing everything you'll need to know about New England at a price lower than that of any comparable guidebook on the shelf. Everything in it was written by one person, the author, who personally visited every lodging and dining establishment, historical site, and amusement. While writing it I had a certain sort of traveler in mind: the one who wants true value for money; the sort who enjoys nice, but not outrageously expensive country inns and excellent, but not overly pretentious restaurants; who wants to poke around in the little hidden corners of New England as well as to see the major sights. You want to have a top-quality vacation, but without paying the top prices which seem to appear at every turn in the road.

I know New England. I've searched through the cities, towns, and villages looking for quaint, charming bed-and-breakfast guest houses, the small places other guides can't afford to uncover. I've sampled the restaurants which local people enjoy, and I keep track of the chefs and the management. I've described these establishments in enough detail that you'll know what you're getting, and what makes one place different from another. There's plenty of information on how to get from here to there, by every possible means, and I've had both the traveler with a car, and the one without, in mind as I wrote. Every major attraction in New England is thoroughly described in this book, plus many of the charming, less-known sights off the beaten track.

If all this sounds sensible and self-evident, think again. These days, some guidebooks are written by committees of editors, others are done entirely through the mail, still others charge money (under one scheme or another) for the "privilege" of being included in their pages, or for stickers saying "Featured in Such-and-such Guide," or for signs to hang out front, or for membership in an "association." The only person who pays me anything is you, the reader—by buying this book. I'm working for *you.*

A BOOK TO READ: The best historical guide to New England is *How New England Happened,* by Christina Tree (Boston: Little, Brown, 1976), "a guide to New England through its history." Ms. Tree's account of New England's progress, from the Vikings to the Victorians, covers all aspects of life in the region—its crafts and social customs, its architecture and industry—and does it in a particularly entertaining and readable style. Bookstore price is currently $7.50, or you can get it by sending a check or money order for $8 to Christina Tree, 15 Whittier St., Cambridge, MA 02140.

Remember that Book Rate is the slowest mail service, so give the postal service adequate time to get the book to you.

INFORMATION IN NEW YORK CITY: Residents and visitors to New York City are lucky, because they can benefit from the services of the **New England Vacation Center**, 630 Fifth Ave., Rockefeller Center Concourse Shop No. 2, New York NY 10020 (tel. 212/307-5780); it's located in Rockefeller Center, between 50th and 51st Sts.

SOME DISCLAIMERS: When I travel around New England looking for the best hotels, country inns, restaurants, and places of amusement, I do my best to keep a secret of what I'm up to, hoping to be treated as any newly arrived customer would be treated, and thus find out firsthand how an establishment is run. Sometimes it's necessary to confess I'm preparing a guidebook—better that than be mistaken for the Mad Bomber as I peer into kitchens, facilities, and rooms. And so the recommendations found in this book are strictly personal, unaffected by reputations or the blandishments of managers. No establishment in this book has paid to appear in these pages, which means that if I get a lot of complaint letters from readers (which I read and answer personally), I can remove any establishment without qualm.

But I hasten to add that if you do not find a favorite place of yours listed in these pages, it's because this is not an exhaustive guide, but rather a selection of some of the best, most convenient, unique, quiet, friendly—in short, *satisfying*—places in New England. They were chosen not according to some inflexible checklist of facilities and luxuries, but with the practical day-to-day needs of travelers like you in mind.

Prices and Inflation

Remember as you use this book that inflation is a fact of life today, and although I tried to present the most complete, inclusive, and accurate price information of any guidebook, prices may change between the time the book goes to press and when you use it. So do check prices when you arrive to avoid confusion.

The prices of rooms, meals, and other expenses given with my recommendations are as accurate as I could make them; if I determined that a price rise was likely between the time of my visit and the time of yours, I figured the rise into the quoted prices. No establishment promised me to keep the prices I quote, and therefore you cannot demand of any establishment that they charge you exactly what is quoted here. When in doubt, a quick telephone call is the best way to determine whether prices have changed or not.

THE FOUR SEASONS: Weather in New England is a much-discussed topic, but it is always surrounded by a certain fatalism, not so much because there's a lot of bad weather, but because it's so unpredictable. My rough, personal survey of weather reports has revealed that the weatherforecasters are wrong a surprising 60% of the time for Boston! But, after all, Boston does seem to have its own weather: a snowfall may cover all New England, but stop short at Route 128, Boston's ring road; or a summer downpour may drench the city while the sun shines everywhere else. However, there are some generalizations which seem to hold true from year to year, and these will affect your plans on when to visit New England.

Spring

Coming very late and staying very briefly, spring tends to be a disappointment. The week or two of spring days in the normal year are a delight, with cool temperatures in the evening and just the perfect degree of warmth during the day, in bright, clear sun. In the countryside the thaw brings "Mud Time," the period between frost and spring planting. Mud Time is the slowest season for tourist facilities, coming after ski season and before summer warmth and school vacations bring out the city folk. Thus many country inns, resorts, and amusements close for a few weeks in April or thereabouts.

Summer

By mid-June, summer is well established and despite the region's northerly and coastal location, it can be pretty hot and sometimes quite humid. When it's 85 degrees (or even up to 95 degrees) and humid, as it often is through mid-September, head for the beaches, the islands, mountains, lakes, and riverbanks. Sailing, along the coast or on the rivers, is choice activity, as is a hike to the top of Mt. Washington, or a week at a beach on Narragansett Bay. But a drive through the Berkshires or along the Connecticut coast can also be very satisfying.

Autumn

This is undoubtedly New England's glory and its finest season, and if you have a choice of vacation times this is the one to pick. Although you may have to forsake swimming, the famous fall foliage is a worthy substitute; it's at its peak usually in late September and early October, starting in northern Maine, New Hampshire, and Vermont and moving southward as the weeks pass. Days are still warm and very pleasant, nights cool but comfortable. City people load their bikes into the car and head for the country, picking up fresh apple cider, pumpkins, and squash on the way home. Fresh cranberries are on sale in the markets all autumn, and although the blueberry-picking season is past, many apple orchards open on a "pick-your-own" basis to provide the energetic with the freshest fruit possible at a very low price. *Everybody* wants to get away for the weekend, no matter where they live. Those who don't want to tangle in the traffic on weekends can take special bus and rail foliage tours from the major cities. Tourist resorts and inns stay open, mostly, through September and often to Columbus Day. Those that stay open all year sometimes close for two weeks or so from mid-October to early December to give the staff a break before the advent of the ski season. By Thanksgiving, everyone's getting in shape for the ski season and shopping for the holidays.

Winter

Winter, as they say, depends: in the winter of 1976–1977, the region had six inches of snow in November, which is very early, for the first flurries usually come in mid-December, when hopes are high that the accumulation will be sufficient for good skiing during the holiday season. Sometimes snow wishes are too well answered, as in the Great Blizzard of 1977–1978, which piled six feet of snow on Boston, closing the city for a week. Ski reports appear in newspapers and the broadcast media, and the special ski condition phones go into operation. January through March is cold and snowy, and the skiing may be quite good through April; gray snow days alternate with brilliant, crisp, sunny days when the air's very cold but the sun's warmth makes it pleasant. Those who aren't skiing take advantage of the cities' cultural season, perhaps escaping to an inn somewhere in the snow-clad mountains for a weekend.

Mt. Washington Weather

None of this applies to Mt. Washington in New Hampshire, of course. This "highest peak in New England" is said to have the worst weather in all the U.S., and New Englanders delight in exchanging horror stories of the latest report: winds of 150 m.p.h. (the record is 211 m.p.h.!), temperatures of minus 40 degrees Fahrenheit, wind-chill factors that don't seem earthly. Regional news media often carry the reports even though they don't really affect anyone but the forlorn weatherforecasters who have to sit through the storm on the mountaintop.

A NOTE ON LODGINGS: In my lodging recommendations, you'll find the full mailing address, with the Zip Code, so that you can write ahead for reservations. Local telephone numbers, and also the toll-free reservation number if the hotel has one, are included. As most of my recommendations will be in the medium-price range, the hotel or motel room you rent (but not bed-and-breakfast or country inn rooms) will normally be air-conditioned and will have a private bath and a TV, usually color. The room may have either one or two double beds in it (single beds are rare), and note that prices are for the *room*, not each bed. To make your life easier, I've figured in the tax as well.

The most economical way to travel is for several people to stay in the same room, and normally a party of five or even six can use the same room. Here's how it works: Two people are charged the regular room rate. Then there is usually a per-person charge for each extra person, but the charge is low. There is also a low cost for rollaway beds. For families there's an extra bonus, because most modern hotels and motels allow children to stay for free with their parents if the parents pay the normal two-person rate and the children use the room's existing beds. So in a room with two double beds, a family of four can stay as cheaply as two. If there are three children and a rollaway bed is necessary, there'll be a small charge (about $5) for it. The age permissible for children under the "family plan" varies.

Sometimes there are other special rates, especially at big-city hotels. Many of the more expensive places try to fill rooms on weekends, when business travelers are gone, by offering special mini-vacation rates for two nights (Friday and Saturday), plus some credit toward meals and drinks in the hotel's restaurants and bars. A $90-a-night double might be $50 per night for the two-day period from 5 p.m. Friday to check-out time on Sunday, with perhaps $20 credit toward drinks and dinners, or maybe a free sightseeing tour of the city. These mini-vacation programs and rates vary from year to year and from hotel to hotel, so it's best to call or write ahead for full details.

Some hotels and motels offer a discount to senior citizens who have proper identification, such as a membership card in the American Association of Retired Persons (AARP). Ask about this if you qualify.

Bed-and-Breakfast Guest Houses: The bed-and-breakfast house, long popular in Europe, is sweeping America as travelers discover that they can pay less, and get more charming accommodations, at a "B&B." Some houses have half a dozen rooms, others only one or two; some serve a full, hearty sausage-and-eggs breakfast, others provide home-baked muffins and rolls; some guest houses provide no breakfast. Rooms can be large or small, with a view or without—in short, nothing is standard. I've given special attention to B&Bs, as they provide the best value-for-money lodgings today. Though I can describe hotel, motel, and inn rooms, which are usually of a certain standard, the only sure way to know what you're getting at a B&B is to look at the room yourself. I've chosen the houses recommended below on grounds of general cleanliness, friendliness, price, location, and charm.

Country Inns: New England is famous for its country inns, delightfully cozy and hospitable places to stay, often with very fine food. You should realize, however, that country inns are no longer the informal roadside "guest houses" that they were a generation ago. Prices tend to be fairly hefty, and requirements for a stay can be complex, very much like those at a resort. For instance, one inn charges $60 for a double room with bath in summer on Monday through

Wednesday nights, but $90 for the same room on Thursday through Sunday. To these rates you must add 5.7% room tax, $3 for the maid's tip (required), and $8 if you use the fireplace in the room. All in, that comes to $75 for the "$60" Monday through Wednesday room, or $106.76 for the "$90" Thursday through Sunday room.

You may have to reserve well ahead for a country-inn room, particularly if you wish to stay during foliage season or when there's some big event nearby. In fact, you'd do well to think of most inns as small resorts, which is what they are.

How to save money? It's simple. City hotels offer weekend packages, as the business trade disappears on weekends. But for country inns, weekends are the busy time. What you want to do is plan your city visits for weekends (or at least partly so), and spend Monday through Thursday out in the country.

Facilities: As mentioned, most modern hotel rooms have bath, TV, and air conditioning, and if they *don't* have any or all of these, I make a special mention of it. Other offerings a hotel or motel can have are free parking, a seasonal or year-round swimming pool (for outdoor seasonal pools, expect to use them only in June, July, and August), and perhaps a sauna, tennis court, or another special attraction. Each of these services will get a special mention, if it exists.

Pets: By far, pets are not allowed in the majority of hotels, inns, motels, and guest houses recommended in this book. Although I've done my best to find highway homes for pets, most places just don't allow them. If a hotel or inn does accept pets, I've mentioned this in the text. No mention of pets means no pets are accepted.

ADVANCE RESERVATIONS: In high summer, it is possible you won't be able to find just the room you want, in the establishment you want, unless you make a reservation ahead of time. Surprisingly, this is true most often of the **high-priced establishments,** few of which are mentioned in this book. But it may be true of small inns and guest houses as well, because they *are* small, and the crowds are large. Reservations are more important for some areas than others. For Cape Cod, Nantucket, Martha's Vineyard, the Berkshires, Bar Harbor, Newport and Mystic, they're important. I suggest you read the text for each town you plan to visit, and assess the need.

To pin down your reservation, you'll have to mail an amount of money as a deposit. Ask about details when you call to inquire about reservations.

AN INVITATION TO READERS: Like the other books in the Dollarwise series, *Dollarwise Guide to New England* hopes to list the establishments that offer the best value-for-money. In achieving this goal, your comments and suggestions can be of tremendous help. Therefore, if you come across a particularly appealing lodging, restaurant, store, even sightseeing attraction, please don't keep it to yourself. In fact, I encourage you to write to me on any matter dealing with this book. Every now and then a change of management, staff, or ownership will affect the quality of an establishment, and if you find this is the case with any recommended place, let me know so I can look it over extra carefully for the following edition. And if you found a suggestion of mine particularly good, or found the book helpful in general, I don't mind hearing that either! Finally, you might want to share your extraordinary experiences with other readers: "Go to this museum on weekdays only, it's less crowded and admission is half price."

You have my word that every letter will be read by me personally, although I find it well-nigh impossible to answer each and every one. Send your notes to Tom Brosnahan, c/o Frommer/Pasmantier Publishers, 1230 Avenue of the Americas, New York, NY 10020.

The $25-a-Day Travel Club—How to Save Money on All Your Travels

In just a few paragraphs, you'll begin your explorations of the attractions of New England. But before you do, you may want to learn about a device for saving money on all your trips and travels; I refer, of course, to the now widely known $25-a-Day Travel Club, which has gone into its 21st successful year of operation.

The Club was formed at the urging of numerous readers of the $$$-a-Day and Dollarwise Guides, who felt that such an organization could provide continuing travel information, and a sense of community to value-minded travelers in all parts of the world. And so it does!

In keeping with the budget concept, the membership fee is low and is immediately exceeded by the value of your benefits. Upon receipt of $14 (U.S. residents), or $16 (Canadian, Mexican, and other foreign residents) by check drawn on a U.S. bank or via international postal money order in U.S. funds to cover one year's membership, all new members will receive by return mail (book rate) the following items:

(1) The latest edition of any *two* of the following books (please designate in your letter which two you wish to receive):

Europe on $25 a Day
Australia on $25 a Day
England and Scotland on $25 a Day
Greece on $25 a Day
Hawaii on $35 a Day
Ireland on $25 a Day
Israel on $30 & $35 a Day
Mexico on $20 a Day
New Zealand on $20 & $25 a Day
Scandinavia on $25 a Day
South America on $25 a Day
Spain and Morocco (plus the Canary Is.) on $25 a Day
Washington, D.C. on $35 a Day

Dollarwise Guide to the Caribbean (including Bermuda and the Bahamas)
Dollarwise Guide to Canada
Dollarwise Guide to Egypt
Dollarwise Guide to England and Scotland
Dollarwise Guide to France
Dollarwise Guide to Germany
Dollarwise Guide to Italy
Dollarwise Guide to Portugal (plus Madeira and the Azores)
Dollarwise Guide to Switzerland (to be published March 1984)
Dollarwise Guide to California and Las Vegas
Dollarwise Guide to Florida
Dollarwise Guide to New England

Dollarwise Guide to the Southeast and New Orleans
(Dollarwise Guides discuss accommodations and facilities in all price categories, with emphasis on the medium-priced.)

How to Beat the High Cost of Travel
(This practical guide details how to save money on absolutely all travel items—accommodations, transportation, dining, sightseeing, shopping, taxes, and more. Includes special budget information for seniors, students, singles, and families.)

The New York Urban Athlete
(The ultimate guide to all the sports facilities in New York City for jocks and novices.)

Museums in New York
(A complete guide to all the museums, historic houses, gardens, zoos, and more in the five boroughs. Illustrated with over 200 photographs.)

The Fast 'n' Easy Phrase Book
(The four most useful languages—French, German, Spanish, and Italian —all in one convenient, easy-to-use phrase guide.)

The Adventure Book
(From the Alps to the Arctic, from the Sahara to the southwest, this stunning four-color showcase features over 200 of the world's finest adventure travel trips.)

Where to Stay USA
(By the Council on International Educational Exchange, this extraordinary guide is the first to list accommodations in all 50 states that cost anywhere from $3 to $25 per night.)

A Guide for the Disabled Traveler
(A guide to the best destinations for wheelchair travelers and other disabled vacationers in Europe, the United States, and Canada by an experienced wheelchair traveler. Includes detailed information about accommodations, restaurants, sights, transportation, and their accessibility. [To be published March 1984.])

Marilyn Wood's Wonderful Weekends
(This very selective guide covers the best mini-vacation destinations within a 175-mile radius of New York City. It describes special country inns and other accommodations, restaurants, picnic spots, sights, and activities— all the information needed for a two- or three-day stay. [To be published May 1984.])

(2) A one-year subscription to the quarterly eight-page tabloid newspaper—The Wonderful World of Budget Travel—which keeps you up to date on fast-breaking developments in low-cost travel in all parts of the world bringing you the latest money-saving information—the kind of information you'd have to pay $25 a year to obtain elsewhere. This consumer-conscious publication also provides special services to readers: **The Traveler's Directory** (a list of members all over the world who are willing to provide hospitality to other members as they pass through their home cities); **Share-a-Trip** (offers and

requests from members for travel companions who can share costs and help avoid the burdensome single supplement); and **Readers Ask ... Readers Reply** (travel questions from members to which other members reply with authentic firsthand information).

(3) A copy of **Arthur Frommer's Guide to New York,** a newly revised pocket-size guide to hotels, restaurants, nightspots, and sightseeing attractions in all price ranges throughout the New York area. (4) Your personal membership card which, once received, entitles you to purchase through the Club *all* Arthur Frommer publications (*including* the *Adventure Book,* which is available to members at $9.50), for a third to a half off their regular retail prices during the term of your membership.

So why not join this hardy band of international budgeteers and participate in its exchange of travel information and hospitality? Simply send your name and address, together with your membership fee of $14 (U.S. residents) or $16 (Canadian, Mexican, and other foreign residents), in U.S. currency to: $25-A-Day Travel Club, Inc., Frommer/Pasmantier Publishers, 1230 Avenue of the Americas, New York, NY 10020. And please remember to specify which *two* of the books in section (1) above you wish to receive in your initial package of members' benefits. Or, if you prefer, use the last page of this book, simply checking off the two books you select and enclosing $14 or $16 by check drawn on a U.S. bank or via international postal money order on U.S. funds.

Chapter I

GETTING THERE

1. Getting to New England
2. Getting Around New England

HOW TO TRAVEL to New England depends on several things; the time you have to spend, the thickness of your vacation wallet, the distance you must travel, and whether you're coming alone, with a partner, family, or group. Although you may already have decided how you'll travel to New England, I'd suggest you look through these pages in any case—perhaps some of the facts and figures will prove useful. If you're planning to go by some kind of public transport, check the appropriate chapter of this book which deals with your chosen destination to see what local transport to that spot is like. Remember also that airlines, bus lines, and the Amtrak rail network all have special excursion and family plans which can save you a good deal of money. But you must call them for current details and schedules—a special fare offered during the busy summer months may not be available in the spring or autumn; a discount on a ticket may be offered only if you travel late in the evening, or on a weekday, and this applies to all means of travel: air, bus, or rail.

1. Getting to New England

BY AIR: For the person with a limited amount of time (the normal two-week vacation) who is traveling alone, flying to New England has obvious advantages: it's the quickest way to go and is not all that much more expensive than other means, and it may be cheaper than some. When planning for a flight, be sure to ask about the special fares which may be applicable. For instance, you save nothing by buying a regular round-trip ticket over buying two regular one-way tickets (the round-trip fare is exactly twice the one-way fare), but you save a considerable amount by buying a round-trip excursion ticket good for a certain amount of time (usually a weekend or a 30-day period). You may have to fly at certain times to qualify for these tickets, perhaps early in the morning, late at night, or on certain days of the week. Check on these requirements when you go to buy your ticket. Remember that Night Coach fares (for planes that depart late in the evening) are lower than normal fares, and you can save money by flying Night Coach both ways, although you won't save as much as by buying an excursion ticket.

These days, air fares are so complicated and they change so frequently that only by calling your travel agent can you get an idea of the fare structure. Besides the basic regular one-way fare, you're sure to find half a dozen bargain, special-interest, or excursion fares, and you will almost certainly qualify for one of them.

BY RAIL: Trains are often looked upon as the poorer cousins of the airplane and the automobile, and they do have their disadvantages: they are slower than a plane, often more expensive than taking the car. But there are advantages to train travel as well. You see the cities and the countryside from a train, while an airplane shows you only clouds. There's room to get up and walk around on a train—much more room than in a bus, car, or plane—and on the long-distance trains restaurant and bar cars, and even sleeping cars, can turn the vehicle into a hotel-on-wheels. Trains can give you a sense of ease, and of being in limbo for a while, which might be just the way to start your vacation. Here are some facts and figures on getting to New England by train:

First, Amtrak offers a **U.S.A. Rail Pass,** similar to the popular Eurailpass, which for a set amount allows you unlimited train travel for a certain period of time. The passes are good on all Amtrak and Southern railway lines and on some lines in Canada as well. Travel is by coach class, but by paying the appropriate surcharge (which any passenger with a normal ticket would also have to pay) you can travel first class, using the Metroliner trains, parlor cars, and sleeping cars. Amtrak ticket agents or any travel agent can give you details on how to buy a U.S.A. Rail Pass.

In addition to the U.S.A. Rail Pass, Amtrak offers special reduced-rate round-trip excursion fares to various points and for special reductions. Call them for details. Information given below is subject to change, so be sure to check with Amtrak.

Sample Rail Fares

To Boston from:	Coach Fare One-way
Atlanta	$165.50
Chicago	$132
Dallas	$246
New Orleans	$231.50
New York	$ 35.50
San Francisco	$361
Washington, D.C.	$ 72

Remember that meals are *not* included in these prices; you must pay for meals on the train when you receive them, or carry your own food.

BY BUS: Virtually all cities and towns of any size have public transport connections with New England; every major U.S. city seems to have at least one bus a day which heads off for New York City, from which connections can be made for Boston or other points in New England. Many are through buses, meaning that you won't have to change until you get to New York. The bus has advantages: it's a bit faster than the train, a lot cheaper than the plane, and has great flexibility as there are buses to practically everywhere. Disadvantages are that buses are as cramped as planes, meals are at rest stops (unless you pack food), and even on through buses you'll find yourself heading frequently into the stop-and-go of city traffic—transcontinental buses may pull into 20 cities or more.

The two big companies, **Trailways** and **Greyhound,** both offer time-travel passes, good for unlimited travel.

From New York's Port Authority Bus Terminal (tel. 212/564-8484), Eighth Avenue and 41st Street, various lines run to the different parts of New England:

Bonanza Bus Lines (tel. 212/594-2000 or 212/564-8484): Bonanza's routes include ones which go to Albany, N.Y., via the Berkshires (Great Barrington, Stockbridge, Lee, Lenox, and Pittsfield) from New York City; and also routes from New York City to Cape Cod (Falmouth, Woods Hole, and Hyannis) via Hartford and Providence. During the winter months, service to Falmouth and Woods Hole (for the ferries to Martha's Vineyard and Nantucket) is via connection at Buzzard's Bay, Massachusetts. Bonanza also operates in conjunction with Greyhound Lines between New York City and Providence and Newport, R.I., and New Bedford, Mass. Buy your tickets in New York's Port Authority Bus Terminal at the Greyhound Ticket Plaza.

Greyhound Lines (tel. 212/594-2000): Greyhound, in conjunction with Bonanza, operates buses from New York City to Hartford, Springfield, Worcester, New Haven, New London, Westerly, Providence, and Cape Cod. The Boston service has a dozen buses daily, leaving on the hour from 8 a.m. to 6 p.m., and then at 9 p.m. The direct trip to Boston takes about 4¾ hours. From Boston, connections are made to points in Maine, New Hampshire, and Vermont.

Trailways (tel. 212/730-7460): Trailways has service to New Haven, Hartford, Springfield, Boston, and points in New Hampshire and Maine. Trailways buses will take you directly to Portland, Me., or to the Mt. Washington Valley ski resorts at North Conway, Glen, Jackson, Pinkham Notch, and Wildcat Mountain. For Lake Winnipesaukee, get off at Wolfeboro or Alton Bay. The Portland, Me., bus goes via Portsmouth, New Hampshire, and the Maine coastal resorts of Ogunquit, Kennebunk, Biddeford, and Old Orchard Beach. There is also a service to Amherst, Mass., and service between Springfield, Mass., and New York City via Hartford and New Haven. Fourteen buses a day travel between New York and Boston, three of them being direct express service.

Vermont Transit Lines (tel. 212/594-2000): Vermont Transit operates in conjunction with Greyhound to serve Vermont's ski and vacation regions as well as Montréal, P.Q., and several points in New Hampshire.

Sample Bus Fares

To Boston from:	One-way Fare	To Boston from:	One-way Fare
Atlanta	$146.95	San Francisco	$275
Chicago	$145.10	Toronto	$ 90.80
Dallas	$225.50	Vancouver	$275
Montreal	$ 58.20	Washington, D.C.	$ 78.40
New Orleans	$204.90		
New York	$ 40.70		

IMPORTANT NOTE: You rarely have to pay these "standard" fares! Most of the time there will be an excursion fare or a "ceiling" price for the trip you want. As of this writing, it is impossible to spend more than $99 for a one-way trip anywhere on the Greyhound system, even if you go from coast to coast. Trailways has a similar "ceiling" fare. Call for details.

Round-trip fares, by the way, are normally about 5% less than two one-way tickets.

BY CAR: Coming to New England by car obviously has lots of advantages, but few people think of the disadvantages of car travel when they plan their vacation: costs including gas, tolls, and parking fees, etc., plus the expenses you'll have for lodging. If you still decide to take the car, here are some useful tips on getting to New England.

If you don't plan to visit New York, the best way to skirt it is on Interstate 84 from Pennsylvania. This connects with I-87 (New York State Thruway, a toll road), and also with the Taconic State Parkway, a very beautiful highway which goes north to the western end of the Massachusetts Turnpike (I-90, a toll road). I-84 itself goes east after these intersections, straight to Hartford and Boston. You can branch off from I-84, on Conn. 34, to get to New Haven, and then the Connecticut Turnpike (I-95, a toll road) will take you straight to New London, Newport, Providence, and Cape Cod.

If you're starting from New York, go north from the city to the Saw Mill River Parkway and then to I-84; I-84 is not subject to tolls, and therefore this route out of New York will cost you only the toll on the parkway, whereas any other route—with bridges and toll roads—will cost more and save neither time nor distance.

2. Getting Around New England

Good public transportation and a network of Interstate highways make getting around New England very easy. The region, like Europe, is compact, and visitors from the wide open spaces out west may be surprised to find that no two points in New England are more than a comfortable day's drive apart: for example, from New Haven, Conn., to Montpelier, Vt., is a mere 200 miles. A train from New Haven to Boston takes only about three hours.

Details of available public transportation will be given along with lodging, restaurant, and sightseeing recommendations in each chapter, but here are some guidelines:

BY AIR: The large cities (Boston, Providence, Hartford, etc.) all have good air service provided by the larger domestic airlines. Deregulation of the airline industry has brought about the birth of numerous regional airlines in New England, and it is now possible to fly between most of the larger cities, even in this small region. There are also many connections by regional carrier to New York City.

The regional airline structure is still in a very fluid state, with routes being added and dropped, companies opening up and closing down or merging. With this in mind, I'll give you a list of some useful carriers and their destinations—subject to change. More detailed information is provided near the beginning of each chapter or section with air service.

Air Florida (tel. toll free 800/327-2971), in conjunction with **Gull Air** (see below), provides service from Boston to Nantucket via Hyannis.

Air North, P.O. Box 2326, 1150 Airport Dr., Burlington, VT 05401 (tel. toll free 800/451-3432), connects Vermont and northern New York state with Boston and Washington (National). The route between Boston and Burlington (Vt.) is the most popular. They also serve White Plains, (N.Y.).

Air Vermont, 1795 South Williston Rd., South Burlington, VT 05401 (tel. 802/863-1110, or toll-free 800/322-9300 in Vermont, 800/343-8828 outside

Vermont). Air Vermont cities are New York (JFK), Long Island, Hartford/ Springfield, Albany, Burlington, Newport (Vt.), Berlin (N.H.), Portland, Boston, Worcester, and Nantucket.

Atlantic Air (tel. 203/386-9000, or toll-free 800/972-9830 in Connecticut, 800/243-9830 outside Connecticut). Atlantic Air provides service from Bridgeport, Ct., to Martha's Vineyard and Nantucket; also to Bedford, (Mass.), Boston, Philadelphia, and White Plains.

Bar Harbor Airlines (tel. toll free 800/732-3770 in Massachusetts, 800/ 343-3210 in New York and New England except Massachusetts), one of the older and better commuter lines, flies to many points in Maine: Auburn/ Lewiston, Augusta, Bangor, Bar Harbor, Portland, Presque Isle, Rockland, and Waterville; and also to Manchester, N.H., Boston, Worcester, Hartford/ Springfield, Albany, and New York City (La Guardia and JFK).

Command Airlines, Dutchess County Airport, Wappingers Falls, NY 12590 (tel. 212/656-5577 in New York City, 617/423-5750 in Boston), serves Albany, Boston, New York City (La Guardia and JFK), White Plains, and also Lebanon, N.H.

Gull Air, Barnstable Municipal Airport, Hyannis, MA 02601 (tel. 617/ 771-1247, or toll-free in Massachusetts only, 800/352-7191), provides service from Hyannis and New Bedford to Nantucket and Martha's Vineyard. In conjunction with Air Florida (tel. toll free 800/327-2971) it has scheduled summer service between Boston and Nantucket, via Hyannis.

PBA (Provincetown–Boston Airline), P.O. Box 639, Provincetown MA 02657 (tel. 617/349-6331, or toll-free in Massachusetts only, 800/352-3132), is one of the oldest and best of the regional carriers in New England, serving Boston, Provincetown, New Bedford, Hyannis, Martha's Vineyard, Nantucket, and New York City (La Guardia).

Precision Airlines, Springfield-Harkness State Airport, North Springfield, VT 05150 (tel. toll free 800/451-4221 in New York and New England), connects Vermont with Boston, New York City (La Guardia), and other points, flying among these cities: Rutland, Montpelier, and the Springfield (Vt.); Pittsfield (Mass.); Manchester, Keene, Lebanon (White River Jct.), and Laconia (N.H.).

Trans East International Airlines (formerly New York Air Commuter), a division of Starflight International Airlines, 1919 Broad Hollow Rd., Farmingdale, NY 11735 (tel. 212/895-4332, toll-free in New York state 800/ 732-9683, in other states 800/645-9679). Trans East cities are New York, Newark, Boston, Providence, Nantucket, Martha's Vineyard, Hyannis, Hartford, White Plains, Atlantic City, and Long Island.

Will's Air (tel. 617/771-1470, or toll-free in Massachusetts only, 800/352-7559), using small aircraft, flies nonstop from Boston to Nantucket, and also nonstop on the Hyannis–Nantucket and Boston–Hyannis routes.

BY RAIL: Amtrak operates trains connecting Boston with Springfield, Mass., Pittsfield, Mass., and Albany, N.Y.; Hartford, New Haven, New London, and Mystic, Conn.; Providence, R.I.; and (via Springfield) Brattleboro, White River Junction, and Montpelier, Vt., and Montréal, Québec. There is no interstate train service northeast of Boston, but there are connecting buses from Boston's South Station to Portsmouth, N.H., and major cities and towns in eastern Maine. Trains on routes between Boston and points south and west are fast and frequent; but to get to points in Vermont from Boston, connections are not good, and service is infrequent.

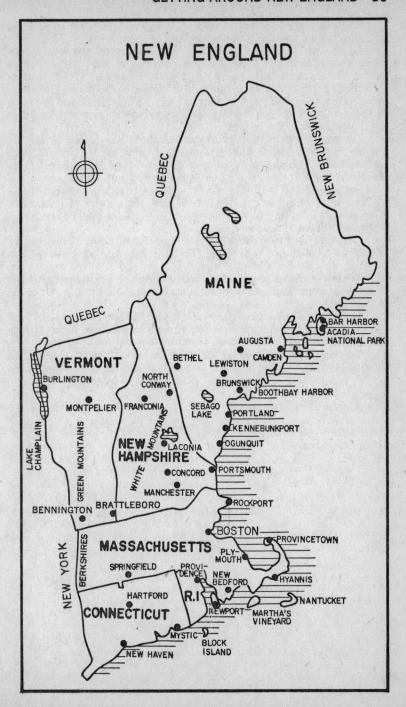

NEW ENGLAND

BY BUS: Bus service is quite good in New England. Here are some of the major companies and the areas they serve:

Greyhound: Buses between Albany, N.Y., and Boston, and some Massachusetts cities along that route; buses between Boston and points in eastern Maine, and Montréal, Québec City (by connecting carrier), and the Canadian Atlantic Provinces. Greyhound also runs to Worcester and Springfield, Mass.; New Haven, New London, and Hartford, Conn.; Providence and Westerly, R.I.; and, of course, New York City. Greyhound buses connect with local lines for points on Cape Cod as well.

Trailways: Besides the big cities of Hartford, New Haven, Worcester, Framingham, and Boston, Trailways operates to most major cities and towns in New Hampshire, and to a number of cities in central Massachusetts; they also go to Portland, Me., and points along the Portland–Boston route.

Bonanza: This is the line to take for western Connecticut, western Massachusetts, central Connecticut, Rhode Island, and southeastern Massachusetts. They also run to Albany, N.Y., and several points on Cape Cod: Buzzards Bay, Falmouth/Woods Hole, and Hyannis.

Cape Cod Bus Lines: From Hyannis, Cape Cod runs out to Provincetown via Route 6A and also U.S. 6, the Mid-Cape Highway, six buses daily in summer.

Englander: From Boston's Greyhound Terminal, Englander runs buses along Massachusetts Route 2 to Williamstown in the Berkshires, thence to Albany, N.Y.

Peter Pan: Their main business is on the route between Springfield and Boston, but they also operate buses from Bradley International Airport (Hartford) to Springfield, South Hadley, Northampton, and Amherst, Mass.

Vermont Transit: Theirs are the routes between Montréal, Québec, and Boston, covering most of Vermont and several large towns in New Hampshire.

Chapter II

INTRODUCING MASSACHUSETTS: BOSTON

1. Arrival and Orientation
2. Getting Around
3. Hotels
4. Restaurants
5. Sights
6. Shopping
7. Nightlife

"BOSTON IS THE HUB of the Universe," or at least that's what many people remembered Dr. Oliver Wendell Holmes as saying. Actually, his statement about his beloved city was less ambitious: "The Boston State House is the Hub of the Solar System." No matter, because to Bostonians their city is still The Hub, the center of the world. And though outsiders may quibble about its being the Hub of the Universe, they must accept the fact that Boston is and always has been the capital of New England. The Pilgrim Fathers settled on the shores of Massachusetts Bay in the 1620s, and the other great cities of the six-state region were offshoots from this early colony: Thomas Hooker, the man who founded Hartford, went there from Cambridge in 1636, and about the same time Roger Williams fled the area to found Providence. The pattern of arriving in Boston and then pushing on into the hills beyond was to be a permanent feature of New England life, and consequently today the city is a rich mixture of ethnic neighborhoods, almost a little United Nations. Immigrants from all over the world arrived at Boston's docks, and later established communities of their own within the city. From these communities second-generation immigrants would then move out across the state and across the nation.

What gives Bostonians the idea they're special? Well, theirs was the first large town in the region, first in resistance to British measures which brought on the Revolution, and first in science and culture during the 19th and early 20th centuries. And in 1960 their favorite son became president of the United States. Their city is the home of the Celtics, the Bruins, the Red Sox, as well as the Boston Pops and countless other types, famous and infamous.

Although Greater Boston today is home for over half of the six million people of Massachusetts, the city of Boston itself is a fairly small area with a population of something over 600,000. But if one adds in the populations of the neighboring cities such as Cambridge, Somerville, Charlestown, Chelsea, Brookline, and so on, the total comes to about 3,000,000. And yet Boston is one of the most "livable" and manageable cities in the world, with the economic and cultural advantages of a great city, but with some of the spirit and ease of a small town. It's a delightful place, and Bostonians know it.

1. Arrival and Orientation

The easiest way to approach a city is to pave the way ahead of you with money: porters, taxis, personal tours. But with a modicum of the right information and a few tips, arrival can be just as smooth, and besides saving money, you'll see the city through your own eyes rather than someone else's.

ARRIVAL BY AIR: Boston's **Logan International Airport** is one of the busiest in the country, but it is well organized, and has the advantage of being very near the center of the city, as airports go. After you get your bags, look for the signs to buses, taxis, and "Limo," and after a few steps you'll see the stops. The **Massport Shuttle Bus** (run by the Massachusetts Port Authority) runs the airport loop, which costs 50¢ in exact change and has a porter at busy stops to load your luggage. You drop your bags at the back door and then board at the front. The bus goes to all the terminals and to the MBTA "Airport" subway stop, where you can take a Blue Line train downtown. The subway into town costs 60¢, and a person in a booth will make change for you except during late-night hours. At this writing, the Blue Line subway cars are some of the most antiquated in the system, and they rattle and squeal into the city's center like banshees on wheels. But the ride takes only ten minutes once you board the train. A few of the hotels listed are within a few blocks of the Government Center stop, but for most places you'll have to change from the Blue Line at Government Center to Green Line trains bound for Boston College, Cleveland Circle, Riverside, or Arborway (all of which pass near the hotels recommended). For Cambridge, take the Green Line one stop from Government Center to Park Street and change to the Red Line for Harvard. It's a fairly long haul to Cambridge, with two subway transfers, and you may want to use the Share-a-Cab service instead (see below).

The **Airways Transportation Company's** limousines (10 Gainsborough St.; tel. 267-2981) will take you from the airport (all terminals) to any downtown hotel and bus terminals for $3.25 per person plus 50¢ per bag for every bag over one (one bag is carried without charge, others cost). The limos operate every day from 7 a.m. to 10 p.m., running every half hour and stopping at the stops marked "Limo" outside each terminal. Buses and limousines run to other points in Massachusetts, New Hampshire, and Maine; for information on them, call the **Massport Dispatcher** at 567-5400, or visit the Massport transportation desk (Share-a-Cab) in each terminal.

A taxi from Logan Airport to downtown Boston will cost between $7 and $10 for the ride, plus 60¢ toll, plus excess baggage charge (if any), plus tip. Figure $9 to $12 all together. To get to Cambridge, the best way is by **Share-a-Cab.** A dispatcher tries to arrange (within 15 minutes) for three or four people to use the same cab to a common destination at a fixed price—to Cambridge, it's $5.75 per person. If the dispatcher can't find other people to share a cab with you after 15 minutes, you'll want to take a cab alone or proceed by other means. Share-a-Cab service also operates to 138 other suburban communities, including Lexington, Concord, Wellesley, and Sudbury.

If you are going directly to New Hampshire, Vermont, or Montréal, call **Vermont Transit** (toll free 800/451-3292) for rates and schedules to these places right from Logan Airport. **Bonanza** (tel. 617/423-5810) goes from Logan to Providence, R.I., a 1¼-hour trip, daily every hour on the half hour from 8:30 a.m. to 10:30 p.m., with a final daily trip at 11:45 p.m. South Shore & Cape Cod Limo (tel. toll free 800/343-7540) runs four trips a day from Logan airport to Plymouth, Sagamore, and Hyannis.

ARRIVAL BY TRAIN: All Amtrak trains operate into and out of **Boston's South Station** (tel. 617/482-3660), the terminus for Boston, and also the **Back Bay Station** which is several blocks from the Prudential Center and Copley Square. If you plan to stay in a Back Bay hotel, get off at Back Bay Station (next-to-last stop) and then walk (if the hotel is fairly close and your luggage light), or take a short cab ride. If you plan to stay downtown or in Cambridge, go to South Station, the end of the line, and transfer to the Red Line subway inbound, "Harvard." In two stops you'll be at Park Street for downtown hotels, and if you stay on the Red Line to Harvard you'll end up in Harvard Square.

ARRIVAL BY BUS: Boston's masterplan calls for all bus and train termini soon to be located in a grand South Station Transportation Center, at Amtrak's South Station. Many local, commuter, and regional bus lines already operate from South Station, and **Trailways of New England** (tel. 482-6620), 555 Atlantic Ave., is located in its own terminal in Dewey Square, just across the street from South Station. They offer service to and from Maine, New Hampshire, Connecticut, Rhode Island, and Massachusetts. Want to find you way there from downtown? Look for the towering silver Federal Reserve Bank building, which resembles mightily an enormous truck radiator. Washboard? Cigarette machine? Anyway, it's right in Dewey Square.

Greyhound Lines (tel. 423-5810) has its own terminal at 10 St. James Ave., near Park Square, the theater district, and the Public Garden. Information on service to Portland, Me., can be obtained by dialing 542-3520; to New York City, 542-2380; to Hartford, 542-2991. At the Greyhound Terminal, you're only two blocks from the Arlington (Green Line) subway station.

ARRIVAL BY CAR: The easiest and fastest, but not the cheapest, way to enter Boston by car is via the **Massachusetts Turnpike** ("Mass Pike"), which goes right through the Back Bay to connect with the **John F. Fitzgerald ("Southeast") Expressway.** There are exits at Prudential Center and Chinatown (Kneeland Street). For downtown points you can get onto the Expressway going north from the end of the Mass Pike and exit at State Street for downtown or at Haymarket for Government Center.

The Southeast Expressway (few people call it the Fitzgerald Expressway) is also Route 3 as it comes up from the South Shore (Cape Cod and Plymouth). It's the main commuter route from everywhere south of Boston, and is traveled very heavily; at rush hours there are frequent tie-ups. When it gets right into Boston around Haymarket, the road is sometimes called the "Central Artery." The Central Artery is subject to frequent attacks of arteriosclerosis.

Two divided highways skirt the Charles River toward Cambridge, the faster and busier one being **Storrow Drive** on the southern bank, the more scenic being **Memorial Drive** in Cambridge on the northern bank of the

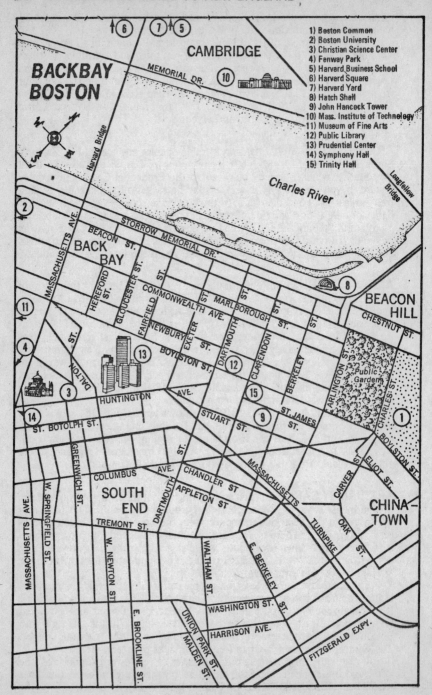

BACKBAY BOSTON

CAMBRIDGE

MEMORIAL DR.

1) Boston Common
2) Boston University
3) Christian Science Center
4) Fenway Park
5) Harvard Business School
6) Harvard Square
7) Harvard Yard
8) Hatch Shell
9) John Hancock Tower
10) Mass. Institute of Technology
11) Museum of Fine Arts
12) Public Library
13) Prudential Center
14) Symphony Hall
15) Trinity Hall

Charles River

Longfellow Bridge

Harvard Bridge

BACK BAY

BEACON ST.

STORROW MEMORIAL DR.

BEACON HILL

CHESTNUT ST.

MASSACHUSETTS AVE.

HEREFORD ST.

GLOUCESTER ST.

FAIRFIELD ST.

COMMONWEALTH AVE.

MARLBOROUGH ST.

EXETER ST.

DARTMOUTH ST.

CLARENDON ST.

BERKELEY ST.

ARLINGTON ST.

CHARLES ST.

Public Garden

NEWBURY ST.

BOYLSTON ST.

DALTON ST.

HUNTINGTON AVE.

ST. JAMES ST.

STUART ST.

BOYLSTON ST.

ST. BOTOLPH ST.

GREENWICH ST.

COLUMBUS AVE.

CHANDLER ST.

APPLETON ST.

DARTMOUTH ST.

MASSACHUSETTS

TURNPIKE

CARVER ST.

ELIOT ST.

CHINA-TOWN

SOUTH END

TREMONT ST.

W. SPRINGFIELD ST.

MASSACHUSETTS AVE.

W. NEWTON ST.

WALTHAM ST.

E. BERKELEY ST.

OAK ST.

WASHINGTON ST.

HARRISON AVE.

E. BROOKLINE ST.

UNION PARK ST.

MALDEN ST.

FITZGERALD EXPY.

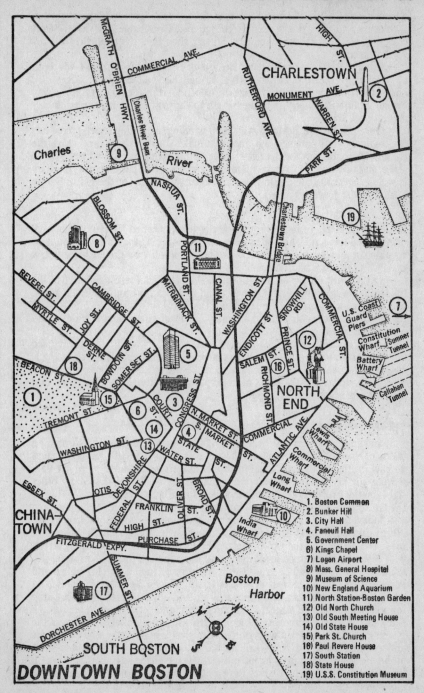

DOWNTOWN BOSTON

1. Boston Common
2. Bunker Hill
3. City Hall
4. Faneuil Hall
5. Government Center
6) Kings Chapel
7) Logan Airport
8) Mass. General Hospital
9) Museum of Science
10) New England Aquarium
11) North Station-Boston Garden
12) Old North Church
13) Old South Meeting House
14) Old State House
15) Park St. Church
16) Paul Revere House
17) South Station
18) State House
19) U.S.S. Constitution Museum

Charles. Take either one to go between Boston and Harvard Square, and go all the way to the Larz Andersen Bridge and Cambridge's Boylston Street (recently renamed John F. Kennedy Street), then turn right (north) for Harvard Square.

Coming from the north, enter Boston on I-93 or U.S. 1 (from I-95), both of which converge on the Mystic River Bridge (also called Tobin Bridge; toll), and at the southern end of the bridge the Central Artery/Southeast Expressway begins. Follow signs on the bridge to get to Storrow Drive for the Back Bay or Harvard Square.

Once downtown, Boston's warren of winding, confusing streets, most one way, will try your patience, but once you make your way to a hotel, park the car and try to forget it for the rest of your visit. Driving downtown makes little sense, and driving to Harvard Square even less sense (the parking problem there is worse). Take the car out to go to Lexington, Concord, or the North Shore, but otherwise leave it parked.

ORIENTATION: In its earliest days, Boston was called "Trimountain," for the three hills around which the settlement was built. At that time Trimountain was almost an island, connected to the mainland only by the narrow natural causeway called "Boston Neck."

In the 19th century an ambitious development plan resulted in two of the hills being leveled and the dirt moved to fill in around Boston Neck; the marsh and bogs which were filled in to make the Back Bay soon became a prime residential district with a Manhattan-style grid of streets and a wide, shady central boulevard called Commonwealth Avenue.

From the time when Trimountain had only a few winding pathways, the city has grown to be a maze of twisty streets difficult to get through in a car, easy to get lost in on foot. We'll try to make the maze more comprehensible for you by describing the city's more important sections and what you'll find in them when you stroll through.

The North End

Starting at the very northeastern tip of Boston's peninsula, the North End is one of the city's oldest quarters. The graves in **Copp's Hill** burying ground go back to the 1600s, and **Old North Church,** from the tower of which Paul Revere got his famous two-lantern signal, dates back to 1723. Many other sights on the **Freedom Trail** (described below) are here. In successive centuries, the North End has been the first landing point for many waves of immigrants, and today the four- and five-story brick buildings packed close around the North End's narrow streets are occupied mainly by Italian families who have made the North End their own. **Salem Street** is the quarter's shopping street, with several Italian groceries featuring all the imported products necessary to the old country's cuisine, as well as a half dozen Italian butcher shops and vegetable stands. The street is always lively, and on Saturday it's closed to traffic so pedestrians can enjoy the stroll up and down it, perhaps with a stop for a glass of wine and a meal at the small restaurant with a few tables on the sidewalk. **Hanover Street,** one block southeast and parallel to Salem, is the North End's main street, always dotted with groups of men standing on corners and passing the latest news—all in Italian, of course. The best and most authentic espresso and cappuccino in Boston is served in the Italian cafés which line the street, and if you plan to have a cup, stop first at one of the delectable bakeries or pastry shops on the street for a treat to go with it.

Haymarket

Most of the costermongers in Haymarket's Friday and Saturday open-air produce market are oldtimers from the North End, and no wonder—a three-minute walk under the Central Artery via a special passage unites the two areas. The pushcarts and stalls in the market are heirlooms passed down from father to son, or sold at a very high price, because the market is so profitable that a family can live all week from the money made on the two market days.

Faneuil Hall Marketplace

Haymarket's open-air stalls may be packed on Friday and Saturday but across the street at Faneuil Hall Marketplace, shops and vendors are hard put to serve the crowds every day of the week. This phenomenally successful restoration of Boston's historic Quincy Market, North Market, and South Market buildings is not only beautiful and historically important, but also just plain fun. The Marketplace deserves its own restaurant guide for the dozens of places to buy the snacks, lunches, or elegant dinners which are housed here; you can buy sausage, cheese, pastries, Turkish figs, freshly baked French or Italian bread, wine, and on and on for your own picnic as well. Go to buy, or to eat, or just to look.

Waterfront

East of Faneuil Hall Marketplace and south of the North End is Boston's Waterfront, another area in which restoration has brought new life and vitality. The solid old brick and granite buildings which once served as warehouses for India and China traders have been modernized and converted to offices, shops, and apartments, and a fine waterfront park brings picnickers, Frisbee-throwers, kids on bikes, and anyone out for a walk. Lewis Wharf, Commercial Wharf, Long Wharf, and all the rest are well worth a stroll. The New England Aquarium and brand-new Marriott hotel are at the southern end of the "new" Waterfront.

Government Center

All of the quarters mentioned above touch on Government Center, a bureaucrats' corral surrounded by striking modern buildings housing city, state, and federal offices and dominated by the **City Hall,** placed in the midst of a brick-paved plaza which covers several acres. City Hall has the central Visitors' Information booth; and the plaza, with its sunken fountain, is a focus of outdoor activities in summer—free concerts, plays, and exhibits. This used to be Scollay Square, the city's tenderloin section close to the rundown waterfront and peopled by sailors and students out for a good time in the burlesque houses and bars which were planted thick as mushrooms.

South of Government Center is the city's **financial and commercial heart,** centered on State Street, Milk Street, Devonshire Street, and the surrounding ways.

Beacon Hill

Due west of Government Center is Beacon Hill, last of the three hills of Trimountain and now the very exclusive residential section with a surprisingly European ambience. The crown of the hill is Bulfinch's great **State House,** topped by its gold dome; the building is the home of the "Great and General Court of Massachusetts Bay" (the state legislature). Be sure to take a walk around Beacon Hill and its famous **Louisburg Square,** where some of the most attractive houses are situated. Today, besides Boston's Old Money, Beacon Hill is home for a good number of students and young professional people as well.

Boston Common

South of Beacon Hill is Boston Common, the city's "central park," with a Frog Pond—filled with splashing children in summer and skaters in winter—statues and monuments, walkways, and benches. Park Street Station, at the Common's southeastern corner (intersection of Park and Tremont Streets), is the heart of the "T," Boston's subway system, and also a gathering place for soapbox orators, one-man bands, religious zealots, panhandlers, mimes, and hawkers who will want you to join fringe political groups. The grass on the Common may look pretty worn in late summer, but not so the grass in the **Public Garden,** right next to the Common to the west. The Public Garden's flower beds and lawns are kept with meticulous care, and the famous **Swan Boats** (run by pedal-power) which slowly cruise sightseers around the pond may be aging, but they get a fresh coat of white paint each spring.

Downtown Crossing

Southeast of the Common is the city's downtown shopping district, a pedestrian zone called Downtown Crossing; take the subway to Washington Station at the corner of Winter and Washington Streets, and you can enter either of the two big stores, **Jordan Marsh** or **Filene's,** without even leaving the subway station. But walk south on Washington Street and soon you'll be in the **Combat Zone,** dead during the day but roaring in the evening and on into the night, its nudie bars and girlie shows doing a brisk business most nights of the week.

Chinatown

The jumble and juxtaposition of Boston's neighborhoods is surprising, and perhaps most of all when one discovers Chinatown right on the edge of the Combat Zone, east of Washington Street. Dozens of very presentable Oriental restaurants, groceries, businesses, and churches are packed into the area around Beach Street, Tyler Street, and Harrison Avenue. Like the North End, Chinatown is a place where the language of the old country may greet your ears more frequently than English.

Back Bay

West of the Public Garden is the large section called Back Bay, with Commonwealth Avenue as its residential axis, Boylston Street its axis of business and pleasure with office buildings, restaurants, clubs, and shops. Walking west on Boylston Street in Back Bay will bring you to **Copley Square,** one of Boston's most genteel areas, bounded by the classic **Boston Public Library,** the elegant **Copley Plaza Hotel,** and Henry Hobson Richardson's famous **Trinity Church** built in the late 1800s. A modern intruder on this gentility is the striking mirror-glass shaft of the **John Hancock Tower.**

Prudential Center

Even farther west along Boylston Street is the **Prudential Center,** Back Bay's first large-scale redevelopment scheme, with the Prudential Building ("the Pru") as its centerpiece, flanked by the mammoth **Sheraton Boston**

Hotel, several blocks of luxury flats, and stores such as Lord & Taylor. Also in the Pru complex is the **John B. Hynes Civic Auditorium,** one of Boston's largest halls and the scene of everything from rock concerts to the boat show.

Huntington Avenue and the Fens

After the Pru Center, Huntington Avenue (which runs along the Pru's southern side) passes the **Christian Science Center, Symphony Hall, Northeastern University,** and the **Museum of Fine Arts** on what might be called Boston's "Cultural Highway." The Back Bay Fens sound uninviting, but actually this unappetizing name designates the first links in Frederick Law Olmsted's "Green Necklace," a chain of green parks, copses, and waterways for the residential districts of Back Bay, Roxbury, and Brookline, stretching for miles from the green banks of the Charles River to the **Arnold Arboretum** way to the south.

Kenmore Square

The westernmost part of Boston proper is centered on Kenmore Square, at the intersection of Commonwealth Avenue, Beacon Street, and Brookline Avenue; **Boston University** is just a block or two west from the square, and thus Kenmore's life is dominated by its student denizens, who flock to its cafeterias, book and record stores, movies, and clubs. On the Boston skyline at night, you can always locate Kenmore Square by the illuminated "gusher" on the White Fuel sign, or by the huge red Citgo delta.

Outlying Districts

Although the city of Boston is fairly large, it is dwarfed by Greater Boston, officially termed the Metropolitan District, which consists of a dozen other cities as well as some outlying sections of Boston proper. **Charlestown,** north of the tip of Boston peninsula, is dominated by the **Bunker Hill Monument** obelisk; *Old Ironsides* is berthed nearby in the old Boston Navy Yard. East Boston, to the northeast, is reached by two tunnels: **Callahan Tunnel** runs north, **Sumner Tunnel** runs south, and the big industry here is Logan International Airport. South Boston, southeast of downtown, is separated from the city proper by the Fort Point Channel. "Southie" is the city's Irish bastion, and here St. Patrick's Day is the national holiday. (*Note:* If someone mentions the South End, they're referring to the residential district just south of Back Bay. The South End and South Boston are, confusingly, completely separate places.)

West of Boston is **Brookline,** a large, mostly residential city and the former home of the Kennedy family. On the northern banks of the Charles River, **Cambridge** got most of the riverfront land, while **Somerville** had to be content with a mere foothold. The banks of the Charles from the Charles River Dam (topped by the Museum of Science) all the way to Harvard are covered in grass and trees, and, in summer, the grass is covered with sunbathers, picnickers, readers of paperbacks, and listeners to portable radios. The **Charles River Esplanade** is the river's edge of Beacon Hill, and is perhaps the loveliest part of the Charles's banks, with its marina for small sailboats, the **Hatch Memorial Shell** for summer concerts, a bikepath, and lots of benches.

Several Bird's-Eye Views

The best way to become familiar with Boston's layout is to hover above it in a helicopter. The next best way is to climb to the top of one of the city's tall buildings for the view. Whereas a helicopter ride might be expensive, the skyscraper observatories won't bust your budget.

Take the Green Line (any car you see except North Station or Lechmere) to the Copley Station for the **John Hancock Observatory** (tel. 617/247-1976), 200 Clarendon St. at Copley Square. The ticket office entrance is on the corner of Trinity Place and St. James Avenue. This, the tallest building in New England, has selected landmarks picked out for visitors by using special telescope-like viewers. Several audio-visual shows outline Boston history and the makeup of the modern cityscape. Hours are Monday through Saturday, 9 a.m. to 11 p.m., year round; on Sunday in summer (May through October), hours are 10 a.m. to 11 p.m.; in winter, noon to 11 p.m. Last tickets are sold at 10:15 p.m. Adults pay $2.25; children and seniors, $1.50.

The **Prudential Building** (tel. 617-236-3318), 800 Boylston St., centerpiece of the Prudential Center, has a **Skywalk** on the 50th floor with a full-circle panorama of the city. It's open from 9 a.m. to 11 p.m., Monday through Thursday; until midnight on Friday and Saturday; 10 a.m. to 11 p.m. on Sunday. Admission is $2 for adults, $1 for children (5 to 15) and seniors. A floor above is the Top of the Hub restaurant and cocktail lounge (with live entertainment), and you can see the city for free when you buy a drink or a meal. To get to the Pru, take a Green Line "Arborway" car to Prudential Station, or "Boston College," "Cleveland Circle," or "Riverside" cars to Auditorium Station.

The least expensive way to survey the city is from the **Customs House Tower,** the Italianate building bearing a clock and rising to dominate State Street near the Central Artery. (Take the T Blue Line or Orange Line to State Street Station.) Enter from State Street between 9 a.m. and 3 p.m., Monday through Friday, and contact the federal protective officer on duty for access to the observation deck. The view is different here from the insurance towers in Back Bay: here, you're right above downtown. Acrophiliacs may want to do the Customs House *and* one of the insurance towers.

VISITORS' INFORMATION: Before coming to Boston, call 617/267-6446 or write the **Greater Boston Convention & Tourist Bureau,** Prudential Plaza West, P.O. Box 490, Boston, MA 02199, and they'll send you a free copy of *Boston ByWeek* (the calendar of events) and information on weekend specials at city hotels. For a fee of $3 they'll send you an even bigger information packet.

If you call the State of Massachusetts at 617/727-3201 or (outside Massachusetts) toll-free 800/343-9072, and leave your name and address, they'll send you a Massachusetts Vacation Kit.

The city's main tourist information desk (tel. 617/725-4765) is the **Boston City Hall Visitor Hospitality Center** in City Hall (Green Line to Government Center). The office has brochures outlining walking tours, handy city maps, and information on current events. The City Hall Center is open Monday through Friday, 9 a.m. to 5 p.m.

Much of Boston's historic downtown area is now part of a National Historical Park, and so the National Park Service maintains an **Information Center** (tel. 617/223-0058) at 15 State St., Boston, MA 02109. Walking tours are available in the summer. The Information Center is open daily, 9 a.m. to 5 p.m. You'll see park rangers here and there at historic spots, ready to help with directions or information.

On Boston Common (Green Line or Red Line to Park Street Station), at the intersection of Tremont and Winter Streets just a few steps from Park Street Station, there's the **Freedom Trail Visitor Center,** open year round, 9 a.m. to

5 p.m. (tel. 267-6446). Come here to get maps and booklets describing the Freedom Trail and other visitor information.

Other information desks are set up at the Massachusetts State House on Beacon Hill (open business hours Monday through Friday), at the Prudential Center, at the John Hancock Tower in Copley Square (open every day including weekends), and at **"Where's Boston"** across from Faneuil Hall in the new 60 State St. Building. *Where's Boston,* a very fine audio-visual show about the city, is a must when you visit. Produced by an exceptionally talented group of Boston artists, the show was made for the Bicentennial Year but proved so successful it was continued indefinitely. Shows are continuous seven days a week, from 10 a.m. onward, beginning on the hour. Current prices are $3.50 for adults, $2 for children 12 and under and senior citizens. For current recorded information, call 367-6090.

Publications

The best calendar of current happenings for free is *Boston By Week,* available at visitors' information desks and in hotel lobbies. It's a complete listing of the best plays, sports events, concerts, special exhibits, and programs. Another way to get current news of current offerings is to buy a copy of one of the city's alternative weekly tabloid newspapers, such as the *Boston Phoenix.* These routinely have theater, concert, cinema, and lecture listings, as well as information on poetry readings and performances at coffee houses, jam sessions, and some of the most fascinating "Personals" ads in the country. These weekly tabloids can be bought at any newsstand or from street hawkers. If you are near a university, go to the student center where the newspapers are often distributed at no charge.

Guided Tours

A guided bus tour is the easiest way of all to get acquainted with the city and its landmarks, and the price for such an introduction is reasonable. The **Gray Line** (tel. 426-8805), 1205 Statler Office Bldg., 20 Providence St., offers 16 tours of New England, one a tour of Boston and Cambridge. Their Tour No. 1 takes three hours, covers 18 miles, and includes many Freedom Trail sights, Beacon Hill, Bunker Hill, and *Old Ironsides,* Harvard, and MIT Tours leave every day at various times and cost $10 for people 13 years and older; free if you're 12 or under. Contact them by phone or at the sightseeing desk of one of the larger hotels.

Boat Excursions: A novel way to get acquainted with Boston is by taking a cruise in the harbor and Massachusetts Bay. **Bay State & Provincetown Steamship Co.** (tel. 723-7800) operates vessels which tour the waters of Boston. Cruises take 1½ hours (three cruises a day); the price is $3 for adults, $2 for children under 12. A 55-minute cruise of Boston's Inner Harbor is also available with the option of going ashore at the Charlestown Navy Yard. There's also a cruise to Nantasket Beach. In addition to these cruises, short trips at lunchtime (12:15 to 12:45) are a refreshing break from city life and cost only $1 per person. Sandwiches and beverages are for sale on board. Call for exact schedules. These boats depart from 20 Long Wharf, opposite the Chart House Restaurant, near the Aquarium (Blue Line) subway station. Offices are at 66 Long Wharf.

The M/V *Provincetown II,* also operated by Bay State-Spray, journeys to Provincetown from Boston daily in late June, and throughout July and August, with one trip a day sailing from Boston about 9:30 a.m., arriving Provincetown at about 1 p.m., then departing P-town at about 3:15 p.m. to arrive back in Boston before 7 p.m. The M/V *Provincetown* also makes the voyage on weekends in May, early June, September, and October. For more details, see Chapter VI, Section 10, "Provincetown."

2. Getting Around

THE T: Boston's subway and bus system is being revitalized and improved, and substantial progress has been made to date. You'll find the T (short for Massachusetts Bay Transportation Authority, or MBTA) the best way to get around downtown and Back Bay. At this writing, fares are 50¢ on buses and 60¢ on the subway, but note this: on several lines (most notably the Green Line) the cars surface and serve as trolleys after they leave the central part of the city. When a car emerges, the first stop above ground is free, but in most cases after that you must pay an extra fare based on the distance traveled *when you get off.* If you catch one of these trolleys inbound, you pay the entire fare to your destination (which may cost more) when you get on, and then there's nothing to pay later. Buses which go to outlying communities (Salem, Marblehead, etc.) charge 50¢ to $3 for the ride. All fares are on an *exact-change* basis: on buses and trolleys you *must* have the exact fare; at subway stations there are change booths open during service hours.

Subway lines are color-coded: the **Red Line** goes from Harvard Square through the central station at Park Street and then on to the suburbs of Quincy, Braintree, Dorchester, and Mattapan; the **Green Line** goes from Lechmere Square in Cambridge through Park Street and downtown and then out to the western suburbs. I'll mention the line—Red, Green, Blue, or Orange—and the appropriate station for most of the sights mentioned in this book, and thus speed your way to your destination.

The **MBTA Information Booth** is in Park Street Station. For information by telephone, call these numbers: for Route Information, 722-3200; for MBTA commuter railroad schedules to places north and west of Boston, 617/227-5070 or toll free 800/392-6099. To points south, 617/482-4400 or toll free 800/882-1220. When in doubt, the central MBTA switchboard number is 722-5000.

Hours of Operation: Times on subway and bus lines vary, but you're pretty sure of being able to take the T Monday through Saturday from 5 a.m. up to 12:30 a.m. After that, be prepared to take a cab, unless you get the final trip time from an officer of the line, and meet the schedule. Sunday hours are 6 a.m. to 10:45 p.m. for trains, 7 a.m. to 7 p.m. for buses.

Subway Pickpockets

Any big-city transportation system has its pickpockets, and Boston is no exception. The *modus operandi* is for a group of four or five such types to ride the trains or buses together so the stolen wallet or purse can be passed from one to the other, thus protecting the one who actually lifted it. Watch for people who continually bump people and crowd toward the doors at a stop, and then "decide this must not be the place," and move back in; they'll be carrying coats or raincoats (whatever the weather) to conceal a light-fingered hand and also any prizes they may take. If you see one in action and challenge him or her, the reaction will be aggressive defense—"Who are you calling a pickpocket?"—and then a quick exit.

If you should be so unlucky as to have your pocket or purse picked, call one of the numbers listed in the White Pages under "Mass. Bay Transportation

Authority, Lost and Found" (the number will depend on the subway line or bus you were on); try a few days later as well, as wallets are often found, minus cash, and turned in.

TAXIS: An ad which runs perpetually in the *Boston Globe*'s "Job Opportunities" classifieds begins, "Sooner or later you'll be a cab driver." There are many long-time professional drivers, of course, but there are also many part-time, out-of-town students, and beginning drivers who may or may not know their way around. There are also those who may know their way around but who will get "lost" because you're paying them by the mile. Such is life in a big city. It could be worse: you could be driving your own car, watching its fenders being bent, battling for parking places. There's no charge for normal luggage, but there is a surcharge for trunks. If you've got a complaint against a driver, get his Hackney Carriage medallion number, and his name and number (from his permit, posted in the cab), record the date and time of the occurrence, and call the Boston Police Department's Hackney Carriage office at 247-4475. Medallions, or permits to operate cabs, cost in the tens of thousands of dollars, and drivers or companies will do a lot not to lose one.

DRIVING: Boston drivers are famed for being slow of wit and heavy of foot. Traffic control is often minimal, leaving each to fend for her- or himself. It's not so much that Boston drivers are aggressive as that they're thoughtless and inconsiderate. There is a widespread belief that stop signs have no meaning, and that red lights, especially late at night, are mere bagatelles. Although there is a required state vehicle inspection, you may run into five or six cars with inoperative brake lights during even a short drive across town. Horror statistics: A fairly expensive late-model car with full collision insurance can cost its owner up to $2000 a year in insurance premiums alone. One reason is that Boston is the stolen car capital of the U.S.

Parking is definitely a problem if you want to do it on the cheap. Downtown parking costs an outrageous $8 or $10 for three hours. For the visitor unfamiliar with the city, I'd suggest the large **Boston Common Underground Garage,** entered from Charles Street between the Common and the Public Garden. Here the rates are moderate, and there's a free shuttle bus to take you to nearby points. If you stay for some time in Boston, do not accumulate a backlog of unpaid parking tickets: cars are towed and held hostage until the tickets are paid. By the way, you will see every No Parking zone in the city parked solid almost all the time. It's done, here and in Cambridge, but a few of the scofflaws come back to find their cars towed away or securely locked in place by the big yellow "Denver Boot" (so named after the city that originated its use). The price to get the car back is about $80 plus the cost of overdue tickets.

BIKES: Boston is a good town for bicycling: the hills are gentle, the views are better from a bike, and there are marked bike paths and a new bikeway running from near the center of town along the beautiful Esplanade and the south bank of the Charles River all the way to Harvard Square. Bring a strong lock or heavy chain to prevent theft, especially if you have a ten-speed. Perhaps the greatest advantage of biking in Boston and Cambridge is the ease and cheapness of parking: any lamppost will do, and it's free. You can rent bikes in Boston or Cambridge. Rental shops are listed in the Yellow Pages under "Bicycles— Renting." You can also rent mopeds, but these cost about three times as much as a bike, require a hefty deposit, and have more potential for problems than a simple bicycle.

3. Hotels

The best way to get to know Boston is to stay right downtown, where the action is. Boston has a very fine selection of downtown hotels, and each one seems to have something special to recommend it. But the pleasure of staying downtown is not without its price, for the U.S. Department of Commerce has found that Boston is the most expensive city in the contiguous United States to live in—even Honolulu is now cheaper, and only Anchorage is more expensive. The cheapest presentable double room costs about $65, and they go up from there to over $100, not counting luxury suites. Besides that, Boston's a popular destination, and hotels are sometimes booked solid. But consider that being downtown saves considerable transportation time and some expense, and allows you to spend *all* your time enjoying the city rather than spending an hour or more on the roads to the suburbs during rush hours.

Still, my job here is to save you money on your travel expenses. Let's examine how that can be done without sacrificing the conveniences or comforts you desire.

First of all, if you want to stay right downtown, by all means *plan your visit for a weekend!* A double room at the luxurious Hotel Meridien, right in downtown Boston, costs a *minimum* of $140 during the week. But if you sign up for a two-night stay on Friday and Saturday, you'll get that same room for less than $90 per night, plus a bottle of champagne, breakfast in bed, the morning's newspaper, and free parking. Similar "weekend specials" are offered by the city's other luxury hotels, and many are even lower in price. By all means, schedule your Boston visit for a weekend. It even makes sense to detour out of town—to Salem and the North Shore, to Cape Cod, or to Old Sturbridge Village—in order to arrive in Boston on Friday afternoon or evening. (By the way, country inns and resorts are most crowded, and highest in price, on weekends; so it makes sense to visit the country places during the week.)

Another way to save money is to try a bed-and-breakfast room. Several agencies will make reservations and arrangements for you, and they're all listed below. By staying in a bed-and-breakfast room, you can pay a half or even a third of the downtown hotel price, and make new Bostonian friends in the bargain.

Finally, there are the hostelries on the outskirts of town. If you have a car and are willing to stay in Salem, Lexington, Concord, or some other suburban location, you can save 25% to 50% of the cost of a downtown room.

If all else fails, and you arrive in Boston on a weeknight, you should at least attempt to get a reduction. Call a few hotels, ask them to quote room prices, and then ask if there are "corporate rates." Sometimes the "corporate rate" is a password for "discount," and if the hotel has lots of rooms to spare, you'll get a lower price. Be sure to tell them how many nights you want to stay, because it's easier to bargain for two or three nights than for one.

Here, then, are descriptions of Boston's hotels. Just for your delectation, I'll describe a few of the luxurious, grand old places you might want to patronize as a special treat. Following these are details on the city's very comfortable, moderately priced establishments. Finally, you'll find some hints on low-budget lodgings, just in case you're running over your budget.

THE TOP HOTELS (Doubles $100 and up): My favorite of the grand old Boston hotels is the **Copley Plaza,** right on Copley Square, Boston, MA 02116 (tel. 617/267-5300 or toll-free in the U.S. 800/225-7654 or 225-7643). The attractions are the hotel's grand style and original touches: a quiet cocktail lounge which is in fact a comfy club library complete with oil portraits and brass-nailed leather chairs; the striking, ornate, elegant Café Plaza, in which the ceilings are heavily gilded, the mantelpieces are marble, and the maître d' a soft-spoken and very suave man in a tuxedo; and Copley's, a mirror-laden brass-rail bar serving drinks and sandwiches, with trompe l'oeil paintings on the mirrors and doors. Single rooms are $100.42 to $121.56; double or twin rooms run $116.27 to $137.41; suites are $185 to $528.50. A rollaway bed is $10. Valet parking is $5; overnight parking in the nearby enclosed garage is $4. By the way, the hotel is not really sedate as a rule, for genteel group and business meetings are held here frequently; it is not noisy and crowded, but neither is it filled with gentle old ladies wearing lavender.

Anyone who's ever come to Boston has considered staying at the **Parker House,** School and Tremont Streets, Boston, MA 02107 (tel. 617/227-8600 or toll free 800/228-2121), an old standby which capitalizes on its antiquity, showing off its wood paneling, ornate gilded ceilings, and leather-upholstered furniture. The rooms, although fairly small, are decorated very tastefully with reproductions of antiques. The dining room, **Parker's,** is a haven of quiet, shining crystal and silver, heavy mirrors, and thick carpets. Lunch here might be $16 to $25, dinner about $35 to $45. Downstairs from the lobby is Dunfey's Last Hurrah, an eye-catching collection of Tiffany lamps, 1890s bars and booths, brass globe-top lamps, pictures of turn-of-the-century prize fighters, and the like. The Last Hurrah is where many office workers in the nearby government and financial districts come for lunch or after-five cocktails that are served with hot and cold hors d'oeuvres (on the house). The 500 rooms at the Parker House are priced at $122 to $143 single, $137.50 to $164 double or twin.

"What a perfect place for a hotel!" That's how the **Bostonian Hotel,** Faneuil Hall Marketplace, Boston, MA 02109 (tel. 617/523-3600 or toll free 800/343-0922), introduces itself. It's true: next to Faneuil Hall, Government Center, the weekend open fruit-and-vegetable market, the North End's Italian shops and restaurants, the Bostonian is in the midst of the action. Modern with colonial accents, the hotel boasts tiny balconies overlooking Faneuil Hall on most rooms. It's a small, low-rise (four-floor) luxury hotel with 155 rooms priced at $95 to $138 single, $111 to $154 double. Honeymoon rooms with Jacuzzi tubs and fireplaces cost somewhat more. Kids under 12 stay free.

A Glance at the Luxury Line-up

The aforementioned are by no means Boston's only luxury hotels, they're just the ones which I think convey a special spirit of the city. In the range of $125 to $160 per night for a double room, you'll also find these excellent places:

The **Hotel Meridien Boston** (tel. 617/451-1900 or toll free 800/223-9918) is Air France's elegant hostelry housed in the handsome former headquarters of the Federal Reserve Bank of Boston, in the heart of the financial district.

The **Boston Marriott Hotel Long Wharf** (tel. 617/227-0800 or toll free 800/228-9290) is a new luxury hotel with traditional lines, right on the waterfront next to Faneuil Hall Marketplace.

The **Ritz-Carlton Hotel** (tel. 617/536-5700 or toll free 800/225-7620) is Boston's *grande dame* in the luxury class, with careful service and a prime location right next to the Public Garden.

The **Colonnade Hotel** (tel. 617/424-7000 or toll free 800/223-6800) concentrates on modern luxuries and European-style service in a location near Symphony Hall and the Prudential Center.

The **Sheraton-Boston Hotel and Towers** (tel. 617/236-2000 or toll free 800/325-3535), the enormous lodging right in the Prudential Center, has two hotels in one: the convention-oriented Sheraton Boston, and the more genteel and select Sheraton Towers.

The **Back Bay Hilton** (tel. 617/236-1100) and the **Westin Hotel Copley Place** (tel. 617/262-9600 or toll free 800/228-3000) are new additions to the luxury line-up, in an ultramodern complex built right next to traditional Copley Square in the Back Bay.

THE UPPER BRACKET (Doubles for $75 to $100): Lower in price than the luxury hotels, these "Upper Bracket" places still offer all the services, such as air conditioning, parking garages, color televisions, room service, restaurants and bars, and downtown locations. Many also have those marvelous money-saving weekend specials. Be sure to ask about them when you call for price information or reservations.

A well-located, upper range hotel in downtown Boston is the **Howard Johnson "57" Park Plaza Hotel**, 200 Stuart St., Boston, MA 02116 (tel. 617/482-1800 or toll free 800/654-2000). The 350-room hotel is only two blocks from Boston Common and the Public Garden, and right near the Greyhound bus terminal, in a multipurpose complex of buildings which includes a parking garage, two cinemas, and a lounge and restaurant. This is one of the more luxurious establishments in the Howard Johnson chain, and it even boasts a year-round swimming pool and a sauna. Business meetings provide a big part of its clientele, both because of the new facilities and because of its very central location. A single person pays $73.92 to $84.56; two in a double bed pay $84.48; two persons in two double beds pay $95.13. Charge for an extra person is $6. Children under 18 can stay for free if their parents pay the normal two-person rate; the hotel gives discounts to senior citizens with ID cards; and there are facilities for handicapped persons.

Enjoy the pleasures of the Prudential Center without paying the premium prices at the center's high-rise hotel by staying at the **Hotel Lenox**, 710 Boylston St., corner of Exeter, Boston, MA 02116 (tel. 617/536-5300 or toll free 800/225-7676). Here you're right in the same block as the Pru, and rooms cost $70 to $90 single, $85 to $108 double. The "average" rooms in that rather wide range of rates cost $86 single, $95 double; an extra person is $10, and children stay free with parents. Delmonico's restaurant features Gibson Girls, fresh flowers on the tables, and everything from veal scallopine to chocolate mousse. An English-style pub is open for lunch, supper, and late-night snacks (till 2 a.m.). Besides these two restaurants, the Lenox makes up for its being an older hotel by providing its rooms with individually controlled air conditioning, color TV, coffee-makers, and soundproofed walls. Besides being right in the Prudential Center, the Lenox is right next to the new addition to the Boston Public Library, and only a block from Copley Square.

The **Holiday Inn** at Government Center, 5 Blossom St., Boston, MA 02114 (tel. 617/742-7630), just off Cambridge Street, between Government Center and Longfellow Bridge across the Charles River, is a high-rise haven slightly out of the center of things. It's several blocks from Government Center, and then several blocks again from Government Center to the Boston Common. But prices are not too bad in this very new and modern building, and facilities are good: swimming pool (summer months only), free covered parking, and a penthouse restaurant. Rooms cost $72.93 to $84.56 single, $83.50 to $95.13 double. Within the same complex as the 300-room hotel are two cinemas, a supermarket, and rows of shops. Children under 18 stay free with their parents.

Boston's famous Statler Hilton is no more, but in its place—actually, in the very same building—you'll find the **Boston Park Plaza Hotel.** The new management performed a complete renovation of all the 960 rooms. At the far end of the lobby from the entry is a great fireplace, now hidden in a café. The hotel has all the services one could desire, including, within the same building, restaurants, piano bar, garden lounge, and 30 of the airline offices in Boston; it is near the Greyhound bus terminal, a scant block from Boston Common, and 15 minutes from Logan. Prices are: $68.71 to $95.13 for single rooms, $81.39 to $107.81 for double rooms; rollaways are $12.68. Children stay for free with their parents. All rooms have air conditioning, color TV, AM-FM radio. The airport limo stops here, but if you're driving, you can park for free. The Boston Park Plaza (tel. 617/426-2000 or toll free 800/225-2008) is at 50 Park Plaza, on Arlington Street, Boston, MA 02117, easily within walking distance of most attractions. The nearest T stop is Arlington.

The **Howard Johnson's Kenmore Square,** at 575 Commonwealth Ave., Boston, MA 02215 (tel. 617/267-3100 or toll free 800/654-2000), is perfectly situated if you're visiting Boston University and well placed for most everything else. A modern motor lodge with indoor swimming pool, restaurant, and ice-cream parlor, its location allows you to hop right on a Green Line train for the short ride to Park Street Station on Boston Common. Room prices are $60 to $82 single, $69 to $90 double. Kids up to 18 stay free, seniors get discounts, and lots of special money-saving package plans are offered. Call for details.

The **Sonesta Hotel,** 5 Cambridge Parkway, Cambridge, MA 02142 (tel. 617/491-3600 or toll free 800/343-7170), is actually closer to downtown Boston than to Harvard Square. A short trundle across the Charles River Dam by the Museum of Science brings you right to Beacon Hill. Though the Sonesta has almost 200 modern rooms with views of the river and of Beacon Hill, it's adding a huge new annex. Rooms right now are priced at $85 to $91 single, $95 to $102 double.

MODERATELY PRICED HOTELS (Doubles for $50 to $75):

Perhaps the best bargain in the area of the Prudential Center, Symphony Hall, and the Christian Science Center is the **Copley Square Hotel,** 47 Huntington Ave. at the corner of Exeter Street, Boston, MA 02116 (tel. 617/536-9000 or toll free 800/225-7062). Like most of the older hotels in Boston, its rooms have been carefully refurbished and maintained, and are very comfortable. The hotel's management divides its rooms into three categories: standard ($50.74 single, $63.42 double); superior ($56.02 single, $68.71 double); and deluxe ($61.31 single, $73.99 double, $89.85 for family suites suitable for two, three, or four persons). All of the rooms are equipped with a TV, a coffee-maker, and air conditioning. All rooms also have private bath. This is a full-service hotel with a bar, restaurant, and coffeeshop; $5 overnight parking; limousine service from the airport at $3.25 per person; and a family plan (children under 14 stay free). In the winter months when trade is down the people at the Copley Square Hotel are liable to offer special budget rates—write and ask about them, detailing your plans. The hotel is a short block from Copley Square, the Prudential Center, and Boylston Street.

The **Midtown Hotel,** 220 Huntington Ave., Boston, MA 02115 (tel. 617/262-1000 or toll free 800/343-1177), was once known as the Midtown Motor

Inn. Since the Christian Science Center was built right across the street, it has grown and prospered to a full-fledged hotel. It still has some of the motel advantages, though: plenty of parking on the lower level of the split-level structure, an outdoor swimming pool, and a steam room, plus a coffeeshop and restaurant. All rooms have the usual services—color TV, air conditioning, etc.—and kids under 18 can share their folks' room for free. Rates are $66.59 single, $71.88 double.

The **Howard Johnson's Motor Lodge Fenway,** 1271 Boylston St., Boston, MA 02215 (tel. 617/267-8300 or toll free 800/654-2000), is near Fenway Park, home of the Boston Red Sox during baseball season. The Museum of Fine Arts and the Gardner Museum are also close by, and public transportation easily gets you to the city's other sights. Prices are moderate for a city hotel: $54 to $70 single, $65 to $80 double. As usual at Hojo's, kids under 18 stay for free, senior citizens get discounts, and package plans bring the price down on numerous occasions.

Yet another Howard Johnson's Motor Lodge is located just south of the city at 5 Howard Johnson's Plaza, Boston, MA 02125 (tel. 617/288-3030 or toll free 800/654-2000). If you're coming from or going on to Plymouth and Cape Cod, the site on the Southeast Expressway (Route 3) at Exit 16, Andrew Square, couldn't be better. Though you're several miles from downtown, you're quite close to the Kennedy Library. Parking at the motor lodge is free, and rooms cost $60 to $68 single, $66 to $76 double. Kids under 18 stay free.

The **TraveLodge Boston** is actually in the neighboring city of Brookline, at 1200 Beacon St., Brookline, MA 02146 (tel. 617/277-1200 or toll free 800/255-3050). The 190 rooms in this residential neighborhood are clean and fairly quiet, with clock radios and color television sets. Public transportation will take you the several miles into town fairly easily. Single rooms are priced at $60, doubles at $70.

BUDGET LODGINGS (Doubles for $30 to $50): It's no simple task
to find a truly inexpensive, respectable room in Boston, but still it can be done. You'd be well advised to reserve your room in advance, to make sure you can nail down that low price.

Bed-and-Breakfast Services

An interesting alternative to commercial lodgings is the bed-and-breakfast room. These are spare rooms or even apartments in private homes, rented to travelers at moderate rates. Bed-and-breakfast services will take your reservation, describe accommodations and prices, and give directions to your lodging. All this is best done in advance, but don't be afraid to call one of the following services if you arrive in town without a reservation.

New England Bed and Breakfast, Inc., 1045 Centre St., Newton Centre, MA 02159 (tel. 617/498-9819 or 244-2112) will find you a room in a private home for $22 to $28 single, $30 to $48 double, with a small breakfast included.

A similar service is operated by **Bed and Breakfast Associates Bay Colony, Inc.,** P.O. Box 166, Babson Park Branch, Boston, MA 02157 (tel. 617/872-6990, 10 a.m. to noon and 1:30 to 5 p.m.). For $1, they'll send you a directory describing various rooms hosted by the service. Prices range from $27 to $48 single, $32 to $59 double, continental breakfast included.

Also try **Bed & Breakfast Brookline/Boston,** P.O. Box 732, Brookline, MA 02146 (tel. 617/277-2292), which, like the other services, has rooms for rent in Boston, Cambridge, and Brookline. Prices here are $32 to $43 single, $44 to $55 double. A small breakfast is included, of course.

City Cousins Bed & Breakfast, P.O. Box 194, Concord, MA 01742 (tel. 617/369-8416), operates out of suburban Concord, but places travelers in homes located in Boston, Cambridge, and the suburbs. Their list runs to some 60 rooms priced at $28 to $43 single, $39 to $59 double, breakfast included. Reserve in advance.

Greater Boston Hospitality, P.O. Box 1142, Brookline, MA 02146 (tel. 617/734-0807), makes reservations for private homes, two-family homes, apartments, private city clubs, small inns, and condominiums in Boston, Brookline, Cambridge, Charlestown, Needham, Newton, and Wellesley. You can write, or call 24 hours a day.

Room Rentals

Beacon Guest House, 248 Newbury St., Boston, MA 02116 (tel. 617/262-1771 or 266-7276), will arrange a daily or weekly room rental for you, with or without private bath or kitchenette, for around $100 to $125 per week single, $140 to $165 per week double. Most of their rooms are in apartment buildings located in Back Bay, on Marlborough Street, Park Drive, Beacon Street, or Newbury Street.

Inns and Guest Houses

Two of the better guest houses are side-by-side in Brookline, not too far from Coolidge Corner, and right on the Green Line subway (Cleveland Circle). The Green Line car will take you right to Park Street Station in downtown Boston.

The **Beacon Inn,** 1087 Beacon St., Brookline, MA 02146 (tel. 617/566-0088), is an old brownstone town house converted into a small inn. Rooms are very tidy and appealing with most of the elegant old decoration (marble fireplaces, cast-iron stoveplates, detailed woodwork) intact. You might get the front parlor (Room No. 1), any of various sitting rooms or bedrooms, huge and ornate or small and simple. Rates vary for each room but are about $32 for a double with shared bath, $40 for one with private bath. This includes a television and wall-to-wall carpeting. The office is open from 3 to 9 p.m. If you prefer a shared bath, try to get a room where the bath is on the same floor so you don't have to climb steps.

Anthony's Town House, 1085 Beacon St., Brookline, MA 02146 (tel. 617/566-3972), is a turn-of-the-century brownstone town house with various rooms (private bath or shared bath) for $21 to $26 single, $32 to $42 double.

Close to Kenmore Square and Boston University is **Northeast Hall,** 204 Bay State Rd., Boston, MA 02215 (tel. 617/267-3042), run by Mrs. Caroline Muzichuk. This fine old Back Bay row house is on a quiet street of dormitories and residences, handy to the subway's Kenmore Station (Boston College or Beacon Street Green Line trains). Rooms all share bath, and rent for $12 to $16 single, $21 to $26 double (twin beds only), $32 triple. If you have a car, Mrs. Muzichuk can arrange for parking.

BUDGET MOTELS ON THE OUTSKIRTS (Doubles for $30 to $50): The **Terrace Motel,** 1650 Commonwealth Ave., Boston, MA 02135 (tel. 617/566-6260), is in the Brighton section, a half block off Commonwealth Avenue, two miles west of Kenmore Square. The subway's Green Line "Boston College–Commonwealth" cars go very near the motel from downtown Park

Street Station. The 75 rooms here all have air conditioning, private bath, color TV, and kitchenettes (you bring the utensils and flatware) for $37 to $44 single, $44 to $53 double or twin; children under 16 stay for free, unless you need a rollaway bed, which is $3. Otherwise, an extra person pays $5. If you're driving, take Exit 18 from the Massachusetts Turnpike, and go one mile southwest on Commonwealth Avenue (Route 30).

Although it's preferable to stay downtown and not get snarled in Boston traffic, high hotel prices in the center of the city drive many people to consider alternative lodgings farther out. Luckily, Boston has three representatives of the budget-price **Susse Chalet** motel chain. Prices at Susse Chalet are standard in two types of motels: in the cheaper motor lodges, a single is $25.05, a double room is $29.28, and rooms with two double beds rent for $28.22, or $31.39 if there are three or four people. In Susse Chalet Inns, rooms are larger, equipped with a lounge-chair and prices are $3 higher per room. The toll-free reservation number for all three Susse Chalets mentioned below is 800/258-1980 (in New Hampshire, 800/572-1880).

Nearest to the center of Boston is the **Susse Chalet Motor Lodge** (tel. 617/287-9100), in Dorchester at 800 Morrissey Blvd., Boston, MA 02122 (Exit 17, 19, or 20 off the Southeast Expressway). Next closest, and convenient for visits to Cambridge, Lexington, Concord, and Sturbridge, as well as Boston, is the **Susse Chalet Motor Lodge and Inn** (tel. 617/527-9000), 160 Boylston St., Newton, MA 02167, on Route 9 in Newton, three miles east of Exit 55E from Route 128/I-95. If you're coming from Providence or Cape Cod, there's the **Susse Chalet Motor Lodge** (tel. 617/848-7890) in Braintree on Route 3 (Southeast Expressway) at Union Street.

THE YMCA: The budget haven of Back Bay is the Boston **YMCA** (MBTA: Symphony or Northeastern U.), 316 Huntington Ave., Boston, MA 02115 (tel. 617/536-7800). The building, about equidistant from Symphony Hall and the Fine Arts Museum, looks like an Italian Renaissance palace and holds 174 rooms, open to both men and women. Rooms are simple, of course, but they cost only $16.91 single, $23.25 double per day. The Y has its own inexpensive cafeteria, and a parking lot. The pool is open year round, of course, as are other facilities. Rooms at these prices and in this good location go quickly, so it's advisable to write in advance for reservations. Only written reservations are accepted. Children under 17 cannot stay at the "Y."

THE YOUTH HOSTEL: Boston has a newly renovated 100-bed youth hostel in Back Bay near the Prudential Center, Berklee College of Music, and Boston University. Called the **Boston International Hostel**, 12 Hemenway St., Boston, MA 02115 (tel. 617/536-9455), it's open to persons of all ages according to the policies of the American Youth Hostels. Those with a hostel card pay $6.25 for a bed in a four-bed dormitory room; without a card the charge is $8.25. To get there, take a Green Line subway train ("Boston College," "Cleveland Circle," or "Riverside") to Auditorium Station, then walk west on Boylston Street one block to Hemenway Street. The youth hostel is near the intersection of Hemenway and Haviland Streets.

4. Restaurants

Dining possibilities in Boston are virtually limitless. The city's array of restaurants includes at least one representative of every notable cuisine in the world, and usually more than one—in the Boston area there are over 150

Chinese restaurants alone. Most of Boston's restaurants take advantage of the fresh seafood which comes to the docks daily, whether the specialty is seafood or not.

For my recommendations, I've tried to help you choose from this bewildering array by sticking to restaurants in Boston proper and excluding the many fine places in the suburbs on the notion that you won't want to fight your way to an unfamiliar town and unfamiliar streets, but would rather spend your time in Boston. Also, I've chosen favorites, places which I've found satisfactory in every way, every time I've been there, and in which I've always felt I've gotten my money's worth. Remember that the many very fine hotel restaurants, lounges, and coffeeshops are covered along with the hotel itself in the preceding section; the good restaurants and coffeehouses in Cambridge are described in the chapter on Cambridge, but it's good to remember that most of them are within walking distance of the Red Line's Harvard subway station, and the trip can be made from central Boston in 10 or 15 minutes. The good restaurant in the Museum of Fine Arts, the best place for lunch if you're seeing the MFA or the Gardner Museum, is described along with the museum itself in the sightseeing section.

As for price ranges, the categories given below will tell you what you *have* to spend to get a meal in any one of the restaurants in that category; you may, of course, spend a good deal more than the minimum figure. If, say, you visit an Upper-Bracket restaurant, you'll spend at least $35 or $40 per person for dinner, and probably a bit more: a rule of thumb is to almost double the price of the main course to figure the entire cost of the meal, so if you order a tenderloin steak for $18, expect to spend another $15 to $18 on appetizer, dessert, beverages, tax and tip, or $33 to $36 altogether. In Budget restaurants the formula is more like half again as much of the platter price: $6 for a spaghetti dinner plate, and then another $3 for a glass of wine or dessert, tax, and tip. Use this formula regularly and you'll avoid the uncomfortable feeling that you're dining beyond your means.

In the more expensive establishments, it's good to call ahead for reservations if they'll take them—many Boston places do not. This is true especially on weekends and holidays, of course. And when you call, ask whether they honor your credit card, and what parking arrangements are.

Massachusetts has a meal tax of 5.7% added to every meal check over a minimal amount.

A Real New England Clambake

Whether on the beach around a driftwood fire, at a backyard cookout, or in a restaurant, chances are you'll encounter the traditional clambake during your stay in New England. The true clambake takes place on the beach, starting with the digging of the clams, but the backyard and restaurant versions are good substitutes provided you observe the rituals properly.

The three essential courses are steamed clams, corn-on-the-cob, and lobsters. Here's a recipe: take one very large pot, fill with clean seawater, and place on the fire to boil. Put live lobsters in the bottom, then a layer of seaweed, then ears of corn, more seaweed, and finally a layer of "steamers" (small clams for steaming). When the clams open, they're ready for the ceremony of eating steamers.

Take a clam, open it completely, and lift out the meat. The "neck" is black and covered with a wrinkled black membrane. Shuck the membrane off (you pick up the knack for this by about the fifth clam), hold the clam by the neck, and dip it in "clam broth" (seawater that has had clams steamed in it—even in a restaurant you'll be provided with it). The "broth" is strictly for dipping, not for drinking; the dip washes any sand off the clam. Next, dip in the melted butter provided, and then enjoy.

When you've had your fill of clams, it's on to the buttered ears of corn, and finally to the lobsters. Eating a lobster is an art in itself. Read on, and I'll give you full instructions.

How to Eat a Lobster

Restaurants will prepare lobsters in any number of elaborate ways, but to a true New Englander there are but two ways to cook a lobster: you boil it or you broil it. To broil, take a live lobster, make a straight cut underneath from head to tail, and place cut-upward under the broiler.

Boiling is even easier. Plunge live lobsters in boiling seawater, and let cook until they turn bright red. When you take them out they'll be very hot, and full of hot water too. Give the lobster a few minutes to cool, and you're ready to begin.

Hold the body in one hand and the tail in the other and twist the tail off. Stick a fork into the tail meat and pull—the whole delicious morsel should come right out. The tail is the largest meaty portion of the lobster, but there's lots more.

Each claw should be broken (claw-crackers are always provided) and the meat taken out, even from the joints which connect the claw to the body. This is the most delicious part, a real delicacy.

In the larger lobsters (1½ pounds and over), you'll find tender little bites in other places too. Twist the four "flippers" off the end of the tail and chew out the delicate meat inside. Twist off each small leg: in the knuckle next to the body there's a nugget, and you can chew tender meat out of each segment in a leg.

Diehard lobster-lovers (I'm one) go even farther. Take the body apart, and behind where each leg was attached there is a good bit of meat. Of the innards, the gray-colored liver (called "tomalley") is edible—chefs sometimes use it in sauces. If you find a waxy red substance, that's roe (eggs), edible but not choice.

By now you will have discovered that eating lobsters is not a refined pastime. The image of the lobster as an item in haute cuisine is justified by its delicious flavor. But simple boiled lobster cannot be improved by even the most creative chef, and eating it should not be an exercise in etiquette. A picnic table, with a newspaper covering to catch the shells, is the perfect setting; a seaside lobster shack is the best location.

THE TOP RESTAURANTS ($35 and up): Any dispute over a city's "best" restaurant is liable to be hot and lengthy, for the simple reason that personal preferences favor certain types of surroundings, service, and cuisine.

Prime of place on Beacon Hill must go to **Another Season,** 97 Mt. Vernon St., between Charles Street and Louisburg Square (tel. 367-0880). Small and friendly, with a marvelous feeling of informal elegance, Another Season is one of those places where the chef puts her personal touch on classic recipes, then makes the rounds of the tables to see how diners have liked them. The wine list is very fine, the cuisine even finer, the service just as good. Get a reservation, then go with about $30 or $35 to spend for each diner, and you'll find the experience worth far more. Lunch is served from noon to 2 p.m. Tuesday through Friday; dinner is from 6 to 10 p.m. Monday through Saturday.

Ben Thompson, the architect largely responsible for saving and restoring Faneuil Hall Marketplace (they were going to build a modern shopping mall!), created a fascinating trio of dining and drinking establishments at the **Landmark Inn,** 300 North Market Bldg. in Faneuil Hall Marketplace (tel. 227-9660). Centerpiece for the trio is the **Wild Goose,** an expensive dining room specializing in fairly exotic and very pricey dishes such as—of course—wild goose, suckling pig, and venison. You may have the most interesting dinner of your life here, but you'll pay upward of $40 or $50 for the privilege. Or you can cut the price in half by coming for lunch.

Several years ago, a group of Boston businessmen organized an exclusive club, called the Bay Club, in an aerie atop the Sheraton World Headquarters at 60 State St., right next to Boston's Old State House. At lunchtime it's the Bay Club, open to members only, but in the evenings the multilevel dining room and lounge with the three-story-high glass wall becomes the **Bay Tower Room** (tel. 723-1666), open to all. On the mezzanine level is a cocktail lounge (open 4:30 p.m., with last call at midnight every day except Sunday) with a band for dancing (Monday through Saturday, 8 p.m. to midnight). Dining is on two levels below, and every table has the same marvelous view of the Customs House Tower, the bay, Logan Airport, and the hills beyond.

Dinner is served from 6 to 9:30 p.m. every evening but Sunday, and a jacket-and-tie dress code is in force. The food is very good, but the service surpasses it. As to the menu: it's long and inclusive, expensive but not outrageous. You can start with fresh caviar or with a simple soup. Fish and shellfish, fowl, and grilled meats are all featured; specialties are braised sweetbreads with goose liver and asparagus, roasted duckling with broiled apples, and breast of chicken with foie gras in a Madeira sauce. The bill, per person—tax, tip, and wine included—will be about $50. Have reservations.

The **Café Budapest** (tel. 734-3388), 90 Exeter St., is underneath the Copley Square Hotel (not to be confused with the more deluxe Copley Plaza Hotel) right at the edge of the Prudential Center. The menu includes Hungarian, French, and American dishes; the luncheon menu is a shorter version of the dinner menu, with prices being the same. At dinner, try the szekely goulache, made with center-cut pork chops, kielbasi, and home-fermented sauerkraut, or perhaps tournedos Rossini; sauerbraten, wienerschnitzel, and steaks are always offered. If you don't want the trouble of choosing, take "Pot-Pourri" dinner for two, complete with soup, salad, pastry, and coffee, at $40; a similar mixed-grill dinner for two is slightly more. Should you want to keep your lunch light, have the luncheon daily special, which might be milk-fed veal, with soup, salad, pastry, coffee, rolls, and butter for $12; or order à la carte, the pancakes stuffed with mushrooms or the beef goulache. If you don't eat too much at first you'll have room for the exquisite and sinfully rich dobos torte, a many-layer cake made with chocolate, honey, nuts, and other fine things.

With tax and tip, and a bottle of wine, dinner at the Café Budapest can run to $40 to $50 per person, but you will leave feeling that every penny was well spent. Lunch is served daily from noon to 3 p.m.; dinner is served from 5:30 to 10:30 p.m. weekdays, until midnight on Friday and Saturday, and from 1 to 10:30 p.m. on Sunday.

The genteel atmosphere of the **Ritz-Carlton Hotel** (tel. 536-5700) is a good place to spend money on a fine lunch or dinner. From its location at 15 Arlington St. (at the beginning of Newbury), the second-floor dining room of the Ritz looks out over the Public Garden and its trees and beds of flowers, or snow scenes, as the case may be. Elegance is all around: gold tracery on the cream-colored ceiling, lofty many-paned windows surrounded by blue-and-white print drapes, crystal chandeliers, and sconces, potted plants, a tinkling piano, and the most refined service imaginable. The menu changes (and is reprinted on heavy stock) daily, but a typical luncheon menu might offer you roast duckling with cherries, médaillons of beef with mushrooms, a thin veal cutlet in chive butter, or perhaps a selection from the cold buffet, or an omelet. The lunchtime minimum for food is $10. At dinner the selection is even more extensive: start with the green turtle soup made with sherry, or Louisiana shrimp with a cocktail sauce, and then go on to a roast leg of spring lamb, or lobster prepared with whisky, or a prime piece of sirloin. For dessert, have one of the several dessert soufflés which are first a dream, then ambrosia, then a fond memory. Such a repast will cost $40 to $50 per person, with wine. You can have lunch at the Ritz daily from noon to 3 p.m.; dinner from 6 to 10 p.m. weekdays, to 11 p.m. on Friday and Saturday, and from 6 to 10 p.m. on Sunday. The dress code is enforced at all times, of course.

MODERATELY PRICED RESTAURANTS ($18 and up): Because the largest number of recommended restaurants is in this price bracket, I've divided them up according to location and specialty. Here then are the best of the midrange dining establishments:

On Beacon Hill

What about a cozy little Beacon Hill restaurant with small dining rooms and a pretty brick patio? **Tiger Lilies**, at 23 Joy St. (tel. 523-9229 or 523-0609), is just the place. Lunch is served (11:30 a.m. to 3:30 p.m.) every day but Saturday; arrive for dinner any day from 5 to 9 p.m. (10 p.m. on Friday and Saturday). You'll love the patio, verdant and cool on a warm summer day. One of the romantic dining rooms has a Tudor fireplace for chilly nights. I had lunch: chilled honeydew melon soup, breast of chicken with tarragon mayonnaise, a chocolate mousse, and coffee, plus a half bottle of French muscadet, and the total cost was $24. But I could have eaten very well, with a glass of wine, for half that amount so don't be scared. At dinner you might spend $25 to $30 per person, all in. Service is super.

Rebecca's, 21 Charles St. (tel. 742-9747), has lots of strong points. A favorite of the young and beautiful, up-and-coming Beacon Hill set, it is also convenient for visitors to downtown shopping areas and tourist attractions. The food is continental, upbeat, and carefully prepared, interesting without being excessively exotic. Prices are moderate, considering that this is an attractively modern place serving fine cuisine, and a full dinner with a good bottle of wine will cost about $25 per person, lunch a good deal less. You can even do what those Beacon Hill sophisticates do: buy the same food at the take-out counter, and have the classiest picnic lunch in Boston. Rebecca's is open 7:30 a.m. to midnight; the take-out store closes at 9 p.m.

In the Landmark Inn along with the very expensive Wild Goose restaurant are two much less expensive places featuring equally interesting fare. Seafood specialties are served in the Landmark Inn's basement eatery, **Thompson's Chowder House.** Don't expect boring fish and chips or filet of sole here, but rather a delightful culinary discovery. Both lunch and dinner are served. For a bowl of truly fabulous seafood chowder, a glass of wine, tax, and tip, expect to pay $10.

The **Landmark Café**, last of the trio, has indoor and outdoor seating, burgers, steaks, and spare ribs, and entertainment in the evenings. It's open from 11:30 a.m. to past midnight.

Faneuil Hall Marketplace and the Waterfront

One of several Boston restaurants which has resisted change over the years is the venerable **Durgin-Park Market Dining Room** (tel. 227-2038), in the South Market building of Faneuil Hall Marketplace. Durgin-Park's menu boasts that it was "Established before You were Born," and adds, somewhat unnecessarily, that "Your grandfather and great-grandfather may have dined with us, too." As you mount the stairs to the dining room, it crosses your mind that you must have taken the wrong stairway and entered some "employees only" door, for there before you is all the dishwashing machinery and hard-working kitchen help, and right next to this, the kitchen itself with cooks and waitresses scurrying here and there. To left and right are large, plain rooms with steam pipes running about on the ceiling, and several sets of long tables covered in white or red checked cloths. The menu, plainly printed with daily specials notices stapled to it, bears pithy reminders and warnings such as "wash room downstairs" and "We are not responsible for any steak ordered well done." To understand Durgin-Park, one must hark back to its beginnings as the mealroom for the sturdy types who wrestled with whole animal carcasses and crates of produce when Quincy Market was a farmers' and butchers' market, and Faneuil Hall's ground floor was populated by greengrocers, coffee and tea merchants, and hog butchers. A century ago these hearty and hungry fellows would pound up the steps to Durgin-Park for their noontime supper at the end of a working day which began at 4 a.m., and what they wanted was beef. What they got was a cut of prime rib so massive it filled the large plate and hung over the edge onto the table. Of course, the prices have changed since those days, but the dining room's decor and its food have stayed the same: the prime rib (while it lasts, for this is the specialty) is just as huge, and costs $14.50. *Fresh* lobster stew (emphasis theirs) is $10, a roast stuffed duck costs $7.50, and lowly "frankfort and beans" is $3.75. Clams, oysters, and fish are in the $6 to $10 range. Remember, gigantic portions are the rule here, and doggy bags are available. Oh, yes: you can have cocktails at the dinner table, and these usually cost $2. Be warned that on weekends for dinner the restaurant is usually very busy, and no reservations are accepted. Perhaps the best time to go is at lunch, referred to as the "dinner bill," when prices are considerably lower (for smaller luncheon portions, of course) and the tables not so crowded. But be sure you get to the restaurant between 11:30 a.m. and 2:30 p.m. for the low-priced lunches.

Also in the Faneuil Hall Marketplace, and perhaps the finest place to dine outdoors is **The Café at Lily's** (tel. 227-4242), in Quincy Market. Actually, there are two Lily's establishments in Quincy Market, **The Bar at Lily's** (a major gathering place for the young, beautiful, and single) and, on the other side of Quincy Market, the Café. In warm weather, tables are set out in the promenades on either side of Quincy Market, and the glass "walls" are lifted into the glass roof to produce a spacious sidewalk-café atmosphere. Luncheon sandwiches run $3.75 to $5.75; a hearty plate of Boston baked beans and knockwurst is $4.85; or an elegant scallop dish named coquille chablis costs $6.75. For a very light, diet-conscious lunch, there are salads as well. Lily's is extremely pleasant in summer if it's not too busy (try a late lunch to avoid the jam); in winter the tables can't be put outside, but the greenhouse—like the main dining area—is almost as good under its glass roof.

Seaside, not to be confused with Cityside, is at the seaside end of the South Market Building, well known to Boston's young, glamorous, and beautiful professional set. Lunch is the prime time for dining, seeing, and being seen, although in fact Seaside stays busy all day. Sandwiches built on elaborate

recipes, complex and delicious salads, omelets, and quiches make up the mid-
day bill of fare, with prices ranging from $4 to $8. Besides the natural-wood
tables, Seaside has a bar at which you can sit to have a drink, or a sandwich,
or both. The view doesn't really reach to the sea, but the tall windows allow
plenty of light to come in—and besides, the most fascinating views at Seaside
are right in the restaurant.

Back Bay: Newbury and Boylston Streets

The two principal shopping and business streets in the Back Bay have a
tremendous number of places to nosh, snack, eat, lunch, or dine. Keep this
section in mind when you make the rounds of Newbury Street galleries.

Newbury Street holds a French restaurant of long standing. It's the **Du
Barry French Restaurant** (tel. 262-2445), 159 Newbury between Dartmouth
and Exeter Streets (Green Line to Copley). Dinner entrees usually include filet
of sole Grenobloise ($8) and daube of beef bourguignon ($8.50), frog legs are
to be had, as are even less frequently seen delicacies such as rabbit sauteed in
white wine, beef tongue in a madeira sauce, and veal kidney "sauce Bercy."
These very moderate prices include potato and vegetable. At lunch the several
platters are priced at $3.50 or so; entrees range from $3.50 to $9; or a light lunch
of soup, salad, bread, and butter need cost only $3.50, plus tax and tip, of
course. In good weather, the outdoor patio and enclosed terrace are the choice
places to dine—walk through the restaurant to reach them.

Perhaps the best all-around café on Newbury Street—and certainly the
nearest thing to an authentic European café in Boston—is the **Café Florian,**
85 Newbury St. (tel. 247-7603), where you can sit at sidewalk tables or in the
air-conditioned rooms down one flight and have a glass of wine ($1.40), import-
ed beer ($2.75), or a cup of truly excellent Viennese coffee ("kaffee Wien mit
schlag"); for a snack, add on a pastry from their pastry tray, a sandwich or a
bowl of soup, a plate of cheese and bread or an antipasto and cheese plate, or
even a full meal. Service is quick and friendly, coffee comes in ten different
varieties, priced from 85¢ to $1.85. There are several kinds of tea, and a small
but select wine list. The Florian is open from 11 a.m. to 11 p.m. Monday
through Thursday; on Friday and Saturday nights it stays open until midnight,
and on Sunday it's open for brunch from noon till 6 p.m. On Newbury Street,
this is my favorite.

At the intersection of Newbury and Berkeley Streets is the Boston branch
of San Francisco's **Magic Pan Crêperie** (tel. 267-9315), a pleasant restaurant
with both sidewalk café tables and indoor dining rooms. Here the famous
French pancakes, or crêpes, can become a full meal: chicken divan crêpes, with
chicken, broccoli, cheddar cheese, a rich sauce, and salad, cost $5.45; similar
pancakes with ham, called palacsintas, are about the same; a steak plate with
mushroom crêpes is a tops of $8.50. By far the best value, though, is in the daily
special dishes. The Magic Pan is open Monday through Saturday from 11 a.m.
to midnight, Sunday from 11 a.m. to 10 p.m., in summer, slightly shorter hours
in winter. There is another branch of the Crêperie in the Faneuil Hall Marketplace, second floor of the North Market.

A good place for lunch, dinner, or an evening's sipping and prowling is
Friday's, 26 Exeter St. at the corner of Newbury (tel. 266-9040), just a block
from the Boston Public Library, and two blocks from Copley Square or the
Prudential Center. The space next to the sidewalk has been covered by a
greenhouse-like shaded glass canopy. Two dozen different kinds of burgers are
priced at $4.75 to $6.50; salads that'll do for a meal cost $5; omelets with
crabmeat and artichoke, or other interesting combinations, are slightly more.

There are several Mexican specialties. The menu is the same for lunch and dinner, and in my opinion the items are a bit overpriced for what you get, but then it's a lively place and you're paying to be in the "in place." Friday's is open from 11:30 a.m. to midnight on weekdays, 11:30 a.m. to 1 a.m. on weekends.

For Seafood

Legal Seafoods (tel. 426-4444) is a Boston institution, a no-nonsense operation which prides itself on freshness and reasonable prices. The restaurant in the Boston Park Plaza Hotel off Park Square (subway to Arlington) is big but nicely broken up, light and attractive. The menu is encyclopedic, listing close to 100 items, but this is for reference: when fresh stocks run out, that's it for any particular fish. Start with a shrimp cocktail or oysters on the half shell, go on to scrod, bluefish, Mako shark, sea trout, etc. Have a glass or two of wine, and you can expect to pay about $18 for your dinner. Choose carefully and you can spend $12 or so; have lobster, salmon, or scallops, and your bill will be more like $25. Hours are Monday through Thursday from 11 a.m. to 9:30 p.m., on Friday and Saturday to 10 p.m., on Sunday from noon to 9:30 p.m. Note that there is often a waiting line, especially long on weekends; also, that you pay when you order—an odd but time-saving custom. No reservations accepted.

Several Boston seafood restaurants are legendary by this time, and none is more so than **Jimmy's Harborside** (tel. 423-1000), on Fish Pier, which is at the end of Northern Avenue (no. 248), due east of downtown Boston across the Fort Point Channel (Red Line to South Station, then a no. 7 bus, "City Point–South Station"). Enter the place, and pass a sign that announces: "Suitcoats after 5, No Dungarees," and you come to a realm of nautical paraphernalia, plush carpets and chairs, a boat-shaped bar surrounded by little cocktail tables. The menu for lunch always has a daily special which includes chowder (fish or clam) or lobster bisque, entree, salad, potato, dessert, and coffee, all for about $6; luncheon entrees alone cost $4 (for the cheapest sandwich) to about $8. At dinnertime, you might be offered *two* fresh "chicken" lobsters (the small females, weighing about a pound apiece), with french fries and salad, for $16, or soft-shell crabs done in garlic butter ($12.50), or perhaps a swordfish shish kebab ($7.25). The menu carries several delicious Greek specialties as well; add $3 or so to these entree prices and you can have an appetizer, salad, potato, dessert, and beverage too. The wine list runs to almost 100 items, four of them Greek. Jimmy's Harborside, "Home of the Chowder King," is open from 11:30 a.m. to 9:30 p.m. every day but Sunday.

Perhaps you have missed the 6 to 9 p.m. dinner hour, and the seafood you crave is getting more and more difficult to find as restaurants close for the evening. The place to go in such a case is **The Half Shell** (tel. 423-5555), 743 Boylston St., almost across the street from the Prudential Center. At the Half Shell, you can order seafood until 1 a.m. The restaurant has two rooms: on the right, a bar with tables, more for those who want seafood with their drinks; on the left and to the rear, a room for those who want a drink with their seafood. Main courses include bouillabaisse, broiled swordfish kebab, fried and boiled seafoods, and lobster dinners. Prices range from $6 to $13. For a late-night supper, just have the clam chowder: portions are big, and the flavor excellent. Besides late-night dinners, you can have lunch here from 11:30 a.m. to 4 p.m. daily.

Italian

It's extremely difficult to choose among the many good Italian restaurants in Boston's North End, but were I forced to do so, I would choose **Felicia's** (tel. 523-9885), because it's what an Italian restaurant should be: shelves of wine bottles festooned with imitation grapes, dark oil paintings along the walls, cozy booths with white tablecloths topped by red shake-cloths, heavy curtains under a valance giving that touch of old-world elegance. The waiters all seem to be young, good-looking Italian men from the North End, always smiling and gracious. The specialty of the house is chicken verdicchio, a boneless breast of chicken cooked with lemon, mushrooms, and artichoke hearts in verdicchio wine ($8.50), but there's also shrimp marinara ($9.75), and beef scallopine à la Marsala ($10.50); pastas are in the range of $4.50 to $8. Felicia's serves dinner only, and it is very popular on weekends. To find it, walk along Hanover Street and take the first right turn onto Richmond Street. Felicia's is at no. 145a. Open the door onto the stairway with its shining brass-rail bannisters, and hope there's no line waiting for tables.

A North End Italian favorite is the **Café Paradiso** (tel. 523-8875), 225 Hanover St. (take the T to Haymarket). Service is from Sunday through Friday, noon to 11:30 p.m., on Saturday from 4:30 to 11:30 p.m. The storefront restaurant is attractively done with several standard Italian restaurant items, but it's the food you're after. If you like veal, have it here. The various Italian classics made with veal cost $8.25 to $11.50; chicken dishes are slightly less. Antipasto and pasta plates cost $3.75 to $5.75, and the inexpensive wines, by the carafe or the bottle, will not break your budget. Service is a bit slow, and as no reservations are taken you may have to wait outside a bit on busy weekend evenings. But the wait has to do with the Café secret. Only three people work here: the chef, the assistant, and the waiter. Everything is cooked to order. You can see into the kitchen. It's all delicious. Plan to spend about $18 per person, with wine, tax, and tip.

Chinese Dim Sum

The **Imperial Tea Room,** at 70 Beach St. in the heart of Boston's small Chinatown (tel. 426-8439), has been around for a long time, but has only recently been recognized for what it is: the best place in town for dim sum yum chai. The classic meal of Chinese hors d'oeuvres is served every day of the week from 9:30 a.m. to 3 p.m. The best time to go is between 10 and 11 a.m., or after 1:30 p.m. on weekdays. Other times the crowd is dense. Most of the patrons here are Chinese residents who know a good thing or, rather, things: spare ribs, water-chestnuts in gelatin, pork dumplings, tofu (soybean cake), green sugar-cane leaves stuffed with sweet rice, pork and quail eggs, even fried duck feet. Sit in the upstairs room for dim sum. The à la carte restaurant downstairs is not as good. The system is this: you pick what you like from the carts which appear in a steady stream throughout the morning and afternoon. Each plate on the cart has about three portions of the item (so it's good to do dim summing with two friends). When you've had enough, the waiter counts up the plates (75¢ or $1.25 apiece) and gives you the bill, which will be very low (about $8 per person) considering the amount and quality of the food.

After dim sum, what? Walk a block along Beach to Oxford Street, turn right, and a few doors down on Oxford is the **Wai Wai** ice cream shop. Downstairs in the shop are three tables, a stove, scoops of ice cream (my favorite is coconut, 55¢ a scoop), and the makings of Wai Wai's famous Red Bean Drink. Made with red kidney beans, milk, and sugar, it's delicious, loaded with protein, and cheap at 85¢. With a scoop of ice cream, it can make a light lunch/dessert for little over a dollar.

Thai

"Last time I was in Bangkok, I ate at this great little restaurant. . . ." That may not be an often-heard phrase in your circle. Few Americans have a close familiarity with Thai cuisine, but anyone in Boston can rectify that lamentable situation with a trip to **Bangkok Cuisine,** 177a Massachusetts Ave., just down from the corner of Boylston Street, near Prudential Center (tel. 262-5377). Clear soups made with scallions, shrimp, and hot peppers, savory dishes of duck with pineapple, spices, and Oriental vegetables and mushrooms—once you've tried the food here, you may indeed want to take off for Bangkok. The restaurant is small, long and narrow, always busy, not romantic but bustling. Have soup or an appetizer, a main course based on seafood, pork, beef, or chicken, a dessert, and a bottle of Thai beer, and you'll pay about $15. A warning: Soups are marked "moderately hot," but in my experience they are very spicy-hot (and very good). Bangkok is open for lunch (11:30 a.m. to 3 p.m.) and dinner (5 p.m. to 10:30 p.m.) Monday through Friday, for dinner only on Saturday and Sunday.

Mexican

Boston's prime Mexican restaurant is the **Casa Romero,** 30 Gloucester St. (tel. 261-2146 or 247-7451). The entrance to the restaurant is actually off Gloucester Street, in an alley between Newbury Street and Commonwealth Avenue. The Casa Romero is a very nicely and authentically decorated dining place, with colorful tiles which greet you as you enter, and lots of Mexican art objects here and there (including many pieces of modern and ancient pottery). The restaurant is open for dinner only from 5 to 10 p.m. Sunday through Thursday, to 11 p.m. on Friday and Saturday. The menu has such desirable dishes as mole Poblana, the famous chicken-in-spicy-chocolate-sauce dish from the city of Pueblo ($11), or puerco adobado (pork in orange sauce, with tamarind and smoked peppers; $11.25). An interesting choice is the plate with taco fixin's which allows you to roll your own. It should be noted that this restaurant serves an authentic Mexican cuisine and not an Americanized version. Parking is available several blocks away in the Prudential Center garage.

Since the **Sol Azteca** (tel. 262-0909) opened, crowds have flocked to its door at 914a Beacon St. in Boston, very near the Brookline town line. The word got around quickly among devotees of Mexican food that the guacamole, enchiladas (rojas, verdes, or Suizas), the tacos, and tostadas were authentic, delicious, and moderately priced. Dinner starts with a basket of tortilla chips and a hot sauce dip and perhaps a bottle of Dos Equis or Superior Mexican beer. The combination plates ($8 to $10) are the best buys, bringing you a little of everything, to the point where you will probably have no capacity left for dessert. When I last dined here with four friends, the total bill for a no-holds-barred feast came to $68, or $17 per person, tax, tip, and many bottles of cerveza included. On Friday and Saturday, especially during college term, it's really crowded, and no reservations are accepted. Get there early. By T, take a "Cleveland Circle" car on the Green Line, and get off at the first stop above ground.

Inexpensive Mexican food on expensive Newbury Street? Yes, at **Acapulco,** 266 Newbury St. (tel. 247-9126), an attractive little restaurant done in brick, butcher block, and Mexican crafts. An inexpensive meal might consist of gazpacho, a tostada, flan for dessert, and a glass of guava juice to drink, all for $7. At the other end of the scale, you could order taquitos, crispy buñuelos for dessert, and drink Dos Equis Mexican beer, and pay exactly twice as much. Cheapest of all? Have just a combination plate, very filling, and only $3.75. You can order meatless meals, or dishes put up to take out. Acapulco serves Monday through Saturday from 11:30 a.m. to 11 p.m., on Sunday from 3 to 11 p.m. In summer, enjoy the outdoor patio tables.

Greek

Pleasant surroundings, good food, and very reasonable prices draw tired Boston visitors at **Aegean Fare** (tel. 723-4850), with several branches in Boston. The original establishment is at 539 Commonwealth Ave. in Kenmore Square, but you're more likely to be visiting the one in Faneuil Hall Marketplace. Everyone's favorite Greek treats are on the menu: souvlaki sandwiches ($3.50, or as a dinner $5.50), "Gyro" slices (doneri, lamb, or beef grilled on a vertical spit, $5.75), dolmathakia (stuffed vine leaves, $4.50), or roast lamb for $6. Not just a "little Greek place," Aegean Fare also features American dishes and New York deli-style sandwiches and such. Aegean Fare seems to be open all the time, from early in the morning until early in the morning again, closing for only a few hours; it's open every day.

The top spot for Greek cuisine in the theater district is the **Athens Olympia**, at 51 Stuart St., not far from the corner of Tremont (tel. 426-6236). It's a big place, with dining rooms on the second floor. The rooms are brightened by Greek-style murals, pillars with Ionic capitals, and white tablecloths on the comfy booth tables. Taramasalata and dolmades are good as starters (red caviar puree and stuffed vine leaves), or for something unusual, try the saganaki, which is hot cheese in olive oil. The main courses include calamari (squid), moussaka, and other Greek classics, but for a taste of them all, order the Ariston ala Olympia, a combination plate with chicken, baked lamb, vegetables, and rice for $7.50. For dessert, only baklava ($1.75) will do. The Olympia is open from 11 a.m. to 11:30 p.m., till 9:30 p.m. on Sunday (they're closed on Sunday in summer). Theater-goers will like the huge, clearly visible clock over the door, good for not missing curtain times.

BUDGET RESTAURANTS (Meals about $5 to $8): It's not difficult to dine inexpensively in Boston. The variety and cuisine make it possible to eat pleasantly for $5 to $8 per day, or less. But the restaurants recommended below are not just for those on a very slim budget. No one wants haute cuisine at every meal—few people's livers can stand it, in any case. For those times when you just want a quick and inexpensive meal, but one that's wholesome and delicious, try one of these places, arranged below according to location:

Budget Seafood

Boston's **No Name Restaurant** (tel. 338-7539) has actually been a top name in Boston seafood for almost half a century. It's hardly a "secret little Boston restaurant," as everyone has known about it for years, and it's still the best place to get seafood at bargain prices. The No Name started out as a rough-and-ready eatery for fishermen working on the pier, and the prices are not a great deal higher than when those hearties—who know the price of fish—used to dine here in droves. Most plates cost $5 to $8, whether it be salmon, lobster, bluefish, or scrod. The cooking is rough-and-ready, the service is bringing-your-food, it's noisy, and there's always a waiting line—but it's fun, and the prices can't be beat. To get there, take Northern Avenue off Atlantic Avenue, and when you see a guard in a booth on the left, ask him to point it out—it's down the wharf behind him, no sign. Closed Sunday.

Along Newbury Street

Budget-minded readers will be glad to know that Newbury Street is not all expensive and exotic. At the **Raleigh Restaurant** (tel. 536-9198), 116 Newbury, for example, a filling bowl of beef stew is only $2.50, a Yankee pot roast only $3.85, and a filling, cool Greek salad only $1.95. Needless to say, the surroundings are not plush, but rather standard cafeteria Formica, and the service not smooth—unless *you* are smooth, because it's self-service—but there are a few tables set out on the sidewalk in good weather, and here you can enjoy Newbury Street people-watching for a fraction of what it would cost at many of the other restaurants on the street.

Another low-budget choice slightly farther along at no. 135 is the **Travis Restaurant** (tel. 267-6388), where a slice of pie à la mode and a cup of coffee will total only $2.50, a hamburger is $1.95, and large salad plates (with tuna, ham, etc.) are $3.50. The small tables on the sidewalk out front are not fitted with umbrellas, and the interior is the familiar lunch counter and stools (with some tables as well), and it's serve yourself, inside and out. The Travis, by the way, is open Monday through Saturday from about 7 a.m. to 4:30 p.m., so it's not the place to plan to go for dinner or a late snack.

In the North End

The North End has over a dozen Italian restaurants, but it seems as though there's always room for one more if the food is good and the price right. That's the situation at **The Pushcart** (tel. 523-9616), 61 Endicott St. (Take the passage under the Central Artery from Haymarket and cross at the lights to the beginning of Salem Street; don't start down Salem Street, but turn left and walk a block, and the restaurant is just around the corner to the right.) Taking its name from the costermongers' carts a block away in Haymarket Square, the Pushcart serves the sort of food the fruit-and-vegetable sellers enjoy: lasagne ($4.25 at lunch), eggplant parmigiana, or a huge lunch of a veal cutlet, eggplant parmigiana, and spaghetti for $5.25. At dinner the pasta dishes cost $3.50 to $5, from spaghetti marinara to linguini with shrimp in a clam sauce; entrees are in the range of $4.50 to $7.50, and a hearty end-of-the-sightseeing-day dinner of two pork chops with vinegar peppers and potato with mushrooms is $7.25. The small brick-and-shingle facade hides one small dining room with bright yellow tables and black wooden chairs with yellow seats. Note the special hours: lunch is served Tuesday through Saturday from 11:30 a.m. to 3 p.m.; dinner is served only Thursday through Saturday from 5 to 10:30 p.m.

Boston's most famous pizza place is **Pizzeria Regina** (tel. 227-0765), 11½ Thatcher St., at the corner of Thatcher and North Margin Streets—if you have trouble finding it, just ask anyone in the North End, for the pizzeria is a center of community life here. Besides its very congenial neighborhood atmosphere, the Regina is special because it's one of the few pizzerias I've run into where one can order beer or wine to go with the pizza. Old dark-wood booths with Formica tables, and a small bar for the solitary lunchers, make up the interior, which is anything but fancy. The pizzas, however, are very fancy, for the cooks know the secret of making a good one: the best imported cheese and tomato sauce, and a few dashes of real olive oil. All pizzas come in small or large sizes, and a small pie will feed two moderately hungry people for lunch for as little as $3.75. That price is for a small cheese pizza, but others in the $4 to $5.75 range come with mushrooms, anchovies, sausage, and the like. The top price is for the Regina Special, everything on a large pizza for $9.75, and this should easily feed a party of four. Beer and wine are served. There is a 99% guarantee that you will be unable to find a parking place near the Regina, and so they've arranged that their customers can park in the lot next to Polcari's (at the southern end of the Charlestown Bridge) for free. Have your ticket validated by your waitress at the Regina.

In Faneuil Hall Marketplace

Good seafood in simple, small surroundings is the formula at **The Salty Dog,** in the basement of Quincy Market (Green or Blue Lines to Government Center). The tiny restaurant is a bit hard to find: facing the front of Quincy Market, with your back to Faneuil Hall, walk to the right of the market facade and just under the southwest corner of the market is the stairway down to the Salty Dog. Fresh fish is sold here to go (lobsters as well) or you can stay and have fish and chips ($4.25), clams on the half shell (a half dozen for $3.75), or any one of several fried or baked fish plates for about $7. Service is hardly elegant, for your food comes in paper containers and you eat with plastic utensils, but the food is very good. The oyster stew seems expensive, but you'll find at least a half dozen whole, succulent oysters in each bowlful. Draft beer and wine are served. Besides the oyster bar, which is usually full, the Salty Dog has a small room behind the stairway with several tiny tables and another bar or counter. In warm weather, tables are set up outside the restaurant's entrance. This tiny place is open from 11:30 a.m. to about 10 p.m. daily. Note that as the emphasis is on fresh fish, they may run out of certain items near the day's end as that day's fresh shipment is used up.

Chinatown, Near the Shopping District

Stories are always in circulation about "this great little Chinese place," and the description is usually of a restaurant in which the decor is not much but the food is delicious, and the bill for a feast is so low as to cause a double-take. Well, Boston has a number of such great little Chinese places, and my favorite is the **Golden Gate** (tel. 426-5022), 66 Beach St. in Chinatown (Red Line to Essex). The decor might best be described as small-town quick-lunch, complete with jukebox (Chinese and Western hits), but the food is very good: egg fu yung, a fine broccoli, beef, and rice, a big dish of pork with pineapple. My wife and I recently had lunch here with two friends, ordered whatever we desired, had food left over, and paid a bill of $20 for all four, tip included. For a morning snack, come in for Chinese pastries and tea, served from 10 a.m. to noon; the Golden Gate is open daily from 10 a.m. to 1 a.m.

Along the Freedom Trail

You're tromping along the Freedom Trail, trying to do it in a few hours, and you just want a quick bite for lunch? Join the be-suited business types grabbing a snack at the **Steaming Kettle,** corner of Cambridge (or Tremont) and Court Streets, very near the Government Center Station (also at 235 Washington St. and 100 Summer St.). The huge kettle over the door has been belching steam for years and years, and inside the waitresses dispense steaming coffee or tea, lemonade or milk, and sandwiches such as hot roast beef, frankfort and beans, or bologna at prices between $1.25 and $2.50 to stand-up customers at the shelf-like hardwood counters that line the walls. If it's breakfast you're after, the coffeeshop upstairs is open from 7:30 a.m. to 3:30 p.m.

5. Sights

THE FREEDOM TRAIL: The sights of revolutionary Boston are linked together by the Freedom Trail, an ingenious idea which makes it easy for any visitor to find all the important colonial and revolutionary landmarks. Starting from the Park Street MBTA station on Boston Common, a red line painted on the sidewalk or a double row of bricks laid in the sidewalk leads past the **Massachusetts State House**, **Park Street Church**, the **Old Granary Burying Ground**, **King's Chapel**, the **Old State House**, the **Paul Revere House**, **Old North Church**, and *Old Ironsides* (U.S.S. *Constitution*), as well as other sights. Except for *Old Ironsides,* the trail passes all the important things to see in a mile and a half; *Old Ironsides* is across Boston's Inner Harbor in Charlestown, 2½ miles away, best reached by bus or car.

There is a bus that follows the Freedom Trail: **Hub Bus Freedom Trail Shuttle** (tel. 776-0630). Arrangements for the bus vary with time of year, summer being the time when service is best and most frequent. Fare is $4.50 per adult ($2 per child 12 or under) for a day pass entitling you to hop on and off the buses as often as you like; buses run about every 45 minutes from 10 a.m. to 4 p.m. Buy your tickets right near the **Freedom Trail Information Center**, 617/267-6446. The Information Center, on Boston Common near the Park Street Station, also hands out maps of the trail and brochures with facts about the sights. Here's a quick rundown so you'll know what there is to see (numbers are keyed to our map):

Boston Common (12)

This park in the center of Boston was the colonial town's "common pasture land," to which any citizen's cows could be brought. The pasture ordinance is still in effect, so they say, but no one seems to take advantage of it—as though with all the picnickers, sunbathers, soap-box orators, street buskers and pitchmen there'd be any room left for a cow quietly to graze!

State House and Archives (13)

The Massachusetts State House dominates Beacon Hill and the Boston Common, its gold dome shining and visible for miles. It was designed by Charles Bulfinch, Boston's most famous and best loved architect, and built at the end of the 1700s. This is where the Massachusetts General Court (legislature) sits today; in its Archives (which you can visit) are curious and famous documents relating to the history of the colony of Massachusetts Bay and the early republic.

While you're up here on Beacon Hill, take a detour off the Freedom Trail and explore the back streets of what was once (and in many ways still is) Boston's wealthiest and prettiest residential neighborhood. Wander down the little "mews" (lanes behind the houses) where once the horses and carriages were kept, and don't miss **Louisburg Square,** a tiny private park which is Beacon Hill's gem. The beautiful old colonial and Federal houses extend to the base of the hill at Charles Street, and down toward the 19th-century developments of Back Bay.

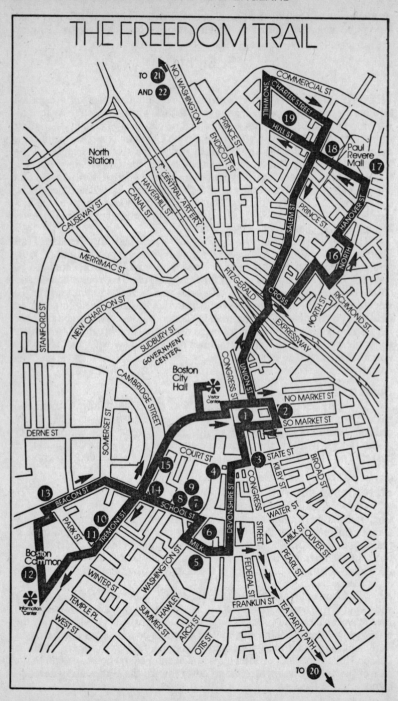

THE FREEDOM TRAIL

Park Street Church (11)

Right next to Park Street Station is this tall-steepled, graceful church designed by Peter Banner and built in 1809. Take a look inside, so you can compare this early 19th-century church with the earlier churches farther along the Freedom Trail.

Old Granary Burying Ground (10)

Some of the American Revolution's most famous figures, from John Hancock to Crispus Attucks, are buried in this cemetery which took its name from a nearby granary, now long gone. Take a walk through—you'll constantly be surprised and delighted by the names, dates, and mottoes on the finely carved headstones.

King's Chapel (14)

The building dates from 1754, and in its interesting career changed from being an Episcopal church to a Unitarian meetinghouse. Services are held here, as are lectures and concerts as well.

Site of the First Public School (9)

Established in 1635, this is where it was.

Statue of Benjamin Franklin (8)

Most people remember the story of Franklin getting off the boat in Philadelphia with very little money and two loaves of bread for sustenance to begin his famous career, but some people forget that he was coming from Boston, his birthplace and childhood home. This statue by Richard Greenough (1856), in front of the city's old headquarters, pays tribute to Boston's famous son.

Old Corner Bookstore (7)

The *Boston Globe* bought and restored this famous house, and now uses it as the office for taking classified ads. The house itself dates from the early 1700s, but its fame began when it became a gathering place for famous American authors in the 19th century. At that time, bookstores were also publishers, and Messrs. Ticknor & Fields, who ran the Old Corner Bookstore, published and drank coffee with the outstanding literary men of the age, including Longfellow, Hawthorne, and Whittier. Walk in for a look at the exhibits of first editions, some furnishings, and a curious page from a 19th-century edition of the *Boston Globe* which attempted to predict what society would be like in 100 years.

Old South Meeting House (6)

New England churches frequently call their buildings meetinghouses rather than churches, and it's from this that the Old South Meeting House gets its name, even though it was used for town meetings as well. (Old North Church, from which the lanterns hung to signal Paul Revere, is a different building farther along the Freedom Trail.) Built in 1729, the meetinghouse saw its most famous meeting on December 16, 1773, when a group of colonials in Indian dress set out from here to throw the Boston Tea Party. Of the exhibits—old documents, currency, furniture—perhaps the most interesting is a plaster-and-wood scale model of the Town of Boston in 1775, which gives you a very clear idea of the size and layout of the town, and helps your imagination recast the events of the Revolution in their proper setting.

The Old State House (4)

The charming brick building dates from 1713, and was built to house the colonial government; after the Revolution it was known as the State House, and after the present State House was built in 1795, this one became the Old State House (206 Washington St.). Washington addressed the citizens of Boston from its balcony. Now that it's hemmed in by giant buildings on all sides, much of the dignity it must have held for colonial and revolutionary Americans is lost. Inside, a museum holds period costumes, portraits, and a good selection of nautical artifacts, from antique sextants to eight very fine scale models of ships and some dramatic paintings of great ships as well. Two nine-minute videotape shows provide historical information. There's an entry fee to the museum of 75¢ for adults, 50¢ for senior citizens, 25¢ for children. Hours are 9:30 a.m. to 4:30 p.m. every day.

Boston Massacre Site (3)

Here, near the Old State House, British soldiers fired into a crowd of colonials protesting what they saw as excesses by the British government. The incident must have happened much as the tragic killings happened at Kent State University during the Vietnam War protests: unarmed civilians expressing their resentment by throwing curses and stones at armed soldiers who were confused as to how they should respond.

Faneuil Hall (1)

Faneuil Hall (pronounced FAN-yool) was built by the Town of Boston in 1742 with money given by Peter Faneuil; designed by John Simbert, it was later enlarged by Bulfinch (1805). The ground floor has been devoted to shops since the building was built; the second floor was—and is—used for public meetings; and the third floor houses the headquarters of Boston's most famous chowder-and-marching society, the Ancient and Honorable Artillery Company. Entrance to the second-floor meeting hall is from the east side; National Park Service guides are on hand to tell you all about the building: the huge painting dominating the front of the hall, they will tell you, is of Daniel Webster speaking on the virtues of a close union of states (as opposed to States' Rights). The speech was given in Washington in 1830, not in Faneuil Hall, but the painting must have inspired hundreds of less talented, although perhaps equally long-winded, orators. Entrance to the hall is free.

The area around Faneuil Hall has recently been rebuilt and restored, and it is a nice change from the boldly modern buildings nearby. (For details on shopping in Quincy Market, next to Faneuil Hall, see the separate Shopping section.)

While you're here in Faneuil Hall Marketplace, be sure to stop by the **Bostix** kiosk (tel. 617/723-5181 for a recording), right next to Faneuil Hall, to see what shows, concerts, and theater performances are on sale at half price. Usually the half-price seats are for today's (or tonight's) performances.

Paul Revere House (16)

A small clapboard dwelling in Boston's North End, surrounded by crooked cobbled streets, the Paul Revere House, 19 North Square (tel. 523-

1676), is the only house left in Boston which was built in the 1600s. Paul Revere moved in about a century after the house was built, and he lived here during the Revolutionary period. The house would be interesting even if the great patriot had never set foot in it, with its quaint weathered exterior, small windows, and wide floorboards. But furnished in colonial style and equipped with an ingenious handrail/barrier which guides you through the house and gives you information on Revere's life at the same time, the house is worth more than an hour's lecture on Revolutionary history. Admission costs $1.50 for adults, 75¢ for seniors and students, 25¢ for ages 6 to 17. No photography is allowed inside the house. Hours are 10 a.m. to 4 p.m. in winter, 9:30 a.m. to 5:30 p.m. in summer. Take a look around North Square, the small cobbled-and-gaslit space near the Revere House, and perhaps rest from your walk on one of its benches. This part of town, the North End, is now very Italian in character—you can hear the local dialect of the mother tongue in the surrounding streets.

Old North Church (18)

You can see by the church's location why it was a good place from which to give a signal. The code, as every schoolchild knows, was "one if by land, two if by sea," and it was two lanterns hung in the tower that started Paul Revere and William Dawes on their fateful night rides to warn the Colonials that British troops were heading out from Boston to search for hidden arms. On April 18, 1975, exactly 200 years from that historic day, President Ford inaugurated the American Revolutionary Bicentennial in Old North Church by lighting a third lantern (hanging at the front of the church). The church is the oldest church building in Boston (1723), and is today officially known as Christ Church, Episcopal. A walk around inside turns up many curiosities which bear on the history of Boston and the United States: memorial plaques to famous men, nameplates on the very high pews. The tall graceful windows of Old North Church are exceptionally fine. After your visit, it's good to drop the requested (not required) donation in the box near the door. Visitors are also welcome for Sunday services at 9:30 a.m., 11 a.m., and 4 p.m.

Although it's hemmed in by houses and shops on all sides, Old North Church does have a set of tiny terraces and gardens on its north side, open to the public. The small formal garden and the fountain are good to refresh your spirit on a hot day, and the memorial plaques set into the walls are, in some cases, delightful. One reads:

1757–1923
Here on September 13, 1757
"John Childs who had given public notice of his intention to
Fly from the steeple of Dr. Cutler's church, performed it to
The satisfaction of a great number of spectators"
In 1923 the year of the first continuous flight across
The continent this tablet has been placed here by
The Massachusetts Society of the Colonial Dames of America
To commemorate the two events.

The question that comes to mind: would it not have been faster to dispatch John Childs from the steeple to Lexington and Concord by air, rather than Dawes and Revere by land, on that historic night in 1775?

U.S.S. Constitution (22)

The *Constitution (Old Ironsides)* is still commissioned in the service of the U.S. Navy and could in theory be called to the defense of the country should the need arise. She still gets under way once a year, on the Fourth of July, when she's taken a short distance out into the harbor to fire a 21-gun salute. The dock here is right on a former navy base; sailors in 1812 period uniforms will take you through the ship and explain her workings to you free of charge. But the ship is not the only exhibit here: the nearby **Museum** ($2 for adults, 50¢ for kids 6 to 16; under 6, free) houses many artifacts dealing with the *Constitution's* history and her 40 battles at sea (all won), besides a "Life at Sea" exhibit, showing what shipboard life was like in 1812. The Boston Navy Yard National Historic Site also offers programs on the yard and the American Revolution every hour in Building No. 5 (between the ship and the museum). Nearby in the Bunker Hill Pavilion another audio-visual show will help you relive the Battle of Bunker Hill, fought only a short distance from here. Admission to the show, the "Whites of Their Eyes," is $2 for adults, half price for senior citizens and children 16 and under. The pavilion has public rest rooms as well. To get to these attractions, and to Bunker Hill with its monument, cross the Mystic River (Tobin) Bridge (toll) or the Charlestown Bridge (free) nearby and follow the signs to the U.S.S. *Constitution.* Bus 93 ("Sullivan Square via Bunker Hill") from Haymarket Square will take you fairly close to Bunker Hill and Boston Navy Yard for 50¢; it runs about every half hour, more frequently during rush hours. You can walk to *Old Ironsides* from Haymarket in about 25 minutes, using the Charlestown Bridge.

Boston Tea Party Ship and Museum (20)

Strictly speaking, this is not on the Freedom Trail, but on a separate excursion called Harborwalk. The events it recalls are very much a part of colonial Boston's struggle for independence. Take the Red Line to South Station, walk north on Atlantic Avenue one block past the new Federal Reserve Bank (looks like a mammoth space-age radiator), turn right onto Congress Street and walk a block to the water, and there's the ship at Congress Street Bridge. A shuttle bus operates daily May through October from the rear of the Old State House on the Freedom Trail (corner of Devonshire and State Streets), or from the Harborside entrance to Faneuil Hall Marketplace. What you see here is the brig *Beaver II,* a full-size replica of one of the merchant ships looted by the "Indians" on the night of the tea party raid, and a museum with exhibits outlining the "tea party." At the nearby Tea Party Store you can buy some tea and throw it over the side of the *Beaver* into Fort Point Channel, although I doubt that this will make the water any more potable. The ship and museum (tel. 338-1773) are open from 9 a.m. to dusk (about 8 p.m. in summer, 5 p.m. in winter) every day except three major holidays, at $2.25 for adults, $1.50 for children 5 to 14; special family rates available. Complimentary tea is served—iced tea in summer, hot tea in winter.

MUSEUM OF FINE ARTS: The great Greek temple at 465 Huntington Ave. houses one of the world's greatest collections of artworks, second in the country only to New York's Metropolitan. Boston's Museum of Fine Arts (tel. 617/267-9300) is a wonder, a vast collection of beautiful things in a beautiful building. Many pictures you may have admired for years through prints and photos in art books are here: Gilbert Stuart's *Athenaeum Head* portrait of George Washington; Renoir's *Le Bal à Bougival;* Burne-Jones's *The Love*

Song; Whistler's *Girl in a White Dress;* works by Van Gogh, Gauguin, Degas, lots of Monets; *Death of Maximilian* by Manet; and works by Japanese, Chinese, European, medieval, Renaissance, and baroque masters are all well represented. A fine collection of Paul Revere silver, several rooms taken from French châteaux, full-size Japanese temples, a ninth-century Spanish chapel, Egyptian mummies, Assyrian seals—the list goes on to the treasures of almost 200 galleries. The way to find what you want is to pick up a floor plan as you enter; you can't possibly see even a fraction of it all, so pick out a few areas or rooms to concentrate on, and enjoy. Before you go, call 267-9377 (or A-N-S-W-E-R-S) for a recording of current special exhibits. If you need the help of a person, call 267-9300, ext. 363.

The entire museum is open normally Tuesday through Sunday from 10 a.m. to 5 p.m. (closed Monday), Wednesday evening till 10 p.m. On Thursday and Friday the main building closes at 5 p.m. but the West Wing stays open till 10 p.m. Admission is $3.50 for adults, free for those under 16 years, $2.50 for seniors. If you come on Saturday from 10 a.m. till noon, you can get in for free; if you visit when only the new West Wing is open, the fee is $2.50.

The museum's restaurant is located in the West Wing. Lunch is served daily from 11:30 a.m. to 2:30 p.m. (except Monday); dinner on Wednesday, Thursday, and Friday from 5:30 to 8:30 p.m. Surrounded by glass, the dining room is ultramodern and attractive. The menu is often keyed to special exhibits —Chinese dishes predominated when the impressive Chinese bronzes were on display—and the prices are moderate. You can figure $8 to $10 for lunch, $15 to $18 for dinner. The wine list is short, good, and fairly priced.

For snacks and pick-me-ups, head for the café below the restaurant.

To get to the museum, take a Green Line "Arborway" or "Huntington Avenue" car and get off at the second stop above ground. Want to save some money? Get off at the first stop above ground ("Northeastern University") and walk the three blocks to the museum. If you do this, you can take one of the cars mentioned, or a "Northeastern University" car.

ISABELLA STEWART GARDNER MUSEUM: If you have a full day when you visit the Museum of Fine Arts, plan to spend at least a few hours of it at the Isabella Stewart Gardner Museum nearby (tel. 734-1359), at 280 The Fenway (walk west from the Museum of Fine Arts around its parking lot to the Fenway; turn left and walk two short blocks). "Mrs. Jack" Gardner early developed a love of art, and with her considerable wealth and the services of Bernard Berenson she set about to build an outstanding collection which now includes almost 300 paintings, almost as many pieces of sculpture, close to 500 pieces of furniture, and hundreds of works in textiles, ceramics, and glass. Most of the holdings are from the great periods of European art, but classical and Oriental civilizations are also represented. Not the least of the exhibits is the house itself, which she had built to hold the collection in 1902. "Fenway Court" is not much to look at from the outside, but inside it is Mrs. Gardner's vision of a 15th-century Venetian palace, with many doors, columns, windows, and the like, which were brought from Europe and assembled around an open court topped by a glass canopy. The court is always planted with flowers, in bloom summer and winter, and several fountains bubble merrily at one end. Upstairs in one room is a dramatic portrait of "Mrs. Jack" herself, displayed with various masterpieces above a floor covered in tiles from Henry Mercer's Moravian tile and pottery works in Pennsylvania. Along a corridor nearby, look for mementoes of Mrs. Gardner's years, including letters from many of the great and famous of the turn of the century. The suggested admission is $1, but lesser amounts are acceptable. It's open in July and August, Tuesday through Saturday from 1 to 5:30 p.m.; September through June the hours are the same, plus it's open Tuesday evenings till 9:30 p.m. Except for July and August, free concerts of chamber music are given on Thursday and Sunday at 4 p.m. and Tuesday evening at 8 p.m.; they're usually very well attended, so go early and claim a seat. The museum has a nice café serving light meals as well.

OTHER GALLERIES: Perhaps it's the amalgam of college faculty, art-conscious Old Guard families, and artists themselves that makes Boston such a good place to go browsing in galleries. Whatever the cause, Boston is rich in exhibitions of painting, sculpture, and the more recent vehicles of artistic expression such as textiles and welded metal. Prime among Boston galleries is the **Institute of Contemporary Art** (tel. 617/266-5151 for a recording, 266-5152 for a person), 955 Boylston St., across the street from the Prudential Center (Green Line's "Boston College," "Riverside," or "Cleveland Circle" cars to Auditorium Station). The institute is a beautifully modern place inside a historic structure of Richardsonian style. Shows may be anything from an exhibit of New England photographers' work to works in various media by Claes Oldenburg, or perhaps a show of the outstanding works by modern artists which are in Boston private collections. Special events include video programs, musical concerts, and Friday noontime lectures (free coffee and dessert provided by ICA). All exhibitions change about every six to seven weeks. The ICA is open Tuesday through Sunday (on Tuesday, Thursday, and Friday from 11 a.m. to 7 p.m., on Wednesday to 8 p.m., on Saturday to 6 p.m., and on Sunday from noon to 6 p.m.; closed Monday). Admission is $2 for adults, $1 for senior citizens and students, 50¢ for children. Free admission on Wednesday, and for all members.

The institute never has works for sale. Those interested in browsing and perhaps buying—without any obligation to do so, of course—should pick a day to stroll down **Newbury Street,** where a good many of Boston's better galleries are located. Highlights and dining possibilities for such a stroll are covered in a separate section on "Newbury Street" in this same chapter. Other streets with galleries and antique shops are **Charles Street** at the base of Beacon Hill, and **Boylston Street.**

Boston City Hall, the Boston Public Library in Copley Square, and other public organizations and private corporations sponsor shows from time to time. See the tabloid weeklies such as the *Boston Phoenix* for full listings of what's currently available, or contact the Department of Public Relations (tel. 266-5152) with your questions.

There's often an interesting exhibit in the lobby of the **Boston Architectural Center** (tel. 536-3170), 320 Newbury St. at the corner of Hereford Street (Green Line to Auditorium). The show will be connected in some way with architecture, whether it be the life and work of Henry Mercer, the turn-of-the-century Pennsylvania tile maker, or a collection of neon signs from many cities and many decades. The hours are Monday through Thursday, 9 a.m. to 10 p.m., Friday and Saturday to 5 p.m. (Sunday from 11 a.m. to 5 p.m. only in the winter season). Shows are always free, and if you're strolling along this part of Newbury Street, at least take a look through the windows to see what's on.

MUSEUM OF SCIENCE: Nobody ever has a bad time when they visit Boston's famous Museum of Science, Science Park (tel. 617/742-6088), because there are so many things to see and do, and of such a variety, that each person's tastes and expectations can be gratified. Children are especially delighted here, for they can walk around a real steam locomotive (out front), and into a full-size model of the Apollo Command Module; they can play with a Wang computer, see themselves on closed-circuit TV, and push buttons to start dozens of various exhibits and demonstrations ranging from fluid dynamics to the human circulatory system. Stand next to a full-size model of the Lunar Lander, and right beside it a replica of America's first rocket launcher built by Dr. Robert Goddard of Auburn, Mass., in 1926; or walk around a tremendous replica of *Tyrannosaurus rex.* See how baseball pitchers throw a curveball, and hear them explain their techniques; watch the counter on the World Population Meter click off another birth every second or so; or learn how to make herbal textile dyes from common plants and weeds. Special exhibits include the Hayden Planetarium with celestial shows on various themes daily. The Museum of Science costs $4.50 for adults, $3 for children 5 to 16, students with IDs, and senior citizens. Friday night rates are $2.25 for adults, $1.50 for all others. There is an extra charge for the planetarium (buy your ticket early for this, when you enter the museum). Hours September through April are Tuesday through Thursday from 9 a.m. to 4 p.m., on Friday to 10 p.m., Saturday to 5 p.m., Sunday from 10 a.m. to 5 p.m. Hours May 1 through Labor Day are Monday through Thursday from 9 a.m. to 5 p.m., on Friday to 10 p.m., Saturday to 5 p.m., and Sunday from 10 a.m. to 5 p.m. During school months, open on Monday holidays and vacation weeks. Parking in the museum's own garage costs several dollars. Besides the rooftop Skyline Cafeteria, there's a Friendly's sandwich shop within the museum.

To get to the Museum of Science, take the Green Line toward Lechmere to the Science Park Station.

THE KENNEDY LIBRARY: Boston's latest attraction is the museum at the John F. Kennedy Library which opened on October 22, 1979. This dramatic chalk-white building, designed by the distinguished architect I. M. Pei, sits on a peninsula on Dorchester Bay. The landscaping of Cape Cod roses, sea grass, and weeping willows serves to harmonize the building with the peninsula, harbor islands, and sea. The library features an exhibition which is introduced by a 30-minute movie on the late president's life. Then, arranged in chronological order, it displays JFK memorabilia from his christening dress, *PT-109* uniform and flight jacket worn when president, to papers relating to the Bay of Pigs and Cuban Missile Crisis. There is a recreation of the Oval Office as it was when he was president, and his desk and rocking chair. The library is open daily from 9 a.m. to 5 p.m. except Thanksgiving, Christmas, and New Year's Days. Admission is $1.50 but free for those 15 and under. Take the MBTA Red Line (Ashmont) to Columbia Station. For additional information write to the John F. Kennedy Library at Columbia Point, Dorchester, MA 02125 (tel. 617/929-4523).

OTHER MUSEUMS: Boston has a score of other museums, each very rich in its presentations, and the best of these are outlined below:

Boston Children's Museum

Children's Museum (tel. 617/426-8855) is located at Museum Wharf, 300 Congress St., on Boston's waterfront near the Boston Tea Party ship and a short walk from Faneuil Hall Marketplace. The museum, an old brick-and-timber warehouse, is a kid's delight, for this is where the whole idea of "hands-on" exhibits began. Kids can clamber through City Slice, a three-story cross-section of a house and street; assemble spinning tops in a real factory; celebrate Japanese festivals in Japanese Home; and challenge the computer to a game of tic-tac-toe. On Giant's Desktop everything is twelve times normal size. On Friday evenings and during Boston school vacations and holidays the museum presents the best in local entertainment for children—jugglers, musicians, magicians, and mime. From July 1 to Labor Day the museum is open daily from 10 a.m. to 5 p.m., Friday till 9 p.m. During the rest of the year the museum is open Tuesday to Sunday from 10 a.m. to 5 p.m., Friday till 9 p.m., closed Monday except Boston school vacations and holidays. Closed Thanksgiving, Christmas, and New Year's. Admission is $4 for adults, $3 for children 2 to 15 and senior citizens. Free admission to all on Friday from 6 to 9 p.m. By public transportation take the Red Line to South Station.

Black Heritage Trail
You can take a Black Heritage Trail walking tour. Pick up a free walking-tour folder at the National Park Service Visitor Center, 15 State St.

NEW ENGLAND AQUARIUM: It seems fitting that a sea-conscious city such as Boston should have a major aquarium, and it has exactly that in the New England Aquarium (tel. 742-8870), on Central Wharf off Atlantic Avenue and two blocks from Faneuil Hall Market in the newly redeveloped waterfront area (look for the twin Harbor Towers apartment buildings, or take the Blue Line to Aquarium Station). Pride of the aquarium is the largest glass-enclosed saltwater tank in the world, and this and other exhibit tanks are stocked with over 2000 species of marine life, from electric eels to sharks. In the ship *Discovery* moored next door, dolphin shows are put on daily for aquarium visitors (call for current show times), and there is a "talking" harbor seal in the outdoor pool on the plaza. The variety of fishes is truly astounding, and the shapes, colors, and forms which evolution and adaptation have produced in these creatures really give one a sense of the richness of the marine environment. The mechanical shark seen in *Jaws* may be squeaking through the waters off Martha's Vineyard, but the real sharks are on view here. The price of admission includes all exhibits, including the dolphin shows, plus daily films, multimedia presentations, and audio tours on aquatic subjects; it's $5 for adults, $3 for children 5 though 15. For senior citizens, servicemen, and college students with IDs, it's $4. On Friday from 4:30 to 9 p.m., the charge is $3 for everyone. Hours are Monday through Thursday from 9 a.m. to 6 p.m., on Friday to 9 p.m., on weekends to 7 p.m., but these may change a bit from season to season.

ARNOLD ARBORETUM: Ever since this 265-acre park was given to the city by James Arnold in 1880, Bostonians have been going here to enjoy the peacefulness of the park and the more than 6000 flowers, plants, and shrubs from various parts of the world which make up the Arboretum's "living collection." Spring is a fine time to catch the first blossoms like the lilacs, early summer brings the rhododendrons, and all through the warm months the scents here will bring back any nose dulled by the city air.

The Arnold Arboretum is maintained jointly by Boston's parks department and Harvard, which uses it as an open-air classroom in botany. It's open to all and sundry from sunrise to sunset every day, free of charge. You can get there easily by taking the Orange Line to Forest Hills, or the Green Line to

Arborway (the Orange Line's probably faster). For 24-hour information, call 524-1717.

THE CHRISTIAN SCIENCE CHURCH CENTER: In 1866 a devout New England woman experienced quick recovery from a severe accident, attributing her cure to a glimpse of God's healing power as taught and lived by Jesus. Thereafter Mary Baker Eddy devoted the remainder of her long life (1821–1910) to better understanding, practicing, and teaching Christian healing; to founding the Church of Christ, Scientist; and establishing the church's periodicals, including the renowned international daily newspaper, the *Christian Science Monitor.*

Today the Christian Science religion has branch churches in some 57 countries, with headquarters in Boston, site of the denomination's Mother Church, built in 1894. Next to the church stands the Christian Science Publishing Society, home of the *Monitor* and other Christian Science publications. Two new church office buildings and the Sunday School complete the Church Center. The whole complex, near Symphony Hall at the intersection of Huntington and Massachusetts Avenues (MBTA: Auditorium), is a new Boston landmark since it was given an architectural unity several years ago. Trees and benches, a magnificent long reflecting pool, and stretches of smooth brick roadway leading to interesting vistas make the area well worth a walk around, and it's right between two other landmarks, Symphony Hall and the Prudential Center. Tours are arranged for free, or you can visit the various buildings on your own: the Mother Church is open Monday through Saturday from 10 a.m. to 4:15 p.m., on Sunday from noon to 4:15 p.m. The Publishing Society building is open Monday through Friday from 8 a.m. to 4 p.m., on Saturday and holidays from 9 a.m. to 4 p.m., on Sunday from noon to 4:45 p.m.; and tours are given weekdays at 9:30 a.m., 11 a.m., and 1:30 and 3 p.m. (tour takes 45 minutes). You can inspect the bold architecture of the Sunday School building from noon to 3 p.m. on Sunday, but tours on other days are at 10:30 a.m. and 1:45 p.m. only. During the winter (November to April) the hours are slightly shortened. For exact times and tours call 262-2300.

The main points of interest are the plaza and reflecting pool, the exterior of the Mother Church and its grand extension where services are held, and the Publishing Society's Mapparium and elegant Reading Room. You can take a tour which lasts 15 to 25 minutes through the Mother Church, or just take the elevator up to see the auditorium. This huge chamber is the main inner space of the church, which is built on the plan of a Byzantine church with its great dome and two semidomes.

The star attraction at the Publishing Society building is the Mapparium, a room-size globe of the world, made of stained glass and viewed from the inside; you walk in and find yourself at the center of the earth, so to speak, with all the countries and continents spread around you. As interesting as this strange map itself are the acoustics of the room, for being inside a glass ball does strange things to sound. On the other side of the Mapparium is a reception room, a place of comfortable armchairs and sofas, dark wood paneling, marble doorways, and great gentility. The church's newest addition is a multimedia Bible Exhibit, located in the Colonnade Building, displaying rare Bibles and a giant Plexiglas map. This is open Monday through Saturday from 10 a.m. to 5 p.m. and Sunday from noon to 5 p.m. (closed Tuesday).

6. Shopping

Like New York, Washington, and other great American cities, Boston has its special places to buy things, whether you're in the market for the mundane or the exotic. Bremner Wafers and brie, cut-price Levi's, live lobsters, and objets d'art are all readily available. The most exciting way to shop is to plunk some mad money in your pocket and set off to roam the stores. Here are some of the prime locales for getting rid of that money.

DEPARTMENT STORES: The two Boston giants are **Jordan Marsh Company** and **Filene's,** located cheek-by-jowl in the downtown pedestrian shopping district on Washington Street (Red Line or Orange Line to Washington) called Downtown Crossing. Jordan's is a large department store with a vast assortment of items for sale, everything from baubles to bar stools. "Jordan's Great Basement Store" is admittedly great in terms of size, but it is outdone in popularity by neighboring Filene's Basement, which has become a New England legend. Stories circulate about women changing clothes right between the dress racks to try things on, of the crowds one must fight, of the "automatic reduction" policy which dictates that if an item is not sold in a certain amount of time, it is simply given away just to get rid of it. Well, the basement has become a bit more refined now that it's famous, and the prices in many cases are similar to those in any of the big new suburban discount stores. As for the automatic reductions, they're still in operation, but few items reach the date when they're given away, and if they do it's usually because they're too torn or ugly or useless to be bought, and even so they're given away to charity (like Goodwill Industries, for example) as a tax write-off, and not to you. But the basement is still busy, often crowded, and it's because people know that there's a *good chance* they'll run into something that suits them at a very good price. Don't "go to Filene's Basement to buy a pair of shoes," but rather go dig around in the shoe bins and see what there is in your size, and at a good price—you may find something which it makes good sense to buy. And look through the other clothes departments, accessory counters, and various sections—a $400 outfit with a marked-down $40 price tag could very well be waiting there for you.

Surplus merchandise from famous stores such as Lou Lattimer's in Houston and Saks in New York comes frequently to Filene's Basement, with such classy labels as I. Magnins and Saint Laurent. Don't be disappointed if you don't find anything. Come back in a few days, for the stock moves incredibly fast and new shipments arrive daily.

FANEUIL HALL MARKETPLACE: The **Faneuil Hall Marketplace** is a whole complex of buildings including Faneuil Hall and **Quincy Market,** flanked by the **North and South Markets** on either side.

Quincy Market is the centerpiece of this imaginative and fantastically successful redevelopment venture by the Rouse company with the guidance of Cambridge architect Benjamin Thompson. For years the area was a rundown waterfront slum, with only the 19th-century-style butchers' shops and provisioners to provide life. The early plan was to have the buildings razed to the ground and replaced with a modern shopping center, but architect Thompson changed the thinking to conservation, and the result is a beauty. Behind Faneuil Hall, the market is busy with crowds of customers from sunrise to sundown every day of the week. A granite block pavement is spread between Faneuil Hall and the market's pillared classic Greek facade, and inside, the long main hall stretches for a city block on two floors. Downstairs the shops sell food, from a carry-out snack to a full picnic-style meal, to a pound of camembert for the kitchen at home. On a recent stroll through Quincy Market I noted the following items for sale (partial list): a dozen kinds of bagels right out of the oven on the premises, an infinite array of deli sandwiches, southern fried chicken, shish kebab, subgum chow mein, Baby Watson cheesecake, German blutwurst, French brie, Châteauneuf-du-Pape, live lobsters, mixed nuts, cold cuts (domestic and imported), rumpsteak, fresh doughnuts, and, at the clam bar, a half-dozen cherrystone clams opened and ready to eat. The wings of the market are of glass, and shelter restaurants, drinking places, and singles hangouts patronized by the good-looking and well-to-do from the business, financial, and government offices nearby. In the basement are various shops selling fish, meat, health foods, imported delicacies. On the second floor, the emphasis is on crafts and exotic imports—rugs from Persia, jewelry from India, baskets from China and Mexico. There's a fine flower shop in a very handsome all-glass building in front, on the granite pavement, and benches set out under the trees between the market and the adjoining buildings.

About the best purchase you can make here at Faneuil Hall Marketplace is tickets to the theater, concerts, ballet, shows, etc. **Bostix,** in a kiosk right next to Faneuil Hall itself, sells half-price seats for today's performances, and this is the only place in the city where you can buy them. Plan your nightlife while you're here, rather than coming all the way back. Cash only for same-day, half-price seats—that's the policy.

Street buskers and musicians are always on hand to entertain in the market promenades, and a genial mounted policeman draws scores of children, all wanting to pat his mount's nose. The whole complex is an all-year, day-and-night carnival you shouldn't miss, open for free. For restaurant details, see the restaurant section, above. To get to Faneuil Hall Marketplace, take the Green or Blue Line to Government Center, or the Blue or Red Line to State Street.

NEWBURY STREET: Boston's famous street of boutiques, galleries, and cafés runs from fashion to funk. It starts at the intersection of Arlington and Newbury, right next to the Ritz-Carlton, and the shoppers' and strollers' delights continue for half a dozen blocks. Shops sell everything from the sublime (and expensive) to the ridiculous (and expensive); galleries can be chic or somewhat traditional. Cafés are good and bad, expensive and cheap, and all possible permutations of those four qualities. Serious shoppers and gallery-goers should pick up two useful brochures, available at information booths (City Hall, Boston Common, Boston Public Library) entitled *The Newbury Street League Map,* which gives a list of most of the shops and some of the cafés along the street, their specialties, addresses, and phone numbers; and *Map of the Newbury Street Art Galleries,* which gives brief descriptions of the 30 galleries on the street, times of operation, special services, etc.

Newbury Street starts at the Ritz, and the shops in the first two blocks are, naturally, the most expensive. Furs, jewelry, art objects, and the like predominate. **Emmanuel Church,** just down from the Ritz in the same block, lends a cool note of English Gothic and ivy to the polished-brass-and-marble of some of the shops. By the way, the church sponsors a variety of musical and theatrical programs—jazz, chamber music, choral recitals, puppet shows—and advertises current offerings on a wooden signboard in the side doorway.

Streets in the Back Bay were laid out in a grid and the cross-streets which run north-south were given names with initial letters running from **A** to **H:** Arlington, Berkeley, Clarendon, Dartmouth, etc., so it's easy to know how far you are from the start of Newbury Street at Arlington Street. The second cross-street, then, is Berkeley, and in the block between Berkeley and Clarendon is still more Gothic church architecture, this time in the form of the **Church of the Covenant** (Presbyterian), a bit plainer than the nearby Emmanuel. Organ recitals are held regularly at the Church of the Covenant, and usually a sign in the glass case will give the time: "Tuesday at 12:15," or whatever's current when you pass by. Two of the most famous stores on Newbury Street are located in this area, **Brooks Brothers** for men's wear, and **Bonwit Teller's** (in the old Boston Museum of Natural History Building) for women's fashions. **F.A.O. Schwarz,** the famous New York toy store, has a branch in Boston, at 40 Newbury and also in the Prudential Center.

7. Nightlife

Forget everything you've ever heard about things being "banned in Boston," for at night in this big city it seems as though anything goes. The opportunities for evening activities are bewildering in their variety, and because of all the students in town, nightlife is very active, available, and—in many cases—not all that expensive. This section will give you some idea of what's going on, with details on a selection of the better things to see and do.

Bostonians have been known to call their city "The Athens of America," —they did this even before the city had a sizable Greek population. The reason, of course, is Boston's lively cultural and artistic life. It could fairly be said that on any given day of the year one could take a pick of a dozen or more lectures, concerts, or dance and theater offerings, and at least a few of these would be free of charge.

The best way to find out what's on tonight is to look in the listings: *Boston ByWeek* (a brochure arts schedule at information booths, hotel desks, and depots), or the tabloid "alternative" weekly newspapers: the *Boston Phoenix* is most easily available. Each one has an arts and entertainment section with reviews and advertisements for the current hot topics, and also a listings portion (classifieds and notices in the back of the arts section) which gives the latest information on the club and coffeehouse scene, poetry readings, and so forth. Look under headings such as "Music," "Lectures," "Theater," "Poetry," and "Lounges." When the university is in session (fall and spring semesters), Harvard publishes its own *Gazette,* available for free from the Harvard University Information Office, Holyoke Center, Harvard Square. The paper includes listings of a great many films, lectures, discussions, gallery shows, plays, and concerts taking place at Harvard, many of which are open to the general public. The other great universities in the area also publish similar calendars, yours for the asking.

NIGHTCLUBS AND SINGLES BARS: The Boston area has over 75 colleges and universities, which give downtown nightlife a particularly lively character; a lot of graduates get to like the town so much they settle down here, and so Boston's crew of "young professionals" is also very large and very conspicuous in the clubs.

The Department of Commerce says that Boston is the most expensive city in the country except for Anchorage, and yet a night on the town won't kill your budget: drinks are mostly $2 to $3; beer or a glass of wine, $1.50 to $2. One of the favorite drinks of the modern "light" imbiber is a white wine spritzer, wine mixed with sparkling mineral water or club soda, and it's relatively inexpensive.

Boston is covered with clubs, from the North End waterfront to Kenmore Square, but if I were asked to choose the top ones, here's what I'd pick:

The **Hub Cap Lounge** (tel. 536-1775) has nothing to do with automobile parts. It's name comes from its location, "capping the Hub" at the top of the lofty Prudential tower in Prudential Center (subway: Green Line to Auditorium or Prudential). The view is panoramic, breathtaking, wonderful. The combo is cool, as are the drinks, as are the patrons. If you don't succeed in meeting someone interesting here, no matter—the view is worth it.

The **Up & Up** (tel. 267-3100) gets its name from its glassed-in elevator which takes you to the top of the Howard Johnson's Motor Lodge at 575 Commonwealth Ave., just past Kenmore Square going west (MBTA: Green Line "Boston College" cars to the Sherborn Street stop). The Motor Lodge is no skyscraper, but still the view of the Charles River, and of the lights and activity in Kenmore Square, are entertaining enough to keep you interested when you've stopped dancing. Live music nightly, and no cover charge.

The music at **Friday's**, 26 Exeter St. (tel. 266-9040), is recorded, but the people are very much alive and sociable. You can have a full meal here, a sandwich, or just a drink in the sumptuous Victorian atmosphere. The routine is to cluster at the small bar under the glass canopy—which will be pretty crowded—and when you inevitably bump into someone interesting, move on to one of the small tables in the dusky interior. Friday's stays open till midnight weeknights, till 1 a.m. on Friday and Saturday.

Boston's all-time success story, the **Faneuil Hall Marketplace** (MBTA: Green Line or Blue Line to Government Center) is a riot of activity morning, afternoon, and evening, with buskers and street musicians outside (in good weather), and a host of clubs and restaurants. For happy hour, you can't beat the crowd which gathers at **The Bay at Lily's** in the Quincy Market Building: beautiful, young, well dressed, smooth, and with some money to burn. Sometimes it's hard to find a place at the bar or at one of the tables, but then again, asking to share a table is the perfect ice-breaker. Happy hour (5 to 7 p.m.) and after is the time when Lily's is most closely packed, with a piano player to provide accompaniment for the social action.

Daisy Buchanan's (tel. 247-8516), 240a Newbury St., at Fairfield (MBTA: Green Line to Copley or Auditorium) is a favorite with the professional sports set and young Newbury Street sophisticates, making for an interesting mixture in the closely packed room. The music is recorded, the action is live. Drinks and light meals.

Lulu's (tel. 338-9572), 3 Appleton St., is just the sort of place one would expect to find authentic New Orleans jazz, but there's also the bonus of real Louisiana cooking as well. Like Basin Street, Appleton Street is on the fringes of the downtown entertainment section: take the MBTA Green Line to Boylston and walk (if you're up to it) five blocks south on Tremont; watch it, for Tremont takes a 90-degree right turn by a cylindrical brick church and then crosses over the Mass Pike, and Appleton Street is a block past this crossing, on the right. Descend to a largish room with a sunken dining area with deep-red flocked wallpaper and a crimson velvet baldachin over the small band platform and dance area. The Lulu White Band holds forth here Friday and Saturday, and the music is the real thing. So's the food: hot filé gumbo, red snapper en papillote (with shrimp, scallops, white wine sauce), or roast loin of pork in black prune sauce. But you don't have to dine, or pay a cover, to enjoy the soulful beat, and drinks are not overpriced. Music is on 7 p.m. to 1 a.m. Tuesday through Thursday; an hour later (till 2 a.m.) Friday and Saturday; and from 1 to 4 p.m. and 7 to 11 p.m. on Sunday. Lulu's is closed Monday.

Discos and Dancing

Top disco honors go to **Jason's** (tel. 262-9000), at 131 Clarendon St. in Back Bay. Jason's is a fairly swanky place—everyone dresses up to come here, and there's even a dress code to keep denim out and let jacket-and-tie in. The people are as good-looking as the clothes they wear, and upward mobility is as prevalent as disco gyration. It's crowded all day, every day from happy hour (5 to 7 p.m.) with free hors d'oeuvres, to 2 a.m. Jason, you may recall, was the dude who went in search of the Golden Fleece with his Argonauts, and as though to recall the legend, Jason's is built in a labyrinth of split-levels around pools, banana trees, hanging plants, tables, and various bars. The dance floor is big. You can drink, you can dance, and you can dine here as well.

Two establishments covered above in the Restaurant section deserve a reminder here. At **Scotch 'n' Sirloin**, on North Washington Street near Haymarket (tel. 723-3677), there's live rock on Wednesday and Sunday and a D.J. at other times for dancing. Cover charge is a moderate $2.50. If you drop in at the **Bay Tower Room** Monday through Saturday evenings after 8 p.m. and before midnight, you can dance to a combo in Boston's poshest watering place for no more than the price of a drink.

OPERA AND SYMPHONY: Although Boston does not have a proper opera house, the indefatigable Sarah Caldwell arranges for her **Opera Company of Boston** to perform in a downtown theater, and she and her company have gained fame nationwide for their ability to overcome all sorts of obstacles and stage memorable performances. Big-city opera companies are undergoing a period of great instability, mostly financial, and so we will not predict that you'll be able to see this-or-that opera in this-or-that hall; rather, call the Opera Company of Boston (tel. 426-5300), 539 Washington St., to see what's up, or watch for the ads in the newspapers. Seats may be expensive, but usually there are cut-price student tickets for sale within two weeks of any performance; get to the office the first day they go on sale, and be prepared to wait in line.

Often the Metropolitan Opera Company comes up from New York for several performances; watch the newspapers for an announcement.

Boston's universities have been known to put on operas, such as the very successful—if amateur—performance of Smetana's *The Bartered Bride* staged at Tufts several years ago with costumes and the basso flown from Czechoslovakia for the occasion. Again, watch for such special one-time events in the newspaper listings.

The **Boston Symphony Orchestra** preserves a reputation for excellence and innovation which it has had for over a century. The formal symphony season runs from September through April, with performances in Symphony Hall (tel. 266-1492). The hall was designed (1900) by McKim, Mead, and White, who carried out one of the earliest known scientific acoustical studies for such a structure, and their careful work has been an outstanding success for over three-quarters of a century.

Symphony tickets are sometimes difficult to get, but the following tips will make the task much easier. First of all, normal ticket sales begin 28 days before any specific concert at the Symphony Hall Box Office, open 10 a.m. to 6 p.m. Monday through Saturday. If you have no luck with these, try to get Rush Seat tickets which go on sale for $4.50, one to a customer, for Friday and Saturday concerts. Ticket sales begin in the Huntington Avenue Lobby of the hall at 10 a.m. on Friday and at 5:30 p.m. on Saturday. Failing that, you can loiter outside the door on the night of the concert and try to buy any "extras" which others have bought in advance, but which they can't use. Otherwise, Wednesday evening Open Rehearsals at 7:30 p.m. are almost as good as concerts. Tickets cost $5, and include an informal discussion of the pieces to be rehearsed (usually that weekend's concert works) which begins at 6:45 p.m. in the Cabot-Cahners Room at Symphony Hall. Tickets for Open Rehearsals are unreserved —sit wherever you like.

The Boston Pops

Many members of the BSO stay on for the **Boston Pops.** At Pops, the music is just that: the most popular and lighter pieces in the symphonic repertoire performed in a café atmosphere. The floor in Symphony Hall is cleared of seats, and café tables and chairs are brought in, the hall is festooned with boughs and garlands of flowers, and champagne and hors d'oeuvres are served at the tables. The program is always a full and varied one, with a major work and lots of "Pops Extras," unlisted numbers thrown in for fun, many of them catchy orchestral arrangements of current hit tunes. Pops season starts when the symphony's season ends and goes through late July. As this is graduation season, many Pops performances are bought up *en bloc* by colleges; call Symphony Hall. An easier way to spend an "Evening at Pops" is by going early to one of the several summer concerts given for free by the Boston Pops in the Hatch Memorial Shell, on the Charles River Esplanade (Red Line to Charles Station). The finale to the Esplanade season is the traditional Fourth of July performance, which always ends with Tchaikovsky's *1812 Overture,* accompanied by a battery of cannons and followed by a mammoth display of fireworks over the river.

Tanglewood

After Pops season, the indefatigable members of the orchestra move out to the Berkshire hills in western Massachusetts for the **Berkshire Music Festival** at Tanglewood in Lenox, Mass. (for administration, tel. 413/637-1600; for tickets, tel. 413/637-1940). Again, these performances are very heavily attended, and it's best to go early to get a good seat (you can sit inside the "Music Shed" or on the lawn outside, depending on how much you want to spend for a ticket); even more important than going early to the concert is to get a room reservation nearby, unless you plan to drive out and back (over three hours one way) the same day.

Other Concerts

Two well-known music schools offer frequent concerts by students, faculty, and visiting groups of performers. The **New England Conservatory of Music,** 290 Huntington Ave. (tel. 262-1120, ext. 257), has frequent concerts, many of them free, in its performance halls which include Jordon Hall. The conservatory is located one block from Symphony Hall, on Huntington Avenue at Gainsborough Street, close to the Boston YMCA and Northeastern University (Green Line's "Arborway" or "Northeastern U" cars to Symphony Station, or to the first stop above ground). A monthly calendar of events is available on request. The other school is the **Berklee College of Music** (tel. 266-7455 for a recorded schedule, or 266-1400 for a human being), which has a Recital Hall at 1140 Boylston St. for small ensembles, and the Berklee Performance Center at 136 Massachusetts Ave. (near the corner of Massachusetts Avenue and Boylston Street) for larger groups. There's also the Berklee Concert Pavilion, an urban amphitheater, for outdoors events. Take the Green Line's "Boston College," "Cleveland Circle," or "Riverside" cars to

Auditorium Station for both places. Both halls are fairly near the Prudential Center.

Few Boston institutions predate the venerable **Handel and Haydn Society** which has been giving choral concerts in Boston since 1815. The society's season runs from September to May, with all performances in Symphony Hall. The society, older even than the Boston Symphony Orchestra, has a closely guarded reputation for high excellence in its performances. For information on its concerts, call the Symphony Hall box office (tel. 266-1492), or the Handel and Haydn Society, 158 Newbury (tel. 266-3605).

Concert Music Cruises

Young Bostonians are crazy for both boats and serious music, and a firm called **Water Music, Inc.,** 12 Arrow St., Cambridge (tel. 876-8742), has put the two together—specifically, the M/V *Fiesta Clipper* and various small classical music groups—to make the "Concert Cruise." Twice, at 6:30 p.m. and 7:30 p.m., the M/V *Fiesta Clipper* leaves for a twilight tour of Boston Harbor and Massachusetts Bay, with its own prominent local musical group on board. Cruises operate Thursday, in summer only, and the musical group is different each week. Tickets are $4.75 per adult, $3.75 per child or senior, for the 1½-hour cruise; add 75¢ if you want preferential seating. Food such as quiches, pâté, salads, and sandwiches can be purchased on board, as can wines, beers, and cocktails. Call for current schedules, musical programs, prices, and boarding information.

Cheap Seats

An outfit called **Bostix** (tel. 723-5181 for a recording) sells all kinds of tickets to all sorts of events in Boston and beyond. Buy a ticket to almost anything in eastern Massachusetts here. You'll pay the regular price plus a small service charge. This is a useful service.

But the real excitement at Bostix is the sale of tickets at half price on the day of performance. Theater, concerts, shows, etc., are put on a "daily list" of half-price offerings, and you must stop by the Bostix kiosk next to Faneuil Hall in Faneuil Hall Marketplace (subway to Government Center, Green Line or Blue Line) to read the list—they won't give you the list over the telephone. For same-day, half-price seats you must pay in cash, no refunds or exchanges; for advance bookings you may pay with a check drawn on a Massachusetts bank. No credit cards are accepted at all.

JAZZ, FOLK, ROCK:
Modern music is all over Boston, but except for a few clubs downtown and a few coffeehouses in Cambridge, performers do a gig here or there and then disappear. The very big names usually play in the **Wang** (formerly Metropolitan) **Center** (tel. 542-3600), 270 Tremont (Green Line to Boylston); in the **Hynes Civic Auditorium** (tel. 262-8000) at the Prudential Center (Green Line to Auditorium); in the **Boston Garden** (tel. 227-3200), below North Station (Green Line to North Station); or in one of the university halls.

The Jazzboat and the Dreamboat

Besides operating a concert music cruise, **Water Music, Inc.** (tel. 876-8742), has come up with weekly cruises featuring jazz musicians ("the Jazzboat") and various other groups from swing bands to a Caribbean steel band ("the Dreamboat"). At this writing, the Dreamboat leaves on Tuesday, the Jazzboat on Wednesday, and the Concert Cruise on Thursday; Jazzboat and Dreamboat sailings are at 7:30 and 9:30 p.m., and cost $7 for one cruise. Call for the latest information, and then get your tickets by mail from Water Music, Inc., 12 Arrow St., Cambridge, MA 02138, or pick them up from one of the outlets they'll tell you about.

THEATER: Boston's taste in theater runs the gamut from previews of Broadway musicals to the most experimental of experimental. The offering is so rich and varied it would be impossible in this small space even to give an idea of the range available: groups will pop up here and there, struggle to survive, and in the meantime put on fine performances, and then fail financially and disperse, having left many theater-goers with a lasting impression. I would stress that people interested in the theater should not limit themselves to the possibilities outlined below, but should take the trouble to seek out the new groups performing in odd places, for they're often at the frontier.

Nevertheless, if you have only a little time to spend in Boston and you'd like to take in a play or a musical, here are some hints:

The **Next Move Theater** (tel. 423-5572), 1 Boylston Pl., is perhaps the city's most interesting and talented theater group. For all its technical excellence, it's a homey sort of place where the actors stand near the door as you enter and as you leave, greeting the audience and exchanging comments on the plays. Boylston Place is a tiny alley off Boylston Street, midway between Tremont and Charles Streets, across from Boston Common. By subway, take the Green Line to Boylston.

The old-line theaters with musicals and plays slated for Broadway are all downtown near the Green Line's Boylston Station: the **Colonial Theater** (tel. 426-9366), 106 Boylston St. right near the station; the **Shubert Theater** (tel. 426-4520), 265 Tremont St., and the **Wilbur Theater** (tel. 423-4008), 246 Tremont, are both two blocks south along Tremont Street from the Boylston Station.

Good drama is the rule at the **Charles Playhouse** (tel. 426-6912), 74 Warrenton St., right down behind the Shubert and Wilbur Theaters and the Bradford Hotel (Green Line to Boylston; Warrenton is parallel to Tremont one block west, but it's only a block long). Comedians perform nightly in the **Comedy Connection,** and the **Charles Cabaret,** in the same building, seems to want to break the record for the longest run of *Shear Madness.*

Besides these, the universities have a great many drama offerings, usually at fairly low prices; and during the summer the city of Boston and other organizations sponsor outdoor performances in City Hall Plaza, other public squares, and along the Charles River Esplanade. (See also the section on Cambridge.)

DANCE: Dance is not quite as prominent in Boston's arts scene as, say, theater or music, but the energetic **Boston Ballet Company** (tel. 542-3945), 553 Tremont St. (Green Line to Copley), is active all year. In winter there is the regular ballet season; in summer the troupe seems to be everywhere, putting on performances in the city's squares and parks, and along the riverbank. Watch for notices and times in the papers.

CINEMA: Movies are a big part of Boston's nighttime entertainment picture, and the hot-topic big releases are always crowded during the first few weeks.

But besides major releases, silent movies, oldtimers, and bestsellers of the recent past are always available. Prices range from $4.50 per seat to free admission.

The local listings will let you know what's on tonight. What you may find of help is directions on how to get to the principal movie theaters. Remember to check out Cambridge movies as well, listed separately in the Cambridge section. Here are the prime movie houses in Boston:

Beacon Hill (tel. 723-8110), 1 Beacon St. at Tremont Street, near King's Chapel and the Parker House Hotel; Green or Red Lines to Park Street, or Green or Blue Lines to Government Center.

Charles (tel. 227-1330), 195a Cambridge St., next to the Holiday Inn near the corner of Cambridge and Blossom Street; Green Line to Government Center, or Red Line to Charles.

Cheri (tel. 536-2870), Dalton Street opposite Hynes Memorial Auditorium in the Prudential Center complex; Green Line's "Boston College," "Cleveland Circle," or "Riverside" cars to Auditorium, turn left out of the station, left again down Boylston, and look right.

Cinema 57 (tel. 482-1222), 200 Stuart St., in the tall Howard Johnson's "57" Hotel in Park Square; Green Line to Boylston Station, then walk along the edge of the Common on Boylston Street to the intersection with Charles Street and turn left—it's right in front of you in the middle distance.

Coolidge Corner (tel. 734-2500), 290 Harvard St., in suburban Brookline, take the Green Line's "Cleveland Circle" car along Beacon Street to the junction with Harvard Street, called Coolidge Corner.

Exeter Street Theatre (tel. 536-7067), 26 Exeter St., near Copley Square; Green Line to Copley, then walk one block southwest toward the Prudential Center, and turn right onto Exeter Street, and the theater's a block down on the right-hand side.

Nickelodeon Cinemas (tel. 247-2160), 666 Commonwealth Ave. near Kenmore Square, is actually slightly off Commonwealth on Cummington Street, behind Boston University's School of Public Communications; but you'll see the cinema's big sign as you walk west along Commonwealth from Kenmore Square.

Paris Cinema (tel. 267-8181), 841 Boylston St., very near Prudential Center; Green Line to Copley, Auditorium, or Prudential.

Pi Alley (tel. 227-6676), 237 Washington St., near Government Center; Orange Line to State, or Green or Blue Lines to Government Center.

The Opera House (tel. 426-5300) has two entrances: 163 Tremont, Green Line to Boylston, and the Tremont entrance is across the street from the subway station, a few doors down; or 539 Washington, Red or Orange Line to Washington, enter two blocks down on the right across from Lafayette Place.

Saxon (tel. 542-4600), 219 Tremont St.; Green Line to Boylston Street, and then a half-block walk south away from the Common on Tremont.

Wang Center (tel. 542-3600), 270 Tremont St., near Stuart Street; this is often booked with concert groups or plays rather than movies; Green Line to Boylston, then south (away from the Common) on Tremont Street right into the honky-tonk for two blocks, and the Wang Center is on the left.

In addition, the **Museum of Fine Arts** has a film series with screenings each Friday evening, often on subjects linked to other events in the museum. Call 267-9300, extension 445 or 446, for details, times, and prices.

Free Movies

Lots of films are shown for free in Boston, or very nearly for free—the college film series at many Boston colleges often charge as little as 25¢ to 50¢

for admission. Newspaper listings may or may not have information about college film series, and indeed the movie to be shown, place of screening, and even date and time may change without notice except for a few mimeographed flyers stuck up here and there on the campus. Still, try calling one of the college switchboards and asking about "the film series." For Harvard, check the *Gazette,* a weekly information sheet about the university available for free in the University Information Office, Holyoke Center, Harvard Square.

More dependable and predictable than the college film series are the films shown fairly regularly by these institutions, all for free:

Boston Public Library (tel. 536-5400), various films shown in the lecture hall and at the library's branches throughout the city. Take the Green Line to Copley.

Institute of Contemporary Art (tel. 266-5151), 955 Boylston St.; various films usually having to do with modern art or artists; see "Galleries" for transportation details.

SPORTS: Especially in summer, Boston is alive with outdoor activities: the Charles River is dotted with sailboats every day the breeze comes up, joggers and bikers huff and puff along the Esplanade, the roar of the Red Sox fans rises from Fenway Park. Every autumn tickets to the Harvard-Yale game are grabbed up like passes into heaven, and while the aristocrats are urging Harvard to fight fiercely, the Boston Bruins and their opponents for the day are probably doing just that with their hockey sticks. Hockey is such a part of Boston's cold-weather life that in winter you may see a lot of kids with schoolbooks in their hands, but you'll see a lot more with hockey sticks. Here's a rundown on the major sports; parking is tough to find and expensive on game nights:

Baseball

The **Red Sox** play at Fenway Park (Green Line's "Riverside" car to Fenway Station, then follow the crowd!), and if you buy your tickets a few days before the game, you can get them at the nearest ticket agency (Ticketron, Bostix, and the like). Call 267-2525 for Red Sox information.

Basketball

The famous **Boston Celtics** play in Boston Garden (Green Line to North Station), a large hall that has nothing to do with Boston's Public Garden. Call 523-6050 for the latest info.

Football

The **New England Patriots,** affectionately called "The Pats" in these "pahts," play at Schaefer Stadium, Route 1 in Foxboro, Mass., some 30 miles southwest of Boston. Several Boston bus companies run special buses to the games; try calling Bonanza (tel. 423-5810) or Peter Pan (tel. 482-6620); for information on Patriots games, call 262-1776.

Hockey

The famed **Boston Bruins** battle it out with all comers at Boston Garden (same as basketball, above), and tickets are often sold out very early. Catch 'em when they take on Montréal, and you've got a spectacle. Call 227-3200 for information.

Horseracing

Suffolk Downs is New England's only thoroughbred track. The track is located in East Boston on McClellan Highway (Route 1) about three miles from Logan International Airport. Take the Callahan Tunnel if you're driving, or take the Blue Line subway to Suffolk Downs Station. Admission is $2.75 for the grandstand, $3.75 for the clubhouse, and $2 for senior citizens. Post time is 1 p.m. every day except Tuesday and Thursday. Call 567-3900.

THE COMBAT ZONE: Police hate it, politicians want to get rid of it, sailors revel in it—the several blocks of Washington Street between West Street and Stuart Street (Green Line to Boylston or Orange Line to Essex) are perhaps the most "un-Boston-like" part of Boston. No grand old traditions here except that of "the oldest profession"; no lofty artistry unless one can call nude dancing art. The Combat Zone, as it is known to all, is Boston's tenderloin: several blocks of prime downtown real estate full of strip shows, "naked college girl revues," porno films, and generally sleazy diversions. Despite its sinister name and gamy appearance, the Combat Zone is not a wildly dangerous place to stroll through, and many of the bars and clubs and movie houses are safe enough to enter if you follow a few simple rules. First, don't go late at night; things are hopping by early evening, and you might as well see this part of the world around 8 or 8:30 p.m. rather than later. It's brightly lit and there are lots of police around. Second, don't go alone; anything's better than being a loner, whether you go with a date, a threesome, or a small group. In most places women are as welcome as men. Third, watch your wallet or purse. And finally, if you want to try out a place, go by gut feeling: some places are fairly attractive and seem safe enough; others look pretty bad, with all sorts of types hanging around. Walk around for a while until you find an acceptable place. And if all this seems terrifying, remember the people who own the Combat Zone places are interested in selling you movie tickets, drinks, and not in ripping you off so you never come back again; and they'd rather not have any trouble that'll bring the police, so they'll usually treat customers pretty well.

Chapter III

ACROSS THE CHARLES

1. Cambridge
2. Lexington
3. Concord

AS PAUL REVERE sped through the countryside along another road, William Dawes made a famous midnight ride which took him from the banks of the Charles through the communities of Cambridge (once called Newtown), Lexington, and Concord. Boston's expansion, like America's, was westward toward the mountains, and these important communities west of the city were large enough to play a significant role in the Revolution.

Today the cities of Cambridge, Lexington, and Concord are linked by Battle Road, a designation given by the National Park Service, which harks back to that historic day when Revere and Dawes rode out, followed by troops of Redcoats. The story of Battle Road and the events of that day in 1775 are clearly told in the exhibits at Minuteman National Historic Park in Lexington and Concord, but before looking at revolutionary history, let's take a look at the home city of Harvard College, which is much older than the Revolution.

1. Cambridge

Cambridge means Harvard to most visitors who come to Boston, and although Harvard is not the only thing in the city of Cambridge (MIT's there too, after all), it is certainly the city's most important institution. Harvard Square, at the intersection of Massachusetts Avenue and John F. Kennedy Street (formerly called Boylston Street), is a crossroads which teems with evidence of a hundred lifestyles, from the stuffily academic to the loosest in drop-outs.

Cambridge has its own collection of hotels, restaurants, and sights to see, examined below. The MBTA's Red Line subway connects Harvard Square to Park Street Station on Boston Common. Service is the fastest, most frequent, and most comfortable in the system and the journey normally takes about 15 minutes from turnstile to turnstile. As of this writing, the Red Line is being extended past Harvard Square. The work is a major project, with streets being torn up and traffic rerouted as the mammoth tunnels and new stations are built. It may be completed by the time you arrive, but you should not be surprised to find a few inconveniences in the square.

At press time there are two "Harvard" subway stops, about 100 yards from one another. "Harvard/Holyoke" is right in Harvard Square. The temporary "Harvard/Brattle" station is in nearby Brattle Square, next to the Harvard Motor House hotel. Use either one.

Those staying in Boston's Back Bay section might find it easier to walk to Massachusetts Avenue and catch a no. 1 bus ("Harvard-Dudley"), which goes past MIT, through Central Square directly to Harvard Square, the last stop.

WHERE TO STAY: Guidelines for Cambridge hotels are similar to those mentioned for Boston. There is no reason why you shouldn't plan to stay in Cambridge during the length of your Boston visit. Remember to consider your means of transportation when you choose a hotel in Cambridge.

Remember also that bed-and-breakfast organizations serving the Boston area serve Cambridge too. See the Boston hotel section for details.

Unrivaled queen of Cambridge hotels, and perhaps the most dramatic hotel in all of Boston, is the Aztec-pyramid **Hyatt Regency Cambridge,** 575 Memorial Dr., Cambridge, MA 02139 (tel. 617/492-1234, or toll free 800/228-9000). True to the dramatic design tradition begun by the first Hyatt hotel in Atlanta, the Hyatt in Cambridge has a central atrium, a grand interior space rising from ground floor to top floor, planted with trees and hanging vines and surrounded with mezzanine walkways to the rooms. Of the several restaurants in the hotel, Johan's on the Terrace is on the mezzanine one flight up from ground level, and diners thus can enjoy the atmosphere of the central atrium, with its greenery and fountains. The Pallysadoe Bar, just off this mezzanine, has a good view of the Charles River.

But the most spectacular feature of the hotel is right at the top. Take one of the crystal-shape glass elevators that slide up the wall of the central atrium to the Spinnaker on the top floor. Open for lunch and dinner, the Spinnaker affords a panoramic view of Boston, Cambridge, and the Charles. Once you're seated on a plush sofa with your table before you and plants all around, take in the view at once, because it will change quickly: the entire dining area is on a revolving disc which moves very slowly so that the perspective is always changing. Now, for all this innovative design and luxury you might expect to pay a good bit, and indeed you do: the cheapest single rooms are $94.07; the cheapest doubles, $120.50 (weekend rates of $75 are offered, based on availability). Prices for the superior, deluxe, and luxury categories are higher yet, rising by about $13 from one category to the next. Children under 18 stay for free; an extra person in a room is $10.

The Hyatt Regency's main dining room is called the Empress (tel. 492-1234), surely Boston and Cambridge's most elegant and expensive Chinese restaurant, with a view of the river from the 14th floor and entrees ranging from fish cooked in a wok for $12 to Peking duck for $28 per person. One might venture to say that even the Chinese empress never had it so good. The Empress is open for dinner only from 6 to 11 p.m., on Sunday for brunch from 11:30 a.m. to 3 p.m. and for dinner from 6 to 10:30 p.m.

The **Howard Johnson's Motor Lodge** in Cambridge, 777 Memorial Dr. (tel. 617/492-7777, or toll free 800/654-2000), is a 14-story, 205-room establishment. Here, which floor your room is on determines its price. Furnishings are clean and modern, and some rooms have small balconies, but otherwise the difference in the rooms is what you can see from them: Boston and the Charles, straight across the Charles, up the Charles River to Harvard (this is the prettiest view, in my opinion), and a city view of Cambridge. Pick your view and your floor (the higher the room, the higher its price) and you can predict accurately what the price will be. City-view rooms on the lower floors are $60.25 single, $66.59 double; on the higher floors and with a river view, the prices are $72.93 single, $83.50 double. The higher price rooms in these groupings have two double beds; lower price rooms have one double. Extra-person charge is $6; children under 18 stay for free, and there are special rates for senior citizens. The hotel is quite comfortable and well run, and has as special offerings a swimming pool (mid-June to Labor Day), a paddle tennis court (year round), all color TVs, free parking, a restaurant and bar, and a pleasant brick-and-dark-wood interior. Note that around the time of any Harvard special events (freshmen registration, Harvard-Yale game, Homecoming, graduation, and the like) rooms here are at a premium and should be reserved well in advance. Car or taxi must be used to get to and from Harvard Square or downtown Boston.

The Howard Johnson's has a fine Japanese steakhouse, called Bisuteki, with moderate prices. Sit at one of the traditional steel griddles, sip a cocktail, sake, or Japanese beer, and watch as the chef deftly cuts and cooks chicken, steak, and shrimp in the twinkling of an eye. An entire meal of shrimp (as an appetizer), soup, salad, rice, vegetables, tea, and ice cream with mandarin orange, will cost only $9 if you have chicken as the main course, $11 to $13 if you have steak. You can't go wrong here.

Without a doubt, the most convenient hotel to Harvard and Harvard Square is the **Harvard Motor House,** 110 Mt. Auburn St., Cambridge, MA 02138 (tel. 617/864-5200). Note that this hostelry is not really a hotel but actually a motel, with only the facilities of a motel: air conditioning, ice machine, vending machines, and free continental breakfast served in the lobby. Parking is free, and a parking place—any parking place—near Harvard Square is a very good thing to have, so this is one of the Harvard Motor House's main advantages. The new, temporary Harvard/Brattle subway station is right next to the motel, and the convenience of the trains to Boston is yet another thing in its favor. Rooms are modern, all have TV, and are rented for $61.31 single, $71.88 double, $79.28 triple; rooms for four cost $86.67; children under 16 stay free. Some rooms have views of Brattle and Harvard Squares.

At 1234 Soldiers' Field Rd., Boston (Brighton), MA 02135 (tel. 617/254-1234), is the local **Ramada Inn,** a good deal more expensive than the nearby Charles River Motel but with more services offered. For $53.91 to $64.48 single, $62.36 to $72.93 double, you get a small swimming pool (open from Memorial Day to Labor Day) and a large restaurant, besides a selection of rooms with views of the river and the steeples and cupolas of Harvard in the middle distance. In fact, room prices are computed on the basis of the view, the front river-view rooms on the higher floors of the building being the most expensive. Children under 18 stay for free; an extra person costs $8; an extra bed, $8. The restaurant is decorated in an appropriate crewing motif, with a full-size scull complete with oars suspended from the ceiling, and pictures of famous crews on the walls. Lunch here is about $3 to $6, with sandwiches for only about $3 to $4; dinner prices are $5 to $12 for most entrees, seafood perhaps a bit more.

The **Charles River Motel,** 1800 Soldiers' Field Rd., Boston (Brighton), MA 02135 (tel. 617/254-0200), is not in Cambridge, strictly speaking, but it offers advantages to visitors to Cambridge who have their own cars. Fairly quiet atmosphere, larger-than-average rooms, and lots of free parking are among the advantages, but the prices are the biggest advantage of all: $42.50 single, $53 double for an air-conditioned room and bath with color TV. The motel has no pool and no restaurant, but there are several restaurants within walking distance. It does have a cocktail lounge. If you're driving, get to the south bank of the Charles River and go west to Soldiers' Field Road, which is in a way the extension of Storrow Drive. Follow signs to Newton, dip down for an underpass, and then a mile or so later look to your left for the pillared southern mansion-style facade of the red-brick motel. You can get to the motel by bus from Central Square in Cambridge: take a no. 64 ("Oak Square") bus. Although the Charles River Motel is several miles from Harvard Square, Soldiers' Field Road allows you to speed to the center of town in only ten minutes. By the way, children under 12 stay for free here.

An older hotel not far from Harvard Square is the **Sheraton Commander,** 16 Garden St., Cambridge, MA 02238 (tel. 617/547-4800, or toll free 800/325-3535). Garden Street runs from Harvard Square past Cambridge Common to Radcliffe, and the Commander is just about equidistant (a ten-minute walk) from either campus. Most of the guest rooms were totally renovated recently, and the decor in the public rooms tends to the high-brow colonial—the "commander" for whom the hotel was named is George Washington; a bronze statue of General Washington stands in the entry garden, to the right of the doors. Rooms cost $79.28 to $102 for one, $89.85 to $112 for two, with suites from $158.55 to $237.83; children under 18 stay for free. Although there is free parking at the hotel, the lot is small, and you may have to leave your keys at the desk so the doorman can jockey the cars around to best advantage.

The **Cambridge Holiday Inn,** 1651 Massachusetts Ave. (tel. 617/491-1000), is a 15-minute walk from Harvard Square along busy Massachusetts Avenue. Not a wildly attractive building, it is functional, even comfortable, with a small swimming pool for the warm months and a homey restaurant off the lobby, and, of course, free parking. If you stay here, you can walk to the subway and be in downtown Boston within 30 minutes from when you close your room door. Single rooms cost $60.50 to $66 and doubles are $66 to $71; kids under 19 stay for free; extra persons and rollaway beds are charged $6 apiece. No view to speak of here.

The best budget buy *for men only* in Cambridge is the **YMCA,** 820 Massachusetts Ave., Cambridge, MA 02139 (tel. 617/876-3860), just out of Central Square (MBTA: Central). The 140 rooms here are basic, but cost only $15.86 single, $30.65 double per night, $53.91 to $60.25 single, $73.99 to $84.56 double per week; almost all are single rooms, with only a few doubles. The building is air-conditioned, and you have use of the pool, gym, and the TV in the public rooms. If you have a car, you will have to park in a commercial lot by the night or have the YMCA help you rent a space for one month ($40). Note that the Y is full most of the time, and reservations are not accepted, so it's best to arrive at the front desk at 1 p.m. for the best chance to get a room that night. Once in, you can stay as long as you want, of course.

WHERE TO DINE: Cambridge, in its woolly way, is even more cosmopolitan than Boston, and this is well demonstrated in its restaurants. Cannelloni to couscous, wonton to weisswürst, Cambridge has it. Some of the best places to have a good, inexpensive lunch or a light supper are Cambridge's coffeehouses, almost all of which serve food as well as coffee, tea, and hot chocolate. And finally, there are the ice cream shops of Harvard Square, worthy of a list unto themselves.

Moderately Priced Restaurants

The **Peacock** (tel. 661-4073) is a short distance out of Harvard Square at 5 Craigie Circle, corner of Craigie and Berkeley Streets, one block southwest of the intersection of Concord Avenue and Craigie Street (follow Garden Street along the south edge of Cambridge Common, bear right on Concord Avenue for about two or three blocks, then left on Craigie—a 13-minute walk from the square). The restaurant is in the basement of an apartment building, and is nicely decorated with pale-yellow walls, white trellises, and yellow tablecloths —not formal enough to be stiff, but elegant enough to provide the right atmosphere for the fine food: a pâté maison ($2.50) to start, then maybe sole Anatole ($8.50) or chicken flambé ($7.25), or if you're hungry, a sirloin steak in béarnaise sauce ($10). Salad is $1 extra, and there are always a half-dozen simple delicious desserts costing $1.50 to $2.50. The Peacock has several advantages over the square's other fine restaurants: it's a short walk, which means that only those really interested in fine food will make the effort—no crowding by expense-account types; its decor is simple, with emphasis on the food and wine; and its location allows prices to be kept at a very reasonable level. We recommend the Peacock highly. It's open Tuesday, Wednesday, and Thursday from 5:30 to 10 p.m., Friday and Saturday to 11 p.m. Reservations are suggested.

So far as I can see, the only problem with **Roka,** 18 Eliot St. (tel. 661-0344), near the gas station on John F. Kennedy Street, is finding a place to sit. The booths and the sushi bar at this small, attractive Japanese restaurant are usually filled, more so at dinner than at lunchtime. Come a bit early, beat the crowds, and treat yourself to classic Japanese sushi and sashimi, or order a set-price meal to be thrifty. You'll spend $12 to $16 per person for dinner with tea, a bit more if you order beer or wine. Lunch is served from 11:30 a.m. to 2:30 p.m. Monday through Saturday; dinner is on every night from 5:30 to 10 p.m. (11 p.m. on Friday and Saturday).

The classic place for Chinese food in Cambridge is the **Joyce Chen Restaurant** (tel. 492-7373), at the intersection of Rindge Avenue and Route 2/16, not far from Fresh Pond. The address is 290 Rindge Ave., and if you're driving, go north on Massachusetts Avenue from Harvard Square for about 1½ miles, then turn left onto Rindge Avenue at a set of lights; follow Rindge Avenue to its end at Route 2/16, and the restaurant is on your left. By bus, catch a no. 83 "Rindge Avenue—Central Square" bus in Central Square, Cambridge, for the 15-minute ride. Buses run about every half hour, more frequently at rush hours.

The restaurant is simple in design and decor, but very attractive. It is on several levels, and the top one has a number of Chinese art objects on display which are worth looking at. The food is just plain delicious. Her famous moo shu pork (shredded pork, eggs, noodles, vegetables, and exotic flavorings; $5) is served in translucent Chinese pancakes—you roll one up like a crêpe. Another special dish is the beef with black mushrooms ($7.50). Sweet-and-sour dishes come in either Cantonese or Mandarin styles, priced in the $6 to $8 range. Peking duck costs $23.75. One of the best things about the cooking here is that each plate is prepared individually, and can be made to suit your taste: normal, hot, very hot, or super-hot; with or without monosodium glutamate. Joyce Chen Restaurant is open every day of the week from noon to 10:15 p.m.; it stays open until 11:15 p.m. on Friday and Saturday evenings.

Matsu-ya has the best Japanese and Korean cuisine in Cambridge, and perhaps in all of Boston. An unpretentious place at 1770 Massachusetts Ave. (tel. 491-5091), about ten blocks north of Harvard Square, Matsu-ya has room for about five dozen diners, and you can sit in booths or at low Japanese-style tables on a raised platform. Decoration is traditional but subdued, depending on simplicity for a harmonious effect; waitresses wear beautifully patterned kimonos. Pleasant as the surroundings are, they are outshone by the food, which has a subtlety of flavor too seldom found in any restaurant, Eastern or Western, and rarely found in Oriental restaurants where MSG and garlic are used lavishly. If you like steak tartare, you'll love yukhae, morsels of choice raw beef flavored with sesame seeds and oil; more familiar dishes, such as pork sukiyaki ($7.50), are prepared right at your table and cooked to your specifications (nothing theatrical about this, no flaming braziers and such, and the food is served exactly when it is *à point*). Cheaper, but equally delicious, is sweet-and-sour beef ($6). Tea, rice, and chopsticks are served automatically. Other drinks and Western eating utensils are available. Wine and beer are served. A filling and very delicious meal for two, with tax and tip included, may come to $16 complete. This is one of the best restaurants in Boston in my opinion: pleasant and restful decor, attentive service, delicate food, and moderate prices. Matsu-ya is open for dinner only Tuesday through Sunday from 5 to 10 p.m., to 11 p.m. on Friday and Saturday.

The würst restaurant in Harvard Square is of course the **Würsthaus** (tel. 491-7110), at 4 Boylston St., right in Harvard Square. Inside, a long bar and several rooms of booths and tables provide a nearly German atmosphere, and prices for the würsts—knackwürst, bratwürst, blutwürst—are moderate, mostly in the $4.50 to $7 range, and that includes sauerkraut, black bread, and butter. World travelers craving the exotic beer of some far-off land will probably find it here, as the Würsthaus tries hard to include on its "beerlist" just about every foreign beer you've ever heard of and dozens you never knew existed; they're priced at $1.80 to $3.90 a bottle. Hearty sandwiches are made here ($1.10 to $4.25). Lunch is served from 11 a.m. to 3 p.m., dinner from 4 to 9 p.m. every day but Sunday, when the dinner menu is offered all day, from 11:30 a.m. on.

Every college freshman reads about Grendel, the dragon which threatens the hero of the ancient English epic *Beowulf,* but anyone in Harvard Square—freshman or not—can frequent **Grendel's Den,** 89 Winthrop St. (tel. 491-1160), a restaurant noted for its reasonable prices and large portions. Grendel's is behind a tiny patch of grass off Boylston Street at Mt. Auburn Street, one block south of Harvard Square toward the Charles River: a huge sign on the roof leads the way. The cellar of the red-brick building is the "den," furnished with a fireplace for cold winter nights, and dark-wood tables. Grendel's is actually two restaurants in one. Besides the basement Den, there is a Grendel's Upstairs, with a glassed-in terrace overlooking busy John F. Kennedy Street. In the Den, the menu is simpler and cheaper: chef's salad, or spinach-and-mushroom soufflé, or perhaps chicken tandoori priced about $3.50 or $4. The Den serves alcohol too. Upstairs, the variety is greater, encompassing omelets, salad plates and salad bar, kebabs, and such exotica as alu chole, a spicy Indian vegetable dish. Prices are a bit higher upstairs too.

The **Club Casablanca** (tel. 876-0999) is chic, attractive, and well regarded in its cuisine. Nominally at 40 Brattle St., it's actually entered from an alley behind the Truc building—look for the Café Algiers, walk down the passage past the café, and you'll come to the Casablanca's entrance. Upstairs are the glassed-in dining rooms—modern, clean, attractive. Brunch is served daily till 4 p.m., lunch till 5 p.m., then the menu changes to café supper till 11 p.m. A good lunch might be one of smoked trout with horseradish, followed by fettucine carbonara with a garden salad, for which you'd pay a total of $10. Cheaper? Order the daily special of soup, main course, and dessert for $5 or $6. You can spend $16 to $18 on a dinner of salmon mousse, veal citron or veal with artichokes, or the fish of the day; but you can also dine for half that if you choose carefully.

What about where the students go? One place is the **Swiss Alps,** 114 Mount Auburn St., (tel. 354-1366), behind the Harvard Motor House hotel. Slip into a booth (or hike up to the roof garden in good weather), order a pitcher of beer, and then peruse the menu. Besides the predictable sandwiches and student necessities such as burgers, you'll find a few Swiss specialties: fondue for two at $11, a raclette casserole made with potatoes, onions, cheese, and white wine ($6.75), or my favorite, the croûte au fromage (cheese and egg casserole; $5.25). The Swiss Alps is open long hours, daily, befitting a student place.

About the best pizza in Harvard Square is at **Regina's Pizza**, 8 Holyoke St. (tel. 864-9279), beside the Holyoke Center building. Regina's is the same outfit famous for its pizza in the North End (Boston's Italian quarter) since the 1930s. A small cheese pizza starts at $3.25, and a large Regina special with everything is $9.75, with a full range in between. Beer and soft drinks are served. Hours? Monday through Saturday from 11 a.m. till 1 a.m., on Sunday from noon till 1 a.m.

For Seafood

Dolphin Seafood, on Massachusetts Avenue between Remington and Trowbridge Streets (tel. 354-9332), near where Massachusetts Avenue intersects Mt. Auburn Street, is only six blocks from the square. Upstairs in a split-level complex of shops, the Dolphin's decor is plain and functional, with the seafood being given all the attention. A big plate of steamers (steamed clams) with butter costs $3.25 as an appetizer. Fried squid is a specialty (the chef is Portuguese), but there are always alternatives such as bluefish and whatever else is fresh that day, each costing $5.25, and coming with potato, salad, rolls, and butter. If you're lobster-happy, order twin lobsters with steamers or mussels, from $9.95 to $12.95, depending on the season. Wine and beer are served at reasonable prices. The Dolphin is good, and thus it's busy—go for an early or late lunch or dinner.

Budget Meals

Many places in Harvard Square serve hamburgers and other sandwiches, but undoubtedly the best value-for-money is to be had at **Elsie's**, 71a Mt. Auburn St. (tel. 864-0461), at the corner of Holyoke and Mt. Auburn Streets, a block from the square. Elsie's is nothing fancy, but the prices, for quantity and quality received, have never been rivaled in Harvard Square: mainstay is the roast beef special, which comes with Bermuda onion and "Elsie's Special Russian Dressing," for $2.15; the turkey deluxe ($2.15); the Elsieburger (a double hamburger; $1.70); and the thick-cut Rumanian pastrami-filled landsman ($2.50) are other features. The "Fresser's Dream" (from the German *fressen,* for an animal to feed) is a gigantic pile of four different meats, each of which could make a sandwich by itself, for $3.75. Pastries, knishes, yogurt cones, and a very good potato salad are other items available. Here's an insider's money-saving tip: Elsie's sells "Meal Tickets" for $10 which give you credit worth $11 on the purchase of food, and if you pay with a Meal Ticket you escape the 5.7% Meals Tax—a double saving! Just hand the waiter a $10 bill and say, "Take it out of a Meal Ticket."

Taking its name from Harvard's famous Yenching Library, the **Yenching Restaurant**, 1326 Massachusetts Ave., at the corner of Massachusetts Avenue and Holyoke Street (tel. 547-1130), has the best Chinese food in the square. Furnishings are simple but bright and tasteful, and the food is authentic and good. If you are not very familiar with Chinese cuisine, be sure to ask the waiter how a certain dish is prepared so as to avoid surprises such as too much garlic or red pepper. Most of the surprises here are very pleasant, however, the greatest being the price of the daily luncheon buffet—only about $4—which attracts a large crowd about 12:15 each afternoon. A hearty bowl of soup is brought to you after you're seated, and when it's finished the buffet line is next. The dinner menu is long but not encyclopedic, offering Szechuan shredded pork, Mandarin sweet-and-sour fish, and a whole Peking duck (order in advance). The average evening meal might come to $10. Service is quick and attentive. The Yenching is open for lunch and dinner every day, but the special luncheon buffet is served Monday through Saturday till 2:30 p.m. only.

Harvard Square has one very unpretentious and inexpensive Mexican restaurant called **La Piñata** (tel. 354-8400), at 16 Eliot St., second floor (Eliot is the short, curved connector between the Mt. Auburn/Brattle Streets intersection and John F. Kennedy Street). La Piñata began in Davis Square, Somerville, and did so well its owners decided to open a branch in Harvard Square, with slightly higher prices to compensate for the higher overhead. Still, prices are very, very reasonable: the popular guacamole plate with lots of tortilla chips costs $2.75, black bean soup is $1.50; tacos, tostadas, and enchiladas are $1.75 each, or a combination plate with all three with rice and refritos (refried beans) is $5.25. Bring your own beer or wine, and the waiter will supply you with glasses and an opener. La Piñata is nothing fancy, with a minimum of decoration—just some Mexican woven pieces tacked up as wall hangings, lots of white paint, and red-and-white check tablecloths.

The half-dozen restaurants in **The Garage,** a sort of mall bounded by Kennedy, Mt. Auburn, and Dunster Streets, are all moderate-to-inexpensive in price. **Souper Salad** is an attractive lunch-or-light-supper place, with interesting spaces in which to sit, an upbeat menu, and prices to suit any appetite or budget. Nearby is **Baby Watson,** noted above all for its desserts. Baby Watson cheesecake is Boston's best known. But for economy and nutrition, nothing beats a Baby Watson stroller—that's a souvlaki-type sandwich made from various ingredients rolled into a soft round of pita bread. Strollers cost $2 to $3, and are made with vegetables, hummus, turkey, roast beef, wheatmeat, tofu, ham, tuna, etc. Pick one, then take it for a stroll through the square.

READER'S RESTAURANT SELECTIONS: "**Formaggio,** in The Garage next to the Coffee Connection, serves gourmet sandwiches as a main order; in the morning and evening espresso and cappuccino are available with 'continental' cuisine. Formaggio's real forte is its cheese counter, with probably the most comprehensive selection in New England.

"Also, the **Pâtisserie Française** on Boylston across from the Galleria is famous for café au lait and featherlight almond croissants. Try the seafood crêpe when it's available. On Sunday mornings, this is the place to be; bring your paper, but be prepared to wait for a table" (Christopher Plummer, Cambridge, Mass.).

Expensive Restaurants

Of the several good restaurants in the top price range in Harvard Square, first place goes to **Harvest,** 44 Brattle St. (tel. 492-1115), for its food, service, location, and ambience. Harvest is hidden away down the tunnel which penetrates the four-story glass building that houses Crate and Barrel on Brattle Street, and its location allows it to have the most pleasant outdoor luncheon area in all Cambridge. Open for lunch and dinner every day from 11:30 a.m. to 2:30 p.m. and 6 to 10 p.m., until 10:30 p.m. on weekends. Closed Sunday at 3 p.m. Harvest offers a good selection of very interesting and meticulously prepared dishes: at lunch, a vegetable mosaïque pâté to start, then poached sole with oysters and caviar, and for dessert a chocolate marquise, for example. For dinner you might find mousseline of three fishes, breast of pheasant with black currants and cassis, and fresh pastry; the extravagant can order lobster and sweetbreads with sorrel. The price-conscious will be able to dine very well for $20 at lunch, for $35 to $40 in the evening.

A perennial favorite of Cambridge diners is **Ferdinand's**, at 121 Mt. Auburn St. (tel. 491-4915), two blocks from the center of the square and only a door down from the post office. Large dining rooms and small ones, plain ones and fancy ones are all part of the same establishment. Service is attentive and smooth, and the menu tends strongly to the French, with concessions to the local passion for seafood. For lunch, entrees range from $5 to $6.50, and include salad and beverage (a glass of wine, or coffee or tea); at dinner many of the familiar classic French dishes are in evidence, such as duck à l'orange ($13), sole meunière ($10), or, for beef lovers, a fine entrecôte ($14). Lunch is served Monday through Friday from 11:30 a.m. to 2:30 p.m., to 3 p.m. on Saturday; dinner is served nightly from 5 to 10 p.m., an hour later on Friday and Saturday. Sunday is brunch day (noon to 3 p.m.), and Sunday dinner is on from noon to 10 p.m.

COFFEEHOUSES: An intellectual center will have its coffeehouses, dedicated to serving that beverage which stimulates thought and aids conversation. Harvard Square has a good selection of coffeehouses, all of which serve light meals, desserts, ice cream, and beverages besides coffee. Each draws a special clientele, and you can spend a very pleasant day or two hopping from one to another of these, testing them out to find the one which suits you best. Here is a rundown of the best places:

It is generally agreed that the finest and most delicious coffee in Harvard Square—and the widest selection—is to be had at the **Coffee Connection**, 36 John F. Kennedy St. (formerly Boylston Street), in the complex called The Garage, at the corner of Kennedy and Mt. Auburn Streets, one block from the MBTA station. Although light meals are served here, such as a breakfast of juice, croissant, and coffee ($3.65), or lunch/supper dishes of quiche, salad, yogurt, and the like, the star of the show is the coffee. Why is it so different here? Because the approach to the brew is similar to that taken with fine wine: green (unroasted) coffees are ordered from the finest bean-growing areas of the world, are carefully stored, roasted on the premises twice a week, ground and brewed to bring out the best qualities in each coffee or blend of coffees, right at your table. The different characteristics of the various brews are described in the menu. Note that some coffees are very strong and hearty, others are smooth and mild—but the flavor in both is delicate, well rounded, and delicious. The cheapest way to have good coffee here is to order the coffee of the day, usually 75¢; other selections go up to and slightly over $1.70. Black and herbal teas are also available. Surroundings here are modern and attractive, light and airy, with a raised sitting area and a nearby counter where coffee beans and teas can be bought in bulk to take home. By the way, there's an entrance to the Garage at the corner of Dunster and Mt. Auburn Streets as well.

Harvard Square's most obvious café is **Au Bon Pain,** 1360 Massachusetts Ave. in the Holyoke Center building next to the Cambridge Savings Bank (tel. 491-1523). In summer the little square in front of the café is filled with tables and chairs; in winter you can see all the tasty croissants, baguette sandwiches, and pastries through the huge plate-glass windows. Buy your breakfast, lunch, or supper at the counter, and then find an unoccupied table. Croissants cost from 65¢ (plain) to $1.60 (ham and cheese). Sandwiches such as roast beef or brie cost about $3.

The **Café La Ruche,** 26 Dunster St. (tel. 497-4313), is a light, attractive, modern place with two tiny sidewalk tables and self-service. Go for croissants and coffee at breakfast, or the specialty—salads—at lunchtime. Tortellini, Niçoise, shrimp, Greek, garden: choose your salad and you'll pay from $2 to $5.50 for it, depending on your hunger.

The **Blue Parrot**, 123 Mt. Auburn St., is a Cambridge institution, having been around for a longer time than most coffeehouses in the square. It's usually filled with a mixed crowd mostly of college or graduate-school age, and its claim to culinary renown comes from its crêpes ($2.25 to $3.75), especially the ones with spinach and ham but also the exotic ratatouille crêpes or fresh mushroom crêpes. On any given day several of the house specials will be offered, including Greek spanikopita (spinach, feta cheese, and the thin filo bread; $5.75) or perhaps North African couscous (steamed cracked wheat topped with chicken, vegetables, and chickpeas; $5.50). The selection is good, and somewhat exotic, and portions are of just the right size to make a satisfying but inexpensive lunch. Wine and beer are served, by the glass or bottle. Coffee seems almost to be forgotten in the myriad of exotic things to eat, but not really: 18 different types are offered, priced from 65¢ to $1.75 a cup.

Another coffeehouse in the square to feature live entertainment is **Passim**, 47 Palmer St. (an alley running between the two buildings of the Harvard Coop). You can stop into Passim for a cup of coffee (varieties priced from 85¢ to $1.75), or for an antipasto plate or a cheese sampler as a light lunch for about $5. Spend some time at the small gallery which displays the work of local artists, or look for a bauble among the glass cases of interesting objets d'art from all over the world which are on sale here. But the big attraction at Passim is undoubtedly the evening performances by folk, blues, and jazz musicians of greater or lesser fame. Passim opens for business at noon, and shows begin somewhere around 7:30 p.m. Call 492-7679 for more information.

The crowd at **Algiers**, 40 Brattle St., in the complex of shops called Truc under the Brattle Theater, is usually lively and unorthodox, bright-eyed and interesting. The two subterranean rooms are often full, and when the weather's nice there's service at a tiny outdoor area along a passage at the side of the theater. Many people come just for coffee and conversation, or to meet new people. Lunches tend to the Arabic, of course: a selection of sandwiches made up with flat Arab bread is offered at $2.50 to $4 apiece, and there are soups, iced drinks, and desserts as well. Coffee costs $1.15 (espresso) to $1.75 (mocha espresso with whipped cream), and is served from 9:30 a.m. to 12:30 a.m. The morning hours make Algiers the place to come for a midmorning cup of coffee and a break to read the newspaper or to plan the day's activities. Enter either by a door and stairway to the left of the Brattle Theater entrance or through the theater entrance itself: from the vestibule of the theater, another stairway descends to the Truc complex, and the Algiers.

It is said that Longfellow, who lived only six blocks away, wrote his famous poem about a Cambridge blacksmith whose shop was on Brattle Street: "Under the spreading chestnut tree/ The village smithy stands/ The smith, a mighty man is he,/ With large and sinewy hands." The spot the smithy occupied is now taken by the **Blacksmith House**, 56 Brattle St., a café and bakery. In summer, the large terrace in front of the house is set with tables; in winter, the coffee lovers have to settle for a nice upstairs room in the house furnished with small wood tables and spindle-back chairs. Coffee costs 60¢ (15¢ for a refill), but the stars of the show are the German- and Austrian-style pastries such as Wiener torte, sacher torte, Mozart torte, Linzer torte, apfel torte, each one $1.90 a slice. Other types of *kuchen*, and also brioche and croissants, are made daily too. The Blacksmith House does as big a business selling cakes and pastries to go as it does selling coffee to stay.

Harvard Square's wooliest of intellectual coffeehouses is the **Café Pamplona**, at 12 Bow St., five short blocks east from the MBTA station along Massachusetts Avenue. Nothing disturbs the current of conversation here, for there's no telephone, no music, no live entertainment. Various kinds of coffee are served, from the inexpensive espresso (90¢) to the mocha, a rich coffee-and-chocolate topped with real whipped cream ($1.85). Most coffees start from a very dark-roast bean, and are therefore quite strong. From 11 a.m. to 3 p.m., gazpacho, toasted sandwiches, and other light lunch items are prepared, and in summer the tiny terrace beside the Pamplona's entrance stairway is furnished with tables, chairs, and umbrellas (the indoor café is in a basement). In winter the atmosphere is that of a group of high-brow troglodytes, and invariably the next table to yours will be occupied by someone writing a poem, or music, or translating some abstruse language. The Pamplona is tiny, and you may have to wait for a seat. It's open from 11 a.m. to midnight or 1 a.m., with a dinner break from 6 to 8 p.m., when it's closed.

ICE CREAM: From a short study of Harvard Square shops, it might appear that the two most valued commodities hereabouts are the Xerox copy and the ice cream cone. Ice cream is almost a cult object in Cambridge, and the virtues of the various shops and their selections of flavors are a frequent topic of debate, and even fierce loyalty. The eating of ice cream is by no means limited to the summer months, and in fact only one or two people thought it unusual that cones should be seen along Massachusetts Avenue during the bitter days of the winter of 1976-1977. Herewith, a guide for the discriminating cone-oisseur:

Once upon a time, a local fellow decided to open an ice cream parlor which served only ice cream made from **cream** and things like vanilla beans, fruits, and other natural ingredients. He set up shop in Somerville, and the lines of passionate devotees soon stretched around the block.

That's the legend behind the legendary Steve Herrell, founder of Steve's Ice Cream. He later sold the business and retired to the mountains for a breather, but then returned to open another shop, **Herrell's**, at 15 Dunster St. (tel. 497-2179), along similar lines. Just around the corner from the Cambridge Savings Bank in Harvard Square, Herrell's is the ultimate of local ice cream shops. It's located in a former bank building, and you can devour your cone or dish in the vault, now walled with mirrors. Flavors change somewhat from day to day, and all cost the same except for Chocolate Pudding, a supercharged chocolate ice cream so rich you won't believe it—this costs slightly more.

As for **Steve's Ice Cream**, at 31 Church St. (tel. 497-1067), it is now famous from coast to coast, still producing top-quality treats, still attracting hordes of faithful devotees. The Harvard Square location has been added to the original shop at 191 Elm St. (Davis Square) in neighboring Somerville. The solution to unhappiness on any hot summer day is a cone from Steve's; winter days too, for that matter.

Dowager of Harvard Square ice cream stores is **Bailey's,** near the beginning of Brattle Street, just west of the Harvard Coop. Flavors are authentic, portions are large, and the standard price is 85¢. Bailey's is Harvard Square's only real candy store as well, serving Bailey's own chocolates for $1.75 a quarter pound; and at the small marble tables under Tiffany lamps at the rear, sandwiches and light luncheon plates are available from midmorning until 11 p.m. every day.

Modern and bright, **Brigham's** is a Boston tradition dating back to 1914. Brigham's is the best place in the square to get an ice cream cone anytime—store hours 7 a.m. to midnight. Besides a standard lunch-counter menu of lunch and dinner offerings, Brigham's has a complete bacon-and-eggs breakfast, orange juice, toast, home fries, and coffee included, for $3.65. Brigham's is located just north of the Harvard Coop on Massachusetts Avenue, right in the center of Harvard Square.

Bailey's and Brigham's have been in the square for a long time. The most recent challenger to come into the field in a large way is **Baskin-Robbins,** 1230 Massachusetts Ave. at the corner of Bow Street and Massachusetts Avenue, several blocks east along Massachusetts Avenue from Harvard Square proper. Thirty-one flavors are sold. They'll make you an ice cream cake, sundaes, shakes, banana splits, freezes, and ice cream sandwiches.

Elsie's Deli, mentioned under restaurants, sells yogurt cones under the brand name "Frogurt" (frozen yogurt) for 70¢, one of the best ice cream bargains in the Square.

WHAT TO SEE AND DO: Harvard Square is the heartbeat of Cambridge, a place where all styles of life commingle in a wild, busy carnival atmosphere. When you arrive at Harvard subway station on your Red Line train from Boston, you'll walk up the station's dingy stairs and out into a funky and fertile world right at the center of America's most staid and most prestigious institution of higher learning.

Harvard

The first college founded in the British colonies, Harvard was established in 1636 by the Great and General Court of Massachusetts Bay, the colonists' assembly. John Harvard, a clergyman, gave his library, his farm, and a sum of money to the fledgling college, a generous gesture which has earned for his name worldwide fame. From that early beginning, Harvard College grew into Harvard University, a huge educational establishment with an endowment of over $1 billion.

The university sponsors tours of its most historic sections during the summer, and during the school year when school is in session (that is, no tours during Christmas recess, spring vacation, etc.) Most of the tours depart from the **Harvard University Information Center,** 1352 Massachusetts Ave., in the Holyoke Center building, the tallest building in the square. During the months when school is in session, tours depart Monday to Friday at 11 a.m. and 3 p.m. from Byerly Hall, across Garden Street from Cambridge Common, in the Radcliffe Yard. Saturday tours leave from the Information Center at 10:30 a.m. Summer hours are 10 and 11:15 a.m., and 2 and 3:15 p.m., Monday through Saturday; on Sunday at 1:30 and 3 p.m., all from the Information Center. The tours last about one hour and are free.

Harvard University Museum

On Oxford Street, this is the largest and most varied of the museums at Harvard. To get there, ask your way to the Science Center and Memorial Hall, then walk between these buildings to get to Oxford Street; walk north on Oxford, and the third building on your right is the University Museum, identified by a sign. Actually, the huge and rambling building houses four museums in one. Here are the high points of each:

Botanical Museum: The world-famous collection of glass flowers is the big attraction here. The incredibly delicate and detailed glass replicas of flowers which grow all over the world were made in the days before color photography allowed a botanist to make teaching aids easily and cheaply with only a camera.

HARVARD SQUARE

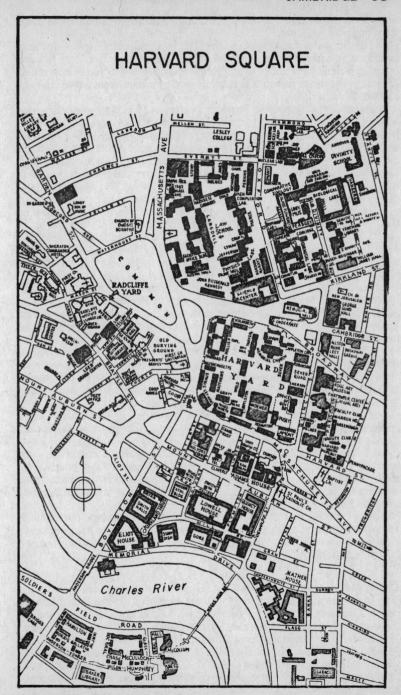

The variety of "flowers" on view and the craftsmanship which it took to make them are truly amazing.

The Botanical Museum has other displays and dioramas on the stair landing as you enter the University Museum. These change from time to time, but may include such things as an exhibit of cross-breeding in the cultivation of corn, or the various narcotic substances used by primitive peoples in different parts of the world.

Museum of Comparative Zoology: Despite its forbidding name, this museum is a favorite with children, for it's loaded with stuffed animals of all kinds, from a tiny hummingbird to a towering giraffe. Sharks, ostriches, hippopotami, and zebras abound, as do the exotic beasts from exotic places: tapirs, lemurs, quetzals, and aardvarks. The museum is a product of that 19th-century rage for natural history which sent Harvard men all over the world in search of specimens to use in scientific teaching. Don't miss the full-size whale skeletons, in the same high-ceiling room that houses the giraffe.

Peabody Museum of Archeology and Ethnology: Many of the exhibits in the Peabody Museum have been given a more modern presentation than is generally found in the University Museum. The collection is very impressive indeed. Statues (authentic as well as fiberglass copies) from the Indian civilizations of Central and South America are accented by wall-size photographs of jungle scenes. Copies of the giant stelae and zoomorphs from Quirigua, Guatemala, and Copan, Honduras, dominate the exhibit, but some of the most interesting artifacts are the items of gold jewelry and household artifacts in the glassed-in wall displays. Notes and extracts from diaries posted here and there give you an idea of what it was like being one of the first archeologists to discover and study these fascinating works of art.

Although the Central American display is the grandest, the Peabody has several other displays—on China, the American Southwest, Polynesia—which are worth seeing. Unless you have lots of time in Cambridge, or plan to return, perhaps the best thing is to pick only one or two exhibits to concentrate on, rather than boggle your mind with all there is to see here.

By the way, the Peabody Museum Shop is one of Cambridge's most fascinating places. Handicrafts and folk art from all over the world are on display and on sale, at reasonable prices. Don't miss a look through, at least.

Geological and Mineralogical Museum: This museum, one of the four scientific museums located in the University Museum building, houses an internationally important collection of rocks, minerals, ores, and meteorites. Exhibits include an unusually comprehensive systematic mineral collection, minerals from New England, gems, and meteorites.

All of the different museums in the University Museum are open from 9 a.m. to 4:30 p.m. Monday through Saturday, and 1 to 4:30 p.m. on Sunday. Admission: adults, $1.50; children (15 and under), 50¢. Monday it's free, except for national holidays.

The Busch-Reisinger Museum

This museum of Central and Northern European art is a little Teutonic gem of a building, complete with clock tower, just north of Memorial Hall, at the corner of Quincy and Kirkland Streets, open from 9 a.m. to 4:45 p.m. Monday through Saturday (closed Sunday, and also Saturday during July and August). The collection is not limited to any one medium, but runs the gamut: you'll be struck by the "Golden Gate," or main doorway, of the cathedral of Freiberg, of which a full-size replica is on display. Tapestries, statuary, paintings, and several cases of exquisite Meissen china and porcelain statuary are always on view, and several rooms are devoted to changing exhibits as well, perhaps on the order of "Early Twentieth-Century German Painters," with works by Kokoschka, Klimt, and others.

The Busch-Reisinger, which looks from the outside as though it could be a church, is in fact equipped with an organ. Recitals are given regularly during the academic year, usually on Saturday afternoons, but call 495-2338 to check on the exact time. The museum is free (donations accepted); there's a small charge for the recitals.

The Fogg Art Museum

This Harvard Museum ranks as one of the more important collections of painting and sculpture in the Boston area. Founded in 1891, the Fogg has long served as the center of art study at Harvard. A new addition is scheduled to open in late 1984. The Fogg is on Quincy Street between Harvard Street and Broadway, east of Harvard Yard, and is open Monday through Friday from 9 a.m. to 5 p.m., on Saturday from 10 a.m. to 5 p.m., on Sunday from 2 to 5 p.m., for $2. As you enter, the mood for your visit to the galleries is set by the interior court, copied in Italian Travertine from an Italian church. Sometimes exhibits are set up in the court; during the academic year concerts are given here (for free) most Sunday afternoons—ask at the desk for a schedule. The museum's permanent collections include Chinese, Japanese, Korean, and Indian works, a fine collection of English silver, classical and Near Eastern art, and 19th- and 20th-century Parisian art. Shows of other works from the museum's holdings are set up periodically, and are very well done. Ask at the desk for a list of current shows, or call 495-2387 to find out what's on.

A Walking Tour

The Cambridge Historical Commission (tel. 498-9040), located in Cambridge City Hall Annex, 57 Inman St., in Central Square, puts out a fine little brochure called the *Old Cambridge Walking Guide,* available for free. The brochure has a map and a description of the 30 sights and buildings to be seen along the walk, each marked with a sign giving the place's name and the number corresponding to that in the brochure. You could walk through the tour route in about an hour if you didn't stop to look closely at any one place, but it's best to plan at least a few hours, for you'll want to visit some of the buildings.

The Longfellow House

Those interested in 19th-century Cambridge will want to see this house at 105 Brattle St., which is now a National Historic Site (open 10 a.m. to 4:30 p.m. daily, 50¢ admission; kids 16 and under, and seniors 62 and over, free). Although the house was built by one Maj. John Vassall in 1759, and was for a time Washington's headquarters (he and Martha celebrated their 17th wedding anniversary here), most of the furnishings are left from the time of Longfellow. Henry Wadsworth Longfellow lived here for 45 years, first as a boarder—the house had by this time been turned into a boarding house—and then as its master. Soon after he and Fanny Appleton were married, Fanny's father bought the house for the young married couple. From 1837, when Longfellow moved in as a boarder, until his death in 1882, this was his home. Virtually all of his belongings and furnishings are still here, as he left them when he died, for the house was occupied by his descendants until 1950. It's an elegant and beautiful house, and yet still warm and homey, a treat to walk through. The

National Park Service guides who take you through are friendly and very knowledgeable. By the way, restoration on the house is still under way, and won't be completed for some years yet, but it is worth the time to see it nevertheless.

Longfellow House sponsors a concert series in the summer months. Concerts are held every two weeks, on Sunday afternoons, on the lawn, and are free and open to the public. For exact information on dates, times, and programs, call 876-4491.

Theater

Touchstone of theater in Cambridge is Harvard's **Loeb's Drama Center** (tel. 547-8300), 64 Brattle St., corner of Hilliard, home of the American Repertory Theater. This resident professional company performs a variety of works year round in a rotating repertory. For six weeks in the autumn and spring, the ART steps aside as Harvard/Radcliffe undergraduates take the stage. Tickets for the ART productions cost $7 to $18; those for the Harvard/ Radcliffe Dramatic Club presentations are $3.50 to $4.50.

The **Tufts Arena Theater** (tel. 381-3493), on the Tufts University campus in Medford, has lots and lots of plays both winter and summer, for $1 to $6 a ticket. From Harvard Square, take a no. 96 ("Medford Square") bus, and get off at Talbot Avenue; walk up Talbot about a block, and the theater is on the left, behind the chemistry building.

The other outstanding college theater in the area is not really in either Cambridge or Boston. It's the **Spingold Theater** (tel. 894-4343) on the campus of Brandeis University in suburban Waltham. It's best to have a car for this one, as it's a long haul by public transport unless you catch the MBTA Commuter Rail train from North Station in Boston or Porter Square in Cambridge to Roberts Station/Brandeis University. Tickets range from $3.50 to $10.

Cinema

Although Boston has a lively movie nightlife, Cambridge has its own group of theaters, many of which tend to be slightly more "far out" than some of the mass-market houses downtown. If you're staying in Boston but want to go to a cinema in Cambridge, the Red Line to Central (for Central Square) or Harvard (for Harvard Square) will take you within an easy walk of the house you're looking for. Here are Cambridge's major film houses:

Brattle Theater (tel. 876-4226), 40 Brattle St., one longish block from the Harvard subway station; the Brattle specializes in nostalgia and American and foreign classics.

Central (tel. 864-0426), 425 Massachusetts Ave. near Central Square, features a mixed bag for the MIT clientele so near at hand.

Galleria (tel. 661-3737), 57 Boylston St., two blocks from the Harvard subway station down toward the river; the Galleria usually has one of the hotter big films of the season, playing to a packed house until it gives out (the film, not the house).

Harvard Square (tel. 864-4580), 10 Church St., right in the square; the most popular films with the college crowd which have been released in the past few years are repeated at intervals of a few weeks; this is where you go to see it if you missed it two or three years ago, or didn't want to pay the high price when it was a hit; seats are low-priced, especially before 6 p.m. (call for exact times). There are also two other auditoriums for first-run showings.

Off the Wall (tel. 354-5678 for a recording, 547-5255 for a human), 15 Pearl St. near Central Square; a phenomenon in itself, Off the Wall may have anything from a bunch of very short skin flicks to seven exquisite short children's films from Europe. The walls are gallery space for local artists, and there are tables and chairs available here too. From the Central Square subway station, the theater's a bit of a walk toward the river, first on Massachusetts Avenue, then on Pearl Street.

Orson Welles (tel. 868-3600), 1001 Massachusetts Ave.; just about equidistant between Central and Harvard Squares on the main street which joins the squares, the Orson Welles has three movie theaters. It is Cambridge's most renowned film house, with a great variety of types of films, but chosen by devotees of the film medium rather than of the box office; a good number of innovative films are featured.

Free Films: Get hold of a copy of the Harvard *Gazette* (free) from the Harvard University Information Office (tel. 495-1000), Holyoke Center, Harvard Square, just across the street from the subway station in Harvard Square. The *Gazette,* published only when Harvard is in its fall and spring semesters, lists all the university activities, including quite a few films for free or for a very low price.

2. Lexington

Lexington was the home of the first Minutemen to die from British bullets in the Revolutionary War. Although they were not the first Americans to die for their country (victims of the Boston Massacre hold that honor), nor even the first to offer spirited resistance as the Minutemen of Concord did, the eight Lexington Minutemen who fell on Lexington Green served their country well. For without the battle at Lexington, the Concord Minutemen might not have been determined to offer strong resistance to the British force.

Americans in the colonies had always had virtually total control over their own destinies, and so when the government in London tried to levy taxes which the colonists did not approve, the colonists' anger was aroused. To show who was boss, troops were sent from England and quartered in the homes of the colonists, further stirring up their anger. As it looked more and more that a head-on collision might occur, the colonists, led by Samuel Adams and John Hancock, began stockpiling arms and ammunition, especially cannons. Hearing rumors of these stockpiles, General Gage, the British commander in Boston, prepared to send out a body of troops to scour the countryside and destroy the stockpiles so as to nip any armed resistance to London in the bud. But the colonists' spy network found out about the plan, and as the troops mustered late at night in preparation for the expedition, Paul Revere and William Dawes galloped through the darkness to alert the patriots.

The "alarm system" was so efficient that the Lexington Minutemen, led by Capt. John Parker, turned out shortly after Revere arrived at midnight, but there were no British troops in sight. The patriots returned home or retired to the Buckman Tavern near Lexington Green, ready to appear again the minute they heard the sound of the drum.

About daybreak the British column finally arrived in Lexington, and the 100-or-so Minutemen drew themselves up in soldierly order on the Green. Nobody knew what would happen. The Minutemen knew only that a much larger force of some 600 soldiers was coming to search their homes, and although it would have been folly to try to stop them, they could still show that they didn't like it and perhaps worry the British a little; the British soldiers knew only that men with rifles were waiting in a position of defiance to keep

the soldiers from doing their duty. When the forces finally came face to face at Lexington Green, officers on both sides seemed to think it would be just as well if everybody kept calm—everybody had a lot to lose—and not to fire a shot. Captain Parker, perhaps fearing capture of his men, ordered them to disperse peaceably; but this only encouraged the British to try and round them up, and some of the soldiers took after the Minutemen. Somehow the running added a sense of alarm to the situation, and a shot rang out. Whether it was a patriot defending himself and his friends, or a British soldier "out to get the rebels" and excited by the chase, the identity of the man who fired the first shot is still a mystery. But other shots followed, of course, and soon eight Minutemen lay dead, and ten others were wounded.

The "battle" was more like a troop riot, and once the British officers regained control of their troops, they started marching them out of town. The Minutemen took their wounded to Buckman Tavern to treat them. It all took less than a half hour. Word was rushed to Concord, where Minutemen assembled for the later events of the day knowing that they might be the next martyrs.

GETTING THERE: The National Park Service has organized most of the interesting historical sites in Lexington and Concord into **Minuteman National Historical Park,** and those with their own car can pick up the Park Service's *Minute Man* brochure which has a sketch map of Battle Road and most of the sights to see. Coming from Boston in a car, take U.S. 3 to Mass. 2, then a road with two route numbers, 4/225, into the center of Lexington. An alternative route subject to tolls is to take the Mass Pike west to Route 128, exiting at Exit 44, "Bedford Street," for Lexington.

Public transportation to Lexington is good, but note that it is not possible to go directly from Lexington to Concord by public transportation. To Lexington, the easiest way is bus 528, "Hanscom Field-Harvard," which leaves Harvard Square on the 45-minute ride every hour during the day, every half hour during rush periods; no night or Sunday service. An alternative route is a commuter train from North Station to Waltham (every 20 minutes during rush hours, every 1¼ hours during the day, every hour in the evening, every two hours or more on weekends), and then bus 525, "Lexington-Waltham," to your destination—buses run every hour during the day, no evening or Sunday service.

WHERE TO STAY: Although Lexington will most likely be a day trip for you, here is a lodging suggestion in case your itinerary indicates a night in the Minutemen's town.

Whether driving or busing, the **Battle Green Motor Inn** (tel. 617/862-6100) is a convenient place to stay, only a few blocks from Lexington Green at 1720 Massachusetts Ave., Lexington, MA 02173. The 90 units here are modern and comfortable, grouped around a long central court dotted with young trees and potted plants. Rooms have color TV and air conditioning, and you can park your car in a covered lot free of charge. Rates are $42 for a double bed (one or two persons), $48 for two beds. From the inn you can easily walk to the Green and to all the historic sites.

WHERE TO DINE: Lexington has a small selection of restaurants, many good for breakfast or a sandwich. **Brigham's,** about three blocks from the Green on Massachusetts Avenue in the main shopping district, is the local reincarnation of the chain which has stores all over Boston and Cambridge. Ice cream, breakfasts, and sandwiches are their forte; either item will be in the $2 to $3 range. **Baskin-Robbins,** an ice cream and sandwich place, has similar values.

The best value in a full restaurant is, believe it or not, Chinese. It's the **Peking Garden** (tel. 862-1051), 27 Waltham St. (several doors down from the intersection of Massachusetts Avenue and Waltham Street), again right in the main shopping district. The cuisine is Mandarin and Szechuan; the hours are Sunday through Thursday from 11:30 a.m. to 9:30 p.m., Friday and Saturday to 10:30 p.m.; and the special bonus is the Chinese buffet served every Monday, Tuesday, and Wednesday evening from 6 to 9 p.m.—all you can eat for $9.50 (children under 10, $5.50), and the food is delicious and varied. Two or more can order the Special House Dinner at other times ($10.75 per person), and receive a varied and bounteous selection of dishes. Besides the evening buffet, the Peking Garden hosts a luncheon buffet Monday through Friday from 11:30 a.m. to 2:30 p.m.—all you can eat for an astoundingly low $5. Wine, beer, and drinks are served.

Right across the street from the Battle Green Inn is **Bel Canto** (tel. 861-6556), a fine place for lunch or a light supper. One of their deep-dish pizzas ($6 to $8, depending on ingredients) will feed 2½ hungry people—that figures out at $2.40 to $3.20 per person. Calzones, the hearty alternatives to pizza, cost $3.50 to $4 apiece.

For a fancier restaurant with continental cuisine, try **Versailles** (tel. 861-1711), located at 1777 Massachusetts Ave. (the main road through town). You can dine very reasonably at lunchtime if you have their soup of the day and salad for about $3.25. At dinnertime, for a full repast, plan to spend more like $20 to $30 per person. Versailles is only a block or so from Lexington Green, so stroll by and see what's offered today.

Cory's (tel. 861-7549), 18 Waltham St., is only a few steps from the traffic lights on Massachusetts Avenue. Its colonial decor is the setting for lunch service Monday through Friday and dinner every day of the week. Filling sandwich plates at lunchtime range from $4.50 to $6; full dinners can be had for $30 to $40.

A Real Bargain for Lunch

Let's say you have a big family, or a big appetite; it's lunchtime on a weekday (Monday through Friday) during July or August; and you're already straining your travel budget, but you want to eat well. Here's what you do: during the aforementioned period, from 11:30 a.m. to 2:30 p.m., find your way to the **Middlesex Regional Technical Vocational School,** only a few minutes' drive east of the National Historic Park Visitors Center. At the Vocational School, one of the major subjects is cuisine, and they sponsor a public cafeteria which serves the products of the students. Portions are generous and prices are surprisingly low, given the quality of the food. Remember, these young people are out to be professionals, and they put their best efforts into the preparation under the guidance of their teachers. You may never get a better meal for twice the price.

For Breakfast, Etc.

Although you can patronize the **Pewter Pot Family Restaurant,** 1710 Massachusetts Ave. (tel. 862-9761), right next door to the Battle Green Motor Inn, for lunch or dinner, I think of it as the best place in town for breakfast. The hot coffee comes quickly, the standard breakfast fare is offered at very good rates, and the location is convenient. There are a variety of muffins and muffin mixes to take back home too. Should you go here for lunch or dinner, don't expect to spend much. Whole meals based on fish and chips, boneless fried chicken, or any of a dozen other items cost $6 or less. They even have a special children's menu of foods kids prefer, priced very reasonably.

WHAT TO SEE: When you approach Battle Green and come up to the Minuteman statue (erected in 1900), you'll feel the great historic significance of the spot. Battle Green is really where it all began: the ivy-covered monument on the southwest part of the green marks the burial spot of seven of the eight Minutemen killed on the memorable day, April 19, 1775. The boulder which sits incongruously on the soft grass of the Green marks the place where the Minutemen drew up in a double rank to face the British grenadiers.

The Lexington Village Green looked much different then than it does today. The meetinghouse, or town church, was located near where the Minuteman statue stands; as it was mid-April, and the Green was in the center of town traffic, it may have been pretty muddy rather than "green." The best time to visit Lexington's historic sights is, of course, on April 19, when the townfolk reenact the famous confrontation with festivities, musketry drill, and fife-and-drum corps. But any day after April 19, until the end of October, will do instead. Note that most of the happenings and places mentioned below are closed between November 1 and April 18.

First thing to do is go to the **Chamber of Commerce Visitors' Center,** 1875 Massachusetts Ave. (tel. 862-1450), just off the Green near the Minuteman statue and next door to Buckman Tavern. Here, every day between the hours of 9 a.m. and 5 p.m. (10 a.m. and 4 p.m. in winter), you can pick up a sketch map of the town, and brochures and information on the sights. More important, you can inspect the diorama, or scale model, of the Battle Green and the events of April 19, 1775: the Minutemen in their farmers' clothes scattering before the long files of crack troops dressed in brilliant colors. The diorama is well worth seeing (it's free, too); historical accounts and explanations of the battle accompany the display.

Besides the Battle Green, several early buildings figured significantly in the battle, and they are today maintained by the Lexington Historical Society (P.O. Box 514, Lexington, MA 02173). All three are open April 19 to October 31, and each tour costs $1 for adults, 25¢ for children 6 to 16 (children under 6 enter for free); an adult combination ticket good for all three houses is on sale at Buckman Tavern for $2.25.

Of the houses, **Buckman Tavern** (1709) is the most important. Here, in the taproom, many of the Minutemen waited out the time between that first midnight call to muster and the final arrival of the British forces at daybreak. After the battle, the wounded were brought here and laid out on the tables for treatment. The tours are given by young ladies well versed in their subject, which encompasses not only the events of the battle, but ranges much more widely, covering a great number of topics on life in the colonies at the time of the Revolution. They'll tell you about the construction of the tavern, about the people who came there to stay, or to have a drink, or for a reception or tea; what and how they ate and drank, how they cooked, slept, and kept warm in unheated rooms. The tavern has an excellent collection of utensils, tools, and implements from the period, "time- and labor-saving devices" which show a good deal of Yankee ingenuity. The tour is well worth the price of admission. The tavern is open 10 a.m. to 5 p.m. daily except Sunday, when the hours are 1 to 5 p.m.; in high summer, the hours are extended to 8 p.m.

The **Munroe Tavern** (1695) was to the British what Buckman Tavern was to the Colonials: a headquarters and a place to care for the wounded after the battle. Today, it's furnished with antiques and battle mementoes, and is open to the public on the same basis as Buckman Tavern. It's a walk (or a short drive) from Battle Green, southeast along Massachusetts Avenue at no. 1332, about seven blocks; the tavern will be on your right.

The third significant house is the **Hancock-Clarke House** (1698), which was the parsonage of the Rev. Jonas Clarke at the time of the battle, and it was with Clarke that John Hancock and Sam Adams, the two "rabble-rousers" most wanted by the British authorities, hid themselves during the uncertain days before the battle. Clarke's house was the first place Paul Revere headed for when he heard of the British plan to march out into the countryside. Revere actually came to Clarke's house twice to warn Adams and Hancock, on April 15, just after hearing that the British were about to do something, and again on April 18, the night the British troops moved out. Hancock-Clarke House is open at the same times and with the same admission fees as Buckman Tavern. It's located at 35 Hancock St., only about a block north of Battle Green.

Several other sights in Lexington are worth a look. Gravestone-rubbers will want to head for **Ye Olde Burying Ground,** just off Battle Green by the church, on its western side. The oldest stone dates from 1690. Another way to get into the spirit of the day of battle is to visit **Cary Memorial Hall,** several blocks southeast of the Green along Massachusetts Avenue, between the town offices and the police station. Here you can see Sandham's famous painting *The Battle of Lexington,* and also statues of John Hancock and Samuel Adams.

Lexington has a new, ultramodern gallery for historical displays of Americana, the **Museum of Our National Heritage.** Built by the Scottish Rite Masons in 1975, there are four galleries exhibiting photograph collections, documents, artifacts, and works of art and industry. Lectures and films are scheduled frequently as well, and may deal with anything from Ohio Amish quilts to early maps of the New World. Call for current offerings and details. The museum is at 33 Marrett Rd. (tel. 861-6559), near the intersection of Routes 2A and 4/225, a short way from the center of Lexington on the road to Boston. It's open Monday through Saturday from 10 a.m. to 5 p.m., on Sunday from noon to 5:30 p.m. during April through October; in winter they close at 4 p.m. Monday through Saturday (Sunday hours don't change). Admission is free.

3. Concord

Concord today is a busy, important town, less of a Boston suburb than is Lexington. It is a beautiful town filled with tall, old trees, graceful houses and mansions, and a rich history that goes beyond the events of the Revolution. Besides the historical sites encompassed by Minute Man National Historical Park, Concord offers a look at the lives and times of America's great 19th-century writers and philosophers: Emerson, Thoreau, Hawthorne, and Louisa May and Bronson Alcott.

GETTING THERE: Those with their own cars should come via Lexington along Route 2A, following the signs which read "Battle Road." Along this route passed the British troops going out to Concord to search for arms stockpiled illegally by the Colonials. A Visitors' Center has been set up a short distance past the intersection of Route 2A and 128, and this is the place to get a map and brochure of Battle Road.

By public transportation, there's no way to go along Battle Road unless you're in a sightseeing tour bus. But train service between Boston and Concord is quite good.

By Train

On weekdays, 20 trains a day leave Boston's North Station for the 40-minute trip to Concord, and on Saturday there are 12 trains; on Sunday, 8. The trip costs $2 one way for adults, half fare for children under 12 and senior citizens. The train can also be boarded at Porter Square in Cambridge (go north on Massachusetts Avenue from Harvard Square for about a mile, and the station is just past the big Sears Roebuck store, under the iron bridge). Call 227-5070 for the latest detailed schedule information. The train arrives at Concord's Depot, which is about five blocks from the town green.

WHERE TO STAY: What there is to see in Concord can be seen in a day, but the town is very fine, and you may want to spend the night.

The nicest place to stay is the **Hawthorne Inn,** 462 Lexington Rd., Concord, MA 01742 (tel. 617/369-5610), directly across the road from "The Wayside," Nathaniel Hawthorne's house. The location, although a mile or two from the town center, is convenient to Orchard House, the Alcotts' home, as well. Single rooms cost $52.85, doubles are $74, tax and continental breakfast (with home-baked goods and fresh fruit) included. An extra person costs $21.14. The inn has pleasant gardens with a tiny fountain, and rooms decorated with period pieces, antique beds, original works of art, and nice homey touches like hooked rugs. Only five rooms here, so reserve early—it's extremely nice.

Right on the town green in Concord is the **Colonial Inn,** 48 Monument Square, Concord, MA 01742 (tel. 617/369-9200). Although the main building of the inn dates back to 1716, and is therefore a smallish, colonial-size hostelry, several new and modern additions have been unobtrusively added, giving the inn a total of 60 rooms. Most of these are decorated in colonial style, but with recently made furnishings. Only 12 original rooms are available to guests, and these are the ones most in demand. If you call or write ahead for reservations, you might ask for one of these, and the manager will do his best to put you in one, but he cannot guarantee any given room to any given guest. Rooms in the main inn, mostly with bath, cost $47.57 to $68.71 single, $52.85 to $68.71 double; in the new Prescott Wing, where rooms have bath and individually controlled air conditioning, prices are a few dollars higher for some rooms, or $89.85 for a suite with parlor. Housekeeping rooms are also available should you be planning to stay a while, for $84.86 to $105.70. An extra person in a room costs $5. The Colonial Inn's restaurant (see below) has a very good reputation.

WHERE TO DINE: Everybody can find a suitable place to have a meal in Concord, no matter what his or her budget.

Restaurants

For my taste, the nicest place to dine in Concord is at **A Different Drummer,** 86 Thoreau St. (tel. 369-8700), upstairs in the Concord train depot about five blocks from the town green (Monument Square). The decor is modern, Scandinavian inspired, with primary colors matched by plain white, and accents in smooth-finished wood and rough boards. Lunch is always a good value, while dinner is more elegant and moderately expensive. The daily luncheon specials might include a seafood quiche with salad ($5), or even veal piccatta with salad ($6). At dinner, feast on freshly shucked clams or oysters for an appetizer, then have sauteed veal marsala perhaps, or scallops, or a steak. With dessert, coffee, tax, and tip, a four-course meal will be about $20 per person. Add a few dollars for wine. A Different Drummer is open every day in summer for lunch and dinner (11:30 a.m. to 3 p.m. and 5 to 9:30 p.m.), closed Monday. Early fall through late spring, the door is open here on Sunday.

Concord's old reliable dining place is the Colonial Inn's **Merchants' Row Dining Room,** (tel. 369-9200) which, as you can guess from its name, is a favorite with business people who work or visit Concord. Although the inn and its dining room have not been exactly preserved from colonial times, the flavor of that era is here, and the surroundings are comfortable and atractive. All three meals are served: breakfast from 7 to 10 a.m.; lunch on Monday to Saturday from noon to 2:30 p.m.; dinner on Monday to Thursday from 6 to 9 p.m., on Friday and Saturday from 6 to 9:30 p.m., on Sunday from noon to 8:30 p.m. Sandwiches in the Tap Room or in the dining room cost $3 to $4, luncheon platters are in the $5 to $8 range. At dinnertime these prices (and the size of the portions) are increased by about $5.

Sandwiches and Light Meals

Concord has a prosperous business life of its own, and office workers here frequently buy sandwiches to take out. Sandwich shops abound, a good situation for you as a cost-conscious tourist. With a little walking, you can pick up all you need.

Walden Sandwiches, 20 Walden St., makes up a variety of sandwiches fresh when you order. All are priced under $3. The shop has a few little tables for customers, and an air conditioner. From the intersection of Main and Walden Streets, walk along Walden, past Woolworth's, and look down the little passage on your right—there it is.

Across the street at 31 Walden St. is **Le Café,** open for lunch and tea (11:30 a.m. to 4 p.m.) Monday through Saturday; Sunday brunch is from 11 a.m. to 2 p.m. Simple and attractive, the café has white walls hung with works by local artists, some small tables, and a counter at the back from which you take your meal. Quiches (hot or cold), salads, sandwiches, cakes for dessert, coffee, tea, and soft drinks make up the menu. A big slice of ham quiche, salad, and iced tea cost me $4.50.

Right next door is a wine-and-cheese shop which will supply your picnic needs admirably.

For breakfast especially, or for a light meal anytime, there's a **Brigham's** restaurant, at 9 Main St., right near the town green (tel. 369-9885). Fixed-priced breakfasts are featured, plus sandwiches, and also the ice cream for which Brigham's is famous.

WHAT TO SEE: Begin your walk around Concord at the town green, officially called Monument Square, complete with obelisk inscribed "Faithful Unto Death." The little church facing Main Street, **St. Bernard's** (Roman Catholic), is particularly pretty when seen from a short distance down Main Street. Of the other buildings on the Green, the most historically noteworthy is the **Wright Tavern** which, being right on the road in from Boston, was one of the first places the British stopped to search for arms. Several shops and firms' offices are located in the tavern today, and you're welcome to walk in and look around during business hours. The **Concord Chamber of Commerce** (tel. 369-3120) maintains an office in the basement (enter from Main Street), open from 9 a.m. to noon Monday through Friday; free brochures, information, and maps are available. Another office is a few blocks away on Heywood Street (off Route 2A). Also, you can take questions to the front desk of the Colonial Inn.

Minuteman National Historic Park

The park encompasses many of the most important sites having to do with the first Revolutionary War battle at Concord. There's a Visitors Center located in the Buttrick Mansion, north of the center of Concord, on the other side of North Bridge. A large parking lot near North Bridge is often full during the summer, and if you have a good parking spot in town, and a few extra minutes, walk the half mile to the bridge and admire Concord's lovely old houses as you go.

After the events in Lexington, the British officers headed their men quickly off to Concord, afraid—no, certain—that since shots had been fired and men killed, there'd be a great deal more trouble coming. Of course, the Minutemen in Concord knew of the Lexington battle shortly after it happened and long before the British troops arrived at 7 a.m. The Minutemen kept an eye on the British as they entered the town, waiting for whatever was to happen. When a force of Regulars was sent to stand guard over Concord's North Bridge, the Minutemen retreated before them, crossing the bridge and taking up a position on a hilltop nearby, where they awaited reinforcements from nearby towns.

Meanwhile, in Concord a polite and not-too-thorough search was being carried out; some arms were found, in particular a number of gun carriages, which were brought out and burned. The Minutemen saw the smoke, assumed the British were burning the town, and began to advance in revenge. The Regulars retreated across the bridge and began firing at the Minutemen, who fired back and pursued them until they fled. It was here at the North Bridge, then, that the Minutemen fired the "shot heard 'round the world."

Soon afterward, the British troops began the return to Boston, but Minutemen kept up a constant sniper fire on them all the way back to Boston, which enraged the Regulars and goaded them to murder some of the innocent persons they met along the way of their march. The bitterness left on both sides by the events of April 19, 1775, would soon bring war to all the British colonies in North America.

Walk across the placid Concord River on the Old North Bridge (a modern reproduction of the kind of bridge which spanned the river in colonial times), and it is easy to imagine, even to half see, the way things happened on the day of the battle. At the far (western) end of the bridge is Daniel Chester French's famous Minuteman statue, the pediment inscribed with Emerson's famous poem. On the near (east) side of the bridge, take a look also at the plaque on the stone wall commemorating the British soldiers who died in the Revolutionary War.

The Old Manse

After visiting the bridge and the Visitor Center on the far side, turn back toward town. Right next to North Bridge, slightly nearer to the center of town, is the Old Manse, Concord's most famous house. It was built in 1769 by the Rev. William Emerson and was lived in by his descendants for 169 years, except for a three-year period when young Nathaniel Hawthorne and his bride Sophia lived here. Hawthorne's residence here gave him material for several later stories. The house today is filled with the spirit and the mementoes of their short stay, and of those of the Emerson clan. Admission costs $2.50, $1 for ages 11 to 16, 75¢ for children 10 and under, but this includes a guided tour. You can phone 369-3909 for group rates with reservations. The Old Manse is open every day except Tuesday and Wednesday from June 1 to October 31, from 10 a.m. to 4:30 p.m. (on Sunday and holidays from 1 to 4:30 p.m.). Open weekends only, mid-April to June.

Transcendentalist Associations

Concord was the center of a philosophical and social movement which, although small in scope, had important effects on American thought and literature. Emerson, Thoreau, Bronson Alcott, and others were all friends living in Concord during the period from about 1836 to 1860. They were aware of the philosophical upheaval going on in Europe at this time, and were encouraged to break away from the Unitarianism which had been their belief. Although they never published a manifesto detailing their beliefs, their creed at this time was that each man has a part of God within himself, and by being sensitive to the dictates of that part, can do what is good and right. Nature had a large share in this belief as well, for the Transcendentalists thought true harmony in life could only be achieved by communing closely with nature and coming to understand it. This, perhaps, was the basis for Thoreau's period of retreat at Walden Pond.

The Transcendentalists got together and tried out their beliefs by buying a farm and living with nature there (1841-1847). The Brook Farm experiment, although it failed, has been an example down to our own times. (The farm was in West Roxbury, now a posh suburb of Boston.) Hawthorne lived on Brook Farm for a while, and he and his friend Herman Melville were both affected by Transcendentalism.

The best way to learn about the Transcendentalist movement is to read Ralph Waldo Emerson's works. While you're here in Concord, you can also visit his house and those in which other adherents of the movement lived, and also go out to Walden Pond and see the place where Thoreau's famous cabin stood. Here, then, are the sights of Transcendentalist Concord:

On your way back from the Old Manse, by Old North Bridge, take a detour up the hill, east off Monument Street before you reach the town green, to get to **Sleepy Hollow Cemetery.** Author's Ridge, on top of the hill, has the graves of Hawthorne, Thoreau, the Alcotts, and Emerson. Emerson's grave, you'll notice, is marked by a great uncarved boulder, very natural and without religious symbolism.

Starting from the town green, most of the Transcendentalists' homes are east along the Lexington Road (Route 2A); Thoreau sites and memorabilia are, appropriately, off by themselves, in another direction.

The **House of Ralph Waldo Emerson,** 28 Cambridge Turnpike, is at the intersection of Lexington Road and Cambridge Turnpike, a ten-minute walk from the green. The house was a center for meetings of Emerson and his friends, and still has a great number of his furnishings and effects. It's open Thursday through Saturday from 10 a.m. to 4:30 p.m., Sunday from 2 to 4:30 p.m., from mid-April through October; open Wednesday also during July and August. Cost is $2 for adults, $1 for children 6 to 17. Children under 6, free.

Across the street from Emerson's house is the **Concord Antiquarian Museum** (tel. 369-9609), which transports the visitor back in time to the early 17th century, when the town of Concord was founded. The guided tour of the museum covers the 15 period rooms arranged in sequence from the 17th to the mid-19th century and illustrates the response of the craftsmen to the increasing refinement of taste.

Special exhibits include the lantern which hung in the spire of the Old North Church in Boston on the night of Revere's famous ride, Ralph Waldo Emerson's study, Henry David Thoreau's belongings used at Walden Pond, and a collection of early powderhorns including the one worn by the model for Daniel Chester French's Minuteman Statue at the Old North Bridge.

The museum is open year round on weekdays and Saturday from 10 a.m. to 4:30 p.m., and on Sunday from 2 to 4:30 p.m. A guided tour lasts about 45 minutes; phone to arrange a group tour. Admission is $3 for adults, $2 for senior citizens, and $1 for children 15 and under.

Continuing east along the Lexington Road, a short drive will bring you to **Orchard House,** home of the Alcotts during the period from 1858 to 1877. Bronson Alcott, while he started life as an itinerant gizmo salesman, had as his life's passion the reform of traditional education methods. His open and natural approach to education was not appreciated in cosmopolitan centers like Boston, but was perfectly congenial to transcendentalist Concord. Here he was ultimately commissioned as superintendent of schools, and he opened a "School of Philosophy" in a building in his backyard. The house itself is a must for anyone, especially a child, who has read Louisa May Alcott's *Little Women.* It's open early April through October from 10 a.m. to 4:30 p.m. (on Sunday, holidays, and after September 15, from 1 to 4:30 p.m.). Admission (and the requisite tour) costs $2 for adults, $1 for kids.

The **Wayside,** just a few steps east of Orchard House, is actually the house described by Louisa May Alcott in her famous book, although today most of the furnishings are those of Margaret Sidney, who wrote *Five Little Peppers.* Hawthorne also lived here. You can visit the house Thursday through Monday (*not* on Tuesday or Wednesday) in April through October, on a 30-minute guided tour from 10 a.m. to 5:30 p.m. (last tour starts at 5 p.m.). Admission is 75¢ for adults; free for children under 16. Tours are limited to ten persons.

Sights dealing with Thoreau's life are west and south of Concord's town green. The **Thoreau Lyceum** (tel. 369-5912) is a Thoreau "learning center" which includes a library, museum with artifacts dealing with his life, and a replica of Thoreau's Walden cabin. There is also a bookstore carrying old as well as new books by or about Thoreau. It's at 156 Belknap (pronounced bell-nap) St., and is open 10 a.m. to 5 p.m. weekdays, 2 to 5 p.m. Sunday, closed on national holidays (on Monday, January through April), and on April 19; admission is $1 for adults, 50¢ for those 8 to 18.

You can visit **Walden Pond,** where Thoreau had his hut from 1845 to 1847, by driving out Walden Street (Route 126), which leaves the center of Concord from Main Street near the Green. After crossing Route 2, look for signs on the right not far from the intersection; park and walk to the site of his hut, marked by a pile of stones. The path circling the lake provides an interesting and refreshing walk; fires and alcoholic beverages are not permitted at any time. The main parking lot by the public beach costs $2 per carload in summer; the beach itself is free.

In a Canoe on the Concord River

After you've taken the standard walking tour of Concord, see the town again, adventurously, by renting a canoe for a paddle up the Concord River. The **South Bridge Boat House** (tel. 369-9438), west of the center of town at 496-502 Main St. (Route 62), will rent you a canoe for $4.50 per hour, $18 per day on weekdays, or $5.50 per hour, $25 per day on weekends. In two hours or so you should be able to make your way down to Concord North Bridge and back, depending on the strength of your paddling arms. The grand houses and gardens which grace the riverbanks alternate with patches of field and wild shrubbery to make a serene and lovely landscape. The boat house is open from the beginning of April into November until the first snowstorm.

A Visit to a Winery

Not too far from the center of Concord is **Nashoba Valley Winery,** Damonmill Square, Concord, MA 01742 (tel. 617/369-0885), where you can sample not grape wines, but traditional New England fruit wines. Nashoba Valley seeks to revive the practice of making and enjoying dry and semisweet apple wines and those made from pears, peaches, blueberries, and combinations of these fruits which seem particularly suitable. Any Friday, Saturday, or Sunday from 11 a.m. (but before 6 p.m.), clear your palate and head southwest on Route 62 out of Concord, past the South Bridge Boat House mentioned above; continue on Route 62 after crossing Route 2, and look for the winery on the right-hand side of the road.

A Side Trip to Longfellow's Wayside Inn

Thirteen miles along the Sudbury Road (which starts from Main Street in Concord) and U.S. 20 West will bring you to the Wayside Inn (1700), South Sudbury, MA 01776 (tel. 617/443-8846). The inn was made famous by Long-fellow's poems telling *Tales from a Wayside Inn,* and now boasts of being the oldest operating inn in the country. Bought by Henry Ford in the early 1920s, it is now a private, nonprofit operation, and all proceeds from the guest rooms and restaurant are put toward its upkeep and restoration. The inn has ten rooms with bath and air conditioning (but no radio or TV), eight twins and two doubles, which rent for $31.71 single, $37 double, tax included. Rooms one through eight are of modern construction and traditional decor; rooms nine and ten are in the old, original part of the inn, and are very quaint. These two are the most in demand, particularly from April to December. Should you want to stay at the inn, it's wise to make reservations as far in advance as possible, even a month or two, but if you can't make them, call up in any case and see what vacancies they might have.

There was a fire in the inn around 1955 and it was heavily damaged (as you can see in the old kitchen), but restoration work was done well and the rooms are worth seeing even if you don't plan to stay for the night. A short tour of the inn is available for 50¢ per person, for free if you drop in for a meal. Lunch is served from 11:30 a.m. to 3 p.m., dinner from 5:30 to 9 p.m., Sunday dinner from noon to 8 p.m.

Besides the inn itself, you should explore the grounds and surroundings: the beautiful formal garden near the inn, the reconstructed barn across the road, and the **Grist Mill** a short (15-minute) walk away, farther down the road. The Grist Mill, a pretty and romantic stone building, is a replica of the mills which used to dot the New England rivers and streams. It is in a beautiful spot, with a copse of pines nearby, and although it's not 100% authentic (the mill wheel is made of heavy-gauge steel), it is worth a look and a walk around. The flour ground here is used in the Wayside Inn's kitchens, and is for sale at the inn's shop. By the way, the Martha-Mary Chapel, on the road between the inn and the Grist Mill, is a typically New England meetinghouse which Ford had built to be rented out for weddings. The chapel and the Wayside Inn are very popular with wedding parties and honeymooners.

Chapter IV

THE MASSACHUSETTS NORTH SHORE

**1. Salem
2. Marblehead
3. Gloucester, Rockport,
and Cape Ann**

NORTH OF BOSTON are many of the towns which brought great wealth to the Massachusetts Bay area in the 18th and 19th centuries. Ships from these Essex County towns would sail to China and Africa, and return several years later with cargoes so rich that everyone involved in the voyage became wealthy overnight.

The gracious houses and public buildings constructed during this era are still here to be seen, and Salem's museums hold a treasure of mementoes and artifacts from the maritime boom. Marblehead and Rockport are still important as yacht harbors and excursion points, but all three towns now make their living primarily from the land: as "bedroom" communities for Boston, and as vacation stops for Bostonians and those who come from farther away.

1. Salem

Think of Salem, think of witches. Although the fame of Salem's witch trials has spread around the world, the town's place in New England history comes from its maritime industries—shipbuilding, warehousing, chandlery, and trade. In the late 1700s, ships from Salem sailed the world, many dealing in trade from the Orient, especially spices, silks, and other luxury goods. The wealth of the Indies brought great prosperity to the town, enabling its citizens to build and decorate fine mansions and impressive museums.

As for the witches, it has never been proved that there were any in Salem! The witch-hunt took place in only one year (1692), and the score of people executed met that fate because they would *not* admit to being witches—many of the less courageous "admitted" being witches so that they wouldn't be executed. The whole affair reached a point of absurdity at which everyone was calling everyone else a witch, and then it fizzled out. Salem would like to forget it all, no doubt, but the rest of the world enjoys remembering this quaint and bizarre episode.

Salem today is a pretty town, with many of its old houses (dating back to the 1600s) and 19th-century mansions intact and in good repair. Part of the downtown section has been restored and closed to traffic as a fine pedestrian mall, and more restoration work is in progress. The **Peabody Museum,** the **Custom House** (National Maritime Historic Site), and the **Essex Institute** have brilliant displays of Salem's (and America's) maritime history. And painters, writers, and patrons add an active artistic element to this very cultured city, well worth a day-trip or even an overnight stop.

GETTING THERE: Driving, the best way to Salem (and neighboring Marblehead) is to take the Mystic River Bridge (also called Tobin Bridge) and U.S. 1; when it intersects with Route 16, follow 16 toward Revere Beach and Route 1A. Route 1A North becomes Lafayette Street in Salem. (For Marblehead, take Route 129 off 1A in Swampscott, and follow it right into Old Town, Marblehead.)

Note: It's only fair to warn you that street and highway signing on the North Shore seems to be particularly bad. Routes are filled with turns, and signs are confusing or missing—you will probably find yourself lost more than once. Resign yourself to stopping and asking the way, not once but several times.

By Bus

Salem is served by MBTA bus 450, which leaves from the parking garage next to Haymarket subway station; the trip, under good traffic conditions, takes 40 minutes. Buses leave every 15 minutes during rush hours, every hour during the day Monday through Saturday, every 90 minutes on Sunday.

By Train

Commuter trains run from Boston's North Station to Salem, Beverly, and Rockport. The trip to Salem takes about 30 minutes; trains run about every 20 minutes during rush hours, every half hour during the day, every hour at night and on weekends. Call, toll free, 800/392-6099 for schedules.

TOURIST INFORMATION: The **Salem Chamber of Commerce** maintains several information booths around the city. The main one is in the **Old Town Hall,** 32 Derby Square, Salem, MA 01970 (tel. 617/744-0004), open Monday through Friday from 9 a.m. to 5 p.m. (Derby Square is off the Essex Street Mall, about a block from the Peabody Museum.) Another information booth is in the lobby of the show *Voyage of the India Star,* and this one is open Sunday through Tuesday from 10 a.m. to 5 p.m., Wednesday through Saturday to 9 p.m. The *Voyage* show is on Pickering Wharf, the renovated waterfront area you'll surely be visiting. Yet another booth is in Riley Plaza, near the station for commuter trains from Boston, open Monday through Saturday from 9 a.m. to 5 p.m., on Sunday from noon to 5 p.m. The **National Park Service** maintains a Visitor Information Center in the Central Wharf Warehouse on Derby Wharf, in the Salem Maritime National Historic Site. This is open every day from 10 a.m. to 4:30 p.m. Derby Wharf is just east of Pickering Wharf.

WHERE TO STAY: Luckily for travelers wanting to spend a night in Salem, the town has several excellent, moderately priced hotels right in the center of town.

The **Salem Inn,** 7 Summer St., Salem, MA 01970 (tel. 617/741-0680), is on Summer Street near the intersection with Essex Street, only a half block from the Witch House and two blocks from the Peabody Museum. It's a lovely old restored brick mansion with 14 nice-size, beautiful, and comfortable rooms (with continental breakfast) priced at $53 to $64 double, or $69 to $80 for a two-room suite with kitchenette; an extra person pays $7.50 per night. Rooms have queen- or king-size beds, antique fireplaces, and telephones. The price differential for rooms depends on plumbing: all rooms have private bathrooms, but the baths for the less expensive rooms are across the hallway from the room itself.

The **Hawthorne Inn,** "on the Green," 18 Washington Square West, Salem, MA 01970 (tel. 617/744-4080), at the corner of Essex Street and Hawthorne Boulevard, is easy walking distance to all the sights in town. The inn is in fact a good-size hotel, recently beautifully restored with lots of fine wood paneling, brass chandeliers, and new paint. The lobby and public rooms (including the Tavern and the restaurant, called the Main Brace) use these elements to achieve a simple but very elegant decor; it's echoed in the rooms with the use of smaller brass chandeliers and wing-back chairs, but otherwise the rooms are modern and decorated in solid colors to keep them bright and cheerful. Rates are moderate: $50.74 to $68.71 single, $57.08 to $79.28 double, suites for $105.70; $8 for each additional person; children under 12 free in their parents' room. In the Main Brace (open for breakfast, lunch, and dinner Monday through Saturday), luncheon plates cost about $4 to $7; dinner, about $15. The Tavern serves the traditional Sunday brunch until 7 p.m.; in the evening from Wednesday through Saturday, there's live entertainment in the Tavern.

Guest Houses

Other than these, Salem has several guest houses charging somewhat less than the inns, but without the inns' central location. Two of these are located within a block of one another on Lafayette Street, three-quarters of a mile from the center of town; both are converted mansions. The **Fairfield Tourist Home,** 248 Lafayette St., Salem, MA 01970 (tel. 617/744-1471), is the more traditional of the two, providing double rooms without bath for $36. The **Coach House Inn,** 284 Lafayette St. (tel. 617/744-4092), is a bit flashier outside, but the rooms are decorated in 19th-century style. Doubles here range from $42.28 to $79.28, the higher prices being for rooms with baths.

For those who are traveling in a group of four or six, this place is especially ideal, though not to the exclusion of smaller parties. The **Stephen Daniels House,** 1 Daniels St. (tel. 617/744-5709), was built in 1667, with a wing added in 1756. It is owned today by Mrs. Katherine Gill, who has furnished it in antiques of the period and virtually turned it into a time machine which takes you back to the Salem of witch-hunting and sea-captain days. Canopied four-poster beds, walk-in fireplaces hung with pots and kettles, low beamed ceilings, and a delightful little terrace garden make it a real showpiece. Prices for the rooms are $31.71 single, $52.85 double, or $89.85 for four in the two adjoining rooms. All rooms have private baths. Be sure to call or write ahead for reservations.

WHERE TO DINE: Salem has lots of interesting restaurants, large and small. The **Lyceum,** 43 Church St. (near the corner of Church and Washington; tel. 745-7665), manages to be both large and small at once. The building, as its name implies, was once at the center of the city's cultural life, and Alexander Graham Bell, who once lived in Salem, gave the first public demonstration of the telephone in its halls. Today the various halls and chambers are all part of the restaurant, but each has been given a distinctive character, and so the Lyceum seems more a collection of restaurants than one large one. In the main room downstairs (to the left as you enter), food is mostly French and local seafood; the variety of dishes available borders on profusion: a pâté with truffles, onion soup, nine different kinds of salads, a dozen types of omelets, quiche, eight kinds of crêpes, and an all-star list of entrees featuring coquille St. Jacques (scallops baked in white wine sauce), frog legs, and beef Wellington. Dinner here will cost $16 to $20. Sunday brunch (11 a.m. to 4 p.m.) has its own special menu, in addition to this.

In the Pub, the menu consists mostly of sandwiches, with some salad plates with meat, fowl, or fish. The evening menu here is similar to that in the main dining room. In good weather, find your way to the terrace out back in the courtyard looking onto the building named One Salem Green.

The **Beef and Oyster House,** 143 Washington St. (tel. 744-4328), right behind the Old Town Hall information booth, seems to have half a dozen dining areas including a bar, lounge, dining rooms, and sidewalk café overlooking the Old Town Hall. The menu is eclectic, the prices are low, and the management wants your business. The various daily special platters, priced from $3 to $6, are guaranteed to be served in five or ten minutes. The daily luncheon buffet (eat all you want) costs a mere $4.50 per adult, $3 per child. Eat here any day, from 11 a.m. to the wee hour of 1 a.m.

Eight Cuisines in One Place

What if you're undecided as to the sort of food you'd like? All you know is it should be quick, good, and inexpensive. The place for you is **The Galley,** in Pickering Wharf, which is one of those groupings of take-out eateries utilizing a common dining area. You buy your food, served on disposable tableware, from the Bavarian strudel place, or the Greek souvlaki-and-salad place, or the Italian pizza-and-sub shop, the New England–style raw seafood bar, the Chinese fast-food, etc., and then you sit at a table in the common dining area. Prices are about the lowest you'll find.

For Waterfront Dining

The **Chase House,** on Pickering Wharf (tel. 744-0000), offers lunch and dinner every day from 11:30 a.m. to 11 p.m. All the air-conditioned dining rooms share a nautical motif and a view of the waterfront activity; a nice outdoor deck is good for cocktails and light meals. Seafood is the heavy on the Chase's menu, as one might expect. At lunch a filet of fish is $3.50, and I would figure you'd spend $5 to $8 for the full meal. Dinner is fancier, and the oysters, scallops, lobster, and varieties of fish will probably tempt you to spend $15 to $20 per person. Kids and seniors get a price cut on some items.

Special Fare

Should you be in Salem for a while, and if you have a group of friends, you can have a private party, tea, or dinner at the **Stephen Daniels House,** mentioned above under accommodations. Mrs. Gill will cook up a full feast, to be eaten next to a crackling fire (in cold weather) at a long rough-hewn antique table, for about $19.50 per person; you bring your own drinks and wine. The price, if you think it over, is competitive with an evening in a restaurant; the surroundings and personal service at the Daniels House are unique. Call 744-5709 to make arrangements.

Just in case you find yourself, on some hot summer day, dreaming of an ice cream cone, I'll include a mention of **Sweet Scoops,** in the Hawthorne Inn building at the corner of Hawthorne and Essex Streets. It makes its own ice cream in the old-fashioned manner using, of all things, real cream without stabilizers, artificial flavors, texturizers, etc.

Just soup and a sandwich? That's the bill of fare at **Soup du Jour,** 7 Central St., Derby Square (tel. 744-9608). Soups come by the cup, small bowl, or large bowl, and the small bowl of thick, stew-like minestrone I had was very filling. With a sandwich such as the Porky (ham, lettuce, and Swiss cheese melted on a roll), and a soft drink, the bill was $5.75. Quiche, a salad bar, desserts, herbal teas, and cocktails are served. Look to the big old school blackboard for daily special meals at very good prices.

WHAT TO SEE: A number of houses in Salem have been preserved from the 1600s, and are furnished with antiques and open to public view. But before you visit them, go to the **Original Salem Witch Museum,** 19½ Washington Square North (tel. 744-1692), next to Salem Common at the intersection of Brown Street, Hawthorne Boulevard, and Washington Square North. The Witch Museum is not really a museum—there are no artifacts on display—but rather a sound-and-light show relating the history of the infamous witch trials of 1692. It's open seven days a week from 10 a.m. to 5 p.m., to 7 p.m. in July and August; admission is $2.50 for adults, $2.25 for seniors, $1.50 for kids 6 to 14, free for kids 5 and under. Shows every 30 minutes.

17th-Century Houses

Visit one or more of these, as you have the time, to see what life was like in one of the earliest towns in the United States:

Witch House (tel. 744-0180), the former home of Jonathan Corwin, the judge in many of the witch trials, stands at 310½ Essex St., corner of Essex and North Streets, and is open March through November from 10 a.m. to 5 p.m. daily. Adults pay $2; children, 75¢.

Goult-Pickman House (tel. 745-1638) is the oldest house in Salem still standing (built 1638). Life-size mannikins people the house, dressed in costumes of the period, matched to a historical narration. The house is on Charter Street, near the corner of New Liberty Street; open daily year round, 10 a.m. to 6 p.m. in summer, to 5 p.m. in spring and fall, in winter by special arrangement. Admission: adults pay $2; children, $1.50; 6 to 12 years old, $1; under 6, free. (*Note:* If you plan to visit both the Witch Museum and the Goult-Pickman House, you can buy a special reduced-rate ticket to the two sights at either place.)

The House of the Seven Gables, 54 Turner St. (tel. 744-0991), which served as the setting for Hawthorne's novel of the same name, is now one of a group of four houses administered jointly. The four—House of the Seven Gables (1668), Hooper-Hathaway House (1682), Hawthorne's Birthplace (c. 1750), and Retire Becket House (1655)—are open from July 1 through Labor Day from 9:30 a.m. to 6:30 p.m. Guided tours of three of the houses cost $3.50 for adults, $1 for those 6 to 17 years old. During the rest of the year you can visit the House of the Seven Gables from 10 a.m. to 4:30 p.m. daily (except for major holidays). Adults get a $1 discount off-season. Ample free parking.

The Essex Institute

The institute is a historical society dedicated to the preservation, study, and exhibition of historical works and artifacts dealing with Essex County. The collection of artifacts ranges from rare early newspapers to entire houses, restored and furnished with authentic antiques. Just about anyone who comes to Salem finds something of interest here: the historian of American trade and culture uses the library, nautical buffs want to see the relics of the China trade, those interested in architecture and decoration take the tour through one or more of the institute's half-dozen Salem houses which date as far back as 1684. Children are fascinated by the unique collection of dolls, doll furniture, and toys from earlier times. There's a lot more here than one can see on a day-trip to Salem, but an hour spent in one of the institute's 13 buildings, particularly in the main building at 132-134 Essex St. (tel. 744-3390) and the adjoining houses, is a must for any Salem visitor. Here is a list of some of the special collections you can look over: clocks, ceramics, military uniforms and weapons, dolls and toys, glassware, buttons, silver and pewter, lamps and lanterns, sculpture, tools, costumes from earlier centuries, and bits and pieces from the China trade, as well as a very good collection of Massachusetts works of art including paintings and furniture. Several galleries and exhibition rooms have changing shows, so the return visitor should check to see what's new. The Essex Institute is open year round, Tuesday through Saturday from 9 a.m. to 4:30 p.m. in winter (November 1 to May 31), Sunday and holidays, 1 to 5 p.m. The museum portion stays open until 6 p.m. from June 1 to Labor Day, Monday through Saturday. Admission for adults is $2 to the museum, $2 per day to the library, and $1.50 to each of the institute's houses; children from 6 to 16 get in for half price, seniors for a slight discount. A combination ticket, good for all the buildings, can be bought for $6 for adults, $4.50 for seniors, $3 for children; the ticket is good until all the houses have been seen—it doesn't run out in a day. The library and offices are open Monday through Friday from 9 a.m. to 4:30 p.m. (closed weekends and holidays).

Peabody Museum

When a group of Salem sea captains and world travelers formed the East India Marine Society in 1799, their charter included provisions for "a museum in which to house the natural and artificial curiosities" brought back from their worldwide travels. This was the genesis of the Peabody Museum, America's oldest museum in continuous operation.

In 1824 the society and its collections moved to grand new headquarters in East India Marine Hall. Since then, four annexes have been added. The most recent, a bright and modern climate-controlled wing, was opened in 1976 and is used primarily for special temporary exhibitions. The Peabody has a research library and a photograph library of one *million* pictures.

The museum's major collections are in New England maritime history, the practical arts and crafts of the East Asian, Pacific Islands, and Native American peoples, and the natural history of Essex County. Maritime collections include portraits of captains, pictures of ships, scale models, figureheads, old navigation instruments and tools, scrimshaw, prints, and gear from the whaling era, plus porcelain, paintings, furniture, and silver from Salem's China trade. There's even a reproduction of the saloon (main cabin) of America's first ocean-going yacht, *Cleopatra's Barge,* built in 1816 by a member of the East India Marine Society. The Ethnology Department has superb collections of objects from everyday life in primitive Polynesia, Micronesia, and Melanesia. A similar collection from preindustrial Japan is rated the best in the world.

The Peabody charges adults $2 for admission, half price for children 6 to 16, $1.50 for senior citizens and students with an ID card. It's open daily from 10 a.m. to 5 p.m., on Sunday from 1 to 5 p.m., with a free guided tour at 2 p.m., Sunday only. Look for the Peabody on the Essex Street pedestrian mall, corner of Liberty Street.

Salem Maritime National Historic Site

In 1937 the National Park Service took over the Custom House, where Nathaniel Hawthorne once worked, and nearby Derby Wharf, one of the city's busiest trade centers, as a basis for the Maritime Site. First thing to do is to pick up free copies of the National Park Service's materials about the site, which have a sketch map and directory of the buildings as well as short histories of the prominent Derby merchant family and of the adventures of several famous Salem vessels, both merchantmen and privateers. These accounts are very well written, and are just the thing to get you in the mood for a tour of the Custom House and wharf.

The Custom House is open from 8:30 a.m. to 5 p.m. every day. Admission is free.

The National Park Service guides are very well informed, as usual, and will take you on a tour back to the Bonded Warehouse to show you what cargoes were like and how they were handled, measured, and weighed. These tours are scheduled daily from March to November. **Derby House,** built for the shipping magnate Elias Derby by his father, Capt. Richard Derby, in 1762, is shown by a free guided tour. The tours are of high quality, limited to eight people at a time, last about 30 minutes, and cover Derby family and Salem maritime history. The West India Goods Store, right next to Derby House, is again open for business and selling teas, coffee (beans and brew), spices, and other treasures from the East.

Whale-Watch Trips

You can take a boat out of Salem harbor on a harbor tour or whale-watching expedition. **Barnegat Transportation Co.,** Pickering Wharf (tel. 617/745-6070), will take you out aboard the *New England Star,* Tuesday through Sunday, on either of two daily trips. Snacks, soft drinks, beer, and mixed drinks are available on board. The *Island Star* goes on harbor tours.

Pier Transit Co., 66 Dearborn St. (tel. 617/744-6311), operates the *Miss Salem* from Central Wharf on Derby Waterfront on whale watch and harbor tours. You can also pick up the *Miss Salem* from Salem Willows Amusement Park.

For the Children

Something for the children? Follow the signs out of the center of town to **Salem Willows Amusement Park,** northeast of downtown. If you have less time, take the **Salem Trolley,** a recreated oldtime vehicle which makes tours of the town every day between 10 a.m. and 4 p.m. for $3 per adult, $2 per child. Tours leave from Riley Plaza, where the railroad station is; you can buy tickets at Salem Trolley Corp., 57 Wharf St., Pickering Wharf (tel. 744-5463).

The aforementioned Witch Museum is a sure favorite with kids, but the witch industry is more elaborate, as you might guess. There's also the **Witch Dungeon,** 16 Lynde St., near Washington Street (tel. 744-9812), just half a block from the western end of East India Mall. Reenactments of the witch trials, a recreated dungeon, and a replica of Old Salem Village are among the exhibits.

For Jazz, A Special Place

Ask any well-known jazz musician to tell you about the North Shore and you'll hear about **Sandy's Jazz Revival,** 54 Cabot St. in Beverly, (tel. 922-7515), next city to the north of Salem. Sandy's is a Boston-area institution by now, and whenever a famous name is around, the sounds will be coming out of Sandy's. Check the papers for latest talent, or call for information.

2. Marblehead

What Salem was to merchantmen a century ago, Marblehead is to yachts today. Summer and winter her beautiful perfectly sheltered harbor is full of white boats bobbing on the water, or in drydock, or heading out to sea. But it's not only yachtsmen who come to Marblehead. This is without doubt one of the prettiest and best kept towns in the country, and people love to come up from Boston on the weekend just to walk the streets and windowshop, or have a bowl of chowder in one of the several good restaurants. They also come for a look at *The Spirit of '76,* the famous painting made even more famous during the Bicentennial celebrations, which is hung in Abbot Hall, Marblehead's Town Hall. If you plan to go to Salem, make the detour to Marblehead for at least an hour or two, or for a meal or even overnight.

GETTING THERE: The trip by bus between Marblehead and Boston means a transfer at Lynn. The commuter trains between Boston and Salem (see Salem section) stop at Lynn, and buses 441 and 442 run between Marblehead and Lynn's Central Square about every half hour during rush hours, every hour other times, but note that only no. 442 runs in the evenings and on Sunday. The bus trip between Lynn and Marblehead takes about 25 minutes.

WHERE TO STAY: Should you really want to get into the spirit and soul of this beautiful seacoast town, you'll have to spend the night. Possibilities are limited, but very attractive. I suggest that you try to plan your visit for a weekday, and that you call ahead for reservations, especially in July and August.

The most charming of Marblehead's places to stay is the **Pleasant Manor Inn,** 264 Pleasant St. (Route 114), Marblehead, MA 01945 (tel. 617/631-5843). This grand Victorian mansion has been converted into a charming inn with a nice lawn, lots of parking, and a tennis court for guests' use. The high-ceiling rooms are furnished in many cases with four-poster beds and dark-wood trim, and many have beautiful marble fireplaces which, alas, can't be used for insurance reasons. The inn can accommodate about 35 people in 14 rooms, many with private baths recently installed. Although rooms do not have TV or air conditioning, the antique charm and high ceilings make up for the lack of them, along with other extra touches, such as coffee-makers in each room and a hall refrigerator for beverages. Rates are $35.94 single, $42.28 double in a room without private bath, or $40.17 single, $46.51 double in a room with bath; cots for another person cost $7. Off-season, rates go down for guests who plan extended stays. By the way, Dick and Takami Phelan, who keep the inn, will be glad to show you the room where Amelia Earhart slept when she visited Marblehead—it's on the third floor.

There is a recommendable guest house right downtown in Marblehead. It's **The Nautilus**, 68 Front St., Marblehead, MA 01945 (tel. 617/631-1703), run by Mrs. Ethel Dermody. This typically small Marblehead house is in great demand because of its waterfront location, and so it's advisable to call ahead for reservations, particularly on weekends in summer. Until present renovations are completed (by 1984), only four rooms are available. Otherwise, the usual eight rooms are very cozy and homey, and cost $42.28 to $44.39 double per night, $158.55 to $169.12 per week; a cot for an additional person costs $6. Bathrooms are not in the rooms but nearby, and a small fridge is in the hall for guests' use. One or two rooms have sea views, and are in great demand. Parking is a problem downtown, but Mrs. Dermody will recommend places without danger of towing or tickets. The Nautilus is right across the street from the Driftwood Restaurant, which is by the Municipal Parking Lot on the water at the end of State Street.

WHERE TO DINE: Marblehead has a conspicuous lack of very posh, expensive dining places, but a wealth of little bistro-style places with good food and lots of atmosphere. Pay particular attention to the hours of operation, given below for each restaurant, as some of them tend to be unusual.

The Big Place

About the largest and most elaborate of Marblehead's restaurants is **The Landing**, on Clark's Landing, off Front Street, down on the water (tel. 631-1878). Here you'll find an English-style pub, and dining rooms with a view of yacht-filled Marblehead Harbor. Catering to the boating crowd—which includes early morning amateur scallop and lobster hunters—the Landing is open for every meal, every day. If you can't make it for a hearty breakfast, come for a simple lunch of fish and chips ($5.50), or something fancier if you prefer. A good dinner choice is the Fisherman's Platter ($13) of sole, shrimp, clams, and scallops, with salad, vegetable, and potato. For a real chow-down of this sort, with wine, expect to pay $20, more if you choose one of the fancy dishes or a Marblehead lobster.

The Smaller Places

At 15 State St., between the center of Old Town and the waterfront, a sign announces that you have come to the **Sail Loft.** A lot of people who are not interested in buying sails pass right by, not knowing that the Sail Loft (tel. 631-9824) is the most popular restaurant in Marblehead. Local people call it Mattie's, and it's the closest thing to a cozy English pub in town. Without trying to copy those congenial English drinking places, it has captured the atmosphere of conviviality. Downstairs there's a long bar and a number of tiny tables, café curtains, a blackboard menu, and rustic wood touches. Steaks and seafood served in a cheerful, informal atmosphere are the mainstay at Mattie's Topside (upstairs) and dinner may normally run about $12; but there are always daily specials such as seafood Newburg which, with a glass of draft beer, make a fine meal for less than $8. Mattie's Sail Loft bar is open from 10 a.m. to midnight Tuesday through Saturday, closed Sunday, and meals are served from 11:45 a.m. to 2 p.m., and from 5:30 to 10 p.m.

The Driftwood café, 63 Front St., next to the Municipal Parking Lot near the intersection of State and Front Streets on the water, is right out of a storybook about hearty New England fishermen and boatbuilders. Its barn-red clapboard exterior is matched inside with red-and-white checked tablecloths and a long lunch counter. At 5:30 a.m., when it opens, the fishermen troop in for coffee, eggs, and ham, and for talk of the day's weather and prospects for the catch; later in the day they may return for a bowl of chowder or a portion of "fried dough," a Driftwood specialty served with butter and maple syrup. Breakfast at the Driftwood can cost in the range of $2.35 for two eggs; the clam chowder is $1.25 to $1.75; sandwiches are $1.85 to $3; and fish or seafood plates are in the $5 range. The Driftwood's a piece of the real Marblehead. *Note:* Although it opens very early in the morning, it closes for the day around 4 p.m.

Budget-minded readers low on cash but high on hunger should head for the **Sandwich Shop,** 75 Washington St., behind the Old Town Hall. It has an established reputation for serving the best subs in town, small (about $2) or large (about $3, depending on ingredients). Regular sandwiches are also offered, most costing $2; any of these can be eaten with a soft drink right in the shop, or wrapped up for the walk to Fort Sewall and a sea-breeze picnic.

Nancy's Incredible Edibles, 78 Front St., across the street from the town landing, is a fine place for light meals and snacks. Have a thick sandwich or a bowl of meaty chili, then a slice of apple or pecan pie or a scoop of ice cream, and you'll pay about $4. Consume your purchases right at Nancy's, or enjoy the weather (if it's good) across the street by the water. Summer hours are from 7:30 a.m. to midnight daily.

The literary-minded who have a free hour in Marblehead in the evening spend it at the **King's Rook,** a very European-style coffeehouse on State Street not far from the intersection with Washington. Coffee is in the $1 range, depending on the type, of course, and the atmosphere—provided by captain's chairs, small wood-plank tables, low-beam ceiling, tin lamps, and watercolors on the walls—is yours at no extra charge. Many couples find it a romantic place. The front window always has a stack or two of yellowing *New York Times Book Review* magazines in it, and you can shuffle through them, or bring your own copy to add to the pile.

WHAT TO SEE AND DO: Walking around, window shopping, and admiring the buildings and the rugged coast are the best things to do in Marblehead's "Old Town" section. Here are some landmarks to seek out as you go:

Abbot Hall dominates the town from a hilltop, readily visible as you ride into Marblehead—you can hardly miss its brick clock tower. Go to the hall and ask the way to the Selectmen's Room (town council) to find that marvelous patriotic painting, *The Spirit of '76.* While you're there, take a look at the deed by which the Indians transferred ownership of the land to the European newcomers in 1684. Abbot Hall is open year round during business hours; in summer the hours are extended to 7 a.m. to 9 p.m. weekdays, 9 a.m. to 6 p.m. on Saturday, and 11 a.m. to 6 p.m. on Sunday and holidays.

Down the center of Old Town, near the intersection of Washington and Hooper Streets, are two old Marblehead mansions open to the public for a fee. The **Jeremiah Lee Mansion,** owned by the Marblehead Historical Society, was built by a wealthy maritime merchant and furnished with the best things money could buy in 1768—before the Revolution. The style is Georgian, of course, and the furnishings are from all over the world. Admission charge is $2.25 for adults, $1.25 for children 10 to 16, younger children free; it's open for visits from mid-May to mid-October, Monday through Saturday from 9:30 a.m. to 4 p.m.

The **King Hooper Mansion,** more or less across the street from the Lee Mansion, is a smaller house and older, having been built in 1728, with a Georgian extension added in 1745. Now owned by the Marblehead Arts Association, it costs $2.25 for adults, $1.25 for children, to see, and is open from 1 to 4 p.m. every day but Monday.

After a walk in the "downtown" part of Old Town, make your way down to the waterfront and **Crocker Park,** on a hill at the western end of Front Street. Relax on one of the benches and admire the panoramic view of the harbor and the town. Bring a sandwich, or buy one in the Sandwich Shop, and have a picnic here. The view is unforgettable.

From Crocker Park walk east along Front Street, past its little restaurants, boatyards, and houses built on the rocks, to **Fort Sewall.** The fort is an earthwork fortification first built in the 1600s and later "modernized" in the late 1700s to include barracks and half-buried buildings which still remain. The fort is right at the mouth of the harbor, and offers a commanding view of the water and of Marblehead Neck, at the other side of the harbor's mouth, dominated by a light. This is another good picnic place, especially for those with children, who will love playing within the fort with little risk of falling into the water.

When you're ready to leave Fort Sewall, walk back along Front Street, turn right on Franklin, then right again on Orne Street to get to **Fountain Park** and **Old Burial Hill,** where the town's first meetinghouse (church) was built (it's gone now) and where ancient gravestones mark the places of many of Marblehead's earliest inhabitants and Revolutionary War dead. Orne Street east of Fountain Park leads to the beach.

3. Gloucester, Rockport, and Cape Ann

When Bostonians tell you they're taking a trip to the Cape, they mean they're heading south to Cape Cod. But there is another cape that attracts weekend and summer visitors from the metropolis: Cape Ann, just over an hour's drive or train ride north of the city.

Though few out-of-towners are familiar with Cape Ann, many have heard of Gloucester and Rockport, the picturesque seaport towns with a fascinating, almost legendary, history of struggle and communion with the sea. Gloucester and Rockport both lie on Cape Ann, Cape Cod's less dramatic cousin to the north.

If you look closely at the map, you'll notice that Cape Ann is in fact an island connected by bridges to the mainland, as is Cape Cod (since construction of the Cape Cod Canal). The bays, inlets, harbors, and coves of Cape Ann lend a variety to the landscape and shoreline which has long attracted vacationers, especially in the summertime.

GETTING THERE: For a visit to Cape Ann, I'd suggest you tour by private car, using Rockport as your base. The drive up the coast from Salem is of exceptional beauty. Don't worry, though, if you have no car. There's train service to Gloucester and Rockport, and Cape Ann has its own Cape Ann Transportation Authority local buses which run among the towns and villages.

By Car

I'll describe the coastal road, Route 127, from Salem through Beverly, Magnolia, Gloucester, and Rockport. Starting from Marblehead, you must first go to Salem. Leaving from Boston and heading directly for Cape Ann, you'll save time by taking Interstate 93 north to I-95/Route 128. Follow I-95 North/ Route 128 East, and when the highway divides, stay on Route 128 (I-95 will head north, toward Maine). For the coastal drive, follow Route 128 until you see signs for **Manchester.** This town is right on the water, and on the coast road, Route 127. Head for Manchester.

If you stay on Route 128, it will deposit you, quickly, right in downtown Gloucester. Between Gloucester and Rockport are two loop roads. Route 127 takes you to Rockport through the middle of Cape Ann, then loops around the northern and western shores to return to Gloucester. Route 127A, on the other hand, takes you up the eastern shore of the cape before reaching Rockport. If you get lost, don't worry. In a short while, some loop will bring you back to one or the other town.

By Train

Boston's MBTA trains (tel. 227-5070), operated by the Boston and Maine Corporation, leave the downtown North Station 12 times a day (eight a day on weekends) for Manchester, Harbor Station, Gloucester, and Rockport. The ride takes about 1¼ hours to Rockport. Children's, senior's, and family fares can save you money, as can travel during off-peak hours (basically, that's before 4:30 p.m. from Boston, and after 8 a.m. from Rockport, on weekdays; all weekend trains are off-peak).

ALONG THE COAST: Manchester is a tidy little North Shore town peopled by old New England types and many professionals who commute into Boston by train. Should you visit during the summer, you can take advantage of **Singing Beach,** half a mile from the train station (center of town) along Beach Street. If you drive, you'll have to pay a parking fee. If you walk, you swim for free. **White Beach,** off Ocean Street, has the same arrangement and the same facilities: bathhouse and snackbar.

A Country Inn

A mile south of the center of Manchester on Route 127 is the **Old Corner Inn,** 2 Harbor St., Manchester, MA 01944 (tel. 617/526-4996). When you see it by the roadside, you may well agree that this looks "just the way a small country inn should look": a white clapboard house (1865) with a nice porch and yard, interesting detail in the decoration of the public rooms, and nine guest rooms, each one different. The building once served as the summer residence of the Danish consul, but you can now sleep where he did for $41 to $59 double per night. Rooms come with shared or private bath (some with nice old tubs), a TV set if you want one. The inn serves brunches and dinners on weekends.

MAGNOLIA: Three miles northeast of Manchester along Route 127 brings you to Magnolia. Once a humble fishing village, Magnolia is now a lush and wealthy town. Lavish "summer cottages" built by the rich during the 19th century have been insulated, and heating installed, so that they can be used as year-round principal residences. The scenery is wonderful.

The town center is quite pretty, and less than a mile past it lie Rafe's Chasm and Norman's Woe, two natural features you may want to inspect. **Rafe's Chasm,** a dramatic cleft in the shoreline rock, is just opposite the reef of **Norman's Woe,** which figured in Longfellow's poem "The Wreck of the

Hesperus." Should you want to spend some time in this lovely setting, there's a good place to stay the night.

An Inn

The **White House,** 18 Norman Ave., Magnolia MA, 01930 (tel. 617/525-3642), is a fine old Magnolia house with an unobtrusive residential wing attached. In the wing are ten motel-style rooms with complete facilities: private baths, television sets, air conditioning. Guests receive passes for the use of a private beach; Rafe's Chasm, Norman's Woe, and Hammond Castle (see below) are all close by. Right across Route 127 is **Lexington Avenue,** a short and interesting street of shops, ice cream parlors, and small café-restaurants. Rooms at the White House cost $53 double in high season.

Hammond Castle Museum

Just after heading out from Magnolia along Route 127, signs will point to the right, down Hesperus Avenue, to the Hammond Castle Museum 80 Hesperus Ave. (tel. 283-2080). A mansion built on the plan of a European storybook castle complete with turrets, battlements, towers, and a dramatic setting, the castle is now a combination museum, gallery, concert hall, café, and gift shop open daily from 10 a.m. to 4 p.m. (till 9 p.m. on Wednesday in summer). Admission costs $3 for adults, $2 for seniors, $1 for kids 6 to 12.

Among the outstanding sights in the castle is the mammoth organ, with almost 9000 pipes! A new console is being installed as of this writing, and the organ should be performing at its powerful best by the time you arrive.

If you tour the castle during the summer (July and August), note that Wednesday evening is the time for **candlelight tours** of the eerie halls and chambers. Dinner is served in the rooftop café on this night, as well.

GLOUCESTER: After Hammond Castle, it's only three miles to Gloucester along Route 127. Herperus Avenue rejoins the highway and takes you into town through West Gloucester and across the little drawbridge. Just before the drawbridge, however, you may want to stop for some . . .

Tourist Information

Stop at the little shanty on the sea side of the road just before the drawbridge, which is the **municipal information booth.** They furnish maps, brochures, information on special events, and listings of accommodations. Another such booth is in the **Fitz Hugh Lane House** (1849) on Rogers Street in downtown Gloucester. Otherwise, the **Cape Ann Chamber of Commerce,** 128 Main St., Gloucester, MA 01930 (tel. 617/283-1601), will be happy to help you with information for any town on Cape Ann.

Gloucester's History

The Pilgrims founded Plymouth in 1620, and three years later fishermen founded Gloucester (1623). The marvelous natural harbor and the plentiful fishing grounds made that early settlement a fisherman's paradise. Almost four centuries later, it still is.

Gloucester prides itself on being the birthplace of the schooner (1713). At one time it was an important shipbuilding town. Like many others on the New England coast, it profited from the wealth of forests inland, the plentiful fish, and the richness of trade. Over the years Gloucester lost so many of its sons to the ravages of the sea that the town thought it fitting to set up a memorial to them. The **Gloucester Fisherman** is one of New England's most famous statues, with its plaque which reads, "They That Go Down to the Sea in Ships, 1623–1923."

The sea is still Gloucester's provider, and the "fishing boats out of Gloucester" still head for open water early each morning. You'll see some of these sturdy little boats, festooned with all sorts of nets and rigging, down in the harbor. Fish-packing plants at quayside process the catch as soon as it's brought in.

Another maritime industry has become important in recent years: whale-watch tours. You might want to take yours from here (see below).

Where to Stay and Eat

Motels dot the roadsides around Gloucester, and **East Gloucester,** on a peninsula southeast of Gloucester proper, is an artists' colony and summer resort. But I'll stick with my earlier recommendation that you make your base in Rockport. If you're convinced that Gloucester is the place to stay, try the **Gray Manor,** 14 Atlantic Rd. (Bass Rocks), East Gloucester, MA 01930 (tel. 617/283-5409). A nice big summer house has been converted to a guest house only a few minutes' walk from Good Harbor Beach. Most of the lodging places in East Gloucester cater to weekly and monthly guests, and Gray Manor is no exception. You'll find various efficiency apartments renting by the week, but also some guest rooms which go for $43 to $48 double per day. Late May through late June, and Labor Day through the end of October, off-season rates are in effect. Gray Manor closes for the winter.

Gloucester's all-purpose eatery is the **Blackburn Tavern,** 2 Main St. (tel. 283-9108), right in the center of town. Several dining rooms provide for various crowds at various times of day, though none requires that you be dressed up. Lunch and dinner are served every day except Sunday, when it's brunch only. Seafood platters, steaks, chicken, sandwiches, and assorted burgers are all available. Depending on where you dine, whether you have drinks or not, and whether the nightly entertainment has begun, you'll pay anywhere from $4 to $12 for hearty fare.

What to Do

Signs direct motorists along Gloucester's **Scenic Tour,** covering the Harbor Cove, Inner Harbor, and Fish Pier, as well as to the famous statue of the **Gloucester Fisherman** by Leonard Craske.

If you're lucky enough to be in Gloucester late in June, ask about the **Festival of St. Peter,** the highpoint of which is the Blessing of the Fleet. Several hundred boats make up Gloucester's important fishing fleet, and the blessing pays tribute to them.

Those who have already visited Hammond Castle (see above) may want to drop in for a look at the **Gloucester Fishermen's Museum,** at Rogers and Porter Streets (tel. 283-1940), for a close-up look at the history and daily life of "America's first fishing port." Movies, slides, displays, and aquariums are yours to examine Monday through Saturday from 10 a.m., to 4 p.m., for $2 per adult, $1 per child, $5.50 per family.

A great "summer cottage" turned museum is **Beauport,** the Sleeper-McCann House on Eastern Point, the peninsula across the bay from downtown Gloucester (tel. 283-0800). The house, now under the care of the Society for the Preservation of New England Antiquities, was built by Henry Davis Sleeper, a prominent art and antique collector of the 1920s. Sleeper, also an interior designer, worked for years to make Beauport a showplace. It still is. You can take the hour-long tour Monday through Friday, May 15 to October 15, from 10 a.m. to 4 p.m.; also on weekends from mid-September through October 15, 1 to 4 p.m. Admission costs $4 per adult, $2 for children 6 to 12, $3.50 for seniors.

On your excursion down to Beauport, you'll want to stroll through East Gloucester's **Rocky Neck Art Colony.** The winding streets offer interesting glimpses of the harbor, and every other house seems to be an artist's studio. You'll see signs asking you to park *before* you enter the narrow streets. Take advantage of the lot next to the signs.

Finally, you might want to take your **whale-watch cruise** out of Gloucester. The Daunty Fleet (tel. 283-5110) leaves Rose's Wharf, 415 Main St., morning and afternoon daily during the summer season, on weekends in spring and fall. It's a good idea to call for prices and reservations.

ROCKPORT: North of Gloucester is the small seacost town of Rockport, famed as an artists' colony and, well, just as a very picturesque place. It's been a long time now since Rockport was a village of hearty, independent fishermen and their wives, living by their daily struggle with the sea, and today you're likely to see ten times as many day-trippers as you are to see colorful village types. But Rockport's popularity means that there are now lots of good places to stay and to dine, and if you decide to stay overnight here, you'll notice that as the evening wears on the streets become calmer and the village takes on something of its slow, antique pace.

If you drive to Rockport, parking conditions downtown are sure to be very tight anytime in summer, so find a nice back street, or use the town-supported parking lot rather than getting snarled in the press of traffic downtown. The town lots charge several dollars per day for parking, but offer a free shuttle bus from the lot to downtown Rockport. This isn't a bad deal, considering the gasoline and frustration you'll waste trying to find a legal spot to park downtown.

Where to Stay

Downtown: For many years now the **Peg Leg Inn,** 18 Beach St., Rockport, MA 01966 (tel. 617/546-2352), has been a haven for visitors to Rockport, and the original inn has now expanded to include six buildings with 36 rooms altogether, many with views of the water. The decor varies from room to room and building to building, but as the houses of the inn are a century or two old, emphasis is on Early American, with such modern luxuries as private baths and TVs added. The rooms are kept as neat as the white clapboard houses they're in, and cost $37 to $59 double ($5.50 for an extra person) in high season, mid-June to Labor Day; in spring and autumn prices are $32 to $44 double, and from November 1 to the end of April rates are a low $33. The difference in price depends on the size of the room, and the view it has of the water. The Peg Leg Inn is a short walk from the center of the town, but is also a good deal quieter, because of this location, than it might otherwise be. To get to the Peg Leg, drive to the center of Rockport and then north, staying as close to the water as possible, and you'll end up on Beach Street.

The **Beach Knoll Inn,** at 30 Beach St., Rockport, MA 01966 (tel. 617/546-6939), overlooks the town's "Back Beach," just a few blocks north of the center of town. The original building of the inn is several centuries old, and was once a haven for smugglers who brought their contraband in from the boats— presumably under cover of darkness—and through a tunnel which led to a stairway behind the fireplace! Not that you'll find anything so dramatic going on at the inn today; rather, it's a placid place away from the bustle of downtown. In the summer season, a double room with private bath and water view costs $59 ($48 without the water view). Discounts are in effect if you stay more than two days, and also during the off-season. Of the five guest houses along Beach Street, The Beach Knoll Inn has the best water views.

The **Cove Hill Inn,** 37 Mt. Pleasant St., Rockport, MA 01966 (tel. 617/ 546-2701), is one of Rockport's most reasonably priced places to stay. There are only ten guest rooms, but this makes for a cozy, congenial atmosphere. Prices are $26 to $55 double, and this includes continental breakfast. An extra person in the room pays $5.

The **Tupper House,** 24 Main St., Rockport, MA 01966 (tel. 617/546-3465), is a big, handsome white house in a large lawn just up the hill from the center of town. Only three rooms are rented to guests, but if you get one, you'll pay $38 double, $5 for an extra person.

On the Outskirts:

The **Seven South Street Inn,** 7 South St., Rockport, MA 01966 (tel. 617/546-6708), is a tidy, 20-room mini-complex with a swimming pool and a welcome variety of accommodations. Single rooms are available, for instance; without private bath, they go for $20 to $27 per night. Doubles are priced at $33 to $52, depending partly on whether you have private bath or shared bath. The charge for an extra person in the room is $8.50. All these prices include continental breakfast. Cottages and efficiencies are for rent as well. South Street, by the way, is Route 127A east of town, so if you're coming up 127A from Gloucester, you'll go right by the inn.

For a modern motel, try the **Sandy Bar Motor Inn** (tel. 617/546-7155), on the road into town (the official address is 173 Main St., Rockport, MA 01966). The modern, colorful rooms here, equipped with color TV, air conditioning, and all the luxury features, are only the beginning of the story. Besides these the motel has an indoor swimming pool, a whirlpool bath, a sauna, tennis courts, and a coffeeshop. Rates are a simple $62 per double room from late June through Labor Day, and $45 throughout the rest of the year. It might be good to make reservations in the busy summer months.

Where to Dine

The first thing you should know is that Rockport is a *dry town.* No liquor, wine, or beer is served in its restaurants. You may bring your own, and setups will be provided, but you must plan in advance, of course.

The T-Wharf in Rockport is just opposite "Motif No. 1" and Bearskin Neck. As you stroll off the main street out onto the T-Wharf, glance right and you'll see **Ellen's Harborside Restaurant** (tel. 546-2512), Rockport's all-around eating place. Ellen's has incredibly long hours: from 5:30 a.m. until late at night, so you can go for breakfast, lunch, dinner, or a late-night snack. Lots of daily specials are on the menu, or you might order an assorted fried seafood plate ($7), or a boiled lobster (the best kind) for the same price. Sandwiches range in price from $1.50 to $4; there's a children's menu. Ellen's manages to be everything to everybody.

For many years the standby in Rockport for dining has been **Oleana-by-the-Sea,** 27 Main St. (tel. 546-2049), not far from the center of town. With a tinge of Norwegian atmosphere, Oleana emphasizes the seafood of the area, and adds a Norwegian bakery just for fun. The decor is simple but attractive, as though the decorators wanted you to concentrate on the views of the Atlantic which are to be had from many of the tables. The soup is billed as homemade, and is quite good; seafood entrees generally run about $5 to $8, but the daily special will always save you money, and may be haddock in a cheese sauce, with potato and vegetable for about $6. For dessert, a Norwegian pastry with strawberries and custard is a good choice. Oleana is open almost year round; in June, July, and August they're in service seven days a week from 11:30 a.m. to 8 p.m. The bakery and coffeeshop next door is open from 7 a.m. to 4 p.m., serving coffee and fresh-baked muffins for $1, and luncheon sandwiches for about $3.

An interesting place to take in the sea view is from the granite porch of the **Old Harbor House,** on Bearskin Neck. Sandwiches here go from the lowly tunafish ($2.75) to the lofty lobster ($7.50), with lots in between, or they offer a platter of cheese, bread, and fruit slices for $4.50. Teas, coffee, and their own cranberry punch are served as refreshment, and a sign proclaims that the area is off-limits to cigarette smokers.

What to Do

First thing every visitor does after arriving in Rockport is to take a stroll down **Bearskin Neck,** the narrow peninsula jutting into the water off Dock Square, the town's main square. Here you'll find lots of quaint shops and art galleries to draw your attention, and many good views of the water and of the town.

Other strolls in town are also rewarding, and local brochures will urge you to take a photograph of the red fisherman's shack called "Motif No. 1," apparently named for its popularity among the first picture painters who moved to Rockport. Actually, it should now be named "Motif No. 2," as the original shack was swept away in the great storm of 1978, and a new one built from scratch. In the interests of originality, I suggest that you try to be the first person to have visited Rockport *without* seeing this unimportant landmark. Take my word for it, the thing is now famous because it's famous because it's famous, etc. Rather, go visit the artists themselves in nearby Rocky Neck; see them at work there and browse through their galleries.

For **swimming,** walk along Beach Street north to Front Beach and Back Beach, or wander (in your car or on your bike) north along the coast to **Pigeon Cove,** about two miles north (a half-hour walk).

You can go farther than Pigeon Cove by car or bike. In fact you can make a loop of Cape Ann on Route 127 via Pigeon Cove, Folly Cove, Plum Cove, Annisquam, and Lobster Cove, ending in Gloucester.

Castle Hill, the Crane Estate: Not far from Rockport is the fabulous hilltop mansion built by Richard Teller Crane, Jr., who made a fortune in plumbing and bathroom fixtures early in this century. The house, in a style from the time of King Charles II, is surrounded by extensive gardens and deer parks. You can take a tour of the house and grounds on certain Fridays and Saturdays during the summer; or you can visit for a crafts fair, concert, or theater performance and get a look at the estate that way. First thing to do is to find out what's scheduled, by contacting the Castle Hill Foundation, P.O. Box 283, Ipswich, MA 01938 (tel. 617/356-4070).

Chapter V

. . . AND THE SOUTH SHORE

1. Plymouth
2. New Bedford
3. Fall River

OF THE MANY COMMUNITIES on the South Shore of Massachusetts Bay, Plymouth is easily the most famous. Crowds of visitors make the pilgrimage every summer to see one of the places where this country began. Due south of Boston on Buzzards Bay is New Bedford, one of the region's best known towns during the whaling era, home of Melville's Captain Ahab of *Moby Dick* fame. The whaling museum and the ferry to Martha's Vineyard are the big attractions in New Bedford today. And in Fall River, on the border with Rhode Island, battleships and submarines are waiting to be visited and toured by nautical buffs.

1. Plymouth

Plymouth is famous because of a small and rather unimpressive boulder. But when visitors come to look at Plymouth Rock, they are coming not because the rock is much to look at—its only notable features are a crack and the date "1620" engraved on it—but because Plymouth, as the landing-place of the Pilgrims, is a symbol for the ideal of religious freedom and the quest for a better life.

Besides the Rock, which will take you about five minutes to inspect, Plymouth has lots of other sights and exhibits dealing with Pilgrim and early American history: a collection of historic houses, a full-size replica of the Pilgrim ship *Mayflower*, an authentic recreation of an entire Pilgrim village complete with living inhabitants, a wax museum, and still more. Many people make Plymouth a day trip, stopping here on their way from Boston to the Cape or vice-versa, but should you want to stay overnight in the Pilgrims' town, there are several attractive lodging possibilities.

GETTING THERE: Plymouth is served from Boston and Hyannis by buses of the Plymouth & Brockton Street Railway Company. About two dozen buses a day run in each direction between Plymouth and Boston; about 16 buses a day run from Hyannis to Plymouth and back. In Boston, buses leave from either the Greyhound Terminal at 10 St. James Ave. (tel. 423-5810) or from the Essex Terminal next to Amtrak's South Station (tel. 749-5067). In Hyannis the P & B terminal (tel. 775-5524) is at Elm Street. In Plymouth, the P & B Terminal is on Sandwich Street near the intersection with South Street (tel. 746-0378), but a few buses stop only at Standish Plaza. The trip between Boston and Plymouth takes one hour and 20 minutes; between Hyannis and Plymouth, 40 minutes.

INFORMATION: The Town of Plymouth maintains an **Information Booth** (tel. 617/746-4734) and **Accommodations Service** on North Park Avenue. Samoset Street (Route 44) is the road you take east from the highway (Route 3), and Samoset turns into North Park after you cross Court Street (Route 3A). Look for the booth on your right just as the road jogs to the right. They'll help you find a room if you don't have a reservation or if you'd like to see what's available.

There is a **Regional Information Complex for Visitors** on Route 3 at Exit 5. For information, call 617/746-3377.

WHERE TO STAY: Right downtown are two motels with similar names and identical management, the **Governor Bradford** (tel. 617/746-6200), right on the waterfront street, and the **Governor Carver** (tel. 746-7100), on Summer Street at Town Square, Plymouth, MA 02360. Both are about the same distance —two blocks—from Plymouth Rock. The Governor Bradford has a little fish-shaped outdoor pool and two tiers of modern rooms, each having individual heat/air conditioning units, two double beds, TV, and coffee-makers. The Governor Carver is a three-story inn with 82 rooms all with two double beds, a pool, and the other features of the Bradford, plus a restaurant and lounge. Rates at the two inns are similar and change depending on the season of the year: mid-June to mid-October, singles are $46.51 to $57.08, and doubles run $57.08 to $67.65; mid-October through November, $46.51 to $50.74 single, $46.62 to $61.31 double; December through March, $42.28 to $46.51 single, $46.51 to $52.85 double; and April to mid-June, $46.51 to $50.74 single, $46.62 to $61.31 double. Children under 14 stay in their parents' room for free. Package plans are available.

One of the better bargains is to be found at the **Cold Spring Motel**, 188 Court St. (which is Route 3A), Plymouth, MA 02360 (tel. 617/746-2222). Although a bit out of the center of town—it's about a half mile to the Rock— the surroundings of grass lawns and large trees make up for the small distance. Nineteen rooms and cottages, many paneled in pine, are for rent. All have air conditioning, electric heat, color TV, and parking at the door. A picnic area with fireplaces is provided for guests' use. Although there's no restaurant at the motel, there's one almost across the street in the small shopping plaza. The rate structure at present is quite complex because of the several types of accommodations (rooms with double beds, twins, cottages with two bedrooms sleeping four). Single rates are $35; double, $41; two bedroom cottages $47; $3 for each extra person, $4 extra per cot. These are the in-season rates; in April, May, and October, prices are a dollar or two less. Note that the Cold Spring Motel *closes* in winter; exact dates vary from year to year.

The tiny **Blue Anchor Motel**, 7 Lincoln St., Plymouth, MA 02360 (tel. 617/746-9551), has only four units, and thus there's a good chance it'll be full in busy periods, but it's worth considering because it is on a quiet street next to Plymouth's town hall and only a short walk from the center of town. It's very much a ma-and-pa place, informal and friendly, with comfy rooms renting for $27.48 to $44.39, depending on the unit and the number in your party. Rates are about $2 less per room off-season. From the center of town, go south on Sandwich Street from the post office. The third street on the left is Lincoln.

Down near Plimoth Plantation, several miles south of the center of Plymouth, is the **Pilgrim Sands Motel,** Warren Avenue (Route 3A), Plymouth, MA 02360 (tel. 617/747-0900). The bonus here, besides proximity to Plimoth Plantation, is the beach which you'd normally have to pay $3 to $5 ($3 weekdays, $5 weekends) to enjoy, but which is free for motel guests. There's an indoor and outdoor pool and spa as well, and all the modern amenities including all-tile bathrooms. After a day's walking in the sun it's great to take a swim and then sit looking out to sea, before going to bed to be lulled by the sound of the surf. All rooms have two double beds and cost $50.74 to $58.14 off-season, $57.08 to $71.88 in season (mid-June to Labor Day), the higher rates for air-conditioned oceanfront rooms. Open year round.

WHERE TO DINE: Plymouth has a number of snack places, sandwich shops, and restaurants, and although it's not noted for a wide range of culinary styles, the town will be able to fill your needs.

For a good, dependable seafood restaurant which serves meat and fowl as well, you can't do much better than **Mayflower Seafoods** (tel. 746-1704), on Fish Pier, five blocks north of Plymouth Rock (you can see it from almost anywhere along the waterfront). The Mayflower is actually several restaurants in one, and capitalizes on the fact that the town's fishing fleet docks virtually at its back door. Go to that back door and you can get seafood to take out (already cooked) or served on a platter to eat there, and prices are cheaper than in the Mayflower's Fishermen's Dinners Room which you enter from the street rather than from the wharf. The specialty is complete dinner platters with seafood as the main course: a filet of sole dinner is slightly over $8, one with baked stuffed lobster is $16 (the most expensive thing on the menu). At lunchtime, the prices are much less for the platters, and while servings are smaller they're still generous, and prices are between $3.50 and $7.50. The Mayflower is open daily at 11:30 a.m., closed Monday except when Monday is a holiday. Behind the Mayflower are several other seafood restaurants.

Walk up North Street, which starts from Water Street between *Mayflower II* and Plymouth Rock, and two blocks up at the corner of Main and North is the **Sandwich and Deli Shop,** a modern place in an ancient house once occupied by Gen. John Winslow (see the plaque on the North Street side). Sandwiches and salad plates cost from $1 to $2.75. The shop has Gay '90s touches and good air conditioning.

For an elegant and higher price lunch or dinner, drive south on Sandwich Street, which becomes Warren Avenue (Route 3A), to the beach just past the turnoff to Plimoth Plantation, and park in the lot of **Bert's Restaurant** (tel. 746-3422). Air conditioning keeps you cool and the view of the ocean, plus a decor accented with various pieces of ships' paraphernalia, make you think (almost) that you're out to sea. The menu features seafood but offers chicken and beef as well, most entrees being in the range of $9 to $14 and full dinners (with appetizer, vegetable and potato, salad, dessert, and coffee) cost $2.50 more. Bert's has lots of parking, and is right beside the entrance to the public beach ($3 entry fee weekdays, $5 weekends).

Bert's is open for breakfast and lunch as well as dancing in the evenings.

WHAT TO SEE: Sightseeing in Plymouth means Pilgrim lore: what they looked like, how they dressed, how they lived from day to day. The many exhibits here make it possible to get a very clear picture of what arrival in America meant to these early pioneers.

The Pilgrims have a special place in American history not only because they were very early settlers, but also because of their reasons for settling here. First they had left England for Holland, so that they could practice their beliefs and rites freely. However, noting the loss of their English character, they decided to seek another haven where cultural influences would not be so strong. Having received permission from London, they sailed for America in 1620. Actually, they had hoped to arrive at a point south of Plymouth, but after being blown off course they ran into Cape Cod; shortly after making Cape Cod, they sailed to the point where Plymouth stands today. The place where they debarked is marked by **Plymouth Rock.**

Today the Rock is sheltered by a monumental enclosure. Just as the Rock marks the beginning of the Pilgrims' adventure in America, so it can serve as the beginning point for your tour of Plymouth. Follow the road signs to find the Rock, and after your look at it, head for the attractions nearby.

Right next to Plymouth Rock is a replica of the sort of house the Pilgrims first built in the New World. Entrance to the house is 10¢, and while there's not much to see inside, you can best imagine what it'd be like to live in so tiny a house when you're actually inside it. Remember that in the 1600s people were not as tall as average Americans today.

The Mayflower

The fact that the Pilgrims were smaller people will be brought home more forcefully when you tour the *Mayflower II,* a replica of the original ship built in England in 1955 and sailed across the Atlantic to Plymouth in 1957. How, you are sure to ask yourself, was it possible for 127 people—even small ones—to fit themselves and all their baggage for setting up a new town into the tiny rooms and onto the tiny decks of this little boat? And how could they stay on it for 2½ months? The only answer which comes to mind is "by courage and dedication," and it's for that the Pilgrims are admired and remembered. Guides on the *Mayflower II* will tell you about the boat's workings and will answer questions; display panels on the dock and an excellent leaflet given to you as you enter will explain other details of nautical lore. *Mayflower II* is only a few steps from Plymouth Rock, and is open April through November from 9 a.m. to 5 p.m.; in the busiest months of July and August the ship stays open until 6:30 p.m. every night. Admission is $2 for adults, $1 for children, but *note:* a special combination ticket sold between Memorial Day and Labor Day is good for the *Mayflower II,* Plimoth Plantation, Pilgrim Hall, and six of the restored houses in Plymouth. If you plan to visit the shop, the Plantation, Pilgrim Hall, and at least two of the houses, it's worth buying the special ticket.

Pilgrim Hall

Seeing how the Pilgrims lived in the earliest of America's colonization is what Plymouth is all about. You can see exhibits like *Mayflower II* and the early huts to give you an idea, or you can see the actual Pilgrim furniture and huge oil paintings featured in Pilgrim Hall, 75 Court St., at the corner of Chilton and Court Streets. (Court Street, Main Street, and Sandwich Street are all different names for different sections of the same street.) The oldest historical museum in the United States, Pilgrim Hall was built in 1824 to house artifacts the Pilgrims used, a library for research into Plymouth's early history, and galleries for the monumental paintings depicting important events in Pilgrim history. In the Lower Hall, the slide show puts the Pilgrim experience into the perspective of the times, surrounded by the exceptional furniture of Brewster and Bradford and the rest and the arms and armor they brought with them. In the Main Hall above are the paintings, the relic of a 17th-century transatlantic ship, and the magnificent pewter, Delftware, and woodenware the Pilgrims and their descendants treasured along with the tools and cookware of the Indians who lived beside the Pilgrims. Many of the items identified as *Mayflower* cargo, such as the wicker cradle of the first English child born in New England, are on display. Pilgrim Hall (tel. 746-1620) is open from 9:30 a.m. to 4:30 p.m. every day, all year, and costs $2 for adults, $1.50 for seniors, and 25¢ for children 6 to 15.

Plymouth National Wax Museum

Even more lifelike than Pilgrim Hall's paintings are the tableaux at the Plymouth National Wax Museum, 16 Carver St. (tel. 746-6468), at the top of the hill across the street from Plymouth Rock. The hill is Cole's Hill, where the first Pilgrim cemetery was established and where the first victims of the frigid New England winter were laid to rest. The museum's scenes trace the history of the Pilgrims from persecution in England through the move to Holland to the trip across the Atlantic and the foundation of the settlement at Plymouth. Soundtracks add to the vividness of the scenes. The Wax Museum is open from 9 a.m. to 5 p.m. in spring and fall, to 9:30 p.m. in summer; admission is $3 for adults, $1.50 for children.

Plimouth Plantation

Most lifelike of all the representations of early colonial life is Plimoth Plantation, a living outdoor museum with inhabitants in period dress. Plimoth Plantation, modeled after Sturbridge Village, is "the living folk museum of 17th-century Plymouth," and represents a Pilgrim village as it may have looked in 1627. Historical research was done to determine every aspect of the village, and the result is as close as could be achieved: it's surrounded by a fortification (stockade), the small houses have thatched roofs and kitchen gardens, the women in period dress may be seen spinning thread or cooking, the men tending the fields or hewing logs to make planks. The people who "live" in Plimoth Plantation are known as "interpreters," and that's what they do for you: interpret the daily activities of a different era to make them comprehensible today.

Plimoth Plantation is a nonprofit educational outdoor museum, open April through November from 9 a.m. to 5 p.m. every day; tickets are sold until 4 p.m. (it's hardly worth entering if you have less than an hour to look around). Admission costs $5.25 for adults, $2.75 for children 5 to 13 (under 5, free), but this includes free parking, films and slide shows at the theater, indoor exhibits on early life, gift shop and bookstore, a snackbar, and a picnic area.

The Forefathers' Monument

This is the sort of grand statue-and-pedestal one would expect to see on a central boulevard in a world capital, but instead it stands on Allerton Street, off Samoset (U.S. 44), in a small park—follow the signs on the road. Designed by Hammet Billings of Boston and erected in 1889, the monument is composed of a great granite statue of Faith, surrounded by smaller figures of Liberty, Law,

Education, and Morality. The monument is impressive, and it's interesting to speculate about the date it was erected, and the thoughts of those who planned and constructed it. The view from the little park, by the way, is very fine; a small cast-iron outline map near the base of the monument traces the outline of Cape Cod, which you can see on a clear day.

Plymouth's Old Houses

Of the antique houses in the town, several are of particular interest. The **Harlow Old Fort House,** South and Sandwich Streets, is a working reproduction of a household of the 1600s, and you can see costumed guides doing the daily chores of that era. The **Jabez Howland House,** on Sandwich Street just south of the town brook, is the only house in Plymouth still standing where some of the first Pilgrims lived. **Sparrow House,** near the **Jenney Grist Mill** on Summer Street and next to the town brook, is the oldest house in Plymouth; the mill is a reconstruction of an early American water-powered mill, and it grinds grain into flour which is sold to visitors. **Spooner House,** behind the Wax Museum on North Street, is an old Plymouth house which was inhabited by the same family, the Spooners, for two centuries. All of these houses are open to the public at a charge of $1 for adults, 25¢ for children; all are on the combination ticket. Entrance to the Grist Mill is free.

Pilgrim Progress

At 5 p.m. on Friday in August a group of Plymouth citizens dressed as Pilgrims honor the memory of their forefathers by recreating the procession to church. The number of persons, their sexes, and ages have been matched to the small group of Pilgrims who survived the first winter in the New World. When you see the procession you may be amazed at the small size of the group that started it all.

READER'S SIGHTSEEING SUGGESTION: "We visited the surprisingly interesting, free exhibition called **Cranberry World** (tel. 617/747-1000), sponsored by Ocean Spray Cranberries, Inc. Pictures, displays, and films tell one everything he ever wanted to know about cranberries but didn't know who to ask! We were offered a free cranberry drink, a small snack and a recipe sheet" (Diana Harper, London, England). [*Author's Note:* Cranberry World is north of Plymouth Rock on Water Street, a ten-minute walk; open April through November every day from 9:30 a.m. to 5 p.m.]

2. New Bedford

New Bedford, like Fall River, owed part of its living to textiles, but its fame rests on its history as a whaling port. Herman Melville set his American classic, *Moby Dick,* in New Bedford as the logical spot to begin a whaling epic, and so it was. During the heyday of whale-oil lamps, New Bedford had about 400 ships out scouting the seas for the monster denizens. A ship might be out at sea for several years, and when it returned to port it could have thousands of barrels of whale oil in its hold. The story of what whaling was all about—how the ships were manned and equipped, how the search went, how the men pursued and killed the whale, and then butchered and rendered it to make the oil—is all told in New Bedford's famous **Whaling Museum** on Johnny Cake Hill.

Today New Bedford's historic waterfront downtown section is undergoing extensive renovation and restoration. A pedestrian shopping mall complete with trees, benches, and music in the air—called **Melville Mall,** appropriately —has been completed and it does much for the town. East of the mall, going down to the water's edge, the **Custom House** and many merchants' buildings are being restored, cobbled streets are being uncovered or restored, and the center of the city is taking on an appearance much like it had during its 19th-century heyday. Right in the middle of the restoration area is the Bristol County Development Council's **Tourist Information Office,** 70 North 2nd St., New Bedford, MA 02744 (signs throughout town point the way; tel. 617/997-1250). They're open from 9 a.m. to 5 p.m. Monday through Saturday, 1 to 5 p.m. on Sunday, and are very helpful with maps, brochures, and touring suggestions.

STAYING IN NEW BEDFORD: This is one of those cities lucky enough to have a bed-and-breakfast service. **Pineapple Hospitality,** 384 Rodney French Blvd., New Bedford, MA 02744 (tel. 617/997-9952), will take your reservation and provide details on your room. You'll stay in a New Bedford home, receive a continental breakfast the next morning, and pay $21.14 to $38.05 single, $28.54 to $62.36 double, depending on accommodations. Many of the homes participating in the service welcome young children.

Why the pineapple, you ask? In New Bedford's nautical heyday, ships would bring this tropical delicacy back home at the end of a voyage. A pineapple set out in front of the house meant the occupants were at home, receiving visitors, celebrating the success of the voyage.

THE WHALING MUSEUM: At 18 Johnny Cake Hill in the heart of the Historic Waterfront District, the museum complex of seven buildings covers the block between William and Union Streets. It's open from 9 a.m. to 5 p.m. on Monday through Saturday and 1 to 5 p.m. on Sunday. Admission for adults is $2, $1 for kids 6 to 14. Inside, the first thing which will confront you is the largest ship model in the world: a replica of the bark *Lagoda* made to exactly one-half the ship's original size. Rigging, tryworks, whaleboats, and other equipment are all in place, and you can walk about the model at will. The family who owned and operated the *Lagoda* donated the model, and the building to house it, to the museum. Around the walls of the museum are old photographs and drawings explaining the whaling industry, and many other rooms in the museum hold collections of other whaling lore: cooperage, chandlery, operation of the counting house, brokerage and banking, insurance, and articles of glass, china, and pewter brought home from whaling and trading voyages. A gallery exhibits dozens of paintings done on whaling themes. Perhaps the most beautiful exhibit besides the *Lagoda* is that of the scrimshaw, the delicate, intricate articles of carved whalebone and tooth which the whalemen made to while away the long hours at sea. The artistry displayed is almost breathtaking, and the ingenuity very revealing of quick and sensitive minds. It wouldn't be far wrong to say that without understanding whaling, one couldn't understand 19th-century New England; and the place to find out about whaling is certainly New Bedford.

In summer, a whaling film is shown daily at 10:30 a.m. and 1:30 p.m. Also, free walking tours of the Historic Waterfront District leave the museum at regular intervals between 10 a.m. and 3 p.m. For more information, call 997-0046.

Other Whaling Memorabilia

Across the street from the Whaling Museum is the **Seamen's Bethel** (tel. 992-3295), a chapel constructed in 1832 "for the moral improvement of sailors," and immortalized in *Moby Dick.* By giving a donation you can explore the Bethel. And several blocks away, at Pleasant and William, the **Public Library** has displays of whaling books and pamphlets. Open 9 a.m. to 9 p.m. Monday through Thursday, to 5 p.m. on Friday and Saturday, closed Sunday and holidays, from May 1 through Columbus Day only.

A NOTE ON PARKING: Metered places on the street are liable to be filled, but right near the Whaling Museum and the old section of the city is a parking garage run by the city, which charges a moderate 25¢ per hour, up to a tops of $2 per day. From here you can easily walk to everything there is to see.

THE FERRY TO MARTHA'S VINEYARD: M/V *Schamonchi* carries passengers (no cars) from New Bedford to the island of Martha's Vineyard three or four times daily in summer for $6.50 one way, $12 round trip for adults; for kids under 12, $3 one way, $5.50 round trip. For schedules and information, call 617/997-1688 in New Bedford, or 617/693-2088 in the island town of **Vineyard Haven.**

3. Fall River

In the mid-19th century, Fall River was a boom textile town. Because of its natural harbor, ample waterpower, and a moist climate ideal for working thread, it became a world textile-weaving center. Huge mills made from blocks of the local granite were built everywhere, making an awesome scene of industry and wealth. But in the 20th century the textile business began moving to the South, and Fall River's industry foundered.

Prosperity has returned to Fall River, and now many of the impressive granite mills produce finished apparel; others turn out rubber products, foods, and paper. The town's new Government Center, built on the airspace over Interstate 195, is a symbol of Fall River's resurgence, and adds its impressive appearance to that of the great mills.

WHAT TO SEE: Most people pass through Fall River on their way from Providence to Cape Cod or from Boston to Newport, and when they do, the thing they stop to see is **Battleship Cove,** permanent berth of a number of impressive craft. The U.S.S. *Joseph P. Kennedy, Jr.,* a World War II destroyer, is here, and also the submarine U.S.S. *Lionfish.* But the star of the exhibit is the mighty U.S.S *Massachusetts,* the battleship berthed here as a memorial to Massachusetts men and women who were killed in World War II. From I-195, follow the signs for Battleship Cove (sometimes just the silhouette of the battleship is on the sign). The exhibits are open May to October, every day from 9 a.m. to 5 p.m.; November through April, every day from 9 a.m. to 4:30 p.m. There's a **Marine Museum** nearby which is open year round, Monday through Friday from 9 a.m. to 5 p.m., Saturday and Sunday from 2 to 5 p.m.; open evenings in summer till 8 p.m. Tickets to all the ships and the museum (four tickets in one) cost $4 for adults, $2 for kids, 50¢ for "tots"; servicemen in uniform pay $1.75.

The combination ticket allows you to tour both above and below decks on all the ships. For lunch, you can have a meal or a snack in the wardroom of the U.S.S. *Massachusetts.* Other facilities at Battleship Cove, under the impressive I-195 bridge, are a snackbar, a Tourist Information Office with free hotel reservation assistance service, and toilets.

Should you not want to lunch in the wardroom, the **Gangplank Restaurant** nearby should be able to take care of you. A building with a panoramic view of the river and Battleship Cove, it's open for lunch Monday through Saturday from 11 a.m. to 4 p.m., for dinner Monday through Saturday beginning at 5 p.m.; Sunday brunch is served in the lounge from 11 a.m. to 3 p.m., and dinner (best to have a reservation) from noon. The Gangplank's bar has a nice view of the highway bridge, the dining room is large, airy, and orderly, with black-jacketed waiters and hatch-top tables. Luncheon entrees include crabmeat, club, and "overstuffed" sandwiches ranging in price from $3 to $6. At dinner, seafood entrees run about $10 to $12, but you can have chowder at the Raw Bar—all you can eat—for $6. Steaks and chicken dishes are offered as well. In the bar, there's entertainment (perhaps an alto sax and piano playing snappy old favorites) after 5 p.m., and room to dance to the music.

As for Fall River's other claim to fame, that's the celebrated Lizzie Borden murder trial in 1892, in which Lizzie, a young Fall River girl, was tried for chopping up her parents with an axe: it's good to remember that the poor girl was acquitted. The guilty party was never found.

CAPE COD

CAPE COD IS A WORLD of its own. This 70-mile-long arm of sand curled into the Atlantic was formed by glacial action and was given its name by an early (1602) visitor to the New World, Bartholomew Gosnold. The Pilgrims first landed in the New World at Provincetown and drew up the Mayflower Compact before heading on to the mainland at what would become Plymouth.

Strictly speaking, Cape Cod is an island separated from the rest of Massachusetts by the Cape Cod Canal, a deep waterway built from north to south across the base of the cape in the early part of this century. Two graceful bridges span the canal, one at Bourne to the south (Route 28), one at Sagamore to the north (Route 6), and both are very busy in the warm months. Just before crossing either bridge, look for the little information sheds established by the Cape Cod Chamber of Commerce, open from 9 a.m. to 7 p.m. every day during the summer. Maps, booklets, motel brochures, and tabloid newspaper "current listings" are all yours for free, and if you need a room reservation, they'll help you get one.

1. Getting There

Cape Cod was once a seafaring man's domain, and although it's still possible to get there by boat, the rail, bus, air, and road routes make it easy to get there any way you choose.

BY CAR: Coming from New York and Providence, take I-195 to Route 28 South and cross the Bourne Bridge if you're heading for Falmouth and Woods

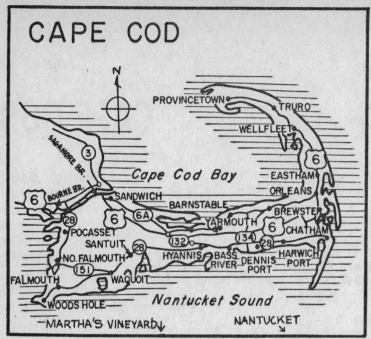

Hole; if you're going to Sandwich, Hyannis, or other cape points, don't take the Bourne Bridge, but take U.S. 6 East just before the Bourne Bridge, and this will take you to the Sagamore Bridge, where you cross the canal. Coming from Boston, the Southeast Expressway (I-93) will take you right to Route 3 which goes straight to the Sagamore Bridge. If you're on your way to Falmouth and Woods Hole, stay on I-93 past the intersection with Route 3 and take Exit 66 for Route 24 South. This beautiful superhighway changes numbers and becomes Route 23, then Route 28 before taking you right over the Bourne Bridge.

BY RAIL: Cape Cod's first crowds of summer visitors came via rail from New York and Boston, and such service may soon again be available. Until it is, take a train to Providence or Boston and connect there with a bus to Cape Cod. In Providence, the bus and train stations are only a block apart.

The **Cape Code & Hyannis Railroad, Inc.** (tel. 617/771-1145), runs excursion trains on the route between Hyannis and Falmouth via Sandwich and Buzzards Bay. In this case, getting there is all the fun; though they do have one-way fares, the train trips are more in the nature of tours, taking in lots of interesting sights (super for kids) along the way. Fares range from $6 to $12 for adults, $3 to $7 for children, depending on the station where you board.

BY BUS: Bus service to the cape from New York, Providence, and Boston is good, fast, and frequent. Here are the details:

From New York: **Bonanza** (Greyhound ticket counter in Port Authority terminal; tel. 212/564-8484 or 212/594-2000) runs buses via two routes, along the coast or via Waterbury and Hartford. In high summer, there are two through buses a day from New York all the way to Provincetown at the tip of the Cape, and a good number of other buses going as far as Hyannis where you can transfer for other points.

From Providence/Newport: From Providence, catch the Bonanza bus (about six a day) to Hyannis, or the two a day going to Provincetown. The trip takes less than two hours to Hyannis. Bonanza's headquarters are at Box 1116, Annex Station, Providence, RI 02901.

From Boston: Plymouth & Brockton St. Railway Co. has buses which leave from the Greyhound Terminal (tel. 617/423-5810) and the South Station (Amtrak) Terminal (tel. 617/749-5067). The trip to Hyannis takes 1½ hours.

South Shore & Cape Cod Limo Service (tel. toll free 800/343-7540) makes four trips a day between Boston's Logan International Airport and Hyannis, with stops at Sagamore, Plymouth, and three other points. Reservations are strongly advised.

BY AIR: PBA (Provincetown–Boston Airline, Inc.) has Boston–Provincetown, Boston–Hyannis, New York (La Guardia)–Hyannis flights. For reservations or information, call 617/567-6090 in Boston; 617/771-1444 in Hyannis; or 212/247-0088 in New York City (within Massachusetts they have a toll-free number: 800/352-3132). Flight service is quite frequent during the busy summer season, but curtailed in winter.

Air Florida (tel. toll free 800/327-2971) also has commuter service between Boston and Hyannis, with two daily flights in each direction.

Hyannis and the islands of Martha's Vineyard and Nantucket are linked by PBA, and by **Gull Air** (tel. 617/771-1247; in Massachusetts only, toll free, 800/352-7191).

BY BOAT: Bay State & Provincetown Steamship Company (tel. 617/723-7800 in Boston) operates the M/V *Provincetown II* on a run from Boston to P-town every day from late June through July and August until Labor Day; there's one daily sailing leaving Boston's Commonwealth Pier about 9:30 a.m., arriving P-town at about 1 p.m., and returning from P-town (about 3:15 p.m.) to Boston (arriving before 7 p.m.). A round-trip ticket for an adult costs $18, or $13 for kids under 12; the one-way fare is $12; for kids, $10. Senior citizens get discounts. On weekends in May, early June, September, and October, the M/V *Provincetown* is also in operation on this route.

TRANSPORTATION ON THE CAPE: Route 6, the Mid-Cape Highway, is the fastest way to travel from the "Upper Cape" (the part you first come to by land) to the "Lower Cape" (the narrow portion north of Orleans to Provincetown). But Route 6 is not necessarily the prettiest way to go; if you have the time, travel one of the smaller, scenic roads instead.

Cape Cod Bus Lines, 11 Walker St., Falmouth (tel. 548-0333), and at the Greyhound Terminal in Hyannis, Center and Elm Streets (tel. 775-5524), has buses to all the larger towns on the Cape. **Southern Massachusetts Bus Lines,** operating from Hyannis, 68 Center St. (tel. 771-3100 or 771-3101), runs buses to Dennisport, Harwichport, and Chatham.

Transportation to the islands of Martha's Vineyard and Nantucket is covered in the sections on Woods Hole and Hyannis.

2. Falmouth and Woods Hole

Falmouth is a pretty town which has grown rapidly in recent years but which has managed to preserve a lot of the charm of a rural New England town. A city park next to the library, a well-preserved Village Green, and magnificent tall trees along Main Street make the downtown section attractive, and manicured lawns and white clapboard houses dress up the side streets. The town has one very pleasant historical inn, several good beaches, and daily ships to Martha's Vineyard.

A few miles past Falmouth to the south is Woods Hole, home of world-famous Woods Hole Oceanographic Institute; car ferries depart from Woods Hole for Martha's Vineyard several times daily in summer.

TOURIST INFORMATION: The **Falmouth Chamber of Commerce,** P.O. Box 582, Falmouth, MA 02541 (tel. 617/548-8500), operates an Information Office downtown off Main Street in the Lawrence Academy building. Look for a short street called Academy Way. If they can't answer your question, it's probably not about Falmouth.

WHERE TO STAY: Falmouth has dozens of motels, mostly expensive and somewhat sterile though modern and comfortable. For the true flavor of Falmouth, however, I'd recommend the moderately priced small inns and guest houses. I've included descriptions of the best of the larger places as well. When inquiring about room prices, be sure to ask about reductions for stays of a few days or more. A room costing $40 for one night may well cost $35 per night if you stay two or three days.

Guest Houses And Inns

Falmouth is rich in guest houses, which is not surprising. The way to spend a week or two by the sea, at moderate cost, is to rent a room in a private home. Lots of houses is **Falmouth Heights,** southeast of the center of Falmouth proper, are devoted to renting rooms for about $35 to $40 double, with a shared bathroom. If you specifically request it, your room may have a view of the sea. But before describing the guest houses, you should know about two charming inns right downtown near Falmouth Green.

Downtown: A few steps from the Falmouth Historical Society is the **Palmer House Inn,** 81 Palmer Ave., Falmouth, MA 02540 (tel. 617/548-1230), very near the Green and the center of town. Each of the eight guest rooms in this turn-of-the-century Victorian house has a private bath, and a full breakfast is included in the room price of $48. If the perfect location doesn't get you, the stained glass will. By the way, the Palmer House is owned by the same people as the Michael Ames Inn on Falmouth Heights Beach (see below).

Mostly Hall, 27 West Main St., Falmouth, MA 02540 (tel. 617/548-3786), is only steps from Falmouth Green, the Katherine Lee Bates house, and the beginning of the bicycle path to Woods Hole. The charming old house was built in 1849 as a wedding present for the bride of Capt. Albert Nye. These days you can stay in any of five guest rooms for $37 to $46 double with shared bath, or $53 to $58 double with private bath; these rates include a full breakfast and the inevitable tax. For getting the real flavor of Falmouth, Mostly Hall can't be beat.

Along Grand Avenue: The guest houses of Grand Avenue in Falmouth Heights differ only slightly in price, accommodations, sea views, and charm. During the summer season your selection may well have to be made on the basis of availability.

Head down Falmouth Heights Road, which skirts the eastern side of Falmouth Harbor, and soon you'll see Grand Avenue bearing off to the right. It then makes a loop south and east, running along Falmouth Heights Beach before heading back to rejoin Falmouth Heights Road. Heading in this direction, house numbers go in descending order.

The **Island View Guest House**, 375 Grand Ave., Falmouth Heights, MA 02540 (tel. 617/540-1080), is as tidy as can be. You'll notice its circular driveway with a little fountain right at the corner of Vernon Street. The rooms here all share baths, and go for $40 per night, tax included.

The **Michael Ames Inn**, 313 Grand Ave. at Gertrude Avenue, Falmouth Heights, MA 02540 (tel. 617/548-1230), has recently been refurbished and the plumbing modernized so that all rooms now have private bath and rent for $48 to $59 double, tax and continental breakfast included. If you pay for four nights, the fifth is free; pay for five and you get a week.

The **Grafton Inn**, 261 Grand Ave., Falmouth Heights, MA 02540 (tel. 617/548-9292), is right across the street from the main beach area, with snack stands and restaurants conveniently nearby. Rates here are $38 double for a room with private bath.

Hastings by the Sea, 28 Worcester Park Ave., near Grand Avenue, Falmouth Heights, MA 02540 (tel. 617/548-1628), is a few steps off Grand Avenue but still offers many water views. Rooms have fans (though the sea breeze usually makes them unnecessary), nice furnishings, and prices that go down the longer you stay: $37 double with shared bath for one night, and several dollars' reduction on the nightly rate if you stay more than one.

The **Gladstone Inn**, 219 Grand Ave. South, Falmouth Heights, MA 02540 (tel. 617/548-9851), is at the corner of Montgomery Avenue, across the street from the beach. A glassed-in veranda shares the sea view, and this is where you can have your continental breakfast or a cool drink. Prices for a room with shared bath are $19 single, $32 double.

The **Moorings**, 207 Grand Ave. South, Falmouth Heights, MA 02540 (tel. 617/540-2370), is across from Falmouth Heights Beach, and some rooms have views of Martha's Vineyard. Morning coffee is served, most rooms have private baths, and rates are between $32 and $42.50 double.

Moderately Priced Motels

My favorite in Falmouth and perhaps on all Cape Cod is the **Elm Arch Inn**, off Main Street, Falmouth, MA 02540 (tel. 617/548-0133). Although originally a private house, the inn has been taking paying guests for over a century—50 years under the present management. The location couldn't be better: right in the center of town, a few steps from the library park, and yet back off Main Street in peace and quiet. The inn's 24 rooms are furnished in colonial-style pieces, many handmade, and are just plain charming. Several have private baths, others have running water and a bath down the hall. In Richardson House, the new addition to the inn, there are private baths throughout. Rooms with twin beds and bath cost $33.82 to $42.28 in season, $29.60 and up off-season; double bed and bath is $31.71 to $42.28, $27.48 and up off-season. Rooms with running water cost $23.25 to $25.37 single, $27.48 to $29.60 double, $31.71 to $33.82 twin in season; several dollars less per room off-season. No meals are served, but the inn offers free coffee in the mornings, in season. Note that the rooms do not have air conditioning, but that a good cross-breeze usually makes it unnecessary anyway; the living room has a color TV. Although you're a 20-minute walk from the beach here, the inn has its own small pool, bordered by a lush lawn and large trees, and a big screened patio for summer evenings.

For those who want a panoramic view of Falmouth harbor, there's the **Studio Motel,** 113 Falmouth Heights Rd., Falmouth, MA 02540 (tel. 617/548-1513). The arrangement here is the common house-turned-to-inn; the house is near the shore, but the new harborfront units are the ones with the views. In season, these cost $53 double; efficiency apartments (with cooking facilities, that is) are more. Rooms in the house are $37. All rooms have private bath and air conditioning, and morning coffee-and-doughnuts are on the house in season. The Studio has a fine lawn with umbrellas under which you can sit and watch the boats sail in and out. Here, you're a short walk from the dock for the *Island Queen* to Martha's Vineyard; the center of town, with the Village Green, is within walking distance.

The **Shore Haven Motor Lodge** is the place for those who want to be near the beach but not too far from downtown. It's at 321 Shore St. (between Main Street and the water), Falmouth, MA 02540 (tel. 617/548-1765), right on the beach. Rooms vary in type and price. The lodge itself is actually an old waterfront mansion converted to take guests. Rooms are clean and pleasant; they rent for $21.14 to $44.39 in season, $14.80 to $29.60 off-season, the higher prices being for rooms with private bath. Some of the "motel units" have cooking facilities, and rent for $301.25 per week in season, $206.12 off-season, double of course. The Shore Haven also has five duplex cottages which can accommodate four to six people. In my view, if you're staying only a day or two, take the rooms in the lodge. Open Memorial Day weekend until about September 15.

The **Shore Way Acres Motel** is more a resort than a motel, with two pools (indoor and outdoor), extensive grounds covered in lush grass, flowers, and trees. It's midway between downtown and the beach on Shore Street (tel. 617/540-3000)—you'll first come across its centerpiece, the stately old white clapboard lodge, dripping with wisteria. Behind the lodge are several attractive buildings with rooms and the glassed-in pool building. Saunas and an exercise room are included among the facilities. The rates here are somewhat of a tangle, and depend on the building you stay in, the time of year you stay, the length of your stay, the number of beds you use, and whether or not your room has kitchen facilities. In general, double rooms with bath cost $47 to $66. In season and on holidays, the minimum reservation period on weekends is three nights.

WHERE TO DINE: Falmouth is not a culinary mecca, although it does have a few quite decent eateries, some good for breakfast or a light lunch, others for a more formal dinner. Best all-around is the **Town House Restaurant,** 275 Main St. (tel. 548-0285), across the street from the town library. First thing you'll notice as you enter is a colorful tartan rug; wood wainscoting and barn boards dress the walls, and liberal use of brick gives the restaurant a rustic but warm feeling. At lunchtime there are soup-and-sandwich specials, a bowl of the soup of the day plus a choice of sandwich for $2.25. In the evening, omelets are $4; a king crabmeat salad, $4.95; and the Mariner Platter (sole, clams, scallops, shrimp, and onion rings) is $7.95. Be sure to inspect the seascape in watercolor painted by a local artist. Note that the Town House is open from the first of May to mid-October *only:* hours are 11:30 a.m. to 2 p.m. and 5 to 8:30 p.m. weekdays, to 9 p.m. weekends off-season. From July 1 through Labor Day hours are 11:30 a.m. to 10 p.m. daily.

For Elegant Dinners

Falmouth's finest place to dine is undoubtedly **The Regatta** (tel. 617/548-5400), at the southern end of Scranton Avenue, overlooking the mouth of Falmouth's long harbor. Open late May through mid-September only, and only for dinner every evening from 5:30 to about 10 p.m., the Regatta offers "informal waterfront dining with a touch of the gourmet." You'll want to be dressed neatly, if informally, and you should bring $30 to $35 per person to spend. But what a meal! Start with gravlax, the lightly cured salmon, or a chilled lobster and sole terrine; then proceed to finely prepared seafood, veal, beef, or chicken, and finish up with a chocolate truffle cake with raspberry sauce, or perhaps hand-dipped chocolate strawberries. The price estimated above will probably cover a bottle of wine, tax, and tip. Call for reservations.

For Lighter Fare

Downtown in Falmouth at 170 Main St., in the shopping district, is **Happiness Is . . .** (tel. 540-5234), a great place to drop in for soups, salads, sandwiches in Syrian pocket bread, yogurt, or ice cream. For $3.50 complete you can buy a bowl of clam chowder and a filling sandwich. It's only a block from the library.

WHAT TO SEE: Falmouth is a very pretty town, and walks through the beaches, and the older sections of town and along the Village Green are a must. For a detailed map, or for other information, send for the 68-page brochure from the Chamber of Commerce (P.O. Box 582, Falmouth, MA 02541), or call 617/548-8500.

During the summer season the **Falmouth Historical Society** has offerings in its lovely old mansion on Palmer Street, just off the Village Green (open Monday through Friday, 2 to 5 p.m.; admission is $1 for adults, 50¢ for children). For the price of admission you get to see the house next door (Conant House) and walk in the formal garden between the two. The people at the Historical Society will be careful to point out that the white Congregational church on the Green is equipped with a bell cast by Paul Revere.

Falmouth's local-girl-made-good is Katharine Lee Bates, the poet who wrote "America the Beautiful." Her house, furnished in 19th-century pieces, is at 16 Main St., and is open to visitors during the season, Monday through Friday from 2 to 5 p.m. ($1 for adults, 50¢ for children), under the auspices of the Falmouth Historical Society.

One of America's—and the world's—most exciting experiments in ecological living is being carried out at the **New Alchemy Institute**, 237 Hatchville Rd., in Hatchville (North Falmouth), MA 02536 (tel. 617/563-2655). The latest, or sometimes the most ancient, cultivation methods are being researched and adapted to fit the world of the future. The success which the New Alchemists have had in growing nutritious vegetables and fruits year round, using wind and solar energy, without chemical fertilizers or pesticides, is amazing. You have to see it all to believe it, and you can do it by dropping in any Saturday, May through September, for an educational session. Sessions start about noon —call for details.

WHAT TO DO: A prime Falmouth activity is to rent bicycles and take the bike path down to Woods Hole (see below). The Falmouth Bikeways Committee of the Chamber of Commerce publishes a pamphlet-map showing bike routes and beaches, and giving the addresses of shops which rent bicycles. Ask at the Information Office mentioned above, or call the Chamber at 548-8500. By biking to a beach you avoid paying the several dollars for parking, and you can put the money saved toward the rental fee.

Besides bicycling down to Woods Hole, Falmouth's greatest outdoor attraction is its coastline. The **town beach** is down at the end of Shore Street (best to walk, as parking can be a problem). The water can be very chilly except in July and August, but otherwise the beach is fine, with no dangerous undertows or currents, and a view of Martha's Vineyard in the distance.

Reputedly the best beach in Falmouth is called **Old Silver Beach**, several miles to the northwest of downtown Falmouth. If you have a bike, that's the way to go even though it's a distance, because it will cost you $2 to park when you get to Old Silver. In a way, the parking fee is not so bad, for it helps the town keep the beach clean. A headland and several jetties set the beach off into sections; the town runs a **Clam Bar** which sells sandwiches, fried clams, and soft drinks, and offers changing rooms. The crowd at Old Silver is spirited, young, and sun-hungry.

The town of Falmouth sponsors free **band concerts** down at the Falmouth Marina on Thursday evenings during the months of July and August. Try to make it to at least one concert; it's a real oldtime event.

ACROSS TO MARTHA'S VINEYARD: Falmouth's own *Island Queen,* Falmouth Heights Road (tel: 617/548-4800), built 1974, carries passengers and bicycles only (no cars) from Falmouth Marina to Oak Bluffs on the island. It does not operate year round, but sails three times a day in each direction during early June and late September (five times a day on weekends), and seven times a day in each direction from mid-June through the first week in September. Adults pay $7.50 round trip ($4 one way); children under 13 pay $4 round trip; children under 5 sail for free. Bicycles are taken at a charge of $4 round trip. The voyage takes about a half hour, and is usually quite smooth and comfortable. A refreshment bar on board serves snacks, sandwiches, soft drinks, beer, and cocktails. There is even a moonlight cruise on Tuesday and Thursday evenings in July and August.

For car ferries to the islands, you'll have to go to Woods Hole or Hyannis (see those sections for full particulars).

WOODS HOLE: When the Emperor of Japan visited the United States in 1976, one of the places he requested to visit was Woods Hole. Being a marine biologist himself, he was interested to see one of the world's great centers for the study of sea life, the **Woods Hole Oceanographic Institute (WHOI).** In a sense, the institute is the town, for its buildings, and that of its sister establishments, take up most of the space at the tip of a tiny peninsula, leaving room for only a few streets of fine old houses, a few small boatyards, a restaurant or two, and the car ferry docks to Martha's Vineyard and Nantucket islands.

The institute has no exhibits open to the public, but the U.S. Department of Commerce's National Marine Fisheries Service maintains an **aquarium,** on Water Street (the town's main street) down at the end of the peninsula—follow Water Street through the town, and just after it turns right the aquarium is on your left. It's open from mid-June to early September, 10 a.m. to 4:30 p.m. daily; free.

Where to Stay

Staying overnight in Woods Hole is not particularly cheap, although it can be very pleasant. The **Sands of Time Motor Inn** (tel. 617/548-6300), just outside the downtown section on the main road to Falmouth, has a fine view of the harbor and is only a short walk from the ferry docks. A unit of motel rooms overlooks the water, while a huge old shingled house behind it serves as lodge. A small garden and swimming pool are fitted into the hillside between the two. In the motel rooms, prices are $65.53 to $68.71 double in season; all these rooms come with private bath, color TV, and two double beds (extra person charge, $5). In the shingled "inn," rooms are lower in price, except the ones with working fireplaces and color TV, and all the inn rooms have a view of the water. The inn rooms are quite nice and flawlessly maintained, with crystal doorknobs, bright new paint, and sparkling bathrooms. A grandfather clock inhabits the pretty entranceway. None of the rooms in the Sands of Time's several buildings has air conditioning, but the breezes off the water usually render this unnecessary.

Sharing the hillside with the Sands of Time is the **Nautilus Motor Inn** (tel. 617/548-1525), a larger establishment with more facilities and slightly higher rates. Room prices are determined by the room's location, view, decor, and facilities, but all have private bath, color TV, and air conditioning. Prices off-season are $42.28 to $65.53; in season, $65.53 to $80.33 (extra person, $4 to $6). Here you have a pool and sundeck, tennis courts, and patches of grass at your disposal, plus a restaurant called the Dome (full dinners in the $9 to $16 range).

Where to Dine

A few restaurants near the ferry docks specialize in big, rich seafood dinners at substantial prices—just what you don't want before taking a boat ride if there's any chance the water may be a bit rough, so I recommend that you have a light lunch at the **Fishmonger's Café**, on Woods Hole's main street just before the little bridge, on the left (official address, 56 Water St.). Lunch and dinner specials are written on the blackboard and sandwiches are available anytime. Grilled fish with rice and herb butter is $5.50; a good clam chowder is $1.25 a cup, $2.25 a bowl. The atmosphere is rustic, with rough wood tables, a matchboard ceiling, board floors, and sea breezes wafting in through the windows. Heavily patronized by local people and visitors to the institute, you may hear Japanese or Spanish being spoken as foreign biologists discuss their countries' marine problems and opportunities. Service is fast, which is what you need if you have to catch a ferry. The Fishmonger's Café is open from 7 a.m. to 10 p.m. daily, except on Tuesday (11:30 a.m. to 10 p.m.) and Sunday (8 a.m. to 10 p.m.).

CAR FERRY TO THE ISLANDS: The **Woods Hole, Martha's Vineyard and Nantucket Steamship Authority**, P.O. Box 284, Woods Hole, MA 02543 (tel. 617/540-2022), operates car-carrying ferries between the points listed in their name, and also Hyannis. Schedules change several times a year, so it's best to call in advance for full current information. In fact, if you plan to ship your car, you *must* have a car reservation. You can get one by calling the number above. Ferries from Woods Hole to Vineyard Haven or Oak Bluffs on Martha's Vineyard Island leave about six times a day in winter, 12 times a day in summer, on the 45-minute trip. Fares are $7.50 round trip for adults, half price for kids 5 to 15, free for kids under 5. Bikes go for $2.50 one way. Autos cost

$21.50 one way in season. From Woods Hole to Nantucket Island, boats run from January through March and mid-June through mid-September. Adult one-way fare is $8 (same arrangements for kids as noted above); bikes cost $4 and cars are $45.50 one way.

It is possible to take your car from Woods Hole to Martha's Vineyard, and then, later, from the Vineyard to Nantucket, or vice-versa. Return to the mainland is either to Woods Hole or Hyannis. (See Hyannis section.)

Parking Fees at the Docks: If you don't plan to ferry your car over, and you don't ride a bike or take the bus to Woods Hole, figure on paying $4.50 to park your car for each *calendar* day ($9 if you leave your car overnight). It is virtually impossible to find a free, legal parking place in Woods Hole in summer or for overnight unless you stay at a motel and use their lot. The Steamship Authority has a dockside lot charging these fees, and also a large lot in Falmouth, with free shuttle bus service to the Woods Hole docks. In late July and all of August you can often save yourself some time by planning to park in the Falmouth lot, because the dockside lot is almost always full.

The Woods Hole ferry docks are served by Plymouth & Brockton Street Railway buses to Boston and by Bonanza lines to Providence and New York. *Important note:* Although bus schedules leaving Woods Hole are designed to work in conjunction with ferry arrivals, often the ferry is late, and *the bus does not wait.* Do not take the last ferry of the day from the islands to Woods Hole (or to Hyannis) and depend on getting the last bus out—you may in fact be able to do it, but it's not dependable. Take an earlier ferry.

3. Sandwich

Sandwich calls itself "the oldest town on the Cape" (incorporated 1639), and it is certainly one of the most beautiful and serene. Much of the vacation traffic to the Cape rushes past it on the way to Provincetown, leaving Sandwich to those few who appreciate it. The town holds its appeal both winter and summer, for although it has beaches, its antique stores and gracious old houses also draws visitors. Other attractions are **Heritage Plantation, Dexter's Mill,** and the **Sandwich Glass Museum,** which holds a fine collection of the interesting glassware once made here.

WHERE TO STAY AND DINE: Route 6A between Sandwich, East Sandwich, and Barnstable has several groupings of motels—one to fit every taste, it would seem. Of the motels on Route 6A, my favorite is the **Spring Hill Motor Lodge,** East Sandwich, MA 02537 (tel. 617/888-1456), which is 2½ miles east of the center of Sandwich. The motel is set back from the road, and a small stand of pine trees is in the front yard, enclosed by a wooden fence which supports more roses (in season) than one would think possible. The place is modern, but built in a traditional style congruent with the Cape's architectural style. Rooms are of the standard motel type (including TV), simply but comfortably furnished, many of the rooms having two double beds and little refrigerators ($4 per day extra if you use it). The season runs from the last week of June through Labor Day, when prices are $42.28 to $44.39 for a room with one double bed (one or two persons), $46.51 for two double beds (for two persons). An extra person in the room costs $5. A two-bedroom suite is offered which costs $52.85 to $63.42 in season. All rooms are air-conditioned. Rates go down before and after high season, and go down again in deep winter, when the charge for staying is only $25.37 for one double bed, $29.60 for two.

A bit closer to town is another good choice, the **Country Acres Motel,** P.O. Box 307, Sandwich, MA 02563 (tel. 617/888-2878). It's open all year, is slightly older than the Spring Hill Motor Lodge, and has a wide range of different rooms as well as a swimming pool. At the Country Acres you can get a room with twin beds, rooms with one double bed or two, or housekeeping cottages complete with kitchen. All rooms have TV, and some (which cost a bit more) have air conditioning. Rates vary with the season of the year and with demand, but are like this: $29.60 for a room with double bed in midwinter, $34.88 to $42.28 for the same room in high summer (late June, July, and August). The motel is eight-tenths of a mile from the center of Sandwich, and the units are arrayed perpendicular to the highway, which makes for less street noise.

Those watching their budgets and yet possessed of a great hunger will want to know about the **Sagamore Inn** (tel. 888-9707), on the Sandwich-Sagamore line on Route 6A (you come to the inn after the Sagamore Bridge, before the town of Sandwich). The decor is not fancy: wooden booths, a stamped-tin ceiling, a Budweiser sign next to the highway. The waitresses are all hometown women, the clientele local families, and the food is hearty, savory, and delicious, the portions huge, and the prices low. The cook's inspiration is Italian cuisine, and so you can find spaghetti dishes for $5.50 to $8, seafood for $7 to $10, sandwiches for $1.25 to $6.25, and such treats as a medium-size antipasto plate for $4. Everyone here is friendly and pleasant and out to make you happy.

WHAT TO SEE: Sandwich is an old-fashioned town true to its traditions, a very pleasant place to live or to visit. A walk downtown will give you clues to its character right away; backyard shops for artisans working in wood, leather, wrought iron, clay, or oil-on-canvas; graceful church steeples; small, well-groomed parks; comely old houses, many with the date of construction posted over the front door. Sooner or later your walk will bring you by **Yesteryears Doll and Miniature Museum** at Main and River Streets (open daily May through October from 10 a.m. to 5 p.m., on Sunday from 1 to 5 p.m.), housed in what was once the town hall and First Parish Meetinghouse. Literally hundreds of fascinating antique dolls, dollhouses, and toys as well as many other domestic articles are on display, and exhibits change from time to time. The museum is nonprofit, but charges admission to defray expenses: $2 per adult, $1 per child under 16, $1.50 for seniors.

From Yesteryear's it's a short walk to the **Dexter Mill,** at the end of a lovely mill pond (complete with ducks), and next to a cool, splashing mill race and an old pump. The mill (1654) was fully restored in 1961, and is not just a picturesque attraction, although you can go in (daily from 10 a.m. to 5 p.m., on Sunday from noon to 5 p.m.) and see the wooden mechanisms at work. The mill actually grinds corn and you can buy bags of fresh meal the same day it's ground. (Admission is 75¢ for adults, 50¢ for children.)

Across from Sandwich's Greek revival town hall is the **Sandwich Glass Museum** (open daily from 9:30 a.m. to 4:30 p.m., April 1 to November 1; admission is $1.50, special group rates available). Sandwich was a major glass-producing town from 1825 to 1888, and although it specialized in the new process of pressing glass in a mold, it also produced blown, cut, etched, and enameled products as well. A brilliant collection of this American glassware is on display, and dioramas and pictures show how it was made. Glassmakers' tools and other articles of Sandwich memorabilia are also part of the museum's collection. The glass museum is the only one of its kind on the Cape.

Perhaps Sandwich's most famous attraction is the **Heritage Plantation** of Sandwich (tel. 888-3300), a mile from town on Grove Street. Another of the museums in which New England abounds, Heritage Plantation specializes not in any one era but has exhibits from all periods of American history. The automobile collection, 34 cars dating from 1899 to 1936, is one of the most popular things to see. Another collection is of firearms and tin soldiers, and still others show American crafts and the tools used to perform them. The buildings and grounds of the plantation are an attraction in themselves, all being reproductions of early-style buildings set in gardens and nature areas covering 76 acres. The plantation is open from mid-May through mid-October, and one ticket ($4 for adults, $1.50 for kids; 5 and under, free) admits a visitor to the grounds, all exhibits, and any of the periodically scheduled shows, concerts, and other activities.

Sandwich has several old houses open to the public for a fee, the most well known of which is **Hoxie House,** on Route 130 along the shore of Shawme Pond (the mill pond). The house dates from the end of the 1600s, and has been restored and furnished with articles of that period. The house is open from 10 a.m. to 5 p.m. daily in season, and you can buy a combination ticket good for admission here and at the Dexter Mill.

The town's beaches include **Town Beach,** the most westerly, and then, in order heading east, **Spring Hill Beach, East Sandwich Beach,** and over the line in Barnstable, **Sandy Neck Beach.** They all have toilets and places to park, and the bay side of the Cape has generally warmer swimming than the ocean side. Look for signs to the beaches on the side roads left (north) off Route 6A between Sandwich and Barnstable.

4. Hyannis

Hyannis gained national fame during the presidency of John F. Kennedy because of his summer home in nearby Hyannisport. Some of the town's growth and perhaps a good portion of its honky-tonk dates from that time, and although curious or devoted fans of the late president still stop to look at the town or to visit its memorial to JFK, the attractions in Hyannis these days are commercial. Should you need the services of an airline, department store, supermarket, or foreign auto parts warehouse while on the Cape, Hyannis is the place to come. If you don't need these things, there are many nicer places on the Cape to spend precious vacation time.

TRANSPORTATION: Specifics on schedules and routes are given above in this chapter's first section, "Getting There." Here's what you'll want to know about Hyannis's facilities:

Airport: The airport is right in town, a short taxi ride from the bus stations or downtown. Several companies offer small planes for charter.

Bus Stations: Greyhound/Bonanza and **Plymouth & Brockton buses** all use the same terminal at Elm and Centre Streets (tel. 617/775-5524). **Southern Massachusetts Bus Lines** uses a terminal a half block away at 68 Centre St. (tel. 617/771-3100 or 617/771-3101). **Cape Cod Bus Lines** has its main terminal in Falmouth, and uses the Greyhound terminal in Hyannis for its trips to Yarmouth, Dennis, Brewster, Orleans, Eastham, Wellfleet, Truro, and Provincetown. **Peter Pan Bus Lines,** which has routes from Hyannis to Amherst, Northampton, Holyoke, Springfield, and Worcester in the summer, uses the Plymouth & Brockton (Greyhound/Bonanza) terminal.

Boat Docks: Hyannis has two main docks, at the foot of Ocean Street for fishing and cruise vessels, and at the foot of Pleasant Street for the passenger and car ferries to Nantucket on the Steamship Authority's boats (tel. 617/771-4000). The docks are about five blocks from the bus stations. (Many buses connecting with ferries take passengers right to the dock.)

WHERE TO STAY: A choice area of motels and guest houses is down Sea Street, off Main Street south toward Keyes Memorial Beach. The most expensive and luxurious place to stay in this area is just off of Sea Street on Gosnold Street. The **Captain Gosnold Village**, P.O. Box 544, Hyannis, MA 02601 (tel. 617/775-9111), is a collection of different types of housing units spread through large and well-kept lawns and copses of trees. Guests have the use of a heated pool, children's playground, shuffleboard, and picnic tables. From late June until Labor Day, motel rooms cost $41.22 to $51.79 (suitable for two, three, or four people); efficiencies are $54.96; a one-bedroom cottage, $72.93; other cottages higher; and $5 for an extra person. Off-season rates are $12.68 to $16.91 lower per room, 25% to 40% lower per cottage. Also, discounts for longer stays (over a week) can save you money during off-season periods. Rooms are paneled, carpeted, equipped with a refrigerator, TV, and coffeemaker, and all have private baths. The beach is a ten-minute walk away.

The **Sea Breeze by the Beach**, 397 Sea St., Hyannis, MA 02601 (tel. 617/775-4269), is very close to Keyes Beach, and has both motel rooms and cottages equipped with TV, private tiled baths, and (in a few rooms) a view of the ocean. A fully equipped kitchen is available for guests' use. Rates vary with the size of the room, number of beds, and similar features, but a normal double costs $39.11 in season; a larger double with a queen-size bed and sea view would cost several dollars more. Recommended.

Sea Street has at least six guest houses varying from ones with very simple rooms-only to those which offer a bit of atmosphere and service. The **Sea Witch Inn**, 363 Sea St., Hyannis, MA 02601 (tel. 617/771-4261 or 775-3608), is the fanciest such guest house on the street, about equidistant from Main Street and Keyes Beach—you'll recognize it by a big red sleigh in the front yard. The lawn is large and lush, shade trees rise here and there, and the inn is painted an appropriately nautical blue-and-white. Rooms here cost $19.03 to $31.71 per day for two people in a room; most rooms are in the $19.03 to $23.25 range. If you rent by the week there's a reduction, as there is if you come in months other than July and August. For longer stays, the Sea Witch has a studio apartment and a cottage for rent by the week.

The **Harvard Guest House**, 37 Harvard St., Hyannis, MA 02601 (tel. 617/771-3458), is a private house with some of Hyannis's lowest rates: $10 to $12 per person in a double room. As there are only a few rooms here, call early for reservations.

Bouchard's Tourist Homes and Apartments, 83 School St., Hyannis, MA 02601 (tel. 617/775-0912), has several buildings and therefore a larger number of rooms at tourist-home prices, plus some apartments for long-term stays. Lowest price is for a room without running water which shares a tub-and-shower bathroom with one other room; cost is $21 single. For $37 two people can have a room with washbasin; for $41 there are rooms with color cable TV, air conditioning, twin beds, private tub-and-shower bath, even a private entrance. Off-season rates for the rooms (after Labor Day until the last week in June) can go as low as $10 to $14 a day for two.

One of Hyannis's better places to stay is at **Hills**, 530 W. Main St., Hyannis, MA 02601 (tel. 617/775-0344), a charming inn. Rooms all have two double beds, which is a bonus for families, and also private baths. On weekends, a room rents at $47.57 double, plus $5 for each extra person—that means a family of five can stay for $52.85 total, or $10.57 per person. On weekdays rates are much cheaper: $31.71 double. Right next door is the famous Hills Dining Room (see below).

WHERE TO DINE: Hyannis has a good number of restaurants, most of them serving the same things in the same surroundings at the same prices (with food of the same quality). All the national chains, from Burger King to Howard Johnson's, have representatives here, and while serviceable these places are hardly atmospheric. If you've just landed in Hyannis from New York and you want to dive into New England's gustatory pleasures right away, seek out:

A Hyannis institution, **Hills Dining Room**, 530 W. Main St. (tel. 775-0344), is a family-run business which specializes in good traditional recipes made the hard way: baked right in the kitchen, or fixed with vegetables from their own garden. Everything is as fresh as possible, and the staff takes all day to prepare it—dinner, from 5 to 9 p.m. (noon on Sunday), is the only meal served, but a lighter sandwich menu is available also in the Lounge until 11:30 p.m. Chicken, veal, seafood, steak, each in a delicious no-nonsense style, make up the main courses. The desserts are a special delight—don't go if you must resist such temptations. The price will be a reasonable $9 to $15 for the entire meal.

Right on Main Street, at no. 415, in the center of the shopping district, is the **Asa Bearse House Restaurant** (tel. 771-4131). The house's big old porch is a favorite Hyannis spot for cocktails; the crowd usually moves to the front-lawn terrace if the weather's fine. The luncheon menu lists lots of sandwiches, but the special lunch-of-the-day—something like a quiche or fish dish—is only $5, including salad and rolls. At dinner the menu turns exotic, to escargots ($3.95), and familiar, to steaks ($13 to $14). Open daily 11 a.m. to 10 p.m. for food, till 1 a.m. for drinks in season; closed Sunday off-season. The original 1840 barn in back, opened in 1981, is hailed by *Yankee* magazine as "the most beautiful room on Cape Cod."

Harvard Square's **Würsthaus** (tel. 771-5000) has a branch in Hyannis, in the Cape Cod Mall. Boasting the "world's largest selection of foreign beers," the Würsthaus is the place to find Mexican Dos Equis and Israeli Gold Star as well as Löwenbräu and Beck's. A long list of sandwiches ($2.25 to $5), salad plates, side orders, and desserts keeps the light-lunch and late-night crowds happy, while for hungrier diners there are steaks ($6.95 to $11) and moderately priced fish. The Würsthaus specializes in Bavarian-style food and is open for breakfast, and then until 1 a.m. daily.

WHAT TO SEE: Many visitors to Hyannis stop to see the memorial to President Kennedy, a stone structure bearing the presidential seal and a small fountain, on Ocean Street right along the water. Hyannisport and the **"Kennedy compound,"** noted in news stories while the late president vacationed here, are not far from the monument. None of the buildings is open to the public.

Also along Ocean Street are **Kalmus Park** and **Veteran's Park**, with their respective beaches, bathhouses, and snackbars. Go down to the south end of Sea Street for **Orrin Keyes Memorial Beach.** Besides swimming facilities, Keyes Beach has a little platform on top of a dune from which you can take a look at the sweep of the beach.

Big-name stars and bands are booked into the **Cape Cod Melody Tent,** at the West Main Street Rotary in Hyannis (tel. 775-9100). The season goes from early June to one week after Labor Day, and runs the gamut—from Bob Hope and Tony Bennett all the way to Crystal Gayle. Tickets are priced differently depending on the show, but most run in the $10 to $18 range, with Thursday matinees, early Saturday evening, and weeknight performances being the less expensive ones in that order. Tickets can be charged by calling the box office.

You'll have to drive to get to the **Cape Playhouse** (tel. 385-3911), on Route 6A in Dennis, but if you do it will be to see a famous actor or actress in a well-known play. The plays (and actors) usually change every week, so call to see what's current. The season runs from early July through Labor Day, with performances each evening (except Sunday) at 8:30 p.m., plus matinees on Wednesday and Thursday at 2:30 p.m. Tickets are priced from $8 to $15. The playhouse has its own restaurant, open for lunch, dinner, Sunday brunch, and after-theater snacks. Also here is the **Cape Cinema,** home of first-run movies and of a mammoth, 6400-square-foot mural of the heavens by Rockwell Kent.

FERRIES TO THE ISLANDS: Two firms operate ferries to the islands of Martha's Vineyard and Nantucket from Hyannis, each operating from a different dock. Here are the details:

Woods Hole, Martha's Vineyard, and Nantucket Steamship Authority (tel. 617/540-2022 for car reservations; the number in Hyannis is 617/771-4000) runs cars and passenger ferries from Hyannis's Pleasant Street docks (follow the signs in town). No direct service is run between Hyannis and Martha's Vineyard by this firm—you have to go via Nantucket. The Steamship Authority's boats run four times daily to Nantucket in summer, less frequently off-season; the trip takes about two hours and costs $8 for adults, half fare for kids 5 to 15. Auto-ferry space must be reserved in advance; in high summer it costs about $45.50 to ship a car one way from Hyannis to Nantucket. In high summer, one ferry is run in each direction between Martha's Vineyard and Nantucket, taking about two hours and costing $7.80 per adult (kids pay half fare), $45.50 per auto. The ferries are large, comfortable, and equipped with lunch counters and bars. Note that if you park in the dockside lots you'll have to pay $4.50 per calendar day for the privilege. *Special Note:* When returning to Hyannis from Nantucket, don't plan on taking the last ferry of the day and meeting the bus to Boston or New York, for the ferries are often delayed and *the bus does not wait.* To be safe, catch a ferry well ahead of the last bus trip scheduled from Hyannis. If you find yourself in a jam because of ferry mix-ups, you can always take another line (see below) or fly.

The **Hy-Line** (tel. 617/775-7185) has several swift passenger-only boats which depart from Hyannis's Ocean Street docks for Nantucket ($8 for an adult, half price for a child) and Martha's Vineyard ($7.50 for adults, half price for kids). Round-trip rates of $15 and $7.50 apply, and although no cars are carried on the Hy-Line's boats, you can take your bicycle over for $4 one way. These boats operate May though November only. By the way, if you sign up for a same-day round trip, you'll have to tell them which boat you plan to return on, and they'll stamp your ticket with the boat's departure time. Otherwise, you must take your chances with standby status.

5. Chatham

Chatham was once the railhead for Cape Cod, and the trains that brought vacationers in and took fish, salt, and shoes out also brought the opportunity for wealth. Chatham is therefore a graceful community with many big old houses and a few grand hotels on the Victorian scale, an easy pace, friendly people, and pleasant vistas all around.

The town maintains an **Information Booth** on Main Street in the center of town (tel. 617/945-0342) during the summer season. It's run by citizens who know the town inside and out, and has available brochures on places to stay, copies of menus from local restaurants, and information on activities.

WHERE TO STAY: Chatham seems to have at least one kind of every accommodation imaginable, so you should have little trouble finding a place you'll like by skimming down this list:

The **Chatham Bars Inn,** at the corner of Chatham Bars Avenue and Shore Road, Chatham, MA 02633 (tel. 617/945-0096), is a true bit of old Chatham, a huge rambling, gracious resort hotel with many attractive nonhousekeeping cottages on the property all operated on the American Plan (rates include meals). Enter the inn by the motor entrance, bear to the right, and you'll enter the parlor, with its highly arched ceiling, lots of windows looking onto a shady veranda, and wicker furniture for cool sitting on warm summer days. The lobby is also grand, large, and spacious, and a stairway out the front door tumbles down the hillside to the road and beyond it to the inn's private beach. Boating, tennis, and golf on the inn's own nine-hole course are other services offered. The staff is large, friendly, well trained, and soft-spoken. Of course, proper dress is required at dinner: jacket and tie for men, pantsuit, summer cottons, cocktail dress, or long dress for women. All three meals are included in these rates: $184 to $230 per couple per day, tax and service included, for a double with bath. If these figures look high, remember that, on the average, one pays $60 to $80 for a luxury motel room, plus two breakfasts, two lunches, and two good dinners, which often brings a normal vacation day's expenses to about $160 per couple. The Chatham Bars Inn is pricey, yes, but it's also a bit of history brought up to modern standards of comfort and service, and we doubt that you'd be disappointed here.

Accessible only by car is the **Pleasant Bay Village Motel,** P.O. Box 772, Chatham, MA 02633 (tel. 617/945-1133), on Route 28 several miles north of town in the section called Chathamport. The motel is about as pleasant as you'll find, located on six acres of very carefully kept grounds, evergreen hedges, trees, bushes, and cascades of roses along the front rail fence. The motel's buildings are scattered through the grounds, and there's a heated pool, badminton, shuffleboard, and Ping-Pong, besides just lounging in the sun, to keep you occupied. The motel has a breakfast room (light lunches served as well). Rooms are modern with paneled walls, private baths, wall-to-wall carpeting, and cable color TV, and most have two double beds. In season (last week in June to Labor Day), motel rooms cost $62 for one double bed, $72 to $92 for rooms with two double beds of ever-increasing size and luxury.

For those who prefer an inn right in the middle of things, the **Chatham Wayside Inn,** 512 Main St., Chatham, MA 02633 (tel. 617/945-0259 or 945-9738), is worth a look. It's right in the center of town, and although the original structure is quite old, the dining rooms and chambers have been updated to meet modern standards of hotel comfort. Besides the rooms in the inn proper, an annex has a number of motel-type rooms to offer. The inn's restaurant is open seven days a week, and is very popular with the townfolk ("Rotary meets here"). Rooms at the Wayside cost $53, in season or out.

In the way of a fairly luxurious motel, Chatham offers the **Hawthorne Motel,** 196 Shore Rd. (tel. 617/945-0372), just up the bank from the beach.

The Hawthorne looks brand-new although it was built over a decade ago. Rooms are simply and attractively decorated, mostly in solid colors, and all rooms are equipped with color TV, a small refrigerator, and large windows (picture windows in those with a sea view). Green lawns roll down the bank from the motel to the private beach reserved for its guests. All the motel rooms are air-conditioned. Rates are $54.96 to $61.31 double per day in high season (late June to Labor Day), the higher prices being for rooms with a good view. Efficiencies are $58.14 double, and a two-bedroom cottage costs $95.13 per day for two, plus $10 for each extra person. Children count as extra guests when staying in the same room. If you get a room with a sea view at the Hawthorne, chances are you'll be able to see Chatham's fishing fleet come in during the afternoon, as the town's Fish Pier is just a short distance away to the north.

Close to the downtown area without being right smack in the center is **The Moorings Motel and Motor Lodge,** 326 Main St. (tel. 617/945-0848). The Moorings consists of a grand old Chatham house, its carriage house, with an annex of motel units attached, a cottage, and another building housing efficiency units. The complex once belonged to a retired admiral, and now serves well as a hostelry. Furnishings and styles of rooms vary with the building you stay in, the ones in the guest house being more traditional and Victorian, the ones in the modern motel annex being modern but decorated in the colonial style. Prices vary as well, the rooms on the upper floor of the carriage (or coach) house costing $40.16 to $44.39, those in the guest house being $54.96 to $65.53. The motel rooms are $54.96; the efficiencies are $369.95 to $528.50 per week. The Moorings doesn't have a restaurant, but continental breakfast is available. Off-season rates are in effect during spring and fall.

Near the Moorings, and therefore near the downtown area—a five-minute walk—is the **Cranberry Inn,** 359 Main St. (tel. 617/945-9232), very much like a large guest house in looks and atmosphere, but including a restaurant. Prices are very reasonable: $30.65 for one or two people in one double bed, $33.82 for twin beds. Off-season, rates are $23.25 and $26.43, respectively. All rooms have running water, some adjoining rooms have private baths; check the bed to see if it's to your liking. The Cranberry Inn is open from mid-May to the end of October.

Another inn downtown in Chatham is the **Town House Inn,** 11 Library Lane, off Main Street (tel. 617/945-2180). There are 16 rooms here with private bath, plus a new six-room lodge. All the rooms are decorated differently, but with great taste and thoughtfulness, even to using hand-hooked rugs rather than wall-to-wall carpeting so that the beautiful old floors can be seen. All the rooms have refrigerators, color cable TV, and individual thermostats. Some have waterbeds. Rates in season are $68.71, $79.28, and $89.85 for a double with bath. An extra person costs $5. A two-bedroom cottage rents for $819.18 per week in season. You can get breakfast at the inn if you wish.

A nice cozy guest house out toward the water and also only a few minutes' walk from the center of town and a shopping center is the **Bow Roof House,** 59 Queen Anne Rd. (tel. 617/945-1346), run by the Joseph Mazulis family. The main house is that of an old sea captain, and many rooms still have the fireplaces (not working now) that were installed to keep out the chill of those winter blasts which roll in off the water. A large living room with rough timbered ceiling and large fireplace is here for guests' use, and just through the door from it is a terrace with tables and umbrellas for a glass of wine (BYO) or tea in the evening. Rooms will cost about $32 double with private bath and continental breakfast, once present construction is completed. If you go in summer, the bank in front of the house will be a riot of wildflowers, and the two yuccas by the door may be in bloom.

WHERE TO DINE: Chatham has a good assortment of restaurants in different price ranges, each with its own ambience. It's easy to find one you like.

The **Impudent Oyster,** on Chatham Bars Avenue just off Main Street (tel. 617/945-3545), has a long and eclectic menu perfect for those evenings when you don't know what sort of cuisine to choose. Chinese, French, Italian, and Mexican-style dishes, each with a different local touch; sandwiches and elegant main courses; seafood and meats—all share the menu. The oysters, by the way, are freshly shucked. Plan to spend $18 to $40 per person for a nice dinner with wine. Dress neatly, but not formally, and call for reservations.

The **Garden Café** (no phone) is in the Swinging Basket Mall, a small collection of shops at the intersection of Chatham Bars Avenue and Main Street. Set near numerous fascinating browsing places, the café is a fine place for a sip, a snack, or a supper (11:30 a.m. to 9 p.m.). For instance, their ploughman's lunch of cheeses, fresh fruit, and French bread costs $5; soups, salads, sandwiches, and wines are served as well.

If you're staying in Chatham and you'd like to walk to dinner, try the **Chatham Wayside Inn** (tel. 945-0259), at 512 Main St. Although the inn is old, the dining rooms are a comfortable blend of modern furnishings and colonial touches. Local people throng here every day, so it's best to have a reservation. Try their fried native oysters ($9), prime rib of beef ($15), or any of the seafood plates priced at $8 to $13, salad, rolls, and butter included.

The young and golden and the young and hip have dinner at the **Chatham Squire Restaurant** (tel. 945-9785), near the intersection of Main and Chatham Bars Avenue. The bar in the room to the left is semifunky, with license plates from a dozen states nailed to a huge rough ceiling beam, the dining room to the right is nicely furnished with Pennsylvania Dutch–style wooden benches and tables. It's a big place, attractive and well tended, and with an interesting menu: for lunch perhaps a "crock o' chowder" with crackers ($3.50) or a salad plate ($3 to $4.50); at dinnertime their seafood of the day is $10, soup or appetizer included. To do it up right the New England way, order a lobster, steamers, and corn on-the-cob.

The **Cranberry Inn** (tel. 945-9232) at 359 Main St. serves dinners in one recently remodeled dining room decorated with wrought-iron furniture, wooden captain's chairs, and a strawberry-colored wallpaper. You feel as if you're at mother's in the kitchen here, especially when she comes out with a Yankee pot roast dinner for only $8. Have a cocktail before dinner if you wish.

A light lunch, New York style, is available at the **Town House Pantry,** 599 Main St., right downtown. The lightest of lunches, a toasted bagel with cream cheese, is 75¢, and prices rise from there: Greek salad, $1.50 to $1.95; croissants stuffed with ham, cheese, tuna, etc., and dozens of sandwiches for $1.35 to $4, the latter being a lobster club sandwich (yes, it exists!). The Pantry is small, cheerful, high-quality, low-priced, and large windows keep it from being claustrophobic.

Most people, both young and old, go to the **Chatham Ice Cream and Sandwich Shoppe,** Main Street at Chatham Bars Avenue, for ice cream. The place looks like the typical summer-resort ice cream shoppe, complete with sunburned help, a long counter, and a number of wrought-iron tables and chairs painted white. But the cones (80¢ and up) are just the beginning for they serve sundaes and also light but adequate lunches: gazpacho is $1.50; various burgers and sandwiches, $2 to $3. If it's midafternoon and you can't justify lunch, just buy a small cone and take it across the street to the New England Gallery, an attractive group of art galleries and gift shops set among garden walks and open to all for a stroll.

Budget Seafood

The **Chowderworks**, 739 Main St. (tel. 945-2019), is just that: a chowder "factory" which specializes in quahog (hard-shell clam) chowder and seafood chowder and lobster bisque, with small, medium, and large servings priced accordingly. They'll pack chowder to go, too. Hungrier? Order their lobster salad, or one of the other salads, plus a loaf of homemade bread (you keep what's left of the bread after you've finished with lunch). You can even buy littleneck clams and oysters one by one. Look for the Sign of the Sail—that's the Chowderworks, too. Only soft drinks, milk, coffee, and tea served, as far as beverages go.

READER'S RESTAURANT SELECTION: "A new restaurant in Chatham is the **Trifles à Café,** a small restaurant with a deck and picnic tables that caters to serving breakfast and light lunch. It has an assortment of sandwiches, soups, salads, and desserts, as well as quiche Lorraine. The place is most casual, but the food is all freshly made and delicious. It is located off Main Street in the public town parking lot behind the Information Booth" (Melanie Petit, Chatham, Mass.).

WHAT TO SEE: There's quite a lot to see and do in this venerable New England town.

The Light and the Fish Pier

The light is the first place to go in Chatham. Go east on Main Street and turn right (south) on Shore Road to the light. The lighthouse is right next to the Coast Guard Station; on the other side of the street is a place to park while you look at the view, some pay telescopes, and down below, a fine beach. The first light was erected on this point of land in 1808, and the present lighthouse dates from 1878, just over a century ago.

The view is very pleasant, looking out to sea across Nauset Beach (the sand bar, actually a peninsula, you see out in the water). The cool sea breeze in summer and the nautical blast in winter make one think it incredible that Rome is at almost exactly the same latitude (but 4200 miles away) as Chatham. The pier (Main Street east to Shore Street, then left/north) is interesting in that it is operated by the town for licensed Chatham fishermen. Chatham is very proud of its fishing fleet of small boats, which the town fathers boast brings in the freshest fish around. The boast has some truth to it, for the use of little boats means that the catch must be brought home every day, whereas larger boats can stay out to sea for several days, refrigerating their catch on board.

The time to go down to the pier is between 3 and 6 p.m. (aim for 4). You'll see the fleet come in and unload, and you can buy the day's catch right after it comes off the boat. Those who'd like to do it themselves can rent a boat at Fish Pier for a day's hunting for bass, bluefish, and tuna out at sea.

Beaches

The town of Chatham has public beaches ($3 a day, $15 a week, $25 the season) at **Oyster Pond,** only a few blocks from the center of town south on Stage Harbor Road from Main Street; and a bit farther out at **Harding's Beach** —follow Main Street (Route 28) west from the center of town for about two miles, and turn left (south) on Barn Hill Road to Harding's Beach Road. Lifeguards and toilets are at both beaches, but no bathhouses.

The Bird and Wildlife Sanctuary

Chatham is a particularly good place for seeing birds, for **Monomoy Island,** south of the town, has been a National Wilderness Area since 1970. Over 300 different species of birds have been spotted on Monomoy. May is the best time to see birds in their mating plumage, and starting in late July many birds begin to be seen in winter plumage. The only way to get to Monomoy is by boat from Chatham. Full details on current offerings are available from the town's information booth on Main Street (tel. 617/945-0342).

Band Concerts

One of the nicest things about Chatham in July and August is the schedule of band concerts (every Friday evening at 8 p.m.) in **Kate Gould Park,** just past the Wayside Inn on Main Street. Everybody comes to the concerts, and on a typical Friday evening the crowd may reach into the thousands. Most of the musicians in the town band are year-round residents of Chatham who live and work in the town and enjoy providing a little free entertainment for their fellow citizens and visitors once a week.

Theater

The **Monomoy Theater,** on Main Street, not far west of the intersection with Old Harbor Road (tel. 945-1589), is the summer-stock operation of Ohio University, and offers a different play each week during July and August. Performances are given Wednesday through Saturday, and the current play is advertised on flyers around town and in the local newspapers. Season tickets are available, should you be spending the summer in Chatham.

Historical Sites

Chatham has its share of antique buildings open to the public, each highlighting a separate part of the town's interesting past. The **Atwood House and Museums** are run by the Chatham Historical Society and feature over 2000 exhibits including an outstanding shell collection, a good number of pieces of Sandwich glass, and a crewel bedspread which took townspeople six years to make. Also on display at the house is a set of French lighthouse lenses used in the Chatham Light from 1923 until recently. Atwood House is open Monday, Wednesday, and Friday from mid-June to mid-September, 2 to 5 p.m., except holidays. Admission is $1 for adults, 50¢ for students, free for children accompanied by adults.

Chatham's **Railroad Museum** is located in the old station on Depot Road (take Old Harbor Road north off Main Street, and Depot Street is a short distance up on the left). The station was built in 1887 by the Chatham Railroad Company, and turned into a museum in 1960. Among the railroading exhibits is a real caboose, once used by the New York Central until that company gave it to the museum. The museum is open Monday through Friday from 2 to 5 p.m. during July, August, and early September. It's staffed with townspeople who act as volunteer guides, and admission is free.

Chatham also has an old **Grist Mill** open to the public daily except Tuesday, July and August only. Entrance is free, but donations are accepted. Sometimes corn is ground between the mill's stones if the wind is sufficient. To find it, take Cross Street south off Main Street to Shattuck Place, which winds down to the mill.

6. Yarmouth

The stretch of Route 6A between Sandwich and Yarmouth is a lush panorama of bogs and marshes, distant views of dunes and the sea, birds calling and fluttering, the winding road dotted with antique shops, craft shops, art galleries, and other businesses, including lots and lots of real estate offices. Eventually the road leads through Yarmouthport.

WHERE TO STAY: Yarmouthport has several fine inns and guest houses, with good variety in prices and accommodations. It's a nice place to spend the night. Here's a description of the places as you'll encounter them going from west to east through town on Route 6A.

A Guest House

Marimac on the Cape, 101 Main St., Yarmouthport, MA 02675 (tel. 617/362-4496), is a comfy guest house with a nice big porch and yard, walking distance from numerous shops. Rooms cost $38 for twin or double beds, shared bath, and continental breakfast; an extra person pays $10. Off-season rates are quite a bit lower, of course.

A Stagecoach Stop

In Yarmouthport there stands the **Old Yarmouth Inn,** 223 Main St. (P.O. Box 212), Yarmouth, MA 02675 (tel. 617/362-3191), dating from 1696. Originally a stagecoach stopping place, the inn today offers both meals (in the original inn) and lodging (in a grand Greek revival manor next door). The adjacent house, newly acquired, offers five two-room suites (from $63.42 to $84.56). The inn bills itself as the "oldest inn on the Cape," and it's open year round now, with eight guest rooms (two with private baths, six semi-private). The 14 rooms in the manor have all been renovated nicely and supplied with elegant antique-style furniture and TV. Each large room is different: many have one double bed and cost $42.28; others have two double beds and cost $52.85; and one room (no. 12) has *four* double beds and thus can sleep eight people for $52.85. All rooms have private bath, and an extra person costs $4. A continental breakfast of juice, toast, and coffee is included in the price of all the rooms, and high tea (4 to 5 p.m.), wine, and cheese will be served in the tavern room.

In the original inn are four dining rooms tending to the modern, but with old time touches, such as the four fireplaces open for use during the fall months. All are air-conditioned. In the hall as you enter a sign says "No dungarees or shorts after 5 p.m." At lunch (noon to 3 p.m.) prices hover around $5 to $6 for a meal such as a Yankee pot roast, a combination salad plate, or an escalloped shrimp pie à la crème. At dinner there are substantial things such as prime filet mignon ($16), chicken Cordon Bleu ($11), and the innkeeper's special (jumbo shrimp, scrod, and native Cape scallops broiled with a seasoned dressing; $12). Appetizers are extra, but otherwise this price includes vegetable or potato, salad, and home-baked bread. Domestic and imported wines are available for $10 to $15 a bottle. The dining rooms are closed Monday, Tuesday, and Wednesday from November through December 31.

Inns

The **Colonial House Inn,** Main Street (Route 6A), Yarmouthport, MA 02675 (tel. 617/362-4348), dates from the 1730s, but has grown in a fascinating manner since first being built. For instance, the rear addition is actually a house that was floated over from Nantucket in the 1820s. Other construction over the centuries has given the inn space for 12 rooms with private bath priced from $46 to $54 double. The inn is right in town, with its own noted restaurant.

Despite its name, the **One Centre Street Inn** (tel. 617/362-8910) is on Main Street (Route 6A), also called the Old King's Highway. But the entrance is around to the side, on Centre Street, right in the middle of Yarmouthport. For simple good taste, the inn is first choice in this town. There are only four guest rooms; baths are private or semi-private; full breakfast is included in the price: $61.50 to $72. This is my favorite sort of hostelry: small, congenial, thoughtfully and finely furnished with taste but without pretention, walking distance to the activities of the town, friendly owners. Need I say more?

WHAT TO SEE AND DO: Across the street from the Old Yarmouth Inn is the **Parnassus Book Store** in a building which started life as a church and later became the local incarnation of the A&P grocery chain. No charge for browsing.

Just down Route 6A from the inn, a minute's walk east, is the U.S. Post Office, and behind it are the **Botanic Trails** of the Historical Society of Old Yarmouth. The trails are open from 10 a.m. to 4 p.m. seven days a week between the beginning of June and sometime in October, 50¢ admission for adults, 25¢ for children. Note that these are not formal "botanical gardens," but rather trails through particularly beautiful wild areas of Yarmouth's land and marshes. Local flowers and trees, plants, and geological features are on view, and maps and trail booklets available at the gate house where you pay your admission will tell you all about what there is to see.

Near the Botanic Trails is the **Baggs Hallett House,** built by a captain in the China trade, who later tired of its low six-foot ceilings and colonial design and had the house cut in half from side-to-side. He sold the front half to somebody else, and went away to sea, leaving his wife with plans and instructions for construction of a Greek revival front. The kitchen in the back of the house is the original, still with the low ceiling. The house has been restored by the Historical Society and furnished with items from the attics and parlors of Yarmouth. The wallpapers are English reproductions of colonial designs. The Baggs Hallett House is open on weekdays from July to September, 1 to 4 in the afternoon; admission is $1 for adults, half price for children. At other times of the year, call 362-3021 for an appointment to see it.

The **Winslow Crocker House,** open June through September on Tuesday through Thursday, and Sunday from noon to 5 p.m., can be seen for $1.50. The rooms in this Georgian house are furnished with 17th- to 19th-century collections.

Yarmouth has a beach which is, by law, free and open to the public, as terms of the bequest which gave it to the town. It's **Grey's Beach** at the end of Centre Street (turn north off Route 6A), and as you go down to the beach, note the cemetery on your left with graves dating from 1639. Picnic tables, toilets, nice lawns, and parking facilities are all available at the beach, and a wooden walkway stretches a good distance out across the marshes, and is pleasant to stroll along even if you don't feel like a swim.

As you come into the town of Dennis, start looking for a cemetery and a white church, and as you come to them look for Old Bass River Road. Turn right onto this road and follow signs for eight-tenths of a mile to the **Scargo Hill Tower.** Park at the base of this stone structure surrounded by oak and pine, and climb the iron staircase inside to the top (not far) for a view that will tell you what the Cape is all about. On a clear day you can easily see Province-town, the white blade of the Cape beaches cutting the deep blue of Cape Cod Bay. The Cape itself appears as a huge green scimitar, a sea of green trees with little white or silver-gray shingled houses poking through here and there. At the foot of the hill which holds the tower is Scargo Lake, and west is the outline of Barnstable Harbor. The tower was given to the town of Dennis in 1929 by the Tobey family, who had had ancestors living in Dennis since 1678. Follow the same road back to Route 6A.

7. Brewster

Brewster is another of the picturesque little towns along Route 6A. A country store, several fine churches, and a Town Hall make it look like many other pleasant Cape towns, but Brewster's different in the number of note-worthy museums and exhibitions situated in the town or nearby. It also has, after days of seeing nothing but seafood on a menu, a restaurant that serves different kinds of schnitzel.

WHERE TO STAY AND DINE: The **Inn of the Golden Ox** (tel. 617/896-3111) is on the outskirts of Brewster on Route 6A at Tubman Road, Brewster, MA 02631, which is technically about 1360 Main St. The inn was built in 1828 as Brewster's First Church, Universalist, and now serves visitors both food and lodging. It's run by Charles and Ruth Evans, and Mrs. Evans's family comes from the Pennsylvania Dutch country, which explains the German emphasis. There are two dining rooms with old wide-board floors and rustic furniture, and a little cranberry-glass candle lamp on each table. The menu is in German with English translations, and the price includes the full meal, from vorspeisen (perhaps lentil soup or a Dutch herring salad) to nachspeisen (creamy cheese-cake, apfelkuchen, or even sacher torte mit schlag). In between are the special-ties of the house such as sauerbraten or the würstplatte of various German sausages; or the schnitzels, from the familiar wienerschnitzel (breaded veal cutlet) to schnitzel Oskar (veal cooked with shrimp, white asparagus, and béarnaise sauce). Dinners cost about $15 to $25.

The Inn of the Golden Ox also has four old-fashioned rooms with shared bath to rent. The rooms are homey and nice, the beds a bit soft, and the price $31.71 double in season, $26.43 off-season, which is anytime other than Memorial Day to Labor Day. The restaurant serves dinner only (5:30 to 9 p.m.), and is closed Monday in summer, Monday and Tuesday in September and October; at other times during the year, dinner is served only on Friday, Saturday, and Sunday. It's good to call for reservations. By the way, breakfast is available for guests who stay overnight if they request it the night before.

Just west of the intersection of Routes 6A and 124 South in Brewster is the **Old Manse Inn**, 1861 Main St., P.O. Box 833, Brewster, MA 02631 (tel. 617/896-3149), a lovely old white building surrounded by tall trees. The nine guest rooms in this former sea captain's house rent for $55 double during the high season (July and August), $48 in spring and fall, $40 in winter. Breakfast and dinner are served in the inn's cozy dining room, which is convenient if you just want to relax and not wander out for meals.

If you follow Main Street west from the Old Manse Inn, and then bear left onto Stony Brook Road, you'll soon come to Brewster's most captivating sight. Read on.

WHAT TO SEE: Brewster is proud of its **Old Grist Mill and Herring Run,** on Stony Brook Road near the intersection with Satucket and Run Hill Roads. The waterwheel, still in good working order, powers the grinding machinery inside the mill. You can watch the whole process at work, and buy freshly ground corn meal, from 2 to 5 p.m. on Wednesday, Friday, and Saturday afternoons in summer. Upstairs there's a small museum with artifacts from the "Factory Village" which occupied this site over a hundred years ago.

The mill is now part of a park owned by the town of Brewster. Wander around the millpond, certainly one of the most romantic and picturesque locales on all of Cape Cod. If your visit falls during mid-April to early May, watch for the run of alewives (herring) which surges upstream from the ocean to freshwater spawning grounds.

Sealand of Cape Cod is right on Route 6A in West Brewster (tel. 385-9252). It's open year round and features a crew of performing dolphins as well as an aquarium with horseshoe crabs, loggerhead turtles, moray eels, otters, seals, sea lions, and any number of different fish. There are three large buildings and several outside pools set in a tree-filled park. The trick is to hit one of the performance times. Late June through Labor Day these are at 10 a.m. and 1:30, 3, 4:30, and 7 p.m. In early and mid-June the times are 11 a.m. and 1, 3, and 5 p.m. In September, October, and May there are shows at 11 a.m. and 1 and 3 p.m. Monday through Friday; on Saturday and Sunday times are 11 a.m., and 3 and 5 p.m. Note that October 1 to June 1 Sealand is closed every Wednesday. November through April regular shows are held on weekends at 11 a.m., 1 and 3 p.m., on weekdays at 1 p.m. Tickets for adults are $5.50; children 5 to 11, $3.50; 4 years and under are free.

The **New England Fire and History Museum,** on Route 6A in Brewster, has a collection of hand- and horse-drawn fire engines, plus a motor-driven one which children are allowed to climb on. Other firefighting paraphernalia—hats, shouting trumpets—and engravings and photographs are on display, with a new diorama (dialogue-display) of the Great Chicago Fire as well; and there is an apothecary shop and blacksmith shop modeled on old-fashioned lines. The museum is open mid-June through Labor Day every day from 10 a.m. to 5 p.m.; from mid-September until Columbus Day, weekends only from 10 a.m. to 3 p.m. Admission is charged (under 6, free), with free parking.

Those interested in Cape Cod's flora, fauna, and ecology will want to visit the **Cape Cod Museum of Natural History,** on Route 6A, open from 10 a.m. to 5 p.m. Monday through Saturday; 12:30 to 5 p.m. on Sunday during the summer. Closed Monday during the winter, and Sunday and Monday January through March. The museum organization was founded in 1954 to preserve the wildlife and plant life in the area around Stony Brook and its marshes, to study this land, and to teach others about it. Nature walks, a lecture program, and children's classes are held the year round.

8. Orleans and Eastham

Orleans owes its name and its fame to French connections. Known as Nauset since its earliest settlement in 1644, the townspeople changed the name to Orleans in 1797 when the town was separated from neighboring Eastham and incorporated. The Duke of Orléans had made a visit to Cape Cod, and the town was named in the French nobleman's honor.

Orleans's other French connection was as close as can be without moving continents. In 1879, Orleans was physically connected by underwater telegraph cable with the town of Brest in France, almost 4000 miles away. You can still see the telegraph station where the cable came ashore before continuing overland to New York.

In its day Orleans has made its living through fishing and shellfishing, clothing manufacture, agriculture, and production of salt from seawater, not to mention trade in contraband. During the Revolutionary War, Orleans sent men and supplies to aid the Revolutionary forces. In the War of 1812, the town refused to pay $1000 "protection money" demanded by the British enemy. A landing force was sent ashore from H.M.S. *Newcastle,* and the town militia quickly convinced the Redcoats that it was probably a good idea to return to the ship, which they did. Needless to say, Orleans kept its $1000. When a German submarine broke the surface off Nauset Beach during World War I, the townspeople again demonstrated their coolness in the face of danger. The sub released a few torpedos at some coal barges, and everybody turned out to watch the show.

Today, Orleans is known as the midpoint between the Cape Cod Canal and Provincetown, a good place to stop for a meal or a night's rest.

WHERE TO STAY IN ORLEANS: You really have quite a choice of places to stay in Orleans, as motels and inns are the town's business.

Inns and Guest Houses

The Nauset House Inn, P.O. Box 774, East Orleans, MA 02643 (tel. 617/255-2195), is actually in East Orleans, nearer to the beach than to the Mid-Cape Highway. Once you get on Beach Road in East Orleans, you'll come to the inn on the right-hand side as you head east. The setting is bucolic and relaxing, the inn nestled into lush surroundings, yet only a short distance from the beach. The 14 rooms range in price from $44 to $58 double, the higher priced rooms having such features as a balcony or sitting area or private bath. Single rooms rent for $32; an extra person pays $8. Full breakfasts (for a few dollars each) are served every morning. This is Orleans's most charming place to stay.

Also on Beach Road in East Orleans, but well before the aforementioned Nauset House Inn, is the **Captain's Quarters** (tel. 617/255-9060), a nice big house being restored by Roy Thurston. Three rooms are rented at the moment, for $25 or $30 each (double). You should have a car for this one. Look for 22 Beach Rd., East Orleans, MA 02643, on the left-hand side of the road a few hundred feet past the big yellow Barley Neck Inn (a restaurant).

The **Orleans Inn of the Yankee Fishermen** is on Route 6A, Orleans, MA 02653 (tel. 617/255-2222), right near the Orleans-Eastham rotary intersection of U.S. 6 and 6A. It's a huge, rambling inn right on the Town Cove which affords its cove-front rooms a fine view of the water and surrounding marshes. The inn is most famous for its restaurant, but it rents modern, neat, clean rooms with new tile baths for $48 double on the cove side, $43 on the highway side, which can be a bit noisy. Off-season, these rates go down by about $10 per room. The rooms are simple, no Olde New Englande touches (authentic or otherwise), but they're very comfortable. Take my advice and rent one on the cove side. The inn is open all year. Some pets are accepted; check with the manager.

Motels

The **Orleans Holiday Motel** (tel. toll free in Massachusetts, 800/451-1818; out of state, 800/451-1833) is on Route 6A, Orleans, MA 02653, just past the intersection of 6A and 28 as you're driving northeast. Bright and modern, the Orleans Holiday has contemporary motel rooms of high quality, all with tiled bath and shower, color cable TV, air conditioning, picture windows, and a balcony-walkway. There's a fine large pool surrounded by lounge chairs and equipped with a slide and a new backyard garden and picnic area. Most rooms have two double beds and rent for $54.96 double; $6 for an extra person from late June through Labor Day. Several rooms in the unit behind the motel's Pancake Maid Restaurant (open for breakfast and lunch) are larger than normal, newer, and a bit more luxurious. Off-season rates are $33.82 double, $4 for an extra person. Weekly rates and a two-night package, including breakfast, for $42.94 a night (double) are offered off-season.

Yet another motel near the intersection of 6A and 28 is the **Cove Motel,** on Route 28, Orleans, MA 02653 (tel. 617/255-1203). The rooms here are modern and soundproof (not that there's all that much noise in the Cove's area), the layout of the motel is quite nice, and it has its own heated pool. The motel's restaurant, with a view of the town cove, serves breakfast and lunch. All in all, it's a very pretty and comfortable place. The rooms rent for $52.85 to $73.99 in high summer, depending on whether you want one or two double beds, a water view, and air conditioning. (The cheapest room is a tiny nine by ten feet; the average-size room costs $55.) In "shoulder season" these rates go down to $31.71 to $40.17, and off-season they're a low $22.20 to $31.71. These prices are for two people; add $4.23 to $5.29 for each extra person.

WHERE TO DINE: Kadee's Lobster & Clam Bar (tel. 255-6184) is right next to the East Orleans Fish Market on Beach Road, and indeed these two establishments share the same telephone and management. That should tell you the fish, lobsters, and clams are fresh and moderately priced. What's left to say is that you dine in attractive rustic rooms or under a colorful umbrella on the pretty deck; or you dine wherever you like, having bought your chowder, fried fish, or boiled lobsters from the take-out window. The take-out is marvelously inexpensive, of course. But the dining room and deck are delightful: have kale soup, corn-on-the-cob, steamers, fish, or order the full clambake ($14) of lobster, steamers, and corn-on-the-cob. To find Kadee's, follow Beach Road east toward East Orleans, and watch for it on the left-hand side of the road. It's open from 11:30 a.m. to 10 p.m. every day.

The **Orleans Inn of the Yankee Fishermen** (tel. 255-2222) is a very popular restaurant in Orleans serving both lunch and dinner. A big fieldstone fireplace graces one of the dining rooms, and both have a fine view over the town cove. The luncheon menu has a number of seafood entrees for $6, and sandwiches for $2.25 to $3 and up. At dinner they offer, among other things, a roast stuffed loin of pork ($8), Cape scallops (when available, $8.25), and roast duckling ($9). The Orleans Inn also has a water-view lounge for before-dinner cocktails, and the whole place is within easy walking distance of all motel suggestions. It's open year round.

Something less formal? The **Lobster Claw** (tel. 255-1800), right next to the Pancake Maid near the Orleans Holiday Motel on Route 6A, is open for lunch and dinner from April to October. Fishnets cover the restaurant's ceiling, and sea-blue booths and natural-wood tables and chairs crowd the floor. Upstairs is a lounge and raw bar. The menus are in the shape of lobster claws (why not?), and they list fish and seafood plates priced at $5.50 to $8.50, lobsters for about $11 to $13 (in season), and daily specials such as soft-shell crabs with french fries and coleslaw for $8. There's a special children's menu. The Lobster

Claw is not very far from the big Orleans traffic circle, and is thus a good place to stop if you're just passing through.

WHAT TO SEE AND DO: Orleans has a rare sight: a museum in the building erected to house the American terminus of a transatlantic cable from Brest, France. Laid in 1879, the cable's terminus came to Orleans in 1891, and the **French Cable Station Museum** remains much as it was when the cable was still in use. Among other important messages, word of Lindbergh's arrival in Paris was transmitted via the cable; the cable was in use until 1959. Today the museum is open in July, August, and the first week in September on Tuesday through Sunday, 2 to 4 p.m., at $2 for adults, $1 for children 7 to 17; 7 and under, free. It's located at Route 28 and Cove Road.

Several good **beaches** are a short distance from Orleans. Remember that Atlantic-side beaches will invariably be cooler for swimming than the beaches on Cape Cod Bay.

Nauset Beach, a stretch of sand ten miles long, is a town beach of Orleans and therefore is subject to a $4 ($5 on weekends) parking fee (use of bathhouse and other facilities included) per day; permits for a week or more also available at reduced prices. The surfing's not bad at Nauset, and a section of the beach is reserved for that activity.

Skaket Beach, on Cape Cod Bay, has less surf, but warmer water and a gently sloping beach. It's operated by the town, has lifeguards, parking places, and a bathhouse, and there's a $3 charge.

Pilgrim Lake is a freshwater swimming spot run by the town. A sand beach runs into the clear water, and a lifeguard is on duty during the summer season. No charge for use of the facilities.

EASTHAM: Eastham's main attraction is the Salt Pond Visitor Center of the Cape Cod National Seashore (see below). Right across the street from the Visitor Center is the quaint and attractive **Eastham Historical Society Museum.** Look for the curious gateway, made from the jawbones of a huge whale. The museum, once a schoolhouse, dates from 1869.

Just south of the Salt Pond Visitor Center on U.S. 6 is the oldest windmill on Cape Cod (1793), a favorite place to stop and take a photo. From the windmill, take a sidetrip west to **First Encounter Beach,** where the Pilgrims first met the Indian inhabitants of the Cape back in 1620. A plaque on a boulder up the hill just north of the parking lot commemorates the meeting which, apparently, was anything but cordial. You can visit the boulder plaque for free, but if you want to park and use the beach during the summer, you'll have to pay the town's beach use parking fee.

A Motel in Eastham

Although I prefer to recommend inns and guest houses in towns, leaving you free to explore Cape Cod's communities on foot, often the best centrally located hostelries are full in high season. If you don't mind driving to see the sights, stay at the **Best Inn** (tel. 617/255-1132), P.O. Box 446, Eastham, MA 02642, right on Route 6. The Best Inn is right next to the more expensive Sheraton Inn, and has comparable facilities at moderate prices: picnic groves and barbecues, a heated swimming pool, and rooms with air conditioning, TV, and baths with tub-and-shower. Prices from late June to Labor Day are $50 single or double, $3 for each extra person. For a month on either side of the high season, rates drop by about 33%; in April and May, prices are less than half the high-season ones. The motel is closed November through March.

9. Cape Cod National Seashore

To preserve intact the particular wild beauty of Cape Cod, Congress established the Cape Cod National Seashore in 1961. It's administered by the National Park Service and includes something less than 27,000 acres of beach, dunes, marsh, forest, and glacial ponds. Acquisition of land for the Seashore is still going on, and so much private property is found in and around the Seashore. Within the Seashore, which stretches for 50 miles from the southern tip of Nauset Beach all the way to Provincetown, there are four developed areas for visitors:

NAUSET AREA: The **Salt Pond Visitor Center** is at Eastham on U.S. 6, and it's here you'll find interpretive exhibits and pamphlets, guide leaflets to the nature trails, rest rooms, picnic areas, and **Coast Guard Beach** and **Nauset Light Beach,** open for swimming. Several bicycle and bridle trails lead from the Visitor Center to the beaches through the pretty woods, marshes, and dunes. Be sure to enter the Visitor Center building and take in the picture-postcard view of Salt Pond, below.

MARCONI STATION AREA: The Seashore's headquarters is here near Wellfleet, and also an interpretive shelter at the site of Marconi's wireless station, the first in the United States; a nature trail; and Marconi Beach, open for swimming. The Great Island Trail is in a separate area southwest of the town of Wellfleet.

PILGRIM HEIGHTS AREA: Between North Truro and Provincetown, this area includes an interpretive shelter dealing with the Pilgrims and the Indians, nature trails, a picnic area, and, nearby, Head of the Meadow Beach, open for swimming.

You'll also see signs pointing the way to Highland Light, with its picturesque lighthouse and ocean observation point. On a nearby hill are several radar installations which look surprisingly like enormous golf balls. And then there's a golf course, right below.

PROVINCE LANDS AREA: A Visitor Center outside Provincetown on Race Point Road provides information and exhibits dealing with the Seashore and its natural treasures, with a schedule of programs at the amphitheater in the evening. Two beaches, a picnic area, a natural trail, and a bicycle trail are here as well.

10. Wellfleet

Cooking lobsters and corn-on-the-cob at a beach picnic, meeting friends downtown at the lunchcounter for a midmorning's lazy second cup of coffee, running errands barefoot or in rubber thongs—if you've enjoyed that sort of an easy summer atmosphere, Wellfleet will bring it back to you. Although a number of motels on U.S. 6 take in travelers heading for Provincetown, Wellfleet is mostly a town of "steadies," people who come every summer for all summer. But it does have a few inns and restaurants worth a look should you find it good to stop here.

WHERE TO STAY: Not far from the center of Wellfleet is the **Holden Inn,** P.O. Box 816, Wellfleet, MA 02667 (tel. 617/349-3450), open July and August only. The inn consists of three buildings of very nicely kept rooms, all different, most with twin beds. One room, for instance, is paneled all in cedar, and is very handsome. No meals are served, and rates vary with the plumbing: doubles with shared bath are $31.71. Doubles with private bath are $37. Several of the rooms are furnished with some antique pieces. To find the Holden Inn, from Route 6 take a left at the Wellfleet Center sign, a left at the sign to the pier; the inn is on the right.

Of the motels out on the highway (U.S. 6), my favorite is the **Mainstay Motor Inn** (tel. 617/349-2350), P.O. Box 295, South Wellfleet, MA 02663. The 28 units here are very modern but done in accord with the Cape's architectural tradition using weathered wood. Each of the rooms is paneled and has two double beds, tiled bath and shower, and TV. There's a nice pool too. Continental breakfast, included in the room price, is the only meal served. Rates are $52 to $60 for a double in season (last weekend in June through Labor Day), $6 for an extra person.

Few "outsiders" know about the **Billingsgate Motel** (tel. 617/349-3924), P.O. Box 778, Wellfleet, MA 02667, because it is not on any beaten path. But its location on Mayo Beach Road, down by the town dock, is a major advantage because of the quiet that prevails. A modern and simple motel structure, the Billingsgate is set at the back of a fine lawn behind a split-rail fence. The eight rooms all have sea views and are constantly cooled by sea breezes. In July and August (till Labor Day), rooms cost $48; off-season (June, September, October), rates are $39 for a double. An extra person pays $2. To find the Billingsgate, simply follow signs to the town dock and then follow the road around to the right.

WHERE TO DINE: The **Wellfleet Oyster House** (tel. 349-2134) takes its name and its menu from the renowned Wellfleet oyster. It's just off Route 6 on East Main Street, the road into town, overlooking a small pond. Owned by Tony and Nonie Castelo, the restaurant is in an early Cape house (built 1750) with wide-board floors and old paintings on the walls. Nonie will probably greet you at the door, while Tony performs as chef (he was with Whyte's of Manhattan for 27 years before coming to the Cape), preparing each dish to order. Have oysters as an appetizer, or as a main course, broiled, in a stew, Casino, or Rockefeller. The menu lists two dozen other seafood entrees, including seafood curries, paella, shrimp, sole, and lobster. For meat-eaters, there's prime rib, sirloin, and steak tartare. Most entrees are priced from $8.75 to $15, and as each includes relish tray, salad, vegetable, potato or rice, garlic bread, and coffee or tea, the entree price is virtually the dinner price (add 5.7% tax, tip, and cost of drinks). The restaurant is open each evening from 6 to 10 p.m., March through November (weekends only in off-season).

Down by the town dock is **Captain Higgins' Seafood Restaurant** (tel. 349-6027), with views of the pier and the harbor. Hours are noon to 3 p.m., and 6 to 9 p.m., and when last I visited, one could have a daily evening special of Wellfleet bluefish for $9.50. With a half dozen Wellfleet oysters on the half shell and a bottle of wine, two people can dine here for $40, wine, tax, and tip included.

The **Bayside Lobster Hutt** (tel. 349-6333) is hardly an exotic place—unless you come from far away. Wellfleet regulars and visitors come into this old oyster shack for a summer picnic-style self-service lobster dinner consisting of live boiled lobster—you pick 'em from the tanks—corn-on-the-cob, steamed clams, and the like. A 1½-pound lobster, easily a huge meal for one person, with corn, costs about $13. Fish and chips is $5.50, and other seafood dinners are in between these extremes in price. Informal, fun, and good food. The Lobster Hutt, on Commercial Street, on the way to the town dock, is open for dinner daily from Memorial Day through September, for lunch during July and August.

Wellfleet's best place for a quick breakfast, good lunch, or inexpensive and tasty dinner is **The Lighthouse** (tel. 349-3681), on Main Street right in the center of town. It's Wellfleet's hometown eatery, and everybody meets everybody else here during the day, for brunch or for a cocktail out on the screened-in "deck." The atmosphere is very informal, the service by young local girls quick and friendly. Breakfast such as french toast, juice, and coffee is $3.75; at lunch, sandwiches such as grilled ham or bacon, lettuce, and tomato are offered. Complete seafood dinners in the evening run $9.50 to $11; if you want the main-course plate only, it's $8 to $10. When you're searching for the Lighthouse, look for the little model of its namesake over the front door.

WHAT TO SEE: As most of Wellfleet's crowd is permanent for the summer, not as many things are available for the transient visitor. Note the town clock in the steeple of the First Congregational Church, which, Wellfleetans proudly say, is the only clock in the world that rings ship's time. The beaches are mostly reserved for permanent or all-summer residents (you need two different permits to swim there, and if you're passing through it's not worth getting them), but **White Crest Beach,** and **Cahoon's Hollow Beach,** off U.S. 6 on the Atlantic coast, are open to day visitors for $2. And you can always go south on U.S. 6 a short distance from Wellfleet and turn left (east) to the Marconi Beach in the National Seashore. At the beach is an ocean overlook and an interpretive shelter explaining the activities of the Marconi Wireless Station, the first in the United States, which was on this site. The Atlantic White Cedar Swamp nature trail starts from here as well.

The Massachusetts Audubon Society operates the **Wellfleet Bay Wildlife Sanctuary** (P.O. Box 236, South Wellfleet, MA 02663; tel. 349-2615), 700 acres of woods and marshland which you can see on your own or by guided tour. The sanctuary is open all year long and interpretive talks are given in summer. There are also birding tours to Monomoy National Wildlife Refuge. Charge is $1.50 for adults, 50¢ for children. A natural history day camp for children operates in July and August.

The **Wellfleet Drive-In Theater** (tel. 349-2520) is back on Route 6 at the Wellfleet-Eastham town line. The show goes on even if it rains, and in any case, shows start at dusk. The box office opens at 7 p.m.—go early to get a good parking place. On Sunday from mid-April through October, and Wednesday from mid-June to mid-September as well, the Drive-In turns into Cape Cod's biggest flea market, and admission is only a dollar per carload of people.

11. Provincetown

Provincetown is a world unto itself, unlike any other place in all New England. Because it is separated from the rest of the Cape by sand, forest, and marsh, it has something of the ambience of an island, an ambience accentuated by the town's compact size. Out of season, the inhabitants are mostly fishermen, descendants of hardy Portuguese whaling men who came here for the whaling trade a century ago. In season Provincetown is a carnival constantly alive with all sorts of people from all around: New York, Boston, Montréal, Québec, and also Podunk. Artists and writers, the successful and the hopeful, college sophomores and sophisticates, dowagers and down-at-heels all mix and mingle in the evening along "P-town's" narrow streets. The town is at the same time quaint and sophisticated, elegant and tawdry, depending on where you look and how you see.

Of all things, the most important when planning a visit to P-town in late July and August is to *have a room reservation without fail.* It is just not possible to find a room in Provincetown for the six weeks of hectic high season unless you reserve ahead. If you have no reservation, it's best to plan to stay in Orleans, Wellfleet, or along U.S. 6 some distance from P-town and to drive up for the day.

Gay vs. Straight in P-town

Like San Francisco and Key West, Provincetown hosts a large gay community on vacation during the summer. Sexual preference is definitely an element which you'll encounter here. The great majority of establishments— hotels, inns, guest houses, restaurants, cafés, bars, and nightclubs—welcome all customers regardless of sexual preference, regardless whether the proprietor is gay or straight. But in a few places you'll definitely feel out of place if your sexual preference doesn't match that of the proprietor and the majority of customers.

GETTING THERE: You can get to Provincetown by car, by bus direct from New York, Hartford, Providence, points in between, by sea, and by air. Here's the rundown:

By Car

U.S. 6 is divided highway all the way to P-town, where it ends and brings you face to face with a parking problem. *Don't* try to park right in the center of town. Get a space in one of the municipal lots (follow the signs) if you can.

By Bus

In summer, **Bonanza Bus Lines** will take you to Hyannis from New York (Port Authority Terminal, Greyhound counter; tel. 212/564-8484 or 212/594-2000) or from Providence (Bonanza Terminal; tel. 401/751-8800 or 331-7500). In Hyannis, transfer to **Cape Cod Bus Lines** (tel. 617/548-0333). The trip takes eight hours from New York, 3¼ hours from Providence. Bonanza also runs buses from Albany and Springfield, Mass., to Hyannis, where you connect for P-town. In Hartford the terminal is at 409 Church St. (Greyhound; tel. 203/547-1500). From Boston, take a bus to Hyannis or Chatham and then switch to **Cape Cod Bus Lines,** which has six buses a day in each direction, for the rest of the trip. **Plymouth & Brockton** runs four buses daily in summer from Boston to Hyannis which connect within minutes with a Cape Cod bus bound for Provincetown. Similar close connections are arranged for buses coming from Montréal via Boston to the Cape (two buses daily in summer, with additional service on weekends). Note that the bus driver will drop you off near or right at your hotel, if it's out of the center of town, if you ask him to do so. This is a normal service, so feel free to ask.

By Sea

You can take a delightful cruise to Provincetown aboard the M/V *Provincetown II,* operated by **Bay State & Provincetown Steamship Co.,** 66 Long Wharf, Boston, MA 02110 (tel. 617/723-7800). The three-hour cruise costs $12 one way ($10 for children under 12), or $18 round trip ($13 for kids) if you make the round trip all in one day. The ship leaves from Boston's Commonwealth Pier: take the T (subway) Blue Line to Aquarium Station, or the Red Line to South Station, and then cross the Fort Point Channel. Ask for Northern Avenue, walk southeast along it for a few blocks, and Commonwealth Pier will be on your left. The walk from either subway stop takes about 15 minutes.

Here's the schedule: leave Commonwealth Pier at 9:30 a.m., arrive at P-town's MacMillan Wharf right in the middle of town at 12:30 p.m. The return trip leaves MacMillan Wharf at 3:30 p.m. to arrive at Commonwealth Pier by 6:30 p.m. Breakfast, lunch, snacks, cocktails, and refreshments are on sale aboard; a band provides music, and the captain describes the landmarks and sights in passing. The 1100-passenger, 195-foot *Provincetown II* has three decks providing open, covered, and enclosed seating areas.

By the way, MacMillan Wharf is where intercity buses begin and end their runs, and where the Chamber of Commerce operates its information office.

By Air

Yes, Provincetown has its own airline! The **Provincetown-Boston Airline, Inc.** (P.O. Box 639, Provincetown, MA 02657), operates on-the-hour, every-hour shuttle flights every day in summer (fewer in winter) between the Eastern Airlines Terminal at Boston's Logan Airport and the Provincetown Municipal Airport near Race Point Beach. Flying time is 30 minutes.

PBA also operates flights connecting Boston with Hyannis, Nantucket, New Bedford, and Martha's Vineyard, plus flights from New York (La Guardia) to Boston, Hyannis, New Bedford, Martha's Vineyard, and Nantucket—no direct New York-to-Provincetown flights as of this writing, though.

For reservations, fares, and schedules, call PBA at these numbers: toll free, 800/352-3132; in Boston, 617/567-6090; in New York, 212/247-0088; in Hyannis, 617/771-1444; or toll free in Florida, 800/282-3197.

INFORMATION: The **Provincetown Chamber of Commerce** operates an information office (tel. 617/487-3424) at 307 Commercial St. on the town wharf, called MacMillan Wharf. Boats from Boston arrive at this wharf, and the chamber's office is also the stop for intercity buses from New York, Providence, and Boston. Bus and boat schedules are posted here.

WHERE TO STAY: Provincetown's streets are lined with guest houses and inns and motels, and in the six weeks from mid-July to Labor Day every room in every one will be rented. Outside of that time you have a chance of finding a room by arriving in town by late morning or early afternoon. A special note is in order concerning credit cards. Demand for services is so great here that very many hotels and restaurants *do not accept credit cards.* As they get all the business they want anyway, they choose not to bother with the extra expense, delay, and paperwork that cards entail. Also, most lodging places require some

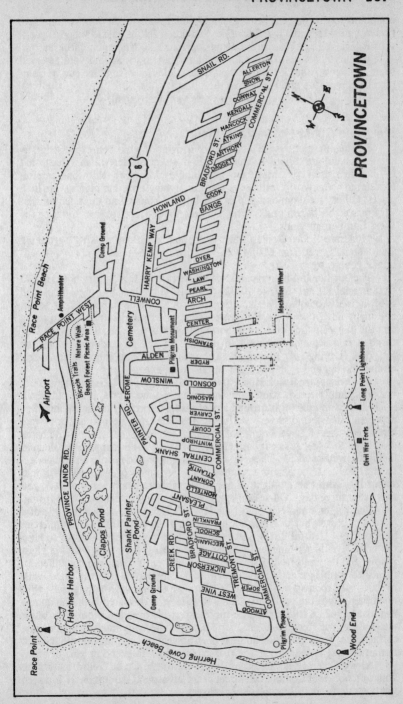

PROVINCETOWN

minimum stay during the peak season period, usually from three or four days (at least, on weekends) to a full week. And you won't be able to fudge it: you'll probably have to pay the full amount for your stay when you check in.

When you set out to hunt for accommodations, or to find your reserved room, remember that P-town is about three miles long from one end of Commercial Street (the main street) to the other.

P-town's ZIP code is 02657, for reservations by mail.

West End Guest Houses and Inns

The quaint, picturesque character of Provincetown is best expressed in its small inns and guest houses. The West End—west of MacMillan Wharf, that is—has the richest concentration of guest houses. Many are really inns, carefully restored with lots of guest rooms, some luxury features, and moderate to high prices. Others are mom-and-pop establishments, simple and unpretentious, at very reasonable bargain rates. First I'll describe the nicer places, and then the West End bargain finds.

Moderate-Priced Rooms: Start your room search by walking west along Commercial Street from MacMillan Wharf, with the street numbers descending as you go west.

The **Anchor Inn** is a gracious, expansive turn-of-the-century house at 175 Commercial St. (tel. 617/487-0432). As with most inns and guest houses in P-town, every room is different, although most have a deck, balcony, or porch, and many have a sea view. Room size, view, and deck determine room price, and the date of your visit is an important factor as well. From Memorial Day through mid-September, expect to pay $50 to $68 for a double room, tax included. (During July Fourth and Labor Day weekends there's a seven-day minimum stay and a $5-per-room surcharge in effect.)

The **Sandpiper Beach House** (tel. 617/487-1928), at 165 Commercial St., is a short and pleasant stroll from the center of town. It's a grand old beach house full of antique furniture and lots of plants (especially hibiscus, philodendron, and ficus), and is very well kept. Facilities include parking, a private beach, and use of a swimming pool. Rooms are equipped with private baths ($50.74 to $63.42), adjacent bath ($42.28 to $59.19, and many have balconies facing the water and TV. These prices are for one or two people; a third person pays $10.57. At the Sandpiper, rates are a bit higher over July Fourth and Labor Day with a seven-night minimum stay required; on Memorial Day, you must stay three days. Off-season rates begin mid-September until late spring.

The **Captain and His Ship** (tel. 617/487-1850) sounds like the title of a Cape Cod novel, but in fact it's a handsome guest house at 164 Commercial St., corner of Central Street, just far enough from the heart of town to keep the noise level low. Shipboard tidiness characterizes the house, its eight guest rooms, and its small front lawn complete with bench. Each room is different, furnished with fascinating Victoriana, and each has a different price; with private bath, rooms are $59.19 to $63.42; with semiprivate bath (shared with one other room) the prices are $42.28 to $51.79; with shared bath, the double rooms are $42.28 to $48.62. The more expensive ones are those with water views, of course. Reductions of $15 to $20 are in effect anytime except mid-June through mid-September; the house is open all year; in high season, a four-night minimum stay is required if you plan to stay on a weekend or part of one.

Along Commercial Street, as you come to the Coast Guard Station on your left, note that Commercial Street bears left around the station. If you keep going straight you'll be on Tremont Street.

Past the Coast Guard Station, at 96 Commercial St., is the very attractive **Captain Lysander Inn** (tel. 617/487-2253), which was built by Capt. Lysander Paine in 1852. A spacious deck in front provides a shady place to sit and watch activity on the street. Some of the 15 guest rooms have private baths, others share a bath; some have views of the sea, several have fireplaces. All have one double bed, and three have a single bed as well. Prices are $43 for a double with shared bath, $53 for a double with private bath in season, about $10 less per room off-season. A third person pays $10. (Tax is already figured in these prices.) Minimum stay of four nights over July Fourth.

Bright, cheerful, comfortable, and well-equipped: that describes the **1807 House** (tel. 617/487-2173), 54 Commercial St. The cedar-shingled main house faces the street, and behind it are several other buildings which hold rooms, studios, and apartments. Names say it all: the Master's Suite, the Artist's Studio, the Cottage Garden Apartment, the Cottage Studio Apartment, the Red Room, the Beige Room, etc. Each is tastefully, attractively done, many have kitchens, and all share the quiet location, free parking, and grassy lawns. Owners Bob Hooper and David Murray will be happy to describe each room for you, and will quote prices such as $37 single, $46.51 double, $54.96 for an apartment, $10.57 for a third person—high-season rates, tax included. In fall, winter, and spring, prices are about $10 lower. Three-day minimum stays on Memorial, July Fourth, and Labor Day weekends.

The Masthead (tel. 617/487-0523), 31–41 Commercial St., lists cottages, apartments, and motel rooms among its accommodations, but you must see the place to appreciate it. All these overnight possibilities are contained in a collection of cozy little cottages which look across flawless green lawn to a private boardwalk, a beach, and the water. Unless you can look in person, it's best to write ahead for a copy of the descriptive sheet detailing the 21 different types of accommodations, from modern rooms through efficiency studios to cottages for up to seven people. In high season (July through Labor Day), the cottages, suites, and efficiencies are rented by the week, anywhere from $369.95 to $729.33 for two people; a few motel rooms rent by the day for $42.28 to $90.90. Mid-September rates are a few dollars lower, but off-season rates (late September to early June) are substantially lower: most accommodations rent for $42.28 double, a few for more, a few for less. Holiday prices are somewhat higher. No pets.

Budget-Priced Rooms: Now let's do that same walk westward from MacMillan Wharf, this time looking for the lowest priced rooms in P-town. While not fancy, these rooms are always comfortable; few have private baths, though.

Mrs. Helen Valentine is the lady who runs **Valentine House**, 88 Commercial St. (tel. 617/487-0839), a very tidy guest house with its own parking facilities and rooms that rent for $26.43 in season, $20.23 off-season, double. Quiet, fairly convenient—an excellent place to stay.

Corea's Guest House (tel. 617/487-0274) is at 5 Cottage St., off Commercial right behind Valentine House. A homey place run by a nice lady, it's comfy rather than classy or chic, but the prices are appealing: $15 single, $25 double (in a double bed), $29 for two in twin beds.

Farther up Cottage Street at no. 16 is the home of **Mrs. Nancy Meads** (tel. 617/487-1494), who rents several clean and neat rooms with shared bath for $28 double. She also has a good housekeeping apartment with separate entrance and private bath for $33. It's very quiet here on Cottage, between Tremont and Bradford.

The Viewpoint (tel. 617/487-1939), 63 Commercial St., is the home of Donald and Joan Morse. It's on the sea side of the street with a beautiful deck and a beach below. The five rooms are modern but simple, renting for $30 to $38 double. Note that reservations are *not* accepted: call when you get to P-town, and if they still have a room, run over and grab it.

Nearby is the **O'Donnell Guest House,** 6 Atwood Ave., a little alley off Commercial (tel. 617/487-0103). John and Marian O'Donnell rent rooms which share a bath for $31.71 (two in a double bed), or $33.82 (two in twin beds), plus a cottage. It has a nice lawn, set back from the street, and free parking.

Elizabeth Doucette's house at 58 Commercial St. (tel. 617/487-0810) has provided rooms for summer visitors for a long time, and some are furnished just as they were when Elizabeth first took in guests decades ago. Don't expect anything fancy, but neither will you have to pay fancy prices. With a shared bath, two pay $27 total; with private bath the price is $3 more.

Tremont Street is parallel to Commercial Street and one block inland (in fact, if Commercial Street didn't jog around the Coast Guard Station, Tremont Street would be the natural continuation of Commercial—see the map). **Bob White's Rooms and Cottages** (tel. 617/487-0482), 21 Tremont St., is actually operated by Mrs. Ethel White, who will show you a twin-bedded room with a TV, sharing a bath, for $26, or a room with private bath and color TV for $35; the cottage goes for $38 per day, double.

East End Guest Houses and Inns

The eastern reaches of Provincetown, along Commercial Street, Bradford Street, and the small cross-streets between them, hold dozens of small inns and a few guest houses. Generally speaking, these are more expensive than the majority of West End places. The location is roughly the same in terms of convenience. You may encounter a bit more noise here, though. Look your room over with this in mind.

Hargood House (tel. 617/487-1324), at 493 Commercial St., is a haven of sophisticated design, almost a showplace, consisting of 17 apartments in four restored Cape houses, three of which are grouped around a central patio overlooking the Hargood's private beach and the water. The character of Hargood House is apparent not only in its tastefulness and good design, but also in the furnishings of the apartments, all of which are high quality, down to the china and stemware in the kitchen cupboards. Most of the apartments have views of the water, some being extremely good. The catch for one-day travelers is that Hargood House rents only by the week in season (last week in June through first week in September), and prices range from $433.37 to $739.90, with many being $528.50 to $591.92 per week. Off-season, rooms rent for two nights minimum (three nights on holiday weekends), and cost $47.57 to $84.56 in an even spread between those two prices. Note that *all* rooms have private bathrooms and kitchens, all with dishwashers, and almost all have sofa beds which allow extra persons ($12.68 a day) to share the apartment.

The **Bradford Gardens Inn** (tel. 617/487-1616), 178 Bradford St. near the corner of Bangs Street/Miller Hill Road, is certainly one of Provincetown's most charming and serene places to stay. Every room in the century-and-a-half-old inn is different, and each has a name rather than a number. In high season, rooms rent from Saturday to Saturday only. All rooms have private baths and TV sets (some color), six rooms have fireplaces as well, and these rent for $67.65 double in season; two small apartments with fireplaces are $62.36 daily; standard double rooms are $62.36. A variety of apartments in newer buildings across Bradford Street from the inn are priced from $72.93 to $99.36. An extra person pays $6 sharing a room, and a 10% reduction is given for stays by the week. Rates include a big breakfast and (for rooms with facilities to use it) firewood as well. If you come to the Bradford Gardens anytime but July and August, rates will be $5 lower per room. And speaking of gardens, the Bradford has 'em, spreading around the house, set with benches, chairs, and even a garden swing. On rainy days, it's easy to stay amused by inspecting the fascinating furnishings owner Jim Logan has collected, or his equally absorbing collection of paintings by local artists. The Bradford Gardens is beautiful, and therefore it is popular: reserve well in advance.

The **White Horse Inn** (tel. 617/487-1790), 500 Commercial St., is a neat and tidy place painted white, with blue shutters and a bright-yellow door. Inside, lots of quaint old pieces picked up in the area were used in decoration to keep the period feeling (the house is at least two centuries old), and every room seems to contain at least five original paintings. The beach is right across the street (guests do have beach rights), and for after-swim, the inn's backyard lawn chairs hit the spot. Doubles with private bath go for $37; with shared bath, $31.71; a twin-bedded room that shares a bath costs $33.82; single rooms are $23.25; and an extra person is charged $5. Off-season, the rates go down; just ask.

Jim Bayard and Les Schaufler's **Asheton House** (tel. 617/487-9966) is one of those immaculately restored, beautifully decorated guest houses found in Provincetown. Each of the seven guest rooms is unique: one has a four-poster bed; another has a fireplace, dressing room, and private bath; yet another has a canopied bed. There's an apartment with bedroom, living room, and kitchen, too. The smallest, simplest room with double bed and shared bath rents for $31.71; most others go for $44.39 and $47.57, although the Suite (with the fireplace) costs $63.52. The apartment rents for $475.65 double per week, $10.57 per day or $52.85 per week for an additional person. All these prices are for summer, and all include the tax. Fall, winter, and spring prices are about 25% lower. Asheton House is at 3 Cook St., just off Commercial.

Motels

A nicely kept motel is the **Cape Colony Inn** (tel. 617/487-1755), at 280 Bradford St. Here, besides clean and well-kept modern rooms, you have a big heated pool, volleyball, badminton, shuffleboard, and a coffeeshop. The Cape Colony has a policy of accepting reservations for a minimum of two nights (three on holidays). Rates for the rooms, all with two double beds (or one queen-size, air conditioning, room phones, and color TV, are $65.53 for two in one bed, and an extra person pays $5.29. There is a suite with two rooms and three double beds, with one bathroom to serve the two rooms, for $78.22 for up to four people. These in-season rates apply from the last week in July to Labor Day. Off-season, from April to closing, rates are $24 to $31 double, $5.29 for an extra person.

The **Shamrock Motel & Cottages** (tel. 617/487-1133) is at 49 Bradford St., at the intersection with Shank Painter Road. A cute little place right near the center of town, it has accommodations of all different varieties: motel rooms, motel apartments large and small, and several cottages capable of sleeping from two to five people. In the motel rooms there are tile baths, wall-to-wall carpeting, and TV. The motel apartments are efficiency units with kitchen facilities. The rooms are $52.85 double in season, $37 off-season; motel apartments cost $52.85 for two, $57.96 to $63.42 for two to five; cottages range from $42.28 for a small studio capable of sleeping two or three, to a deluxe cottage which sleeps five, $57.96 per night. These rates are cut by 40% off-season, and weekly rates both in-season and off give you in effect one free night every week you stay.

The **Moors Motel** (tel. 617/487-1342), Bradford Street Extension (mail address: P.O. Box 661, Provincetown, MA 02657), is right at the tip of the Cape, at the very end of Bradford Street. It is, therefore, a bit out of the center of town, but this has its advantages. For one, the motel's 32 modern, bath-equipped rooms overlook the scenic moors of the National Seashore, and are very near the beach. The weathered wood of this two-decker motel is in the Cape Cod style, and on the second floor a walkway is good for sitting to look at the view. There's a small pool and color TV for those who tire of the view, and a good restaurant (Portuguese and American food) and cocktail lounge connected with the motel. Rates vary almost by the month, but at their highest they're $46 to $56 for two, going down to $26 to $32 in April and October. Note that every room sleeps three people (the third person pays an extra-person rate of $8.50). The higher prices in every case are for the second-floor rooms, which have balconies and the best views. Continental breakfast is included in the high-season rates.

WHERE TO DINE: Provincetown has a bewildering array of restaurants, everything from classy places with *sommeliers* and an ocean view to hot-dog stands with a view of Commercial Street. Some general rules: all P-town restaurants specialize in seafood, often prepared Portuguese style. Most restaurants on the seaward side of Commercial Street, with sea views, are more expensive than those on the landward side. If this is your first experience dining on clams, oysters, or lobster, be sure to read "A New England Clambake" and "How to Eat a Lobster" in Chapter II on Boston.

First I'll describe P-town's best all-around good, moderately priced establishments in the middle of town. Then I'll go on to some special, or elegant, or out-of-the-way places you might want to try.

Moderately Priced Restaurants

The **Grand Central Café** (tel. 487-9116) boasts that it was established in 1968. That might not seem a long run when compared to Boston's century-old Durgin-Park, but for Provincetown it's an eon. Why so long-lived? Because it's got the formula down: good food at moderate prices in attractive, cozy, even romantic surroundings. Stained-glass lamps, wrought-iron fancywork, plants everywhere, a variety of small dining rooms, and an outdoor garden provide the atmosphere, and the sea provides the main courses. Swordfish, lobster, fresh salmon, and scampi are at the high end ($10 to $13) along with the steaks and prime rib, but you can get sole florentine or bluefish for $7.50, and that includes rice, potato or vegetable, salad, bread, and butter. There is a 10% discount on all dinners before 7 and after 10 p.m. Wine and cocktails are served, with late night Happy Hour after 11 p.m. Note that a 15% service charge will be added to your bill, so there's no need to tip. The café is at 5 Masonic Pl. (a little street that starts between 216 and 218 Commercial St.), open from Memorial Day to late September for dinner: early, leisurely, and late-night (till midnight).

Another of P-town's long-lived restaurants is appropriately named the **Old Reliable Fish House** (tel. 487-9742), down the alley at Rear-229 Commercial St. Perched over the water on a well-worn wharf, the Old Reliable opens at 9 a.m. for breakfast starting at $2.95, 11:30 a.m. daily for lunch, at 5 p.m. for dinner, staying open until 10:30 or 11 p.m. The menu is heavy on fish and shellfish, plus some Portuguese dishes, but the special feature here is the pricing structure. Each dish has three prices: for the main course alone (comes with rice or potato, and salad); or #1, which includes soup or appetizer; or #2, which gets you soup *and* appetizer. Prices are low in any case, and you can get the full, four-course #2 fish dinner for as little as $6.50, depending on the fish you choose. Most fish and Portuguese dishes are priced under $8. Ambience is well-worn nautical, youngish, and fun.

Just off MacMillan Wharf at 321 Commercial St. is the **Lobster Pot** (tel. 487-0842), an intriguing establishment combining fish market, pastry shop, and seafood restaurant. Approach the white New England-beach-eatery facade and you'll see the fish market first; the dining room is in the back overlooking the wharf and the water. Open from noon to 10 p.m. every day, the Lobster Pot has a full, medium-priced menu of seafood, meat, and poultry. But the specialty is the clambake, an all-inclusive dinner: New England clam chowder (or Portuguese soup), salad, corn-on-the-cob, steamed clams, fried potatoes, and one whole lobster, boiled or broiled. You can choose the size of your lobster (1¼ to 1½ pounds is best), and the price will depend on its weight. Expect to pay about $20, tax, tip, and a glass of wine included. Now all you have to do is resist ordering one of those desserts you passed on the way in!

Let's conjure up a mood now. It's the evening of a fine, adventurous day, and you want to have a good dinner at some small, very intimate candlelit spot with particularly interesting and delicious food at moderate prices. The place is **Sal's Place** (tel. 487-1279), 99 Commercial St. past the Coast Guard Station in the West End; the day is any day but Monday (closed); the time is 6 to 10 p.m. The food is Italian, and all cooked to order. Tiny wooden tables, Chianti bottles hanging from the ceiling, and a small dining room both simple and romantic; there is also a new larger room on the water, and outdoor dining. First you order, say, fish soup or a shellfish appetizer, then perhaps spaghettini alle Foriana (with raisins, nuts, and anchovies), and then a main course of seafood or perhaps vitello saltimbocca or scaloppine con funghi. On Tuesday several veal dishes are featured; on Friday the specialty is calamari (squid). Appetizers, main courses, coffees, and wine for two at Sal's will bring the tab to about $40, all included. Call ahead for reservations.

Provincetown's most serviceable midrange restaurant is **Plain and Fancy** (tel. 487-0147), at 334 Commercial St. It's open only for dinner, from 5 to 11 p.m., mid-May to mid-September. A highly polished floor matches the sheen on the wood tables, and charcoal drawings or watercolors of Provincetown scenes decorate each wall. A small bar and air conditioning add to the restaurant's attractiveness, but the big attraction is large portions of good food for reasonable prices: seafood dinners for $6 to $8 (but the daily special is always good and usually the lowest priced), meat entrees for a dollar or two more, Wellfleet oysters on the half shell for $3.50. A half-liter carafe of wine is $3.25. You can't go wrong here, as the prices quoted include entree, rice or potato, salad, vegetable, bread, and butter.

For less well-padded readers I suggest the **Cicero Trattoria and Panificio** at 267 Commercial St. (tel. 487-3233). Actually a trio of Italian eateries under one roof, Cicero draws customers in with freshly made cannolis and napoleons, tempts them with Sicilian pizza piled with cheese ($1 the slice), fills them with giant sandwiches made on the bakery's piping-hot bread, or with calzones (dough wrapped around any of a variety of fillings; about $5). In the evening, the trattoria section comes into play, serving a full menu of Italian and seafood specialties, wine and beer, with a view of Cape Cod Bay thrown in for good measure. A simple but delicious and filling meal of *homemade* fettuccine, with salad and garlic bread, will cost under $9; fancier main courses cost more.

Out of Town, On the Moors

The **Moors Restaurant** (tel. 487-3259) takes its name from its location right at the end of Bradford Street Extension, at the junction with Route 6A, on the moors. The dining rooms are positively fraught with nautical paraphernalia, on the walls, on the ceiling, adorning the bar, but somehow it manages to be atmospheric rather than overwhelming. Lunch and dinner are served April through October, every day, and cuisine is pure Provincetown: seafood with Portuguese accents. At lunchtime, you can eat for as little as $4 if you can be contented with a linguiça roll (linguiça is a mildly spicy Portuguese sausage) and a beer; or you can spend a few dollars more for lobster Newburg or something like flounder roll-ups with seafood stuffing. Dinnertime main courses cost, in general, $9 to $13, but for the same price you can order the daily special dinner which includes soup, salad, and coffee. Besides the standard fresh fish and lobster casserole, you might find carangueijo vieira a moda de peniche (scallops and crabmeat in a casserole, made with wine, brandy, and tomato sauce; $12). On Sunday in July and August, come out to the Moors for a jazz brunch from noon to 3 p.m.: hot crêpes and cool live jazz, lots of fun.

Elegant Places

For those times when you don't mind spending a little more, here are some of Provincetown's classier dining places.

One of the most popular dining places in P-town lately is **Ciro & Sal's,** 4 Kiley Court (tel. 487-9803), down at the end of the alley at 430 Commercial St. East. It's open for dinner only (bar opens at 5:30 p.m., dining room at 6) and features Italian haute cuisine, finely prepared pasta, veal, seafood, and chicken dishes. The menu is long and inclusive. An enthusiastic diner could easily spend $50 by ordering all the courses, an expensive entree, and little extras like a side order of mushrooms ($4.50!). But it's equally easy to have the dinner special plate with salad, rolls, and butter for about $10. For a normal dinner with wine, tax, and tip, figure $25 and you'll come away very pleased. Enter the restaurant through the little garden at the end of the alley; have reservations.

The **Red Inn** 15 Commercial St. (tel. 487-0050), is almost at the western end of the street, the town, and indeed the Cape. Perched on a grassy rise, it overlooks the harbor and takes full advantage of the view. A quaint old red Cape building, the Red Inn serves lunch and dinner every day of the year in its quiet location. The dining rooms are refined but not stuffy, with high-backed captain's chairs and nicely set tables. The menu is short and good, specializing in fresh ingredients prepared in the traditional ways: broiled scallops, baked sole or swordfish, baked stuffed shrimp, or stuffed filet of sole (with chopped shrimp and scallops in a light seafood bisque sauce). Pork, lamb, and beef are served as well. The bill will come to $18 to $28 per person, all in.

Poor Richard's Buttery (tel. 487-3259) is the best of the many good restaurants gathered on Commercial Street several blocks east of MacMillan Wharf. Small, tasteful dining rooms, careful service, and a fascinating menu draw the clientele here, most of whom are well dressed, well heeled, and experienced in exotic cuisine. The menu changes frequently, but as you read it (by candlelight, of course) you'll find such things as gazpacho, eggs Kiev, and elegant crêpes; frog legs, bouillabaisse, and boeuf en croûte Wellington; and strawberries with fresh cream for dessert. Fish, shellfish, lobster, and steak are always served too. What you pay depends partly on when you come and how you order. Each night they offer a special three-course menu (with choices) for about $14; another special is the two-for-the-price-of-one arrangement. Specials are most generous early in the week, not on Friday and Saturday nights. Ordering à la carte, you could pay about $45 or so for dinner here.

An Outdoor Café

Want to sit at an outdoor café? The most obvious place to go is the **Café Blasé**, 328 Commercial St. (tel. 487-3810), just east of the center of town. Lots of tables shaded by umbrellas sit out in a courtyard surrounded by flower boxes. Should you want solid sustenance, try a portion of quiche Lorraine, mushroom and spinach, or crab ($5), a huge salad ($4.50 to $6), or the Blazing Blasé Burger made with fresh mushrooms, grilled cheese, and bacon for $5.75. The array of drinks offered is nothing short of astounding, with nonalcoholic specialties such as piña colada, orzata, grenadine, coco rico, guava and mango nectar. Imported and domestic beer, wine by the glass, half liter, or liter, or by the bottle satisfy stronger thirsts. The café is open for breakfast, lunch, cocktails, afternoon espresso, and dinner.

A Budget Find

You people on low budgets, take note! P-town has a restaurant which everyone but locals go right by without a second look, even though it serves some of the best inexpensive food in town. It's called, simply, **Cookie's**, as you will read from the Narragansett beer sign which hangs outside, and it's located on the upper reaches of Commercial Street West at no. 133, corner of Pleasant Street. The kitchen is family-run and the food, like the family, is good and of Portuguese extraction. Peek in for a look at the daily specials on the blackboard: a boiled dinner, complete for $6? A tuna salad plate for $4.25? Or a Portuguese specialty such as peixe em vinho de alhos (marinated fish, fried and served with lettuce, tomato, and french-fried potatoes) for $8? Cookie's is open every day of the week from noon to 10 or 11 p.m. Beer and wine are served.

For Breakfast

Fresh coffee in the morning, yes, but also fresh bread and rolls: find the **Portuguese Bakery**, right down by MacMillan Wharf at 299 Commercial St.—follow the coffee and fresh-bread smells. Not only is breakfast the freshest here, it's the cheapest. Put it together yourself, take it out to the wharf to consume, and you can do it for $2.50 easily.

The Best Pizza in Town

For a slice of the high life, stop in at **Spiritus**, 190 Commercial St., drop $1.25 (about $8 for a whole pizza), and you'll have a sample of the best pizza in P-town. Spiritus has other good things too, like Breyer's Ice Cream, hot coffee, and any of the various essential concoctions which issue from the jets of an espresso machine.

WHAT TO SEE AND DO: Provincetown's an interesting small town to browse around. Although people-watching could keep one amused for days, here are some of P-town's other highlights.

Pilgrim Monument and Provincetown Museum

For a general view, the **Pilgrim Monument** and **Provincetown Museum** (tel. 487-1310), on Town Hill off Winslow Street, give you the best view of the town in both its physical and historical aspects. Both attractions are open during the same hours, and you pay one fee for the two: $2.50 per adult, $1.25 per child. The museum is an interesting potpourri of old fire-fighting gear, costumes, a whaling ship captain's quarters on board, primitive portraits, World War I mementoes, arctic lore, and a sequence of displays on the activities of the Pilgrims in Provincetown, for this is the first place they touched land in the New World. After seeing these you can continue with the Wedgwood, model of a Thai temple, antique dolls, etc. Then head for the tower.

The Pilgrim Monument is copied from the Torre del Mangia in Siena, Italy, and is all granite and 252½ feet high. The cornerstone was laid in 1907 with Pres. Teddy Roosevelt in attendance, and the structure was completed three years later, when President Taft did the dedicating. You may think that there's an elevator in it. Well, there's not, and you'll have to c-l-i-m-b to the top, the equivalent of going up the steps in a 20-story building, to see the view. Most of the climb is on a ramp, not steps, and you can take your time and read the commemorative plaques from New England cities, towns, and civic groups which line the granite walls. The view is worth the climb: Provincetown and all Cape Cod spread out like the maps you've been following.

Both the monument and the museum are open at 9 a.m. The tower can't be climbed less than a half hour before closing, so get there before 4:30 p.m. in high summer, 3 p.m. the rest of the year.

A Walk Around Town

Drop in at the chamber of commerce's information office down by the town wharf and pick up (25¢) the Provincetown Historical Society's pamphlet which tells you all the historic sights and houses in P-town. Check out the Pilgrims first landing place, the monument commemorating the signing of the Mayflower Compact (America's first democratic "constitution"), and the oldest house in town (1746), at 72 Commercial St., open June through October from 10 a.m. to 5 p.m. daily; $1.50 for adults, 25¢ for kids. The house is now the home of artist John W. Gregory and his wife, who will be happy to show you around and explain how it was built by a shipwright from materials salvaged from shipwrecks.

The **Provincetown Heritage Museum**—actually the municipal museum— at Commercial and Center Streets, preserves the town's heritage in its wide-ranging displays. Relics of the fishing industry, Victoriana, and many other items capture Provincetown's history. Especially exciting for children are the antique fire engine, and the *Rose Dorothea,* the world's largest half-scale fishing schooner being built indoors. The museum is open from 10 a.m. to 8 p.m. daily from mid-June through mid-October. Adults pay $1; children under 12 enter for free.

Galleries, Cinemas, and Theater

Latest schedules are published in the local sheet, the *Provincetown Advocate,* and are also available at the chamber of commerce information booth. Galleries dot the downtown streets, often open until late in the evening. The **Provincetown Playhouse** (tel. 487-0955) is active all summer. Take a look at their Eugene O'Neill museum during intermission (he lived and wrote many of his plays in town). The **New Art Cinema** (tel. 487-9222), across from the post office downtown at 212 Commercial St., plays both foreign and domestic first-run films. It's the newest cinema in P-town, blissfully air-conditioned. The **Metro Cinema** is right next to the Town Hall at Commercial and Ryder Streets.

Other Activities

Arnold's (tel. 487-0855), at 329 Commercial St., and **Nelson's** (tel. 487-0034), on Race Point Road, rent **bicycles,** and you can use them in town or on the bike trails in the National Seashore. Drop in at the Seashore's Province Lands Visitor Center for a free guide pamphlet to the trails. Nelson's will also rent you a horse if you make a reservation, and they have guided trail rides through the dunes four times during the day (one hour) and a two-hour ride at sunset. Several companies will take you through the dunes in a four-wheel-drive vehicle on a daylight or sunset tour for a reasonable price. Call **Drifting Sands Dune Tours** (tel. 349-9231) in North Truro for a reservation, or **Art's Sand Dune Taxi Tours,** at the town wharf (tel. 487-1950). What about a sail on a schooner? Several boats make two-hour runs through the waters around the tip of the Cape, giving you a very different view of the land and water. Try the *Hindu* (tel. 487-0659), or the *Olad* (tel. 487-9308); both have sunset cruises. It's best to reserve in advance. The price, like that for all the other activities here, is very reasonable, and won't set you back by even the price of a good dinner. Those who want more action on their cruise can go out with one of the two daily deep-sea fishing voyages that leave from MacMillan Wharf; whale-watching boats also leave from here, especially from mid-April to mid-June.

Should you want to do nothing more active than sit, you can have a local artist do your portrait in pastels while you're sitting. Shops are along Commercial Street near the town wharf, and prices start at $40 for a front view, $15 for the side, $20 if it's to be charcoal; frames and glass are extra and cost $20 and up. The portrait can be done, framed, and wrapped to take home in a surprisingly short time.

But biking, schooner sails, deep-sea fishing, and portrait-sitting can't equal the sense of freedom you get if you sail your own boat out onto Cape Cod Bay. You don't have to own a boat, of course, because Provincetown has **Flyer's Boat Rental** (tel. 617/487-0898), 131A Commercial St., behind Cookie's restaurant. Little Scorpions, larger (14- to 22-foot) sailboats, dinghies with outboard motors, and dinghies with just a pair of oars are all for rent. They'll even teach you how to sail if you don't already know.

Whale-Watching

Believe me, it's a great thrill when you see one of the monster denizens break the surface, spout, sport, and play. You can sight whales from the Coast Guard Station on Race Point Beach, and just with the naked eye you'll see their spouting and their backs roll. But to see them up close is something else, and for that you need to sign up for a whale-watching cruise. Several boats leave on morning and afternoon runs, and give you several hours in which to find and watch the whales. Call the **Dolphin Fleet** (tel. 617/487-1900, or off-season, 255-3857), which by the way has a 99.4% sighting record; or the **Ranger III** (tel. 617/487-1582 or 487-3322) for times, prices, and reservations. Boats leave from the Town Wharf (MacMillan Wharf), and charge about $12 per person. By the way, the whales—which seem to perform expressly for the appreciative crowds on the boats—enjoy the trip as much as you do.

Nightlife

No one who visits Provincetown spends an evening without at least a few minutes' stroll along Commercial Street, for the main drag is P-town's greatest free-entertainment thrill, a circus in a straight line. But to get away from it all, try one of these things-to-do:

Lounges: After the dinner hour, many Provincetown restaurants will have entertainment in their lounges, perhaps a guitarist or pianist, even a violinist. Drop in at any one you see open in late evening, and see what's on. **Ciro and Sal's,** 41 Kiley Court (in the 400 block of Commercial Street), is a popular place, as is the cellar bar below the **Café at the Mews Restaurant,** 359 Commercial St.

Clubs: The Crown & Anchor, 247 Commercial St., is a veritable entertainment supermarket, with a disco at the rear of the parking lot named the Backroom; the front room ("Lobby Bar") on Commercial Street is for live jazz.

Speaking of revues, the **Madeira Room** (tel. 487-0319), at 336 Commercial St., always has something going, usually on the decent side of raunchy, most often very funny. Pass by for a look at their signboard.

Blitz, at 293 Commercial St., downstairs, has live entertainment and disco from 3 p.m. till 1 a.m., and aims at a gay female clientele, although there's often a smattering of others in the crowd. The **Pied Piper,** at 193–195 Commercial St., is a similar place, more into disco. Monday is talent night, however, and if you have any you're welcome to show it off.

Chapter VII

MARTHA'S VINEYARD AND NANTUCKET

1. Vineyard Haven
2. Oak Bluffs
3. Edgartown
4. What to See and Do on Martha's Vineyard
5. Nantucket

THESE TWO ISLANDS are among the eastern seaboard's most attractive and visited resorts. There's something special about vacationing on an island, a particular feeling of isolation, of being apart from the schedules and worries of city life, and this is truly relaxing and therapeutic. Here is a detailed description of Massachusetts's retreats in the Atlantic:

MARTHA'S VINEYARD: To Bostonians and denizens of Cape Cod, it is simply "the Vineyard"; sometimes you'll see the name given as Martha's Vineyard Island, just so visitors know they're in a special place out to sea. The island got its odd name in the early 1600s, when mariner and explorer Bartholomew Gosnold stopped here. It's said he found wild grapes, and it's known he had a daughter named Martha. *Voila!* Today the island actually has a commercial vineyard and a winery producing fine vintages which you can sample and buy. But more of that later.

The Vineyard is not really a part of Cape Cod, and does not look upon itself as such. Vineyard residents are proud that the island is the County of Dukes County, not part of some mainland county, and they guard the anachronistic redundancy of that title very closely. For a long time the Vineyard had its own representative in the General Court (state legislature), and when redistricting made the island a part of the Cape Cod legislative district, the islanders threatened to secede from Massachusetts and become part of another state, one that would allow them their own representative.

Islanders get their exceptional sense of independence from a history of struggle with and mastery of the sea, from the days when whaling brought great wealth to an otherwise poor island. And just about the time the whaling industry declined, the tourist industry began, and Martha's Vineyard found its place in the modern world. Today the big ferries which ply the waters of Vineyard Sound are packed with visitors every day in summer, and also very crowded on weekends in spring and fall.

A WARNING ABOUT RESERVATIONS: In high summer—July and August—you need reservations for everything: space for your car on the ferry, or for a rental car on the island, or for a hotel room, or for a mainland-to-island flight. You can't reserve passenger space on the ferry, so the thing to do is get to the docks 15 or 20 minutes early, buy your ticket, and get in line. If the ferry's passenger capacity is reached, the remaining passengers in the line will have to wait for the next boat. If you don't have a room reservation in an island hotel, there's a direct-line telephone in the Steamship Authority ticket office in Woods Hole for island hotels; you'll have to wait in line to use it. On weekends in high season, chances for finding a room are not good; on weekdays you may find a room for a few nights because of a cancellation, or a gap between reservations. If all else fails, plan to visit the island for the day, returning to the mainland in the evening.

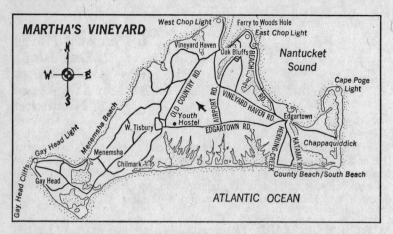

GETTING THERE: For ferries to Martha's Vineyard, see the information in the sections on Woods Hole, Falmouth, Hyannis, and New Bedford. One ferry a day runs between the islands of Martha's Vineyard and Nantucket. When taking a ferry, note which island port—Oak Bluffs or Vineyard Haven—the ferry operates from or to.

Several regional and commuter airlines serve the Vineyard.

Air Florida (tel. toll free 800/327-2971), in conjunction with Gull Air (see below), provides service from Boston to Nantucket via Hyannis.

Atlantic Air (tel. 203/386-9000, or toll-free 800/972-9830 in Connecticut; 800/243-9830 outside Connecticut), provides service from Bridgeport, Conn., to Martha's Vineyard and Nantucket; also to Bedford (Mass.), Boston, Philadelphia, and White Plains.

Gull Air, Barnstable Municipal Airport, Hyannis, MA 02601 (tel. 617/771-1247, or toll-free in Massachusetts only, 800/352-7191), provides service from Hyannis and New Bedford to Nantucket and Martha's Vineyard. In conjunction with Air Florida (see above) it has scheduled summer service between Boston, and Nantucket via Hyannis.

PBA (Provincetown–Boston Airline), P.O. Box 639, Provincetown, MA 02657 (tel. 617/349-6331, or toll-free in Massachusetts only, 800/352-3132), is one of the oldest and best of the regional carriers in New England, serving Boston, Provincetown, New Bedford, Hyannis, Martha's Vineyard, Nantucket, and New York City (La Guardia).

Trans East International Airlines (formerly New York Air Commuter), a division of Starflight International Airlines, 1919 Broad Hollow Rd., Farmingdale, NY 11735 (tel. 212/895-4332, or toll-free in New York state, 800/732-9683; in other states, 800/645-9679). Trans East cities are New York, Newark, Boston, Providence, Nantucket, Martha's Vineyard, Hyannis, Hartford, White Plains, and Atlantic City, plus Long Island.

GETTING AROUND THE ISLAND: There are lots of ways to get around: rental cars (which are best reserved in advance), buses, bikes, or motorbikes. Taxi service is also readily available.

Car Rentals

The big names are here: **Hertz** (tel. 617/627-4728) in Edgartown and at the airport; **Avis** (tel. 617/693-9010) in Oak Bluffs and Vineyard Haven; **Budget** (tel. 617/693-9780) on Water Street in Vineyard Haven; **National** (tel. 617/627-4761) on Main Street in Edgartown.

If these places produce no results, or if you'd rather rent from a small local firm, try these numbers: **Adventure Rentals** of Martha's Vineyard (tel. 617/693-1959 and also a direct line from the Woods Hole Ferry Terminal) specializes in offbeat equipment such as dune buggies, vans, mopeds, four-wheel-drive vehicles, and trucks, but they do rent cars as well. Other firms are **Atlantic Auto Rentals** (tel. 617/693-0480), **DeBettencourt's Car Rentals** (tel. 617/693-0011), **Martha's Vineyard Auto Village** (tel. 617/693-0100), and **Mr. Rent-a-Car** (tel. 617/693-3173).

Bikes and Motorbikes

Rental agencies abound, and you can barely descend from the ferry without coming across one. Prices are all competitive, and a three-speed bicycle should cost in the range of $6 to $10 for a day's rental; motorbikes and mopeds are a good deal more, in the range of $25 to $30, and entail greater responsibility and more chance of breakdowns. I think the island and the bicycle were made for one another, and islanders have even helped this relationship along: there's a fine bike path between Oak Bluffs and Edgartown, right along the beaches. No need to reserve bikes in advance, for there are always plenty to go around.

Bus

Island Transport Bus Service operates school-bus-type vehicles between the Vineyard's various settlements every half hour or so, with stops near the various ferry docks. Prices vary according to distances traveled; round-trip tickets are always sold at a discount over the normal two-single-trip fare, so ask for a round-trip ticket if that's what suits your needs. The cheapest fare is Vineyard Haven to Oak Bluffs (50¢), and fares can be several dollars for longer trips.

ORIENTATION: The island's three principal towns are **Vineyard Haven**, the commercial center where many of the mainland ferries dock; **Oak Bluffs, a** Victorian resort community of ornate "gingerbread" houses, a marina, and several grand old wooden hotels; and **Edgartown**, the county seat and main tourist attraction—clearly the prettiest town on the island. I'll list the recommended hotels, restaurants, and things to do by town.

1. Vineyard Haven

Vineyard Haven is a nice enough town, with a main shopping street a few blocks up from the docks, and a state lobster hatchery nearby; but Oak Bluffs and Edgartown are the choice places to stay overnight, so I'll concentrate on Vineyard Haven's several restaurants which you might patronize on your way through.

WHERE TO STAY: Should you stay overnight here, the **Vineyard Harbor Motel** (tel. 617/693-3334), P.O. Box 1609, Vineyard Haven, MA 02568, near the edge of town on the coast road to Oak Bluffs, is modern and comfortable, with color TVs, wall-to-wall carpeting, and refrigerators in all rooms; some have kitchen facilities as well, and many have a fine ocean view. In-season rates are $68.70 to $74 for a harbor-view double room, $58.15 to $63.45 without the view; the higher price includes kitchen facilities. A two-room apartment is $79.30 for four people, and the Penthouse, complete with view, fireplace, and private deck, is $74. An extra person is $9 per day. In spring and fall, these rates are $15 to $20 less per room, and in winter the rates are less than half those of high summer.

WHERE TO DINE: The finest place to dine in town, and one of the more expensive, is the **Black Dog Tavern** (tel. 693-9223), at the water end of Beach Street, right down next to the yacht marina. Its location and good food bring in the yachting crowd, and this keeps the quality high. A large screened porch overlooking the harbor and marina is the choice place to sit, and you must come early to get a place there. No reservations are accepted, so get there by about 6 p.m. for dinner. I had clams casino, roast half duckling with lingonberry sauce, and fresh-baked apple pie for dessert, and with coffee, tax, and tip the total was $24. The Black Dog is open year round except in January and February, seven days a week, from 6:30 to 11 a.m., 11:30 a.m. to 2:30 p.m., and from 5:30 to 10 p.m. There's a $3 minimum at dinnertime; bring your own wine or beer, as Vineyard Haven is a dry town. And be dressed something like a yachtsman—the dress code is loose, but it's there.

The **Café du Port,** just a block from the docks at the intersection with Main Street, is a cute little place with a small indoor dining room and a good number of little tables set outside under large awnings. It's the perfect spot for dinnertime seafood dishes at about $6.50 to $9.50, meat dishes a bit more. Homemade desserts here too. Open from Memorial Day weekend until Labor Day weekend.

Popeye's Chowder Bar, on Main Street, is a recreation of an old tavern restaurant with a long wooden salad bar and lots of small tables. A bowl of chowder ($2.25) is a light lunch in itself, or pay for the Soup and Salad Special ($4.50) for a more substantial meal. In the evenings (after 5), the short but select seafood dinner menu comes into effect. My favorite from the seafood list is the seafood kebab of scallops, shrimp, and swordfish ($9.25); a trip to the salad bar and baked potato are included in the dinner price.

The **Hungry "U" Sub and Pizza Shop** on Union Street (just up from the docks) is open from 10:30 a.m. to 9 p.m. daily, serving the perfect things for a budget-conscious traveler's lunch. Pizza is only 95¢ a slice, and submarine sandwiches range from the Kitchen Sink (that's with everything) to steak and peppers. For dessert, go right next door to the **Great American Ice Cream and Candy Company** for one of their delicious cones.

READER'S PICNIC SUGGESTION: "You can pick up gourmet picnic supplies at the **Vineyard Cheese and Gourmet Shop**, on Main Street. For the more basic things (and lower prices), **Cronig's Market** is right across the street. Coming up from the docks, turn right onto Main Street" (Marta Fry, Boston, Mass.).

2. Oak Bluffs

It's odd that this community, which began as a tent camp for summer meetings of the Methodist church, should be one of the two "wet" towns on Martha's Vineyard, but so it is. Although the camp meetings are still the most important part of the summer's activities here (your hotel will have a schedule), many other nighttime pleasures are available as well, including movies, penny arcades, and an antique merry-go-round called "The Flying Horses." During the daytime, stroll straight in from the ferry docks and along the shores of the marina for a view of the fantastically ornate Victorian "gingerbread houses" which face the marina.

WHERE TO STAY: The **Attleboro House**, at 11 Lake Ave. (P.O. Box 1564), Oak Bluffs, MA 02557 (tel. 617/693-4346), is in that marvelous row of ginger-bread houses, next to the old Wesley, which faces the sheltered harbor. If you arrive by Hy-Line boat, you'll be able to spot Attleboro House before you even debark. The house's wide verandas are well furnished with rockers and fine views. Rooms are spartan but tidy, and fully in the spirit of Oak Bluffs; in fact the house is on land owned by the Methodist Campmeeting Association, so guests must agree to refrain from "rude or loud behavior." Only a few rooms have washbasins; none has private bath; and though there are plenty of clean sheets and towels, maid service is strictly do-it-yourself. Single rooms cost $26.50, doubles are $42.50. Here, and at the Wesley (below), you're living right within Oak Bluffs' history.

Left from Oak Bluffs' gingerbread heyday is **The Wesley**, P.O. Box 1207, Oak Bluffs, MA 02557 (tel. 617/693-0135), a rambling wooden place with old-fashioned rooms at old-fashioned prices: from the Steamship Authority docks walk straight inland toward the marina, and the Wesley is a few blocks down on the left. Rooms here are in the main building or in one of the nearby houses, and may be plain, with only a dresser, bed, chairs, and closet, or may be a bit "better dressed," but all are quite clean and presentable; some have fairly good views of the town and the water. Rates, including continental breakfast, are $25 to $30 per night for a single, the higher price being for a room with private bath; or $30 for a bathless double, $49 for a double with bath. An extra person costs $7, and these rates include a continental breakfast of juice, muffins baked in the Wesley's kitchens, butter, jam, and coffee—as much as you like. The Wesley also handles a number of harbor-view apartments on East Chop ($225 a week). The Wesley has been run by the same family—the Chases —since 1879, and the service could not be more friendly or efficient.

Similar to the Wesley in ambience, and even more ornate architecturally, is **Nashua House** (tel. 617/693-0043), Oak Bluffs, MA 02557, across the street from the post office, where rooms with a bit more decoration than the Wesley's go for $30.65 single, $42.28 double, with a shared bath. Being smaller than Wesley's, Nashua House is a bit harder to find a place in, so write or telephone early. Note that there's a coin-op laundry just across the street from Nashua House.

Lucille's Guest House (tel. 617/693-1944), on Circuit Avenue down at the end of the commercial section, is an Oak Bluffs home with several rooms for rent by the day or week. A large room with private bath can sleep up to four people, and costs $43 double ($48 if you use all four beds). It even has a little refrigerator. Other rooms are smaller, less elaborate, and less expensive.

WHERE TO DINE: For some reason Vineyard Haven has a good number of good restaurants, and Edgartown has its share, but in Oak Bluffs the fare is less than inspired. Of course, resort towns always present problems to the visitor in search of a fine dinner: the crowds must be fed, and customers will continue to come whether the food is great or not, because they must eat. But you won't go to bed without your dinner in Oak Bluffs.

The place that packs 'em in is **Giordano's,** at the corner of Circuit and Lake Avenues. The large, modern, brightly lit dining room is filled every night of high summer with the hungry and the thrifty filling themselves with the inexpensive Italian cuisine that's been offered here since 1930. Elegant it's not, and although it's a bit noisy, the service is efficient, the food is filling, and the price is reasonable: a full dinner special with chowder, potato, vegetable, coffee, and dessert can cost $6 (entree of baked ham), $6.75 (pork chops), or $9 (sirloin steak). The à la carte items are also reasonably priced, the pizzas and spaghettis being in the $4 to $6.25 range. Cocktails, house wines sold by the half liter and liter, and bottled wines are available. There may well be a line of the value-minded waiting to get in, so it's good to arrive early.

Just a snack or breakfast? The **Old Stone Bakery and Coffee Shop** is right next to the post office, and besides bread and danish you may find French butter cookies or apple fritters. Coffee is always served. At lunchtime they may be serving clam chowder. Hours are from 7 a.m. to 5 p.m. daily.

3. Edgartown

Undoubtedly the prettiest and most picturesque town on the island, Edgartown is the place most people want to stay when they come to Martha's Vineyard, and so the selection of rooms is fairly good. Whether your taste calls for a resort hotel with golf course, a modern motel with a sea view, or a colonial inn, Edgartown has what you want.

Besides being the residential center of the island, Edgartown has many good restaurants, most of the island's finer shops and art galleries, and street after street of attractive houses. Many of the houses were built by whaling captains with the profits of their voyages, and these same profits provided the funds to build the Methodist church (1843) on Main Street. In more recent times, Edgartown came to national prominence as the place where the movie *Jaws* and its sequel were filmed, and many island residents made the daily stroll down to the harbor to look at the small mechanical shark in its special rack, covered by a canvas tarpaulin.

WHERE TO STAY: For many years visitors to Martha's Vineyard have been staying at the **Daggett Houses** (tel. 617/627-4600), Edgartown, MA 02539, on North Water Street at Daggett Street. A collection of historic houses, the rooms are tastefully furnished, several are of very good size, and some have good water views—the larger rooms and those with views are the more expensive ones. All rooms have king-size, double, or twin beds, and private bath; some rooms, good for groups of friends or large families, are arranged in suites sharing a bath. There are even a few housekeeping rooms with kitchen, and a Garden Cottage with three double rooms down by the water. Prices for the 25 rooms in three different houses are $65.71 to $105.70 (most rooms run $89.85) in summer, with a one-week minimum stay required; off-season, rates are from $47.57 to

$89.85 (most rooms at $68.71). A full country breakfast is included with the price of the room. The original Daggett House has its own dock, and a "Chimney Room" said to be Edgartown's oldest tavern, now used for the breakfast service (ask them to show you the secret stairway here). Daggett House II is across the street, and is equally nice, and guests at either house may use the lawns and beach. Needless to say, Daggett Houses are a popular place to stay, and so it's best to write well in advance to get the type of room you desire.

Edgartown's most charming and elegant inn is the **Charlotte Inn** (tel. 617/627-4751), South Summer Street, Edgartown, MA 02539, a unique hostelry combining the services of an inn, a fine art gallery, and a very good French restaurant called Chez Pierre. Rooms here are all given a personal touch with furnishings—some antiques—selected by the owners, and thus the best way to select a room is to see several, although this is often difficult as many are sure to be occupied. The rates are in keeping with the elegant atmosphere: doubles run $79.28 to $142.70 in season (mid-June to mid-October); for a month on either side of high season, rates go down to $47.57 to $103.59 double; and during the winter they become $33.82 to $50.74 double. Continental breakfast is included. Children 12 and under pay $4 for a cot in their parents' room. Even if you decide not to stay at the Charlotte Inn, stroll by some evening to admire the graceful house, the very good gallery, and perhaps the garden-terrace dining at Chez Pierre.

The **Edgartown Inn** (tel. 617/627-4794), North Water Street, Edgartown, MA 02539, has been hosting famous guests for well over a century, including the likes of Daniel Webster, Nathaniel Hawthorne (who wrote *Twice Told Tales* here), and (Sen.) John F. Kennedy. The inn is thus a place of contrasts: in the rooms, 19th-century decor competes with the modern tiled baths, and in the parlor, a portrait of Hawthorne hangs glowering at the color TV. There are 12 rooms in the inn proper, which cost $52.85 to $68.71 from June 15 to Labor Day, $37 to $49.70 off-season. In season they may not take reservations for less than five days.

Rooms in the "Captain's Quarters" out back do not have private baths, and rent for $31.71 in season; also, several rooms in the old barn attached to the inn are sometimes rented for about $9 per person—take a look at these before you rent. The Edgartown Inn serves country breakfasts in its quaint, cozy breakfast room, old-fashioned and neat as a pin: a deer head, a fine ship model, and the only "colonial" ceiling fans we've ever seen add to the decor. Whether a guest at the inn or not, you can have the full breakfast here for $4, a continental breakfast of homemade cakes and breads baked everyday for $2.50.

The **Shiretown Inn** (tel. 617/627-4283), P.O. Box 921, Edgartown, MA 02539, is on North Water Street, right downtown. Two fine old houses and several buildings in the back enclose a nice little garden patio and make up not only an inn, but also a restaurant and bar. All rooms have private baths, whether in the Captain's Houses or in the modern motel-style Carriage House out back, and rates vary according to which building the room is in and how many people it will hold. Rooms in the Captain's Houses are quite expensive; in the Carriage House, doubles are $53. Off-season rates are about $20 per room less, but note that the Shiretown Inn is open only from late May through September. The restaurant in the pleasant patio dotted with trees and flowers is open for breakfast and dinner.

The **Colonial Inn** (tel. 617/627-4711), North Water Street, Edgartown, MA 02539, looks like Edgartown's answer to the huge rambling Victorian hotels of Oak Bluffs and elsewhere, although to keep with tradition on North Water Street, this one is covered in cedar "shakes" (shingles) and many windows have shutters like those of the sea captains' houses. The advantages at the Colonial, besides its central location and numerous rooms with sea views, are its large number of rooms and varied rates. Double rooms with private bath are most expensive ($63.42 to $73.99), but if you choose a double with connecting bath—that is, shared with one other room—the price drops to $58.14, and if you don't mind walking to a bath down the hall, a double is only $47.57. Children under 12 stay for free off-season, $15 apiece in season; an extra person pays $15 off-season, $25 in season. Room rates off-season are $7 to $10 less per room. The Colonial has its own restaurant and bar, and is open from late May to mid-October.

Although the **Kelley House** (tel. 617/627-4394) boasts that it has been "an Edgartown tradition since 1742," when you stay here it is in very bright, modern surroundings. Private baths, color TV in each room, and central air conditioning are some of the modern conveniences, while the furniture is mostly colonial in inspiration. If you stay in the main building, rooms are $89.85 to $95.13 single, $100.42 to $110.99 double; in the new wing, rooms are $110.99 single, $116.56 double; an extra person pays $10. Note that these rates don't include service charge. The Kelley House is open all year, and off-season rates are a good deal lower. For reservations, write to the Kelley House, Kelley Street, Edgartown, MA 02539. The Kelley House has its own restaurant, and is located just off North Water Street right downtown.

Edgartown's most immaculately kept guest house has got to be the **Captain Fisher House** (tel. 617/627-5544), at the corner of North Water and Winter Streets, Edgartown, MA 02539. The lawns and gardens are as carefully tended as are the beds and bathrooms. Although it's right smack in the center of Edgartown, the shady grounds allow guests to relax away from the busy activity of the street, even to stretch out in a hammock out back. Rates, if you are fortunate enough (or reserve early enough) to get a room, are $68 for two each night, with a discount in winter during periods when it's open for business. In season they may not take reservations for less than five days or one week. Be sure to admire the magnificent holly tree at the south corner of the house.

Of the guest houses in Edgartown, the **Captain Henry Colt House** (tel. 617/627-4084), 26 North Summer St. (P.O. Box 302, Edgartown, MA 02539), is one of the nicest and most congenial. The house is kept very well, the proprietress, Mrs. Berube, is very helpful to her guests, and the street is quiet though very close to the center of town. Rooms are doubles with bath ($52.85 to $58.14) or with shared bath ($37 to $42.28); an efficiency apartment which can sleep four people costs $84.56. These rates are for the summer, from mid-June through mid-September; off-season, reductions are in order, and the size of the reduction depends on demand. No meals are served, but the town's restaurants are all within two or three blocks.

For Longer Stays

A group of two to four people wanting to stay on Martha's Vineyard for a few weeks should look into the **Edgartown Lodge** (tel. 617/627-8069 or 693-9451), corner of Church and Winter Streets (P.O. Box 1104, Edgartown, MA 02539), a small building of efficiency apartments not far from the center of town. Each apartment sleeps two in luxury, four in comfort, and is complete with kitchen, utensils, linens—all you'll need. During the summer the apartments rent for $350 to $390 weekly, which makes the daily per-person rate only $12.50 to $14 if four share the flat. Off-season, rooms rent on a two-night minimum stay for considerably less. Call for reservations.

Vineyard Preferred Properties (tel. 617/693-9451), P.O. Box 1104, Edgartown, MA 02539, will set you up with a one- or two-bedroom rental unit, all electric and heated, for about $145 per week in April, about $325 in June or September. In high season, prices are higher and the units are rented well in advance. Write early if you want the busy months.

Budget Lodgings

The **Jonathan Munroe House** (tel. 617/627-5536; P.O. Box 1165, Edgartown, MA 02539) is at 100 Main St. not too far from the center of town (no visible street numbers here). It's a house converted to receive guests, which is exactly what it does, placing them in quaint and homey rooms, nicely done, and charging them $31.71 in July and August, $21.14 at other times of the year, for a double room. The six rooms share two upstairs baths. The **Horn o' Plenty Guest House**, 100 Main St., is run by the same people who have the Jonathan Munroe; this house has a common room with television, and parking on the premises. The six rooms share two baths, and are somewhat smaller, priced accordingly at $31.71 double. Both houses provide tea and coffee for free, and each has a refrigerator for guests' use.

How long it will last is anyone's guess, but there is, as of this writing, a rooming house in which you can get a tiny single room for $19.03, other singles for $26.03, and double rooms for $31.71. There is one room for three at $47.57. All share the hall baths. These rooms could all use extensive repairs, but when they receive expensive attention, the prices will treble. They're in the **Charles Marchant House** (tel. 617/627-4489; P.O. Box 303) on Main Street, almost opposite the big white-pillared Methodist church. The Charles Marchant is owned and run by a whaling captain's granddaughter who has been an island resident for many, many years.

The Nearby Youth Hostel

Martha's Vineyard has a youth hostel in West Tisbury (tel. 617/693-2665), actually one mile east of West Tisbury on the road to Edgartown. The hostel's affiliated with AYH (American Youth Hostels), and it's good to be a member; it's also good to have reservations in July and August. With your reservation, plan to arrive between 5 and 8 p.m., and bring your own sheets and towels (blankets provided).

WHERE TO DINE: Edgartown—and the island in general—can boast a large number of eateries, plain and fancy. I couldn't possibly list them all in the limited space here, and in fact an all-inclusive list would be more bewildering than helpful. Although I can heartily recommend the establishments below as delivering good value-for-money, you will no doubt want to do some exploration of your own. Let me warn you that there are a number of clip joints—I got clipped for large amounts in several while doing the revision work for this book. It's fairly simple to avoid clip joints by following this rule: never sit down to dine in an expensive restaurant which is almost empty. Better still, pass by your intended dining spot the evening before you plan to dine there, and look at the crowd. On a rainy weekday evening, even good places may be emptyish; but any place that has only two or three tables occupied on a weekend night has got to be flawed.

Of Edgartown's restaurants, one of the most elegant and congenial is certainly **Chez Pierre** (tel. 627-8947), in the garden and glassed-in terrace of the Charlotte Inn on South Summer Street. It's open for lunch, dinner, and

Sunday brunch in season. The white tables and chairs set out among the trees, vines, and flowers on a patio surrounded by trelliswork provide the perfect place for a warm-weather evening's repast; in bad weather, the terrace room is almost as good, with lots of windows and skylights. The menu reads like a list of ambrosias: fresh island seafood marinated in lime juice with shallots, or a pâté of chicken livers with cognac and herbed croutons to start; then a main course of two sauteed boneless quail with wild rice, mushrooms, and Madeira wine sauce, or perhaps sauteed island scallops in wine. A green salad, choice of cheese, dessert, and coffee are included in the dinner price, as is the appetizer. Dinner prices, tax and tip included, range from $25 to $38—well worth it. Prices at lunch are a good deal less.

As Edgartown is one of the Vineyard's two "wet" towns, you can order wine to accompany your meal. Call for reservations, and ask what the day's special will be.

The Harborside Inn's **Navigator Restaurant** (tel. 627-4321), on the water near the yacht club, offers several dining rooms that are positively choc-a-bloc with nautical paraphernalia, and a bar which is festooned with blocks and tackle, lanterns, nets, and whatnot. Fare tends to the familiar rather than the exotic, such as creamed finnan haddie or sandwiches at lunch ($5 to $6), baked stuffed fish of the day ($11) at dinner. Meats at dinner are in the $12 to $16 range. Open for breakfast (8 to 11 a.m.), lunch (noon to 2:30 p.m.), and dinner (5:30 to 10 p.m.) daily; the bar is open from 11:30 a.m. to 11:30 p.m.

After years of being Edgartown's prime fish market, **Lawry's** (tel. 627-8857) added a modern dining room and became one of Edgartown's prime seafood restaurants as well. Formica tables and red padded benches make the atmosphere bright but simple, and while the restaurant serves sandwiches ($2.75 to $3.50), the seafood is the thing. I recently filled myself (and my wife) with steamed clams ($4.75 for a huge portion which was sufficient for two), then a portion of broiled bluefish and one of fish-and-chips ($7.85 for each). The main courses came with coleslaw, potato, rolls, and butter, and the total bill was $27, tax, tip, and two glasses of beer included. After 5 p.m., all of Lawry's food can be taken out too. Service is fast and the friendliest in town. Highly recommended.

The Wharf (tel. 627-9966), right down by its namesake in Edgartown, is good for any meal, any time of day. Simple, airy, attractive surroundings, air-conditioned on the hot days, are the place to enjoy a cold beer or glass of wine with, say, a crabmeat salad. Such a luncheon treat will cost about $7. Lots of other seafood is served, or you can serve yourself, at lower prices, from the Wharf Landing carry-out counter. A deck with tables and chairs is your do-it-yourself dining room.

The **Seafood Shanty**, on Dock Street at Kelley Street, is a favorite with the younger crowd because of its atmosphere and its very reasonable seafood prices—not to mention a fine harbor view. At lunch (noon to 3 p.m.), something elegant such as a seafood Newburg crêpe is $5.75, but the fish-of-the-day is even less, and sandwiches a lot less. At dinner, fish main courses run to $8.50 to $11, or you can have a steak, or chicken, or a huge salad if you prefer. Dinner is served daily from 5:30 to 10:30 p.m.

Perhaps the cheapest prices in expensive Edgartown are found at **The Quarterdeck**, down near the Chappaquiddick ferry dock, in front of the Seafood Shanty. Though seafood is slightly higher in price, they've got the cheapest hamburgers and sandwiches in town.

Martha's Restaurant, across the street from Edgartown's Town Hall on Main Street (tel. 627-8316), has one dining room downstairs, another upstairs near the raw bar. The menu is interesting and varied, with everything from bluefish through fettuccine to sushi. Sunday brunch is a tradition. Prices are on the high side, with many dinner entrees selling for $12, which means a full dinner with wine will cost about $25, perhaps a bit less. Stick to Mexican specialties and cut the price in half.

For Breakfast or a Snack

The same **Old Stone Bakery and Coffee Shop** you may have patronized in Oak Bluffs has a branch in Edgartown on Water Street across from the Captain Fisher House. As in Edgartown's sister city, the Old Stone is the perfect place for a light breakfast of freshly baked rolls, danish or pastries, with coffee. For picnics, it's a prime supplier of good, fresh bread.

4. What to See and Do on Martha's Vineyard

The most delightful thing about Martha's Vineyard is that it is its own entertainment, and one can often be fully satisfied just strolling along past picket-fence houses, swimming at the many beaches, or biking past the marshes, forests, and island heath. But should you wish a little directed, purposeful activity, you will not be at a loss. First thing to do is to find out what's on currently in the way of festivities and special events. There's an **Information Desk** in the Steamship Authority's dockside ticket office in Woods Hole, so you can find out some things even before getting to the island. But once on the Vineyard, pick up a copy of the island's tabloid newssheet called *The Grapevine,* or *This Week on Martha's Vineyard* (a pull-out section of the paper). Here you'll discover a list of the church-sponsored white elephant sales, musical concerts (many free), lectures, dances, movies, tournaments (kite-flying, fishing, Ping-Pong), community sings, and the like. The island's most important to-do is the annual **Regatta and Around-the-Island Race,** held on a weekend in late July (hotels are extra-full then).

TOURS: The **Gay Head Sightseeing Company** (tel. 617/693-1555) operates daily sightseeing tours of the island, including the Vineyard's six towns and two villages, the sea captains' houses (from the outside), and even a stop at the multicolored cliffs at Gay Head. The trip takes about 2½ hours, covers 56 miles, and costs $8 for adults, half price for children. Tours leave the ferry wharves after the arrival of the ship, and from the traffic circle in Oak Bluffs.

THE THOMAS COOKE HOUSE: The Dukes County Historical Society, at the corner of Cooke and School Streets in Edgartown, operates the island's most interesting museum in the former Thomas Cooke House (1760s). All the artifacts in the refurnished house came from Vineyard houses, including scrimshaw, china, glass, paintings, and nautical paraphernalia. In other buildings on the grounds, various types of boats which played a part in the island's history can be seen, and there's a special tower to hold the Paris-made lens (1854) which revolved in the Gay Head lighthouse from 1856 to 1952. A guided tour of the museum costs $1 for adults, 50¢ for children under 16. During the summer, the museum is open from 10 a.m. to 4:30 p.m. except Sunday and Monday and holidays; in off-season visits to the library can be made on Thursday and Friday from 1 to 4 p.m., on Saturday from 10 a.m. to noon and from 1 to 4 p.m.

THE HANSEL AND GRETEL DOLL MUSEUM: A fine collection of dolls and girls' tin toys, many of them valuable antiques, is on display at this museum, on New York Avenue between Oak Bluffs and Vineyard Haven. China, bisque, or parian heads are on doll bodies of cloth or leather, and many dolls have the original dresses made for them. The collection is in a private home, and is open to the public from 10 a.m. to 5 p.m. in July and August, for 75¢ admission; other times by appointment (call 693-9285). It's a bit difficult to spot the museum: going from Oak Bluffs to Vineyard Haven, look for signs saying "Dick's Bait and Tackle Shop," and "Fishing Tackle," on the left-hand side of New York Avenue. The museum is in the same small house, its sign much less prominent than the others.

THE STATE LOBSTER HATCHERY: The Massachusetts State Lobster Hatchery is just outside Vineyard Haven on the road to Oak Bluffs, and is open from 9 a.m. to noon and 1 to 3 p.m. daily, except Sunday, free of charge. Here thousands of tiny lobsters are raised on pieces of quahog (clam) meat to keep from devouring one another until they are judged capable of fending for themselves in the chilly waters of the Atlantic.

A VINEYARD ON THE VINEYARD: Martha's Vineyard now has its own real vineyard, and you can visit it. **Chicama Vineyards** (tel. 693-0309) is southwest of Vineyard Haven off State Road on Stoney Hill Road, in West Tisbury. The 33 acres are planted in vinifera varieties such as Cabernet, Chardonnay, Chenin Blanc, Pinot Noir, Riesling, Zinfandel, and others. It's obviously a serious effort, in operation since 1971. Visit during Friday and Saturday afternoons in April and early May; daily except Sunday from 10 a.m. to 5 p.m. from mid-May to August (in July and August, 1 to 5 p.m. on Sunday); in October, hours are 1 to 4 p.m. Monday through Saturday. The vineyard is closed July 4 and Labor Day.

BEACHES AND BIKE TRIPS: The **State Beach** on the road between Oak Bluffs and Edgartown is probably the first beach you'll see. It's a fine long stretch of white sand, free and open to the public, with parking along the road. The **County Beach at Katama Bay** south of Edgartown has surf swimming, and is likewise free. The three major towns all have town beaches open to everyone, but the smaller towns and villages reserve their beaches for local property owners, or charge a beach-use fee.

Bicycle riding is fun anywhere on the island as the hills are few and gently sloped, but it's particularly good on the bike path between Oak Bluffs and Edgartown, and on the island of Chappaquiddick, reached by ferry (five-minute trip) from the docks in Edgartown. Wildlife preserves are dotted about Martha's Vineyard, particularly on Chappaquiddick and at Menemsha, Felix Neck, and Cedar Tree Neck. And the excursion to the strikingly beautiful cliffs at Gay Head is a must, but one must have a bit of stamina for this trip on a bike, and you should devote most of a day to it.

You can, of course drive or take a tour to the **Gay Head Cliffs,** which is Martha's Vineyard's top "excursion." Don't expect a dramatic, towering wall of land staunchly resisting the thundering waves: the cliffs are dramatic only when one considers the more-or-less level terrain of the island. But the cliffs and their colors are pretty, and Gay Head is the perfect "goal" for what would otherwise be an aimless meander. You can view the cliffs for free (although you must pay to use the nearby public toilets).

SAILING AND SUCH: The **Harborside Inn** (tel. 627-4321), on Lower Main Street, will rent you a 15-foot Boston Whaler with a 25-hp outboard motor, or a 17-foot Daysailor, or a smaller Sunfish if you like to take to the waters under your own control for a day. The boatyard is open from 8:30 a.m. to 5 p.m. daily. If you don't understand the lingo or the techniques and can't tell a sheet from a painter, they'll even sell you lessons.

An even grander way to sail the seas is aboard the clipper schooner *Shenandoah* out of Vineyard Haven, commanded by Capt. Robert Douglas for the Coastwise Packet Company (tel. 617/693-1699). The *Shenandoah* is no small boat, measuring 108 feet along the rail, built at South Bristol, Me., in 1964. When she's going all out, the *Shenandoah* has all nine of her sails out in a classic square topsail rig, and can do better than 12 knots. You can sail aboard the ship for a week by paying $490 per person, which price pays not only for the adventure, but for food and lodging as well. Call for particulars.

The Vineyard's island sister, Nantucket, is even more of an ocean-going grande dame. More difficult of access (at least in terms of time and price), Nantucket draws an elite crowd willing to pay fairly high prices for lodging and meals. But the crowd is no smaller even though it's elite: prepare for your visit in advance, in high season, by booking reservations.

5. Nantucket

To its year-round inhabitants, Nantucket is not just another resort island off Cape Cod, but a special sea-going world of its own. All the brochures and booklets handed out on the island seem to bear the legend "Thirty Miles at Sea." With its history of whaling, its choppy Indian name, and its people's reputation for hardiness, one might expect to find clusters of peasant dwellings and strong-armed shipwrights making rough island boats, but in fact the opposite is true: Nantucket's Main Street is lined with gracious buildings and towering elms, and the rest of the town boasts street after street of charming and dignified houses from the 18th and 19th centuries. And this is to be expected when you think of the money that whaling brought to Nantucket: before the oil sheiks there were the whale-oil magnates, for whale oil fired the lamps of all New England, whalebone provided the stays for the corsets then in style, and ambergris was the base for perfume, a luxury item.

In 1659, the first colonists came ashore to settle the island, already inhabited by four tribes of Indians. The **Jethro Coffin House,** the first fine house to be built, went up in 1686, almost 20 years after the first whale had been claimed off Nantucket's shores. By the time of the Revolution, Nantucket was already wealthy from the whale-oil trade and contributed greatly to the revolutionary cause, losing over 100 whaling ships and 2000 Nantucketers in the war. Without time to fully recover, the War of 1812 came to the island and again interfered with its prosperity. In another 50 years the age of the sail-rigged whaling ship was at an end, but the same device which put an end to that era—the steamship—brought the beginning of a new era for Nantucket as a vacation destination. In summer, the cobblestones of Main Street are worn down by visitors from Boston, New York, and even farther away, and in winter the islanders go about their business getting ready for the next summer season.

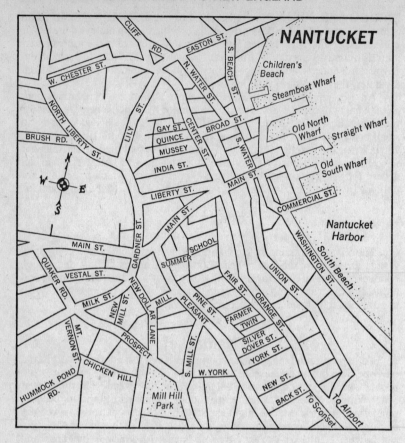

GETTING THERE: Ferryboats carrying both cars and passengers run to Nantucket from Hyannis, Martha's Vineyard, and Woods Hole in summer. (See those sections in Chapter VI for details.)

Flights to Nantucket are operated by several regional and local airlines. From Hyannis, **Gull Air** and **PBA** operate Nantucket shuttle services for which you need no reservation. Just show up, buy a ticket, and board the plane. The fare is $19 one way; the flight takes 15 minutes.

Air Florida (tel. toll free 800/327-2971), in conjunction with Gull Air (see below), provides service from Boston to Nantucket via Hyannis.

Air Vermont, 1795 South Williston Rd., South Burlington, VT 05401 (tel. 802/863-1110, or toll-free 800/322-9300 in Vermont; 800/343-8828 outside Vermont), cities are New York (JFK), Hartford/Springfield, Albany, Burlington, Newport (Vt.), Berlin (N.H.), Portland, Boston, Worcester, and Nantucket, plus Long Island.

Atlantic Air (tel. 203/386-9000, or toll-free 800/972-9830 in Connecticut; 800/243-9830 outside Connecticut) provides service from Bridgeport, Conn., to Martha's Vineyard and Nantucket; also to Bedford (Mass.), Boston, Philadelphia, and White Plains.

Gull Air, Barnstable Municipal Airport, Hyannis, MA 02601 (tel. 617/771-1247, or toll free in Massachusetts only, 800/352-7191), provides service from Hyannis and New Bedford to Nantucket and Martha's Vineyard. In conjunction with Air Florida (see above), it has scheduled summer service between Boston, and Nantucket via Hyannis.

PBA (Provincetown–Boston Airline), P.O. Box 639, Provincetown, MA 02657 (tel. 617/349-6331, or toll-free in Massachusetts only, 800/352-3132), is one of the oldest and best of the regional carriers in New England, serving Boston, Provincetown, New Bedford, Hyannis, Martha's Vineyard, Nantucket, and New York City (La Guardia).

Precision Airlines, Springfield-Harkness State Airport, North Springfield, VT 05150 (tel. toll free 800/451-4221 in New York and New England), connects Vermont with Boston, New York City (La Guardia), and other points, flying amont these cities: Rutland, Montpelier, and Springfield (Vt.); Pittsfield (Mass.); and Manchester, Keene, Lebanon (White River Junction), and Laconia (N.H.).

Trans East International Airlines (formerly New York Air Commuter), a division of Starflight International Airlines, 1919 Broad Hollow Rd., Farmingdale, NY 11735 (tel. 212/895-4332, or toll-free in New York state, 800/732-9683; in other states, 800/645-9679). Trans East cities are New York, Newark, Boston, Providence, Nantucket, Martha's Vineyard, Hyannis, Hartford, White Plains, and Atlantic City, plus Long Island.

Will's Air (tel. 617/771-1470, or toll free in Massachusetts only, 800/352-7559), using small aircraft, flies nonstop from Boston to Nantucket, and also nonstop on the Hyannis–Nantucket and Boston–Hyannis routes.

GETTING AROUND: Nantucket's a small place without the need of a large bus service, but there are several buses run by the **Nantucket and 'Sconset Bus Company** (tel. 617/228-0420): five times daily in summer between Nantucket and 'Sconset, one bus a day to Wauwinet, to the beach at the jetties (leaves every 30 minutes or so), and to other, more distant beaches. Buy tickets, get information, and board the bus at the bus stop on South Water Street, opposite the fire house.

Taxis abound and their rates are: $2.50 for one person within town limits, $1.25 for each additional person; between airport and town, $5 for one person, $1 for each additional person. Other rates are established for trips to the beaches and sights, and are posted in the cab. Bicycles (but no mopeds) are for rent at over a half dozen shops in town. Rates for a bicycle are $6 to $8 a day, and these vehicles do well on this small island (except on the cobblestones of Main Street!). One can ride the seven miles to 'Sconset on a bike path in less than an hour—less than a half hour if you push it. Incidentally, almost any taxi driver will be glad to give you a tour of the island, with rates depending on how much ground you want to cover and time you want to spend.

INFORMATION AND RESERVATIONS: The Nantucket Chamber of Commerce (tel. 617/228-1700) and the Public Relations Committee have done a lot to organize the tourist industry on the island, and information about rooms, tours, and sights is surprisingly easy to get. The **Town Information Bureau** (tel. 617/228-0925) is the place to go for a free copy of the *Nantucket Vacation Guide,* a summertime ads-and-information booklet; they'll also help you find a room for that day if you haven't already reserved one. But note that *they do not make advance reservations for you*—you must do that directly with the establishment concerned. The bureau is not far from Main Street and the ferry docks, at 25 Federal St., and it's open 9 a.m. until the evening hours during the summer, shorter hours off-season.

Reserve in Advance for Summer!

Rooms are hard to find in July and August unless you reserve well in advance, and while you might have a chance of finding a room for a day or two during the week, on weekends it's virtually impossible. If you plan to try to find a last-minute room in those two months, arrive on the island early in the day—fly over and beat the ferryboat crowds—and go straight to the Town Information Booth and ask them what's available in town. During July and August the Information Bureau establishes a toll-free 800-number (from Massachusetts only). It changes each year, so call 800/555-1212 to get the latest number.

Nantucket is well organized and governed, and local residents have various regulations which they want visitors to observe, such as not wearing bathing suits on Main Street, obeying all traffic rules when riding a bicycle, and not camping—whether in a vehicle or a tent or under the stars—anywhere on the island.

WHERE TO STAY: Nantucket Island harbors nearly 100 places to stay, but the real character of the place is best captured in the old whaling merchants' and ship captains' houses converted to inns and guest houses. Many of these are carefully restored, luxuriously appointed, and staffed with professionals; others are run by one person or a couple and are modest but warm and friendly.

The Problem of High Prices

Let me soften the blow, if I can. Nantucket has taken on the character of a posh summer resort in recent years, and a double room in a charming old inn can cost well over $100 if you're not careful. I won't recommend any such expensive places. But even the less classy inns (still extremely nice) charge $65 to $80 for a double room in July and August—and they rarely have an empty room! What's to do?

There is a way to visit Nantucket without invoking Chapter 11. On the outskirts of downtown Nantucket are simple, homey guest houses which rent comfortable, nicely furnished rooms, sometimes with private bath but more often without, for $40 to $55 double per night. The best places give you some breakfast as well. If this sounds like a lot, take my word for it: on Nantucket, in July and August, this is very inexpensive. Even on the outskirts (within a 10- or 15-minute walk of the center), you'll have to reserve a room in advance.

Here are some strategic tips. The farther you go from the center (and no place is much more than 15 minutes' walk from the center), the lower the price. Also, a guest house with a name ("The Poop Deck," "Sea Seasons," etc.) will often be more expensive than one with just an address ("333 India St.") or a proprietor's name ("Mrs. Dunleavey's Guest House"). Any house with a history, that is, any house over a century old, will probably cost more. The least expensive lodgings, therefore, are in a guest house run by a lady who lives in a 40-year-old house on the outskirts of town. If you cannot locate and reserve a room in advance, but you're determined to visit Nantucket, spend the extra money and *fly over early in the morning,* then rush to the Town Information

Bureau (described above) and enlist their help in pinning down a room. By flying you beat the hordes of hopeful room-seekers who will arrive by ferryboat later on.

Nantucket has over 70 guest houses with perhaps 400 rooms—single, double, triple, with private bath and without. I've chosen a good number of these, listed below, to get you started in your July-August room search. I've also described some of Nantucket's charming inns, more expensive than guest houses but less than the $100+per-night places. But before you pick up the telephone, read this:

Notes on Reservations

Although some lodging establishments on Nantucket stay open all year, many operate only between May and October. Any place will give you an off-season discount on room rates if you come in spring or autumn, although the dates vary from one place to the next. In high season (roughly, from mid-June to mid-September), you'll certainly have to send a substantial deposit to hold your room reservation. Minimum-stay requirements may also be imposed during the high season as well.

Here, then, are Nantucket's best guest houses and inns, followed by a few recommendations for hotels, and for lodgings in 'Sconset, across the island.

Guest Houses

Almost all of Nantucket's reasonably priced guest houses charge the same rates: $45 ($47.75 with the tax) for a double room that shares a bath; $55 ($58.32 with tax) for a double with private bath. When you call for reservations, find out if breakfast is included, and if it's rolls-and-coffee or bacon-and-eggs. Ask if the room has a view, or is especially large. Every room is different, and you must know these things to get the most for your money.

The **Hungry Whale,** 8 Derrymore Rd., Nantucket, MA 02554 (tel. 617/228-0793), is exceptional in several ways. Mrs. Johnson, the smiling owner, charges several dollars *less* than most other houses, and includes a hearty breakfast to boot! The location is off North Liberty Avenue.

Mrs. Austin F. Tyrer, 23 India St., Nantucket, MA 02554 (tel. 617/228-1581), owns this big house with pleasant gardens out back, and rents rooms. The location is very handy to the center of town.

Mrs. Elwyn Francis, 31 India St., Nantucket, MA 02554 (tel. 617/228-0538), has two single rooms as well as five doubles which share bathrooms. The location is very good, close to downtown.

The **Nesbitt Inn,** 21 Broad St., Nantucket, MA 02554 (tel. 617/228-0156), despite it appellation and downtown location, is one of the island's lodging bargains, three blocks from the wharf, charging guest house prices.

The **Ivy Lodge & Cottages,** 2 Chester St., Nantucket, MA 02554 (tel. 617/228-0305), at North Water Street, is far enough from downtown to have reasonable prices, close enough to be very handy.

The **Holiday Inn,** 78 Centre St., Nantucket, MA 02554 (tel. 617/228-0199), is obviously not part of the worldwide chain, but rather a pleasant guest house charging normal guest-house rates.

The **"While Away" Guest House** (tel. 617/228-1102) is of the oldtime, gracious guest-house type, with a friendly proprietor (Mrs. Elise Link), a fine old house with bull's-eye windows, and a widow's walk. A blossom-filled garden surrounding the house, a baby grand piano within, and a very good location at the intersection of Gay, Centre, and Broad Streets (officially, 4 Gay

St.), makes the While Away a real find. Prices are moderate: $50 for two without bath, $58.50 for two with private bath, in spotless rooms. When looking for the While Away, try to spot the flagpole in the little park right next door—that will serve as a landmark.

Another group of guest houses is a 10- to 15-minute walk to the northwest of the center on Cliff Road.

Cliff Lodge, 9 Cliff Rd., Nantucket, MA 02554 (tel. 617/228-0893), is a large house with some good views, and closest to the center of this group of houses.

Century House, 10 Cliff Rd., Nantucket, MA 02554 (tel. 617/228-0530), is right across the street from Cliff Lodge; again, the better location in this group.

Cliff House, 34 Cliff Rd., Nantucket, MA 02554 (tel. 617/228-2154), not to be confused with Cliff Lodge, has slightly lower prices.

Inns

India House (tel. 617/228-9043) is slightly over a block from the busy center of town at 37 India St., but that assures that the rooms will not be noisy. Built in the early 1800s, India House has seven cheerful rooms with bath which are priced at $37 single, $52.85 to $68.71 double. Besides its rooms, India House is noted for its dining room. Meals are not included in the room rates; lower rates are in effect in May and after mid-September.

Fair Gardens (tel. 617/228-4258) is the description, as well as the name, of the guest house at 27 Fair St., in a quiet residential neighborhood. Mrs. Murray, the Fair Gardens' owner, designs and makes many of the textiles in the rooms herself. Behind the house is an English-style garden, complete with a Shakespearean herb plot, carefully tended flowers and lawns, and a patio for breakfast or an afternoon's cup of tea. The ten rooms are all unique, most have private baths, and now there are two deluxe rooms in the new Garden House. Rooms are priced between $50.74 and $71.88 double in the old house, $76.10 in the new Garden House; an extra person pays $10.57. All of these prices include breakfast with freshly baked bread, served in the garden in good weather.

The **House of Orange** (tel. 617/228-9287) has seven rooms decorated with an artist's eye for color and harmony, as one of the house's owners is a painter. The rooms are as lovingly furnished and as carefully kept as is the little garden. Some rooms have fireplaces, although, as is often the case, local regulations prohibit guests from using them. Every room is different, from the small single with semiprivate bath ($28.54) through the doubles with semiprivate baths ($52.85 to $63.42). A double room with private bath is tops in price, at $68.71 to $79.28. The House of Orange is open year round. Look for it at 25 Orange St.

Fair Street has its share of houses built by ship captains, but the **Ships Inn** (tel. 617/228-0040) is more a mansion than a house, its three stories looking over Fair Street from a position just opposite the Episcopal church. It was built in 1812 by Capt. Obed Starbuck and occupies the site which once held the birthplace of Lucretia Coffin Mott, the abolitionist and suffragist who was a native islander. The rooms are finished with period pieces and all, except two small singles, have private bath. Those little singles cost $32; otherwise, one person pays $60 for a room, two pay $75, with private bath. Off-season (November through mid-June), rates go down about 30%. The price of a room includes continental breakfast in season. The Captain's Table restaurant is in the basement of the Ships Inn.

Run by the same family as the Roberts House, the **Periwinkle Guest House and Cottage** (tel. 617/228-9267) is very close to the Whaling Museum, at 7 and 9 North Water St., Nantucket, MA 02554. A nice old Nantucket house, the Periwinkle has 18 rooms of various shapes, sizes, sleeping capacities, and bath facilities: doubles with bath are $89.85 daily; doubles with semiprivate bath are $68.71; twin beds with shared bath are $63.42. A few single rooms with shared bath are priced at $31.71 to $37. The Periwinkle—the name is that of a spiral-shape saltwater snail—is open all year, and rates are 25% to 30% lower off-season. By the way, continental breakfast is included in all the above rates.

The **Bartlett House** (tel. 617/228-1139), 14 Gardner St. (P.O. Box 1329, Nantucket, MA 02554), prides itself not merely on the attractiveness of the 150-year-old house and the coziness of its rooms, but on the quietness of its clientele. Only five rooms are for rent, at $31.71 to $58.13 per night, single or double, with a three-night minimum stay. Two of the rooms share a bathroom, all the others have private facilities, although one room's shower is down the hall. Bartlett House has no living room for guests' use, but the garden is most people's first choice of a place to relax in any case. Room prices are among the best in town, and the silence, as they say, is golden.

The **House of the Seven Gables** (tel. 617/228-4706) is a small castle of a place, once the Victorian annex to an even larger old Victorian-era seaside hotel. Actually, Seven Gables and a Tower would be an even more accurate description of this good example of Victorian architectural enthusiasm. As it's not one of those small and quaint Nantucket houses, it has more rooms to offer—ten in all, with nine bathrooms. Continental breakfast is served in July and August, and rates run from $68.71 to $79.28 for a room with double bed and semiprivate bath, or a room with double bed and private bath, or a triple with private bath. Mid-September to mid-June these rates drop by about a third. The location, at 32 Cliff Rd., is a ten-minute walk from Main Street, not as close into town as some other houses; but the area is a quiet residential one.

Martin's Guest House (tel. 617/228-0678), 61 Center St., is a fine old, elegant place on a quiet street. While it can't boast a romantic history of sea-captain ownership, it can boast a good selection of rooms, 12 in all, priced from $50 double (shared bath), through $55 double (semiprivate bath), to $60 to $75 for double rooms with private bath. The Berger family, who own and run the house, will give you the traditionally hearty Nantucket welcome. A sunny living room and porch are open to guests' use, and a complimentary continental breakfast is provided.

The **Anchor Inn**, 66 Center St., Nantucket, MA 02554 (tel. 617/228-0072), is aptly named, considering that it was built (1806) by Capt. Archaelus Hammond, the first man to strike a whale in the Pacific Ocean. The location is good, close enough to the center to be convenient, far enough away to encourage moderate prices. All rooms are charmingly decorated, and have private baths. Rates in high season are $58.32 to $75, depending on the special attributes of the particular room.

Hotels

Nantucket still has a few of the rambling old Victorian-era wooden hotels which used to be found throughout New England, and indeed throughout North America, but which have been disappearing quickly since the advent of the automobile and the motel. Although there are a few motels on the island too, I'll describe the older hotels as they offer accommodations more in keeping with the island's traditions, at prices which are undeniably good value-for-money.

The **Gordon Folger Hotel and Cottages** (tel. 617/228-0313), at the corner of Cliff Road and Easton Street (P.O. Box 628, Nantucket, MA 02554), is just such an old rambling hotel, set on sunny lawns, well kept, but now easily informal whereas in earlier times everyone had to dress for dinner. Open only from mid-May to mid-October, the Gordon Folger charges $21.14 to $33.82 for a single room without private bath, $50.74 to $65.53 for a similar double; rooms with private bath cost $32.27 to $45.45 single, $67.65 to $76.10 double. In the annex, called the Captain's Corners, rooms are $21.14 for a single with semiprivate bath, $50.74 for a similar double- or twin-bedded room; doubles or twins with bath are $63.42 daily; a triple with bath is $76.10. Off-season rates are in effect during the first and last months of the hotel's season. The hotel's restaurant, called the Whale, can provide breakfast, and dinner too.

The **Overlook Hotel** (tel. 617/228-0695), on Three Step Lane, is not far from the Gordon Folger, with a view of Nantucket Harbor. Several long balcony-walkways on the hotel's sea side give guests a view of the town and the water. The hotel's Indian Room provides breakfast. Rooms are old-fashioned but comfortable and thoughtfully done, and prices are moderate: doubles with private bath cost $68.71 to $79.28; with semiprivate bath, they're $58.14 to $63.42. The season is May to October.

The Youth Hostel

Nantucket has a youth hostel three miles from town, affiliated with the AYH, and you must be a member to stay here (you can join up at this hostel, though). The nightly charge is in addition to your membership fee, of course: the price is $5.25 per night and the maximum stay is three nights. Hostelers are segregated by sex in the dormitories. The hostel is open from April 1 through Thanksgiving; for more information, write to AYH, Surfside, Nantucket, MA 02554, or call 617/228-0433.

Lodging in 'Sconset

Should you want to escape the pleasant bustle of Nantucket Town for a few days, you can stay in 'Sconset on the other side of the island, at **The Chanticleer** (tel. 617/257-6231), Siasconset, Nantucket, MA 02564. The Chanticleer is a particularly graceful and lovely place, a dignified house built around a fine rose garden which serves as the famous Chanticleer restaurant in good weather. There are rooms and cottages for rent, all with private bath; rooms cost $87 per day; cottages are rentable by the week only. The Chanticleer is open from June to October, and rates are lower in June and September after Labor Day.

WHERE TO DINE: Meals, like rooms, are fairly expensive on Nantucket, and the press of customers does little to encourage high standards of quality: why go to the trouble of presenting the best possible food when there's no need to attract customers—they'll come anyway because they've got to eat! All the same, you can eat well on Nantucket if you are careful and selective.

Most serviceable and reasonably priced of downtown restaurants is the Quaker House, 31 Center St., corner of Chestnut, in the Quaker Inn (tel. 228-0400). A simple and down-to-earth dining room is the setting for breakfast, lunch, and dinner. Come for waffles ($2.25) or a crab omelet ($6), and many other things beyond the standard bacon and eggs. They feature complete dinners with soup, salad, vegetable, bread and butter, and dessert for $7 (filet of sole) to $10 (crab Newburg); children can order smaller portions of the standard fare. Wine, beer, and real espresso are served.

The **White Dog Café,** on North Union Street, just off Main Street (tel. 228-4435), is on the terrace of the Gaslight Theatre. The tiny patio is crowded with tables, and diners, from 8 a.m. to 10 p.m. seven days a week, chowing down on burgers ($4.50) to the bluefish dinner special ($8). Food and prices are good, but many people come to people-watch, enjoying the café atmosphere.

At 12 Federal St., corner of Federal and India Streets, is **The Boarding House** (tel. 228-9622), with an outdoor patio for luncheons in good weather and a basement dining room for rainy days and for dinner. It's cozy and romantic in the extreme, and the large mural of a surrealistic bunch of asparagus won't disconcert you—now that you're prepared for it. Low lights and soft classical music set the mood for sumptuous repasts: oven-broiled swordfish in béarnaise sauce and pecan butter ($15), tournedos of beef Boarding House ($17), and similar main courses come with salad, potato, and vegetable. At lunch, things are lighter: quahog chowder, herb bread, pâté, salads, and omelets are joined by one or two fish dishes, and several of these courses will come to a total of $10 or less. Wine, beer, and cocktails are served, of course.

The **Captain's Table** (tel. 228-0040), in the basement of the Ships Inn on Fair Street, offers such things as lamb chops, and Nantucket scallops, for about $13. For dessert they may list chocolate mousse or cranberry sherbet with cassis. And don't let the "basement" dining room worry you. It is a supremely warm and cheerful place, with old oil paintings adding grace and beauty to the light-colored walls. The dining room is licensed, or you can have a drink in the Dory Bar, which is usually quite lively.

India House (tel. 228-9043), 37 India St., serves meals in its French country dining room from April 1 through January 1, and the ethic here is of the French variety: effort and finesse is put into the cuisine. The menu is French both in its style and its offerings, for meals here are *prix fixe*—you pay one price, and then choose from a limited number of items for each course. Breakfast costs $7, and is served 8:30 to 10:30 a.m.; dinner is served from 7 to 9:30 p.m., both seven days a week. There's bar service, and a nice patio outside in which to enjoy a cocktail or a pousse-café. Dinner at India House is bountiful and mouthwatering, including a choice of appetizer, a soup, pasta, or pâté, the main course which changes weekly, and salad. If the $16 to $20 price seems a bit high, remember that in any restaurant where the entree costs $8 to $10, there will be at least $7 to $9 to add to the bill for appetizer, soup, and dessert. Reservations are required for dinner.

Want to see where the people who *own* summer houses go to dine? Wander over to **The Mad Hatter** (tel. 228-9667), at 72 Easton St., at the corner of town. Solid food, good and friendly service, a comfortable and unobtrusive Early American decor, and a regular clientele are what make the Mad Hatter, and what give it almost a country-club atmosphere. A piano entertains diners, while big-screen TV flickers in the bar. Monday through Saturday, lunch is served from noon to 2 p.m., with a menu of sandwiches, but always including a fish of the day and something fancier such as coquille of lobster Savannah. But dinner is the main event, and you'll be expected to come in coat-and-tie formality. French onion soup, Bismarck herring, and other appetizers precede a long list of seafood main courses priced about $10 to $16, and a good number of chicken, steak, and chops dishes too. The Mad Hatter is open year round. You can even get breakfast here from 8 to 10:30 a.m. daily (in season). By the way, lunch on Sunday is a buffet for $7.25 per adult, $5 per child.

you won't find any dining with more authentic old Nantucket atmosphere than that which is to be had at **The Woodbox** (tel. 228-0587), 29 Fair St. The two beautiful old dining rooms date from 1709, and the colonial charm has been carefully preserved. The menu is one of classic dishes: beef Wellington, duck in orange sauce, and scampi, with main courses priced at $10 to $16. In chilly weather, fireplaces in each dining room add warmth as well as atmosphere. Dinner is served at 7 and 9 p.m., and you should have reservations. The Woodbox, "Nantucket's Oldest Inn," is closed Monday.

Dinner and a Show

The Skipper (tel. 228-4444), on Steamboat Wharf, is special in two ways: first, it's on the water; second, on evenings from Monday through Saturday at 10:45 p.m. to 1 a.m., the Skipper Singers entertain with show tunes, ballads, and upbeat numbers. The Singers are drawn from two close-harmony singing groups at Harvard, The Pitches and the Krokodiloes, well practiced and stage-wise. The Skipper's menu is a general one, with chicken and beef as well as seafood, priced in the upper reaches of the moderate (for Nantucket) range. During the show, a $3 minimum is invoked.

Budget Dinners

With French-style menus, exotic recipes, and thick steaks abounding, sometimes it seems as though Nantucket harbors no place to have a simple but good and filling inexpensive meal. But if you find your way to **Vincent's Restaurant** (tel. 228-0189), right across the street from the fire house at 21 S. Water St., you'll find unpretentious food at prices which are very moderate for Nantucket: the Tourist Special plate of fish and chips is generous, and costs $5. A bowl of chowder and a fish filet sandwich costs even less, and Italian dishes such as chicken cacciatore and eggplant parmigiana are all about $5 or $6. Seafood plates, with salad, are about $6. In good weather, you can even dine on Vincent's small outdoor terrace, or just have pizza and beer there.

At **The Tavern** (tel. 228-1126), on Straight Wharf at Harbor Square, right by the marina, you may eat at tables set out in the picturesque cobbled square, or on a second-floor balcony overlooking the marina and the activity on the street, or even in a little fleche-topped gazebo in the cobbled square. Drinks are served, as are chili con carne and sandwiches ($4 to $5) at lunch; dinnertime is 6 to 10 p.m., and then you can get fish and chips for less than $8, scampi or a London broil for less than $13. The food is okay here, but the situation is even better.

I'd recommend that everyone pick up a mammoth sandwich from **Henry's Sandwiches** (tel. 228-0123), on Steamboat Wharf, before they get on the boat. Henry's huge sandwiches are made in the best Italian sub/grinder/hoagie/po' boy tradition, and cost about $3. Soft drinks are available, and all can be wrapped to go or consumed post-haste at small tables on the premises. Remember Henry's if you're planning a picnic, or are down to your last $3 plus your ticket home.

The cheapest hamburger in town ($2.25) is served at **The Blueberry Muffin** (tel. 228-9740), 26 Center St., a block off Main. But as you might suspect, the Muffin is a favorite for breakfast treats. Drop by for muffins, pastries, brownies, and coffee, and cut the high cost of breakfasting on Nantucket. For lunch, a bowl of chili ($1.75) is even cheaper than the burgers.

The Big Splurge

The **Company of the Cauldron** (tel. 228-4016), 7 India St. serves only dinner, at one sitting (two on Saturday) —and you *must* have a reservation. Then, the menu is completely table d'hôte, and fixed-price: you have no choice, although if you've called for reservations (as you must), it's presumed you've asked what will be served, perhaps homemade fettuccine tossed with eggplant, capers, and olives, followed by an apple and watercress salad, and then medallions of veal rolled with spinach and mozzarella, served with a parfait of pimentos. In all, two dining together can expect to pay close to $80 with wine. The dining room is small, with kitchen and wine racks in the rear. A harpist plays at dinner. An antique-fancier's collection of old tubs, buckets, and cauldrons serves to show off a cascade of flowers. As you walk to the restaurant, don't look for a sign, but rather for the old copper tub (cauldron?) hanging above the entrance: that is the "sign."

Dining in 'Sconset

Most everyone who gets to Nantucket for a few days has a chance to ride a bike to 'Sconset on the other side of the island. You can go for lunch or dinner: **The Chanticleer** (tel. 257-6231) is noted for its elegant French cuisine and for the charm of its dining area which in summer is a courtyard surrounded by rose-covered trellises under which tables are set. Dinner prices are not low: an appetizer of assorted smoked fish is $5; roast duckling with a baked apple as a garnish is $15; there's delectable Nantucket-raised rabbit with mushrooms, white wine, and mustard sauce. At lunchtime the dishes are equally appealing, and more moderately priced. There's a bar and lounge called the Chanty. This is 'Sconset's most elegant spot, and a meal here becomes a nice memory.

Right by the flagpole at the traffic circle is **Claudette's** food-catering shop (tel. 257-6622), where you can sit at a tiny table on the wood deck and watch the easy activity of the square while drinking coffee, tea, or lemonade. Meanwhile, Claudette will be making you a delicious box lunch for your picnic or bike trip for $4 to $5. Should you want a party or clambake catered, that can be handled as well.

READER'S DINING SELECTIONS: "At **The Whale** (tel. 617/228-0313), in the Gordon Folger Hotel on Easton St. near Cliff Rd., we ate swordfish ($11.75) and stuffed shrimp in a beautiful wood-ceilinged, candlelit room. Service was friendly and careful, down to sherbet between the courses to 'clear the palate.' Dinner for two, with clam chowder, appetizers and wine was $40; it could have been $30 without the wine.

"Also, the **Nantucket Lobster Trap** (tel. 617/228-4041), 23 Washington St., is the place to go for a no-nonsense seafood dinner. The decor is rustic pine with the bar in the middle of the dining room, but the food is good and the service friendly. The seafood platter ($11.50) had an assortment of lightly deep-fried fish, scallops, shrimp, clams, plus half a lobster. There's homemade pie for dessert" (Richard C. Foote, Cleveland, Ohio).

WHAT TO SEE AND DO: Once on Nantucket, your activity schedule will take care of itself. In good weather everyone takes off to the beaches, either by taxi, bus, or bike. For variety, the island offers tennis, golf, horseback riding, movies, antique stores, and art galleries. Sport fishermen should wander down to **Straight Wharf** to talk to one of the charter boat captains about a day's run for bluefish or striped bass. Those who just like being in a boat can rent a sailboat and take sailing lessons at one of the establishments on **Washington Street Extension** or **Steamboat Wharf**. The island's information office on Federal Street will be able to help you out with information on these.

Nantucket's history can keep one occupied for days as well. To run the full gamut, buy a season pass ($4.50) to the exhibits of the **Nantucket Historical Association** on Union Street (tel. 228-1894), which include the famous **Whaling Museum,** the **Peter Foulger Museum,** the oldest house on the island, an old windmill, and seven other historical points of interest. To see them all, paying the individual admissions would cost over $8.50, and the season pass gives you the advantage of being able to browse in a museum for a while, go to the beach, and return to the museum later in the afternoon. You can get your pass at the Whaling Museum on Broad Street, or at any of the other Historical Association buildings.

Another sight worth seeing is the Lightship *Nantucket,* a floating lighthouse and radio beacon transmitter which helped guide ships heading out to cross the Atlantic, and those arriving in the New World after the transatlantic voyage. The ship is moored at Straight Wharf, and is open during the summer from 10 a.m. to 4 p.m.; admission is $1.

'Sconset

The village of Siasconset is called nothing but 'Sconset by islanders—the contracted name is hallowed by tradition. There is nothing to do in 'Sconset but swim at the free public beach, have a meal in one of its eateries, and take a turn through the narrow streets while admiring the low houses and bungalows which sit squatly as though avoiding the violence of the winter storms. 'Sconset is pretty, picturesque, and the best excuse ever for a pleasant seven-mile bike ride along the bikepath which borders the Nantucket Town-'Sconset road. A secret: Wild blueberries abound in the copses by the roadside, and people in cars never get to taste them; late July and early August are the best times for pickin'.

Tours

Tour buses will meet your ferryboat at Steamboat Wharf, ready to take you on a 1¼-hour tour of the island for $5.50 (half price for children). There's no better way to get your bearings, and the short time spent will help you to better organize the few precious days you'll have on the island. If you can't find the tour bus, contact **Nantucket Island Tours** (tel. 617/228-0334), on Straight Wharf, Nantucket, MA 02554.

Walking Tours of the Town

The Nantucket Historical Association, mentioned above, also publishes a number of detailed walking-tour brochures, available from the association or from the Nantucket Information Bureau at 25 Federal St. *Rambles through the Historic Nantucket District* and *Main Street* will fill you in on the town's and the island's colorful past. If you follow these pamphlet guides thoroughly, you'll know more about Nantucket than many natives.

Music

In the past few years, Nantucket has supported chamber music concerts at various times, particularly in the weeks of high summer. Ask at the Information Bureau, or look for notices of upcoming events.

Also, visiting and local bands often give free concerts in the gazebo near Straight Wharf (at the foot of Main Street). The *Weekly Vacation Guides,* available at the Information Bureau, will have listings of times and programs.

Chapter VIII

CENTRAL AND WESTERN MASSACHUSETTS

1. Getting There
2. Sturbridge
3. Deerfield, Amherst and Northampton
4. Lenox and Lee
5. Stockbridge
6. South Egremont and Great Barrington
7. Williamstown and the Mohawk Trail

WEST OF BOSTON spreads a landscape familiar to the early pioneers, a beautiful land of clear lakes and glacial ponds, cool forests and massive granite outcrops. Farming, forestry, and light industry occupy the people of central and western Massachusetts, not to mention the textile and paper mills dotted along its many rivers. Amid this bucolic scenery you'll also find several of America's finest colleges, posh 19th-century mountain resorts, and New England's premier summer music festival.

Wealthy vacationers of the 19th century who loved the sea would get away to Newport, Cape Cod, or Bar Harbor; those who loved the mountains would head for Saratoga Springs, N.Y., or for the storybook New England towns scattered through the low mountains known as the Berkshires in western Massachusetts. The grand residences and hotels of the wealthy remain in Stockbridge, Lenox, Williamstown, and other Berkshire communities, adding to the romance and interest of the area and serving a new purpose as hostelries for the new wave of vacationers. Today the lure of the Berkshires is enhanced by one of the country's major summer musical events, the Berkshire Music Festival at Tanglewood, near Lenox; another Berkshire town draws crowds because of its beauty and its educational opportunities, for Williamstown in the northern Berkshires has been the seat of Williams College since the school was chartered in 1785. Whatever your reason for going, you can't fail to enjoy the lush countryside, the picturesque towns with rows of fine houses, and the acres of manicured greenery.

1. Getting There

From New York City, the Taconic State Parkway provides a very pleasant route to the Berkshires; from other points, I-90 (the Massachusetts Turnpike) and I-91 can be used as the fastest routes to the area. There's convenient public transport as well:

BY BUS: **Greyhound** provides direct service between Boston and Albany via Lee, Lenox, and Pittsfield, Mass., with several buses a day. In addition, they have direct Toronto-New York services with stops in Albany, where transfer can be made to a Lenox-bound bus.

Vermont Transit operates buses between Montréal and New York City, stopping in Albany at the Greyhound terminal, and from there one must transfer for the trip to Lenox. There are also direct buses between Montréal and Pittsfield, Mass., passing through Williamstown; in Pittsfield the transfer can be made for Lenox.

Englander Coach Lines, operating from the Greyhound terminal in Boston, has several buses a day between Boston and Albany, stopping in Williamstown; connecting services are also run between Boston and Providence.

Bonanza Bus Lines has direct Providence-Albany service, with stops in Pittsfield, Lenox, and Lee, and also direct buses between New York City and Great Barrington, Stockbridge, Lee, Lenox, and Pittsfield. Bonanza works in conjunction with **Peter Pan Bus Lines** (which operates from Boston's Trailways terminal) to provide service from Boston to Amherst, Northampton, Holyoke, and Springfield, Mass., and thence to Pittsfield, Lee, and Lenox. By taking a Greyhound bus from Hartford to Springfield, one can connect with the Bonanza bus to these three Berkshire towns as well.

Local buses connect Berkshire County towns and resorts with one another.

The Special Old Sturbridge Village Bus

Peter Pan Tours, 1776 Main St., Springfield, MA 01103 (tel. 413/781-2900), operates special one-day trips from Boston directly to Old Sturbridge Village. The bus fare includes admission to Old Sturbridge Village; the trip leaves daily, all year, at 10:15 a.m., returning by 6:55 p.m. Peter Pan operates from Boston's Trailways Terminal (tel. 617/482-6620).

BY RAIL: Amtrak's *Lakeshore Limited* runs daily between New York/Boston and Chicago, one section leaving Boston in midafternoon and another leaving New York City in early evening. The two sections link up in Albany-Rensselaer and continue on to Chicago. The section from Boston passes through Springfield, and then Pittsfield, Mass., in the evening. The *Adirondack,* traveling between Montréal and New York City, passes through Albany-Rensselaer as well. From that point, arrangements would have to be made to get to your destination by bus.

BY AIR: **Precision Airlines** flies four times daily in summer from New York City's La Guardia Airport (Eastern Air Shuttle Terminal) to Pittsfield, Mass. Call them for details: toll free 800/451-4221. This flight continues to Rutland, Vt., by the way. You can fly from Rutland to Pittsfield, too. Precision Airlines is based in Springfield, Vt.

2. Sturbridge

The creators of Old Sturbridge Village couldn't have chosen a better spot for their "living museum." It's set in the beautiful hills of east-central Massachusetts right where the Massachusetts Turnpike (I-90) intersects with the feeder road to I-86, a major route to Hartford and New York City. Most people who tour New England would pass this junction sometime. Anyone who passes should certainly stop to see Old Sturbridge Village, and perhaps to spend the night.

WHERE TO STAY: Because of Old Sturbridge Village, and because the village of Sturbridge is very near the intersection of two major Interstate highways, motels abound in this town and nearby. Trade is brisk in summer, even brisker during the autumn foliage season, and briskest of all during the three annual Brimfield Flea Market weekends. Nearby Brimfield, eight miles west of Sturbridge on U.S. 20, is a normally sleepy place which springs to life in early May, mid-July, and mid-September. As Brimfield has few hotels and motels itself, those in Sturbridge—and even in Springfield, 35 miles away—are filled to overflowing. If you come at flea market time, have ironclad reservations. The flea markets are in May, July, and September.

During the normally slow months of January through March, several Sturbridge inns and motels band together to offer attractive discount "Winter Weekend" package plans. For details, contact the Publick House, described below.

You should note that the village of Sturbridge, a bona fide Massachusetts colonial-era town, and Old Sturbridge Village, a "living museum," are actually two different places in the same general area. They're only about a mile apart, but the village of Sturbridge's Town Common, or center, is on Route 131, while the entrance to Old Sturbridge Village is on Route 20.

With hotels, motels, and inns in the Berkshires packed to capacity on summer weekends, some visitors and music lovers actually plan to stay as far east as Sturbridge, where rooms are plentiful. Using Sturbridge as a base, a tour through the Berkshires, including a stop at Tanglewood, can be a day's outing.

If you're writing for reservations, the ZIP code for Sturbridge is 01566.

The **Old Sturbridge Village Motor Lodge** (tel. 617/347-3327), formerly the Liberty Cap Motel, is owned by the same people who operate Old Sturbridge Village. The motel is among the most attractive in Sturbridge, with the guest rooms clustered in a variety of buildings designed along colonial lines and positioned as though the motel were itself a colonial town. Sound like Disneyland? It's not. It's attractive, and it's right next to Old Sturbridge Village. From April through November, twin-bedded rooms cost $46.51; rooms with two double beds cost $48.62 for two, $51.79 for three, $54.96 for four persons. Very substantial discounts are in effect off-season. And although the 47 rooms are colonial inspired, they are modern equipped, with color TV, air conditioning, telephones, and private baths.

The **Publick House** (tel. 617/347-3313), on the Common in Sturbridge, is a local institution. Founded in 1771 by one Col. Ebenezer Crafts, the Publick House occupies the original building plus several large (but tasteful) additions, mostly furnished for dining. In the inn, there are 21 guest rooms, including several suites for three or four people. All rooms and suites have private bath, air conditioning, and direct-dial phone. In the adjoining Chamberlain House are four suites with queen-size beds, color TV, air conditioning, direct-dial phone, and living room area; each suite accommodates up to four people.

Double rooms cost $55 to $64; suites are $85 to $93 for two. On holidays and during the busy foliage season, add about $5 to room prices, $10 to suites.

The Publick House people also operate the **Colonel Ebenezer Crafts Inn** (tel. 617/347-3313), at the summit of Fiske Hill. The fine old house was built by David Fiske in 1786, and later converted to an inn. It's gracious, filled with antiques, and small, taking only about 20 people at one time. Rates are good for what you get: continental breakfast, a morning newspaper, and later on afternoon tea; and at bedtime you'll enter your room to find sweets by your bed. It's all included in the rates: $64 to $66 for a double room with private bath; a suite capable of sleeping four or more people costs $68.71 to $79.28 for four. All the rooms are air-conditioned, and while they don't have TV, there's one in the library which you can watch.

The **Sturbridge Coach Motor Lodge**, P.O. Box 502 in Sturbridge (tel. 617/347-7327), is on Route 20 almost opposite the entrance to Old Sturbridge, up on the hill. Although it's obviously a modern two-floor luxury motel, the inspiration for both design and decor is colonial. There's nothing colonial about the swimming pool, though, or the rooms, each equipped with color TV, air conditioning, and private baths with separate dressing room areas. Rates in summer are $52.86 for two in a double bed, $57.08 for two in two beds.

The **Sturbridge Motor Inn** (tel. 617/347-3391) is on the service road parallel to I-86, a quarter mile north of I-86 Exit 3. With 34 rooms, the inn offers air conditioning, color TV, telephone, and an interesting swimming pool nestled among the pines. High-season prices (May through October) are $40.17 to $54.96, single or double. By the way, the mail address here is P.O. Box 185, Sturbridge, MA 01566.

Right near the intersection of Routes 15, 20, and 131, the **Carriage House Motor Lodge** (tel. 617/347-9000) is a modern and attractive two- and three-floor brick motel with 100 rooms, all with air conditioning and color TV, and with a swimming pool. Convenient, attractive, and comfortable, the rooms cost $38 single, $48 double in summer, a bit more on holiday weekends, during the Brimfield Flea Markets Week, and on prime foliage weekends. Winter and spring rates are a few dollars lower.

Budget Motels

Sturbridge has a few small motels which offer special bargains. They're out of the way where few tourists would find them, yet they're convenient to the sights of Sturbridge if you have a car. From Route 20, follow Route 131 through the center of the village of Sturbridge and past its Common, up the hill, and past the Sturbridge Plaza Shopping Center. Just past the shopping center you'll see a sign for the **Green Acres Motel** (tel. 617/347-3496 or 347-3402; P.O. Box 153, Sturbridge, MA 01566), a nice little place down the hill next to the woods (it's quiet!) behind a large white house. The rooms are finished in wood paneling, with picture windows, color TV, phones, and air conditioning, and are kept scrupulously clean. Richard and Sandra Norris, the new owners, can boast a recently installed small swimming pool, basketball court, and coffee machine. But price is the best part: $37 for two in a double bed, $41.25 for two in two beds; an extra person is free. Off-season prices are $26.45 and $29.60, respectively. Cots are $3.

On Route 131, also just past the shopping center, is the **Pine Grove Motel** (tel. 617/347-9673), a small 20-room establishment very similar in accommodations and price to the Green Acres. These two small, local motels are Sturbridge's best-kept lodging secret.

In the other direction, on U.S. 20 west of Old Sturbridge Village, is a real budget find. When you see the sign for Kristine's Kountry Bake Shop, look next to it for the gateway to the **Village Motel** (tel. 617/347-3049), U.S. 20 West, Sturbridge, MA 01566. Pass through the gateway (the road is one way) and after a few hundred feet you'll see the tidy little stucco building set amid emerald lawns. It's quiet here, it's homey, and prices for a comfy motel room are only $26 single, $32 double. You'll love it!

A Guest House

The **Maple Street Guest House** (tel. 617/347-3746), owned by Mrs. Flora Farland, on Maple Street in Sturbridge, has only four rooms: a twin-bedded one with shower and private entrance; one with a double bed and two twins, plus full bath; one with a double bed and bath; and another with twins and a shower. All are neat as a pin, and quiet—Maple is a dead-end street. To find it, leave U.S. 20 and turn onto Route 131, heading for the village of Sturbridge and the Publick House. About a quarter mile from U.S. 20, look for the Federated church and the town library on your left. Turn left just before them—that's Maple Street, and the guest house is down a short way on the left. If you come to the Publick House, you've missed the Maple Street turn.

READER'S SELECTION: "We operate the **Wildwood Inn** (tel. 413/967-7798), 121 Church St., Ware MA 01082. Though it's off the beaten track, we fill up with people visiting Sturbridge and Amherst, who find Ware a convenient stop. If your readers would rather travel the scenic back roads than the turnpike, we know they'll find a friendly welcome and reasonable prices ($31 to $48 double, shared bath, continental breakfast and tax included). Ware is on Routes 9 and 32, 10 miles north of Exit 8 from I-90 (Mass. Pike)" (Margaret Lobenstine, Ware, Mass.).

WHERE TO DINE: Sturbridge abounds in fast-food joints and snack shops, both for the hungry Old Sturbridge Village visitors and for highway passersby. But good places for a full meal do exist.

The **Publick House** (tel. 347-3313), mentioned above, is a Sturbridge favorite, located right on the Town Common on Route 131. It's big: the several dining rooms can handle a large number of diners at once, and yet the scale of an old New England inn has not been lost. The lunch menu lists a few sandwiches, but concentrates on hot main courses or cold meat or salad plates: omelets, chicken Cordon Bleu, broiled fish, and a crêpe plate are all priced about $8 to $10, but the price includes vegetable, potato, assorted relishes, salad, and a bakery basket filled with freshly baked bread and rolls. Dinner is fancier, with main-course prices about $10 to $14; steaks are a few dollars higher. But for such a price you get almost a full meal, with all the extras that are given with a comparable luncheon plate. And the main course could be chicken Eugénie (sauteed breast of chicken on grilled ham with a "poulette" sauce), frog legs sauteed in garlic butter, broiled center-cut pork chops with spiced apples, or even a shrimp, crabmeat, and scallop brochette (shish kebab) in Newburg sauce. The Publick House's wine list is fairly short, diverse, and moderate-to-expensively priced.

The fare at the **Oxhead Tavern** (tel. 347-9994), off Route 20 in the Sheraton Sturbridge Inn, is designed with transients in mind. It's not an elegant restaurant, and doesn't try to be, but it succeeds beautifully in being a roadside tavern. Furnished in rustic colonial, an old-fashioned pub bar is at one end, a big stone fireplace at the other. The menu is well suited to what a roadhouse must provide: various meals at any time of day or evening. Tops in price is a char-broiled rib steak for $11.50, but chicken-in-the-basket ($6) and lots of sandwiches ($3.50 to $6) are cheaper and equally filling. And the ambience really is similar to what you might have found 100 years ago in this town, making allowances for modern dress and speech, of course.

Just past the Sturbridge Coach Motor Lodge on Route 20 (coming from Old Sturbridge Village) is **Brother Jonathan's 1899 Restaurant** (tel. 347-7470), which looks fancy but isn't. The menu for both lunch and dinner features fare such as omelets, hamburgers, quiches, and sandwiches, and interesting combinations like soup with fresh-made bread and a salad from the salad bar. All prices seem to be $4 to $7.50, including big, filling daily special platters. In good weather, the pretty terrace is opened for service.

For an Early Breakfast

You've got a long way to drive, you're up early, and you want to fortify yourself: head for **Anna's Country Kitchen** (tel 347-2320), on Route 131 out of the center of Sturbridge, past the Publick House, past the shopping plaza and the Green Acres and Pine Grove Motels. Anna's, an A-frame lunchroom, opens at 5 a.m. and serves the traditional bacon and eggs along with fresh baked goods until 2 o'clock in the afternoon. Soups, sandwiches, and desserts are homemade, delicious, and inexpensive as well. Breakfast can cost little more than $2; light luncheon platters run $3 to almost $5.

A Sturbridge Institution

Rom's (tel. 347-3349), the Italian-American restaurant on Route 131 across from the shopping plaza, is an all-American success story. Started as a roadside sandwich-and-seafood stand, Rom's now seats up to 700 people in attractive, air-conditioned surroundings. What packs 'em in is Rom's unbeatable formula: good, plentiful food in pleasant dining rooms at low prices. A lunch of soup, broiled halibut steak, potato, vegetable, and coleslaw costs only $4.50; a four-course dinner need cost only $6 to $7, complete. The menu features Italian dishes, steaks, seafood, and traditional meals. Service is seven days a week from 11 a.m. to 9 p.m., on Saturday to 10 p.m.

The original dairy bar/lunchstand is still here, by the way. Food to go, including Italian dishes, is even lower in price.

WHAT TO SEE: Besides the obvious headline attraction in Sturbridge, you might want to have a picnic in **Wells State Park,** a few miles north of Sturbridge (take U.S. 20 east, then Route 49 north and follow the signs). Swimming and camping are available here as well.

Don't miss the chance to pore over trash and treasures at the **Brimfield Flea Market,** held three times a year (see the introduction to this section for details). If Brimfield is not in session, you can still do some browsing in the many shops on U.S. 20 west of Old Sturbridge Village.

Old Sturbridge Village

Old Sturbridge Village (tel. 617/347-3362) is one of the first and greatest of America's outdoor museums. It's a recreation of a New England town of the early 1800s, but it's a recreation formed with the artifacts: buildings and tools, machines and methods of work were all collected and brought together in this beautiful part of the Massachusetts hinterland so that Americans could see from whence their forefathers had come. Like Plimoth Plantation and Mystic

Seaport, Old Sturbridge Village is peopled with authentically dressed "interpreters," folks who perform the tasks of the village's daily life, and explain to visitors how things are done and how things are made. Plan at least a few hours to get into village life.

When you pay your admission fee of $7.50 per adult, $3 per youth aged 6 to 15, you will receive a map and guide which will explain all about the exhibits in the Village. The Village is open throughout the year, closing only on Christmas, New Year's Day, and on Monday from November through March. Hours are 9:30 a.m. to 5:30 p.m. April through October, 10 a.m. to 4 p.m. November through March. Within the Village are several varied places to eat: a bake shop, the Pantry (serving soft drinks), a cafeteria, the Tavern which serves full meals, cocktails, and—from late May to late October—a luncheon buffet.

READER'S SIGHTSEEING SUGGESTION: "About one mile west of Old Sturbridge Village is **St. Anne's Shrine,** with a museum housing one of the largest collections of Russian icons in the United States. I think there are over 60 icons—it's quite impressive" (John L. Franck, Brookline, Mass.). [*Author's Note:* St. Anne's Shrine (tel. 617/347-7338) is on U.S. Route 20 west of Old Sturbridge Village, in the section called Fiskdale on the right-hand (north) side of the road.]

3. Deerfield, Amherst, and Northampton

The Connecticut River cuts through western Massachusetts on its way through Hartford and Essex to Long Island Sound. In colonial times the river provided easy and cheap transport from the interior to the bustling markets of New York and Philadelphia. Today the river valley serves as pathway for Interstate 91, the modern equivalent of the ancient waterway.

Because of this easy access, pioneer farmers and settlers poured into Massachusetts' portion of the Connecticut River Valley very early in colonial times. The alluvial riverbed soil is rich, and white men were farming at Springfield as early as 1636. Remote from the colonial power centers, they suffered from attacks by the French and their Indian allies.

This early settlement gained the region its modern name: the Pioneer Valley. Although it is still a rich farming region, other interests now predominate: Springfield's industrial career started with the construction of an armory there in 1777, and Holyoke and Hadley benefited from abundant waterpower and fostered a paper industry. But to most of the world the towns of Amherst, Northampton, and South Hadley are famous for education. Here in this pastoral setting are five famous colleges and several smaller institutions: Amherst College, Smith College, Mount Holyoke College, Hampshire College, and the **University of Massachusetts.** To the north, Old Deerfield is one of the most gracious, best preserved colonial and Federal towns in the country.

INFORMATION: The region has an area organization, the **Pioneer Valley Association,** P.O. Box 749, Northampton, MA 01061 (tel. 413/586-0321). In addition, each town's chamber of commerce sponsors a visitor information office. In **Amherst,** there's an information booth right on the town common across the street from the bus depot, or you can look to the Chamber of Commerce, 11 Spring St., Amherst, MA 01002 (tel. 413/253-9666). For **Northampton** information, try the Greater Northampton Chamber of Commerce, on State Street (tel. 413/584-1900). In **South Hadley,** the chamber is at 362 North Main St. (tel. 413/532-2864).

WHERE TO STAY: Accommodation in the area is very much geared to college life. Most visitors come on college business, and when big college events such as homecomings, graduations, and major football matches draw big crowds, rooms are scarce throughout the area. Try to plan and to reserve well in advance if you think you'll arrive in a busy time.

In Amherst

Every college town has its college inn, usually a gracious old place with a refined atmosphere and very comfortable—often plush—accommodations. Amherst is no exception, for right on the Town Common stands the **Lord Jeffrey Inn**, 30 Boltwood Ave., Amherst, MA 01002 (tel. 413/253-2576). Named for the town's namesake, Lord Jeffrey Amherst, the Lord Jeff is cozy, colonial, and collegiate, but with all the conveniences: cable color TV, direct-dial phone, individual heating and air conditioning, and, of course, private bathroom. A tavern and dining room can provide food and refreshment. In summer, the Lord Jeff charges $62 to $66 for a single room, or $64 to $74 for a double, tax included.

From the Town Common, head out North Pleasant Street and soon you'll see the **University Motor Lodge** at 345 North Pleasant St., Amherst, MA 01002 (tel. 413/256-8111), on the right-hand side. Up on the hillside above the road, this is an attractive neocolonial place which charges $34.88 single, $51.79 double, for its modern, fully equipped (right down to coffee in the room) motel rooms. The location is good, as you can walk in ten minutes either to Amherst or to U. Mass.

The University of Massachusetts ("U. Mass." for short) has its own major lodging facility for out-of-towners. Within the modern tower named the Murray D. Lincoln Campus Center is the **Campus Center Hotel** (tel. 413/549-6000), with over 100 rooms. Besides the standard luxuries such as air conditioning, color TV, telephone, and private bath, most rooms have wonderful, panoramic views of the campus, the town, and the surrounding farmland. Prices are $35 single, $48 double, $54 triple, tax included. To find the Campus Center, head north on North Pleasant Street, enter the U. Mass. campus, and follow signs to Campus Center Parking, an underground lot right next to the Campus Center.

Northampton Road is the highway (Route 9) between Amherst and Northampton. The road starts at the southern end of the Town Common, and exactly one mile later, after crossing the Amherst town line, it enters a commercial zone. Here, just over the town line on the left-hand side, is the **Amherst Motel**, 408 Northampton Rd., Amherst, MA 01002 (tel. 413/256-8122). Although it's a large-ish place complete with pool, there are just 13 motel rooms; the rest of the space has been converted to apartments. The rooms are fully equipped, including cable TV and Home Box Office, and rent for $36 to $39 double on weekends in summer, several dollars less on nights from Sunday through Thursday.

A bit farther along Route 9 toward Northampton is the local **Howard Johnson's Motor Lodge**, 401 Russell St., Hadley, MA 01305 (tel. 413/586-0114, or toll free 800/654-2000). Although it's very close to Amherst—only a few miles from the Town Common—its mail address is Hadley. Rooms are of the high Hojo standard, some newly remodeled with cathedral ceilings and balconies, and in addition the lodge has a nice big outdoor pool and lots of deck chairs for sunning. All rooms have two double beds and rent for $41.22 to $48.62 single, $51.79 to $59.19 double, tax included. V.I.P., handicapped, and adjoining family rooms also available. Seniors get special rates, and children under 12 can stay in their parents' room for free.

In Deerfield

Deerfield, the village that's virtually a museum, has an inn. Built in 1884 and modernized in 1981, the **Deerfield Inn** (tel. 617/774-5587) has 23 rooms with country-inn decor and all the modern conveniences, plus dining rooms and lounge. The inn is nice, but its location is even nicer: just steps from the houses of Historic Deerfield. Staying here, you can really feel that you're part of a historic community. Room prices are not cheap, though, at $69 to $75. The inn's address is simple: The Street, Deerfield MA 01342. If you're driving, follow the signs to Historic Deerfield. It's about 15 miles north of Northampton on Routes 5 and 10, less than that north of Amherst.

In Northampton

Closest thing in Northampton to the traditional college inn is the luxurious **Autumn Inn,** 259 Elm St., Northampton, MA 01060 (tel. 413/584-7660). From the street you see an attractive brick house, but behind the house are comfortable motel units and a small, very pretty swimming pool. Special attention is given to good-quality furnishings and equipment here; a lounge and dining room provide sustenance. Prices in summer are $44.39 single, $50.74 double, $10 for an extra person; children under 12, $6. Here on Elm Street you're right across the street from Smith College. By the way, Route 9 passes right along Elm Street as it makes its way through Northampton.

Budget Motels Farther Out

In the vicinity of Northampton are two members of the Susse Chalet budget motel chain which offer exceptional value. In the city of Holyoke on U.S. 5, there's a **Susse Chalet Inn** (tel. 413/536-1980, or toll free 800/258-1980; in New Hampshire, 800/572-1880), 1515 Northampton St., Holyoke, MA 01040. Look for the Susse Chalet on the right-hand side as you head south from Northampton, behind a Howard Johnson's restaurant. Susse Chalet Inn rooms are comfortably furnished with all the usual services, yet they cost a lot less than "standard" motel rooms: $24 single, $28.22 double, $31.40 for three, $34.56 for four persons. By the way, the exit to take from I-91 for this Susse Chalet Inn is Exit 17 or 17A.

At Chicopee, near Massachusetts Turnpike Exit 6, is a **Susse Chalet Motor Lodge** (tel. 413/592-5141, or toll free 800/258-1980; in New Hampshire 800/572-1880), Burnett Road, Chicopee, MA 01020. Susse Chalet Motor Lodges, almost as comfortable as the chain's inns, are a few dollars lower in price—and they still have all the conveniences, including TV, air conditioning, ice machine, coin-op laundry, direct-dial phone, even a swimming pool.

WHERE TO DINE: Amherst has several restaurants. The best all-around place to dine, in my opinion, is at **Plumbley's Off the Common** (tel. 253-9586), 30 Boltwood Walk. Everything from salads and burgers through prime rib and fresh seafood is on the menu here, and it's all reasonably priced. The decor is mod-Victorian, nicely done and verging on the formal, with an outdoor patio for fair-weather dining, and a glassed-in terrace as well. Spend as little as $3 for a substantial hamburger, or something like $7.50 for chicken orange whiskey (two boneless breasts of chicken in an orange-and-whiskey sauce), up to

$12.50 for the top-of-the-line steak. Plumbley's hits the happy medium for food, decor, and service. Good hours too: 11:30 a.m. to 1 a.m. (on Sunday from 10 a.m. to 1 a.m.). To find Plumbley's, start from the Town Common, bounded on the north by Main Street. Just off the northeast corner of the Common, past that huge brownstone Romanesque building, is Boltwood Walk (not to be confused with Boltwood Avenue), and Plumbley's.

La Raclette (tel. 253-5927) specializes in the classic Swiss dish of the same name: melted Swiss cheese served with pearl onions, gherkins, and boiled potatoes. They'll serve it to you with soup and salad for $7 at lunchtime, a bit more at dinner. Then there's the fancier fare, such as duck with lemon sauce, but the tone of La Raclette is basically quite informal: lots of light wood, and a modern lunch counter. Lunch and dinner are served every day but Monday, when they're closed. The address is 103 Boltwood Walk, off North Pleasant Street just a few blocks north of Main Street.

Before you get to Plumbley's, you'll pass **Amherst Chinese Food** (tel. 253-7835), 62–64 Main Street, good for lunch or dinner any day but Wednesday (closed all day) and Sunday (brunch only). Your best bet for good, plentiful, inexpensive food is always the local Chinese restaurant, and this is no exception. It's the only place in the area which grows its own vegetables. The Sunday brunch, for example (served 11:30 a.m. to 2:30 p.m.), includes hot-and-sour soup, vegetable lo mein, fried rice, stir-fried vegetables, steamed whole-wheat bread, dumplings, house special chicken, and beef with vegetable—all for $6 per person. A neat-and-tidy pine-paneled lunchroom, the restaurant is open daily except Wednesday from 11:30 a.m. to 2:30 p.m. and 4:30 to 10 p.m., on Friday and Saturday continuously from 11:30 a.m. to 10 p.m.

The **Lord Jeffrey Inn** (tel. 253-2576) offers the most elegant dining in town, serving breakfast (7:30 to 10:30 a.m.), and lunch (11:30 a.m. to 2:30 p.m.) and dinner (5:30 to 9 p.m.), plus Sunday brunch (noon to 2:30 p.m.). Expect to spend $18 to $25 per person for a full dinner, less for a hearty lunch.

The **Top of the Campus Restaurant and Lounge** (tel. 545-0636) is in a unique position atop the Murray D. Lincoln Campus Center of the University of Massachusetts. Here the formula is decent food at decent prices, with that panoramic view as bonus. Note the hours, though: breakfast is Monday through Friday from 7 to 9 a.m.; lunch the same days, from 11:30 a.m. to 2 p.m.; dinner is Tuesday through Saturday from 5 to 9 p.m. On Sunday there's a sunset buffet from 5 to 9 p.m. When college is not in session, more limited hours apply.

In Northampton

Right downtown in Northampton at 140 Main St. is **Beardsley's Café Restaurant** (tel. 586-2699), perhaps the area's best restaurant. It's not a large place, but the Edwardian decor is attractive, not overdone, and makes for sympathetic dining. The menu offers interesting and delicate dishes, many quite fancy. With dessert, tax, tip, and inexpensive beer or wine, the bill for two might come to $45, although you can dine for less and still dine very well. Beardsley's serves lunch Monday through Saturday from 11:30 a.m. to 5 p.m., with a 10:30 a.m. to 3:30 p.m. Sunday brunch; and dinner every day of the week; the kitchen serves from 5:30 to 10 p.m.

A Coffeehouse

Want to visit one of those fertile, funky places found only in college towns? **The Iron Horse Coffeehouse** (tel. 584-0610), 20 Center St., is just a few steps off Main Street right downtown. It's the real thing: a converted storefront with newspaper-readers, poets and proto-poets, and a full schedule of entertainment in the evenings, from the best in the Northeast to nationally known folk, jazz, and blues artists. Drop by, pick up a schedule, and have one of a dozen coffees, such as espresso Tangier (with orange rind and shaved chocolate; 85¢). Light breakfasts, cheese boards, Greek salads, quiche, pecan pie, and fully licensed liquor bar are available 8 a.m. to midnight daily (10 a.m. on Sunday).

WHAT TO SEE: You'll want to take a tour of **Amherst College,** founded in 1821. The Information Booth on the Town Common in Amherst can furnish you with a handy map and guide. The college is all around you. Want more information? Contact Amherst College, Converse Hall (tel. 413/542-2000).

The sprawling campus of the **University of Massachusetts** takes more time to see, but there is a free bus line you can use, and an excellent campus map. Ask at the Information Booth on the Common, or at the Information Desk in the Campus Center (east end of second floor concourse; tel. 413/545-0111). U. Mass, by the way, was founded in 1863 as Massachusetts Agricultural College. Present enrollment on the Amherst campus is about 24,000—compare that to Amherst College's 1500.

Perhaps the prettiest campus of all is that of **Smith College** in Northampton, founded 1871. You can arrange for a tour of the campus by contacting the Office of the Secretary of the College, College Hall 30, Northampton, MA 01063 (tel. 413/584-2700). But the handy *Campus Guide* folder available at information booths may well satisfy your needs. Smith's enrollment is about 2600, predominantly women.

Mount Holyoke College in South Hadley bears the distinction of being the country's oldest women's college, founded in 1837. The campus was designed by Frederick Law Olmstead, who fashioned so many beautiful parks and forests during the 19th century. For a campus tour, call 538-2023. The enrollment at Mount Holyoke is about 1900 students.

For a closer look at the Connecticut River, climb aboard the *Ouinnetukut II* riverboat for a 12-mile, 1½-hour interpretive boat cruise. Geology, ecology, and history of the river are the featured subjects, but the scenery alone is worth the fee: $5 per adult, $2 per child 3 to 14, free for kids under 3; there's a $1 discount for seniors 55 and over. Cruises leave at 10 a.m., noon, and 2 and 4 p.m. Wednesday through Sunday (no cruises Monday or Tuesday) from June 29 to September 5. June 8 through 26, there's no 10 a.m. or 4 p.m. cruise; September 7 through October 10 from Wednesday through Friday cruises are at 11 a.m. and 1 p.m., with an additional 3 p.m. cruise on Saturday and Sunday. To check prices and schedules, write R.R. 1, Box 377, Northfield, MA 01360, or call 413/659-3714. Call to make reservations so that you're sure to get the cruise you want. Buy your tickets at the Northfield Mountain Recreation and Environmental Center, on Route 63 to the north of Route 2, due east of Greenfield (take I-91 north to Exit 27, then Route 2 east, then Route 63 north).

Old Deerfield

About 15 miles north of Northampton and Amherst on Routes 5 and 10 is **Historic Deerfield** (tel. 617/774-5581; P.O. Box 321, Deerfield, MA 01342), a wide street lined with well-preserved 18th-century houses and shops. Unlike

Old Sturbridge Village or Mystic Seaport, you pay nothing to stroll along the Street and admire the nice old buildings and the setting, though there is an admission charge to each house, which includes a 30- to 45-minute guided tour (combination tickets of three houses for $4, or 12 houses for $15, are available). Plan your visit for Monday through Saturday, 9:30 a.m. to 4:30 p.m. or on Sunday 11 a.m. to 4:30 p.m. Then head for the Hall Tavern Museum, across from the Deerfield Inn, for maps, brochures, information, and a short audio-visual show which gives you an overview of the village.

The **Wright House** (1824), beautiful in itself, holds collections of Chippen-dale and Federal furniture, American paintings, and Chinese export porcelain.

The **Flynt Fabric Hall** (1872) houses a large collection of textiles, cos-tumes, and needlework from America, England, and continental Europe.

The **Parker and Russell Silver Shop** (1814) holds the museum's collection of silver.

Allen House (1720) is furnished in items made in Boston and the Connect-icut River Valley.

Stebbins House (1799–1810) is a wealthy landowner's house, with the rich period furnishings you might expect such a grandee to have.

Barnard Tavern (1740–1795) is favorite with children because some of its rooms have exhibits that are okay to touch.

Wells-Thorn House (1717–1751) has Federal furnishings, and a period lawyer's office as well.

The **Wilson Printing Office** (1816) also served as a cabinetmaker's shop.

Dwight-Barnard House (1725) was actually built in Springfield, and moved to Deerfield in 1950. Local furniture and a period doctor's office are the attractions.

the **Sheldon-Hawks House** (1743) was home for the same family during two centuries. Rich Deerfield farmers, the Sheldons were able to buy the best available at the time.

Ashley House (1730) was the minister's residence in old times, and by the look of it, this wasn't such a bad life.

Numerous other exhibits, not included within the Historic Deerfield orga-nization, are also open to view. It's clear one could spend days here, the collections are so rich and varied.

The Eastern States Exposition

Should you be lucky enough to travel in New England after Labor Day, try to hit the Eastern States Exposition (tel. 413/732-2361) in West Springfield. September is fair season, and **The Big "E"** is "New England's great State Fair." Admission to the grounds costs $4 per adult, $3 for those aged 13 to 17, $2 for children 6 to 12, and for seniors. (If you buy your tickets before the fair opens, you can save $1 on the adult fare.) The gates open at 8 a.m. daily, with most of the exhibit buildings opening at 10 a.m. Things don't cool down until everyone's gone home sometime after midnight. What's to do? Look at prize-winning steers, or new ideas in solar living, or crafts; try your hand at games on the midway; stuff yourself with carnival food and snacks; and examine the displays in the New England states' pavilions (one for each state) and in the theme pavilions.

To find the Big "E," though, get off the Massachusetts Turnpike (I-90) at Exit 4 and take Route 5 south; or get off I-91 at Exit 13, and take 5 south. Follow Route 5 to Route 147 west, and then follow the signs to the Exposition. Dates vary with the yearly calendar, but are something like September 12-23 each year.

4. Lenox and Lee

In the 1700s, pioneers spreading through the lands west of Boston came to settle among the fertile fields of the Berkshires. At first the settlement at Lenox was called Yokuntown, after a local Indian chief, but the name was later changed to honor an English lord—Charles Lenox, Duke of Richmond—who was sympathetic to the American Revolutionary cause. Although small industries have at times appeared in the town, it has been predominantly rural and agricultural, and has remained unspoiled. In the 19th century, business tycoons (including Andrew Carnegie) came to admire the tidy farms and streets of Lenox as the perfect place for a summer's retreat, and many farms were bought up by them for this purpose. The houses are still standing for visitors to admire.

If Lenox is the dowager aunt, pristine and correct in her beauty, neighboring Lee is the boisterous 20th-century daughter, lively and more modern, somewhat careless of her beauty.

WHERE TO STAY: The overnight lodging situation in Lenox is not the best. Proprietors of inns and motels bemoan the short season and the incredible press of traffic on Tanglewood weekends, which thins out to less-than-capacity during the week. For most lodging places, prices are high and rooms are in great demand. Some Tanglewood travelers stay as far east as Springfield, and drive to the concert, then back to Springfield. In any case, have reservations for weekends.

In Lee the situation is marginally better, although even the roadside motels fill to capacity on the weekends. Lee is fortunate to have a collection of rooms in guest houses. Reservations for these rooms are handled by the Lee Chamber of Commerce (see below).

Bed-and-Breakfast Services

For a room in a private home, with breakfast, throughout western Massachusetts, you can contact Tim and Mary Allen, who operate the **Berkshire Bed and Breakfast Connection,** 141 Newton Rd., Springfield, MA 01118 (tel. 413/ 783-5111). Rooms are priced at $20 to $46 double, $5 to $10 extra per night for a child or third person in a room.

Somewhat farther afield, the **Hilltown Community Development Corp.,** P.O. Box 17, Chesterfield, MA 01012, publishes a list of bed-and-breakfast houses scattered among the hills and villages between the Berkshires and the Connecticut River Valley (roughly between Lenox and Northampton, Mass.). Write to them for a copy, or ask for it in an information booth in Amherst, Northampton, or towns west of there.

Inns and Guest Houses

The **Garden Gables Inn** is very near the center of town at 141 Main St., Lenox, MA 01240 (tel. 413/637-0193), just off Main at the bottom of Church Hill down its own short private road. The inn's name is appropriate, as you'll see when you drive or walk down the road through the gardens to the large white house with three sharply triangular gables set in its roof. The shape of the house gives you some idea of the rooms, for all are of different shapes and sizes, all have lots of interesting nooks, crannies, and angles. All are furnished differently, and most have private baths; only four rooms share baths. Downstairs there's a cozy low-ceiling living room with rows of books and a fireplace. Rooms are $37 to $79.28 in July and August, with a three-night minimum stay on weekends; the lowest price is for a midweek single room without bath, and the higher price for just the opposite: a large room with private bath on a weekend. There are also two small efficiencies available for $295.96 and $338.24 weekly, in summer. The inn has its own 72-foot swimming pool out back, and a gift shop. You can get breakfast here if you're a guest, for an extra charge. Rates in May and June are dramatically lower, and in September and October many room prices are lower still. Mrs. Marie Veselik, owner of the Garden Gables, welcomes guests all year round.

The **Colonial Guest House,** 59 Walker St., Lenox, MA 01240 (tel. 413/637-0384 or 637-0043), is right next door to the Candlelight Inn in downtown Lenox. A very fine old "summer cottage," it has spacious, airy rooms with simple, attractive furnishings which go with the house and its era. In fact it's the only Lenox summer cottage which hasn't been substantially altered by the addition of private bathrooms, bars, large kitchens, and other modern "improvements." The huge front porch, right in the center of town, is wonderful for people-watching. Of the five rooms, two share an adjoining bathroom; the other three share baths in the hall. Prices are $58 double during the week, $69 double on weekends, in summer. This place is really charming.

Gerhard and Lilliane Schmid's **Gateways Inn,** 71 Walker St., Lenox, MA 01240 (tel. 413/637-2532), is a fine place to stay, but an even finer place to dine. Chef-owner Schmid has won numerous gold medals for his culinary skill, and if you stay at his inn, you get preference for seating in the dining room. The Gateways is quite near the center of Lenox, a grand old white mansion built by Harley Proctor of Proctor and Gamble in 1912. In-season rates are $58 (weekdays) and $90 (weekends) for a double room with private bath and continental breakfast; a small double room with shared bath costs $37 and $53. During July and August there's a three-night minimum stay if you plan to visit from Thursday to Sunday. The bonus here, besides the restaurant, is that guests at the Gateways get to use the indoor pool, tennis court, and bicycles at the Schmid's other inn, Haus Andreas, a few miles away.

The **Candlelight Inn** (tel. 413/637-1555) is known best for its restaurant (described below), but there are some rooms for rent in the big and graceful old house at 53 Walker St., corner of Church, Lenox, MA 01240. Off-season, the rooms go for $58, but in July and August the price rises to $69 to $90 double. The location is excellent, though. Call early for July or August reservations.

Lenox has many other inns and resorts, but the charge for a room can be upward of $100 double per night. With tax and a three-night minimum stay, minimum lodging expenditure for a couple on a Tanglewood weekend can mount to a breathtaking $320! Clearly, it's mostly the well-heeled who stay right in Lenox. Cost-conscious travelers put up in one of the several neighboring communities and drive or bus to Tanglewood.

Lee has numerous guest houses. They're not furnished in antiques like Lenox's inns, they don't have expensive dining rooms, but dollar for dollar they offer the best lodging value in the Berkshires. Exactly what you pay depends on the particular room in the particular private home, but the price will easily be less than half of a room in Lenox. As the rooms are scattered around town, the **Lee Chamber of Commerce** handles reservations. Contact them at 10 Park Pl., Lee, MA 01238 (tel. 413/243-0852).

Motels

The motels in Lee are moderately priced for the area. Try the **Pilgrim Motel,** 127 Housatonic St. (U.S. 20), Lee, MA 01238 (tel. 413/243-1328). The 24 rooms here all have wall-to-wall carpeting, private bath with tub, color cable

TV, and air conditioning. You can even splash in their pool. Prices for the rooms, including tax, are $47.57 ($73.99 Friday and Saturday); winter rates are $29.60 to $42.28.

Another motel not far north of the Massachusetts Turnpike is the **Sunset Motel,** 114 Housatonic St., Lee, MA 01238 (tel. 413/243-0302). Very similar in facilities to the aforementioned Pilgrim, the Sunset charges $34 on weekdays, $69 on weekends, per room in high season. Prices drop dramatically off-season.

North of Lenox on Routes 7 and 20 (same road) are numerous motels, extending all the way to Pittsfield. One of the closest to Lenox proper is also one of the least expensive. The **Susse Chalet Motor Lodge** (tel. 413/637-3560, or toll free 800/258-1980; In New Hampshire, 800/572-1880) has all the standard motel facilities in an attractive hillside location priced at $25 single, $30 for two, $32.50 for three, $36 for four people. These are midweek rates; weekend rates are substantially higher. It's the best value in the Berkshires, but you must reserve early.

WHERE TO DINE: Lenox is not covered with restaurants, as many of the classy places to eat are out in the countryside. But for a snack or a good dinner in town, try one of these:

New and very successful is the **Church Street Café** (tel. 637-2745), "an American bistro" at 69 Church St. Lunch, dinner, and Sunday brunch are served in the small, cozy dining room or out on the pleasant covered deck. Service is personal and informal, and prices are quite moderate for Lenox. I had hot tomato bisque to start (it's often served cold, and is delicious either way); then roast chicken marinated in ginger, garlic, and spices, served with rice and a salad. Apple pan dowdy and espresso finished up, and the bill— including tax, tip, and a half bottle of the house wine—was $20. They make their own pasta here, and country pâté too. Luncheon prices include $4 sandwiches, salade Niçoise for $5.50.

The **Candlelight Inn** (tel 637-1555), 53 Walker St., at the corner of Church Street, is right near the center of town, warm, friendly, and popular with locals and visitors alike. The menu lists a good number of appetizers and a selection of main courses, most of which are continental favorites like duck in orange sauce. Lunch at the Candlelight Inn is served daily except Sunday from 11 a.m. to 2:30 p.m.; dinner every day from 5 to 10 p.m. You don't have to dress up, but you'll feel better if you do. Expect to spend $20 to $25 per person here.

Lenox has a restaurant for the budget-minded which will appeal to natural-foods fans and those who enjoy exotica as well. It's **The Restaurant** (tel. 637-9894), 15 Franklin St., a half block off Main Street near the Mobil service station. The mood at the Restaurant is that of a European bistro: the walls are hung with artistic drawings and photographs, and a fantastically ornate and handsome cast-iron grille (the cover for a heating duct in some mansion's floor?) hangs on one wall in a place of honor. The furniture is simple, made of rough wood, and the atmosphere is relaxed and informal. But it's the menu which attracts the customers: everything from curries to knackwürst and sauerkraut and back again. A large bowl of steamed mussels with vermicelli is $6, or you might have crêpes and a salad. Most of the lunch selections, including a variety of sandwiches, seem to be priced at $5 or less. For dinner, the menu may feature roast duck Cantonese or shrimp de Jonghe (about $9), or for vegetarian diners there may be a vegetable curry or fettucine Alfredo ($7 to $8). The wine and spirits list is small, but well rounded and reasonably priced. Come for lunch from noon to 2:30 p.m. Monday through Saturday (Sunday brunch,

11 a.m. to 2 p.m.), for dinner from 6 to 10 p.m. Monday through Saturday (on Sunday from 4:30 to 9 p.m.).

For Picnics

With so many picnic lunches being consumed on the grounds of Tanglewood, there must be a place that fixes ready-to-go picnics, right? It's **A Moveable Feast,** at the rear of 104 Main St. (tel. 637-1785). The thing to do is call and order, then drop by to pick up something like this: vichyssoise or gazpacho, chicken salad with grapes and walnuts or marinated beef with Oriental rice, then cheesecake for dessert. Fresh bread, napkin, and cutlery are all included in the price of about $7.50. They're open Thursday (10 a.m. to 7 p.m.), Friday and Saturday (to 8 p.m.), and Sunday (to 2 p.m.) only.

WHAT TO DO: The Number One activity in Lenox is, of course, the **Berkshire Music Festival,** the summer season of the Boston Symphony Orchestra. Since 1934 the concerts have been held in July and August on the grounds of a fine estate called Tanglewood, about a mile from the center of Lenox out in the Berkshire hills. Seats in the Music Shed ($6.50 to $40) are difficult to come by, but general admission tickets to the grounds ($4 to $6) are easy to find at Tanglewood. All tickets can be bought through Ticketron. Bring a blanket and picnic lunch, and come early to get a good seat near the Music Shed. Grounds open two hours before concert time. Programs of the concert series are available from the information booth in Lenox, or call the Tanglewood office (tel. 413/637-1940). In Boston, call the Berkshire Music Center in Symphony Hall (251 Huntington Ave.) at 617/266-1492.

When you call for information, be sure to ask about other happenings at Tanglewood, because the Music Festival concerts are not the only thing going on. Over 40 concerts take place during the Tanglewood season, not including the famous weekend BSO concerts. Performers are the young and extremely promising musicians who attend the Berkshire Music Center for study and advanced training. Maestro Seiji Ozawa, now music director of the BSO, was once among this young up-and-coming elite. Chamber music, solo recitals, and full orchestra concerts are all on this 40-program list.

Tanglewood Tips

If you drive to Tanglewood for one of the BSO concerts, here are some tips to make things easier. First, expect heavy highway traffic. Plan to get to Tanglewood proper by 6 p.m. or earlier (the concert begins at 8:30). Bring your picnic lunch—that's what everyone does, and that's why the parking lots fill up early, and that's why no one minds getting there three hours before the concert begins. Expect a tremendous jam of traffic when you leave at the end of the concert. The flood is ably directed by Tanglewood staff, but the exodus takes time nonetheless.

Other Concerts

Tanglewood has begun to sponsor a series of popular, folk, and rock concerts as well as the more lofty Berkshire Music Festival series. When you call 413/637-1600, ask about what's coming up in the **Popular Artists' Series.**

The **Music Inn** (tel. 413/637-2970) has top popular artists of national and international reputation all summer, and the grounds south of Lenox (actually in Stockbridge) always seem to be crowded. Call for current programs and ticket data, and then follow the signs off the highways to the inn.

South Mountain Concerts (tel. 413/442-2106), in nearby Pittsfield, specializes in chamber music, and concerts begin in July and last through the high summer season and on into September. Recently, the grand finale in late September was the Emerson String Quartet—so you never know what kind of (classical) music will be featured until you call. South Mountain Concerts was started in 1918 in a lovely old hall located a mile south of Pittsfield on U.S. Routes 7 and 20. For a printed schedule of concerts, drop a line to the South Mountain Association, P.O. Box 23, Pittsfield, MA 01202.

Sightseeing in Lenox

In Lenox proper, be sure to walk to the top of the hill which is on Main Street (U.S. 7), north of the center of town, to see the "Church on the Hill," a very fine New England Congregational church building erected in 1805.

Otherwise, long walks or a drive around the "back streets" and lanes of Lenox can turn up unexpected sights: tremendous mansions, even small castles, nestled in fine parks and copses of trees, once occupied for a few months in summer by commercial and industrial magnates and their immediate families. Many of the mansions are still in private hands, enjoyed by an ever-widening circle of the descendants of the original builders. Most are not open to the public, except for tantalizing looks from the sidewalk.

Jacob's Pillow Dance Festival

In Lee, a dilapidated barn served as the birthplace, in 1931, of a major American dance festival. Bought by Ted Shawn and renovated for performances, the barn and the festival grew larger and more important over the years, enlisting the talents of Alvin Ailey, Merce Cunningham, and similar lights.

The eight-week Jacob's Pillow season lasts through July and August. Write for a season brochure to: Jacob's Pillow Dance Festival, P.O. Box 287, Lee, MA 01238, or call 413/243-0745. The performance center is ten miles east of downtown Lee, off U.S. 20.

5. Stockbridge

Any way you look at it, Stockbridge is a very beautiful town. Its wide Main Street is lined with grand houses and other buildings each set apart in its own lawns and gardens. Stately trees fill the skyline. Stockbridge is the center of many Berkshire activities, including the **Berkshire Playhouse** (details below) and also once the home of famed painter Norman Rockwell.

The town of **West Stockbridge** is a different municipality altogether, four miles west of Stockbridge and Lenox. The dilapidated town was bought up by developers some years ago and reconstructed, expanded, and spruced up as a real-life Disneyland for shoppers, browsers, and sightseers. Purists may say the town is now like a movie set, but most visitors enjoy their time here, meandering along the short streets, peering in windows and shops, having a meal or a cool refresher. It's all pretty commercial, it's true, but that's the attraction.

TOURIST INFORMATION: The Stockbridge Kiwanis Club maintains an Information Booth on the main street right in the center of town. They'll provide you with pamphlets and brochures, answer your questions, and even help you find an inexpensive room in a private home—but only if lodging conditions are tight. If the local motels are not full, they'll direct you to one of those, as the private-home rooms are more of an emergency measure.

WHERE TO STAY AND DINE: The **Red Lion Inn,** on Main Street in Stockbridge, MA 01262 (tel. 413/298-5545), is a town institution, a huge white frame hotel with a wide front porch. Always bustling with guests and diners in summer, the Red Lion charges its high-season rates on weekends from July through October. Minimum weekend stay is two nights, at $62 (shared bath) or $85 to $100 (private bath) per night, double. On weekdays the rate drops to $47 or $62 for the same double with bath.

The Red Lion is also Stockbridge's premier place for dining. Besides the formal dining room, there's the Widow Bingham Tavern, a rough-hewn and woody place of colonial flavor. The Lion's Den, downstairs, is the cocktail lounge with a sandwich-and-salad menu. Plan to spend about $40 per person for a luxurious beef dinner in the dining room, about $30 in the Widow Bingham Tavern. In summer, there's a pretty outdoor café in back. By the way, the building dates from 1897 when it was constructed on the site of an earlier inn which was completely destroyed by fire.

In the center of Stockbridge, a block from the Red Lion Inn, is the **guest house** of **Mr. and Mrs. William Roy** (tel. 413/298-3448), right on Main Street just north of the inn. Here, double rooms with air conditioning are priced at $32.50 (for a smaller room), and $36.50 (for a larger room), and the bathrooms are shared. During the summer and early fall, weekend rates are higher. It's convenient, pleasant, friendly, and the money you save can be spent having dinner at the Red Lion.

A Guest House Out of Town: Do this: pick up a telephone and call **Mrs. Blodgett** (tel. 413/528-1298), and ask her if she has any rooms available. She owns a pretty house in the country several miles from the center of Stockbridge, and she rents rooms in an annex during the summer. There are only a few rooms, but prices are very good, Mrs. Blodgett is charming, and you'll love it. Be sure to ask for driving directions. They'll be something like this: from the Red Lion Inn, go south on U.S. 7 four miles to a sign which says "To Route 183." Turn right; at the stop sign, turn hard right onto Route 183, then take the next left onto Division Street. Two miles later you'll see a blinker; go another mile and turn right onto Long Pond Road; it's another mile to Mrs. Blodgett's. But call first.

Other Restaurants: For a light lunch in a pleasant setting, try **The Café** (tel. 298-3070), off the main street down a passage just a few doors north of the Red Lion. Soups, salads, sandwiches, wine, and beer are served. Soup and a sandwich might run $7, beverage included; a huge chef's salad the same. The Café is open 11 a.m. to 4 p.m. on weekdays, to 6 or 7 p.m. on weekends.

If you've seen the Arlo Guthrie movie *Alice's Restaurant,* you may recall that the setting was Stockbridge, Mass. Alice's is now called **Sophia's Restaurant** (tel. 298-3216), a haven of low prices in otherwise pricey Stockbridge. It's located behind Nejaime's Market, about a half block north of the Red Lion. The menu offers a vast selection of omelets, breakfasts, Italian and Greek dishes in all price ranges. Greek souvlaki, for instance, is filling, and priced between $3.85 and $5.50. It's almost true that "You can get anything you want/At [Sophia's] restaurant!"

In West Stockbridge

West Stockbridge harbors several establishments offering lodging and meals at lower rates than in Stockbridge proper. These are well worth a look.

The bed-and-breakfast **Thorne House,** on Main Street just south of all the shops, West Stockbridge, MA 01266 (tel. 413/232-7042), is a charming village house from the early 1800s. Three bedrooms (one with a fireplace) and a breakfast-sitting room have been restored for guests' use. They're all very well done, as is the continental breakfast which comes with your room. You pay $48 double for a room with shared bath; there's a two-night minimum stay on summer weekends. Three miles from Tanglewood, a few steps from West Stockbridge, this place is really wonderful.

So many places call themselves country inns these days, even though they have downtown locations, Muzak and color cable TV, bus tours and Jacuzzis. The **Williamsville Inn** (tel. 413/274-6580) is a true country inn, however. It's out in the country, about four miles south of West Stockbridge on Route 41. Some of the 15 guest rooms have fireplaces, some have four-poster beds; all have private baths and fine old furnishings. The inn, built in 1797, has ten acres of grounds, a swimming pool, clay tennis court, and woodland trails. The dining room is well known and well regarded. In July and August rooms cost $72 to $83 double, and a two-day minimum stay is applied on weekends (three on holidays). The address is simply Route 41, West Stockbridge, MA 01266.

If Berkshire lodging prices are making your spine tingle, consider the 17-room **Pleasant Valley Motel** (tel. 413/232-4216), Route 102, West Stockbridge, MA 01266, right near Exit 1 of the Mass Turnpike, a mile or so from town. Soundproof rooms with television, coffee-makers, private baths, and rights to use of a swimming pool nearby are yours for the moderate rate of $38 double Sunday through Thursday, $58 on Friday or Saturday. Not bad.

A Restaurant in West Stockbridge: Over in West Stockbridge for the day, one of the very best things you can do is have a meal at the **Orient Express** (tel. 232-4204), on Harris Street. Light and airy, with wicker furniture, it is an exceptionally attractive place, and a welcome change from the antique-packed dining rooms hereabouts. The "Orient" in the name is Vietnam: appetizers such as mien cua (crab and bean-thread soup) or ga nuong chanh (skewered lemon chicken), main courses of sauteed squid with bamboo shoots, or fresh flounder in a spicy sweet-and-sour sauce. For dessert, the customary lychee or not-so-customary flan finish up nicely. Such a dinner would cost $12 to $15, and if you choose carefully you might even squeeze a glass of sake or plum wine into the price. There are lots of vegetarian dishes too. Open 11 a.m. to 11 p.m., seven days a week. Don't miss it.

WHAT TO SEE AND DO: Stockbridge is rich in historical and cultural attractions. You'll want to visit the **Old Corner House** (tel. 298-3822) in the center of Stockbridge, which has shows of historical memorabilia which change from time to time, and also a large permanent collection of Norman Rockwell paintings. The famed American illustrator did many pictures for magazine covers and posters, and the originals of those paintings, or at least many of them, are housed in the Old Corner House. Admission is $2 for adults, 50¢ for children, and it's open from 10 a.m. to 5 p.m. every day but Tuesday.

Other old houses worth a visit are the **Mission House** (1739), on Main Street, built by the Rev. John Sergeant to carry out his Christian mission to the Indians. The house is a National Historic Landmark, and is furnished in American pieces all dating from 1740 or earlier. It's open from Memorial Day through Columbus Day, Tuesday through Saturday from 10 a.m. to 5 p.m., Sunday and Monday holidays from 11 a.m. to 4 p.m.; open holidays. Admission is $1.40 for adults, 30¢ for children 14 and under.

Naumkeag, on Prospect Hill, was built by Stanford White for Joseph Choate, an American ambassador to Great Britain, in 1886. Many of the sumptuous furnishings are still in place, and there are extensive formal gardens. Take Pine Street from the Red Lion Inn, then turn onto Prospect Street to reach Naumkeag. Hours for the palatial house are on weekends (on Saturday from 10 a.m. to 5 p.m., on Sunday from 11 a.m. to 4 p.m.) from Memorial Day through Columbus Day on weekends and holidays, and from July through Labor Day daily, except Monday. Naumkeag is open from 10 a.m. to 5 p.m. (on Sunday and holidays from 11 a.m. to 4 p.m.). Admission is several dollars. Call 298-3239 for any further details.

Right near Naumkeag is another sumptuous estate reached by the same route via Pine Street and Prospect. From its beginning as an Indian mission in 1734, the estate atop Eden Hill in Stockbridge has seen many additions over the years. Having served as a mansion for the wealthy and as a private school, it is now a monastery for the Marian Fathers, and visitors are welcome to stroll the grounds and take in the impressive buildings and the views of the Berkshire Hills.

Chesterwood

Just a few miles from Stockbridge is Chesterwood (tel. 298-3579), the former summer estate of Daniel Chester French, sculptor of the statue of Lincoln which graces the Lincoln Memorial, and also of the Minuteman statute at Concord North Bridge. French (1850–1931) summered here from 1897 until 1931 and used the studio (built in 1898) near the house for his work. You can visit both the mansion and studio as well as an 1800s barn which has been converted to a gallery featuring exhibits on French's life and work. A lovely period garden, a nature trail laid out by French himself, and a panoramic view of Monument Mountain are unexpected extras to a Chesterwood visit. Admission fees go toward the upkeep of the property, which is maintained by the National Trust for Historic Preservation. Adults pay $3, children pay $1, and seniors pay $2. Chesterwood is open daily from 10 a.m. to 5 p.m. May through October. To get there, drive west on Route 102 from Stockbridge, and follow the signs.

Berkshire Theater Festival

In the Berkshire Playhouse (tel. 413/298-5536) and in a big red barn close by, the Berkshire Theater Festival hosts a series of performances now in its second half-century. From mid-June through August, plays are staged Wednesday through Sunday evenings, and on Thursday and Saturday afternoons. The classic plays with name performers are in the Playhouse proper. The Unicorn Theater Company puts on experimental and new plays in the barn, and throughout the summer special children's theater performances are held.

Hancock Shaker Village

Ten miles north of West Stockbridge along Route 41, then west on U.S. 20, will bring you to the outskirts of Pittsfield, Mass., and Hancock Shaker Village, one of the most fascinating sights in the Berkshires. Here lived—right up until 1960—members of a religious sect noted for their quiet, simple lives, hard work, and quality handicrafts.

"The United Society of Believers in Christ's Second Appearing," "The Millennial Church," more readily known as the Shakers, was a movement begun in 1747 in England as an offshoot of Quakerism. It gained momentum when Ann Lee, "Mother Ann," proclaimed that she had received the "mother element" of the spirit of Christ. Imprisoned for her zeal, Mother Ann and eight followers later (1774) emigrated to the American colony of New York and founded a settlement near Albany. By the time Mother Ann died in 1784, her followers were ready to spread out and found other Shaker communities based on the principles of communal possessions, celibacy, pacifism, open confession of sins, and equality of the sexes. Organization of the communities was into "families" of 30 to 90 people. Work was a consecrated act, which accounts for the high quality of workmanship and design in Shaker furniture and crafts: in effect, every product was a prayer.

Shakers, named for the trembling which came upon them from their religious zeal, believed that God had both a male and female nature. The male was embodied in Jesus, the female in Mother Ann. Though a convert devoted himself and all his possessions to the community, he was free to leave at any time. Celibacy, less than effective in the spreading of a people or a belief, and the onslaught of the 20th century's complex lifestyle, almost put an end to Shakerism after more than two centuries; there are only 12 of the faithful left now, living in a small community in Maine.

One cannot help but admire a gentle fanaticism which feeds on kindliness and good hard work. Shaker products are still copied and admired, because these good people took daily tasks to the level of an art. Twenty of the original Shaker buildings at Hancock have been restored, furnished with artifacts of Shaker life, and staffed with men and women who can explain the Shakers and their lives to you. Hancock Shaker Village, P.O. Box 898, Pittsfield, MA 01202 (tel. 413/443-0188), is open Memorial Day weekend through October from 9:30 a.m. to 5 p.m. every day. Admission is $4.50 per adult, $1.50 for children 6 to 12, $4 for seniors, $10 for a family (two adults and two children under 18). Don't miss it.

Skiing
There are at least six well-known downhill ski areas in the Berkshires. To get information on all of them—**Butternut, Bosquet, Catamount, Brodie, Berkshire East, Jiminy Peak, Otis Ridge**—call one toll-free number if you're in New York, New Jersey, Connecticut, Vermont, Rhode Island, or New Hampshire: 800/628-5030. If you're in Massachusetts, you'll have to pay; dial 413/499-0700.

My favorite area in the Berkshires is **Butternut** (tel. 413/528-2000), outside Great Barrington, Mass. Butternut has won awards for its design and for the concern shown in fitting the ski area and buildings into the Berkshire forests without much environmental disruption or ugliness. It has a good variety of lifts: five double chairs, a triple chair, and a Poma, with a combined capacity of over 7000 skiers an hour; it has a good deal of snowmaking and grooming, and the staff here works particularly hard at its job; and there is a good balance among novice, intermediate, and expert slopes. The other features common to good ski areas are available.

6. South Egremont and Great Barrington
Although it is certainly not a city, Great Barrington is the largest town in the southern Berkshires, a major crossroads and commercial center. Supplies

and services which you might not find in Stockbridge or Lenox will be available here.

Great Barrington was an important town even before the Revolution. The citizenry, angered at Britain's denial of colonials' rights, prevented the king's judges from convening in the courthouse here in 1774. In the 19th century Mr. and Mrs. Edward Searles became the town's benefactors, establishing many public buildings and constructing for themselves an immense mansion in a 100-acre park which nudges right into the center of town. You can visit the "Searles Castle," which is also the site of a summer antiques fair.

WHERE TO STAY: A short ride from the center of Great Barrington are two of the Berkshires' best lodging places.

Jo and Ray Elling run **Elling's Guest House** R.R. 3, Box 6, Great Barrington, MA 01230 (tel. 413/528-4103), which is one mile from the center of town southwest along Route 23. The house, which dates from 1746, is actually more like an inn. The six rooms are all pretty and quaint; those with private bath rent for $47.57, with shared bath for $40.17. An extra person in a room pays $10. The rates go down a few dollars in winter, but whatever the season, a good continental breakfast is included. No credit cards accepted, by the way, and there is a two-night minimum stay on weekends. Quiet, friendly, reasonably priced, this is the best of the Berkshires.

A bit farther along the same road, 2½ miles from the center of town, is the **Seekonk Pines Inn,** R.R. 1, Box 29AA, Great Barrington, MA 01230 (tel. 413/528-4192). As you come from town, look for it on the right-hand side, behind the pines. Linda and Chris Best are your hosts here, and their inn features a nice swimming pool, a garden from which they will sell you fresh produce, bicycles for rent; and in winter, a fireplace in the large living room, besides the cozy rooms. It's not fancy, but clean, neat, the rooms decorated with antiques and old quilts, and moderately priced at $34.88 double on weekdays, $37 on weekends, for a room with shared bath. For the suite with sitting area and room for four to sleep (perfect for a family or couple on a longer visit), and with private bath, the price is $47.57. An extra person pays $7 ($6 in winter).

Besides these fine guest houses, Great Barrington has motels. Numerous establishments are spread along U.S. 7 north of town, and one luxurious place is right in the center.

The **Berkshire Motor Inn,** on Main Street in Great Barrington, MA 02130 (tel. 413/528-3150), is right behind the town information booth and across the street from Searles Castle. The two-story building holds rooms with all comforts priced at $58 double Sunday through Wednesday, $79 on Thursday, Friday, and Saturday nights in summer. An indoor pool, sauna, and central location are the bonuses.

If you have a car, try the **Lantern House Motel,** P.O. Box 97, Great Barrington, MA 01230 (tel. 413/528-2350), which is on U.S. 7 north of town, on the right. Accommodations are quite good, and prices are moderate for the Berkshires in high season: $42.28 to $50.74 on weekdays, $52.85 to $63.42 on weekends.

7. Williamstown and the Mohawk Trail

The home of famous **Williams College** is also one of the prettiest towns in New England, a town of hills and dales and emerald greenswards. Besides the college, Williamstown has a noted theater festival and a fine art museum.

GETTING THERE: Most readers will be circulating through the Berkshires, or southern Vermont, when they visit Williamstown. But if you're coming directly from Boston, contact **Englander Coach Lines** at the Greyhound Bus Terminal, 10 St. James Ave. (tel. 617/423-5810). Englander runs two or three buses daily along the route between Boston, via Fitchburg, Greenfield, and North Adams, to Williamstown and Albany. Headquarters for Englander is 303 Deerfield St., Greenfield, Mass. (tel. 413/773-7316).

WHERE TO STAY AND DINE: Far enough from Tanglewood to avoid the crush, Williamstown is favored with a fine selection of small guest houses and inns, moderately priced motels, and a full-service hotel. You should have little trouble finding the sort of room you want in this charming Berkshire town.

Small Inns and Guest Houses

For thrifty travelers, the **Glen Guest House** (tel. 413/458-4607) is also near the intersection of Routes 2 and 7, with its official address being 13 Cold Spring Rd., Williamstown, MA 01267. Continue south on Route 2/7 from the intersection, and you'll see the large house which is the Glen set in the midst of its large rolling lawn. Mr. and Mrs. Czerwinski have a number of rooms for rent, some with private baths, others without baths. The price for two people is $19.03 to $31.17, depending on the room. The proprietors, who left Czechoslovakia during the Dubcek era, are very kindly and helpful.

My favorite place in all Williamstown is the **River Bend Farm**, 643 Simonds Rd., Williamstown, MA 01267 (tel. 413/458-5504). This old roadside inn and tavern-turned-farmhouse is being restored lovingly by Dave and Judy Loomis. So far there are four rooms to rent to guests, at $27 double. True country-inn feeling without the commercial hype, River Bend Farm is just over one mile north of Williamstown's Information Booth, along U.S. 7; turn left onto the private drive immediately after crossing a bridge over the river.

Downtown next to the Williams Inn and more or less across from the Glen Guest House is the **Victorian Tourist Home**, 1120 Main St., Williamstown, MA 01267 (tel. 413/458-3121), hidden by shady trees. Cool and quiet, the seven rooms here have three shared baths and prices of $22 single, $32 double. The location is excellent, being quiet and secluded, yet walking distance to just about everything.

Motels

Head north on U.S. 7 from Williamstown, and just over a mile will bring you to the **Cozy Corner Motel,** Sand Springs Road, Williamstown, MA 01267 (tel. 413/458-5677). This tidy two-story establishment is run by Mike and Sandy Dolan, who promise that there's "always an Irish smile." Rooms have the standard motel comforts of TV and private bath, and cost $28 to $36 double, depending on season.

Less than a half mile farther north, on the left (west) side of the road is the **Villager Motel,** Route 7 North, Williamstown, MA 01267 (tel. 413/458-4046). The 21 units here consist of motel units and individual cabins set well back from the road, which is not very noisy in any case. Take your pick of a room with one double bed ($34) or two double beds ($38).

Right downtown in Williamstown, cheek by jowl with the Williams Inn, is the **Northside Inn Motel,** a few steps north of the junction of Routes 2 and 7, 45 North St., Williamstown, MA 01267 (tel. 413/458-8107). The Northside is a neat little motel of one and two stories, with a small pool, and rooms equipped with individual thermostats, ceramic tile baths, color TV, and telephones. It's open all year, and charges $35.94 to $38.05 for a double room, the higher prices being for larger rooms with two double beds. For convenience, there's a motel coffeeshop.

The Big One

Fanciest place to stay in Williamstown is the **Williams Inn** (tel. 413/458-9371), right in the middle of town at the intersection of Routes 2 and 7, Williamstown, MA 01267. Although built only a few years ago, the feeling at the inn is like that at any other luxury hotel in a New England college town: full comfort, touches of elegance, colonial atmosphere. There are over 100 modern rooms, all air-conditioned and all equipped with shiny new baths and cable color TVs; an indoor swimming pool and sauna, and live entertainment in the lounge on weekends are extra attractions. Perhaps the greatest attraction of all, though, is the inn's location right downtown, making it within easy walking distance of everything—ideal when the town is just made for walking. Room prices rise and fall with the seasons: April through December the rooms cost $59.19 to $67.65 single, $67.65 to $78.22 double; during the rest of the year, rates are lower. Remember that rooms in Williamstown are more difficult to find during special college functions such as reunions, graduation, and major football games.

A Special Restaurant

Williamstown has a small commercial district artfully hidden away on Spring Street (take Route 2 east—that's Main Street—from the intersection with U.S. 7, and look for Spring Street on the right). Here is where you'll find a tavern, a sandwich shop, and various stores. Follow Spring Street to its end, turn left onto Latham Street, and go down to the "T" at Water Street. Turn right and you'll see the **River House** (tel. 458-4820), 123 Water St. Williamstown's most popular downtown restaurant, the River House is open every day from 11:30 a.m. to midnight. Prices are moderate, the wine and spirits list is long, and the menu has something for everybody. Have quiche, omelet, or eggplant parmesan for lunch, and you'll get a salad, garlic bread, and french fries with it for less than $5. In the evening, complete dinners from soup to dessert are priced from $10 to $15: lots of beef entrees, chops, fish, and several Italian dishes are featured. Special platters for children under 12 and seniors (over 60) are a money-saving extra. Sandwiches and light meals served at all hours.

WHAT TO SEE AND DO: Take a walk around the **Williams College** campus. The college was founded (as a college) in 1793, and named for Col. Ephraim Williams, a colonial soldier and early resident of the area. Although known as a private men's college, Williams has been coed for several years now.

For a small town in the Berkshires, Williamstown has a surprising number of cultural offerings. For instance, the **Clark Art Institute** (tel. 413/458-8109), on South Street, has a very fine collection of the impressionists, and also a good number of paintings by the old masters. The 19th-century French paintings are the strong point of the collection, but you may easily run into a Dürer, a work by Winslow Homer, or something by Memling. The Clark Art Institute is open all year, Tuesday through Sunday from 10 a.m. to 5 p.m. (closed Monday), and admission is free.

Williams College also has a **Museum of Art** (tel. 597-2429) in Lawrence Hall on Main Street, open daily 10 a.m. to 5 p.m. and on Sunday from 1 to 5 p.m., closed Monday admission free. The museum's holdings are eclectic, from modern sculpture through pre-Columbian pottery to European art. Lawrence Hall is a Greek revival building with a rotunda, easy to spot as you stroll along Main Street.

The **Williamstown Theater Festival** is staged during the summer months in the college's **Adams Memorial Theater** (tel. 413/458-8145) on Main Street. The festival has seen over two dozen seasons so far, with many famous performers (all are members of Actors' Equity) taking the stage. Plays are on through July and August. During the college year the theater is used for collegiate productions which are also of a high calibre. For festival information, write to P.O. Box 517, Williamstown, MA 01267.

No matter if the weather is clear or cloudy, stroll over to the **Milham Planetarium** in the Hopkins Observatory Building on Main Street. The observatory itself is the oldest astronomical observatory in the United States. Mid-June through mid-August on two evenings each week the planetarium has free celestial shows; from October through May, when college is in session, shows are on Friday evenings.

Chapter IX

RHODE ISLAND

1. Providence
2. Newport
3. Narragansett Bay
4. Block Island
5. Watch Hill

JUST BECAUSE RHODE ISLAND is the smallest state in the Union, many people assume that this in some way limits the variety of things one can see and do in this corner of New England. Not so. The state's beaches are famed throughout the region, sites and structures of historical importance abound, the cities are pleasant and of manageable size, and then there's Newport—a world apart. In fact, the only real effects the state's small size seem to have are to make the residents feel that they are a part of a very special place, which they are, and to make everything easily accessible to the visitor.

In the 1600s, when New England was being colonized by Europeans, the best solution to a community conflict was for the weaker of the conflicting parties to shove off into the wilderness and found and develop their own community. To save his skin and freely express his beliefs, Roger Williams left Puritan Salem in 1636 and came to Narragansett Bay, followed soon afterward by others who shared his views, or at least knew they would be allowed to disagree. Williams was way ahead of the times in his political, religious, and ethical thinking, and his contribution to the American democratic tradition is very important: in his new community of Providence, a man could think and say what he liked. In the years that followed the founding of Providence, Williams persuaded Parliament to include the settlements of Portsmouth and Newport on Rhode Island with his own Providence Plantation under the same charter—these towns had also been founded by dissenters who desired freedom of thought and speech—thus securing to the colony as a whole the right of absolute liberty in matters of belief. The official name of the state to this day remains "Rhode Island and Providence Plantations."

Today Rhode Island is a manufacturing center, a maritime state, with a lot of rich agricultural land and several industries of importance. But the summer vacationers who come to Rhode Island—beginning with the very wealthy socialites who started the custom in the 19th century—are also an important part of the economy, and the state government does a lot to see that "Little Rhodie" retains the lure it had for those discriminating types who built palatial mansions in Newport, Watch Hill, and other coastal towns.

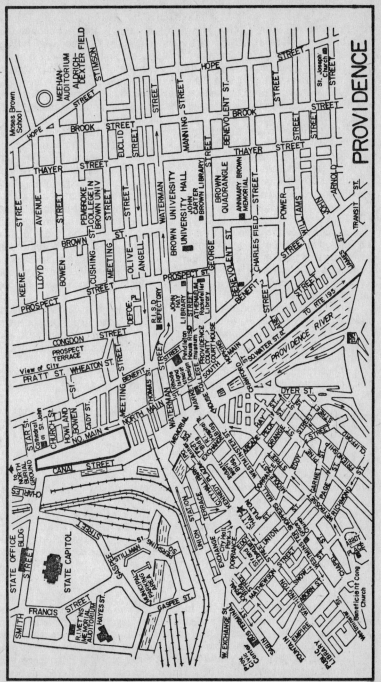

Map courtesy of AAA, the Automobile Club of Rhode Island, and the Providence Journal Company.

1. Providence

Providence is a pretty city. The downtown area is compact enough that a visitor can get off the train, or park the car, and walk to just about everything there is to see and do. The State Capitol, a pleasant and harmonious building of white Georgia marble, crowns a hilltop on the edge of the downtown section. College Hill rises from the east bank of the Providence River, which runs through downtown; Brown University, the Rhode Island School of Design, and a collection of exceptionally beautiful and interesting houses from the 17th, 18th, and 19th centuries give College Hill its character.

The city was founded in 1636 by Roger Williams (1603–1683), who had been minister of the church at Salem, Mass., but whose free-thinking religious ideas had made the General Court banish him from Massachusetts Bay. (He held that the Massachusetts Bay charter was not legal, and that the Puritans should face the fact that they had really separated from the Church of England, whether they chose to admit it or not; and he said that in matters of conscience no civil authority had any power—no wonder the powers-that-be thought him a dangerous man!) Because of his own belief in free-thinking, he dedicated his new settlement of Providence to the proposition that all people should have freedom of conscience. A good number came from Massachusetts, and others came directly from England, to the new colony. Williams had bought the land for the town from the Narragansett Indians, and he remained on very good terms with them, even writing a book on their language which was published and sold in England.

Providence became the first colony to declare independence from England, in May 1776. After the Revolutionary War it took over from Newport the position as the state's most important seaport. It's still an important port, and its industries of textiles, machine tools, rubber, jewelry, and boatbuilding also contribute to its prosperity.

The telephone area code for all of Rhode Island is (401). The sales tax is 6%. Some municipalities levy a room tax (2% to 3%) as well.

GETTING THERE: Getting to Providence couldn't be easier, whether you're going by car or public transport.

By Car

I-95, which in Connecticut is the Connecticut Turnpike, goes right through the center of Providence on its way between New York and Boston; right downtown I-195 branches off to go through Fall River (turnoff for Newport), New Bedford, and then on to Cape Cod. *Note on Parking:* Street parking in Providence is scarce, and meters are checked frequently. The center of town has lots of private pay lots, which it is best to use if you park downtown. Otherwise, park on a side street on College Hill, where there's plenty of shade and no time limit.

By Rail

The station (tel. 401/751-5416) in Providence is smack in the middle of town, almost on Kennedy Plaza. Ten trains a day in each direction pass through on their way between New York and Boston. Travel time from New York is less than four hours; from Boston, about an hour. You could, if you want, take an early-morning train from New York, get off in Providence, and stroll around downtown and College Hill for several hours, have lunch, get back on the train and be in Boston by four in the afternoon.

By Bus

The **Bonanza Bus Station** (tel. 401/751-8800) is a block from the railroad station. (**Greyhound** uses this same terminal.) Bonanza and Greyhound run buses to Providence from New York City, Boston, Newport, Hartford, Cape Cod, Springfield (Mass.), and Albany. Travel time from New York is about four hours; from Boston it's one hour. A bus from Providence to Newport takes just over an hour; to Cape Cod (Hyannis) the trip takes an hour and a half.

By Air

Rhode Island is so compact that one airport handles all the important national flights: **T. F. Green State Airport** in Warwick, just a few miles south of Providence. USAir, American, Eastern, Pan Am, and United fly here. **Newport Aero** shuttles passengers from T. F. Green to Newport and New York's La Guardia. From the airport you'll have to take a taxi to the center of Providence.

WHERE TO STAY: Most people who visit Providence stay in motels on the outskirts of town as these offer the best value and the greatest selection, although staying out of the center entails driving and parking problems. Providence does have a choice place to stay right downtown, plus a few of the familiar and comfortable chain hotels.

Downtown

Right on Kennedy Plaza in the center of Providence is the newly restored **Biltmore Plaza Hotel** (tel. 401/421-0700, or toll free 800/228-2121), Providence, RI 02903. The Plaza was the most elegant hotel in Providence when it was built in 1922, and after the recent $14-million renovation, it's Providence's poshest place to stay once again. Of the 350 rooms and suites, a hundred have their own wet bars and lounge areas; 14 are designed especially for the handicapped. If you knew the Plaza before, you'll hardly recognize it now, as much has been changed, although the outstanding features of 1920s elegance have been carefully preserved. Even the facade has seen a change, for now a glass-enclosed elevator starts from the hotel lobby, penetrates the three-story-high lobby ceiling, and glides up the side of the 18-floor hotel to the top, where L'Apogee (the Biltmore's elegant restaurant, described below) awaits diners. Rooms at the Biltmore, sister hotel to Boston's Copley Plaza, cost $75 to $99 single, $86 to $110 double, with the highest prices going for the luxurious rooms described above. But here's a secret: a handful of small, twin-bedded rooms go for even less. Normally the reservation clerk won't mention these. Ask about them.

Another centrally located hotel is the downtown **Providence Holiday Inn,** at 21 Atwells Ave., Providence, RI 02903 (tel. 401/831-3900), right next to the new Civic Center. The 13-story hotel has 284 rooms, a restaurant, a lounge with live entertainment, and a small indoor pool. Because of its location next to the Civic Center, many of the stars who give concerts in the center stay here, as do conventioneers attending gatherings in the center. The bus and train stations are less than half a mile away. Rooms cost $55 to $68 single, $60 to $73 double; if a couple takes the highest priced room (with two double beds), teenage children or younger can stay in the same room for free—if there's no convention in town.

On the Outskirts

Most of Providence's hotel capacity is on the outskirts of greater Providence, in the neighboring cities of Warwick near the airport to the south, Pawtucket to the north toward Boston on I-95, and Seekonk, Mass., on I-195, the road to Cape Cod. As most of these hotels and motels are right off the highway, it would be good to pick them according to your plans for *tomorrow:* if it's evening as you approach Providence, stay in Warwick and then see Providence the next day; if it's early in the day, tour through Providence and then head out I-95 to Pawtucket if your next stop is Boston, or I-195 to Seekonk if you're headed for Cape Cod. You can call for a reservation while you're seeing the sights in Providence.

Warwick has one of the five **Howard Johnson's Motor Lodges** in the Providence area. This one is at 20 Jefferson Blvd., Warwick, RI 02888 (tel. 401/467-9800, or toll free 800/654-2000), which is at Exit 15 of I-95, near T. F. Green State Airport. There's a 24-hour restaurant, a lounge with entertainment, and a variety of package plans which can save you lots of money, particularly on weekends. Seniors get a discount; kids under 18 stay for free. Rates are $53 to $65 single, $55 to $68 double. Package plans give it to you for less, though.

In Pawtucket your best bet is the local **Howard Johnson's Motor Lodge,** a stone's throw off I-95 (Exit 27) at 2 George St., Pawtucket, RI 02860 (tel. 401/723-6700, or toll free 800/654-2000). One of the more expensive hotels on the outskirts, the lodge charges $47 to $62 single, $55 to $71 double; an extra person is $8. Children under 18 can use their parents' room for free, which means up to four people can sleep for $71. The lodge has an indoor heated pool, a sauna, and an adjacent Hojo's restaurant open 24 hours a day.

In Seekonk, Mass., there are several good lodging possibilities. Note that you have a different telephone area code to contend with if you're calling from Rhode Island. Take Exit 114A from I-195 for these.

A family-run set of motels in Seekonk, operated by the Darling family, are on U.S. 6 near the intersection of Alternate Route 114 (114-A), Seekonk, MA 02771. The **Esquire** and **Town 'n' Country Motels** are right across the highway from one another (tel. 617/336-9000) and share an outdoor pool, open during the warm months. Rooms are brightly painted and have individual air-conditioning units. The motels also share a putting green, coffeeshop, and cocktail lounge, as well as Eileen Darling's Restaurant. Rates for the rooms are $25.50 for one double bed, $30 for two double beds—one of the better bargains in the area.

Next best bet is the **Howard Johnson's Motor Lodge** in Seekonk (tel. 617/336-7800, or toll free 800/654-2000), at the intersection of I-195 and Route 114-A, 821 Fall River Ave., Seekonk, MA 02771. Facilities and rates are very similar to those in the Pawtucket Lodge mentioned above, but rooms with one bed (accommodating one or two people) are cheaper here: $37 to $42 single, $42 to $47 double. In the winter (November through April) special weekend package rates are offered. The lodge has no restaurant of its own, but there are several nearby.

There is also a **Ramada Inn** here, very close to the Howard Johnson's at 940 Fall River Ave., Seekonk, MA 02771 (which is Route 114-A; tel. 617/336-7300, or toll free 800/228-2828). The Ramada is structured and priced very competitively with the Howard Johnson's, with pool, sauna, lounge with live entertainment, and a children's playground, all costing $47 single, $58 double; kids 18 and under stay free.

In the cluster of motels at the intersection of U.S. 6 and Route 114-A is a **Susse Chalet Inn**, at 341 Highland Ave., Seekonk, MA 02771 (tel. 617/336-7900, or toll free 800/258-1980). Susse Chalet is a fairly new budget motel chain in New England offering good, clean, new rooms with all the usual conveniences—TV, air conditioning, a pool (outdoor), an ice machine—but at budget prices such as $28.31 single, $32.56 double, with all rooms having luxuries such as color TV, a reclining chair (in single rooms), and a worktable. The Susse Chalets are particularly good for families because a family of four can stay in a normal room with two double beds for $39, making the cost per person a mere $9.75. The good value at these places is unmistakable.

WHERE TO DINE: Providence's sophisticated university crowd generates a need for good restaurants, and Providence has plenty. Not all of them are up on College Hill, however.

The Biltmore Plaza's rooftop restaurant, **L'Apogee** (tel. 421-0700), is aptly named as it sits atop the 18-story hotel. The menu is classic French-American: steaks and seafood and fowl all elegantly prepared, rich and expensive, with a sweeping view of the city to match. You might start with a half dozen oysters and go on to filet de boeuf Diane (a tenderloin steak, flamed at your table) or to the quenelles (fish "dumplings") which are made here with salmon rather than the traditional pike, and served with a lobster sauce. Strawberries Romanoff are good for dessert, but cakes, tarts, and pastries are less expensive. The wine list runs to 87 items: lots of château-bottled vintages at $25 to $30 and up per bottle, but also plenty of French, German, Italian, and American wines at $12 and $14 a bottle. Expect to spend $25 to $40 per person, all in. Most of the tables at L'Apogee are at window-side, and all have the marvelous view of Rhode Island's gleaming white Capitol. Come for a weekday lunch (noon to 2:30 p.m.), dinner (6 to 10 p.m.), or for Saturday or Sunday brunch (11:30 a.m. to 3 p.m.). You can have a drink in the bar—with that fantastic view—for $2 to $3.

Goddard's (tel. 421-0700), on the ground floor of the Biltmore Plaza, is much less formal than L'Apogee. Here the surroundings are very turn-of-the-century, with globe lamps, wicker furniture, ferns, and awnings to simulate the ambience of a Paris or New York—or Providence—café 80 years ago. Salads, soups, and stews fill the menu, most $5 or less, although there are a few main-course plates. Goddard's is open from 7 to 11 a.m. Monday through Friday for breakfast, 11:30 a.m. to 11:30 p.m. Monday through Friday for lunch and dinner (same menu); from 6 to 11:30 p.m. Saturday, closed Sunday.

Providence consumes almost as much succulent seafood as Newport, and a lot of the best seafood in Providence disappears at **Bluepoint** (tel. 272-6145), an oyster bar and restaurant at 99 North Main St., corner of Elizabeth, just by the rusty iron railroad bridge. The one-room restaurant, with the oyster-and-spirits bar on the right as you enter, is usually filled with a classy young clientele talking and perforating the dart board by the bar, but mostly eating. The clam chowder comes red Provençal (with tomatoes) or New England (with cream and potatoes) for $2. Oysters, a half dozen of any variety of your choice on the half shell, are $3.50; littleneck and cherrystone clams are a bit less. The list of main courses on the blackboard is very short because the daily specials are what most people order. The specials, whether they be squid, grilled prawns, swordfish, bluefish, or scallops, constitute the best and freshest seafood at the lowest price. Dinner will cost about $15 per person here, a bit more if you drink lots of wine or beer, a bit less if you order carefully. Bluepoint is an easy walk from downtown, and is open 11:30 a.m. to 3 p.m. on weekdays for lunch Monday through Saturday, from 6 to 11 p.m. (to 11:30 p.m. on Friday and Saturday) for dinner, noon to 11 p.m. Sunday; and the bar is open from 5 p.m. to 1 a.m. daily.

Good Chinese cuisine is always a delight, but oftentimes this is because it's savory, plentiful, and inexpensive. At the **Ming Garden**, 68 Kennedy Plaza (tel. 751-1700), the food is delicately prepared as well. Rather than the standard Chinese restaurant decoration which makes great use of deep red colors and imported doodads, the Ming Garden's decor is spare and beautiful, with light natural-finish wood and Oriental pictures. Chinese music plays softly in the air. When you first look at the menu, you may be bewildered because of its length, but after you've paged through the sections on chicken, beef, seafood, teriyaki, Cantonese dishes, and combination plates (these last are disappointing), you'll come to the "Deluxe Gourmet" main-course listing. Here, dishes cost about $11—much more than most items in the menu—but for the premium price one gets premium food. The Ming Garden is open Sunday through Friday from 11:30 a.m. to 10:30 p.m. (last service); on Saturday it opens at noon and serves until 11:30 p.m. Liquor is served.

Another fine place for lunch or dinner is about ten blocks from Brown University. It's French in character and French in name: **Rue de L'Espoir**, at 99 Hope St. (tel. 751-8890), and it's open daily except Monday (Tuesday through Sunday, 11:30 a.m. to 2:30 p.m.; Saturday and Sunday brunch served). The menu offers perfect things for a light French-style lunch: several types of quiche, their own pâté, omelets, crêpes, salads, and portions of cheese and bread—all in the $4 to $6 range. Fare at dinner includes filet mignon, brochettes, fish terrines, roast pork loins; prices are a bit higher, with several dinner plates priced at about $6.25 to $9. A full bar is available.

For Light Meals Downtown. . .

For a good light lunch, supper, or snack anytime, try **Duck Soup** (tel. 331-3555), 74 Dorrance St. near the corner of Weybosset, just two blocks from Kennedy Plaza, open from 7 a.m. to 7 p.m. every day (Thursday till 8 p.m., Saturday till 6 p.m.). Duck Soup is Providence's New York delicatessen-in-residence and features fresh bagels and cream cheese ($1.30), New York cheesecake, a selection of soups and sandwiches ($3 to $4), and salads that are meals in themselves. Duck Soup is a small, attractive place decorated in light wood tones with lots of hanging plants. It's pretty crowded (but what a crowd!) between noon and 1 p.m. Wine and beer are served.

For breakfast or lunch, try **Tommy's**, in the Arcade, 130 Westminster St., just after the eastern end of the Westminster Mall. The Arcade building is a sight in itself (see below). It's an extremely friendly place, with a lunch counter, tables and booths, and small "outdoor" tables set out in the Arcade for lunch or afternoon pastry and tea. The decor is modern and comfy, the service is fast, friendly, and considerate, and the selection of sandwiches is encyclopedic: everything from Greek souvlaki to eggplant parmesan (in a sandwich!). Sandwiches cost $2.75 to $5.50, slightly more with french fries and coleslaw. Full breakfasts, and hot luncheon plates are also available, as are pastries freshly made on the premises. Tommy's is open from 7 a.m. to 4:30 p.m.; lunch is served outside from noon onward.

. . .And up on College Hill

Don't let the rather posh exterior of **La Serre**, 182 Angell St., corner of Thayer (tel. 331-3312), put you off. It's even posher inside, with candlelit little tables in the glassed-in sunporch looking onto the sidewalk, and an upbeat inside dining room with mod lights, prints, posters, and flashy colors to charm any RISD student. But the prices are meant to appeal to students and young faculty, and about the most you can spend for lunch or dinner here, even if you have wine or beer, is $15. The most expensive item on the menu is the sirloin or scallops at $7.75; all else is less expensive salads, quiches, sandwiches, omelets, hamburgers, and a few daily special meals (often seafood) priced under $8. Come for lunch (from 11:30 a.m. on; from 10 a.m. for Sunday brunch) or dinner. La Serre stays open until 11 p.m. most nights, till 1 a.m. on Friday and Saturday.

WHAT TO SEE: Preservation and urban redevelopment have done much to make Providence a delightful place to walk in today. The most interesting districts are small enough that you can make your way around on foot. For an expert look at Providence's historical treasures, consider the following:

Walking tours

Every morning from May through October, the Providence Preservation Society (tel. 831-7440) organizes two guided tours, one of College Hill, with special emphasis on the restored 18th- and 19th-century houses along Benefit Street, the sights of South Main Street, and the waterfront. Find your way to 24 Meeting St. at 10 a.m. on Monday through Saturday. The second tour, leaving May through October at 2 p.m. from the third floor of the Three for All Arcade (65 Weybosset St.), will cover the downtown area. Call for information on Sunday tours. Each tour lasts about 1½ hours, and costs $2.50 for adults, $1 for children. Neither tour is available on holidays.

Seeing Providence, Old and New

The place to start touring Providence is **Kennedy Plaza,** in the center of town. Shady trees and benches make the plaza an oasis in the middle of the city, and an equestrian statue of Gen. Ambrose Burnside, the Civil War officer whose long side whiskers were the first "sideburns," watches over the eastern end of the plaza. **City Hall** is at the other end, an agreeable Second Empire building completed in 1878 (go inside to see a wall display of other entries in the competition for the city hall design).

From Kennedy Plaza to College Hill

Go one block southeast from the plaza to reach the **Westminster Mall,** a six-block section of Westminster Street closed to vehicles. The mall is a pleasant place to sit and people-watch, or to stroll down. Just past its eastern end, at 130 Westminster St., is the **Arcade,** which looks like an imaginative bit of urban renewal, but is in fact the creation of Russell Warren and James Bucklin, who designed the building in 1827. For a century and a half some of Providence's better shops have operated in the Arcade. There are three levels of shops topped by a roof of glass panes; one modern addition to the arcade is an elevator to take shoppers to the upper floors. Besides Tommy's restaurant (mentioned above), the Arcade has stores selling antiques, jewelry, rare books, fine tobaccos, cosmetics, and other luxury items. Shops are all robin's-egg blue with gold-lettered signs, and decorative cast-iron balustrades and stairways remind one of the Arcade's early 19th-century construction. Look at both facades—on Westminster Street and on Weybosset—which clearly show that each architect had his own idea of how the facade should look. With two facades, each got his chance to do what he wanted.

Walk through the Arcade from Westminster Street to Weybosset Street, and turn right to get to Providence's historic **"Round Top" Church**—you'll see its golden dome in the distance. The church, officially known as the Beneficent Congregational Meeting House, got its name because of its dome, which is a departure from the usual New England church spire. Finished in 1810, it was influenced by the classical revival then going on in Europe. The interior is as pleasant to look at as the exterior: besides the gracious New England meeting-house furnishings, the Round Top Church has a crystal chandelier consisting of almost 6000 pieces. (Enter by the door on the side, around to the right.)

Now head northeast down Weybosset, past the Arcade, to the intersection of this street with Westminster and Exchange. Here in front of the Hospital Trust Bank activities and shows are held during the warm months, perhaps a Boy Scouts' display of fancy marching or a small (but highly amplified) jazz combo giving a lunch-hour concert.

College Hill

Walk two more blocks east and you will cross the Providence River to the foot of **College Hill.** The hill is the prettiest section of the city, its streets lined with 18th- and 19th-century houses, most of which have been well preserved or restored, many of which bear plaques put up by the Providence Preservation Society giving the builder's name and the date of construction. At the bottom of College Hill, on South Main Street between Thomas and Waterman Streets, take a stroll past the **First Baptist Meetinghouse.** Roger Williams founded the first Baptist congregation in the New World in 1638, but this building dates from 1775. The architect was Joseph Brown, and the steeple—designed from a plate in James Gibbs's *Book of Architecture* representing suggested steeples for St. Martin-in-the-Fields in London—rises to a height of 185 feet. It's one of the outstanding churches in New England, and a guide will take you through for free between the hours of 10 a.m. and 3 p.m. Monday through Friday, and 10 a.m. to noon on Saturday, and at noon on Sunday following the weekly church service. Between November and March, the church is open daily, but guides are available only by appointment. Call 751-2266 for an appointment. The front door of the church will probably be locked, so go around to the right to the side (office) door.

To the left of the church, at 7 Thomas St., is a fantastic old building with half-timbering and stucco bas-reliefs on its facade. This is **Sidney Burleigh's "Fleur de Lys" house,** built by this Providence artist in 1885 (the date is in the stucco). Thomas Street might be called "artist' row," because very near Burleigh's house is the Providence Art Club, at no. 11, which is open from 10 a.m. to 4 p.m. (3 to 5 p.m. on Sunday), with changing shows exhibited in its galleries. The Providence Watercolor Club is also on Thomas Street.

At the intersection of Thomas and Benefit Streets, turn right and go south on Benefit for a block to the **Museum of Art of the Rhode Island School of Design** (tel. 331-6363), at 224 Benefit St. RISD's museum is Providence's finest, and one of the best small museums in the country, with collections from Greece and Rome, China and Japan, paintings by Manet, Monet, Degas, Cézanne, Matisse, as well as by other masters, and a good collection of American painting, furniture, costumes, and modern works of art. Of the choicest pieces in this impressive collection, Rodin's famous statue of Balzac ranks high, as does Monet's *Bassin d'Argenteuil* and the collection of Townsend/Goddard furniture in Pendleton House, an adjunct to the museum. You can see all this for

$1 for adults, 25¢ for children and youths (5 to 18), free for small children. The museum is always closed Monday. *Special note:* Admission is *free* on Saturday. Otherwise, hours are rather complicated. From mid-June through August, hours are 11 a.m. to 4 p.m. on Wednesday through Saturday; the rest of the year, the museum is open Tuesday, Wednesday, Friday, and Saturday from 10:30 a.m. to 5 p.m., Thursday from 1 to 9 p.m., Sunday from 2 to 5 p.m.

The **Rhode Island School of Design** is one of the country's best art, architecture, and design schools (founded in 1877), and it shares College Hill with **Brown University,** a member of the Ivy League (founded in 1764—Brown is the seventh-oldest college in the U.S.). You can visit Brown's University Hall (built in 1770) on weekdays; campus tours begin at 10 and 11 a.m. and 1, 3, and 4 p.m. University Hall is a National Historic Landmark. To get to it, walk up the hill (east) on Waterman Street, cross Prospect Street, and turn into the gates on your right.

RISD, known in Providence as "RIZ-dee," has another attractive building besides its museum dedicated to the display of art. It's the **Woods-Gerry Mansion,** 62 Prospect St., which was built between 1860 and 1864 and now serves as RISD's administration building and gallery for students' works of art. Admission is free and the galleries are open Monday through Saturday from 11 a.m. to 4 p.m., Sunday from 2 to 4 p.m. (except in summer when they're open weekdays only). The big old brick-and-brownstone mansion is empty of its plush furnishings now, but parquet floors and gorgeous marble fireplaces give an idea of what it must have been like, and the high-ceiling rooms with large windows provide perfect space for exhibiting students' efforts: drawings, paintings, sculpture, or what-have-you, all guaranteed to be the most *avant* of the avant-garde. The grounds of the mansion are covered with grand shade trees and rhododendron bushes (which bloom in late June and early July), and dotted with pieces of sculpture and benches for a welcome rest.

Another RISD building open to the public is the **Bayard Ewing Building,** 231 South Main St., which houses RISD's architectural division. Exhibits here change frequently, and feature architectural and industrial design.

Prospect Street is so named because it passes near **Prospect Terrace** (go north a block from Woods-Gerry House to Cushing Street and turn left). From the Terrace, a small park, you can see downtown Providence and the State Capitol, along with a famous but—pardon me—rather wooden statue of the founder, Roger Williams. His grave is here as well. Trees have grown up below and block a bit of the perspective, but the view is still panoramic and impressive.

College Hill has lots of other places to see including many historic houses. Once of the fanciest of these is the **John Brown House** (tel. 331-8575), 52 Power St. at Benefit Street, a late-Georgian, or Federal, building constructed in 1786 and now used as the headquarters of the Rhode Island Historical Society. Proclaimed by John Quincy Adams to be "the most magnificent and elegant private mansion that I have seen on this continent," this restored house-museum reveals the prosperity of post-Revolutionary Providence and houses an outstanding collection of furnishings and decorative arts. The museum gallery at the rear of the house holds changing exhibitions relating to Rhode Island history. John Brown was a merchant whose ships plied the seas both east and west out of Narragansett Bay and ultimately made him a wealthy man. The Brown family, by the way, had been prominent in Providence commerce and industry since the early 1700s. John's brother Moses joined with Samuel Slater to set up the first water-powered cotton mill in America in 1790, now known as Slater Mill (see below). One of his nephews, Nicholas Brown, was a graduate of Rhode Island College, which was later renamed Brown

College (and later, University) in his honor. John Brown House is open Tuesday through Saturday from 11 a.m. to 4 p.m., Sunday from 1 to 4 p.m., closed holidays. Admission and guided tour costs $2.50 for adults, $1 for seniors and students.

The State Capitol

Rhode Island government was conducted in the Old State House (1762), on North Main Street between North and South Court Streets from 1762 to 1895 when the new State Capitol building was dedicated. The Capitol is a pleasant sight, its tall dome floating over the Providence skyline, its white Georgia marble gleaming in the sun. Whether it is "the most beautiful in the country," as the state's tourist brochures claim, might be disputed by admirers of 49 other such capitols, but certainly it is one of the more beautiful. Enter by the portal on Smith Street (Route 44) to see display cases filled with battle flags from the state's proud military units which served in the Civil War, Spanish-American War, and the World Wars. Here also is a cannon which was used in the Civil War and was hit right in the muzzle by another cannon's ball. When the crew tried to charge the cannon again, they put the powder and wad in and first they couldn't get the ball in; then they couldn't get the ball *out*. The gun was retired, but it was only in the 1960s, when the cannon had been here in the Capitol for decades, that someone remembered that the gunpowder charge was still in it! So after 100 years of having been loaded and ready, the Civil War charge was removed. Beyond the cannons is the rich, gleaming marble interior and hallways decorated with paintings of the founding fathers of Rhode Island and Providence Plantations. Free tours of the capitol are offered on weekdays from 9 a.m. to 4:30 p.m. (last tour at 3:30). It's worth seeing.

Sights on the Outskirts

Two more places to visit lie a few miles outside the center of town. **Roger Williams Park** is south of the city on Elmwood Avenue (Exit 17 from I-95), and boasts magnificently restored 19th-century Victorian buildings, the **Charles E. Smith Greenhouses,** a museum of natural history, zoo, and amusement area besides its 430 acres of beautifully kept lawns, copses, lakes, and paths. The park is open to the public for free, and special concerts and programs are scheduled throughout the summer—call 401/785-9450 for the latest information on these. The zoo, by the way, is open every day from 10 a.m. to 4 p.m.

Water-powered cotton and textile mills changed all of New England in the 19th century, and it all started in Pawtucket, a few miles from downtown Providence. In 1793 three enterprising men named Slater, Almy, and Brown set up the first water-powered cotton-spinning factory in America, on the Blackstone River. Today the early mills and the **Sylvanus Brown House** (1758), home of the skilled artisan, make up the **Slater Mill Historic Site.** The mills have many of their old machines in working order, and you can see them in action, such as the water wheel, shafts, and pulleys in **Wilkinson Mill.** Earlier handicraft devices for doing the same jobs are also on display to show you what a breakthrough the machine-filled stone mill was. Besides the permanent exhibits, traveling and temporary displays are set up from time to time, and guided tours interpret the history of the textile industry, and the impact of factories on working conditions. Admission is $2.50 for adults, $1 for children 6 through 14. It's open in summer Memorial Day to Labor Day Monday through Saturday from 10 a.m. to 5 p.m., Sunday from 1 to 5 p.m.; in spring and fall it's open on weekends from 1 to 5 p.m., but closed in January and February. To get there, take I-95 north from Providence, get off at Exit 28, and turn left (under the highway) onto School Street. Cross the Blackstone River and turn right into Roosevelt Avenue, and the site is on your right.

2. Newport

Whatever glittering reports you've had of Newport, they're probably correct, because Newport is a fascinating, diverse place. Palatial mansions, the wealthy yachting set, major naval and Coast Guard installations, tennis tournaments, cocktails on marble terraces in the soft air of a summer's evening, or succulent seafood served in a waterfront restaurant—Newport is all of these.

Newport has enjoyed prominence during two periods in American history: in colonial times it was an important trade center, and so, like Salem, Mass., it has a lovely colonial section right downtown, much of which has been restored authentically in the styles of centuries ago; and in the mid-19th century, it became a resort for the very wealthy, who built what are indeed palaces in another part of town. Newport preserves remembrances of this past while pursuing its future as one of New England's prime vacation destinations: people who own yachts and people who can only afford to look at yachts, people who play tennis and those who watch it, people who live in mansions and others who take guided tours through mansions—they all flock to Newport. Besides the visitors, Newport is home to tens of thousands of Rhode Islanders who take all the glamor and glitter for granted, and who live here year round.

Several things are important to remember when you're planning a visit to Newport. First, it is crowded in summer, particularly on weekends, and when the important tennis tournaments and yacht races are being held. Second, it is fairly expensive (but certainly not outrageous), and prices tend to go up on weekends and when the yachtsmen are around. Third, Newport prides itself on having style, and many visitors will be dressed like movie stars; many restaurants, cocktail lounges, and hotels require "proper" dress at dinner, and perhaps even lunch: jacket, or jacket and tie for men, skirt and top or pants suit, or similar attire, for women.

HISTORY: Newport is at the southern tip of an island which the Indians called Aquidneck, and which the colonial settlers dubbed Rhode Island. As Providence was settled by Roger Williams, dissident from Salem, so Newport was founded by one William Coddington, who decided to strike out on his own from Providence in 1639. The new town soon became famous for shipbuilding, and as soon as the ships were built in sufficient numbers, for trade. The famous "triangle trade," from Newport to ports in the West Indies and Africa would later bring great wealth to the town from the buying and selling of slaves, rum, molasses, and other goods. Because Providence and Newport were founded by dissidents, they became places of refuge for others wishing to worship as they pleased: Quakers from England, Jews from Portugal and Spain, and Baptists all came to Newport in the mid-1600s to find religious freedom. They brought talent and a gift for hard work, and the settlement prospered so that it became the colony's most important town, and one of the New World's busiest ports. The many beautiful colonial homes, the handsome Old Colony House (center of government), Touro Synagogue, and other landmarks attest to the wealth and prosperity of Newport at the time.

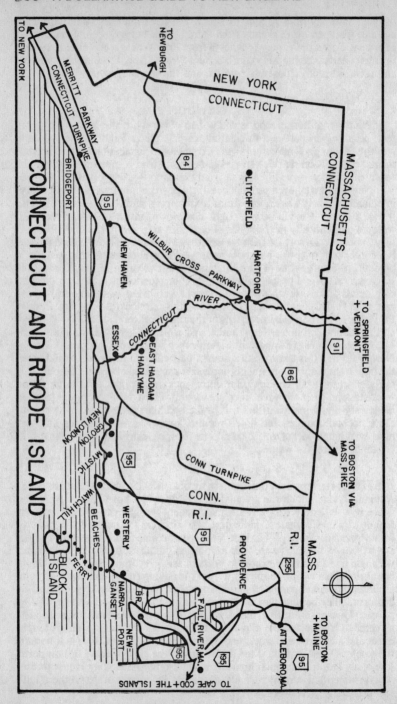

During the American Revolution the British occupied the town and its excellent harbor, and held it for three years. A British frigate, H.M.S. *Rose,* did much to hinder the transport of supplies to the Americans, and spurred them to found the U.S. Navy in retaliation. Despite a French naval blockade and an American siege, the British held onto Newport until 1779, and after this interruption in its social and economic life, Newport never regained its former status as Rhode Island's prime trade center.

Several decades later, however, it achieved prominence in another fashion. Drawn by the beautiful woods and dramatic coastline, wealthy merchants from New York and Philadelphia began to come to Newport to spend their summers. In the mid-1800s, the first of Newport's famous mansions, Château-sur-Mer, was built, and others followed until Newport's Bellevue Avenue and Ocean Drive could boast the highest concentration of summer palaces—and they are *palaces*—anywhere in the world.

Today the city's symbol is the pineapple, a sign of welcome left from Newport's great commercial era when traders back from West Indies with this fruit would put a pineapple outside their warehouses to invite customers to come in and look over the stock. Newport is used to welcoming visitors, and with the hints and recommendations given below, you should have no trouble finding your way around and having a good time without going over your budget.

GETTING THERE: Newport is served by bus, boat, and air taxi service.

By Bus: Bonanza Bus Lines serves Newport, with a terminal slightly out of town at Cote Pharmacy, 104 Broadway (tel. 401/846-1820); Bonanza works in concert with Greyhound Lines, and has frequent daily buses from Boston to Newport (2 hours), Providence to Newport (1 hour), and New York to Newport (5½ hours).

By Boat: There are daily boats between Providence, Newport, and Block Island. See Block Island section for details.

By Air: Several national and regional airlines fly into T. F. Green State Airport in Warwick, and from there you can take a Newport Aero flight (tel. 401/253-5161) to Newport State Airport. Newport Aero also operates to La Guardia Airport in New York. From Newport State Airport you'll have to take a taxi into town.

GETTING YOUR BEARINGS: On the island of Rhode Island there are three main towns: Portsmouth in the north, Newport at the southern end, and Middletown in between. Newport and Middletown are so close that many visitors to Newport stay in motels in Middletown and then drive the mile or two into Newport to see the sights. The two most important streets in Newport are **Thames Street** (pronounced "Thaymz," *not* "Temz"), center of the colonial section, the wharves, and most of modern downtown; and **Bellevue Avenue,** parallel to Thames but south and east of it. Bellevue is the street with many of the old mansions on it. Free maps and information are handed out by the **Newport County Chamber of Commerce** office, 10 America's Cup Ave., Newport, RI 02840 (tel. 401/847-1600). They're open from 9 a.m. to 5 p.m. every day in summer; weekends in winter from 9 a.m. to 4 p.m. Get help here if you're stuck without a reservation and can't find a room. America's Cup Avenue is parallel to Thames Street and runs right along the water downtown. If you'd like them to send you information on Newport, they're ready to do so: send your request to the Newport County Chamber of Commerce, P.O. Box 237TB, Newport, RI 02840.

WHERE TO STAY: There aren't a great many places to stay in downtown Newport, and so at least half of all visitors who come here stay in Middletown. But it's very nice to be right downtown, and I'd recommend that you try to find a place there first. Accommodations in Newport are of two types: fairly expensive modern hotels, costing around—or over—$100 double per night; and charming bed-and-breakfast guest houses. You can guess my preference!

Guest Houses

Other than the expensive downtown hotels, and the expensive inns on Ocean Drive, accommodations in Newport consist of guest houses—private homes which have been converted to hostelries with varying degrees of luxury and charm. It's important to stress that because guest houses offer the most inexpensive accommodations in Newport, and because they are limited in number (and each one of that limited number only has a dozen rooms or less), it is best to reserve a room in advance. But lest I be too discouraging, let me say that it is often possible to find a room on the spur of the moment, and if you're in need, you should try phoning around. It's safe to say that anyone arriving in Newport on a Saturday evening in July or August will almost certainly not find a room available, though. Come during the week, and arrive early in the day for a better crack at what's available.

The **Newport Chamber of Commerce** (tel. 401/847-1600) has a nice long list of bed-and-breakfast guest houses and small inns. Send for it if you have the time; pick one up when you arrive if you don't; or call and ask for their help in locating a room. Note that Rhode Island has a 6% sales tax, and that a 3% Newport rooms tax is also applied to prices in establishments with ten or more rooms.

Two guest houses, perhaps Newport's finest, stand side-by-side on a short, quiet dead-end street not far off of Memorial Boulevard, Newport's main east-west road. The venerable **Bella Vista Guest Manor,** 1 Seaview Ave., corner of Cliff Avenue, Newport, RI 02840 (tel. 401/847-4262), has been a refuge for guests for almost four decades. Rosamond Hendel and Alice Simpson like to make their guests feel like part of the family. The large three-story white shingle house dates from before the turn of the century, when it was built for Governor Franklin of Pennsylvania. It's surrounded by trees and lawns in a residential neighborhood, and is therefore very quiet—all you hear when sitting out on the broad veranda, comfortably furnished with white wicker, are the birds and the surf. Rooms are simply furnished with various pieces old and new, but the beds are always kept in good condition. Prices for the rooms can vary from $31.80 to $42.40 for two off-season to $37.10 to $53 for two in high season. At the Bella Vista, you're only four houses away from the Cliff Walk, and five minutes from the beach.

Right next door to the Bella Vista, across Seaview Avenue, is the **Cliffside Inn,** 2 Seaview Ave., Newport, RI 02840 (tel. 401/847-1811), owned by a painter named Beatrice Pasatorius Turner until about a decade ago. Many of the antique furnishings dating from the time when the house was built as a summer cottage for Governor Swann of Maryland in 1880 are still here, and the house exudes *unfaded* Victorian charm. A few rooms have private showers and rent for $44 to $61 in season (May through October); the others have shower and tub and rent for $66 to $72, depending on furnishings, size, and

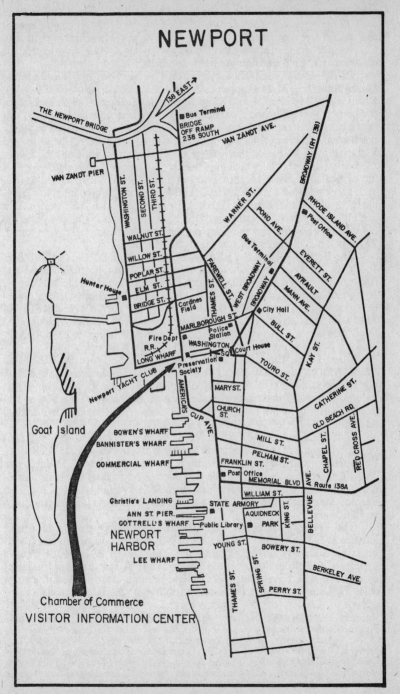

NEWPORT

view. To get to the Cliffside and the Bella Vista, take America's Cup Avenue or Bellevue Avenue to Memorial Boulevard (Route 138A), follow Memorial east to Cliff Avenue, which is before you get to Newport Beach; turn right onto Cliff Avenue and go the two short blocks to Seaview Avenue. As you turn left onto Seaview, Cliffside is on your left, the Bella Vista on your right.

Of the several guest houses downtown in Newport, my favorite is the **Queen Anne Inn,** at 16 Clarke St., Newport, RI 02840 (tel. 401/846-5676), which is a half block off Touro Street at Washington Square, two blocks from the harbor, in the Historic District. The Queen Anne advertises that you can "park your car in our lot and walk to everything," which is true of everything downtown, and even of the mansions if you're a good walker. One of the old Victorian town houses (rather than a wooden summer mansion) the Queen Anne has a dozen rooms which have been totally redone in a cheerful way with lots of nice little antique touches. Prices at present are $37.10 to $58.30 double, and there's one single at $26.50; seven baths are shared. Complimentary continental breakfast is served. The Queen Anne has its own patio and garden. You can't miss the place: headquarters of the Newport Artillery Company and the old Clarke Street Meetinghouse are right across the street. Open year round. There is a minimum stay of two nights all summer.

The **Brinley Victorian,** 23 Brinley St., Newport, RI 02840 (tel. 401/849-7645), is a lovely Victorian house on a quiet street. Follow Catherine Street east from the big old Viking Hotel, and look for Brinley Street on the left (north). Antiques and thoughtful little touches characterize the Brinley, and a home-baked continental breakfast is served. Rates are $59 double with shared bath, $64 to $75 with private bath; there's also a room with kitchen (shared bath) for $70. There's a two-day minimum on weekends, three days on holiday weekends—this is pretty much standard policy in Newport.

Guest House International, 28 Weaver Ave., Newport, RI 02840 (tel. 401/847-1501), is a comfy old house in a middle-income residential district. A block behind the Tennis Hall of Fame on Bellevue Avenue, it's quite convenient to everything, and inexpensive in the bargain: doubles rent for $34 to $55 (shared bath), or as low as $220 per week. Continental breakfast is included, as usual.

Cliff View Cottage, 4 Cliff Terrace, Newport, RI 02840 (tel. 401/846-0885), is convenient to the beach and to Cliff Walk. In fact you can walk along the latter to get to the former; downtown is a ten-minute stroll. Prices in this classy neighborhood are reasonable: $51 double, continental breakfast included. To get there, head for the aforementioned Bella Vista and Cliffside Inn. Cliff Terrace is another of those little dead-end streets off Cliff Avenue leading down to Cliff Walk.

The **Yankee Peddler Inn** (tel. 401/846-1323) has a very fine downtown location at 113 Touro St., Newport, RI 02840. Though you get bed and (continental) breakfast here, you get more than in a simple B&B, as the Yankee Peddler is finely decorated in the old Newport style. A double room with shared bath is $59; with private bath, $80. Suites are more. An extra bed in a room costs $9. Look for the inn at the corner of Spring and Touro Streets.

Readers' Guest House Selection: "For a good bed-and-breakfast accommodation in Newport, within walking distance of shops, docks, and restaurants (and even the beach, if your legs are sturdy), we highly recommend **The Anchorage,** 19 Old Beach Rd., Newport, RI 02840 (tel. 401/849-3479). There are three comfortable air-conditioned guest rooms in this Victorian Gothic house, restored by owners Trudy and Peter Boiani. We paid $45 for a double room with shared bath, and a full American breakfast elegantly served" (Shirley and Martin Burnett, New York, N.Y.).

A Guest House Search List

Because Newport fills up in the summer, and because guest houses have few rooms and tend to fill up, here's an emergency list of names and telephone numbers which will help you find a room when the rooms situation is tight. I'd appreciate reports on new guest houses not described above.

Aboard Commander's Quarters, 54 Dixon St. (tel. 401/849-8393)
Bed and Breakfast, 21 Dearborn St. (tel. 401/846-7716)
Bellevue/New Cliffs, 14 Catherine St. (tel. 401/847-1355)
Calico Cat, 14 Union Ave., Jamestown (tel. 401/423-2641)
Covell House, 43 Farewell St. (tel. 401/847-8872)
Captain Hawkins House, 6 Dean Ave. (tel. 401/846-3734)
LaParles Guest House, 26 Greenough Pl. (tel. 401/846-8124)
Lindsey's Guest House, 6 James St., Middletown (tel. 401/846-9386)
Mount Vernon Inn, 26 Mt. Vernon St. (tel. 401/846-6314)
Spring House, 353 Spring St. (tel. 401/847-4767)
Wayside, Bellevue Avenue (tel. 401/847-0302)
William Fludder House, 30 Bellevue Ave. (tel. 401/849-4220)

Staying on the Outskirts

Middletown has numerous motels which serve tourists and navy personnel coming to visit Newport, many of them located along Route 114, also called West Main Road, which conveniently runs right into Broadway, and then America's Cup Avenue, in Newport.

Middletown is also possessed of a **Howard Johnson's Motor Lodge,** 351 West Main Rd., Route 114/138 (tel. 401/849-2000, or toll free 800/654-2000), Newport, RI 02840. The two-story lodge is new, modern, and large, with all comforts; the restaurant is open 24 hours a day, and of the motels on West Main Road, this is just about the closest to downtown Newport. There's a shiny indoor heated pool, men's and women's saunas, two tennis courts, and plenty of parking. Rates are $58.30 to $69.80 for one or two during summer (May through September). In spring and fall, rates are $46.64 to $59.36 single or double; in winter, $37.10 to $42.40 single, $37.10 to $47.70 double will rent you a room. Accommodations and service are standardized here, and you are sure to get your money's worth.

WHERE TO DINE: As with most things in Newport, dining out here is slightly more expensive than in other New England cities, but with a few hints you'll find it easy to get your money's worth.

Two things to remember: Many restaurants require jacket-and-tie (or at least jacket) formality in the evening; and for the more popular restaurants it's wise to have reservations in advance—even a week in advance if you want a table in one of Newport's "in" places.

Best-Value Restaurants

After a hot morning's sightseeing in Newport, the **Brick Alley Pub and Restaurant** (tel. 849-6334) has just what you want: a cool, shady, quiet place to sit down and have some refreshment. At 140 Thames St., it's right behind the block of shops housing the Chamber of Commerce Information Office. Walk up the passage beside the restaurant and you'll come to a cool, shady courtyard with tables set out. The selection of sandwiches, burgers, salads, and omelets is enormous, all costing about $4 or $5 (for $1.50 more you can have soup and a whack at the salad bar). Open every day for lunch and dinner. There are indoor dining rooms as well.

Another good place for good, moderately priced fare is the **Rhumb Line,** 62 Bridge St. (tel. 849-6950), on the north side of downtown. The menu here goes through the lighter selections and courses all the way to full-course dinners, and there's a full bar. Evenings on weekends, there's live jazz (this draws a crowd—have reservations). Expect to spend about $6 or $7 for lunch (served 11:30 a.m. to 3 p.m.), about $10 to $15 for dinner (5 to 10 or 11 p.m.). Sunday brunch is served from noon to 4 p.m. What's a rhumb line? It's a line on a map or chart showing a constant compass direction straight to the destination. As the name for a restaurant, it could be worse: the same line is also called a loxodromic curve.

Off Bowen's Wharf, but still near the waterfront, **Soups and Crêpes,** at 190A Thames St. (down half a flight) is a shiny bright restaurant specializing in the light lunch or supper made up of the elements which comprise its name. Soups are $1.25 a cup, $1.95 a bowl at lunch and dinner, and include standards such as chowder and vegetable soups, and also crème Olga, the house special, made with fresh scallions and mushrooms. Crêpes in any of various incarnations, omelets, and a soup-and-salad special are priced from $3 to $5. Butcher-block tables, popular music (not loud), and bright colors make Soups and Crêpes a good place for a light meal any day of the week, from 11:30 a.m. to midnight.

For Seafood: You can guess the specialty at the **S.S. Newport** (tel. 401/846-1200), a ship docked on Waites Wharf off Lower Thames Street. The old boat is fixed up nicely but not overfancy, and it's air-conditioned. You can dine in the cool comfort from 11:30 a.m. to 10 p.m. daily, or you can order from the take-out window and eat at the picnic tables. A big fish-and-chips plate to go is an amazingly low $3 (inside it's $4). Lots of sandwiches, clams, squid, and other dishes, even steaks (for $5 to $8), are served, as are alcoholic drinks. You have to walk a bit (or drive) down Lower Thames Street to reach, it, but it's worth the trip.

Nearer into the center of town is **Salas',** 341 Thames St. (tel. 846-8772), on Lower Thames, a half block past the post office. Salas' actually consists of three establishments in one: a fish market and raw bar (open 11 a.m. to 1 a.m.), a brasserie (open for lunch from 11:30 a.m. to 3 p.m.), and the dining room (open from 4 p.m. on for dinner). Lunch could be breaded, fried fish strips with french fries and coleslaw for $3, or any of numerous daily special plates priced from $3 to $5. For dinner there are several set-price meals which offer good value, such as the No. 1 Clambake, a one-pound lobster, clams, corn-on-the-cob, sausage, clam broth, and so forth, for $13.

Slightly Fancier: Lower Thames Street, as you now see, is the place for better food at lower prices. The **Café Zelda,** 528 Thames St., corner of Dean Avenue (tel. 849-4002), adds the simple elegance of a French café atmosphere, plain furnishings of high quality in good taste. The luncheon standards—salads, burgers, quiche—are good and moderately priced, but it's the daily special plates, many featuring crab, which draw the crowds. A bowl of tomato soup, the fish of the day sauteed with almonds and wine, dessert, and a glass of wine could be served to you for $10 or less.

Newport's well-established restaurant is the **Black Pearl** (tel. 846-5264), on Bowen's Wharf right next to the Clarke Cooke House. For lunch and dinner, on weekdays and weekends, the Black Pearl is crowded with the blonde and beautiful, the tanned and handsome. There are actually four places to dine here.

In the Commodore's Room, dinner is served from 6 to 10 p.m., and a jacket is required for men, and similarly suitable dress for women. This is not the busiest of the Pearl's eating places, but rather a refuge from the busy places. Table settings are quietly elegant and include a candle lantern on each table. The decor is subdued and not at all overdone or garish, which is a common fault in many waterfront restaurants. The menu is classic French, with all the familiar dishes of that tradition, and a full meal will cost about $25 with wine. Next to the Commodore's Room is the Tavern, where a jacket is not required, and happy, hungry yachting types press in for a drink, a "Pearlburger," omelets, or perhaps a daily special such as fresh bluefish with lemon caper butter. Outdoors, next to the Black Pearl, are the outdoor bar, a sort of waterfront café, with white metal tables and chairs set out on a patch of white gravel, shaded by brightly colored Cinzano umbrellas, and the Hot Dog Annex.

READER'S RESTAURANT SELECTION: "I found a very good, cheap Mexican restaurant called the **Taco House** (tel. 846-8999) at the corner of Spring Street and Broadway, officially 35 Broadway, in Newport. They have a combination plate for less than $5, soup of the day for less than $1" (Jane Kretchman, Cambridge, Mass.).

Elegant Fare

The **White Horse Tavern,** Marlborough and Farewell Streets, on the north side of downtown (tel. 849-3600), is a Newport institution, serving classic and nouvelle cuisine. The menu is select and somewhat pricey, but the food and service justify all, and the reservation book is crowded with names each night. The quaint dining rooms in the historic house are open for lunch (11:30 a.m. to 3 p.m.) and dinner (6 to 10 p.m.) seven days a week (Sunday is brunch day). You'll spend about $15 for lunch, twice that for dinner. Come well dressed.

You won't find the tourist crowds flocking into **Frick's Restaurant** (tel. 846-5830), and the reasons are several: first, it's off the beaten track at 673 Thames St., almost a mile from the center of town (if you walk, allow 15 to 20 minutes). Second, it's small, with only 11 tables, which means you must have reservations, especially for dinner. But those who come to Frick's (mostly local people) are in for some of the best dining in Newport. Volker Frick, the chef, prepares everything to order. The small dining room, with soft gray walls acting as backdrop for a collection of paintings and drawings, has soft music—classical—playing in the background. Beer and wine are served at Frick's. The restaurant is open seven days a week in summer for dinner from 6 to closing; brunch on Sundays from noon to 3 p.m. The restaurant is closed between November 1 and March 1.

Of the waterfront redevelopment projects completed so far in Newport, the one at **Bannister's Wharf/Bowen's Wharf** is the most charming, and it has a selection of good restaurants. Bannister's Wharf is right next to the Treadway Inn, downtown on the waterfront, and would be West Pelham Street's extension if it were still a street. Poshest place on this very posh wharf is the **Clarke Cooke House** (tel. 849-2900), which has one of the most interesting French menus in Newport (not all frog legs and escargots) and two very different dining rooms. To your left at the top of the short flight of steps is the Dining Room, a very authentic-looking colonial room with rugged ceiling beams (original to the house, which is colonial), wood chairs and tables, gleaming crystal stemware, and tuxedo'd waiters. To the right as you enter is the Candy Store Café, a light, airy, and open room overlooking the wharf and the water—about as different from the dusky colonial room as can be. Plan on spending about $30 per person on a full dinner here (served 6 to 10 p.m.). In the café, a lunch or light supper will cost about $10.

WHAT TO SEE: There is plenty to see in Newport, and therefore during the summer there are also plenty of people here to see it. Parking places are at a premium, although the situation is certainly not hopeless. But why bother? If you are among the readers of this book who live close enough to Newport to make it practicable, why not bring a bicycle, or rent one when you get here? You can't really see the mansions by car as you always have to keep moving (the car behind you will make sure you do), and Newport is small enough so that even an out-of-shape biker can see the town without much of a strain. Several shops in Newport rent bikes, both three-speed (which is all you'll need), and ten-speed, among them **10 Speed Spokes,** 79 Thames St. (tel. 847-5609), around the corner from the Chamber of Commerce. You can also rent a moped (motorized bicycle), but both Thames Street and Bellevue Avenue are straight and flat, and the hill in between them is no Everest, and hardly worth the considerable extra expense of renting one. Other stores renting bikes are **Bermuda Bike Rentals** (tel. 847-2440), on Bowen's Wharf right downtown, and the **B & J Cycle Company** (tel. 846-0773), at 162 Broadway near Washington Square.

Tours

Should you want to get "the lay of the land" before heading out to see individual sights, take a bus tour of the town, Ocean Drive, Bellevue Avenue, and other districts. You don't necessarily have to take a tour which stops and goes through a mansion, although those are offered as well. **Viking Tours,** 182 Thames St. (tel. 847-6921), will take you on a 22-mile Newport tour for $7.50 (kids, $4.50); throw in another $3 and they'll take you through one mansion.

Another way to tour Newport is to rent a cassette tape recorder complete with prerecorded taped tour commentary from **Art's Island Tours,** for rent through the Chamber of Commerce, 10 America's Cup Ave., right downtown on the water (tel. 847-1600). You put a deposit on the recorder, take their map, and walk or ride along the mapped route while listening to the commentary.

The Mansions

Newport boasts mansions of two types these days: those that are now, in effect, museums and are open to the public, and those that are still private summer residences and are most emphatically *not* open to the public. Believe it or not, many of these palatial houses are indeed still privately owned and maintained and lived in. In fact, the wealthy people who live in Newport mansions are also responsible for opening others to the public, for it was through the efforts of the Preservation Society of Newport County, to which many of them belong, that the marvelous houses were preserved. To think that **The Elms,** perhaps the most graceful and charming of the mansions, was to be torn down to make way for a housing development until the Preservation Society bought it, is nothing short of astounding.

Not all of the mansions which are open to the public are owned by the Preservation Society, however. Several notable houses are privately maintained and open to visitors on terms similar to those of the society houses. When visiting the mansions, remember these two rules of thumb: first, figure on at least an hour per house to take it all in; second, don't try to see more than three, or at the most four, houses in one day unless you have a tremendous capacity for absorbing glitter and magnificence. More than three or four tours in one day will leave you dizzy and exhausted. Also, try to visit the mansions on a weekday when the crowds are smaller, saving Saturday and Sunday for Newport's other attractions. If you must go on Saturday, get there early. **The Preservation Society of Newport County,** 118 Mill St. (tel. 847-1000), maintains six Newport mansions, plus **Hunter House** (a colonial house built in 1748), and **Green Animals** (a topiary garden with 80 sculptured trees and shrubs, many in the shapes of animals, in Portsmouth to the north of Newport). A combination ticket covering all of these attractions is available for $18 per adult, $6 per child. Tickets for individual mansions cost $3.50 or $4.50, or $1.25 for children 6 through 11, but as you'll probably be seeing more than one mansion, buy a "strip ticket" good for two mansions ($6), three ($8), four ($10), five ($12), or six mansions ($14). Children's prices are less than half of these. Tickets are on sale at any of the society's mansions. During the summer (May to November) the mansions are open every day from 10 a.m. to 5 p.m. In the spring, in April the four fanciest mansions are open every day; the rest are open Saturday and Sunday at the same times. Note that in July, August, and September several mansions have late hours, and stay open until 8 p.m. Check for which ones are currently open which evenings. During the winter, Marble House, the Elms, and Château-sur-Mer are open Saturday and Sunday from 10 a.m. to 4 p.m.

Admission to any mansion includes a very informative tour through the rooms, and the right to stroll about the grounds at your leisure. Tours are very frequent, and the guides are almost always charming and very well informed. Here is what you'll see:

The Breakers: Certainly the most grandiose of the mansions, and most popular with visitors, is the Breakers, an Italian Renaissance palace built for Cornelius Vanderbilt. It is nothing short of sumptuous, with lavish use of the finest marble. The marble columns in the two-story-high Grand Hall have capitals carved of alabaster. Priceless tapestries, fine mosaic work, irreplaceable paintings, and ornate furniture testify to the wealth of the Breakers' owners and their desire to flaunt it. Hard to believe, the Breakers was built in only two years. It was designed by Richard Morris Hunt, who did a great many buildings in New England, especially in Newport.

Besides the mansion, there is a children's cottage on the grounds (included in the price of admission to the mansion).

The Elms: E. J. Berwind, son of a Philadelphia tradesman, got an appointment to the U.S. Naval Academy, and served in the navy until mustered out with high rank because of an injury. He soon made it big in the coal business, and secured the contract to supply all U.S. Navy ships with coal. With the profits he built the Elms, perhaps the most gracious and pleasant of the Newport mansions. Although it is grand, it is also supremely harmonious, having been modeled on a château in France. The sunken formal garden at the far end of the spacious lawn was designed by a French landscape artist. The Elms is the masterpiece of Philadelphia architect Horace Trumbauer. It was threatened with destruction when a land development firm bought it and planned to build a housing development on the site, but was saved by the zoning laws and the Preservation Society. Few of the original furnishings are left, but the mansion has been furnished with pieces from museum collections and private lenders.

Château-sur-Mer: The first stone mansion to go up on Bellevue Avenue was Château-sur-Mer (1852), built as a home for William S. Wetmore of New York. Wetmore's son, who met Richard Morris Hunt while on a tour of Europe, was responsible for bringing the American-born architect to Newport to rebuild his mansion, and later the mansions of others. (The senior Wetmore had lived in the mansion ten years before he died, and upon his death his son took it over.) The château is very rich Victorian Gothic, and to modern tastes it seems luxurious, but also dark and heavy. Château-sur-Mer has the feeling of being lived in and enjoyed—something which can't be said of some of the other mansions.

Marble House: Richard Morris Hunt threw himself into building this mansion for William K. Vanderbilt, finishing it in 1892. It was modeled on the palace at Versailles, and is therefore decorated pretty much in the style of Louis XIV which was, well, pretty grandiose—you'll see! As in the Breakers, the furnishings in Marble House are all original to the building. Get ready to see the Gold Room, a ballroom decorated with a king's ransom in gold, and the kitchen and the fascinating Chinese tea house.

Kingscote: Kingscote, built in 1839, is the type of "summer cottage" lived in by wealthy visitors to Newport before the great stone mansions were built. First built for G. N. Jones of Georgia by Richard Upjohn, it was later acquired by a merchant in the China trade called William H. King, who gave the house its name. "Kingscote" is coined from "dovecote," so, by analogy, it means "Mr. King's Cottage." A cottage it isn't, for no peasant lived here; but rather a man who appreciated Tiffany glass and a gorgeous dining room.

Rosecliff: Another famous New England architect, Stanford White, built Rosecliff in 1902 for Mrs. Hermann Oelrichs, whose father had made a fortune in the California Gold Rush. The building is modeled on the Grand Trianon, the larger of the two châteaux in the park at Versailles, but was meant to be even more lavish in layout and decor. Its ballroom is the largest one in Newport, and the mansion is still used for summer entertainments as it has been for most of this century.

Besides the mansions maintained by the Preservation Society, several others are open to the public. Grandest of these is **Belcourt Castle,** another creation of Richard Morris Hunt's, done in 1891. Oliver Belmont and his wife, formerly Mrs. William Vanderbilt, had Hunt make them a castle in the style of Louis XIII (1610–1643). Today the castle is filled with appropriate memorabilia: stained glass, armor, silver, carpets. It even boasts a golden coronation coach. Well-informed guides in costume escort the visitor through the beautiful period rooms and explain the collection. Tea is then served. Belcourt Castle is open daily from 10 a.m. to 5 p.m. from April 1 until November 30. Admission is $3.50 for adults, $1.50 for children 6 to 15.

Beechwood, the house of William B. Astor, was built on Bellevue Avenue in 1856. It, too, is open to the public every day from 10 a.m. to 5 p.m.; adults pay $2 (children, half price).

Richard Morris Hunt's **Ochre Court,** a mansion built for Ogden Goelet, styled after a French château. You can visit the mansion any weekday from 9 a.m. to 4 p.m., and admission is free. The **Edward King House,** in Aquidneck Park (which is bounded by Bowery, Spring, William, and King Streets) is now Newport's senior citizens' center. It was built in 1845 on the plan of an Italian villa. The architect was Richard Upjohn. The King House is open weekdays from 9 a.m. to 4:30 p.m. Admission is free.

Want to visit a summer White House? **Hammersmith Farm** (tel. 846-0420), on Ocean Drive, was built by John W. Auchincloss in 1887 as his family's 28-room summer "cottage." Jacqueline Bouvier, daughter of Mrs. Hugh Auchincloss, became Mrs. John F. Kennedy, and after the Newport wedding the reception was held at Hammersmith Farm. President Kennedy and his wife enjoyed visiting the farm when they could find the time, and no wonder. Beautiful rolling lawns and gardens, nature paths and copses of trees—not to mention the lovely old house itself—make the farm a seaside paradise.

Mrs. Auchincloss sold Hammersmith Farm in 1977 to private developers, and it is now being preserved and opened to the public. Guided tours are given daily from April through November 13, 10 a.m. to 5 p.m.; in summer till 7 p.m. The charge is $4 per adult, $1.50 per child.

Newport's Other Sights

The mansions are on everyone's list of things to see in Newport, but there are lots of other things to do as well. Here's a rundown on some other possibilities:

A Walk in Washington Square: Right downtown between Thames and Spring Streets, next to the new Brick Market Place shopping mall, is Washington Square, the center of colonial Newport. At the western tip of the square is the **Brick Market,** a Newport landmark, built in 1762 and designed by Peter Harrison. (The name derives from its use as a market, and its brick construction —no bricks were sold!) Having served variously as a town hall, theater, and crafts center, as of this writing it is undergoing yet another metamorphosis to serve a new purpose. At the other end of the square from the Brick Market stands the **Old Colony House,** center of Newport governmental affairs for 160 years from its construction in 1739 until the Rhode Island General Assembly (which met in Newport in the summer) last used it in 1900. It was from the Colony (later State) House's balcony that the Declaration of Independence was read to Rhode Islanders. In the assembly room is Gilbert Stuart's famous portrait of George Washington. You can go through the building in July and August daily from 9:30 a.m. to 4 p.m.; in other months from 9:30 a.m. to noon and from 1 to 4 p.m. on weekdays, 9:30 a.m. to noon on Saturday.

Historic Houses of Worship: Because Rhode Island allowed so much religious freedom, many religious groups suffering persecution made their way here in early times. Thus Newport boasts a number of firsts. The **Touro Synagogue,** a half block from Washington Square up Touro Street, is the most famous of these. Designed by Peter Harrison (it resembles in some ways his King's Chapel in Boston) and built in 1763, the temple was the spiritual center of Congregation Yeshuat Israel, an Orthodox Sephardic congregation. The temple and congregation prospered along with Newport, but after the British occupation of the town during the Revolutionary War prosperity fled Newport and few of its erstwhile citizens returned. But in the late 19th century, Newport came to life again. The temple reopened in 1883, and has been used for services ever since.

Touro Synagogue (the name comes from a 19th-century benefactor, Abraham Touro, son of the rabbi who presided at the synagogue's dedication) is open to visitors from late June to Labor Day on weekdays 10 a.m. to 5 p.m., on Sunday to 6 p.m.; during other months it's open on Sunday from 2 to 4 p.m., and by special arrangement (call 847-4794). Admission is free, donations are accepted. During the summer, short tours are conducted, and the guide will show you the priceless breastplates and belltops, some from Europe and others made in America, which adorn the Torahs; and also a beautiful Torah made of deerskin and sent as a gift from a congregation in Amsterdam to be the new Newport temple's first Torah in the 1700s. You can also see a copy of George Washington's letter to the congregation, written while he was president in 1790.

The Newport Historical Society is housed today in another early house of worship, the **Seventh Day Baptist Meetinghouse** (1729), the first in America of that sect. The buildings are at 82 Touro St., a few steps from the Touro

Synagogue; they're open Tuesday through Friday from 9:30 a.m. to 4:30 p.m., on Saturday to noon. Take a look at the meetinghouse and its famed pulpit, and also at the Society's museum, which houses paintings, furniture, china, silver, and marine artifacts.

The **Quaker Meeting House,** at the corner of Marlborough and Farewell Streets, was built in 1699, but was greatly modified in the early 1700s and again in the early 1800s. The congregation, founded in 1657, is the oldest of the Society of Friends in this country. The meetinghouse has been restored to look as it did in the early 1800s. Admission is $1.50, and it's open 10 a.m. to 5 p.m. from Monday to Saturday June through September, other times by calling 846-0813.

Of course, Newport has a beautiful old pre-Revolutionary church, this one a real gem. **Trinity Church** (1726), at the corner of Spring and Church Streets (tel. 846-0660), was built from plans by Sir Christopher Wren, and still has the "bishop's mitre" weathervane as it did before the Revolution. The church is full of history: Bishop George Berkeley gave the organ (1733), Washington was known to have worshiped here (pew no. 81), and its famous three-decker "wineglass" pulpit is widely admired. You can get in to see the church Monday through Saturday from 10 a.m. to 4 p.m. in summer (late June to Labor Day), at other times on weekends from 1 to 4 p.m., or at Sunday services at 8 and 10 a.m. Other times, call 846-0660 and make an appointment. Donations accepted.

Other Attractions: Army buffs will want to drop in at the **Artillery Company of Newport,** 23 Clarke St., a few steps from Washington Square. The company got its charter in 1741, and since that time, besides defending Newport, has been collecting military uniforms. You can see this great collection on display from June through September, afternoons from 1 to 5 p.m. on Tuesday through Sunday. At other times of the year, it's open Saturday and Sunday afternoons only. Children are admitted free; adults are asked to give a donation.

The **International Tennis Hall of Fame and Tennis Museum:** This is sure to be of interest to anyone obsessed with the game. It's in the Newport Casino building on Bellevue Avenue across from the shopping center. The Casino (1880) is the perfect location for a tennis museum, as it was here that the first national tennis tournaments were held. The museum has on exhibit trophies, tennis fashions, and displays explaining the evolution of tennis equipment. The 13 grass courts (and 3 indoor courts) are open to the public for play, so bring your racquet and call 849-3990 to make arrangements. The Hall of Fame and Museum are open all year from 10 a.m. to 5 p.m., April through November, and December through March on weekdays from 10 a.m. to 4 p.m. Admission costs $4 for adults, $2.50 for seniors, and $2 for children 6 to 18.

WHAT TO DO: Here are several absolute musts while you're in Newport:

Ocean Drive and Cliff Walk

Take a drive (or ride your bike, if you're in shape) along Newport's ten-mile **Ocean Drive.** The scenery is very beautiful, with low heath, evergreens, stretches of rugged coast, and several smooth grassy lawns maintained as state parks. **Brenton Point State Park** has parking, walking, and picnic areas, and there's a Public Fishing Area with parking nearby. Ocean Drive also gives you a look at some of the yachts sailing on Rhode Island Sound, and at the mansions dotted around the end of the island.

For walkers, the pedestrian equivalent of Ocean Drive is **Cliff Walk, a** path which runs along the shore and along the edge of the "front yards" of the mansions on Bellevue Avenue. Official start of the hour-long walk is off Memorial Boulevard just before Newport Beach, but you can also get to the path by going east on one of the side streets off Bellevue Avenue. By the same token, you needn't take the entire walk, but can head back to Bellevue Avenue at various points along the way.

Fort Adams State Park

On a peninsula jutting into Newport Harbor, this park (tel. 847-2400) offers several attractions. The park is open 6 a.m. to 11 p.m. daily all year, and picnic and fishing sites are open to all. The fort itself, named after Pres. John Adams, is open on a guided-tour basis from 11:30 a.m. to 4:30 p.m., Wednesday through Sunday in the summer (for a fee). Boat-launching ramps, beach with lifeguard, picnic area, and soccer fields are among the services. The fort's defenses are some of the most impressive in the country—so impressive, in fact, that it rarely came under fire. Views of the town and the harbor from hills in the park are well worth the short climb.

Beaches

Newport's beaches are of two types, public (open to everyone for a fee), and private (open to members only, "Keep Out—This Means You!"). Bailey's Beach, at the southern end of Bellevue Avenue, is definitely very private, but **Newport Beach,** also called "First Beach," is public and quite large. It's on the isthmus at the eastern reach of Memorial Boulevard. Second Beach is in Middletown, a bit farther along the same route where the street changes names to become Purgatory Road. Just around the corner from Second Beach is Third Beach, at the mouth of the Sakonnet River, facing east. It may be a bit chilly at any time except July and August.

Gooseberry Beach, on Ocean Drive, is an especially attractive beach, open to the public for a parking fee of $4 on weekdays, $6 on weekends. It's framed by nice mansions on either side, and has interesting rock formations.

Jai Alai

The newest spectator sport and game of chance in Newport is the fast-moving game of jai alai ("high-lie"), familiar to those who have traveled to Latin America. Note first off that minors (under 18) are not admitted because of the betting, and that the season is April 15 to October 10. The Newport Fronton is at 150 Admiral Kalbfus Rd., near the Newport end of the Newport Bridge. Seats cost $2 to $4 and general admission (standing room) is $1, $2 for the lounge and restaurant. Betting is on which player or team will win, and is pari-mutuel as it is at horse and dog tracks. The game is fast and exciting, and the ball (harder than a golf ball) moves at murderous speeds approachiing 188 miles an hour. If you've never seen it before (or bet before), you can get a brochure at the door explaining it all. For seat reservations, call 849-5000 in Rhode Island, or out-of-state, toll free 800/556-6900. There are matinees Monday and Saturday, at which seniors are free; ladies free Tuesday; closed Sunday.

Festivals and Events

Newport seems to have a festival going, one or another, all summer long. For current information on exact dates and offerings, contact the **Newport**

County Chamber of Commerce, 10 America's Cup Ave., Newport, RI 02840 (tel. 401/847-1600), or write for the State of Rhode Island's *Guide to Rhode Island* to: Rhode Island Department of Economic Development, Tourist Promotion Division, One Weybosset Hill, Providence, RI 02903. The *Guide,* a 50-page pamphlet, has a complete list of Rhode Island events and festivals for the current year.

One of the world's great yachting races, the America's Cup Race held every three years or so, took place in the waters off Newport for years. In 1983 Australia challenged and defeated the American defender. The next America's Cup race will be held in Perth in 1987. The major festivals and approximate times are these:

Newport Music Festival: Perhaps the biggest annual event in the town, the Newport Music Festival attracts great crowds to the grand mansions for the many and varied concerts. There are performances morning, afternoon, and evening for two consecutive weekends and the weekdays in between in mid-July. As the capacity of all the mansions and halls is limited, it's best to write for tickets—and to make reservations for a hotel room—in advance. Write to the Newport Music Festival, 50 Washington Square, Newport, RI 02840 (tel. 401/846-1133). They'll send you a list of all the concerts and performers, and the prices of tickets.

The **Kool Jazz Festival** in Newport is held on a weekend late in August, in Fort Adams State Park. Each day from noon to 6:30 p.m., top-name stars perform. The Viking Hotel (tel. 401/847-8100) is usually festival headquarters, where you can buy your tickets (general admission only) for $17.50 in advance, $20 the day of the festival, for each day.

May Breakfasts: May is officially celebrated as Heritage Month in Rhode Island, as "Little Rhody" was the first colony to declare independence from British rule (May 4, 1776). On May Day (May 1), or thereabouts, May Day Breakfasts are held by all sorts of church, civic, and fraternal organizations across the state, and the public is invited to most of them. These can be pretty lavish affairs, and you're sure to get your money's worth. Write to the Department of Economic Development (address above) for a full list of breakfasts throughout the state.

Outdoor Art Festival: The end of July, usually the last weekend, sees Newport's Outdoor Art Festival, when painters, sculptors, and craftspeople display their works downtown and in several parks throughout the city.

Fishing Tournaments: From June to October, tournaments are organized periodically to see who can make a record catch of one of the familiar fish in the waters off Newport. The chamber of commerce can tell you more.

Tennis: The Miller Hall of Fame Tennis Championships are held at the Newport Casino (Tennis Hall of Fame) in July, hosting the top professional male stars. For tickets and information, contact the Hall of Fame, 194 Bellevue Ave., Newport, RI 02840 (tel. 401/849-3990).

3. Narragansett Bay

To get across Narragansett Bay from Newport, you will have to cross two bridges on Route 138: first, the Newport Bridge from Newport to Jamestown Island ($2, payable in both directions), and then the Jamestown Bridge from Jamestown Island to Saunderstown (free). The total fee therefore to cross from Newport to Saunderstown or vice-versa is $2. From Saunderstown, head south on Route 1A (Alternate U.S. 1).

NARRAGANSETT PIER: Route 1A skirts the southwestern shore of Narragansett Bay passing through this famous Victorian resort town, which is also the main town on the peninsula here. Although not quite so famous now, the town is still popular for the same reasons as in an earlier age: beautiful sea views, a fine waterfront promenade, and gracious old Victorian hotels.

Where to Stay

The modern **Atlantic Motor Inn,** 85 Ocean Rd., Narragansett Pier, RI 02882 (tel. 401/783-5534), is a three-story motel set back in a fine lawn and painted in a shady beige and sky blue. The views from the upstairs front porch are panoramic. In season (July and August), a double room on the front costs $53; on the back $47. Off-season, rooms rent for $30.

What to See

Passiing through Narragansett on Ocean Road, you'll drive right under the last standing remnant of Stanford White's mammoth Narragansett casino, "The Towers," built in 1882. The town's chamber of commerce maintains a Tourist Information Office in the base of the seaward tower—park on either side of the underpass arch and walk to the door.

The main beach in Narragansett is north of these hotels and the Towers, about a half mile distant. The parking fee is your admission fee, as usual.

FROM SAUNDERSTOWN TO POINT JUDITH: As you drive south along 1A from Saunderstown, look for signs off to the right (west) which point the way to the **Gilbert Stuart birthplace.** Stuart (1755–1828) was America's most famous portrait painter during the Revolutionary era, and did no fewer than three portraits of George Washington from life, perhaps the most famous of which is the so-called *Athenaeum Head,* model for the portrait of Washington on the dollar bill. (Look for the original of this in the Museum of Fine Arts in Boston.) Stuart was the son of a snuff-maker, but his father had a comfortable living, judging from the house, and the son was able to go to London to study painting with Benjamin West. Period furnishings, snuff-making equipment, and Stuart paintings adorn the house. Open daily except Friday all year, from 11 a.m. to 5 p.m. except from December to February. Admission is $1.50 for adults, 50¢ for children.

Ocean Road (Route 1A) also passes by the **Scarborough State Beach** facilities, very popular on hot summer days although never filled to capacity. Scarborough Beach, like all Rhode Island beaches, works on a system of parking/admission fees, charged *per car.*

Continuing along Route 1A south will bring you to Point Judith and the departure place for Block Island ferryboats.

POINT JUDITH/PORT GALILEE: Jutting southeast into the Atlantic Ocean and dividing Block Island Sound from Rhode Island Sound is Point Judith. The peninsula of Narragansett's southern extremity offers several things to travelers: the car and passenger ferry docks for boats to Block Island, located at Port Galilee; camping and picnic facilities at Fishermen's Memorial State Park, only two miles from Port Galilee; and good sand beaches along the southern and eastern shores of the peninsula. Port Galilee exists for the ferries to Block Island, the Wheeler Memorial Beach, several small fisheries, and a Coast Guard station.

Where to Stay and Eat

The **Dutch Inn,** Great Island Road, Narragansett, RI 02882 (tel 401/789-9341), a motel with a copy of a Dutch windmill over the entranceway, is an interesting place to stay. It's just across the street from the ferry docks and the Coast Guard Station. The rooms have been renovated recently; most rooms have two double beds and cost $38.16 and up single, $71.02 to $81.62 double from June through September; an extra person costs $10, and children under 12 stay free with their parents. Several rooms overlooking the exotic palm-lined indoor pool are a bit more expensive. At poolside the tropical decor is a cocktail lounge with entertainment in the evenings; yet another lounge-cum-bar and a restaurant are nearby in the same building. Besides the pool, a whirlpool bath, tennis courts, an exercise room, and saunas are part of the inn's facilities. If you've arrived early in the morning to catch the early ferry to Block Island and you want a hearty breakfast, this is the place to buy it.

If the Dutch Inn is the expensive place to eat, the **Port Side Restaurant,** to the left of the inn, is the inexpensive place. A lobster and seafood dinner here is a mere $14; a boiled lobster with french fries and coleslaw is a very low $8. House specials are $3.50 to $6; sandwiches are 90¢ to $2.75. The dining room has been remodeled in paneling and picture windows looking out to the water. The food is good and the price right. The Port Side is open from 9:30 a.m. to 8 p.m. seven days a week in summer, and a service window at which you can buy anything on the menu to go opens at about 8:30 a.m. Serves breakfast too.

In the other direction, south along the main street, are several restaurants which cater mainly to the crowd spending the day at the beach. **George's of Galilee Restaurant,** Sand Hill Cove Road, next to the parking lot at the end of the main road, will sell you just the thing for beach-side sustenance: clam cakes, seafood chowder, assorted sandwiches, and more elaborate—but still informal—dinners. You'll pay between $4 and $11, depending on how hungry you are.

The Beach and the Ferry

First of all, be warned that Port Galilee has very few parking places on the street, and that these are usually taken up quickly by the people who work for the fishing companies. Parking for the beach is $2 a day ($3 on weekends and holidays) for Rhode Island residents, $3 a day ($5 on weekends and holidays) for out-of-state cars, but this includes the entry fee to the beach for everyone in your party, and is standard practice at all state beaches in Rhode Island. Whether you park next to George's of Galilee or at the large lots of the Wheeler Memorial Beach several hundred yards east, the rate and arrangement are the same.

For the ferry, parking fees are of the same order, and the lot is across the street and down a few yards from the ferry dock. Note that the restaurants and motel in Galilee have parking lots, but they also put our fierce signs that threaten to have your car towed if your intention is other than patronizing their establishments. It's best to take them at their word, especially if you're going away to Block Island for the day.

4. Block Island

In 1614, a man named Adriaen Block visited a small island off the coast of Rhode Island, but his visit did little more than give the island its name. Slightly over 20 years later, a colonist was found in a boat near the island, presumed murdered by the local Pequot Indians, and this unhappy event precipitated a battle between Pequots and colonists which turned out to be very bloody.

A generation later these bloody events forgotten, settlers from the colony moved onto the island, and the town of New Shoreham (incorporated in 1672) was built. For almost 200 years the people of Block Island lived their quiet lives, fishing in boats from the island's two natural harbors, growing what they could in the sandy and windswept soil. But in the mid-1800s the Age of Steam changed Block Island from a fishermen's outpost in the Atlantic to a summer excursion paradise, with regularly scheduled steamboats bringing residents of the sooty factory cities out for fresh air and bright sunshine. Late 19th-century frame hotels, huge and sprawling, went up to accommodate them, and the island's economy came to depend on tourism rather than fishing, and so it has remained. Most of the island's buildings—houses as well as hotels—date from the late 1800s or the turn of the century; the roads are rough and sandy (nobody has to be in a hurry to get quickly from one end of the island to the other—it's only seven miles); the pace is very relaxed; and the citizens of New Shoreham, which takes up all of the island, have a strong sense of community.

GETTING THERE: During the summer season from late June to early September, Block Island is very accessible, whether you're touring New England by car or by public transport. During spring, autumn, and winter, there's limited service to the island.

By Air

New England Airlines, Block Island's own airline, will fly you over from the State Airport, Westerly, RI 02891, on any of nine daily flights year round for $18, one way, per person. The flight takes 15 minutes. You must have reservations, so call 401/596-2460. If you're on Block Island, dial 5959. The airport is on Airport Road, Westerly, off Route 78.

By Boat

Boats leave for Block Island from four ports during the summer: from Port Galilee (Point Judith, R.I.), the port with most frequent service, there are at least nine daily sailings in each direction from mid-June to early September. The trip takes less than an hour and a half, and costs $4.50 per adult, one way, or $5.75 for a same-day round trip; children pay $2.25 one way, $3 for a same-day round trip. It costs about $26 round trip for a car (driver not included), and you must have written for reservations in advance. The Port Galilee agent is the **Interstate Navigation Co.,** Galilee State Pier, Point Judith, RI 02882 (tel. 401/783-4613). Motorcycles and bikes are also carried. During spring, fall, and winter there are fewer trips, two daily in each direction in May and early June, and late September through October; in winter, there's one trip daily.

Although private car is about the only way to get to Port Galilee, Amtrak trains run to New London and Providence (other docks with ferries to Block Island) and Westerly (for flights); buses run by Almeida and Bonanza go to Providence and Newport.

From New London

In summer (mid-June to early September) there's one trip daily in each direction between New London and Block Island, leaving New London mid-morning, returning from Block Island midafternoon. The trip takes about 2¼ hours and costs $8.25 for adults ($9.25 same-day round trip), and $5.50 for children ($6.50 same-day round trip). A car costs $36 round trip. The boat leaves from Ferry Street, about one-eighth mile from the railroad station. For more information, contact the **Nelseco Navigation Co.,** P.O. Box 482, New London, CT 06320 (tel. 203/442-7891 or 203/442-9553 during business hours). By the way, ferries from New London arrive at New Harbor on Block Island, and you may have to take a taxi to reach hotel and restaurant choices.

MAIL/TELEPHONES: Block Island's ZIP Code is 02807; the telephone area code is 401, the exchange is 466. On the island, you need only dial the last four digits of any phone number.

ARRIVING IN OLD HARBOR: The boat trip is easy enough, plenty of room to sun on the top deck benches, a small bar and snack counter on board. As you approach Block Island the character of the place becomes clear: dunes and white cliffs, low shrubs and grass with a few trees, ponds and hillocks (highest point on the island is 211 feet above sea level). The big old hotels come right down to the harbor, most looking pretty weathered from the stiff breezes and salt air, not to mention the winter storms, which are the norm here. Several of the hotels have vans which will be waiting at the dock to pick up passengers who have reservations, or those who want a room but have not reserved.

WHERE TO STAY: Most people go to Block Island just for the day, or they go for a week or two. All the hotels have weekly rates, and some require that you reserve by the week in July and August; most visitors have hotel reservations before they arrive, although it is often possible (but not certain) to find a room just by coming over and looking around. Of the island's two dozen hotels, inns, and guest houses, here are my favorites:

Marks for all-around best go to the **1661 Inn** (tel. 401/466-2421), on Spring Street, up the hill from Old Harbor. The inn is a large old white house with a panoramic view of the water and beautiful soft lawns. Rooms are small but very pretty, decorated with well-selected period pieces and bright, small-print wallpapers; some have sea views. Rates are $37.10 single, $58.30 to $68.90 double in rooms without private bath, $74.20 to $100.70 double in rooms with bath; $132.50 for the same with a Jacuzzi. These rates include a complete breakfast, and wine-and-cheese hour. There is a 5% discount on stays longer than a week. Winter rates start Columbus Day and end just before Memorial Day weekends. Rates then are $42.40 for a shared bath and $68.90 for private bath; 10% less for singles. This includes mini-buffet breakfast and wine-and-cheese hour. By the way, these prices *include* the 6% service charge and 6% tax. There are only 25 rooms at the 1661 Inn, but they keep a guest house (10 rooms) open year round; or if you're not lucky enough to get either, you can go there for breakfast (8 to 11 a.m.) or dinner at *The Manisses,* mentioned later, also run by the Abrams. Many of the vegetables served at dinner there have been grown in the inn's garden across the street. Block Island seafood—striped bass, swordfish, flounder, clams, mussels—is featured, all of it very fresh and moderately priced, with complete dinners costing $12 to $18. Those tired of seafood can have one of a variety of steaks, or roast Long Island duckling. Extras: A free wine-and-cheese party for guests every evening during high season before dinner; bicycle and snorkeling gear rentals; free taxi service from the docks.

Just up the road from the 1661 Inn at the top of the hill is the **Spring House** (tel. 401/466-2633), a grand old clapboard hotel from the Victorian era, kept very much as it was in Block Island's 19th-century heyday. Chairs for sunning are set out on the lawns and the long veranda, and the views from this hilltop are magnificent. Inside, the 19th-century parlor, complete with grand piano, is almost unchanged from years ago. The rooms come in various sizes, styles, and furnishings, and vary greatly in price. All of the following rates include breakfast and dinner: singles, $45.58 to $55.12 per day, $312.70 to $381.60 per week in high season; doubles, $67.84 to $89.04 per day, $474.88 to $604.20 per week. Cheaper rooms have only washbasins, more expensive rooms have private bath, and the most expensive rooms have private baths, choice locations, views, and furnishings. Many of the lower-price rooms are not at all fancy, but rather plain. Note that the Spring House minibus will pick you up at the dock, and that a jacket is required at dinner. If you call to ask about reservations, ask also about the Block Island Musical Society's "musical evenings," recitals given by native and visiting performers in the grand parlor at Spring House.

The **Surf Hotel** (tel. 401/466-2241 or 466-5990) is another Victorian wood palace, not quite so austerely elegant as Spring House, but rather homey as only a great Victorian wood palace can be homey: cranberry glass hanging lamps, wicker furniture, a great ornate iron stove, and a grandfather clock in the parlor, colonial wallpaper prints in the rooms. A good number of the rooms have fine beach views—the beach is just a few steps away down the hill—and although the hotel is a mere block and a half from the Old Harbor ferry dock, the hotel car will pick you up if you have a reservation. All but three rooms do not have private bath, and during July and August reservations can be made by the week only. For a single, the price is $29.15 per day, $181.50 per week; for a double, $38.50 per day, $242 per week (twin or double bed); an extra person in a room costs $10 a day, $60 a week, and there's no discount for children except for infants. Meals at the Surf Hotel cost $4.50 for breakfast ($27.50 a week). Cooking and service is home-style. Although the Surf Hotel won't take a reservation for less than a week in high season, that doesn't mean they won't rent you a room for a day or two if they have one. Check with them: if they've had a cancellation, or if there's a free room, you can make an arrangement. The hotel is open from Memorial Day to Columbus Day weekends.

The most modern hostelry on the island, most of it built within this last decade rather than a century ago, is **Ballard's Inn** (tel. 401/466-2231), right on the water just to the left of the Old Harbor ferry docks as you get off the boat. There are two parts to the inn, a slightly older building in traditional Block Island style which houses the restaurant and bar, and several rooms with twin beds; and a new motel-style addition, with rooms which have a sea view forming a ring around another group of rooms which, of course, have no view at all. The best rooms at the inn are clearly the sea-view ones, which are modern and decorated in standard motel fashion with two double beds and delightful little sitting porches overlooking the town and the ocean. These rooms cost $58.30 on Sunday to Thursday in season, $68.90 on Friday, Saturday, and holidays; the inside no-view rooms are $53 during the week and $58.30 on Friday and Saturday in season; rooms in the original building are $47.70 on Sunday to Thursday, $56.18 on Friday, Saturday, and holidays. These rates apply whether one or two people stay in a room. An additional person is charged $10 a day; children under 12 must pay $5 a day. Note that although the rooms in the original building and the no-view rooms sleep only two people, the sea-view rooms can hold up to five. Off-season, rooms cost much less (before mid-June and after mid-September). In the new harbor area, Champlin's Marina, which is part of the same operation, is an Olympic-size swimming pool open to inn guests.

Lovers of family guest houses will want to check out the **Gables Inn,** on Dodge Street (P.O. Box 516, Block Island, RI 02807; tel. 401/466-2213), just around the corner from the Surf Hotel and behind the old National Hotel. The Gables is a traditional Block Island house converted to a guest house, and with its companion, the Gables II, it has a good variety of accommodations: single rooms are $28 to $36 daily; doubles are $36 to $44. Most of the rooms don't have running water, but there are bathrooms nearby. The Gables has several advantages over other places on the island: its prices are low, it is open year round (you can get meals here in fall, winter, and spring), free coffee and tea are available throughout the day, and guests have the use of barbecues, picnic tables, a croquet set, and horseshoes for throwing, all in the back yard.

If you're arriving from New London in New Harbor, Block Island, one of the first hotels you'll see is the **Narragansett Inn** (tel. 401/466-2626). The big advantages here are convenience to the New Harbor docks and rooms, a one-minute run across the lawn from the beach. The inn itself is a Victorian three-story house with several new additions. Prices are per person, at $35 to $40 each. The rates include breakfast and dinner and, by the way, a jacket is *not* required for dinner at the Narragansett Inn.

The **Island Towne House Motel** (tel. 401/466-5567) is the newest lodging place on Block Island, and the first one to be built in the past 40 years. The two shingle-clad, two-story buildings are next to the restaurant on Chapel Street, one block to the beach, village, and ferry dock. It offers new and modern rooms, private baths, cable color TV, queen-size beds, and prices of $63.60 double, $11.66 for each additional family member (limit of four persons in a room). Off-season rates available.

WHERE TO EAT: Where and what you eat depends on how you're visiting Block Island. Those over for the day may want only a sandwich or a light luncheon plate, but those staying for a few days or a week will want to try the seafood dinners which are one of the island's strong suits.

In several of the hotels mentioned above meals are available to guests at special weekly rates, and that is undoubtedly the best way to enjoy a full week's meals at a moderate price. At the **Ballard Inn** the requisite seafood dishes are supplemented with Italian fare: chicken cacciatore for $9, or good old pork chops for the same price. The lobsters at Ballard's are fresh from the tank—you choose the one you want—and cost $11 and up depending on size. (*Hint:* Get one large one to feed your party rather than several small ones. It'll save you money.)

A good, general service restaurant open year round, seven days a week, from 8 a.m. to 10 p.m., is the **Island Towne House Restaurant,** not far from the Old Harbor docks, directly inland. It's a modern place with traditional touches, comfortable booths, a small bar, and soft music. Waitresses are very friendly and wear attractive blue-and-white sailor suits. Lunch (11 a.m. to 4 p.m.) is mostly sandwich and seafood plates priced at $2 to $7. For dinner (4:30 to 10 p.m.) the menu is similar to Ballard's, with seafood and some Italian dishes in the range of $6.50 to $10 for the full dinner. The best bargains are the weekly specials, which may include lobster and green salad for only $8. Beer and wine, as well as cocktails, are available.

Joan and Justin Abrams, who own and operate the 1661 Inn, have just finished restoring an 1800s hotel named **The Manisses.** Prices in the dining room are moderate, and the menu at present includes un-Victorian but deliciously satisfying items such as fish pâté, quiches, hamburgers, salads simple and elaborate, and dinners from fish and chips, to broiled scallops, served with salad and potato. Cocktails, wines by the bottle, the half liter, or liter, beer by the pint, half pint, and pitcher are all on sale. The Manisses' 16 guest rooms have also been restored. All rooms have private baths, three with Jacuzzis.

WHAT TO DO: Most people coming to Block Island are looking for an easy schedule, quiet relaxation, time at the beach, bicycle trips, and seafood dinners. The island has a movie theater, the **Empire,** and a number of cocktail lounges, mostly in the hotels. A few small art galleries and craft shops are good for a browse. But beaching and bicycling are the two main activities.

Beaches

You can't miss **Crescent Beach,** to your right as you approach Old Harbor on the ferry. It stretches from the ferry dock for several miles north to the cliffs of Clay Head. It's simply beautiful, although the water is a bit brisk this far out in the Atlantic (it's warmest in late July and August, of course). Crescent Beach is divided into the State Beach, with a bathhouse, which is the section nearest the ferry dock, and Scotch Beach, which is the section farther north. Other beaches are over in the New Harbor area, several small ones on Great Salt Pond, and Charleston Beach facing west on the Atlantic.

Bicycling

It seems as though almost every commercial concern on the island rents bikes in its spare time, and one should not be surprised to find even a Funeral-Parlor-and-Bike-Rental place. Rates are competitive and can be surprisingly low, $4.50 for a three-speed for a full day. Shop around, look at the equipment, and plan your trip before renting. A shortish, pleasant trip is out Spring Street, which becomes Southeast Light Road and passes the lighthouse of that name on Mohegan Bluffs. Turn right onto Pilot Hill Road to get back to town in a short loop, or continue on to Lakeside Drive for a longer loop. Another trip is along Corn Neck Road, heading due north from the Old Harbor area, which goes to the north end of the island.

Fishing

Several marinas on the island have fishing boats for hire, and surfcasting for striped bass and other delicacies is popular. Even if you're alone, the marina hands may be able to get together a party to go out, thereby reducing your costs greatly. For details, call any one of the three marinas at 466-2631, 466-2641, or 466-7790, or the boat rental firms at 466-5547 or 466-2290. All the boat-rental and sport-fishing businesses operate out of the New Harbor.

What Not to Do

Block Island and the town of New Shoreham are really one and the same, and so the local government of the island is the town council. While on the island the town's ordinances are the law, and these prohibit camping (except Scout groups and the like), sleeping overnight in cars or on beaches, riding motorcycles on the beaches, and shellfishing without a license.

5. Watch Hill

Rhode Island is known for its beaches, and some of the finest are along the state's southwestern shore: names such as Misquamicut, Weekapaug, and Quonochontaug identify the built-up areas along the strand. The buildings are usually private homes, or snackbars and restaurants, and much of the waterfront land is privately owned and fiercely guarded. But the state beaches dotted along the shore are open to all at a fee of $1 per car with Rhode Island plates, $2 per car with out-of-state plates during the week, and twice those amounts on weekends and holidays.

As a base for your day at the beach, you could choose no better place than Watch Hill, an old and genteel town at the end of a peninsula between the Atlantic Ocean and the Pawcatuck River. Watch Hill is a sort of Newport-in-miniature, with stately old homes (grand, but not palatial), yachts in the harbor (expensive, but not priceless), and a gentility still strongly felt if slightly faded. It's a quiet town, with fewer than a half dozen places to put up for a night or a week, unless, of course, you own a summer home.

Hartley's Guest House, Larkin Road, Watch Hill, RI 02891 (tel. 401/348-8253), is just up the hill from the carousel at the end of Bay Street—look for signs. This nice big white house with blue trim is open June through mid-September, renting rooms for $26.50 to $40.28 single, $33.92 to $44.52 double, with shared bath; $40.28 to $47.70, for a double room with private bath. Children (5 to 10) can stay with their parents for an additional $12. Two days minimum stay on weekends and holidays. Hartley's is high on a hill overlooking the town and the water. It's a short walk to the beach.

Right in the center of Watch Hill, near the yacht marina, is **Harbour House** (tel. 401/348-8998), Bay Street, Watch Hill, RI 02891, where double rooms in a well-maintained building (shops below, living quarters above) cost $42.40 to $47.70 for two per night, $254.40 to $286.20 per week for two, late May through September. There's a suite which will sleep up to six people for $79.50 nightly, $477 weekly, and several apartments suitable for two to six people which are rented by the week only at $275.60 to $360.40. Price differences are based on the plumbing arrangements: some rooms have full baths, others just toilet-and-washbasin and so forth.

WHAT TO DO: Look at the **merry-go-round** at the end of Bay Street, said to be the oldest still operating in the United States; browse through the shops on Bay Street; walk to **Watch Hill Lighthouse** for the view out to sea; find the harborside statue of Ninigret, Great Sachem of the Narragansett Indians (erected in 1914). Watch Hill is a place to start a romance, or to pursue one; to read and relax, or swim strenuously all day; to do as you please. There are no crowds, no neon signs, no plastic "lifestyles." Watch Hill is a bit of fading glory, which, luckily for those who go there, the rest of the world has already passed by.

Chapter X

CONNECTICUT

1. New Haven
2. Connecticut River Valley
3. Mystic, New London, and Groton
4. Hartford
5. Litchfield Lakes and Hills

CONNECTICUT'S LANDSCAPE is sprinkled liberally with lakes, rivers, and streams. But the state's mighty namesake is the Connecticut River, which springs from the Connecticut Lakes in northern New Hampshire, flows southward forming the boundary between New Hampshire and Vermont, cuts through Massachusetts and Connecticut, finally to empty into Long Island Sound. The great river is navigable as far north as Hartford, a significant fact that was not lost on the region's Native American inhabitants. They were the ones who gave it the name *Quinnehtukqut,* "the long tidal river."

Later inhabitants pasted different labels here. "The Nutmeg State" used to be a popular nickname, coming from the time when itinerant peddlars sold nutmeg from door to door. As often as not, the "nutmegs" were cleverly carved balls of wood. By the time a housewife discovered the fakery, the peddlar was gone.

For obvious reasons, the people of Connecticut prefer the moniker "Constitution State," which reminds one and all that Connecticut was the first American colony to have a written constitution.

Almost three-quarters of the territory in Connecticut is woodland, and drives along the back roads through these forests reveal rich fields of corn, grain, vegetables, and tobacco, but the state's wealth comes not from agriculture, nor from tourism, but rather from insurance and manufacturing. The capital city of Hartford is laden with tremendous buildings which are headquarters for dozens of insurance companies. As for manufacturing, Charles Goodyear, Eli Whitney, Seth Thomas, and Mr. Fuller of Fuller Brush fame were all Connecticut Yankees. In the old days the state's production of buttons, pins, doodads, and kitchenwares gave rise to the breed of men known as Yankee peddlars, who traveled from town to town in horse and buggy, spreading the products of Connecticut's industry far and wide. Today the state's industries are a bit different: Sikorsky makes helicopters, General Dynamics makes atomic submarines, and the rubber companies turn out tires and products such as Naugahyde, the synthetic leather named after the Connecticut town of Naugatuck where it's made.

Although Connecticut has many historic houses and lovely New England villages, the places which are popular with tourists are mostly along the coast:

New Haven, home of Yale University; Essex, a fine old town at the mouth of the Connecticut River; Groton and New London, submarine capital of the world; and of course Mystic Seaport, the exciting and attractive recreation of an old Connecticut maritime village. Hartford, although not what one would think of as a tourist mecca, is a pretty and interesting city well worth a short visit. Besides the attractions of the city itself, it can be used as a base for excursions into the lush farm and woodlands of Litchfield County, in the northwest corner of the state among the Litchfield Hills, Connecticut's "Berkshires."

The telephone area code for all Connecticut is 203.

The state tax on rooms and meals is 7%.

Bed-and-Breakfast, Statewide

Connecticut boasts a bed-and-breakfast service with listings of rooms in private homes throughout the state. It's named **Nutmeg Bed and Breakfast,** operated by Maxine Kates and Phyllis Nova, at 56 Fox Chase Lane, West Hartford, CT 06107 (tel. 203/236-6698). Rooms cost from $25 to $65 per night, double, depending on location and the degree of luxury. For a directory of many houses, send $2 and a self-addressed, stamped envelope.

GETTING THERE: The capital and the southern coastal region are well served by public transport, most of which goes through or originates in the metropolis of New York.

By Air

The state is served by **Bradley International Airport** in Windsor Locks, 12 miles north of Hartford. There's direct one-plane service between Bradley and over 60 other North American airports, operated by Eastern, United, TWA, Delta, American, USAir, Pilgrim, and Altair. Buses leave the terminal for downtown Hartford and for Springfield, Mass., periodically, and limousines shuttle from Bradley to most cities in Connecticut. By the way, the Connecticut Aeronautical Historical Association operates the **Bradley Air Museum** (tel. 203/623-3305) at the airport, with over 30 aircraft, plus engines, accessories, and memorabilia, on display. The collection is open to visitors all year from 10 a.m. to 6 p.m. every day. Admission for adults is $3.50; children (6 to 11), $1.75; preschool children, free.

By Rail

Amtrak runs trains daily from New York to Boston along both the coastal route (via New Haven, Old Saybrook, New London, Mystic, and Providence) and the inland route (via Hartford, Windsor Locks, and Springfield). Stopovers are allowed at no extra charge on most trains, so if you buy a ticket from New York to Boston, the stops in New Haven, New London, and Mystic, or New Haven and Hartford, need cost no more. It is usually possible to catch a train from New York in the morning, be in Mystic by noon, tour the Seaport thoroughly, catch another train around 5 p.m., arrive in Providence by about 6 p.m. and Boston by 8 p.m. The trip from New York to Hartford takes less than three hours; to New Haven, about 1½ hours; to New London, about 2¾ hours; to Mystic, about three hours.

Besides the Amtrak trains, there are frequent commuter runs operated on the Connecticut Department of Transportation's New Haven Line by Conrail

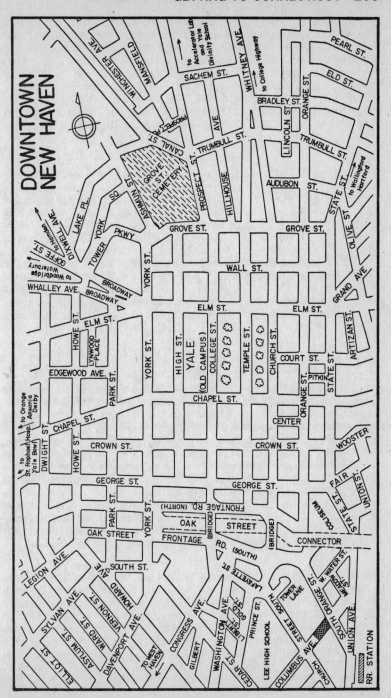

DOWNTOWN
NEW HAVEN

(Consolidated Rail Corporation). These CDT/Conrail trains depart New York's Grand Central Terminal hourly from about 7 a.m. until after midnight on weekdays, with even more frequent runs during rush hours. Service on Saturday, Sunday, and holidays is almost as frequent, with trains at least every two hours. The trip by CDT/Conrail takes one hour and 40 minutes. For exact schedule information, call toll free 800/223-6052 or in New York City 212/532-4900. The big advantages of the CDT/Conrail trains over Amtrak on the trip to New Haven are the convenience of Grand Central Terminal—midtown, right beneath the Pan Am Building—and the great frequency of trains.

By Bus

Greyhound, Trailways, Bonanza, and Vermont Transit all operate daily buses between New York City, New Haven, and Hartford. The trip to Hartford takes about 3 to 4¾ hours, depending on the line and the number of stops en route. Greyhound and Bonanza have services between New York and New London, and on to Providence and Cape Cod. From New York City to New London takes about 3 or 3½ hours, depending on stops. It's difficult to take a bus to Mystic Seaport—the train's the best way to get there.

From Hartford, **Bonanza** has buses to Providence and Hyannis; **Vermont Transit** operates buses to Vermont, New Hampshire, Montréal, and Québec City. All the large lines have buses between Hartford and Boston. In Hartford, the bus stations and the railroad station are all within a block of one another close to downtown. The terminal for Greyhound, Vermont Transit, and Bonanza is at 409 Church St. (tel. 203/547-1500); for Trailways it's at 77 Union Pl. (tel. 203/527-2181).

1. New Haven

This is a town of spires and steeples, of Gothic towers and steel-and-glass towers, very much of the present and very much of the past. While New Haven was founded in 1638, the crucial year in its history was 1718, for in that year Connecticut's "Collegiate School" for the training of young men for the ministry decided to make its permanent and perpetual home in New Haven, ignoring the suits and blandishments of the other notable towns of Hartford and Saybrook. Perhaps the college came to New Haven because a local man offered a good deal of financial assistance, and in fact it was for this assistance that the school's name was changed to honor Elihu Yale.

New Haven has never been the same. Although today it is a town of business and industry—small arms, the telephone company, the county government—it is still more than anything the town where Yale is, and the presence of the great university dominates New Haven's social and cultural life.

INFORMATION: The **New Haven Visitors and Convention Bureau** maintains a year-round Information Center right in the center of town on the Green at 155 Church St. (tel. 203/787-8367), open Monday through Friday from 10 a.m. to 4 p.m. They also operate an information center off Interstate 95 from March 15 to November 15. At little or no cost, they will answer questions, give maps of the bus routes and streets, give literature on the city's attractions; they also provide walking tours, current material on recreational, educational, cultural, and special events in the area. A full-service program is furnished, complete with information packets, registration assistance, and spouse programs.

WHERE TO STAY: New Haven's lodging set-up is similar to that of many American cities: several luxurious hotels right downtown, and a larger number of moderate- and budget-priced motels on the outskirts. I'll describe the most convenient and attractively priced motels first, and then the posh places downtown, finishing up with some notes on motels farther out of town along I-95.

Bed and Breakfast

For one of those wonderful, moderately priced bed-and-breakfast rooms in the New Haven area, contact **Bed & Breakfast, Ltd.** (tel. 203/469-3260), P.O. Box 216, New Haven, CT 06513. You should be able to do better on price here than at a motel, and the room will be more like home.

Wilbur Cross Parkway Motels

Your best bet for a good, moderately priced motel room is the cluster of hostelries near New Haven on the Wilbur Cross Parkway. The parkway is the scenic alternative to the Connecticut Turnpike (I-95). Passing several miles northeast of New Haven, the parkway provides access to the city at its Exits 57 (Conn. Rte. 34, Derby Avenue), 59 (Conn. Rte. 63, Whalley Avenue), and 60 (Conn. Rte. 10, Dixwell Avenue). Motels are grouped at each exit, but the best selection is at Exit 59, Whalley Avenue.

Staying at any of the Exit 59 motels mentioned below, you'll be exactly 3½ miles from the greensward of Yale's Old Campus, the very center of the city. The "Amity Road" bus, no. B-1, will shuttle you between the motels and the center of town. A small shopping center and several restaurants are within walking distance of each motel.

The **Three Judges Motor Lodge,** 1560 Whalley Ave., New Haven, CT 06515 (tel. 203/389-2161), is just off the parkway at Exit 59, on the New Haven side. Modern, simple, and attractive, it's the sort of place Frank Lloyd Wright might have designed had he gone into the motel business. Prices for the well-equipped rooms are quite moderate: $34 for a double-bedded room, $40 for twin beds, tax included.

The **New Haven Motor Inn,** 100 Pond Lily Ave., New Haven, CT 06525 (tel. 203/387-6651), boasts that it can accommodate 1086 people at one time— and at moderate prices. The style here is what you might call "motel Georgian," handsome as well as functional. As you approach the motel (follow the signs from Exit 59), you'll think the place has about 18 rooms. But behind the main building (which is where you register) are several other large buildings boasting 125 rooms in all. You pay $44 to $48 single, $48 to $52 double (tax included) to stay here. Swimming pools, putting green, and restaurant are all on site. The New Haven Motor Inn was once the city's prime place to stay. Although it has lost that primacy—and the glitter that goes with it—it's still a good place to stay.

At Exit 61: Farther north, at Exit 61 North (Exit 62 South) is a **Howard Johnson's Motor Lodge** (tel. 203/288-3831, or toll free 800/654-2000), 2260 Whitney Ave., Hamden, CT 06518. The bonus here, as at many large nationally franchised motels, is that children up to 18 years old can stay with their parents for free. Rooms have color TVs, and cost $50 to $54 single, $53 to $61 double; an extra person in the room pays $5.35.

Downtown Hotels

The **Holiday Inn–Downtown** is at 30 Whalley Ave., New Haven, CT 06511 (tel. 203/777-6221), very near Yale and only a five-minute walk from the center of town. The 160 rooms here are all equipped with color TV, and cost $53.75 double, $62.35 single, tax included. Teenage children can stay free with their parents. The inn has its own "Village Café" restaurant and lounge, with foods from all over the world.

The downtown **Howard Johnson's Motor Lodge** is at 400 Sargent Dr., New Haven, CT 06511 (tel. 203/562-1111, or toll free 800/654-2000), near Long Wharf. Take Exit 46 from the Connecticut Turnpike, I-95. At this posh, hotel-like lodge, you're very close to the Long Wharf Theatre and not far from the center of town. The rooms have king-size beds in some of them, but prices are $52 to $65 single, $63 to $76 double; an extra person pays $9, but kids under 18 stay free. Even higher rates apply at graduation time. Senior citizens get a discount.

Motels in Branford

Nine miles east of downtown New Haven, at Exit 55 on the Connecticut Turnpike (I-95), are several motels which serve visitors to New Haven and those passing through.

The **Sunset Motel** (tel. 203/488-4035) is small, tidy, and inexpensive. For a room with TV, shower, and air conditioner, two people pay $29.03, tax included. Rooms are small, decor is dramatic, but housekeeping is top-notch, and the motel is only a quarter mile south of I-95 on U.S. 1 (look for signs), Branford, CT 06405. Coming from New Haven, get off at Exit 55, and turn left at the first stop sign.

If you get off I-95 at Exit 55 coming from New Haven, turn right at the stop sign to pass underneath the highway and you'll come to the large and luxurious **Branford Motor Inn**, P.O. Box 449, Branford, CT 06405 (tel. 203/488-8314). A U-shaped group of buildings faces U.S. 1 across a wide swath of lawn complete with swimming pool. Scores of guest rooms fill the two-story buildings, each room having air conditioning, direct-dial telephone, cable color TV and Home Box Office movies. Some rooms even have private steambaths. Rooms in the newer annex are several dollars more expensive than those in the older main buildings, and the price structure is further complicated by the size, number of beds, and special features (waterbed, steambath, handicapped, etc.). The cheapest single room goes for $41.93, the cheapest double for $51.60, tax included. The most luxurious, expensive double costs $91.38. Note that children aged 14 or under stay for free with their parents. You'll find a coffeeshop and steakhouse right in the motel.

WHERE TO DINE: New Haven's restaurants are spread throughout the metropolitan area, with no particularly rich concentration right downtown such as one finds in Hartford or Boston. But if you are selective, it is not difficult to find the meal you're looking for, at the price you want to pay, within walking distance of the Green. Part of the problem is that many New Havenites who enjoy dining out belong to private clubs (the famed Mory's is one of these), and thus tend not to patronize restaurants that are open to the general public.

A short walk north from the Green is the **Whitney Winery**, 44 Whitney Ave. (tel. 773-3399), across from the corner of Audubon Street. Light and airy inside, the spacious dining room is brightened with white trellises. The food is equally light and refreshing—the cheese board, for example, made up of cheese (your choice) and fruit, crackers, and vegetables or pepperoni ($4). You can have a cup of soup, or a slice of quiche, and a trip to the salad bar for $3.95, any of many sandwiches for even less. Over a dozen wines are sold by the glass, many more by the bottle; cocktails too. The beer list is international and endless. Hours are long: opening at 11:30 a.m., the main kitchen serves till 11 p.m. weekdays, till midnight on weekends, and after that you can get sandwiches from the bar until 2 a.m. (3 a.m. on Friday and Saturday). Sunday hours are 5 p.m. to 2 a.m.

Just across the street is Yale's "in" place for lunch these days, the **Foundry Café** (tel. 776-5144), 104 Audubon St., near the corner of Whitney Avenue and Audubon. The Foundry was just that, a machine foundry building, until it was recycled into a bookstore, shops, and the café. The one small café room has a bar/lunch counter, a blackboard menu, and some beautiful old inlaid wood chess tables as dining tables. Lunch is the only meal served, and it's on from Monday through Saturday, 11:30 a.m. to 3:30 p.m. Fare is simple but tasty: a selection of sandwiches for $2.15 to $3.75, a lobster salad plate for $5, cheesecake for $1. For the rest of the day and into the evening the Foundry Café is a bar and nightclub. Happy hour, when the hors d'oeuvres are free, is every weekday evening from 4 to 8 p.m., and there's entertainment each evening, with special jazz programs Thursday, Friday, and Saturday. Be warned that there is often a fearful demand for lunch tables at the Foundry Café, so go to lunch early or late rather than right at noon.

Buffet Lunch with a View

The **Top of the Park Restaurant,** atop the Park Plaza Hotel (tel. 772-1700) at 155 Temple St., near Chapel just south of the Green, has a value-for-money buffet lunch. It's served from noon to 3 p.m. Monday through Friday, and for $8.50 (plus tax and service, and beverage, total of $12) you can help yourself at the bountiful buffet table, then take a seat next to a wall of glass overlooking all New Haven. If you're new in town, like good food and plenty of it, and enjoy panoramas, this is for you.

Student Fare

Now for a few of those student eateries which abound in every college town, where prices are low and quantities are high:

Mamoun's, 85 Howe St. (tel. 562-8444), sounds properly exotic, and it is—a real middle eastern coffeehouse serving such dishes as baba ghannouj and hummus, falafel, and shish kebab for $1.70 (sandwiches) to $5.85 (combination plates). Turkish coffee and baklava or halvah are the right desserts at Mamoun's. If you want to drink, you BYO. Mamoun's is open 11 a.m. to 3 a.m., 365 days a year.

For quick lunches, there's **d'Angelo's Subs,** 849 Chapel St. (tel. 865-9291), a half block from the corner of Chapel and Church walking east. The beauty of d'Angelo's is variety—in size, ingredients, and price. All subs come in small, medium, or large sizes for $1.35 to $3.50 (a few, such as the sumptuous crabmeat sub, cost more). Syrian-bread "pokket" sandwiches are made a dozen ways and sold for around $2. Salads, with dressing and Syrian bread, cost even less. No extra charge for sliced tomatoes, onions, pickles, and hot peppers on any sandwich. These prices are great! Benches on the Green provide the perfect dining area in good weather, and if it's raining you can have lunch right in d'Angelo's.

Birthplace of the Hamburger

An audacious claim, to say that **Louis' Lunch,** 261 Crown St., at the corner of Chestnut Ridge Road (tel. 562-5507), was the "purveyor of the first hamburger in the U.S.A.," but so it is.

Louis' started in 1900, serving the first thinly sliced steak sandwich, and then developed the vertically grilled ground-beef sandwich. The beef is still ground fresh daily and grilled in the original antique vertical grills. Served on toast with tomato and onion, the hamburger is also available as a cheeseburger (introduced in 1931) for a bit more money. Threatened by downtown redevelopment some years ago, faithful Louis' fans saw to it that the brick structure was picked up and moved safely to its present location. Many—from all over the world—donated bricks for use in resettlement.

Louis' caters faithfully to New Haven's weekday lunch crowd from 9 a.m. to 4:30 p.m., closed weekends. Coffee and soft drinks are available.

WHAT TO SEE: The center of New Haven, the Green, is also the center of its history, and for a good historical introduction to the Green, stop in at the Information Center (tel. 787-8367) at 155 Church St., on the Green, and rent one of their tapé recorders for $3.50 plus tax. The taped tour will allow up to six people to walk at their leisure through the Green, learning of its history and of the three churches on it.

The churches on the Green have illustrious heritages of design, for Trinity Church is said to have been modeled somewhat on England's York Minster; Center Church and United Church are both said to have sprung from early plans for London's famous Church of St. Martin's-in-the-Fields. Center Church is particularly interesting as it was built on an old burying ground, and today has a crypt under it where you can see over 100 of the early gravestones. Guided tours of the church are offered Tuesday through Sunday.

Yale University

New Haven's prime attraction is Yale. Starting with the first day of classes and continuing whenever classes are in session, Yale sponsors free guided tours of the campus (tel. 436-8330). Tours start on College Street near the Green, at a place called Phelps Gateway, where the university has its information office. Tours are run during the summer months as well, but on a less full schedule.

Yale's campus reminds one right off of England's Oxford, for it's much more Gothic (and neo-Gothic) than, say, Harvard, which is mostly Georgian and colonial in style. Yale's got lots of open, grassy courts and fleched towers. Centerpiece of this English Gothic world is **Harkness Tower,** inscribed with the famous motto which has for generations admonished Yale men to move ever upward: "For God, For Country, and For Yale." Harkness Tower has a lovely carillon, which plays short medleys throughout the day. You can also see the art galleries, the Beinecke Rare Book Library, the Georgian-style Connecticut Hall, and the Gothic-style Sterling Law Buildings.

The Peabody Museum

Yale's Peabody Museum of Natural History is one of those fine, turn-of-the-century collections assembled when American scientists were venturing into all the corners of the world to bring back specimens of terra, flora, and fauna for study and observation by university students. Dinosaur bones, dioramas featuring exotic animals, mineral displays, and the like are all on show, although of course what the museum can show is only a fraction of its vast collections. Besides the permanent exhibits, the museum sponsors special shows, lectures, and films. Admission is $1 per adult, 50¢ per child (5 to 16). The museum, at 170 Whitney Ave., is open from 9 a.m. to 4:45 p.m. Monday through Saturday, from 1 to 4:45 p.m. on Sunday. Free on Tuesday.

Galleries

Opened in April 1977, on the Yale campus is the **Yale Center for British Art** (tel. 432-4594), 1080 Chapel St. near the corner of High Street. The center has a fine collection of works by British artists, and also features regular special exhibitions and concerts. Check *New Haven Info* listings for current offerings or call the center. You can visit and see what the center has to offer from 10 a.m. to 5 p.m. Tuesday through Saturday, 2 to 5 p.m. on Sunday. Admission is free.

Yale's other major art collection is in the **Yale University Art Gallery,** on Chapel Street between High and York. The oldest university art museum in the western hemisphere, the Yale Gallery is justifiably proud of its Garvan Collection of American Furniture and Silver. Anyone interested in 18th-century American silver has got to see the Garvan—it's the best in the world. Along with Van Gogh's masterpiece *The Night Café,* there are paintings by Rubens, Hals, Manet, Picasso, and others. The university's collections form a substantial holding of European, African, pre-Columbian, American, and Oriental art on view daily, Tuesday through Saturday from 10 a.m. to 5 p.m., Sunday from 2 to 5 p.m. There are also Thursday evenings hours from 6 to 9 p.m. during the academic year. Lectures, concerts, films, and special exhibits are always on when the university is in session; see the listings for current events.

Performing Arts

Because of Yale, New Haven has a surprisingly rich cultural life in music, dance, and drama. Each academic year sees concerts and performances by over a dozen excellent groups including the New Haven Symphony Orchestra, the Yale Concert Band, Yale Glee Club, Yale Jazz Ensemble, the Bach Society, the New Haven Civic Orchestra, and the Community Choir. The Yale Repertory Theater and the Long Wharf Theater (a proving-ground for New York–bound plays) get very good reviews each season, as does the Connecticut Ballet Company. New Haven also plays host to visits from the Boston Symphony Orchestra, major concert and popular performers, and groups. Several buildings in and around the campus are foci for these events. The listings recommended above have full information on the current season's performances. Most will be within a few blocks of the Green. Long Wharf is a bit farther out, next to Howard Johnson's, in the wholesale market at 222 Sargent Dr. (Connecticut Turnpike Exit 46; tel. 787-4282).

Nightlife Notes

New Haven must retain its dignity as the seat of Yale University. But that doesn't mean things are dead at night. Try the **Foundry Café,** mentioned above under "Where to Dine," for live music. The **Park Plaza** (see "Where to Stay") has a disco that's more sedate and elegant than wild.

2. Connecticut River Valley

Strictly speaking, the Connecticut River Valley extends all the way from Long Island Sound to northern New Hampshire. It's the lower valley that we're interested in, though. Besides being particularly beautiful, the last 100 or so miles of the river's course has figured prominently in Connecticut history. The small towns retain the charm of a bygone era, and the river's banks are scattered with state parks and forests.

From New Haven, it's about 30 miles along the Connecticut Turnpike (I-95) to Old Saybrook, right at the mouth of the Connecticut River. Cross the river and you're in Old Lyme, a particularly beautiful and charming colonial town. As a base of operations, the prime town is Essex, reached from the Connecticut Turnpike by either Route 153 or Route 9.

ESSEX: This was a shipbuilding and sea captain's town, founded in 1648. At first, life in Essex was centered on farming, but within 100 years the shipbuilding industry grew and brought Essex much greater prosperity. The early name, by the way, was the Indian one of Potapaug, which served to identify the town until well into the 19th century.

Today Essex is one of the most picturesque towns in Connecticut, its old houses well kept, its boatyards and marina bobbing with sleek yachts and power boats.

WHERE TO STAY AND EAT: Essex's fine old **Griswold Inn** (tel. 203/767-0991) is famous throughout Connecticut for its location, food, and lodging. The rooms are quaint and old-fashioned, with low ceilings and exposed rough-hewn rafters, hooked rugs on the floors, perhaps a marble-topped vanity or a similar piece in one corner. All the rooms are air-conditioned, and all have private baths. Price for the rooms: $52 double (both double beds and twins are available). Continental breakfast is included in the rates. Note that in summer it may be necessary to reserve a weekend date two months in advance, so call or write to the Griswold Inn, Essex, CT 06426.

The Griswold's several dining rooms are well done and interesting. At lunch, have the Griswold's own brand of sausages for $5 or $6, or a sandwich for about the same. Luncheon plates are only $1 more. Dinner specialties are hearty, with seafood for $10 to $13.50, steaks and such for a bit more. The wine list is decent, the beer both domestic and imported, and the draft is the English lager named Courage.

The Griswold is known for its Sunday "Hunt Breakfasts," when for $9 (noon to 2:30 p.m.) you can help yourself to unlimited amounts of eggs, bacon, and ham, sausage, grits, fried potatoes, kippers, chicken, lamb kidneys, creamed chipped beef, smelts, or whatever else is offered for the day. Children under 6 eat for free.

Perhaps the finest place to have lunch in Essex is at **The Gull** (tel. 203/767-0916), on the waterfront next to the Dauntless Boatyard. (From the Essex Island Marina, look to the boatyard; a gray building with large second-story windows, a white silhouette of a gull, and the word "restaurant" in blue letters identify it.) The Gull has a clean, bright, modern feel about it, with the nautical colors of white and blue predominating, even to the informal uniforms of the staff: blue jeans with white jerseys, or white jeans and blue jerseys. Two dining areas here. Upstairs is the full menu: I had a caviar egg (although sorely tempted by the more expensive smoked salmon with frozen vodka); then bluefish poached in fish stock, finally strawberry crêpes with sour cream and strawberry ice cream, all for $22, tax and tip included. I could have had veal, beef, or chicken. All main courses come with potato or rice, vegetable, salad, roll, and butter, and you can order just the main course ($9 to $15), or indeed just the appetizer or dessert—no minimum charge. But for lighter meals, the **Laughing Gull** downstairs is the place to go, for here they serve quiches, cabbage rolls, sandwiches, and so on. Nice, inexpensive wine list on both levels. The Laughing Gull is open Tuesday through Sunday, 7:30 a.m. to 10 p.m. and Monday from 5 to 9 p.m.; the Gull (upstairs) serves lunch and dinner every day; Sunday evening is buffet night.

Essex's all-round eatery is the **Light Horse,** at the corner of North Main, Main, and Pratt Streets, in the center of town. Ice-cream-parlor wire chairs and tables, and racks of jams, sauces, and condiments on the wall give the Light Horse its summery atmosphere. Go straight to it if you intend to breakfast in Essex. During the rest of the day, a hamburger on a hard roll is $2.45; other sandwiches and several salad plates cost $3. There's Würzburger beer on tap. Hours are Monday through Friday from 7:30 a.m. to 4 p.m., in summer to 6 p.m.; Saturday from 8 a.m. to 4 p.m., in summer until 6 p.m.; closed Sunday.

One of the most elegant and delightful dining places in all southern Connecticut is a few minutes from Essex in nearby Ivoryton. It's the **Copper Beech Inn,** described a few paragraphs below—read on.

WHAT TO SEE: From Essex Square (intersection of Main, North Main, South Main, and Pratt Streets), walk down Main Street to the end, known as the Foot of Main. You'll pass the Griswold Inn, and, at the end of the street, an art gallery (open 1:30 to 5:30 p.m., Tuesday through Saturday). A bit farther and you're at the river, looking at the boats moored or making their way. The **Steamboat Dock** area is up for restoration, as soon as the money is found. Walk down Ferry Street to the Essex Boat Works and **Essex Island Marina.** If you're dressed in yachting garb and don't mind telling a white lie, walk down to the dock and climb aboard the little shuttle boat. The operator may ask if you have a boat in the marina, or if you're visiting friends on one, to which you answer "yes." He'll ferry you across the narrow channel, and you can stroll around, looking at the boats. The Dauntless Boatyard and the Gull Restaurant are near the mainland part of the Essex Island Marina.

Walk up Pratt Street for a look at the old houses, and then from Essex Square, take a drive out North Main Street to view the fine old mansions. This quick tour leaves out lots of interesting side streets, corners, and crannies of Essex, and if you have the time, you could do worse than poke around town, turning up quaint vignettes and fine river views. To see the inside of an old Essex house, go to the **Pratt House** at 20 West Ave. (west out of Essex Square on Methodist Hill, toward the highway), now owned by the Society for the Preservation of New England Antiquities and open to the public for a small fee during the summer.

The Valley Railroad

On the way to nearby Ivoryton, the road passes the station of the Valley Railroad. You can ride the old steam train five miles upriver to Chester and back. At Deep River Station, if you wish, you can get off the train and onto the riverboat *Silver Star* to motor farther upriver past Gillette Castle (see below). Trains leave four times a day in fall, two times a day during spring, and several times every day beginning at 10:30 a.m. in summer; they connect with the boat for a two-hour combination trip. The train ride alone costs $3.95 for adults, $2 for children under 12; with a one-hour cruise, the prices are $6.95 and $4. Call 767-0103 for the latest information on schedules and fares.

Over in Ivoryton

Ivoryton is a part of Essex for municipal government purposes, but it has a character and history of its own. The name came from the ivory industry set up here by the Comstock family, and many of the ivory keys for America's pianos and organs were made here. The ivory industry is gone, but the company that makes Witch Hazel, that soothing and astringent distillate, is still going strong on the Essex/Ivoryton boundary.

The reason to go to Ivoryton is to dine at the **Copper Beech Inn** (tel. 767-0330) on Main Street. The inn was built as the home of a prosperous ivory merchant, and is now one of New England's most gracious places to dine: tables have fresh flowers and a full French service in silver. The Comstock Room has fine dark-wood paneling; the garden porch is mostly windows and plants, with a floor of quarry tiles and a unique pineapple chandelier. Behind the inn is the **Greenhouse**, a real one set with wicker chairs and small tables, and it's here that cocktails are served. The menus for lunch and dinner are among the best in New England: brace of baby quail, shrimp in beer batter with fruit sauce, rack of lamb persille, filet of beef Wellington with sauce perigourdine—and it goes on to 20 items at each meal, none common, all interesting. Entrees are mostly $13 to $17, with some less, some more. Appetizers such as clams roasted with garlic butter and Pernod, topped with hazelnuts, cost $5.50 at lunch or dinner. The 13 desserts offered (about $3) include Grand Marnier mousse en swans, and the Copper Beech Inn's sacher torte.

Lunch is served at the Copper Beech from noon to 2 p.m. Tuesday through Saturday; dinner is from 6 to 9 p.m. Tuesday through Thursday, to 10 p.m. on Friday and Saturday; Sunday dinner is from 1 to 9 p.m. Note that because of its high standards of cuisine, tables at the Copper Beech are in great demand, and for a weekend it's good to have a reservation a month in advance; for a weekday, two weeks. You may find a place at the last minute, but you will have to take what times are available rather than choosing your own. The Copper Beech also has five fine rooms with private baths decorated in the Colonial Williamsburg style and air-conditioned, for $55 to $85 double per night.

Gillette Castle State Park

Shortly after the turn of the century, an actor named William Gillette realized a lifelong dream by building himself a castle to live in. His stage career, including a very successful period in the role of Sherlock Holmes, had brought him the wealth he needed, and so in 1914 he started. Over five years and a million dollars later, the result was a strange-looking mansion of river stone named "The Seventh Sister," complete with a commanding view of the Connecticut River and its own three-mile-long excursion railroad. Inside the castle, Gillette gave vent to his passion for detail and exotica, bringing furnishings from around the world and specifying in great detail the form which was to be given to the intricately carved oak trim and the ingenious wooden door latches. Today William Gillette's fantasy house is known as Gillette Castle, and it's a state park open to all and sundry. The toy railroad is gone, but forest paths, picnic tables, and river vista spots have replaced it. Tours of the house itself are given from Memorial Day to Columbus Day from 11 a.m. to 5 p.m., at a charge of 50¢ for adults (children under 12, free). Gillette Castle is either

Connecticut's most distinguished medieval castle, or the largest backyard barbecue ever constructed—you decide.

If you're driving, the most enjoyable way to get to the castle is to take the old **Hadlyme ferry,** which takes cars (25¢ for car and driver) as well as pedestrians (5¢) at prices more antique than the fairly modern boat which performs the run. Although the boat is new, the history of the ferry run at this point goes back to 1769, when one Jonathan Warner would drag you across the river for a small fee. Today the ferry is run by the State of Connecticut, and it operates from April through October, 7 a.m. to 7:45 p.m. every day. The trip across the river is made right in the shadow of Gillette Castle, and takes about five minutes, not counting the short waiting time.

Goodspeed Opera

Up the river a few miles from Gillette Castle is the village of **East Haddam** and the Goodspeed Opera House, a riverside Victorian gem built in 1876, and restored recently to serve as the home of the American Musical. Its setting by the river and the bridge is so picturesque that it's worth the ride just to see the exterior, but if you have the time, take a tour of the interior (on Monday in summer only, 1 to 3 p.m.; 50¢ for adults, 25¢ for kids). Best of all, see a play; the specialty is the revival of early musicals and the production of new works. Eight Goodspeed shows have moved to Broadway. Three musicals are offered each season beginning in late April and continuing through early November with performances every day but Monday, and a matinee on Wednesday. Tickets cost $8 to $12 Friday through Sunday, $1 less on other days. For the latest information and ticket reservations, call 203/873-8668.

Right next door to the Goodspeed Opera House is **Gelston House** (tel. 873-9300), a restaurant which coordinates its menus to the performances in the Opera House. It's open seven days a week for lunch and dinner, and dinner all day (noon to 8 p.m.) on Sunday. The luncheon special, with soup and dessert, is only about $6; sandwiches are less; à la carte plates are only slightly more. At dinnertime entrees cost $8.50 to $14.50 and tend to seafood, but also include such things as veal permigiana with spaghetti. Although the building dates from 1853, the interior has been redone nicely with modern materials. A large patio enclosed with small-pane windows overlooks the river, the Opera House, and the bridge. At the rear of the Gelston House, a small beer garden (open in summer) is the place to enjoy a cold beer, a glass of wine, a sandwich. The inside rooms are air-conditioned; the garden depends on the weather.

3. Mystic Seaport, New London, and Groton

Connecticut's maritime life, past and present, is all on view in the area comprising the open-air museum called Mystic Seaport, and the "submarine cities" of Groton and New London. Mystic Seaport is one of the top tourist attractions in New England, drawing very large crowds every day of the summer. The huge open-air "museum" is big enough to handle the crowds, but the capacity of nearby motels is not, and so the prices of rooms very near Mystic are astoundingly high. Even at high prices, though, the motels are packed in July and August, and guests must *prepay* their entire stay! I would suggest, therefore, that you consider staying slightly farther from Mystic if you wish to save money. Using one motel as your base, arrange to see all the sights in the three cities by car.

You can avoid the hotel crush altogether by taking an Amtrak train through this area, getting off for the day at Mystic, where a bus will take you from the station to Mystic Seaport. After your day roaming around the ships, old buildings, and exhibits, board an afternoon train to Providence or Boston (or New Haven, or New York). There's no extra charge for the stopover if you buy a through ticket, and you obviate the need for a room.

INFORMATION: Each of the towns listed below has its own information booths and offices, which I'll mention as I go along. For general inquiries your best bet is the **New England Tourist Information Center,** Olde Mistick Village, Mystic, CT 06355 (tel. 203/536-1641). Olde Mistick Village is the new colonial-style shopping complex just south of I-95 on Route 27, very near Mystic Seaport. The Tourist Information Center is in Building 1.

WHERE TO STAY: Because of the crush of visitors to the area in summer, I'll include below lodging suggestions for the area as a whole. Generally speaking, if you want a lower-price room with fewer frills, try the motels in **Niantic,** for fancier places at higher prices, closer to Mystic Seaport, try **Mystic.** But the coziest places of all are in the quaint village of **Stonington.**

Bed and Breakfast in Stonington

The village of Stonington is five miles east of Mystic, on the water. It's a pretty, traditional New England seacoast village, just the place to stay if you want to escape the crowded highways and modern motels. Stonington's bed-and-breakfast guest-house list is beginning to grow. If you can't get a room at the following places, drop by the **State of Connecticut Tourism Division Information Center** off I-95 southbound at North Stonington. They may be able to help.

The **Pleasant View Guest House,** 92 Water St., Stonington, CT 06378 (tel. 203/535-0055), is owned by Mr. and Mrs. Edwin D'Amico, who rent out a few rooms in their old New England house. Rooms cost $38 to $43 double with shared bath, tax included.

Farnan House, 10 McGrath Court, Stonington, CT 06378 (tel. 203/535-0634), is another large, nice old Stonington house which takes in travelers for $40 double per night, tax included. You share a bath. Farnan House is a bit difficult to find, so call ahead first.

Motels in Niantic

Just off I-95, Exit 74, at the intersection with Route 161, north of the town of Niantic, is a collection of motels with similar facilities and fairly low prices. There's also a **Chamber of Commerce Information Booth,** in a converted railroad caboose, next to the entrance to the TraveLodge motel on Route 161.

The budget star here is, of course, the **Susse Chalet Motor Lodge** (tel. 203/739-6991, or toll free 800/258-1980), East Lyme, CT 06333, where the clean, modern rooms with air conditioning, TV, full bath, and a double bed cost $25.70 single, $30 double; rooms with two double beds cost $33.20 for three, $36.50 for four persons. The motel has an outdoor pool, coin laundry, and other standard motel services.

Nearby is the **Connecticut Yankee/TraveLodge** (tel. 203/739-5483), East Lyme, CT 06333, where rooms start at $36.68, and children under 17 can stay with their parents for free. An outdoor pool is open from May to September; live entertainment Tuesday through Sunday. The TraveLodge has a restaurant where dinner will cost $7 to $12; at lunch the special is "Soup, Sandwich, and

Suds," that is, soup of the day, your choice of a sandwich, and a glass of draft beer for $4 to $5. A Champagne Brunch for $7 is served every Sunday from 11 a.m. to 2 p.m., or you can start your weekday mornings paying $1.75 to $3.

The local incarnation of **Howard Johnson's** (tel. 203/739-6921, or toll free 800/654-2000), P.O. Box 185, East Lyme, CT 06333, is a pretty good bargain at $38.70 to $55.90 single, $45.15 to $62.35 double, or for a family (in the higher-price rooms) during the summer season (late June through Labor Day); April, May, the greater part of June, and September, rates are 10% to 15% lower. Two saunas, an indoor pool, and color TV in the rooms make it a fairly plush place for a reasonable price. Kids under 18 stay free, and there's a senior-citizen discount.

On the Highway

At the Cross Road Exit (no. 81) on I-95, get off for the **Lamplighter Motel** (tel. 203/442-7227 or 442-8142), Waterford, CT 06385, set back from the highway a bit in a wooded area. The Lamplighter still suffers from a certain amount of road noise, but the problem is common to almost all the motels near Mystic, New London, and Groton. The extras here are color TV, full baths, air conditioning, an outdoor pool, a picnic area, and a few holes of mini-golf. In July and August a two-day minimum applies on weekends. Rates are $34.24 to $38.52 for one, $36.38 to $40.66 for two in a double bed, $38.52 to $40 for two in two double beds; the third and fourth persons in a room pay $3 each. For an extra $4, you can have a room with a fully equipped kitchenette. In winter, prices at the Lamplighter fall dramatically.

Motels in Groton

Two motels are at the Route 184 exit from I-95.

The **Windsor Motel** (tel. 203/445-7474) has a good choice of accommodations—some especially good for families—at reasonable prices. Of the 28 motel rooms, six come with complete kitchens; all have TV and air conditioning. The price structure is to your advantage: use only one double bed and you pay only $32.50 to $37; use both double beds and the price is $41 to $52. Children of any age, when traveling with a parent, stay free, so the two-bed price is what a family of four would pay! All these prices include taxes, and all are substantially lower off-season, or for longer stays (a week or more). Swimming pool and tennis courts should be in operation by the time you arrive. The Windsor's address is 345 Gold Star Hwy., Groton, CT 06340.

At the nearby Bet-Nick Motel (tel. 203/445-7458), prices are similar. Off-season for these two establishments is the period from mid-September through May.

Motels in Mystic

The cluster of motels at the Route 27 interchange on I-95 includes several branches of big chains, and several local establishments.

Best buy here is the **Howard Johnson's** (tel. 203/536-2654, or toll free 800/654-2000), P.O. Box 159, Mystic, CT 06355, where, besides their standard rooms with cable color TV, you can enjoy an indoor pool, sauna, and a lounge, with wide-screen cable TV as well as live entertainment (although presumably not at the same time). Children up to 18 can stay free. Prices depend on when you go: off-season rates are lower, but mid-June through September, rates are $42 to $81 single, $45.50 to $81 double. An extra person pays $8.

At the **Ramada Inn** (tel. 203/536-4281, or toll free 800/228-2828), I-95 at Route 27, Mystic, CT 06355, the facilities are similar to the Howard Johnson's—indoor pool, live entertainment, and a playground too. The year-round rates are $42 to $60.20 single, $49.50 to $71 double.

The **Seaport Motor Inn** (tel. 203/536-2621), Mystic, CT 06355, is perched on a rise, surveying the other motels, restaurants, and the Olde Mistick Village shopping area. Again, the facilities are luxury class, but with a bit more thought and style put into the room furnishing compared to the large chain operations. The outdoor pool shares the view of the scene below with rooms. Rates in summer are $59.13 to $64.50 for a double, in winter $47.30 and up, with an extra person, whether child or adult, paying $5.

The **Taber Motel** (tel. 203/536-4904), on U.S. 1 east of Mystic, CT 06355, is more than a motel, actually. Besides its brand-new motel rooms, it can rent you a room in a restored inn (1829), a two-bedroom cottage, or an efficiency apartment. All rooms have private bath, cable color TV, phone, and air conditioning. In high summer, rooms go for $58 to $70 double in the motel, about $10 to $15 less in the inn, continental breakfast included.

WHERE TO DINE: The **Seamen's Inne Restaurant** (tel. 536-9649) is right next to the entrance to Mystic Seaport, and is open daily from 11:30 a.m. to 10 p.m. (on Sunday until 9 p.m.). Besides the interior rooms, decorated—as one might well expect—in congruence with the period of Mystic Seaport (19th century), the Seamen's Inne has a terrace out back with a view of the inlet from the sea. At lunch, the fare is mostly salad plates (about $5), and the special combination of soup, sandwich, coleslaw, and beverage is about $7. Lunch is served Monday through Saturday only. In the evenings and all day Sunday, dinner is served, and the Inne's forte is seafood, with a fairly full dinner costing $16 to $20.

The Seamen's Inne has recently added a **Victorian Oyster Saloon,** the place to go for drinks, freshly shucked clams and oysters, and light meals in the $5 to $6 range.

Within the confines of Mystic Seaport itself is the **Galley,** a fast-food restaurant. Food is ordered from the counter and taken to one of the dozens of sheltered tables. Seafood dinners average $3.50; also included on the menu are hamburger, hot dogs, ice cream, and soft drinks.

Out by the I-95 intersection is the **Steak Loft** (tel. 536-2661), a large barnlike structure suitably rusticized with lots of rough stained boards on the walls and ceilings and small candle lanterns on the tables. In the loft itself, which is two stories high, farm gear is hung here and there to get you in the mood. The bar is here, and there's live entertainment most nights during the summer. The lunch menu has sandwiches and the fish of the day for $4 to $5; at dinner, as the restaurant's name indicates, the specialty is steak: sirloin, tenderloin, steak teriyaki, and such for $8 to $13; seafood is slightly more expensive, but fowl—skewered chicken, for example—is less. Salad and potato are included in the entree price.

In the Olde Mistick Village shopping mall, the **Pioneer Sandwich Shoppe** is open 11 a.m. to 5:30 p.m. Monday through Saturday, noon to 5:30 p.m. on Sunday, and features grinders and sandwiches for $2.50 to $4, platters for twice that amount, and Michelob on tap. Several tables outside on the porch give you a view of the other buildings and shoppers, but beer is served inside only.

WHAT TO SEE IN MYSTIC: Mystic Seaport Museum is impressive. One could return again and again to see the various indoor exhibits, walk through the preserved 19th-century town, or climb aboard one of the venerable sailing ships moored and preserved here. Although it is technically a nonprofit museum, there is much more life to it than just rows of glass cases housing exhibits. While you will see scrimshaw, old tools, watches, clocks, chronometers, navigational instruments, and so on, most of your time will be taken walking through the village and watching the interpreters (staff) do their jobs and explain what they're doing. You will see a half dozen crew high in the rigging of the square-rigged ship *Joseph Conrad,* furling a sail in time to a chantey they sing, with one rope supporting all of them high above the deck. Mystic Seaport is open from 9 a.m. to 5 p.m. daily year round except Christmas Day. Grounds and selected exhibits are open until 8 p.m. from mid-May to mid-September, at $8 for adults, $4 for children 5 to 15; toddlers and military personnel, free. Reduced rates for senior citizens, for groups, and for two-day tickets. To get the feel of the place, the management recommends that you stay at least three or four hours; if you've arrived late in the day, when you buy your ticket, have it validated for the next day for a small extra charge. With your ticket you'll be given a very handsome map of the village and its exhibits, plus a list of the daily events, from special lectures to sea chantey sings. Look at the list first off to get an idea what'll be in action for the hours you're in the village. The museum can be divided basically into three areas: the formal exhibits of various boats, instruments, figureheads, and the like, mostly near the Seamen's Inne entrance gate; the restored village and waterfront area; and the shipyard at the southern end of the grounds where the whaler *Charles W. Morgan,* the last surviving wooden whaling ship in the country, is being restored.

Remember that the crowds are heavy in summer—although the museum seems large enough to absorb them all without too much crowding—and that traffic on the mile-long road from I-95 to Mystic Seaport may be pokey. At Mystic Seaport there's quite a lot of free parking.

Mystic's Other Sights

Mystic has a **Marinelife Aquarium** (tel. 536-3323) at the Mystic exit off I-95 and Route 27. Exhibits include many types of familiar and exotic fishes, and also recreations of their natural habitats. A belukha whale from Hudsons Bay is one of the major exhibits. The aquarium is open from 9 a.m. to 7:30 p.m. in summer, to 4:45 p.m. in winter; closed only Thanksgiving, Christmas, and New Year's Days. Admission is $5.50 for adults, $2.75 for children and senior citizens.

Also at the I-95 Mystic intersection is **Olde Mistick Village,** a shopping center built in the form of a New England village circa 1720. The various shops, banks, bakeries, and so forth are all housed in quaint buildings. The meeting-house (church) is sometimes rented out for weddings. The complex has a **Tourist Information Center** (tel. 203/536-1641) in Building 1, very near where you drive into the center's parking lot. The center is open daily.

On Pequotsepos Road is the **Denison Homestead,** a restored 1717 house which has belonged to one family for 11 generations (open mid-May to mid-October from 1 to 5 p.m. daily except Monday; adults pay $1.50; kids, 25¢). Nearby is the **Denison Pequotsepos Nature Center,** a 125-acre wildlife sanctuary with exhibits explaining the flora and fauna, and several miles of trails for nature walks. It's open April through October, Monday through Saturday from 9 a.m. to 5 p.m., on Sunday 1 to 5 p.m.; November through March, Tuesday through Saturday from 10 a.m. to 4 p.m., on Sunday 1 to 4 p.m.; closed Monday in winter.

Boat Trips on the Mystic River

The 1908 S.S. *Sabino,* one of the last coal-fired passenger steamers in the United States, leaves its dock in Mystic Seaport each evening mid-May through mid-October, for 1½-hour downriver excursions. No Seaport admission is required for the evening voyages, priced at $4 for adults, $2.50 for children 5 to 15. At various times throughout the summer, special music cruises are scheduled, and for a bit more money you can enjoy a lively Dixieland band, barbershop quartet, or sea chantey singer as you steam along. Ask at the Seaport, or write or call ahead (Mystic Seaport, Mystic, CT 06355; tel. 203/572-0711) to find out when the music cruises will be.

The *Sabino* also makes short half-hour waterfront trips for visitors to the Seaport. You must have paid admission to the Seaport, and then tickets cost $2 for adults, $1.25 for children. The trips begin hourly from 11 a.m. to 4 p.m.

WHAT TO SEE IN GROTON: Groton, "The Submarine Capital of the World," makes its living from General Dynamics' Electric Boat Division and from Pfizer pharmaceuticals, besides the naval facilities at the navy submarine base. A warning is in order: Rush-hour traffic (8 to 9 a.m. and 5 to 6 p.m.) in the Groton/New London area is extremely heavy, especially along I-95 and its feeder roads. Make your getaway before 5 p.m., or stay and have dinner till the roads empty out.

No one comes to Groton to see anything but submarines, and there are plenty to see. **Gray Line** of New London–Mystic (tel. 443-1831; on weekends, 447-1727), P.O. Box 828, New London, CT 06320, has several tours through the navy's sub base. A one-hour tour (late June through Labor Day) costs $5 for adults, $2.50 for kids under 12; a special two-hour tour is by reservation only. For a few dollars more you can have a tour of New London, the Coast Guard Academy, several historic houses, and a drive along the Thames (pronounced as it looks, *not* "temz") River. This tour takes 2½ hours.

The inside of a sub is yours to explore in the U.S.S. *Croaker* (tel. 448-1616), a World War II submarine now open to the public at 359 Thames St. (near Fort Griswold on the street running along the Thames's east bank; take the Bridge Street Exit, no. 85, off I-95). The sub is on view from 9 a.m. to 3 p.m. (to 5 p.m. in summer) all year. Admission is $3 for adults, $1.50 for children 12 and under, $2 for seniors; military, free.

While you're down in Groton, see the **Fort Griswold State Park,** at Monument and Park Streets (Monument runs parallel to Thames Street). The heroic, tragic story of the American force which defended the fort in 1781 against the British is told in the museum, open from Memorial Day to Columbus Day. The Memorial Tower (view from the top) was erected for the courageous defenders who fought until overpowered and then perished in the massacre by the victorious British. The state park is open all year, and both the park and the museum are free of charge.

WHAT TO SEE IN NEW LONDON: The major tourist attraction in New London can be found by following the red signs with white lettering dotted throughout the town and at the highway exits.

The **U.S. Coast Guard Academy** (tel. 203/444-8270), on Mogehan Avenue, New London, CT 06320, opens its campus to visitors from 9 a.m. to sunset daily. Admission is free. Start your tour of the grounds at the Visitors' Pavilion (open 10 a.m. to 5 p.m. from May 1 through October). The academy's museum is open 8 a.m. to 4 p.m., weekdays year round, and from 10 a.m. to 5 p.m. weekends and holidays, May through October. A special treat here is a visit to the Coast Guard's training barque *Eagle,* generally in port at the academy in April and May. If you miss the *Eagle,* perhaps you can catch the colorful dress review of the Corps of Cadets, usually held (weather permitting) in April, May, September, and October. For times and dates, contact the Public Affairs Office at the above number.

Ferry to the Islands

New London is a major ferryboat port, with frequent summer sailings to Block Island, Rhode Island, and Fishers Island and Orient Point, N.Y., on the tip of Long Island.

Block Island: See the Block Island section of Chapter IX for full details. The pier in New London is north of the railroad station (tel. 203/442-7891 or 442-9553). Follow the red-and-white signs to the dock.

Fishers Island: Daily ferries go to this New York island a few miles off the Connecticut coast, departing from the dock on State Street. For fares and schedules, call 203/443-6851.

Orient Point, Long Island: The dock for these is on Ferry Street; details from the Cross Sound Ferry Service (P.O. Box 33, New London, CT 06320) are available by calling 203/443-5281, 443-5035, or 443-7394; for reservations from Orient Point, call 516/323-2415, 323-2525, or 323-2743. Cars are carried, and reservations for the 1½-hour cruise are a must in high summer.

Ocean Beach Park

New London's major beach-and-amusement complex is at Ocean Beach Park, near Harkness Memorial State Park south of the city (Exit 75-76 from I-95; tel. 447-3031). Besides the beach, a boardwalk allows strolling to check out other members of the swimsuit set, miniature golf will test your reflexes, amusement rides provide a cheap thrill, and an Olympic-size pool is provided for diving and freshwater swimming. If amusement parks and commercial beaches are your thing, this is one of the best on the coast.

4. Hartford

Hartford is Connecticut's capital, a fairly small (pop. 150,000) and manageable city with an admirable range of attractive architectural styles and a businesslike spirit. It is and has been a city with a good amount of wealth, much of it generated by the tens of thousands of officeworkers who sit in the thousands of offices of Hartford's four dozen great insurance companies and banks. Insurance companies seem to have a penchant for expressing their wealth and prestige through skyscrapers: the Prudential Tower in Chicago, the John Hancock Tower in Boston, and others. Hartford has lots of insurance companies, and therefore lots of skyscrapers. The downtown area has been given a new attractiveness by redevelopment, which has left most of the buildings of great historical value intact.

The city was founded by Thomas Hooker, who left Newtown (Cambridge, Mass.) on foot with a band of followers in 1636 after a dispute with another clergyman over the strict rules which governed the colony of Massachusetts Bay. In 1639 Hooker and others drafted the Fundamental Orders as the legal constitution of their settlement, and it is upon this early document that Connecticut bases its claims as the first place in the world to have a written constitution. Every Connecticut auto license plate remembers Hooker when it proclaims Connecticut "The Constitution State."

TOURIST INFORMATION: The city maintains a Visitors' Information desk (tel. 203/522-6766) in the Old State House, 800 Main St., Hartford, CT 06103, in Old State House Square, right in the center of town. The desk is open Monday through Saturday from 10 a.m. to 5 p.m., Sunday from noon to 5 p.m. There is no short-term parking convenient to the Old State House, so plan to park for the length of your visit in a downtown lot, and then walk to the Old State House to ask questions and pick up maps and brochures. Another traffic note: Hartford is very much a commuters' town, and traffic is very heavy at rush hours. The best day to visit the city is Saturday, when most everything is open and parking is easily available. On Sunday a lot of things are closed.

WHERE TO STAY: Although Hartford has many motels on its outskirts, I'll concentrate on the hotels downtown. Staying in the center of things saves time and driving, and everything in downtown Hartford (except the Mark Twain House) can be visited comfortably on foot. All the downtown hotels have their own parking garages, or arrangements with nearby garages.

Adjoining Hartford's modern Civic Center is the new **Sheraton-Hartford Hotel** (tel. 203/728-5151, or toll free 800/325-3535), Trumbull Street at Civic Center Plaza, Hartford, CT 06103. Here there are over 400 rooms, and the hotel focuses on attracting convention crowds who will be meeting in the Civic Center. An indoor heated pool, a health club with sauna and whirlpool bath, all brightened by a large skylight, make it possible to swim and sun even in the dead of winter. The Cloister Restaurant seems at first a strange thing to find in so modern a hotel: rough wood beams and crude plaster walls, dimly lit with lanterns (albeit electric ones). Although it was undoubtedly thought up by a theatrical designer, it's not badly done. The menu is varied and the prices not too high: veal steak Southern Comfort ($14), suprême of chicken Jurasienne (breast of chicken sauteed and topped with prosciutto and cheese, on a bed of wild rice, $11). Rooms at the Sheraton-Hartford are priced at $70 to $92 single, $85 to $106 double. Pets accepted.

Asylum Street is the principal east-west thoroughfare in downtown Hartford, and at 440 Asylum St., Hartford, CT 06103, is the **Governor's House Motor Hotel** (tel. 203/246-6591). The location is quite good: right next to the Amtrak passenger station, a block and a half from the bus station, and a short four blocks to the Old State House. Although bearing the name of a motel, it's more like a refurbished downtown hotel, and it has the best prices of any downtown hotel: $35 to $40 single, $40 to $45 for two in a double bed, and suites for $50. There's no charge for children under 12 when they stay in their parents' room. Get a room in the front of the hotel and you'll have a view of the State Capitol. This is the best budget buy in town.

Both men and women who are traveling alone have a good place to stay inexpensively in Hartford. The city's modern—almost plush—YMCA, 160 Jewell St. at the corner of Pearl, Hartford, CT 06103 (tel. 203/522-4183), accepts both men and women in its 220 rooms. The location couldn't be better, right on Bushnell Park and only two blocks from the Old State House. The entire building is air-conditioned and the rooms—which are all singles—come in two types: a single without bath but with a TV is $15.75, and a single with a private bath and a TV is $20.05, and the tax is already included in these prices as well. The TVs are color sets, believe it or not. A $5 key deposit will have to be paid at check-in, but you get it back when you check out. These rates go down the longer you stay.

The **Hartford Region YWCA Residence Tower,** is located at 135 Broad St., corner of Broad and Farmington, Hartford, CT 06105 (tel. 203/525-1163), about eight or nine blocks from the very center of town, but only three blocks (up a hill) from the bus and train stations. It, too, is an attractive modern building with sports and classroom facilities, but it accepts only women in its single rooms. The rate structure and accommodations are similar to those at the YMCA, except that rooms do not have TVs: a single without a private bath is $13.98; with private bath and a telephone, the room costs $19.35, tax included. Some of the rooms have very fine views of the Capitol and downtown, and a budget-price cafeteria off the lobby serves meals at money-saving prices. The rooms with bath here are usually in great demand, so if you want one it's best to reserve in advance.

A Budget Motel on the Outskirts

Breaking my "downtown only" rule, here's a motel which offers an exceptional bargain. It's especially well suited for those zooming north on I-91 to Vermont and New Hampshire. At I-91 Exit 27 (Brainard Road) is a branch of the **Susse Chalet Inn** chain (tel. 203/525-9306, or toll free 800/258-1980), where a modern, comfortable (but not plush) room with a king-size bed costs $28 for one person, $32 for two; in a room with two double beds, two pay $32, and three or four persons pay $40. The rates are the same year round, and the motel offers the expected motel features: outdoor swimming pool, air conditioning, TV in the rooms, private bath, coin laundry, ice machine, etc.

WHERE TO DINE: Downtown Hartford's center of attraction is the big modern Civic Center. Many local citizens head here when it's time for lunch or dinner, as the Civic Center holds a good selection of eating establishments in all price ranges.

Civic Center Restaurants

The Civic Center is not just a place for meetings, for besides the auditorium and the shopping arcades, the place is loaded with sandwich shops, delicatessens, and full-service restaurants, at least a dozen in all.

The Promenade in the Civic Center is a collection of bright, modern light-meal counters, each with a different cultural theme. All serve cafeteria style, and when you've gotten your food you sit at a wooden table in one of the seating areas common to all. Most of these eateries are on the Market Level, below the Coliseum (which is on Level I). You'll see **La Crêpe** (tel. 527-3900), which specializes in its namesake; **Shelly's Downtown Deli** (tel. 278-1510), good for breakfast or a deli sandwich any hour of the day or night, seven days a week; **Buon Apetito** (tel. 522-4635), the place for pizza, Italian sandwiches, and daily special platters; **Ludlow's Raw Bar** (tel. 728-5868) is there just to serve clams, oysters, and the chowders made from them; **Ludlow's Restaurant** is a bit classier than the take-your-tray establishments in the same area.

Perhaps the most rewarding dining to be had in the Civic Center—and perhaps in all Hartford—is at the **Rising Sun Restaurant** (tel. 527-2600), on Level I. A tasteful, simple-but-elegant Japanese place, the Rising Sun's chefs prepare the food at your table, before your eyes, on either the hibachi (charcoal grill) or teppanyaki (steel griddle) style. First you start with a hot *oshibori* washcloth to clean your hands. Then have an appetizer of sashimi (raw fish), or shrimps and scallops in tempura butter. Teppanyaki age is a main course of beef cubes, shrimp, and breast of chicken quickly fried on the steel griddle. Entrees cost about $7 at lunch, twice that at dinner (for larger portions). Full meals, therefore, can be $14 or so at lunch, twice that at dinner. Drinks are served. Visit the Rising Sun for lunch, Monday through Saturday, from noon to 2:30 p.m., for dinner starting at 5:30 p.m., going till 10 p.m. (to 11 p.m. on Thursday, Friday, and Saturday). Sunday hours are noon to 3 p.m. for brunch, 5:30 to 9 p.m. for dinner.

Near the Civic Center

Several other fine restaurants are in the immediate vicinity of the Civic Center, and are good for lunch, dinner, or an evening of jazz.

For Lunch or Dinner: Luckily, Hartford has one of those dining places dear to the palate and pocketbook: a good, attractive, inexpensive Chinese restaurant. My favorite is **Song Hays** (tel. 525-6388), 93 Asylum St., just a block from the Civic Center. It offers long hours (11 a.m. to midnight, till 1 a.m. on Saturday nights, noon to 11 p.m. on Sunday), full bar, take-out service, and excellent prices for good food. The special lunch of soup and a plate of chop suey (for example) is only $4.25; other combinations are only a dollar or so more. Prices go up by a few dollars in the evening, but prices in the adjoining Orient Express fast-food outlet remain low.

Hartford's grande dame of restaurants is **The Brownstone** (tel. 525-1171), 190 Trumbull St. at the corner of Asylum and Trumbull Streets, right downtown next to the Civic Center. Brass plaques, lots of brick walls and potted plants, and Victorian-era furniture set the mood at the turn of the century, and a good number of dining rooms, nooks, and crannies give you a wide choice of situations in which to dine. The Brownstone's menu tends to the elegant, such as chicken Oscar ($6.50) for lunch, but less expensive items such as soup-and-salad ($1.95) are also available. At dinner the entrees are heartier and pricier: veal New Bedford, seafood California, and a slice of almond ricotta pie for dessert will set you back $13 to $14. Recoup some of that by visiting the Brownstone's bar, one of Hartford's best meeting places, during happy hour (Monday through Friday, 4 to 7 p.m.) when drinks are $1.25 and beer is 75¢, with complimentary hors d'oeuvres. A disco in the lower level is very active Thursday through Saturday evenings after 9 p.m.

For Supper and Music: A restaurant where the address is the name, that's **36 Lewis Street** (tel. 247-2300), only a few blocks from the Civic Center. (Lewis Street, by the way, is one block west of the Old State House, running between Pearl and Gold Streets.) The lunch and supper menus in this restored town house feature many Mexican favorites as well as sandwiches and quiches. If you're just in Hartford for the day, go here and order the "36 Express," your choice of two items: quiche, salad, soup, one-half sandwich, for less than $4. If you're here in the evening there's almost always entertainment—see the schedule posted on the door.

The **Russian Lady Café** (tel. 525-3003), 191 Ann St., just a half block off Asylum (Ann Street is the western edge of the Civic Center), is right in the middle of things. It takes its name from the 1600-pound solid-bronze statue group atop the building's facade. The statue, executed by the German sculptor Edwin Schulte, was the figurehead of the Rossia Insurance Company for many years, but when the building at Broad and Farmington was torn down to make way for the YWCA, the statue was saved and moved to its present perch. In fact, much of the Russian Lady's decor came from urban renewal: the lamps over the bar are from the ruins of the city's cathedral, which burned down some years ago; the stained-glass windows are from a former Russian Orthodox church. The menu has salads, sandwiches, quiches, and a few hot items such as Texas chili, for $2.50 to $3.50. Borscht is always available, as are draft beer and cocktails. The Russian Lady Café is open Monday through Saturday from 4 p.m. to 3 a.m., and Sunday from 6 p.m. to midnight. There's live entertainment seven nights a week.

WHAT TO SEE: The **Greater Hartford Convention and Visitors Bureau** (tel. 203/728-6789) has organized all the sights in Hartford's downtown into what they call **The Walk,** and a free folder guiding you from point to point along the scenic stroll is available from them at One Civic Center Plaza, or from the Visitors' Information desk in the Old State House. Bushnell Park, the city's central park on the Walk, was laid out by the famous landscape architect Frederick Law Olmsted, the Hartford resident who also landscaped Central Park in New York, the Fenway parks in Boston, and Montréal's Mount Royal Park. Here are the highlights of the Walk:

The Old State House

Pure Bulfinch, the Old State House served as Connecticut's state capitol from 1796 to 1878. You can see the inside Monday through Saturday from 10 a.m. to 5 p.m., Sunday from noon to 5 p.m.; admission is free. On the Main Street side, have a look at the statue of Hartford's founder, the Rev. Thomas Hooker (1586–1647). Compare this Bulfinch state house with the one in Boston, or with the Capitol in Washington, both Bulfinch achievements. Outdoor concerts are often held in the precincts of the Old State House, and three galleries inside hold exhibits which change frequently. Warm weather finds farm markets, festivals, and concerts outside on the large lawn. Visitors Information Center and Museum shop open during regular hours.

The Cheney Building

North on Main Street a block from the Old State House is the mass of Connecticut brownstone built in 1877 by Henry Hobson Richardson for the Cheneys, a Connecticut family of silk manufacturers.

Constitution Plaza

Just east of the Old State House is this plaza, Hartford's triumph of urban renewal. The plaza has nice copses of trees (one of willows), a fountain designed not to splash or spray passersby in the wind, and the elliptical Phoenix Mutual Life building, perhaps Hartford's most striking building. Hartford is particularly rich in works by Alexander Calder, who had his home and workshop in the state. There's one of his mobiles suspended from the ceiling of the commercial banking room in the Connecticut Bank and Trust Company, on the Plaza.

The Travelers Tower

Between Main and Prospect Streets, right next to the Old State House, rises Hartford's tallest observation point, the Travelers Insurance Company Tower (tel. 277-2431). On weekdays in summer from 8:30 a.m. to 3:30 p.m. there are tours to the top of the building, leaving every half hour on the hour and half hour. In the 15 minutes spent at the top, you'll get the best possible view of the entire city, the suburbs, and the surrounding tobacco country. The Travelers Tower stands on the spot where there was once a tavern. It was in this tavern that Connecticut's royal charter disappeared during a dispute between colonials and royal officials, only to be hidden in the cavity of a nearby oak tree, the famous "Charter Oak" incident. Although the king's men ruled Connecticut illegally for a time (they could not find the charter and so destroy the legal instrument of Connecticut's self-rule), the charter survived, and is now on view at the State Library (see below).

By the way, there are 70 steps at the top of the tower which you must climb to get to the observation area. Also note that tours are run off-season, but you must call and make reservations.

Wadsworth Atheneum

This is Hartford's art museum at 600 Main St. (tel. 278-2670), with a fine collection of over 40,000 items of painting, sculpture, primitive and modern art. Don't miss a visit. It's open Tuesday through Sunday from 11 a.m. to 5 p.m.; suggested donation is $2 for adults, half that for children over 13 and seniors. Free on Thursday. As you enter, ask for a guide leaflet to the collections.

Burr Mall

Between Wadsworth Atheneum and the attractive city executive office building, the Mall is a shady, fragrant spot with a fountain and a fine—if incongruously placed—stabile of Calder's called *Stegosaurus* (1971).

Across Prospect Street from Burr Mall, take a look at the interesting buildings: the **Masonic Temple** and the **Hartford Times Building**. The facade for the latter building was once the front of a church in New York, which explains its architecture, odd for a newspaper building!

Center Church and Ancient Burying Ground

Across Main Street from the Travelers Tower is the site of the first church in Hartford, whose pastor was Thomas Hooker (he's thought to be buried under the church). The present church dates from 1807. The gravestones in the cemetery date as far back as 1640.

Bushnell Park

The park has 500 trees of 150 varieties, and is an oasis in the middle of the busy city. The twin-towered Gothic gateway on Trinity Street is Hartford's memorial to its Civil War dead. Be sure to visit the park's **carousel,** one of the finest restored merry-go-rounds you'll ever see, complete with calliope and automatic drums and cymbals. Rides cost 10¢, and it is by no means only children who take advantage of this low price. It has three types of seating accommodation: "Lovers' Chariots" for the unadventurous, stationary wooden horses, and horses that move up and down. Remember to grab at the brass ring. Note that the carousel doesn't operate on Sunday, and you must see it with all the lights on and the music trilling to really get the feeling.

The Capitol and Lafayette Square

Richard M. Upjohn is the architect responsible for Hartford's great potpourri of architectural styles and periods—soldiers in Civil War uniforms standing in Gothic niches, etc. For all that, the capitol is fine to look at. Once it was topped by a statue of *The Genius of Connecticut,* a lady. You can see that statue inside the building, and also the battle flags and memorabilia preserved here. Across Capitol Avenue is the **State Library** and **Supreme Court,** a pretty building housing the paper treasures of Connecticut history, including the famous Royal Charter once hidden in an oak tree. Besides the documents, the library is now the repository of the Samuel Colt collection of firearms of more than 1000 weapons. All together, the collections here make up the **Museum of Connecticut History,** and you can visit it Monday through Friday from 9 a.m. to 5 p.m., on Saturday to 1 p.m., closed Sunday; no charge for admission.

Near the Capitol and State Library, in Lafayette Square, is the **Bushnell Memorial Hall,** where many of the city's concerts, plays, and recitals are held. The interior is of the purest 1930s art deco, a style which has seen a resurgence in recent years. The Vienna Choir Boys or the Boston Symphony—you may find either on the playbill here depending on current schedules. For current information, call the Bushnell Memorial at 203/527-3123.

The Civic Center

This complex of several city blocks follows some of the best modernistic architecture, with fine shopping arcades, lots of open spaces, and mezzanines with hanging plants, small trees in pots growing up a story or two, and meeting rooms, restaurants, and clubs. The thing to do, especially on a hot summer day, is to enter its air-conditioned spaces and wander around enjoying the sights, perhaps stopping for a snack or a meal.

The Mark Twain and Harriet Beecher Stowe Houses

Hartford has a surprising number of palatial houses, most of them still occupied by wealthy families, and anyone in domestic architecture should take a drive through the residential sections northwest of downtown. For a look at two of the city's most impressive houses, drive out Asylum Street and Farmington Avenue about 15 blocks to the Mark Twain House (tel. 525-9317), 77 Forest St. While you drive, look for the art deco steeple of Trinity Church—the Twain and Stowe houses are four blocks past that point, on the left. You can go by bus: catch any one of the following at the Old State House or along Asylum Street: E-1, "Westgate–Health Center,"; E-2, "Unionville"; E-3, "Bishops Corner"; or E-4, "Corbins Corner."

The famous American author from Hannibal, Mo., settled in Hartford in the early 1870s. One of the wealthiest young men in town, Samuel Clemens (1835–1910) had this house designed by Edward Tuckerman Potter. It was finished in 1874 at a cost of $131,000, and is extremely rich in the sort of detail which makes Victorian architecture so much fun to inspect. The author lived here for 17 years, only moving out after bad investments forced him to take a lecture tour of Europe to make some quick money. He loved this place for the best years of his life, and *Tom Sawyer, Huckleberry Finn, Life on the Mississippi, The Prince and the Pauper,* and *A Connecticut Yankee in King Arthur's Court* were all written while he lived here. To see the house you must take the tour, which is just as well for the guides have an encyclopedic knowledge of the house and its occupants. In summer, tours run from 10 a.m. to 4:30 p.m. every day (June, July, and August); September through May, tours are given from 9:30 a.m. to 4 p.m. Tuesday through Saturday and 1 to 4 p.m. on Sunday; closed Monday. The tour takes about 50 minutes and costs $3 for adults, $1.25 for children 16 and under.

In the same complex of buildings, known as Nook Farm, is a house once lived in by Harriet Beecher Stowe, who wrote *Uncle Tom's Cabin*. Although that work was written while Mrs. Stowe lived in Brunswick, Me., the author lived and wrote in this house from 1873 until she died in 1896. Lots of the original furnishings of the author's remain in this Victorian "cottage," and the 40-minute guided tour costs $2.50 for adults, $1 for children 16 and under. Combination tickets for both the Twain and Stowe houses are available too: $5 for adults, $2.25 for children. The Stowe house is open at the same times as the Twain house.

5. Litchfield Lakes and Hills

Northwest of Hartford is tobacco country. The Connecticut River Valley has very good conditions for growing a premium wrapper leaf for cigars, the famous Connecticut Valley Shade-Grown Tobacco. The long barns next to the fields are for drying; and part of the year the crop will be covered with gauze enclosures to protect it from too much direct sun, hence the "shade-grown" name.

A pleasant morning or afternoon can be spent driving through part of the tobacco country on the way to Litchfield, the town from which Litchfield County takes its name. The county is all forest, rivers, and rolling hills, some of the prettiest country in this exceptionally pretty state, and the town of Litchfield itself is certainly among the most beautiful in New England.

Deeper into the northwest corner of the state you will come upon other charming towns, country inns, and resorts nestled in the Litchfield Hills (Connecticut's "Berkshires") and scattered on the shores of clear lakes. This is vacation country. In the charming old town of Salisbury, you're only four miles from the Massachusetts state line, 12 miles from the southern Berkshire town of South Egremont. (For the Berkshires, see Chapter VIII.)

A STOP EN ROUTE: Part-way to Litchfield on U.S. 44 is the **Avon Old Farms Hotel** (tel. 203/677-1651), a good place to have lunch or dinner. The original structure of the inn dates from 1757, although the larger dining rooms have been added in recent years. The biggest bargain for big eaters at the inn is its Sunday brunch, served from 11 a.m. to 3:30 p.m., an attractive buffet spread, from which you can take as much as you like and go back for seconds and thirds for $10 per person. On other days (except Monday, when the inn is closed), dishes will be on the order of broiled swordfish steak, filet mignon, or veal sentino, for $10 to $13.50. This price is for the full dinner with potato, vegetable, and a garden salad. The above prices are for dinner-size portions; at lunch the cost and the portions would be proportionately smaller. The Old Farms Hotel has a decent wine list.

Should you be on your way to the Berkshires and in need of a place to spend the night, the **Avon Old Farms Hotel,** P.O. Box 961, Avon, CT 06001 (tel. 203/677-1651), just across U.S. 44 from the restaurant, has modern rooms with all the trimmings, air conditioning, TV, an outdoor pool, two double beds per room, for $59.92 to $79.18 double, $49.22 to $68.48 single in summer, and about 15% less in winter. Children under 12 stay for free. For these prices you get a hostelry with tennis courts, health club, sauna, coffeeshop, and hairdresser. A 40-room addition was recently completed.

A TYPICAL 18TH-CENTURY TOWN: Connecticut's answer to the pretty Massachusetts towns in the Berkshires is Litchfield, a town which a National

Park Service writer has called "probably New England's finest surviving example of a typical late 18th-century town." The town was incorporated in 1719, and in the following 100 years grew and prospered as a center for small industry and an important way-station on the Hartford–Albany stagecoach route. With this prosperity came the urge, and the wherewithal, to build very fine, graceful houses, which is what the citizens did, making sure that the houses were set well back from the roadway. And while progress in the 19th century robbed Litchfield of much of its wealth—water-powered industry drove Litchfield's small-time craftsmen out of business, and the railroads bypassed the town—the town's decline may have been a blessing in disguise. Today, Litchfield retains its late 18th-century beauty, unsullied by the workers' tenements and textile mills which have changed the face of so many other New England towns.

WHAT TO SEE: At a tiny information booth on the town Green, you can get a free booklet on the town's history, architecture, and activities, complete with a small map. The sightseeing is simple enough: drive down South Street just to get the feel of the gracious neighborhood. Stop at the **Tapping Reeve House** (1773), and take a look at the small, unpossessing edifice beside it, which was the nation's first school of law, established here by Tapping Reeve in 1775 (the school moved into the one-room building in 1784). North Street is as attractive as South Street, and after a drive has given you the lay of the land, park at the Green and stroll along either street to see the houses more closely.

Here are some useful details: Tapping Reeve House and Law School is open from mid-May to mid-October, Thursday through Monday from noon to 4 p.m.; adults pay $1. The **Litchfield Historical Society** (tel. 567-5862) will give you a glimpse into the town's interesting past in many of its aspects, political, economic, industrial, decorative, and artistic. The society is on the Green at the corner of South Street, and exhibits are open mid-April to mid-November, Tuesday through Saturday from 11 a.m. to 5 p.m. The research library is now open year round, Tuesday through Saturday from 10 a.m. to 4 p.m.

The **White Memorial Conservation Center** (tel. 567-0015) is out on West Street (Route 202) a ways and is the state's largest nature center, with plenty of trails for enjoying the flora and fauna, and several prime perches for bird-watching. It's free, and it's open all year; the Museum is open Tuesday through Saturday from 9 a.m. to 5 p.m., and also on Sunday from 11 a.m. to 5 p.m. This displays live animals, a nature library, and exhibits, at $1 for adults and 50¢ for children 6 to 15.

Other Litchfield curiosities: The **Ethan Allen House,** thought to be the one in which the famous patriot and leader of Vermont's "Green Mountain Boys" was born; at the southern end of South Street, in the road's fork. A **milestone** dating from 1787, which informed the traveler that it was "33 Miles to Hartford, 102 Miles to New York—J. Strong AD 1787." The stone stands on West Street, northern side, just at the end of the town Green. And the jail, right on the Green at the beginning of North Street, is connected to the bank next door! Whether it's for the convenience of burglars who wish to escape or police who may nab burglars in the bank is not clear.

Litchfield's Winery

Just outside Litchfield is the **Haight Vineyard** (tel. 567-4045), on Chester Hill Road off Route 118 one mile east of town. This quaint but inviting place prides itself on being Connecticut's first farm winery (established 1975). Besides tastings, you can take the Vineyard Walk, a self-guided tour of the vineyards during which you get to inspect the various types of grapes which make Haight wines.

Some of the favorite wines here are Covertside White and Red, the table wines (the red is very spicy, made with a good amount of the Maréchal Foch French-American hybrid grape), a pure-red Maréchal Foch, a chardonnay and a Johannisberg Riesling. They even make a sparkling wine. Prices are moderate.

The winery is open May through December, Monday through Saturday from 10:30 a.m. to 5 p.m., on Sunday from noon to 5 p.m. In January through April it's open on weekends only. Tours are given Wednesday through Sunday, May through December.

LAKE WARAMAUG: From Litchfield, drive along U.S. 202 south and west for 12 miles to New Preston. Then head north on Route 45, and you'll come to pretty Lake Waramaug. Attractive inns front the lake, as does a state park with picnic and camping facilities.

Heading clockwise along the road which rings the lake, first you'll come upon the **Birches Inn** (tel. 203/868-0229), West Shore Road, New Preston, CT 06777. Heinz and Christa Holl, the innkeepers, preside over this large lakeside house set amid birch trees, overlooking the lake. Guest rooms are in the Guesthouse, a separate building behind the inn, or down on the shore of the lake. With private bath, breakfast, and dinner, double rooms cost $86 to $106 daily, or $215 to $269 per week without meals—a considerable saving. Rooms with kitchenettes, or a lakefront cottage which sleeps up to six people, can be rented by the week.

If you don't stay at the Birches, you might want at least to stop for a meal. A substantial tuck-in of herring in sour cream, chicken Cordon Bleu, sauerbraten, or sole stuffed with crabmeat, plus apfelstrudel for dessert, will cost about $18 to $24, more with wine or beer. As you might expect, the emphasis is on Central European dishes, and the service is personal.

Next landmark on your way around the lake is for campers. **Lake Waramaug State Park** (tel. 203/868-0220), New Preston, CT 06777, has 88 sites open May 15 through Labor Day. You can reserve in advance, but only by mail. Picnic grounds and swimming are here too.

The Inn on Lake Waramaug (tel. 203/868-0563; in New York City, 212/724-8775), just past the Hopkins Inn, New Preston, CT 06777, is actually a resort with all attractions. Indoor swimming pool, tennis courts, air-conditioned rooms, restaurant and lounge, gift shop, buggy rides and water sports (rowing, canoeing, sailing) are among the many offerings. There's even a small launch designed like an old "showboat" for tours of the lake. Even so, the inn retains an antique flavor. Of the guest rooms, only five are in the original inn, the others being in more modern but attractive guest houses. All rooms have baths, and some have working fireplaces. Prices range from $155 to $235 per day for two people, breakfast, dinner, taxes, and tips included.

Finally, not far from where the shore road rejoins Route 45, look for signs which point the way to the **Hopkins Inn** (tel. 203/868-7295), New Preston, CT 06777. This graceful old mansion set on a hill above the lake is most famous for its restaurant, but ten rooms are for rent as well. If you share a bath, a double room will cost $31; with private bath, prices start at $31. Whether you stay or not, have a meal—but also, have reservations. This is a very popular dining spot, especially on Saturday evenings, when reservations are required.

The blackboard menus change daily, but you can be sure of finding interesting, appetizing dishes. I had a difficult choice between clams Casino and smoked salmon to start, and an even harder time choosing among *backhendl* with lingonberries, steamed lobster, weinerschnitzel, or live trout meunière (you can choose your own trout from the tank!). When it came to those Austrian desserts, the choice was impossible. Figure $20 to $22 per person for dinner, with wine. Note these short dining hours: lunch from noon to 2 p.m. and dinner from 6 to 9 p.m. (till 10 p.m. on Friday and Saturday), Sunday dinner from 12:30 to 8:30 p.m. The inn is open April through December every day except Monday; rooms are rented May through October. In warm weather you can dine on the shady patio outside, with a grand view of the lake.

A Visit to a Vineyard

Next door to the Hopkins Inn on Lake Waramaug is the **Hopkins Vineyard,** on Hopkins Road in Warren (tel. 203/868-7954). The quaint red barn winery is open for tours and tastings from Memorial Day to Labor Day from 11 a.m. to 5 p.m., January through April on weekends from 1 to 5 p.m.; otherwise Wednesday through Sunday from 11 a.m. to 5 p.m.

Whoever heard of a vineyard in Connecticut? You'll be telling all your friends about vineyards in Connecticut once you taste Hopkins' fine, dry Seyval Blanc, perfect for a seafood meal at the inn across the street. Wine prices are moderate and quality is high. By the way, the vineyard is not affiliated with the Hopkins Inn, though the vineyard barn was obviously part of the same estate at one time.

NORTH TO SALISBURY: Back on Connecticut Route 45, head north and you're on your way to **Cornwall Bridge,** which is famous for its picturesque covered bridge. **Housatonic Meadows State Park** (tel. 203/672-6772), Cornwall Bridge, CT 06754, is here with camping and picnic areas, north of town on U.S. 7.

You can head north on U.S. 7, then cross westward on Route 112 to pick up Route 41 north to Salisbury; or take Route 4 west from Cornwall Bridge to Sharon, then Route 41 north through Lakeville to Salisbury. The distance is about 16 or 18 miles.

Salisbury is an aristocratic, historic town on the edge of the Berkshires. Late in September there's a big flea market here, and at the height of the fall foliage color the Salisbury Antiques Fair is held in the Town Hall. Come anytime of year, though. The town is pretty, tranquil, surrounded by gorgeous country, and only 20 miles from the heart of the Berkshires' summer and winter activities.

Where to Stay and Eat

Cornwall Bridge is famous for its picturesque covered bridge, and it also has a choice place to stay. The **Cornwall Inn and Motel,** on U.S. 7, Cornwall Bridge, CT 06754 (tel. 203/672-6884), is one mile south of the intersection with Connecticut Route 45. The cozy old inn has a dining room and lounge, and is supplemented by half a dozen tidy motel-style rooms. Constructed in red-barn style, the rooms have all the conveniences such as television and air conditioning, and cost $43 double on weekdays, $55 on weekends. There's a swimming pool. The location is good, out in the country where it's peaceful and quiet. Note that the dining room is closed on Monday.

You can't miss the **White Hart Inn** (tel. 203/435-2511), on the Village Green, Salisbury, CT 06068, right where Routes 41 and 44 meet. A true travelers' inn, the White Hart is a rambling frame place which recently underwent an extensive renovation program. The inn's tavern is a town favorite, and all four of its restaurants are popular with guests, travelers and townfolk alike. The 20-plus rooms here—some in the inn, a few in the colonial Gideon Smith house next door—all have private bath and telephone; most have cable color TV and Home Box Office. Doubles are priced at $47.70 to $58.30. Singles are a few dollars cheaper; an extra person pays $4.50 to $5.50.

You might also put up at the **Ragamont Inn** (tel. 203/435-2372), Salisbury, CT 06068, just off the Village Green on Route 44. You can't miss the inn's two Greek revival facades with awning-covered dining patio between. The Ragamont rents rooms at prices not much different from those at the nearby White Hart. But the emphasis here is on dining as the owner happens also to be a Swiss-trained *chef de cuisine*. On a warm summer afternoon I lunched on vichyssoise, knackwurst Cordon Bleu (who could pass it up?), and pastry, for $10, all in. Fresh fish, the Swiss national dish of raclette, chef's salad, club sandwiches—all these and more were also offered. I caught a glance of the dinner menu (actually, a blackboard) and noted they were serving duck and veal Calvados (that's the apple brandy from France). I'd estimate about $25 for a full dinner with wine, per person.

INTO THE BERKSHIRES: Up here in Connecticut's northwest corner, you're very close to one of America's oldest and finest resort areas, the Berkshire Mountains of Massachusetts. The towns of South Egremont, Great Barrington, Lee, and Lenox have great charm, good restaurants, fine old inns and guest houses, a bewildering array of cultural activities, and more antique shops than you've ever seen before in one area at one time. For details on it all, see Chapter VIII, "Central and Western Massachusetts."

Chapter XI

NEW HAMPSHIRE

1. Hampton Beach
2. Portsmouth
3. Manchester
4. Concord
5. Lake Winnipesaukee
6. North Conway
7. Bretton Woods and Crawford Notch
8. Waterville Valley
9. The Franconia Notch Area
10. Lake Sunapee
11. Hanover

"LIVE FREE OR DIE" says the motto on every auto license plate in New Hampshire, echoing the stirring words of Gen. John Stark, victor at the momentous Battle of Bennington (1777) and a New Hampshire native. New Hampshire folk are still very patriotic in an old-fashioned way, and committed to material progress: modern facilities abound, and the road system is perhaps the best maintained in New England. On a vacation, "living free" in New Hampshire is a snap: mountains, beaches, lakes, amusements, special activities, and good restaurants are all available to the visitor.

On our tour through New Hampshire, we'll look first at the state's seacoast. Yes! New Hampshire has a seacoast—and the charming colonial town of Portsmouth on the border with Maine. Then we'll head north into the state's heart, passing through Manchester, the state's largest city, and Concord, its capital, on our way to Lake Winnipesaukee. From this veritable inland sea, we'll head north again into the White Mountains National Forest and the skiing/hiking center of North Conway, and then even farther north to Bretton Woods. Moving west, the next area we'll cover is that of Franconia Notch, North Woodstock, and Waterville Valley. Finally, we'll visit Lake Sunapee and then Hanover, the hometown of Dartmouth College.

By the way, throughout New Hampshire a rooms-and-meals tax of 6% will be added to your hotel, motel, or inn bill, and you'll also have to pay it every time you have a meal in a restaurant.

New Hampshire's telephone area code is 603.

GETTING THERE: New Hampshirites are committed to highway travel, and so air links and rail lines are played down in favor of bus and car. Amtrak, in fact, has no operations in New Hampshire proper, although it does run along the New Hampshire–Vermont border for a ways, stopping in Brattleboro, Bellows Falls, and White River Junction on the route between New York and Montréal.

By Air

Precision Airlines (tel. toll free in all New England states except Vermont: 800/451-4221; in Vermont, 800/622-4393) flies between Boston and Manchester, N.H., and Keene, N.H., and also points in Vermont. At Boston's Logan Airport, Precision is located at Gate 14, Eastern Airlines terminal.

By Limousine and Bus

Airport limousines run regularly from Boston's Logan airport to many points in New Hampshire. C & J Airport Limousine Service runs daily trips from Logan to New Hampshire's seacoast region and Portsmouth; call these toll-free numbers for schedules and reservations: in New York and New England, 800/258-7111; in New Hampshire, 800/582-7191. Hudson Bus Lines' Airporter Limousine Service goes from Logan to Manchester, Concord, and other southern New Hampshire cities. Call these numbers in Boston: 617/245-5930, 696-9200, or 395-8080; in Manchester, call 603/669-4045.

Concord Trailways (South Main Street, Concord, N.H. 03301; tel. 603/224-3381, or toll free in New Hampshire: 800/852-3317; in other New England states: 800/258-3722) operates buses from Boston through Manchester and Concord to Laconia on Lake Winnipesaukee, and also Weirs Beach; from there the bus continues to Plymouth, North Woodstock, and through Franconia Notch. Trailways also has buses from Boston to Portsmouth, N.H., on the coast, thence to Alton, Alton Bay, and Wolfeboro on Lake Winnipesaukee, and finally to Conway, North Conway, Glen, Jackson, Pinkham Notch A.M.C. Camp, Wildcat Mountain, and on to Berlin. For Trailways schedules in Boston, call 617/482-6620.

Vermont Transit, operating out of Boston's Greyhound terminal (tel. 617/423-5810), has routes from Portland, Me., to St. Johnsbury, Vt., via North Conway, Bretton Woods, and Bethlehem (near Franconia), N.H., besides running from Logan Airport in Boston to the cities of Manchester and Concord, and thence to Mt. Sunapee and Hanover. Vermont Transit also runs buses from Montréal south into Vermont and a few points in New Hampshire, but Montréal visitors will have to transfer at least once to reach most of the vacation locations in the state. Vermont Transit buses depart from the Voyageur Terminal in Montréal (tel. 514/842-2281).

1. Hampton Beach

Many visitors to New England forget that Vermont is the only New England state without a seacoast, and that New Hampshire is in fact a maritime state, even though its coastline is only about 20 miles long. The 20 miles is almost all beach, with some rocky headlands and coves, and four state parks with their own uncommercial stretches of beach. Hampton Beach State Park is the most southerly, and the public parking and bathing facilities here are run in the clean, well-ordered way of state park management. But just north of the state park is the town of Hampton Beach, two streets wide (north along the waterfront, south along the inland street, as far as cars are concerned). Hampton Beach is a riot of closely packed motels and cottages, ice-cream stands and hot-dog stands, penny arcades, and watering places. Lights, glitter, and throb-

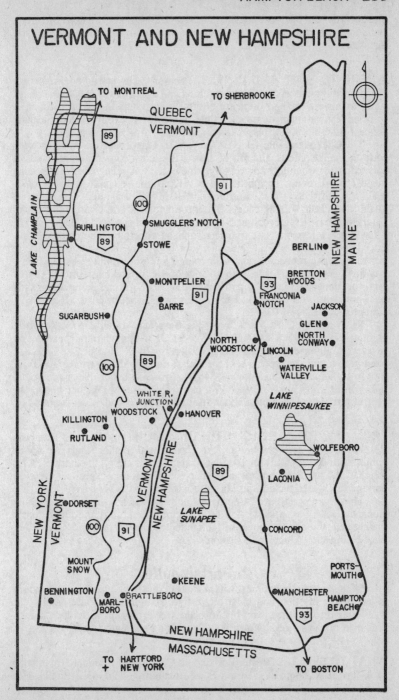

VERMONT AND NEW HAMPSHIRE

bing crowds of the young, tanned, and adventurous make it a nonstop circus, something out of a "beach party" movie, to revel in or abhor as your taste dictates.

WHERE TO STAY AND DINE: The season really starts moving on the Fourth of July weekend, and between then and Labor Day the "No Vacancy" signs are always on, and there are positively no rooms to be had without an ironclad reservation made weeks, or months, in advance. But north of the main concentration are a few places to stay with less of a press of crowds.

The **Chez Marie Inn** (tel. 603/926-7558) is a large vacation house converted to take a few guests, and lots of diners. It offers a good deal more comfort and refinement than most places along the beach, including a very interesting menu (pâté homard, or lobster pie at $12.50, and coquille en casserole—scallops with sherry in a casserole—at $10.50, for example) served in two quaint and cheery dining rooms. The proprietors, Marie Claire and "Dick" Duchemin, have a Québecois heritage, and so the dishes served will also include a few Québec favorites like tourtière (minced pork pie). The daily specials, priced at $8.25 to $11.50, are always a good buy. Wine, beer, and cocktails are served. The two rooms for rent, with color TV, cost $37.45 to $44.94. Even if you don't stay on the beach, stop in Chez Marie for breakfast/brunch (8 to 1 p.m.) or dinner (5:30 to 9:30 p.m. on Friday and Saturday; reservations only on Thursdays, 7 to 9 p.m.). The address is 965 Ocean Blvd. (Route 1A), Hampton Beach, NH 03842.

Right next to Chez Marie Inn is the **Seascape Motel**, 255 Ocean Blvd., Hampton Beach, NH 03842 (tel. 603/926-9153), with modern motel rooms on two levels, all air-conditioned and heated, all with TV and private bath. It's open year round, and rooms rent for $50.88 double, $57.24 triple, $63.60 for four in high season; $40.28 double, $46.64 triple, $53 quadruple in spring and fall. Weekly rates are available. You can walk to the water, but not to the central portions of Hampton Beach itself, from the motel.

FROM HAMPTON BEACH TO PORTSMOUTH: North of Hampton Beach, the state park beaches at **Rye Harbor** and **Wallis Sands** are not as bubbly with activity as Hampton, but to some tastes are all the more pleasant for that. At the state park beaches in New Hampshire, expect to pay a $1 parking fee, which includes use of all other facilities as well.

The drive along Route 1A north to Hampton Beach is very pretty, winding along the coast past a succession of ever more sumptuous and meticulously maintained summer mansions, still inhabited by the wealthy and powerful of New Hampshire, Maine, and Boston.

2. Portsmouth

Of the gracious maritime towns along the New England coast, Portsmouth is one of the prettiest and most interesting. A morning or afternoon spent wandering through the town's historic side streets, perhaps with lunch, tea, or dinner in one of its restaurants, is both relaxing and entertaining.

WHAT TO SEE: The Greater Portsmouth Chamber of Commerce maintains an **Information Booth** at 278 State St., Portsmouth, NH 03801 (tel. 603/436-1118).

Strawbery Banke

Portsmouth's jump from wilderness to settlement started in 1630, when a group of settlers sailed into the Piscataqua River's mouth in search of fresh water and good land. As they climbed up the rise from the shore they found not only good land and water but also acres of wild strawberries, which delighted them so much they named the place **Strawbery Banke.** Today that name serves to identify the center of the city's historic restoration effort, a ten-acre section of colonial and Revolutionary-era buildings brought back to life and peopled with families, craftspeople, and merchants who are not here for show but in fact make their homes and livelihoods right where you see them. The ten-acre Strawbery Banke area (tel. 603/436-8010) is open from 9:30 a.m. to 5 p.m. daily, May through October, at $4.50 for adults, $3.50 for seniors, $1.50 for children 6 to 15. You can rent a casette tape player with a prerecorded tour of the grounds for $2; or you can attend the orientation films (included in the price of admission) shown hourly and then wander about, looking at the 34 houses and buildings, workshops, and artisans' galleries on display.

A walk through Strawbery Banke is educational as well as entertaining, for you'll see how chairs, tables, and cabinets were made besides seeing examples of the work itself; weaving and stoneware potting are explained, and early tools and architectural designs are spread out for your examination. A gallery in the Joshua Wentworth House shows local artists' works from June through August, militia units and fife-and-drum corps parade sometimes, and in the last weekend in June through the first weekend in August the Strawbery Banke Chamber Music Festival is held on Saturday and Sunday evenings (South Church).

Finding the Strawbery Banke section is easy: just follow the strawbery signs, with arrows, posted throughout the town and on approach roads.

Strawbery Banke is the major part of Portsmouth's Old Harbour area, the cornerstone of which is **Prescott Park,** a waterfront park, dock, and amusement area donated to the city by the Prescott sisters in the 1930s and 1940s. Besides being a fine place for a stroll or a rest from walking, the park is the site of the annual Strawbery Banke Children's Art Festival, held on the third weekend in June, and the Prescott Park Arts Festival, during the last three weeks in July and the first three in August. The chamber of commerce information booth (see above) will give you a leaflet detailing all the festivals, concerts, shows, plays, and exhibitions.

John Paul Jones's House

Of the other notable places in this pretty city, none is more notable than the house of John Paul Jones (1758), open from mid-May through mid-October, 10 a.m. to 4:30 p.m. on Monday through Saturday, and 1 to 4 p.m. on Sunday. The stately house, at the corner of Middle and State Streets, was actually a rooming house when Jones stayed in it, a commander whose frigate, the famous *Ranger,* was still being built in a nearby shipyard. The house is now the headquarters of the Portsmouth Historical Society, and you can visit the house and museum by guided tour at $2 for adults, 75¢ for children 6 to 14.

WHERE TO DINE: Portsmouth has more than its share of good places to eat. Here are several which will serve you well for either lunch or dinner.

The **Library Restaurant,** in the Rockingham Hotel at 401 State St. (tel. 431-5202), is a good choice no matter what your culinary preference. The menu lists such varied delights as Long Island duckling, spare ribs cooked with Vermont maple syrup, and calamari fritti (fried squid), along with more familiar fare and money-saving daily special plates. The old rooms of the hotel have been preserved without overdoing the decor; books line the walls. You might spend $18 to $24 for a good, full dinner with wine, tax, and tip, less than half that for lunch. Hours are 11:30 a.m. to 3 p.m. and 5:30 to 11 p.m. (till midnight on Friday and Saturday), Sunday brunch from noon to 3 p.m.

Strawbery Court (tel. 431-7722) is a restaurant specializing in continental cuisine. The restaurant, at 20 Atkinson St., is a fine old colonial house with a glass-in garden room. It is decorated with exquisite oil paintings and a beautiful blue and white tile picture of a nautical scene. The restaurant is open Tuesday through Friday from 11:30 a.m. to 1:30 p.m. for lunch and from 6 to 9 p.m. for dinner, on Sunday for brunch from 11:30 a.m. to 2:30 p.m., closed Monday. For lunch the menu includes such items as assorted quiches, fresh fish du jour, or salade Niçoise, for $5 to $7. For dinner, there is a choice of entrees, and a fixed-price meal: $21 per person, plus tax, tip, and wine. Gracious surroundings, friendly staff, good food, fair price.

The **Puddle Dock Pub** (tel. 431-4731), 38 State St. near Prescott Park, is more than just a fondue restaurant. Being in Portsmouth the decor is of colonial brick and wood, the accents and hangings nautical rather than alpine, which the Swiss dish of fondue usually calls for. The tables are all equipped with fondue pots, and a small outdoor patio dining area in back is pleasant on warm days. Although you can get sandwiches here ($2 to $4), and now a variety of seafood and steak dishes from $7.50 to $10, the specialty is fondue fixings served up for two: the cheapest starts at $12.50; lobster, the most expensive, is $16—but remember, these prices are for meals that feed two persons. For dessert? Fondue again, this time such delicious concoctions as chocolate, raspberry, strawberry, or butterscotch, priced at $5 for two. The Puddle Dock Pub's upstairs' section is the place if you just want a beer or glass of any of 26 wines or a cocktail without a large meal, and there is nightly entertainment.

3. Manchester

Manchester borders the Merrimack River, and the cheap waterpower brought the city wealth in the textile boom of the mid- and late-19th century. The very impressive **Amoskeag Mills** still border the river and the canals in the center of town, the brick facades stretching for almost a mile. The mills are used for various purposes today, including the manufacture of textiles and shoes (plenty of factory-outlet stores in town), and continued use preserves these monuments of American architectural and industrial history.

WHAT TO SEE: Although a business and manufacturing town, Manchester has two points of interest besides the giant mills. The **Currier Gallery of Art,** (tel. 669-6144 or 669-6145), 192 Orange St., is a fine little museum/gallery in a handsome buildng, open free to the public on Tuesday, Wednesday, Friday, and Saturday from 10 a.m. to 4 p.m., on Thursday to 10 p.m., and on Sunday from 2 to 5 p.m. The collection is strong in New England and Sandwich glass, English and American silver and pewter, and colonial and early American furniture. It also has a nice collection of paintings and sculpture from other parts of the world. Degas, Jan Gossaert, and a follower of Meliore are represented along with other masters. A beautiful new wing shows off the collections to best advantage. To find the gallery, cross the Queen City or Amoskeag

Bridge to downtown, and drive along Elm Street (Route 3) to Orange Street. Go east on Orange six blocks, and the gallery is on your left.

READER'S SIGHTSEEING SUGGESTION: "An interesting place to see is the **Budweiser Brewery** on Route 3 (Daniel Webster Highway) in Merrimack, between Nashua and Manchester. The brewery offers a half-hour tour for free. There's a tasting room (limit: three bottles!) and the famous Clydesdale horses" (Robert B. Huggins, Upper Darby, Pa.). [*Author's Note:* The Anheuser-Busch Brewery (tel. 603/889-6631) is reached by taking Exit 8 (Merrimack) from the Everett Turnpike, then Route 3.]

WHERE TO STAY AND EAT: The newest, and the best value, is the **Susse Chalet Inn,** 860 South Porter St., Manchester, NH 03103 (tel. 603/625-2020, or toll free 800/258-1980). The rooms, plainish but tidy and comfortable, are bargain priced at $28.40 single, $32.70 double, $35.85 for three, $39 for four. The Susse Chalet is at Exit 1 from I-293/Route 101.

Should you have to stay overnight on the road, I-293 at Manchester has several chain motels and one local one. **Howard Johnson's Motor Lodge** is at the Queen City Boulevard Exit (no. 4) from I-293 (tel. 603/668-2600, or toll free 800/654-2000), Manchester, NH 03102. Large beds, color TV, an indoor pool, saunas, and a 24-hour restaurant are offered with rooms ranging from $53.95 to $60.31 single, $58.19 to $64.55 double; children under 18 stay free.

At the **Holiday Inn,** 21 Front St., Manchester, NH 03102 (tel. 603/669-2660), there are restaurants, a lounge, an outdoor pool, health club, and rooms for $50.29 to $56.71 double; children, including teenagers, stay free if their parents rent one or more of the pool-view rooms with two double beds. Take the Amoskeag Bridge Exit (Route 114) from I-293 for this one.

READER'S RESTAURANT SELECTION: "The restaurant to go to in Manchester is **Anton's** (tel. 669-0652), off I-293 at Exit 4, Queen City Bridge. While Anton's offers a fairly traditional menu of steaks, seafood, and poultry, a real bargain is the 'Salade de Maurice and Butcherblock Buffet.' At $11 a person, it has to be one of the best values in New England: all you can eat, from soup to dessert. *Have reservations,* though" (Robert B. Huggins, Upper Darby, Pa.).

4. Concord

The capital of New Hampshire is a pleasant little city with an appropriate frontier-mountain feeling. First settled in 1725, the town was called Rumford for the first 40 years; the name later found its way into the title of Count Rumford, inventor of a certain sort of shallow fireplace. Since 1816, Concord has been the capital of the state. Granite, printing, electrical equipment, and leather goods, as well as a surprisingly small amount of state bureaucracy, keep the town going.

WHAT TO SEE: Mary Baker Eddy, founder of Christian Science, was born nearby in the village of Bow. Franklin Pierce, 14th president of the United States, was speaker of the New Hampshire General Court (legislature) as well as being among the town's prominent lawyers, and you can visit his house, which is now a National Historic Site, called the **Pierce Manse** (there are two houses of his in Concord). The Manse, at the farthest reaches of North Main Street, was saved from demolition by a civic-minded group named the Pierce Brigade, and it is open from the first of June through Labor Day (except Sunday and holidays), at $1.50 for adults, 50¢ for children and students. You might want to make an appointment by calling 224-9620.

The State Capitol, called the **State House,** was built in 1819 of—you guessed it—granite, and is the oldest capitol in which a legislature still occupies its original chambers. Inside are proudly displayed the state's battle flags and portraits of its notable military commanders. A statue of Daniel Webster, one of several native New Hampshire boys who made good on a national scale, stands before the building. The small size of the State House will surprise you; compared to the mammoth buildings in Providence, Hartford, and Boston, it seems barely big enough to hold just the governor's staff. But many of the tax-burdened citizens of other states are lured to New Hampshire every year by the low tax rate, kept low in one way by keeping bureaucracy small.

WHERE TO STAY AND EAT: Concord is a town for businesspeople and lawmakers. The **New Hampshire Highway Hotel** (tel. 603/225-6687), Concord, NH 03301, is right on I-93 at the intersection with N.H. 9/U.S. 4/202; here, the layout is extensive, the pool is outdoors, and in addition to the restaurant, coffeeshop, and lounge, it features a Bubble Dining Terrace (out by the pool, enclosed by clear plastic "bubble" panes). The rooms are air-conditioned, and all have private baths and TV. Rates are $33 to $37 single, $37 to $50 double.

5. Lake Winnipesaukee

The largest of the lakes in New Hampshire's Lakes Region is grand indeed: 28 miles long, close to 300 miles of shoreline, 72 square miles of water to swim in or boat on, and almost 300 islands. The name has been translated as "smile of the Great Spirit," and while the lake's irregular shoreline might suggest a wry grin rather than a sunny smile, the lake's large size would certainly do the Great Spirit justice. Summer is when the lake is busiest with swimmers, boaters, waterskiers, and the like, but winter snows draw crowds to the **Gunstock** and **Alpine Ridge** ski areas near the lake's shore.

Laconia is Lake Winnipesaukee's largest town, and business and commercial center. Many of the companies with large shoe factories in the region have factory-outlet stores here where shoes sell at bargain prices. Downtown, the **Belknap** (pronounced BELL-nap) **Mill,** a textile mill built in 1823, has been restored and you can tour it to see its machinery made of wood—gears, cogwheels, and all. The tour takes three-quarters of an hour and costs $2 for adults, 75¢ for children 10 to 18; it's open from 11 a.m. to 2 p.m. every day from mid-June to Labor Day.

WHERE TO STAY: Coming to the lake for fun, people stay in the many motels and inns on portions of the lake's shore near Laconia, or in a small, pretty town such as Wolfeboro, due east of Laconia. Skiers stay at the inns located near the slopes or in a lakefront establishment with winterized cabins.

To get away from the hustle and bustle of the highway, drive along Route 11 and watch for signs pointing out a scenic shore road off to the left. Route 11 has been remade in recent years and is farther away from the lakeshore, while the motels are still along the old road which used to be Route 11. Most of the traffic uses the new road, leaving the old one much quieter.

At Glendale, one of the first places along the old road, you'll see **Glendale Cabins,** R.F.D. 4, Box 46, Laconia, NH 03246 (tel. 603/293-7731). Eileen and Tom Syrko are the friendly owners, and they rent out seven nice cabins complete with screened porches, showers, and such for very reasonable rates: $31.80 double for one night, slightly more on holiday weekends. There's a nice lawn and picnic tables, and the cabins have grand evergreen trees between them. The boat-launching ramp and marina at Glendale are just a few minutes' walk away. The Glendale Cabins are usually open only from the first of May to mid-October, perhaps a bit longer if the weather is nice.

Those looking for quiet, luxurious accommodations with all the conveniences, including color TV and air conditioning, will enjoy the **Belknap Point Motel,** R.F.D. 4, Box 80, Laconia, NH 03246 (tel. 603/293-7511). The Belknap Point has two sections: down on the shore of the lake, a number of modern efficiency units with kitchens and decks reach out almost over the water; and up the steep slope of the hill between the old road and the new (you can enter from either road) are a number of hotel rooms, all with ceramic tile baths, little balconies, and gorgeous views of the lake. The owners have put a lot of thought into decorating the rooms nicely, and they work hard to make sure each guest is comfortable. The Belknap Point has its own swimming area and a grassy patio. Prices for the hotel rooms are $58.30 per day double, $20 a day less off-season (May, early June, September, and October). You can rent a room here for one or two days at $38 a day if there's an opening for that amount of time. The efficiencies down by the water rent by the week. An additional person in a room is $6; in an efficiency, $35.

The **Estate Motel and Cottages,** R.F.D. 4, Laconia, NH 03246 (tel. 603/293-7792), is another of the establishments along the scenic lakefront road. Here there are ten motel rooms in white buildings under red shingled roofs. The rooms look out over a grassy lawn down to the lake; the lake beach and swimming dock are convenient. The Estate is secluded and quiet, and it's best to reserve in advance for one of its rooms: $36.38 double in a normal room, $41.73 for two in one of the three efficiency cottages, lower rates by the week. Rooms have two double beds, TV, shower, and refrigerator; the efficiencies have the same, plus tub-shower combination, a sink and stove, and kitchen utensils. The Estate also has a private dock and places to moor your boat.

WHERE TO DINE: Dinner is the special offering of **B. Mae Denny's** (tel. 603/293-4351), at the intersection of Routes 11 and 11B, Gilford, NH 03246. A large old house has been redone and expanded to accommodate dozens of diners and overnight guests as well. The heavy wood beams and white stucco of the dining room give a rustic, almost Teutonic effect, but the cathedral ceiling keeps it from being claustrophobic. The dining room, bar, and lounge, and 12 guest rooms are all air-conditioned, as is the Redwood Room downstairs. At lunchtime meals are lighter and less expensive than these dinner suggestions which follow: steaks come small, medium, and large, priced from $11 to $14; barbecued pork spare ribs are $9.25. Most inexpensive meals are spaghetti with meat sauce ($7.25), and soup and the salad bar.

The 12 rooms at B. Mae Denny's are comfortable, with air conditioning, wall-to-wall carpeting, TV, and, in most rooms, private bath. Prices are $33.50 to $41 per room.

WHAT TO DO: **Ellacoya State Beach,** on Route 11 southeast of Glendale, is one of the nicest beaches on the lake. The entrance fee is low, there's plenty of parking, and if you go early in the day you can get one of the picnic tables. A snackbar is in operation, and a lifeguard is on duty all the time the beach is open. The slope of the beach is very, very gradual, making it ideal for small children; for more experienced swimmers, a swimming dock floats in the water farther out.

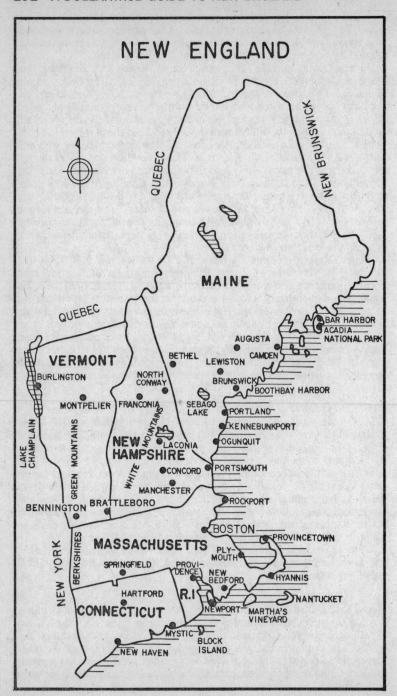

Weirs Beach, on Route 11B near its intersection with U.S. 3, is a town beach with a similar admission charge, free parking at several lots in the town of Weirs Beach (look for the signs to the free lots—everything on the main street is metered). Weirs Beach is known more for its honky-tonk penny arcades, candlepin bowling alleys, pinball machines, fortune tellers, and fast-food stands than it is for the beauty of its beach. These amusements are open during the day and in the evening in summer, and give the town a character which differs greatly from what it once must have been: the grand old turn-of-the-century mansions seen here and there in the town are some of the finest of their genre, with lots of cupolas, turrets, gables, and all the other paraphernalia which make late Victorian architecture so intricate. You can stay overnight at Weirs Beach in one of the hotels, motels, or guest houses, although the low lakefront situation seems to lend a mustiness to most accommodations.

Boat Rides

A number of large boats make tours of the lake several times daily. Most famous is the M/V *Mount Washington* (tel. 603/366-5531), which runs cruises from Weirs Beach three times a day between June 15 and Labor Day, two times a day in early June and September through mid-October. The cruise around the lake takes 3¼ hours and costs $7.50 for adults, half price for children 5 to 12; under 5, free. Breakfast, lunch, and snacks are available on board. You can also pick up the boat in Wolfeboro every day at 11 a.m. The *Mount Washington* also leaves on moonlight cruises on Wednesday, Thursday, Friday, and Saturday evenings from July 1 through Labor Day weekend.

The Alpine Slide and Chair Lifts

During the summer, the ski areas at Gunstock and Alpine Ridge on Route 11A are busy with other things. Gunstock is turned into a giant 500-space camping area with a swimming pool and weekend flea markets plus a chair lift on weekends ($3; kids, $2); Alpine Ridge (tel. 293-4304) has an Alpine Slide, a sport imported from Germany, and now also an Aquaboggan Waterslide. The Alpine Slide is a sort of sled which runs along a concrete-fiberglass track down the side of the mountain. Each person has his or her own sled and can control the speed of descent. It's safe for people of all ages, children included, and has been used by people over 80 years old (over 70, you ride for free). The ski lift takes you to the top of Mt. Rowe, where you get your sled for the ride down. Tickets for both are $3.75 for adults (aged 13 through 69), $3 for children 6 through 12; children 5 and under are free, but must ride with an adult. Books of tickets are available.

Skiing

The two areas near Winnipesaukee and Laconia are **Gunstock** (tel. 603/293-4341) and **Alpine Ridge** (tel. 603/293-4304), Route 11A, Gilford, NH 03246, formerly called Mt. Rowe. Gunstock is the larger of the two, with the more difficult slopes, although Alpine Ridge is in the process of acquiring rights to a very challenging trail. Gunstock has three chair lifts, three T-bars, and a rope tow; the vertical drop is 1500 feet. At Alpine Ridge there is a chair lift and a T-bar. Both areas have snowmaking capacity, restaurants, and lounges.

The settings of both areas are very fine, nestled in valleys off the main road. While Gunstock is the older and more complete (at the moment), Alpine Ridge is putting on a big expansion drive and will have new things to offer soon besides its good restaurant (see "Where to Dine" section above).

WOLFEBORO: Of the other towns on Lake Winnipesaukee, Wolfeboro is certainly the finest. The town escaped the blight which hit such textile-producing towns as Laconia because Wolfeboro never industrialized; and it has escaped the honky-tonk commercialism that has taken over some other lake towns, perhaps because of its "inconvenient" position at the southeastern tip of the lake. So today Wolfeboro is a fine, almost typical, New England town with the requisite Historical Society, white-steepled churches, gracious old houses, and some very good views of the lake.

There is less hustle and bustle in Wolfeboro than in some other lake towns, less to "see and do," but that makes it all the better for those who really want to relax. The M/V *Mount Washington* stops here to pick up and discharge passengers for its tours of the lake (see above under "Weirs Beach" for details); and a good number of the motels and resorts in town have their own stretches of beach. Wolfeboro is proud to call itself "the oldest summer resort in America," because in 1763 Gov. John Wentworth built what is thought to be the first summer house in the U.S. within the town's boundaries.

Where to Stay and Dine

Among the most serviceable of Wolfeboro's hostelries is the venerable **Wolfeboro Inn**, 44 North Main St., Wolfeboro, NH 03894 (tel. 603/569-3016). The inn was built in 1812, and prides itself on giving the "glitter-weary traveler" a comfortable and tasteful place to lodge or to dine. The rooms have some antique pieces, and all but two of the 15 rooms have private bath. Doubles have either one double bed or twins, and cost $48 per night with a private bath; singles are $26 with a private bath; an extra bed is $7. As the inn is often full in high summer, it's best to reserve in advance.

The downstairs rooms of the inn are devoted to dining. The atmosphere is from the era of the inn's construction, with wooden chairs and tables and several fireplaces, including a large brick one in the main dining room. Altogether there are six dining rooms, so take a look around to see which you'd prefer (if there's room to choose!). The menu offers a fairly standard selection of the popular beef, seafood, and fowl dishes, but the daily specials (available at both lunch and dinner) are the best values, and also the most interesting items: swordfish, lobster chunks, and frog legs on rice were offered when I was last there. Sandwiches at lunch are priced at $3 to $4.25; at dinner, entrees with side dishes cost $7.50 to $15, with the daily specials usually being nearer the lower end of that range. When you enter the Wolfeboro Inn, look for the interesting old copper still in the entrance hallway—no doubt *that* has a colorful history!

Staying on the Outskirts

Wolfeboro is surrounded by motels and inns on the outskirts, many of them very nice indeed. Herewith my two favorites:

The **Pick Point Lodge**, 4½ miles north of Wolfeboro off Route 109 (mail address: P.O. Box 220D, Mirror Lake, NH 03853; tel. 603/569-1338), is truly unique. It was formerly a wealthy family's summer estate, and has been converted to accommodate a small number of guests in ten large cottages (up to four bedrooms) and in four rooms in the main lodge. It would be possible to fill pages with the good points of the Pick Point Lodge, but a quick list will give you the idea: cottages are all very comfy and tastefully done, with fireplaces, porches, full kitchens, and, in the larger ones, two bathrooms; the estate is on a 70-acre tract of forest, with several nature trails plotted for guests' use;

guests can enjoy a full half mile of lake frontage, indoor and outdoor tennis courts, a private beach and jetty, indoor and outdoor games, and special cookouts, cocktail parties, and such which are "on the house," and which you can join or ignore as you wish. The hosts, the Newcomb family, are very gracious and solicitous of their guests' well-being and privacy, and couldn't be nicer. Rates for such quality are not low, but are reasonable for what you get; prices given below include the 6% tax. Rentals are by the week only, unless there is a cancellation or the like which leaves a cottage or room open for several days. Cottages range in price from $583 for a one-bedroom to $1219 for a four-bedroom for one week from mid-July through Labor Day weekend; prices for May, June, September, and October are in the range of $344.50 to $848 for a cottage. In the main lodge, rooms cost $84.80 double, light breakfast included. This could easily be the finest place on Winnipesaukee.

READERS' RESTAURANT SELECTION: "The best restaurant in the Winnipesaukee area is **The Woodshed** (tel. 476-2311), east of Moultonboro on Route 109 near Castle in the Clouds. We were there on a Monday night when they had their $9 lobster special, and the place was packed. There's a pleasant lounge in which to spend the inevitable wait for a table. Lighting is strictly by candlelight" (Mr. and Mrs. Wayne Ditmer, Mott, N.D.).

What to Do in Wolfeboro

Several activities in Wolfeboro are worth a special mention.

Dr. Henry F. Libby, a Boston dentist who was born and raised near the shores of Winnipesaukee, devoted the latter part of his life to the study and collection of natural history specimens: fish, animals, and birds. Other interests of his included early Indian lore of the region, and artifacts from the times of early settlers. All these diverse exhibits are brought together in the **Libby Museum** on Route 109 north/west, open from 10 a.m. to 5 p.m. daily except Monday during the summer. Donation is 50¢ for adults, 25¢ for children. The museum is several miles north of the town, even though it's run as a nonprofit institution by the town of Wolfeboro.

Around the turn of the century, Thomas Gustav Plant decided to build himself a retreat in the New Hampshire wilderness. While he was not alone in this—lots of rich men were building lavish estates in the region—his accomplishment is certainly among the grandest. Lucknow, as the estate was named, cost millions of dollars to build; the name comes from a castle in Scotland, and ultimately from a city in India, although the mansion has distinctly Central European touches to it. Today Lucknow is called **Castle in the Clouds** (Route 171, in Moultonboro, N.H.; tel. 603/476-2352), and is open to visitors who pay $4.50 per adult, $2.50 for children from 5 through 11. The grounds are very beautiful, and the view of the mountains and lakes is nothing short of spectacular. Horseback trail rides are available. Castle in the Clouds is open weekends in May and June from 9 a.m. to 5 p.m., daily during July and August to Labor Day from 9 a.m. to 6 p.m., and daily until the end of the foliage season in mid-October from 9 a.m. to 5 p.m. To get there, take Route 109 north from Wolfeboro for 17 miles, turn right (east) onto Route 171, and go three miles to the entrance.

From a station in downtown Wolfeboro, on Route 16 in Wakefield or Route 109 in Sanbornville, you can board a train of the **Wolfeboro Rail Road** (tel. 569-4884), hauled by a Baldwin steam locomotive in high summer, and take a two-hour trip through the lakes and forests. The 24-mile trip costs $6.50 for adults, $4.50 for children 5 through 11. Evening dinner train Thursday through Saturday evenings in July and August.

MOUNT WASHINGTON VALLEY

The area along Route 16 between North Conway and Gorham, including the town of Bartlett on U.S. 302, is organized for tourist reasons as the Mount Washington Valley. The towns of North Conway and Jackson are centers for summer hiking, camping, and biking trips, and for winter skiing at the ski areas of Attitash, Mt. Cranmore, Black Mountain, and Wildcat Mountain. The **Mount Washington Valley Chamber of Commerce** (tel. 603/356-3171) has its headquarters and main information office on Main Street in the center of North Conway, open during business hours and on weekends. They will be glad to help you with room reservations if you've had trouble finding a place to stay, and are in general very helpful indeed.

In addition, **North Country Tours**, P.O. Box 747, North Conway, NH 03860 (tel. 603/356-3212), will help you to make reservations at many inns, resorts, and motels throughout the White Mountain area, at no charge for the service.

6. North Conway

On the edge of the White Mountain National Forest and at the end of Mount Washington Valley, North Conway is the sports capital of the White Mountains. It's not a particularly large town, although the mile or two of motels and eateries along Route 16 south of town do seem to extend the boundaries. But basically one can walk to almost anything except this southern extension by parking downtown, somewhere near the antique railroad station.

North Conway has taken well to its role of mountain town, and the people talk hearty and look healthy. And while some of the businesses are oldtime mom-and-pop affairs, a lot of shops obviously have been citified to cater to the hiking and ski trades. But still the town has not been "taken over" by city people. Perhaps the character and charm of North Conway is best exhibited by the town library building on Main Street not far from the railroad station: although small, it's built of massive granite blocks and has a slate roof which will last forever; it's open to all and sundry on Monday, Wednesday, Friday, and Saturday from 2 to 5:30 p.m.

WHERE TO STAY: North Conway has dozens of places to stay, including a good number of motels along the southern extension of Main Street (Route 16), but I'll concentrate mainly on the small inns in the town, and on those in the neighboring towns of Jackson and Glen.

North Conway's Inns and Guest Houses

Perhaps the best inn to choose in North Conway, from the standpoint of price, convenience, and pleasantness, is the **Cranmore Inn**, North Conway, NH 03860 (tel. 603/356-5502), just off Main Street on the street leading to the Mount Cranmore ski area, and only a few blocks from the Trailways bus stop. The inn is over a century old, although its 25 guest rooms have all been refurbished to meet modern standards of comfort and convenience. Rooms come with private bath for $26.50 single, $33.92 double; with running water in the room and a bath down the hall, the price is $21.20 single, $27.56 double. Several two-bedroom suites (the two bedrooms share one bath) have been added in a modern but suitable and attractive style, and can be rented at a price of $53 for two, $60.42 for three, or $67.84 for four persons. Special family rates apply. For $10 more per person you can have breakfast and dinner at the inn, all home-cooking even to the bread, rolls, and pastries. Meal service is family style, with several choices of appetizer and dessert, but one entree for all. Although all this would make the Cranmore Inn well worth it, there are bonuses: a huge parlor with fireplace, a game room, and a TV room; nice big lawns suitable for games and Frisbee (in summer), and a small swimming pool. From the inn you can walk to the slopes of Mt. Cranmore in ten minutes, and the center of town in five or less. There is an inn service which will meet you at the bus stop a mile south. Note that in winter the rate structure is a bit different: breakfast and dinner are included in the price of the room, and rates vary depending on whether you come during the week or on the weekend. Singles are $26.50 to $37.10; doubles are $47.70 to $58.30. Ski packages for Mt. Washington Valley areas are also offered.

On a quiet back street stands the **Sunny Side Lodge,** Seavey Street, North Conway, NH 03860 (tel. 603/356-6239). It's a big white New Hampshire house with 11 guest rooms—singles, doubles, and dorms—which rent for $12 to $15 per person in summer, depending on the dates and flow of trade. In winter, the standard room-and-two-meals plan applies. Mrs. Cummings is proud of her nice living room (for guests), complete with fireplace. To get to the Sunny Side, turn off of Main Street following the signs to the Mt. Cranmore Skimobile. At the next turn, the signs point left, but you go right, and the lodge is a few houses down on the left-hand side.

Another charming guest house, 1½ miles north of the center of North Conway, is named **Wildflowers,** North Main Street, North Conway, NH 03860 (tel. 603/356-2224). You'll see the sign on the left as you head north, and behind it the big white house with porch posts made of peeled and painted tree trunks. Homey, simple, convenient, friendly, the six bedrooms at Wildflowers rent for $22 single, $28 double, $36 for a double room with two beds.

The **Scottish Lion** (tel. 603/356-6381; outside New Hampshire tel. toll free 800/258-0370) is known more for its dining room and for its British imports shop than for its lodging. But that doesn't detract from the comfort of the rooms, furnished in quaint period pieces and Gaelic touches. Eight rooms in all are here, sharing five bathrooms. Rates include a hearty Scottish breakfast, and the tax, for a total of $42.80 per double room. (See below for a description of the Scottish Lion's dining room.)

The **Cranmore Mt. Lodge** (tel. 603/356-2044), P.O. Box 1194, North Conway, NH 03860, is off the beaten path, which preserves a spirit of quiet and relaxation. A mile and a half from the center of town you'll come to the lodge, which consists of a nice old inn and a modernized barn loft. Rooms in the inn are the best bargains as they share several bathrooms; many rooms have sinks; prices are $31 to $35 for two, including breakfast. In the barn loft, rooms have private baths, color TV, air conditioning, one or two double beds—in short, all the comforts. Prices are commensurate with the degree of luxury, at $45 to $53 for two, again including breakfast. If you're alone, subtract $8 from the double price; if you have an extra person, the charge is $10 more; children under 12 pay half price with their parents. A bonus: Stay four days midweek and the fifth day is free (holidays excluded, of course). Cranmore Mt. Lodge has a 40-foot swimming pool, tennis and basketball courts, Jacuzzi spa bath, trout pond for fly angling, and outdoor barbecues. To find the lodge, turn east at the traffic light in North Conway onto Kearsarge Street; when you can go straight no longer, turn left. This is Kearsarge Road, and the lodge is a mile down.

Hotels and Motels in North Conway

For decades the **Eastern Slope Inn** (tel. 603/356-6321, or toll free in New England 800/258-4708) was North Conway's posh place to stay, a stately white-pillared hotel with a genteel ambience. It closed, but now it's open again, remodeled and more comfortable than ever. Swimming pool, clay tennis courts, a restaurant and pub, a summer theater next door, and a prime downtown location are among the inn's advantages. Choose from rooms in the inn or in the motel-like lodge nearby, or suites, or efficiency apartments. Rooms in the inn cost $26.75 to $85.60, single or double, tax included. Children 12 and under can stay with their parents for free; otherwise, there's an extra-person charge of $8. Suites cost $20 to $30 more than rooms. In the motor lodge, rooms are considerably cheaper: about $10 less than the inn. Additional breakfast included for $14 to $17 more per day. Address for both is Main Street, North Conway, NH 03860.

North Conway's snazziest hostelry, always in great demand, is the **Red Jacket Mountain View Motor Inn,** perched on a slope above South Main Street, North Conway, NH 03860 (tel. 603/356-5411). At the height of the season (summer or winter) its rooms go quickly because of its fairly central location and its luxury accoutrements: a beautiful indoor pool covered by a dramatic wood roof, and an outdoor pool as well; saunas; a game room with billiard, Ping-Pong, and fussball tables, and a shuffleboard court; tennis courts; dining room and cocktail lounge; many rooms with views and balconies, and some rooms with lofts so that a family can sleep more comfortably. Ceramic tile baths, two double beds to a room, color TV, air conditioning and heat, direct-dial telephones, and other luxury touches add to the draw, but it's the views and the convenience that convince many people to stay here. Rates are in accord with the services offered: rooms for two cost $53 to $84.80 per night, or about $16 more *per person* if you want breakfast and dinner. Otherwise, à la carte evening meals in the dining room are in the $10 to $15 range. Make your reservations early, for this is the headquarters for the Volvo International Tennis Tournament every year from mid-July to August.

The **Alpine Motor Inn** (tel. 603/356-2369), North Conway, NH 03860, is right near the Mt. Cranmore Skimobile and the tennis courts used for the Volvo tennis tournament. Rooms are a bit small. Prices vary accordng to size, decoration, and facilities of the room, but range from $27 to $42 with $36 double being about average for a normal weekday in summer.

Staying In Intervale

A mile or two north of North Conway along Route 16 and 16A are several inns and motels also worth considering. Although you won't be able to walk easily to town from here, these establishments have their own restaurants, and you're only a short drive from most of the hiking and ski points.

Off the main road, on scenic Route 16A (a short loop of a few miles) are several more lodging possibilities.

The **New England Inn** (tel. 603/356-5541), Intervale, NH 03845, is the largest (35 rooms) of the establishments on Route 16A, comprising both the inn of that name and the Hampshire House across the road. It's quite a spread, with pools, four-hole golf course, clay tennis courts, and shuffleboard, besides rooms with or without bath in several buildings, costing $35 to $74 *per person;* a normal double room would thus cost about $125 total, per day, 6% tax and 15% service included. A big breakfast and dinner each evening are included in these rates. The one-room cottages for rent here have their own fireplaces and cost between $58 and $66 *per person* for up to four persons, meals included. Besides the inn's pine-paneled dining rooms, there's a lounge. The dining room, named Anna Martin's, is open to the public for all meals and specializes in Yankee cuisine with home-baked breads and desserts.

Just down the road from the New England Inn is the **Old Field House** (tel. 603/356-5478), Intervale, NH 03845, which is in a field, yes, but which is not old. It's hard to tell when you first see it whether this new and modern hostelry is an old building redone from top to bottom or a new building made to look good and last long. Despite its sturdy granite facade and gambrel-roof wings, it is quite new, although meant to conjure up the romantic New Hampshire past. Rooms are all clean and shiny, with paneled walls, beamed ceilings, and colonial-style furniture. The bed arrangements are twins, a double, a queen, or a tremendous king. They also offer an efficiency apartment which overlooks the pool. The room prices are all for two people, including two continental breakfasts: $41.34 for twin beds, $46.64 for two double beds, $47.70 to $49.84 for a king-size bed; there are also two adjoining rooms. You get lots of extras at the Old Field House, such as a heated outdoor pool, laundry facilities, background music, cable TV, a game room, and shuffleboard. The entire place is air-conditioned.

Another place in Intervale is the **Holiday Inn** (*not* a branch of the ubiquitous chain), a large old house converted to take guests (tel. 603/356-9772). There are 11 rooms in the inn itself and two in a nearby cottage, and all cost the same: $35 single, $60 double for room and breakfast, or $50 and $80 for room, breakfast, and dinner. For these prices, which include tax and tips, you get a private bath, a nice living room to meet new friends, a heated pool in summer, or a skating rink and cross-country skiing in winter. The Holiday Inn also offers a three-day summer mini-vacation plan in which you stay three nights, have three breakfasts, and pay $210 for two people, except in the first week of August and Labor Day Weekend, of course.

Staying in Jackson

About seven miles from North Conway going north on Route 16 is Jackson, right at the geographical center of the Mount Washington Valley, and the central point for cross-country skiing in the region. Besides being right in the middle of the downhill ski areas, Jackson has its own ski touring organization—but more of that below. It also has a collection of delightful inns open winter and summer. The **Jackson Resort Association** (P.O. Box 304, Jackson, NH 03846) will send you information, or you can contact the **Jackson/Glen Information Center** (tel. 603/383-9356).

At the center of Jackson is the **Village House**, Jackson, NH 03846 (tel. 603/383-6666), very near the covered bridge leading into the town from Route 16. The nine rooms here have all been redecorated recently, but the antique flavor of the house has been preserved. Most rooms have private bath, and there's a color TV in the living room. Rates include use of the swimming pool, and also a "deluxe" continental breakfast for each person. The basic charges for two are $32 double with bath, $45 double with shared bath. Winter midweek package plans are available.

The **Christmas Farm Inn** (tel. 603/383-4313), Jackson, NH 03846, is just outside the center of Jackson village proper on the road up the hill to the Black Mountain Ski Area. Here the proprietors hold that "Hospitality makes the difference," but one must admit that the resort-style facilities help: the inn has its own pool and putting green (there are two professional golf courses near Jackson), a game room, sauna, lounge, living room, shuffleboard, and a dining room done in early American. The Christmas Inn has no fewer than five separate places of accommodation, from the original inn (built in 1786) to a maple sugaring house converted into two modern rooms good for family accommodations. There are over 20 rooms in all, priced at $89.88 to $111.28 total for two persons, tax, service, breakfast, and dinner for each person included. Children under 12 sharing their parents' room are charged $23.54. There is also a bunkroom (and you can have your kids stay here) for $36.38 per person, two meals included. Weekly and five-day midweek rates are also available, and these can save you several dollars.

The Inn at Thorn Hill, Jackson, NH 03846 (tel. 603/383-4242), is a huge old country house a short way outside Jackson which prides itself on several special features not often found. The baked goods are from its own ovens. As with several other Jackson inns, rooms here are in several buildings, including the inn itself, a nearby modernized chalet, and several cottages. All rooms have private bath. In winter, breakfast and dinner come with the room at a price of $46.64 to $59.36 per person per day in a double. Thorn Hill is one of the nicest, and friendliest, places in the entire Mount Washington Valley.

"If we were not a little out of the way, we could not be so totally out of the ordinary!" That's the way the staff at **Whitney's Village Inn** (tel. 603/383-6886) describes their establishment. Located in a secluded glade by a stream on Route 16B, Jackson, NH 03846, Whitney's is a different place, with fascinating touches: pretty dried flowers in a ski boot, breakfast menu mounted in a frying pan, the tick-tock of antique clocks—delights for eyes, ears, and nose all around. An inn has been on this spot since 1842, but the present place was completely restored in 1980. Rates are complex, as at most resort inns, going up and down according to the season, the room, and the services offered. Bed and full breakfast during normal summer and fall times (not holidays, and not foliage peak weeks) costs from $34 to $84. Add $5 per person and you can have dinner too. A few rooms share baths; these cost $12 per person less than the above rates. These rates already include the 6% tax and 15% service charge. Lots of money-saving package plans are offered—call or write and ask. In summer, tennis, swimming, volleyball, croquet, shuffleboard, and hiking are available. You can even call toll free: 800/225-2550 in the U.S. (800/272-2550 from Massachusetts); 800/463-4755 from eastern Canada.

A Motel in Jackson: The village of Jackson is known for its country inns, and staying in one of these excellent places is a real treat. But—as you've seen—it is not an inexpensive proposition, especially when you add that silly 15% "service charge" as I've done in the prices quoted.

For reasonable prices in this high-priced village, look to the **Covered Bridge Motel** (tel. 603/383-6630), Jackson, NH 03846, an attractive hostelry right near the red covered bridge. The modern units here are designed not to clash with Jackson's forest mood, and prices are reasonable. For a fully comfortable room with bath you pay $36.38 to $47.08 total, tax included, for two in high season, $4 to $8 less off-season. An extra child is charged $2; an extra adult, $5. Special package plans are often put together. Four efficiency apartments rent by the week.

Mountain Hikers' Huts

The **Appalachian Mountain Club,** the organization which has done so much to preserve and maintain wilderness trails in New England, operates several lodging facilities in the White Mountains National Forest. At the AMC's **Pinkham Notch Camp** (tel. 603/466-2727), Gorham, NH 03581, 11 miles north of Jackson on Route 16, people of all ages, whether AMC members or not, can find inexpensive bunkroom-type accommodations and simple but hearty meals. A bunk and breakfast costs $19.50 per adult; bed and supper is $21.75; bed and breakfast and supper is $25.75. Children 9 and under pay half price for the beds and meals, and as a convenience the kitchen will make up trail lunches for $2.25 per person. Note that you must have reservations, and they must be secured by a nonrefundable *per person per night* deposit. If you'd like a room alone, you will have to pay $10 extra for each unused bunk in the room. All these rules seem quite sensible. Note that the 6% tax is already included in these prices.

Besides the Pinkham Notch Camp, the AMC maintains a laudable system of mountain huts along its hiking trails in the mountains. Similar accommodations and meals are provided at similar prices, and with similar reservation arrangements. The huts are attended and trail meals prepared by "hutmen" and "hutwomen," a hearty breed of New England youth who pride themselves on being able to pack on their backs all the supplies needed in the huts—to a weight which would make a normal person stagger—and almost *run* up the mountains with the load several times a week. When you pass a hutman or woman on the trail, look for the record weight he or she is carrying, recorded in ink or with a woodburning iron on the side of the packframe. Special reduced-rate, prepaid reservations ($20 a day for bed, breakfast, and dinner) are available anytime but August. Write for details.

A Quiet Country Inn

Almost a century old, the **Bernerhof Inn** (tel. 603/383-4414), west of the town of Glen, NH 03838, several miles on U.S. 302, has always been a way-station for weary travelers along this major road. Today the owners, Ted and Sharon Wroblewski, concentrate on keeping the quality of the cuisine high and on entertaining their dinner guests, and sometimes diners here don't even know that rooms are for rent. They are, though, with breakfast and at reasonable prices. Depending on the room's size, location, and plumbing, prices are $31.80 to $37.10 double—breakfast included.

READER'S INN SELECTION: "I spent a week at the **Snowville Inn** near Conway (tel. 603/447-2818) in Snowville, and loved every minute of it. I went in July, and the price for a room, and a big breakfast, and a four-course dinner, was $432.50. For two people I guess the price would be something like $600 for the week. They stay open in winter" (Floyd Ostler, Shunk, Pa.). [*Author's Note:* Snowville Inn is on Foss Mountain Road east of Snowville; reach Snowville from Route 153 between Conway and Eaton. Double occupancy rates are $47.50 per person, tax and service. Open year round.]

WHERE TO DINE: As I have concentrated on town and country inns with their own dining rooms for lodging recommendations, you should have little trouble finding hearty, tasty meals for a reasonable price right where you stay. Group dynamics dictate that a kitchen can prepare dinner for a few dozen guests at an inn, and serve it family style, at a price considerably less than if the same number of people came in to order individual and particular meals. Should you want a change of scene or of cuisine, or if you're just passing through, you'll want a few tips on other places to dine.

Keep in mind that virtually all recommended inns open their dining rooms to the general public, and that it is possible to drop in any evening and order a meal à la carte.

Behind Horsefeathers, on Kearsarge Street, is **Le Bistrot at Chez Alain** (tel. 356-5295), a quaint little restaurant in a converted house with a menu straight out of Montmartre and the Ginestets, chef/owners, straight out of France (literally!): pâté maison, moules Provençales (mussels Provence style, with garlic and parsley butter), oysters on the half shell, all as starters. Rack of lamb is the entree for big spenders, escalope de veau aux capres (veal with capers and lemon) is reasonably priced; coquille de poisson Mornay (haddock in a Mornay sauce) is even cheaper, and good. For dessert? The classics: crème caramel, profiteroles, poire Belle Hélène, espresso, and cappuccino. Lunch is served from 11:30 a.m.; dinner from 6 to 9:30 p.m. Closed Monday. Expect to pay about $22 per person here, tax and tip included; more if you order that succulent rack of lamb, or if you share a bottle of wine.

For Scottish specialties, drop in at the **Scottish Lion** (tel. 356-6381), on Route 16 (Main Street) about a mile north of the center of North Conway. Your dinner here comes with hot Scottish oatcakes, nut breads, salad, and Rumbledethumps (potato and chopped cabbage with chives and cheddar cheese, baked). Start with scotch eggs, finnan haddie, or smoked salmon; then go on to a salmon kedgeree, mushroom-and-steak pie, or leg of lamb. They even have Highland desserts—although you may have no room left. You'll send about $15 per person for dinner here, unless you have steak or lobster. Hours: lunch, 11:30 a.m. to 2 p.m.; dinner, 5:30 to 9 p.m. (to 9:30 on Saturday), seven days a week; Sunday brunch/buffet 11 a.m. to 2 p.m. Otherwise breakfast Monday through Saturday is from 7:30 to 9:30 a.m.

At Mount Cranmore

Every ski area has its own restaurant and lounge, or at least a cafeteria, but **The Eating House** (tel. 356-2472) at the base of the Mt. Cranmore Skimobile and a good server's shot from the Tennis Club is not just a place to grab a quick lunch. Here, in an atmosphere of mountain rusticity, you can dine on poulet à la Kiev, coquilles St. Jacques, or tournedos of filet béarnaise, for $9 to $12 per main course. The menu is not encyclopedic but quite adequate, and the selection and preparation of the entrees shows balance and a knowledge of good eating. At lunch they offer a variety of hot and cold platters (hamburgers, seafood crêpes, etc.) for about $3 to $6.50. Despite its rustic decor—heavy beams and posts, dark wood, and the like—the Eating House bespeaks a certain refinement signaled by the deep-blue tablecloths and attractive place settings. Lunch is served from 11:30 a.m. to 2:30 p.m., dinner from 5 to 9 p.m., on Saturday to 10 p.m., and on Sunday lunch is from noon to 5 p.m., dinner from noon to 9 p.m.

Out in the Country

One of the better restaurants in the Mount Washington Valley is out in the country, several miles west of Glen on U.S. 302. The **Bernerhof** (tel. 383-4414) boasts that it has "fine European Cuisine in the Old World Tradition," and the selection of dishes is indeed European. The decor in the several dining rooms is simple and comely—pine paneling and similar—reflecting the owner's Swiss tastes. Besides the Swiss dishes on the menu such as fondue Neuchateloise ($6 at lunch, $7 at dinner), other European preparations are prominent: Hungarian goulash, Holstein schnitzel, and escargots bourguignonnes are but a few. One of the house specialties is the émince de veau au vin blanc (shredded veal sauteed in white wine; $10). Lunch is served from noon to 3:30 p.m. (June through October), dinner all year round from 6 to 9 p.m. Reservations are appreciated.

WHAT TO DO: North Conway is the Mount Washington Valley center for winter sports, but even during the summer there's plenty to do.

Downhill Skiing

The Mount Washington Valley includes five alpine ski areas: Attitash, Black, Cranmore, Tuckerman's Ravine, and Wildcat. Altogether there are 94 downhill trails and 21 lifts, and the slopes range from those for the beginner to those that present a challenge even to some experienced skiers. Many of the inns recommended above under "Where to Stay" offer special ski packages which include lift fees for all five areas.

You can get full free particulars on any or all of these areas by writing to the **Mount Washington Valley Chamber of Commerce,** Main Street, North Conway, NH 03860 (tel. 603/356-3171 or 356-5701).

Here's a rundown on the downhill ski slopes:

Attitash: Perhaps the thing that appeals most to impatient skiers about Attitash (Bartlett, NH 03812; tel. 603/374-2369; toll free snow info: 800/258-0316) is its policy of accepting reservations for its lift on weekends and holidays. Only 1800 skiers can use the area in any one day, which keeps the lift lines moving right along. The lifts are four double chairs with a 4400-skier capacity per hour. The vertical drop is about 1550 feet, and of the 20 trails, four are for novices, ten (up to two miles long) for the intermediate skier, and six (up to three-quarter of a mile long) for the expert. Grooming machines keep the slopes and trails in good condition. Equipment rentals and lessons are available, and the facilities include a restaurant (beer and wine served) and snackbar at the base, plus two warm-up huts. Attitash is open from 9 a.m. to 4 p.m. daily, and charges these prices for its lift tickets: $19 or $20 per adult, $14 for juniors all day on weekends: on weekdays the prices are $16 and $11 all day. Attitash is located several miles west of Glen along U.S. 302. Remember to call for those reservations on weekends and holidays. There is an Alpine slide and Aquahoggan waterslide for $3.75 and $3 a person when the snow melts.

Black Mountain: This is in the Carter Notch area only a few miles from Jackson, and the management prides itself on Black's being a good family ski area. Besides the 14 trails and two slopes on a vertical drop of 1200 feet, there is a pond good for ice skating at the base and a network of cross-country trails as well. Whitneys Inn and the Shovel Handle Saloon are at the base to provide sustenance, and in fact lodging too. The lifts are a double chair, two T-bars, and a J-bar; the trails are rated three novice, six novice-intermediate, and five expert. Ski rentals and lessons are available, there is some machinery for grooming the slopes and trails, and the hours of operation are the regular 9 a.m. to 4 p.m.

Mount Cranmore (tel. 356-5544 or 356-5545): This is the oldest ski area in the valley, dating back to the late 1930s, and its major ski lift, the Skimobile, was one of the first devices (besides legs) to take skiers to the top of a mountain. The Skimobile is a series of little bathtub-like cars running on a track along the ground which haul one person plus skies easily and solidly to the top of the mountain. Besides the Skimobile, Cranmore has three double chair lifts and a Poma, and all together can transport 5000 skiers per hour up the mountain. The vertical drop is 1500 feet, and the slopes run down 2500 to 3000 feet; the 13 trails are mostly intermediate and expert, 1½ to 2 miles long. The snowmaking capacity covers the whole mountain, as does the capability of the grooming machines. Ski instruction is in the Hannes Schneider school; rentals are available. Cranmore operates from 9 a.m. to 4 p.m. daily, and you can walk to it from the center of North Conway in about 15 minutes.

Wildcat Mountain (Pinkham Notch, Jackson, NH 03846; tel. 603/466-3326, or toll free in New Hampshire: 800/552-8952; in New York and New England: 800/258-8902). Wildcat is the major, most challenging area in the

Mount Washington Valley, located on Route 16 about 12 miles or so north of Jackson, right in the National Forest. The views of Tuckerman's Ravine and Mount Washington are impressive, and Wildcat can boast the longest trail in the valley: almost three miles. The 22 trails are just about evenly divided among the novice, intermediate, and expert classifications; the lifts are a 6800-foot gondola with a capacity of 600 per hour, a catapult double chair, a lynx double chair, a snowcat triple chair, and a T-bar; total hourly capacity is close to 5000. Vertical drop is also the greatest in the valley at 2100 feet. Wildcat Mountain has the longest ski season in the valley, and lots of facilities: school, rentals, babysitting service seven days a week, a cafeteria (with beer and wine), and a snackbar at the base, plus a Summit Lodge with a snackbar, and snowmaking and grooming capacity for the whole mountain. Lift rates come in all sorts of divisions and package plans.

Tuckerman's Ravine: Besides the five developed ski areas in the valley, it is possible to ski in the cirque at Tuckerman's Ravine, where the shadows protect the snow long past the time when the snow on other slopes has begun to melt. The special excitement at Tuckerman, besides the challenge of the *au naturel* slopes, comes from climbing the mountain you're going to ski down, for there are no lifts. This is oldtime skiing, with only a run or two a day, and only those with real stamina and strong legs should and will accept the challenge. But going back to the basics is exhilarating, everyone you meet here is your friend, and the fling down the mountain after the climb is a fitting way to end the season. Park in the Wildcat lot, recuperate in their cafeteria or lounge; follow the line of black dots up the mountain to the top.

Cross-country Skiing

All of the alpine ski areas in the valley have some cross-country trails and some are very easy while others are only for experts. The center of the ski touring activity in the valley is in Jackson, where the **Jackson Ski Touring Foundation** (P.O. Box 90, Jackson, NH 03846) spends upward of $70,000 a year to open, maintain, and groom over 125 kilometers of cross-country trails. The foundation is a nonprofit village organization dedicated to encouraging ski touring in and around Jackson, and it has a small office in the center of the village (check here for passes, information, maps; tel. 603/383-9355). There is a nominal fee for the use of the trails. A season membership is available. Clinics, tours, and rentals are all available both in Jackson and in North Conway at the several ski shops. In North Conway, the cross-country areas are at Whittaker Woods, Good Earth Sports, and the Carroll Reed Center.

Other Winter Sports

Because of the state parks, national forest, and private reserves in the valley, lots of other winter sports are popular here. Winter camping is possible, using a tent or the AMC huts, a few of which are open all winter. Note that many areas in the White Mountains have extremely severe weather—this writer has hiked into a blizzard, in a temperature of 14 degrees and winds gusting to 100 m.p.h. on top of Mount Washington, on the last day of *August.* This does not mean you will hit impossible weather, but it does mean you should check with rangers and AMC personnel, and have good equipment and a knowledge of winter camping before you go in.

Snowmobiling is also pretty big in the valley, and rental places in North Conway will rent you a machine by the hour or the day. Ice-skating rinks are maintained by the towns of North Conway, Jackson, and Bartlett. Various ponds and lakes are not bad for ice fishing—the locals will be glad to give visitors tips on the most-visited ice-fishing spots.

Tennis clubs in Glen and North Conway now have indoor courts suitable for winter play, and guest memberships are available. Contact the Mt. Washington Valley Racquet Club or the Mt. Cranmore Tennis Club.

The Ski Areas in Summer

The three largest ski areas, Attitash, Mount Cranmore, and Wildcat Mountain, don't fully close down in summer. Indeed, they are developing full warm-weather recreation programs to keep the visitors coming and the bills paid. At Attitash (tel. 603/374-2369), the lifts keep working to take you up to the top of the Alpine Slide similar to the one described in the section on Alpine Ridge at Winnipesaukee; prices are the same. At the foot of the slide a row of little huts are leased out to workers in the crafts who display and sell their wares in a fleamarket atmosphere, particularly on weekends. At Wildcat Mountain the cafeteria stays open for those wanting a snack before boarding the gondolas for the 25-minute round-trip ride up the mountainside (in operation from late May to late October, 9:30 a.m. to 4:30 p.m. daily except in July and August, when it operates until 5:30 p.m. The area around Wildcat Mountain, and its base camp, are kept immaculate because they're within the National Forest and subject to its regulations.

Mount Cranmore, right in North Conway, has the most activities, however. The Skimobile is in operation daily Memorial Day weekend, and then late June through October to take visitors up the 1500 feet from the base to the summit for $4 per adult, $2 for kids 6 to 12. On certain days, the local hang-gliding school offers demonstration flights from the side of the mountain (you take the Skimobile up to see them). Look for a small sign hung out at the Skimobile base station giving the days. The annual hang-gliding championship meet is held in late August. Mount Cranmore's restaurant, the **Eating House,** is open all summer (see above), and next to the parking lot are several picnic tables in a pine grove next to a clear, cold mountain brook.

But Mt. Cranmore's big summer event is the annual **Volvo International Tennis Tournament,** held in the Mt. Cranmore Tennis Club near the base of the Skimobile at the very end of July and first week in August. Lodging rates go up throughout the town as though this time were a holiday, and it's good to reserve in advance if you plan to occupy a room in town during the tournament. For full information on the tournament call 603/356-5765; or write Volvo Tennis, P.O. Box 428, North Conway, NH 03860. To reserve one of the tennis club's six indoor and three outdoor courts before or after the tournament, call 603/356-3164.

Summer Activities

Besides hiking and camping in the state parks and national forests, the Mount Washington Valley offers many other activities.

Conway Scenic Railroad: Right in town is the romantic old station of this scenic railroad (tel. 356-5251), built in 1874 and restored to its present condition in 1974. For $4 (adults) or $2 (kids 4 to 12) you can buy a ticket for the scenic ride through the mountain country; choose your seat from among those in the enclosed cars or the open-air "cinder collectors." Two steam locomotives and two 35-year-old diesel engines are on hand to provide the power, and if you go a little early you can visit the roundhouse to see where the locomotives are turned around. From early May to mid-June the trains run on weekends only; from late June through late October the trains run every day, rain or shine. Departure times are 11 a.m. and 1, 2:30, and 4 p.m. The trip takes about an hour.

Theater: The Mount Washington Valley Theater Company (tel. 603/356-5776), North Conway, NH 03860, currently performs at the playhouse on Main Street in the Eastern Mountain Sports (EMS) complex. From the end of June through Labor Day they offer a half dozen or so plays. Of course, it's most fun to see the entire series, watching the various members of the company take on different roles every other week, but even if you can't afford to stay in North Conway the entire season, you'll enjoy taking in a play here. The box office opens daily at 11 a.m., and curtain time is 8:30 p.m. sharp.

White Mountains National Forest: A considerable part of northern New Hampshire is included in the White Mountains National Forest, which is not to be confused with a national *park.* The forest does have a number of developed sites, however. Camping areas ($3 to $4 per night, cold running water, and toilets only) are dotted here and there, as are very pretty picnic areas. A maze of trails, both very easy and not so easy, cover a lot of the forest's vast expanse. Signs by the roadside mark the trail's beginning, but don't wander in just for a 30-minute walk if you're not familiar with the area. Instead, buy detailed maps of the trails and a trail guide from the **Appalachian Mountain Club**, 5 Joy St., Boston, Mass., or from the club's camp at Pinkham Notch on Route 16 north of Jackson. The trail guide will tell you all about the trail: how difficult it is, how long it is, the vertical rise, the average walking time, reference points along the way, and what to see as you walk.

Snowmobilers can use parts of the forest, but other parts are restricted, so the best thing to do is to stop at a Forest Service office, or write to the State Bureau of Off-Road Vehicles, Concord, NH 03301, for a snowmobile map of the forest.

Sports: Want to go horseback riding? Call the **Bald Ledge Riding Stables** (tel. 367-4647) on Route 153 in Freedom, N.H., or **Robinwood Riding Inn** (tel. 383-4261) in Jackson. Besides hayrides and sleighrides, there are trail rides ($8 per hour). If you'd rather travel under your own power, rent a canoe for the day or the week from **Saco Bound/Northern Waters** (tel. 447-2177), two miles east of Center Conway on Route 302. The Saco River has lots of smooth and easy areas, and you can go on a Tuesday or Thursday day trip—lunch, guide, and transportation included—for $14 per person. Overnight Trips and canoe pickup service are available too.

A Look at New Hampshire History

Heritage New Hampshire (tel. 383-9776), on Route 16 in Glen, has a variety of lifelike scenes and dioramas with talking figures which outline New Hampshire's history, from the docks of an English port town through the Industrial Revolution at the Amoskeag Mills in Manchester. You can walk at your own pace through the maze of displays, and costumed guides will answer any questions you may have about New Hampshire's history. The price is $4 for adults, $2 for children 4 to 12, and it's open from 9 a.m. to 6 p.m. daily between Memorial Day and Labor Day, and then from 10 a.m. to 5 p.m. until mid-October.

Two Scenic Drives

A private business, the **Mount Washington Summit Road Company**, Gorham, NH 03581 (tel. 603/466-2222 or 466-3988), operates an alpine toll road to the top of the highest peak in the Northeast, 6288-foot Mt. Washington. Start from Route 16 in Pinkham Notch. You can drive your own car (no trucks or campers) to the top of the mountain for $9 car and driver, and $2 for each passenger (kids pay half fare); vans operated by the company will take you to the top and back down again for $10 per person (kids 5 to 12, half fare) if you'd rather not drive. Hours are 7 a.m. to 6 p.m. for the road, 8:30 a.m. to 4:30 p.m. for the van shuttles. The season is normally from mid-May to late October, but remember that Mt. Washington's summit has the most severe weather in the Northeast, and it's altogether possible that the road might be temporarily closed because of snow even in June or September. This, by the way, is only one of three ways to reach the Mt. Washington summit, the others being on foot following the Appalachian Mountain Club trails, or by Cog Railway, described a bit further on in this book.

   The Kancamagus Highway: Route 112 between Conway and Lincoln is known as the Kancamagus Highway; its 33-mile length exhibits some of the finest scenery in the White Mountains, including the view from the 2860-foot Kancamagus Pass. Almost the entire length of the road is within the boundaries of the national forest, and is therefore protected from any development more civilized than a campground (there are six along the road) or a picnic area. The drive is a must: this is White Mountains beauty in its purest form.

7. Bretton Woods and Crawford Notch

   North and east on U.S. 302 from Glen will take you through Crawford Notch to the **Crawford Notch State Park.** The park is a fine place for hiking and fishing, and you can see two impressive waterfalls—the Flume and the Silver Cascades—from the highway. Facilities include a 24-site campground, a picnic area, an information booth, and a shop featuring the products of New Hampshire artisans. The ruins of the **Willey House** hold a mystery and a story from the 1820s, when the road was being cut through Crawford Notch and the Willey family set up house in Crawford Notch to provide for the teams which would pass through the valley. In August 1826, one of the worst storms ever to hit the White Mountains wreaked havoc in the valley, with floods, landslides, wind, and rain which left the Willey House unharmed, but resulted in the deaths of every member of the household.

WHERE TO STAY: At **Bretton Woods Resort,** P.O. Box 18, Bretton Woods, NH 03575, is a ski area and two lodging establishments, the new and modern **Bretton Woods Motor Inn** and the venerable rambling palace known as the **Mount Washington Hotel** (tel. 603/278-1000, or toll free 800/258-0330). The mammoth hotel was the site of the famous Bretton Woods conference of 1943 which established the world monetary system for the postwar period. Although great old hotels of this sort, with their private golf courses, riding stables, playhouses, and the like are almost as rare as dinosaurs, it is heartening to see that this one is still thriving, its gracious service and accommodations open to both the tourist and the conventioneer. The lobby is immense, with a baronial fireplace and lots of color and activity; nearby is a semicircular Conservatory with a dome and many small stained-glass windows. The views of the mountains and the grounds are very fine. There are hundreds of rooms, and they rent with two meals included in the price. All rooms have private bath, and the cost for room and meals is about $81 *per person,* tax and service included. You can save a bit on the weekly rate (about 5%), or by taking advantage of the midweek or weekend package plans. There are small fees for use of the golf course, horses from the stable, tennis court, bicycles, and for children's playroom and babysitting services.

The **Lodge at Bretton Woods** out on the highway (U.S. 302) is an annex of the hotel, and although the hotel operates only from the first of June to mid-October, the lodge stays open both winter and summer. Here the prices are for lodging only, but all privileges open to guests at the hotel are extended to guests at the lodge: a double with bath is $62 per person; children under 14 are free in the same room with their parents. Package plans for four days or more are available.

READER'S LODGING SELECTION: "A lovely place to stay in the White Mountains near Bretton Woods is the **Lakeside Farm Inn** (tel. 603/837-2741), just north of Whitefield, NH 03598, on Route 116. The inn is a beautiful farmhouse with lovely lake and mountain views from most of the rooms. There is a private beach on the lake for guests. We found this to be one of the least expensive places, as the price ($33 to $43 double, tax in) includes a big country breakfast" (Carolyn Farmer, Washington, D.C.).

WHAT TO DO: Certainly the quaintest way to get to the top of Mt. Washington is by the **Mt. Washington Cog Railway** (tel. 846-5404). It's a 3½-mile track along a steep trestle up the mountainside. The locomotive (powered by steam) drives a cog wheel on its undercarriage which engages with pins between the rails to pull the locomotive and train up the slope. In operation since 1866, it's a lot of fun besides being very scenic indeed. At the portion of the run known as Jacob's Ladder, the grade is a surprising 37%, but the little engine pulls along trustworthily despite the steepness. At the top, the average summer temperature is 40 degrees Fahrenheit, and there may be a stiff wind. Stroll to the new Visitor Center for a snack, drink, or souvenir, and then tour the mountaintop: see the displays highlighting the worst of Mt. Washington's weather. If you pick a clear day to ascend to the 6288-foot summit, it will seem as though you can see all the way to Europe!

The Base Station, where you board the train, is six miles off U.S. 302 east of Twin Mountain, N.H. The season is Memorial Day weekend through Columbus Day (Canadian Thanksgiving), with weekends-only runs until late June, then daily starting at 8 a.m., and keeping as close to an hourly schedule as possible. Try to take an early train—perhaps the 8 a.m.—to avoid having to wait in line. From Labor Day through mid-October there are trains daily if weather permits at 10 a.m. and as needed. Fares (round trip) are $18 per adult, half fare for kids 6 to 15; under 6, free if sitting on a parent's lap. Remember to take a sweater or jacket, or both, for the cool weather at the top, no matter how warm it is at the bottom.

8. Waterville Valley

In 1829, a small settlement in a remote New Hampshire valley was incorporated as a town. A few farms, perhaps a small store, and a tiny library—even here in the remoteness of the White Mountains, the symbol of New England's cultural life—that was all there was to Waterville Valley. Today the tiny settlement is still there, deep within the White Mountains National Forest, but a developer with great taste and tact now owns the valley, and dictates what shape the new resort community in this beautiful spot will take. The results so far are very encouraging, almost a marvel: six hotels and several condominium developments under different ownership, all of striking and interesting design, furnished in good taste and staffed with competent, concerned personnel. Two ski areas are handy, a golf course and lots of tennis courts await visitors, and hiking, bicycling, fishing, and snowshoeing are right at one's doorstep. A free shuttle bus connects all the hotels with all the things there are to do. This is a very fine resort indeed.

All the places in Waterville Valley have the same postal address: Waterville Valley, NH 03223, and there is a **Lodging Bureau** which provides free reservations service: call toll free 800/258-8988 on the eastern seaboard south to Virginia and west to Ohio, 800/552-4767 in New Hampshire, and 603/236-8371 for all other areas. Or write to Waterville Valley Lodging Bureau, Waterville Valley, NH 03223, for information.

WHERE TO STAY: The setting of Waterville Valley, in the shadow of Mt. Tecumseh, is very beautiful, and the hotels have been designed to fit in well with the town and the natural beauty. Of the six hotels, the majority are of moderate price, one is expensive, and another is very low-priced.

Queen of the valley's hostelries is the **Snowy Owl Inn** (tel. 603/236-8383), a dramatic structure of weathered wood and shining windows which reflect the trees and mountains surrounding it. The interior, like the exterior, is all of natural wood, with a large stone fireplace for accent in the three-story-high lobby. The rooms are modern, luxurious, and decorated with taste that might have come right out of a design magazine. Many rooms have fine views of the valley and mountains, others of Snow's Brook, the stream which runs by the hotel. Even if you don't have a mountain view, you can get one by climbing the spiral staircase at the top of the lobby to the little observation tower. The Snowy Owl has its own heated outdoor pool, of course. Rooms cost $46 to $64 single, $64 to $93 double (children under 12 free in their parents' room). These are the summer rates: in winter, the rates are about 15% higher.

The **Silver Squirrel Inn** (tel. 603/236-8366) is owned and managed by the same people who own the Snowy Owl Inn, and although the Silver Squirrel is not quite so posh, it is very comfortable. It's right across Snow's Brook from the Snowy Owl, and is near several other inns and the Fourways Restaurant. Prices at the Silver Squirrel are $42 to $58 single, $60 to $88 double; children 12 and under stay free if their parents pay for a standard double room. (There are loft rooms which sleep four people, but in these each person must pay, regardless of age.)

The **Valley Inn & Tavern** (tel. 603/236-8336) is also among the posh places to stay in Waterville Valley. Its attractive design adds to the scenery in the valley, and also provides some unexpected bonuses to guests. For instance, many rooms have small private patios overlooking the valley and mountains; others have small balconies over the forest and settlement. The swimming pool is indoor/outdoor: part is enclosed by the building, but a huge window comes down just to water level, and you can swim underneath it to the outdoor portion of the pool, winter or summer. Heated water makes it useful all year. The Valley Inn has other athletic goodies: a platform (or paddle) tennis club with two courts, free to guests; an exercise room; a sauna; a massage room. The rooms are large, with two double beds, TV, telephone, and of course private bath. There are three types of rooms, differing in views mostly: an economy room is $198 double, tax, tips, and two meals a day included; at the other end of the scale, a deluxe room would cost $30 more per night. Children 6 and under stay free in their parents room. In winter the rates are about $2 higher per room, per night.

Also in the group of inns clustered near the restaurant are the **Landmarc Lodges**, P.O. Box 3, Waterville Valley, NH 03223 (tel. 603/236-8366). Landmarc West is a smaller hotel than the Snowy Owl or Valley Inn, with a personality all its own. In the public rooms you'll find three stone fireplaces, color TV, indoor pool, and Jacuzzi. The 27 rooms themselves have queen-size beds, and each has a pull-out sofa bed or trundle bed; some rooms have lofts with several single beds in addition. All rooms have private baths.

Set off from the more expensive hotels, closer to the ski slopes and tennis courts, is Waterville Valley's most innovative hostelry. It's the rustic, modern **Waterville Valley Bunkhouse** (tel. 603/236-8326), the dream of Patti and John Sava, who believe that skiing and summer outdoor activities in the beautiful valley should not be limited to those who can pay a lot for a hotel. Mr. Sava, an architect, designed the bunkhouse to accommodate young people, families, all-comers. The feeling is of a modern, well-designed mountain hostel, with a big stone fireplace, and lots of rooms, each with six bunk beds. Every room has a window and is constructed of rough boards; the bunks all have covered foam mattresses, but other than this there are no furnishings. Bathrooms are located nearby, and are communal. Guests at the Bunkhouse are encouraged to bring their own sleeping bags or bedding, or they can rent it from the Bunkhouse for a few dollars. The Bunkhouse is divided into men's and women's wings during the very busy times, but arrangements for families, couples, and small groups are usually easily arranged. The 200-odd beds cost $12 midweek, $16 on weekends, *per person,* in summer; during winter it's $15 midweek, $20 on weekends. Hearty, filling meals are cooked in the dining room downstairs, and are available to Bunkhouse guests at a flat charge.

Long-term Stays

Several of the condominium developments in the valley have long-term (by the month or the season) rental rates for those who want an apartment rather than a hotel room. Accommodations range from one-bedroom apartments for one or two people to three-bedroom apartments which can take eight to ten people. Each apartment is completely furnished, including kitchen utensils and dinner service, all linens, and color cable TV. The apartments also rent by the day (two-day minimum) for $164.30 to $381.60 for a weekend, or $275.60 to $651.90 for a five-night ski week. In summer you'll pay $275.60 to $482.30 per week. There are various package and weekly plans, both for normal and holiday periods. For more information, contact **Windsor Hill Condominiums,** Jennings Peak Road, Waterville Valley, NH 03223 (tel. 603/236-8321; in New York, New Jersey, and New England (except New Hampshire, call toll free 800/343-1286).

WHERE TO DINE: Waterville Valley's all-purpose restaurant is the **Fourways** (tel. 236-8331), near the hotels. It's pleasant and modern, if less rustic than the hotels which surround and depend on it. Lunch is served in the winter season only, and includes hearty sandwiches and hot soups as well as smaller portions of several dinner menu items. At dinner, the menu is varied and interesting. Besides the required steak offerings ($10 to $15), there is suprême of chicken Barbara (boneless breast of chicken sauteed in butter and lemon juice, with mushrooms, red pimientos, and lemon rind as a sauce; $9), or perhaps a beef brochette teriyaki, steak au poivre Alfredo, or cannelloni Piemontaise. The daily special dinners give one a choice of entree, and the full meal is about $15 ($10 for children). The wine list goes to almost 100 choices. Enjoy the hanging plants and the views of greenery from the restaurant's windows, and the pleasant, efficient service of its staff, and that will keep you busy so you won't notice the lurid modern variations on the wagon-wheel chandelier which hang from the ceiling in the dining room.

The Fourways has several lounges and the Loggers' Bar. There's entertainment nightly. Some thoughts: The hotels offer meal package plans in many cases, and adopting the plan can save you 20% to 25% on meal costs—you eat in the same restaurant. Also, New Hampshire law is such that hotels cannot have full bars without food service, which means that for a cocktail or glass of wine, or even a beer, you must patronize a lounge as at the Fourways. This is certainly pleasant enough, but it's good to know that hotels do provide set-ups, and you can buy liquor at New Hampshire State Stores off I-93 at Hooksett toll booth, or Ashland, or Plymouth.

Down by the Snow's Mountain lift base station and the tennis courts is **The Finish Line** restaurant. The cuisine is American, international, Italian, and both bottled and carafe wines are available. The simple, modern dining room looks right out to the Snow's Mountain slopes and the tennis courts (and skating rink). In summer there are a few tables outdoors under an awning. Lunch is the busiest time for the obvious reason, when grill plates cost $2.25 to $5, and sandwiches run $2.50 to $4.

WHAT TO DO IN SUMMER: It seems as if they've thought of everything here. First and foremost, the valley is deep within the national forest, so hiking and fishing are easy to find. For tennis, there are 18 clay courts and lessons by a professional staff. The golf course in the valley is nine holes, and not too far away at White Mountains Country Club is an 18-hole course. Guests at the Valley Inn & Tavern can use its paddle tennis courts for free; the general public can use them, day and night, for a fee. Bikes can be rented from the Golf and Tennis Club.

WHAT TO DO IN WINTER: Although snowshoeing, hiking, skating, and general taking of country-mountain air are all possible and enjoyable in Waterville Valley, most people come to ski the trails and slopes of Mt. Tecumseh and Snow's Mountain. **Mount Tecumseh** is the larger and more elaborate of the two, with two triple chair lifts, five double chair lifts, a T-bar, and a J-bar. The vertical drop is over 2000 feet, and there are 34 trails and slopes. Rentals and lessons are easily available, as is a quick meal at the base cafeteria. A Schuss bus takes guests from Waterville Valley hotels to Tecumseh and back. The other area, **Snow's Mountain,** is right in the valley near the hotels of the village, and has three intermediate and beginners' slopes. It's for first-timers and learners, with one double-chair lift and a vertical drop of less than 600 feet. To keep the crowds down, Mt. Tecumseh and Snow's Mountain operate on a limited-ticket basis (no more than a 15-minute wait for the lift on average).

For information about snow at both areas, call toll free 800/552-0388 if you're calling from New Hampshire, or 800/258-8983 if you're phoning from any other eastern state. Lift rates at Mt. Tecumseh are $16 to $20 per adult, $12 to $15 per junior, the higher rate being for weekends; students and senior citizens are granted discounts. At Snow's Mountain, the rates are $13 per adult, $10 per junior. Snow's is open on weekends and during holiday periods only.

Ski packages for two, three, five, or seven nights are offered, and all facilities in the valley participate. Depending on what you want, you can get a package which includes lodging, meals, lifts, lessons, even rental equipment. Prices depend on which hotel you choose, and what options you need to do the sort of skiing you're after. Options are also offered for ski touring (trail fees, lessons, equipment, and lodging) in the packages.

9. The Franconia Notch Area

Interstate 93 comes up from Manchester and Concord to pass through the White Mountains National Forest. The towns of North Woodstock and Lincoln form the center of the developed area within the forest, and it's here that most people come to look for a room, a meal, or any of the other services of civilization. At this point the Kancamagus Highway heads east through the most scenic 33-mile drive in the mountains; north of Lincoln and North Woodstock are several natural curiosities, including the famous **Old Man of the Mountains** at the narrow pass called Franconia Notch.

The area centered on North Woodstock and Lincoln is very rich in possibilities for outdoor activities, especially hiking, camping, picnicking, and skiing at Cannon Mountain and Mittersill in Franconia Notch itself, and Loon Mountain near Lincoln on the Kancamagus Highway.

The local **Visitor Center** is at the intersection of I-93 and the Kancamagus Highway. It is run both by the Lincoln–North Woodstock Chamber of Commerce personnel and also by national forest rangers; hours of operation in summer high season are 8:30 a.m. to 8 p.m., normal business hours at other times of the year.

WHERE TO STAY: Except for one motel right near Franconia Notch itself, I'll keep the recommendations to the center of this area, the towns of North Woodstock and Lincoln.

North of North Woodstock on U.S. 3 is **Woodward's Motor Inn** (tel. 603/745-8141), Lincoln, NH 03251, which describes itself as "a complete family resort open all the year." This is one of the better motels on a strip of motels and restaurants; its 42 rooms are in buildings set back from the roadway behind a scattering of tall pine trees and a small pond. The pool is heated and is a comfortable 30 by 65 feet; guests get to play tennis on the Woodward's own court; and the Open Hearth Steak House is open to motel guests and nonguests alike. All rooms are air-conditioned and have color TVs and telephones; many have two double beds—the traveling family's boon—as well. Rates for high summer are $51.36 double, $55.64 triple, $59.92 quadruple in the motel rooms, all of which have private baths. In foliage season (first two weeks in October) the rates are about $2 higher than summer rates. Ski-season rates are slightly lower than the summer rates. The restaurant, by the way, is open for breakfast and dinner, 7:30 to 10:30 a.m. and 5 to 9 p.m. in season, 8 to 10 a.m. and 5 to 8:30 p.m. off-season; the Open Hearth is open only for dinner. Live entertainment in the lounge provided six nights a week in season.

The **Kancamagus Motor Lodge** (tel. 603/745-3365, or toll free 800/631-1601), Lincoln, NH 03251, on the Kancamagus Highway one mile west of Loon Mountain ski area (take Exit 32 from I-93, then drive east on Route 112), is a modern motel with heated outdoor pool, new rooms in a modern style furnished with private steambaths, wall-to-wall carpet, and color TV. Its attraction is in its location, very close to Loon Mountain and not far at all from the attractions of Franconia Notch. Rates in summer are $42.40 to $47.70 for two in a room, fully air-conditioned; kids under 12 stay free. In winter, a double room is $36.05 to $42.40 for two Sunday through Thursday nights; on weekends it's $42.40 to $53. The Kancamagus has a dining and cocktail lounge.

Right at the center of the Loon Mountain ski action is the **Inn at Loon Mountain** (tel. 603/745-8111), Lincoln, NH 03251, a modern structure with modern hotel rooms containing two double beds and a cable color TV each. Furnishings and decor are fairly simple and attractive enough, and guests have the use (in summer) of the outdoor pool, a game room, babysitting service, and a lounge with live entertainment almost every night. Winter rates are $63.60 single, $93.28 double during the week, $88 single, $116.60 double on weekends, but the price includes breakfast and dinner in the inn's restaurant for each person. In summer, the rates are considerably lower and the traffic a bit lighter, but reservations are a must when there are special activities, such as the annual Loon Mountain Fall Foliage Festival in October and the Gathering of the Scottish Clans in September.

In the town of Lincoln proper, on Route 112, is the **Lincoln Motel,** at 5 Church St., Lincoln, NH 03251 (tel. 603/745-2780), an unprepossessing two-story structure with rooms that constitute one of the best bargains in the area, especially for skiers. Rooms have private bath, air conditioning, and cable TV, and a small kitchenette (bring your own utensils, pans, and dishes) is open to guests. Besides the nine rooms in the motel proper, a nearby house has been converted to take transient guests and thereby increases the chance a visitor on a budget may find a room here. Rates are $26 to $33 double (the higher price for an air-conditioned room), with special triple and quadruple rates and ski package deals. Good, if basic, rooms, decent prices, and Loon Mountain less than two miles away. You'll see the Lincoln Motel from the Kancamagus Highway, set back from the road a half block on the left-hand side as you go from North Woodstock east toward Loon Mountain.

Budget-minded readers will want to consider staying at the **Mt. Adams Inn** (tel. 603/745-2711), on U.S. 3 south of the center of North Woodstock, NH 03262. Dixie Hartle not only operates the inn in which a room can be had for as little as $17 double (share a bath), but she also is in charge of the restaurant which specializes in Polish and American home-cooked food. The inn is open all year round. They also have a homey public lounge with a fireplace and color TV.

The restaurant, open July 1 to October 12, finds both local and out-of-state diners relishing the golombki (stuffed cabbage, at $4.25 for a large plate), or the kielbasa sausage with sauerkraut. A bowl of soup (90¢) and one of these plates makes a very filling meal, but if you're ravenous, you can have the Polish combination plate, with a little—actually, a lot—of each for $5.25. The dining room has unpretentious wood tables and *hard* wood chairs, the service is a bit slow but friendly, and cocktails, wine, and beer are available. Besides the Polish specialties, a good number of standard American dishes are served as well. Children, pets, and hikers are welcome.

READERS' RESTAURANT SELECTION: "We stopped in Plymouth, about 20 miles south of Lincoln, and had a fantastic meal at the **Downunder Restaurant**, 81-C Main St., Plymouth, NH 03264 (tel. 536-3983). The menu is very extensive and reasonable, with veal Oscar for $7, sole Florentine for $5, stuffed pork chops, crab legs, and chicken Kiev at similar prices. They also have interesting, original dishes" (Mr. and Mrs. Robert Davenport, Huntington Beach, Fla.).

WHAT TO SEE AND DO: Franconia Notch State Park is surrounded by the **White Mountains National Forest.** The natural wonders of the park are impressive indeed, including the "notch" (pass, or gorge) itself, the Flume, the Basin, several lakes, and the rock outcrop in the shape of a man's profile which has all but become the state symbol of New Hampshire, the famous Old Man of the Mountains. The state park offers a wealth of outdoor activities: Lafayette Campground, the Appalachian Mountain Club's system of trails and huts, swimming in the mountain lakes, a number of beautiful picnic sites, and two ski areas, one of them with an aerial tramway which operates winter and summer.

The Old Man

The Old Man of the Mountains, also called the Great Stone Face, is one of New Hampshire's most famous features. It was discovered by white settlers at the beginning of the 19th century after having been in the process of formation for thousands of years at least. The profile is formed by several ledges of granite, and in a cubist sort of way the resemblance is quite striking. But don't expect a mammoth face: the face is only about 40 feet high, and it's way up on a cliff 1000 feet above the valley floor. Its grandeur comes not from its size, but rather from its fidelity and its impressive perch high in the sky, gazing out over the mountains. In recent years the state has spent a good deal of money preserving the Face from the ravages of nature, for even granite formations crumble given enough wind, rain, and ice. From the highway parking lot, a path leads down to the shores of Profile Lake, and descriptive plaques tell you all about the Old Man.

South of the Old Man along U.S. 3, some people think that the undulant crest of Mt. Liberty to the east resembles George Washington lying in state. Take a look, and feel free to concur or disagree!

The Basin and the Flume

South of the Old Man along U.S. 3, signs will point to a side road and the Basin, a huge glacial pothole in the native granite, 20 feet in diameter. The hole is at the foot of a waterfall, and was presumably made by the action of small rocks and stones whirled around by the force of the water. It's a cool spot, good for contemplation.

Four miles north of North Woodstock, but still south of the Basin, is the Flume, a natural gorge or cleft in the granite. A boardwalk has been erected along the 800-foot length of the Flume, and for $2.50 ($1.50 for children) you can walk through its cool depths, the granite walls rising to 60 or 70 feet above you, mosses and plants growing precariously in niches here and there. Signs explain now nature formed the Flume, and point out interesting sights along the way. Near the Flume is a covered bridge thought to be one of the oldest in the state, perhaps erected as early as the 1820s.

Cannon Mountain Aerial Tramway

An impressive view of the notch and the mountains is yours if you take the Cannon Mountain Aerial Tramway (Route 3, Franconia Notch; tel. 603/823-5563) to the top of the line. The tramway operates in the summer from the end of May to mid-October, 9 a.m. to 4:30 p.m.; $5 for adults, $2.75 for children 6 to 12, round trip. The tramway station is just off U.S. 3 north of the Old Man, and has its own parking lot. In the weathered shingle building at the base is a cafeteria, should you be in need of a light meal.

Skiing

There are three notable ski resorts in the Franconia Notch area: Cannon Mountain and Mittersill near the Notch itself, and Loon Mountain in Lincoln at the western end of the Kancamagus Highway.

Cannon Mountain (tel. 603/823-5563 or 603/823-5661): Besides the brand-new aerial tramway, Cannon has three double-chair lifts, two T-bars, and a pony lift, all with an hourly capacity of close to 6000 skiers. There are 26 miles of trails and slopes, about a quarter of them novice, another quarter expert, and the remaining half intermediate. The vertical drop is 2145 feet, and besides having snowmaking equipment for the snowless days, the slopes are positioned so that they naturally receive and retain more than the average amount of snow. Cannon Mountain is operated by the state as it is in a state park. Lift prices are $19 per adult, $14 per junior on weekends for a full day. Besides the cafeteria and the base and lounges nearby, there is a ski school, a nursery, and a ski shop where you can rent equipment.

Mittersill (tel. 603/823-5511; snow info, 603/823-7772): This is the junior cousin to Cannon Mountain, with a vertical drop of 1600 feet, and one double chair and one T-bar for lifts. It's open daily, north of Cannon Mountain, off of U.S. 3 on Route 18.

Loon Mountain (tel. 603/745-8111; snow info, 745-8100): Just a few miles east of Lincoln along the Kancamagus Highway brings you to Loon Mountain, a modern ski area with a gondola (four-passenger cars) and five double-chair lifts to take 6400 skiers an hour up the mountain. The vertical drop is 1850 feet, and the longest run is 2½ miles. Loon has a limited-lift-lines policy (make reservations), and top-to-bottom snowmaking capacity. The Inn at Loon Mountain has a restaurant (described above); other services at the base lodge include a cafeteria, lounge, nursery, ski shop, and rental shop. Lift fees are $20 on weekends, and $18 on weekdays. Chair-lift-only tickets are available.

In summer and fall, Loon Mountain's gondolas operate from 10 a.m. to 5 p.m. daily to take visitors on the 7000-foot trip (1800-foot rise) to the summit, at $4 per adult, $2.50 per child, free for age 5 and under. Special family rates available. There are cafeterias at both the base and summit stations. Loon features many special events throughout the summer, like the annual gathering of the Scottish Clans, a two-day traditional Highland Games, held in September. Also a wine festival and arts and crafts festivals. For full information on what's scheduled, write for the flyer *News from Loon,* Loon Mountain, Lincoln, NH 03251; or call 603/745-8111.

Several ski areas offer package arrangements through the **Ski 93 Association,** named because the areas involved are all accessible by using Interstate 93. Bretton Woods, Cannon Mountain, Loon Mountain, and Waterville Valley are among the members, and you can get three-day or five-day cut-price lift tickets. Midweek passes good at all four areas are a real bargain. The association will be glad to help with reservations at area hotels, lodges, and inns. Write to them at P.O. Box 517, Lincoln, NH 03251; or call 603/745-8101. By the way, the 24-hour snow phone is 603/745-2409.

10. Lake Sunapee

Lake Sunapee is a pleasant regional vacation spot in southwestern New Hampshire, not all that far from the town of Hanover, which is home for Dartmouth College. Besides summer sports such as swimming, boating, and canoeing, the area around Lake Sunapee also has its own small ski area in Mount Sunapee State Park. On a trip to Vermont or north to Hanover for a visit to Dartmouth, the shores of Lake Sunapee are a fine place to stop for a night, or even a week.

Of the towns around the lake, Sunapee (sometimes called Sunapee Harbor) on the western shore is the nicest, with a good collection of inns, motels, and resorts. Although in its early days Sunapee held a tannery, grist mill, and several shops for woodworking industries, for many years now it has made its living from summer visitors; and in recent years skiers have brought business to the town in winter as well.

The town of Mount Sunapee, on the southwestern shore, is not really a town at all, regardless of what it may say on your road map. The intersection of Routes 103 and 103B, with a motel and the state park and state beach entrance, *is* the "town." Don't plan to get gas there!

INFORMATION: The **Dartmouth/Lake Sunapee Region Association** (tel. 603/448-3303) is the local information source. Call, or write to them at P.O. Box 246, Lebanon, NH 03766.

WHERE TO STAY: Right near the entrance to Mount Sunapee State Park is the very popular **Mt. Sunapee Motel** (tel. 603/763-5592), Route 103, Mt. Sunapee, NH 03772. The Mt. Sunapee Motel is modern: tile bathrooms, with tub-shower combinations, TV, and twin beds in many rooms. One building has several two-room apartments and studio efficiency apartments, and the swimming pool (outdoors) is shared by all. Summer rates are $36.04 double in a motel room, $42.40 to $44.52 in a two-room unit, $50.88 in a studio with kitchen. The cheaper rate of each pair is for a double bed (twins only in the motel rooms). These rates go up a bit for winter, down a bit for the first two weeks in June, and for most of September (after Labor Day). Make your reservations in advance, for the Mt. Sunapee is a popular place because of its very convenient location.

WHERE TO DINE: In Sunapee Harbor, one restaurant provides a good range of cuisines and prices; near Mount Sunapee State Park, a place with Swiss ambience matches the mountains well.

Sunapee Harbor visitors have been going to the **Woodbine Cottage Restaurant** (tel. 763-2222) for 55 years, and at my last visit it was as popular as ever: several smallish, but bright and cheery rooms with lots of polished blond wood, with pewter vessels and an old rifle hung here and there for effect. Lots of windows provide plenty of light especially on a bright day. At lunchtime, the daily luncheons are priced between $7.15 and $10.55, but that's for a full three- or four-course meal. At dinner, the prices are in the $11.60 to $17.50 range for such favorites as baked ham in raisin sauce, broiled lamb chops, or lobster Newburg. Remember that these prices include appetizer, vegetable and potato, salad, roll, dessert, and coffee, tea, or milk. The Woodbine is open from May 1 through mid-October.

Near Mount Sunapee State Park, the place to go for a light lunch, cocktail, or dinner, is **Schweitzer's** (tel. 863-1820), about a mile west of the state park entrance (the big traffic circle) on Route 103. Schweitzer's, as you might have guessed, has a Swiss ambience, although the food is mostly American. Wood floors, knotty-pine paneling, and rustic-looking tables add to the mountain flavor of the place, red-and-white checkered tablecloths (Swiss colors) make it informal, and a vine-covered terrace like a small beer garden provides a fine place for a cold glass of suds on a warm summer day. Schweitzer's serves lunch, cocktails, and dinner from May through October and from December through March. For lunch you can order something as light as a $2 sandwich, or a full $8 meal; at dinner, full meals featuring wienerschnitzel ($9.75) and sauerbraten ($10.75) are about the only "Swiss" items in evidence, although the menu bears a good, full selection of American dishes at similar prices.

WHAT TO DO: To see Lake Sunapee, there is no better way than to catch the M/V *Mount Sunapee II* (tel. 603/763-4030), which leaves Sunapee Harbor marina at 10 a.m. and 2:30 p.m. every day for tours of the beautiful, very pure lake. The morning tour costs $4 and takes 1½ hours; the afternoon tour is a big longer (1¾ hours) and costs $4.50; kids under 12 pay half fare; kids under 5 ride free. The *Mount Sunapee II* holds 150 people, and the tour is narrated by the amiable captain. Also available for senior-citizen cruises.

In the summer, Sunapee hosts very well-attended flea markets out on Route 103B at the blinking light (between Sunapee Harbor and Sunapee Lower Village). Both buyers and sellers flock to the intersection's roadsides, and everything from craftwork through antiques to junk is available.

The best beach in the area is down near the state park entrance. It's the state park beach, and the entrance fee covers use of changing rooms. Lake Sunapee is a Class A reservoir—the water is about as pure and unpolluted as you'll find anywhere.

Across the large traffic circle from the entrance road to the beach is the entrance to the state park and its gondola to the summit of Mount Sunapee. In summer the price is $4 for adults, half price for children 6 to 12, for the return trip in the four-person gondolas. The trip takes you over 1¼ miles (1450 feet higher up) to the summit at 2743 feet. At the top, there are walking trails (not difficult) to overlooks and to a glacial tarn named Lake Solitude. At the base of the mountain, near the gondola station, is a cafeteria, spacious lawns, hiking trails, and picnic areas, all open to the public at no charge.

Skiing

The Mount Sunapee area (tel. 603/763-4020; in Boston, snow info is 617/338-6922) has five double-chair lifts, a T-bar, a J-bar, and a rope tow, with a capacity of 6000 skiers an hour. The vertical drop is 1500 feet on 23 slopes and trails; in addition, there are ten miles of free ski touring trails, novice and intermediate (tel. 603/763-2356 for info). Ski school, ski shop with rental equipment, a cafeteria and (weekdays) a nursery are all available.

11. Hanover

This small town is the home of one of the country's oldest and most prestigious colleges. **Dartmouth** (named for the earl who was colonial secretary to King George III) was founded in 1769, and its charter gives a hint why it was located in such a remote place: it was meant primarily "for the education and instruction of Youth of the Indian Tribes," and only secondarily for the education of "English Youth and others." Today Dartmouth is more than a small undergraduate college; its graduate schools of medicine, engineering, and business administration are well respected, and the Hopkins Center for the Arts is the cultural focus of the entire region.

In many ways, the college is the town and vice-versa. College buildings of exceptional beauty and grace are scattered or clustered throughout Hanover, and are usually shaded by trees of a prodigious height and girth. Anyone out for a drive would enjoy a walk through the campus, perhaps on one of the guided college tours (free) which leave from the college information booth during the summer at 9 and 11 a.m. and 3 p.m., and from the Hopkins Center at 2 p.m. (no tours on Sunday); in winter, tours depart from McNutt Hall. To order tickets to performances, or to find out what's showing at the Hopkins Center, call 603/646-2422.

In winter, **Dartmouth's Winter Carnival** is the major fun and social event, with special art shows, drama and concerts, an ice sculpture contest, and other amusements.

WHERE TO STAY AND EAT: The prime place in Hanover is the **Hanover Inn** (tel. 603/643-4300), Hanover, NH 03755, right in the center of town. Some rooms have views of the lawns and buildings of the college. It fills up quickly at major college events such as matriculation, graduation, and the big football games played at home. Decor is colonial, to fit in with the rest of Hanover, but the shiny new bathrooms and color TVs show modern comfort has been given great consideration. Most of the rooms have twin beds, but there are a few double beds. Single rooms cost $79 to $99; doubles, $85 to $106—the higher prices being for the larger and slightly newer rooms in the west wing.

The Hanover Inn's formal dining room is supplemented by a lovely out-door patio, under an awning, in summer. The feeling is very much that of an exclusive country club. At lunch, sandwiches are only about $4, but full lunch-eon meals (the daily specials) can be had for $10; ordering à la carte, an entree at lunch would cost $7.50 to $10. The dinner menu offers a good and balanced selection of well-known meat, fish, and fowl dishes: start with a smoked oyster cocktail, and then have anything from half a broiled chicken to a steak, and the total bill will be $25 to $32 per person. The waitresses in black uniforms with white trim are silent, efficient, and friendly, waiting attentively at their stations when all the diners have been served.

North of Hanover several miles on Route 10 is the **Chieftain Motel**, Lyme Road, Hanover, NH 03755 (tel. 603/643-2550). Friendly, clean, and reason-ably priced are words that describe the family-run Chieftain, but in addition, the motel is large and well situated, with views of trees and lawns from most of the rooms. Rooms have TVs and private baths, and rent for $30 single, $38 to $44 double, tax included.

South of town two miles is another congenial motel, the neat and simple **Sunset Motel**, Route 10, West Lebanon, NH 3784 (tel. 603/298-8721). The Sunset's rooms are equipped with two queen-size beds, and you pay $34.24 to $37.45 for two; $3.25 for an extra person.

As for dining, the rage these days is **Peter Christian's Tavern** (tel. 643-2345), 39 South Main St. Step down a few stairs from street level into the perfect college hangout: dark, rustic, woody, with a bar, booths, and tables. The food is good, filling, and reasonably priced as you might expect.

READER'S RESTAURANT SELECTION: "We were pleasantly surprised at **Than Wheeler's Restaurant** (tel. 802/295-9717) in White River Junction, Vermont. By far it was the best restaurant on our trip. Two sisters own it, and serve only a few main courses. My husband had chicken almondine, I had lasagne; both were extremely good, and less than $6" (Mrs. Eda Richards, Whittier, Calif.).

SAINT-GAUDENS NATIONAL HISTORIC SITE: Augustus Saint-Gau-dens (1848–1907) is among America's greatest and most renowned sculptors.

Like his contemporary Daniel Chester French (1850–1931), Saint-Gaudens had a country abode where he completed some of his most famous and beautiful works. French's studio in the Berkshire town of Stockbridge (Mass.), and Saint-Gaudens' in Cornish (N.H.) bear this in common: they allow you to get very close to the work, spirit, and life of a great American artist.

The **Augustus Saint-Gaudens National Historic Site** (tel. 603/675-2175), Exit 8 or 9 from I-95, then U.S. 5 to Windsor, Vt. and New Hampshire Route 12A north, is open every day from mid-May through October, 8:30 a.m. to 4:30 p.m.; November to mid-May, Monday through Friday only, from 8:30 a.m. to 5 p.m.; admission costs 50¢.

Saint-Gaudens first came to Cornish from New York City in 1885, got to like it, and bought the house—an old tavern—in 1891. Besides the artist's house, you can visit his studios (the **Little Studio** was where he did most of his work) and galleries. Among the sculptures on view are copies of "Grief," his memorial for Marion (Mrs. Henry) Adams, and "The Puritan." Also, the "Diana" which was perched atop the old Madison Square Garden was brought here after the Garden was razed.

The grounds of the estate are a gorgeous slice of New Hampshire countryside, well set up for walks. On a few occasions in high summer, concerts are given (for free) on the lawns. Call for details.

MAINE

THERE IS SOMETHING quintessentially American about this rugged and sparsely populated state, the largest in New England. It's as though the vast forests of the north and the jagged coastline of "downeast" Maine are the last American frontier, rich in natural resources but waiting for people equally rugged to tame them.

Although there are still areas of wilderness in Maine, some of the state's potential was exploited long ago, soon after its discovery by Europeans. When the French and English came to these shores, they found miles and miles of virgin white pine forest, just the thing for masts, boards, and planks for the king's navy, and these forests were cut and cut until little remains of the original, virgin growth. The tremendous white pines have been replaced by other varieties, and lumber products again yield a good deal of the state's economy.

Besides her forests, Maine has great stores of granite for building, but they're mostly untapped as yet. Although agriculture is difficult because of the rocky soil and the short growing season, Maine potatoes are known and used throughout the eastern United States. Maine's fishermen yearly pull great quantities of fish, scallops, shrimp, and the famous lobsters from the freezing Atlantic waters. But the largest industry in Maine these days is the vacation trade: campers, hikers, and fishermen in the mountains and lakes, yachting and summer residents in the beautiful old coastal towns. Good food—especially the fresh seafood—and clean air draw the crowds from Boston, Montréal, and New York, and life in the southern coastal towns is lively and interesting from mid-June through Labor Day, after which the visitors become those looking for the quiet of Indian Summer and the autumn foliage season. Most resorts close up by the last week in October.

Of the vacation areas in Maine, certainly the most popular is the southern coast, where pretty towns such as Ogunquit, Kennebunkport, Boothbay Harbor, and Camden provide an atmosphere either restful or lively, cultural or natural, as you like it. Next in popularity comes the famous old resort of Bar Harbor, which is a good ways "downeast." The crowds these days come to commune with the rugged beauty of **Acadia National Park.** Finally, a smaller number of hardy souls head into the hinterland among the mountains, forests, and glacial lakes for a piece of the outdoor life.

Meals and rooms in Maine are taxed at a rate of 5%, so look for this tax to be added to your bill each night, and at mealtimes. The telephone area code for the entire state is 207.

GETTING THERE: Amtrak does not operate in Maine, but its trains do connect with buses at Boston's South Station that will take you north into the state. If you're driving, be aware that the Maine Turnpike (I-95) is a toll road. U.S. 1 or its scenic alternate route, 1A, parallels the Maine Turnpike all the way to Brunswick, and while it's a bit slower, it costs nothing. Besides, it's more scenic, and in my opinion no other highway in the entire country could possibly have as many flea markets, antique shops, and white elephant sales as does U.S. 1 in Maine, all the way from Kittery to Ellsworth. Weekends are the best times to catch them, but in July and August any day will do. *Note:* If you're heading for Ogunquit, take the exit from I-95 soon after you cross the state line at Kittery—follow the signs for U.S. 1 and the "shore" or "scenic" route through York, and this will save you a toll. And now for some tips on traveling by public transport:

By Bus

Greyhound Lines operates buses from Boston all the way to St. Stephen, New Brunswick, stopping at Portsmouth, N.H., Ogunquit, Kennebunk, Portland, Brunswick, Bath, Wiscasset, Camden, Bangor, and Ellsworth (for Bar Harbor). Two buses daily make the trip all the way to St. Stephen, another goes as far as Ellsworth and then runs down to its final stop at Bar Harbor. There are direct buses along this route from New York with a rest stop in Boston. Greyhound also runs between Montréal and Bangor, and there are connecting buses between Ottawa, Toronto, and Montréal, and between Bangor and Bar Harbor. One can also change at Bangor to go south along the coast. The Montréal-Bangor/Bar Harbor bus goes through Bethel, Me., but presently only on Saturday runs does it stop there. In conjunction with Autobus Fortin Poulin, Greyhound runs between Québec City and Portland, Me.

Trailways also operates along the Maine coast from Boston as far as Portland, stopping at Portsmouth, N.H., Ogunquit, Kennebunk, and the other coast resort towns.

Vermont Transit works in conjunction with Greyhound and Voyageur to operate on routes between Boston and Portland, and from Portland west to North Conway, N.H., Bretton Woods, Bethlehem, N.H., and St. Johnsbury, Barre, Montpelier, and Burlington; in Burlington, connections are made to or from Montréal.

C & J Airport Limousine Service operates those long airport limousines between Boston's Logan International Airport and points along the Maine coast, including Ogunquit and Kennebunk. In Ogunquit their terminal is at the Dunaway Municipal Building right in the center of town; in Kennebunk it's at the Kennebunk Inn. Places in the limousines are best reserved in advance.

By Air

Maine is served from the rest of the country by several airlines. Long-distance connections to Portland and Bangor are best made through **Delta Airlines,** which has local telephone numbers in most big cities and toll-free numbers for each state. In Boston, the number is 617/567-4100; from other points in Massachusetts, call toll free 800/962-3500. Delta flies between Boston, Portland, and Bangor about six times a day.

Bar Harbor Airlines (tel. toll free 800/732-3770 in Massachusetts, 800/343-3210 in New York and New England except Massachusetts), one of the older and better commuter lines, flies to many points in Maine: Auburn/Lewiston, Augusta, Bangor, Bar Harbor, Portland, Presque Isle, Rockland, and Waterville; and also to Manchester, N.H., Boston, Worcester, Hartford/Springfield, Albany, and New York City (La Guardia and JFK).

Air Vermont, 1795 South Williston Rd., South Burlington, VT 05401 (tel. 802/863-1110, or toll-free 800/322-9300 in Vermont, 800/343-8828 outside Vermont), cities are New York (JFK), Hartford/Springfield, Albany, Burlington, Newport (Vt.), Berlin (N.H.), Portland (Me.), Boston, Worcester, and Nantucket, plus Long Island.

1. Ogunquit

The Indian name means "beautiful place by the sea," and it holds true even today, because Ogunquit's town fathers have ensured that the town remains tidy and picturesque despite its tourism development. Visitors feel welcome in the town, whether they're strolling along Ogunquit's picturesque "Marginal Way," a path along the rocky coast; relaxing at the Ogunquit Beach; or dining in one of the many excellent restaurants. At Perkins Cove, a tiny peninsula is festooned with the quaint low waterfront shops and shacks from Ogunquit's fishing-village heyday. Right along U.S. 1 is the **Ogunquit Playhouse** (tel. 207/646-5511), presenting summer stock selections from late June through Labor Day. Ogunquit has been a summer resort for over a century, and it is no wonder that people come back year after year.

INFORMATION: The chamber of commerce maintains an information office at the junction of Main and School Streets (P.O. Box 751, Ogunquit, ME 03907), a block south of the center of town, and as Main Street is U.S. 1, you will come to the office as you enter the downtown area. It's open during business hours in the summer season (tel. 207/646-2939).

WHERE TO STAY: Having been a summer resort for so many years, Ogunquit today has a good selection of accommodations in all price ranges, from the extravagant to the inexpensive.

It seems as though every place in town rents rooms, from the gas station to the gift shoppe. Many are on U.S. 1, however, which is busy with traffic. If you don't find what you want among the following selections, search along Shore Road toward Perkins Cove, where it's quieter.

For over a century vacationers have been driving up to the top of Bald Head Cliff, a few miles southeast of Ogunquit, to stay at the **Cliff House** (tel. 207/646-5124), Ogunquit, ME 03907. Originally, one stayed in the large old house perched on the cliff, 90 feet above the surf, but now the house is overshadowed by several large and very modern motel units, all with a view of the sea. Extensive pine-covered grounds, a heated outdoor pool, and tennis courts add to the lure of the Cliff House's remote location and its view. The rooms are luxurious, with tub/shower combination baths in each, picture windows for the sea view, color TV; some are air-conditioned. From July 1 through Labor Day, they cost $79.80 to $90.30 double; in April through June, and September through November the range is $40 to $71.40. Efficiency units are rented by the week in high season. Note that the Cliff House offers special mini-vacation package plans off-season (April through June and September through November). Cliff House provides free transportation into town, to the beach, and to other points of interest in and around Ogunquit.

Ogunquit's modern, "almost downtown" motel is the attractive **Country Squire Motel,** on U.S. 1 at Bourne's Lane, Ogunquit, ME 03907 (tel. 207/646-3162), just four blocks or so from the center of town. The inspiration is colonial, with an arched portico along the front of the motel, bay windows in each room, pots of plants, and colonial-style furniture. The facilities are another matter, however, for each room has a tiled tub/shower, heat and air conditioning, color TV, and uncolonial wall-to-wall carpeting. The Country Squire is open only from mid-May to mid-October, like most Ogunquit lodging places, and charges lower rates for the off-season months of May, June, September, and October: $29.40 to $35.70 single, $33.50 to $40 double; an extra person costs $4.20. In July and August, rates are $42 to $47.25 single, $47.25 to $52.50 double, and an extra person costs $6.30. These are the rates for one- or two-night stays; if you stay three nights or more, a reduction of $2 per room per night is in order off-season, $4 per room per night in season. Get a reservation early.

When you first see the **New Englander,** 46 Shore Rd., Ogunquit, ME 03907 (tel. 207/646-2136), you'll think I've made an error in telling you that it has 28 rooms, half of them being modern motel style. All you see as you enter is a lofty tree, a semicircular drive, and a fine old white New England mansion with long porches on both the first and second floors. Well, half of the New Englander's 28 rooms are in the mansion, all modernized and redecorated, of course, and costing $40 to $55 in season with private bath, $33 to $38 with semiprivate bath; the modern motel rooms, hidden in a rear annex of the mansion, cost $57 to $64 in season for two with bath and TV. Reductions of 15% to 40% are in effect off-season.

Two blocks from downtown on Shore Road in Ogunquit is the **Sea Chambers Motor Lodge,** 37 Shore Rd., Ogunquit, ME 03907 (tel. 207/646-9311). The two- and three-story motel is right down near the water and also has its own heated pool and tennis court. You can walk from your room and get right on Marginal Way, the path along the rocky coast. The whole establishment is quite modern, and all rooms have bath, color TV, air conditioning, balcony, and twin beds or two double beds; most rooms have good sea views. In-season rates for late June through Labor Day are $68 to $83 double, with an extra person paying $10.50.

Want to turn back the clock a bit? The **Old Village Inn,** 30 Main St., Ogunquit, ME 03907 (tel. 207/646-7088), has been must restored of late, and now has 12 nice high-ceiling suites with an old-fashioned air and modern conveniences priced at $64. There's TV in the parlor, or you can sit around a warm fire should the weather be chilly. Several parlors, decorated with tapestries and old pieces, are open to guests staying at the inn or dining in its restaurant (see below).

Of Ogunquit's cozy Victorian seaside hotels, the **Colonial Inn** (tel. 207/646-2438 or 646-3993), just south of Obed's Lane on Shore Road (P.O. Box 895, Ogunquit, ME 03907), is the notable survivor. These days it's brimming with life, having been renovated by Chet and Sheila Sawtelle. The Colonial's 45 rooms cost $31.50 to $47.25 single (the higher price being for rooms with private bathroom); and $38.85 to $52.50 double, in this case—as all doubles have private bath—the higher price is for the rooms with the best ocean views. From May to late June and after Labor Day until Columbus Day, rates are about 30% lower. The Colonial has a elevator and, more important, a spacious veranda in the turn-of-the-century fashion, the perfect place for sitting, viewing, reading, napping. Free morning coffee is brewed every day. By the way, continental breakfast is included in the rates.

Of the several guest houses on Shore Road near the turnoff to Perkins Cove, my favorite is the **Hayes Guest House** (tel. 207/646-2277), 133 Shore Rd. (RR1, Box 12, Ogunquit, ME 03907). Mrs. Elinor Hayes is very kind and friendly, and has decorated her five rooms and two apartments with interesting old pieces such as a rope-frame bed made in Maine (now with a box spring, of course!), old sea chests, and patchwork quilts. Both twin and double beds are available. With private bath, a room is $42, or $40 with semiprivate bath. The apartments rent for $63 per night and $367.50 a week. Guests have use of a refrigerator and the coffee-maker; all rooms have air conditioning and TV. It's a charming place, and she's a charming lady, and here you're within walking distance of Perkins Cove with its restaurants, shops, and galleries.

WHERE TO DINE: The prime place to dine in Ogunquit is surely the **Clay Hill Farm** (tel. 646-2272), on Agamenticus Road, two miles from downtown Ogunquit. Richard Perkins, of "Poor Richard's" fame, has teamed up with Robert Maurais to turn an old country farm into a very fine restaurant. The farmhouse has been converted into several large dining rooms with lots of windows and a very comfortable air. Seafood and steak are featured. Start with clam chowder or vichyssoise and go on to broiled scallops or haddock, or perhaps a sole stuffed with lobster; with dessert, wine, tax, and tip, you'll pay $24 to $28. The chef's special each evening costs about $10, and these prices include vegetable, potato, and rolls. Before and after dinner you can relax in the lounge and enjoy the piano entertainment provided. With its country breezes and atmosphere, its small farm animals and garden providing some of the restaurant's supplies, and its easy pace, it's no wonder the Farm is a favorite with the Ogunquit Playhouse crowd. Clay Hill Farm is open in season (June to September) Monday through Saturday from 5:30 p.m. to 1 a.m. (kitchen closes at 10 p.m.), and for Sunday brunch from noon to 6 p.m.; in winter, you can have dinner here on Thursday, Friday, and Saturday during the same hours, or the Sunday brunch. Call for reservations, winter or summer. To get to the tavern, go south on Main Street (U.S. 1) from the blinker in the center of Ogunquit for three-tenths of a mile, to a blinker at a crossroads next to the Post Road Inn; turn right—this is Agamenticus Road—and go 1.8 miles to the tavern, which will be on your right.

In Ogunquit, everybody goes to **Barnacle Billy's**, in Perkins Cove, and the reason is clear: good prices, good food, and good service as only you yourself could provide. The routine here is to enter, choose what you want from the blackboard menu, pay the cashier and get a slip, and submit the slip to the counterperson; then wander off into Barnacle Billy's waterfront dining room done all in pine with tables and chairs to match, and a hardwood fire going in the big stone fireplace if it's September. The view of the marina and the cove is as good as the food: a 1¼-pound lobster for $8.50 (heavier ones for a dollar or two more), steamed clams, corn-on-the-cob, salad, and garlic bread are all available. When the weather's fine, you can even order at a window on the flagstone terrace and have your meal while sitting in the sunshine, either on the terrace or on a deck a flight up, both terraces being right next to the Finestkind

Boat Dock. Free parking for customers right across the street. Billy's is open May to mid-October, 11 a.m. to 11 p.m., more or less, depending on the crowds.

Right downtown in Ogunquit, one of the town's busiest dining spots is the **Old Village Inn** (tel. 646-7088), 30 Main St., and as it's so busy, be sure to call or stop by and make reservations before you dine. It's popular because of its location, and because of its several low-ceiling dining rooms with their heavy beams barely six feet from the floor, all decorated with old crockery; a fireplace lends a cheery glow in cool weather, but if the weather's fine, you'll want to dine in the inn's glassed-in conservatory amid the flowers and plants. At dinner, have the delicious lobster bisque to start, then a seafood dish such as seafood imperial or perhaps roast duckling; the fish of the day is always a good choice; such a meal will cost $20 to $25. Steaks will cost more. And for dessert, my choice would be the homemade cheesecake and strawberries. At lunch/brunch, entrees are $5 to $6. Lunch/brunch is served from 10 a.m. to 3 p.m., dinner from 5:30 to 9 p.m.; a small bar provides for the thirsty.

The **Trolley Stop** (tel. 646-9596), on Main Street (U.S. 1) just north of the center of town, specializes in dishes leaning to the French and prepared with a special bit of care and ingenuity. For instance, the onion soup has a dash of cognac added, and besides the chilled shrimp offered as an appetizer you can get "skillet shrimp" as well. Most entrees are in the range of $11 to $16. After dinner, the pastry tray is yours to choose from, or there are parfaits, or you can go all the way and have the Trolley Fudge Sundae, and finish off with Irish, Jamaican, or Parisian coffee. Dinner is served daily from 5:30 to 10 p.m., cocktails until 1 a.m., and there's live entertainment every night during the summer. By the way, the Trolley Shop has a sister restaurant in Portsmouth, N.H. You'll want to dress up to dine at either one.

One of Ogunquit's more interesting places to dine is **Gypsy Sweethearts** (tel. 646-7021), 18 Shore Rd., only a few blocks from the main crossroads in the center of town. Bright and simple decor, young and friendly staff, and an encyclopedic menu of good things at low prices make it a popular place for breakfast (7:30 a.m. to noon) or dinner (5:30 to 10 p.m.). Strawberry crêpes, eggs Benedict, bloody marys, pancakes, and omelets are on order. Spend $2 or spend $4 for breakfast, as you like. Dinner is fancier, with wine, beer, and cocktails, swordfish and sirloin steaks, both charcoal-broiled; or escalope of veal, shrimp and mushrooms. Prices for main courses are $7.50 to $11—very reasonable for a resort.

Ogunquit is prepared for New Yorkers who come north for the summer, or others in search of good corned beef, bagels, and the like. **Einstein's Deli,** at the corner of Shore Road and Route 1, has all these delights and lots more, besides several dining areas and a take-out service (tel. 646-5262).

WHAT TO DO: First thing to do is stop in at the town's information office and pick up a map, and then take off to walk **Marginal Way.** Start next to the Sachem Hotel and you'll come out right at Barnacle Billy's in Perkins Cove, a mile or so away. The Atlantic, the rocky coast, the gulls wheeling overhead, and the smiles of the other walkers you'll meet are all part of this Ogunquit institution, and all are a treat whether the sun is shining, or it's misty, or even if there's a gale coming.

Next thing to do is call the **Ogunquit Playhouse** (tel. 207/646-5511) to get seats for a performance, which will no doubt feature a star or two of national reputation.

Some lazy afternoon, be sure to leave time for a stroll around the shops and galleries of **Perkins Cove,** the picturesque old fishing village section of town.

One can get to know the sea in Ogunquit by going down to Perkins Cove and, next to Barnacle Billy's, the dock of the **Finestkind boats** is located. Each hour during the day (except Sunday) the lobster boats set out to cruise the Maine coast, hauling in the lobster pots and the day's catch. You can go along and have the process of lobstering explained while you view the coastline and the fishing grounds, all at $7 for adults, half price for children. Make reservations, if you like, by calling 207/646-5227, or just drop down to the docks for more information.

Auto buffs can visit the **Wells Auto Museum** on U.S. 1 in Wells, just north of Ogunquit. From mid-June to mid-September, you can view the 1907 Stanley Steamer, a rare 1912 Pathfinder Roadster, a 1918 Pierce Arrow, and other classics for $2.50 per adult, $1 for each child above the age of 6.

2. Kennebunkport

The several communities with similar names—Kennebunk, Kennebunkport, Kennebunk Beach—are clustered together on the Maine Coast and constitute one of the most popular vacation areas on the coast.

Of the towns, Kennebunkport is perhaps the most interesting. As its name implies, Kennebunkport was the waterfront part of the Kennebunk area. It's been a resort for years, drawing both the well-to-do and the student crowd living on summer earnings. Prices for rooms and meals tend to be a bit high, but for most people the price is not so important so long as they can just find a room open in this delightful Maine town.

WHERE TO STAY: Kennebunkport has every sort of lodging, from the inexpensive guest house to the luxurious classic inn. I've concentrated on these quaint and charming places, with the occasional hotel or motel selected just in case that fits your mood.

Guest Houses

The **Fairview Lodge** (tel. 207/967-2074; off-season, 617/664-4865), P.O. Box 1288, Kennebunkport, ME 04046, is an inexpensive place to stay. The big old house on Ocean Avenue has its gracious downstairs rooms packed with Oriental carpets, curious and beautiful objects in glass and wood, and many other items picked with a careful and artistic eye. Everything (or almost) is for sale, although there's certainly no pressure to buy. The rooms, while very plain and without running water, are a bargain: $21 off-season, $36.75 in season, for two, with a shower down the hall.

Among the smaller and more modest inns, the **Green Heron** (tel. 207/967-3315), on Ocean Drive very near the Colony, has been a dependable Kennebunkport hostelry for years and years. This nice old house has been converted to hold ten guest rooms, and a cottage out back can hold an additional four people. Furnishings are simple but quite comfortable, and there's a cheery breakfast room with lots of big windows overlooking the water. These rates include a good breakfast: $30.45 to $36.75 double in season, $28.35 to $35.70 off-season. All of the rooms have private baths, with tubs and showers. The beaches are within walking distance. The Green Heron's mail address is P.O. Drawer 151, Kennebunkport, ME 04046.

Of Kennebunkport's guest houses, certainly the most pristine is the **Chetwynd House** (tel. 207/967-2235), Kennebunkport, ME 04046, with only four rooms and one small efficiency apartment. The house is immaculately clean, which allows you to admire the fine wide-board floors of a rich honey color, and all the very decent furnishing, including many four-poster beds. Extra pleasures at the Chetwynd House include a full breakfast with your room, the use of the tables and chairs in the garden, perhaps for a lunch of lobsters from the pound or an evening's glass of wine, and here you're only a few blocks from Dock Square and the center of town. One room ($68.25) has private bath; the other three share two baths ($44 to $54.60). Chetwynd House is on Chestnut Street, the street off Ocean Avenue opposite Arundel Wharf—the street is not marked, but Chetwynd House is a short distance up on the left, and is marked clearly by a sign.

Inns

Kennebunkport's inns come in all shapes and sizes, from the rambling old seaside "cottage" to the magnificently restored sea captain's mansion. Here are the best examples:

The **Maine Stay,** Maine Street, Kennebunkport, ME 04046 (tel. 207/967-2117), actually calls itself a "motel" because the up-to-date rooms are in a tidy addition to the big Maine house on this shady street. But there is absolutely no relation between a modern highway motel and this charming place, surrounded by gardens and lofty trees, right in the center of town. Rates are $58 double in season. Though the rooms are equipped with all the modern conveniences, the spirit—and the welcome—are those of a cozy inn. Walk to everything in town.

At **The Breakwater** (tel. 207/967-3118), Kennebunkport, ME 04046, the situation is almost as good as the Colony's because that latter grand establishment is right next door. But prices are distinctly lower: $33.10 to $42 double in season in the Breakwater building, $50.40 to $63 in the Riverside building, which is open year round and is more modern with suites next door. Off-season rates are 25% to 30% lower, from mid-May to late-June and after Labor Day until mid-October. Continental breakfast is included in these prices. For dinner, the Breakwater has one of the best restaurants around (see below).

The **Captain Jefferds Inn,** P.O. Box 691, Pearl Street, Kennebunkport, ME 04046 (tel. 207/967-2311), is one of those old sea captains' houses so immaculately restored that it made the cover of *House Beautiful.* The house was beautiful, but the owners have improved upon it with unusual antiques, lots of them, and comfortable furnishings. Single rooms cost $47.25 and doubles are $57.75 to $71.40, including tax and a country breakfast; there's a two-night minimum stay from July through October. Besides being everything a quaint inn should be, the Captain Jefferds House is just off Ocean Avenue, walking distance to everything in town.

Kennebunkport has a very special place to stay, and you should consider it. The **Captain Lord House,** P.O. Box 527, Kennebunkport, ME 04046 (tel. 207/967-3141), was built in 1812 by a naval captain whose sailors were blockaded in Kennebunk Harbor by the British. With nothing better for his men to do, Lord put them to work to build him a sumptuous mansion, and the master craftsmen who built his ships did an impressive job. Today, after years of benign neglect, the mansion has been meticulously restored down to the matched oak boards in the floors and the gold-leaf wallpaper. The Captain Lord Mansion is once again a luxurious house, with antiques everywhere, private baths all around, and working fireplaces in 10 of the 15 rooms, and you can stay here for $67.20 single, $77.70 to $88.20 double (the highest price doubles are the ones with the fireplaces). A third person pays $25 in the same room. A full homemade breakfast in included in these rates. If you've ever dreamed of staying in a work of art, a treasurehouse, or a National Historic Landmark, stay here, for the Lord Mansion is all three. Driving from Dock Square down Ocean Avenue, keep glancing to your left and soon you'll see the stately yellow mansion topped by its cupola/observatory at the back of a rich greensward a block long: Captain Lord meant this first sight of the mansion to be impressive, and it certainly is.

Hotels

The **Nonantum** (tel. 207/967-3338) is a very well-kept, classic 19th-century resort hotel, with comfortable and charming public rooms, lawns and a swimming pool, a waterfront location, and even a motel annex. The price, including breakfast, dinner, and tax, for a double with bath, is $102 to $113 with one double bed; a few dollars more with two double beds; rooms with running water (bath nearby) are $80 to $91, depending on whether you want a double or twin beds. Look for the Nonantum on Ocean Avenue, a half mile from town.

Those who want to be smack in the middle of town, right next to Dock Square, should consider **Austin's Inn-Town Hotel** (tel. 207/967-4241), P.O. Box 609, Kennebunkport, ME 04046, right next to the Kennebunk River and the dock. The Inn-Town is a new and modern hostelry within an older style building, and all rooms have private baths; it's possible to fit three, four, or even five people in several, which is good for traveling families to note. A room with a double bed is $40; with a double, a single, and a convertible sofa you pay $47.25; for two double beds and a sofa the charge is $50.40. There's free parking for guests on the dock right next to the hotel.

On Kennebunk Beach: The **Seaside** (tel. 207/967-4461 or 967-4282) near Kennebunk Beach at Gooch's Beach, Kennebunkport, ME 04046, is a variety of lodging establishments all in one. Peaceful, dignified, friendly, and immaculately kept would describe any of the accommodations and staff here. In the 1756 inn, twin bedrooms cost $53.55 to $61.95 all with private bath; in a tasteful and luxurious motel-style unit of two stories, rooms are $80.85 to $86.10 in July and August, $57.75 to $65.10 in June and in September after Labor Day, even cheaper in the cold months. Cottages capable of sleeping three to seven persons cost $472.50 to $735 per week in season, about half price off-season. The Seaside is a very fine place, and thus has lots of guests who return year after year. Reserve early to get the room you want.

WHERE TO DINE: Like any good resort town, Kennebunkport has a selection of restaurants in all price categories. Here are the ones I like best:

The **Breakwater** (tel. 967-3118), not far from the Colony on Ocean Avenue, is a restaurant and inn (in that order) which is thought of highly by local people and visitors alike. The dining rooms are elegant without being overly formal, and from the sunporch—which is a dining room—one gets a beautiful view of the sea. It's difficult to know which facet of the Breakwater is the most enchanting: the decor and ambience, the staff, or the cuisine. Certainly the dinner menu is tempting, and the prices very sensible. Main courses, which come with baked potato or rice, salad, and a small loaf of bread, are arranged according to price category. Thus for $8 you can order a beef kebab, or baked haddock; then for $9.25 there are broiled scallops. The prices and delicacies proceed to $10 or $13 (swordfish, roast prime rib), with the lobster clambake priced according to the day's market. Soups and appetizers, vegetables, and beverages are all priced separately. The food is of the best. Have reservations, but be sympathetic when they tell you they can't reserve specific tables (the ones with the sea view are the hot ones).

The **White Barn Inn** (tel. 967-2321), on Beach Street across from the Franciscan Monastery in Kennebunkport, is a real barn converted to a restaurant. Everything that was found during the cleaning and renovation of the barn was hung on the many rafters and beams for effect, or so it seems. The menu includes snails, or chowder, or chicken livers wrapped in bacon, or baked stuffed lobster or shrimp, and marinated lamb kebab or veal piccata. Prices for entrees are generally $9 to $16.50, and this includes rice pilaf or potato, vegetable, and salad. Of the desserts, the homemade pie of the day or hot fudge puff would be my choice. Dinner is served at the White Barn from 5:30 to 9:30 p.m. Beach Street (or Beach Avenue), by the way, is parallel to Ocean Avenue but across the inlet from it, to the south; if in doubt, ask for the St. Anthony Monastery, and the White Barn's very near, on the other side of the street.

Convenient to Dock Square, and good for a moderately priced supper, is the restaurant called **Arundel Wharf** (tel. 967-3444), off Ocean Avenue a short distance from Dock Square. Walking to the restaurant across its parking lot, the gulls will be squealing overhead; as you enter you'll see a modernistic "funnel" fireplace, a beamed ceiling, and several windows with water views, for the Arundel is indeed on a wharf by the Kennebunk River. The staff here are young and friendly. For lunch there are mostly sandwiches ($3.50 or $4) with a few platters offered, but for dinner you can have a vegetable casserole, broiled haddock, or even lobster pie, for $7 to $11.

The Arundel's name comes from the fact that Kennebunkport was once named Arundel after England's Earl of Arundel; in fact, it bore that name all through the better part of its maritime prominence, changing it only in 1821. Arundel Wharf is open daily from 11:30 a.m. to 3 p.m. and 5:30 to 9:30 p.m. (10 p.m. on Friday and Saturday).

Near the huge old hotel named the Colony is another restaurant which does a good business, **The Landing** (tel. 967-4221), off Ocean Avenue. The decor is nautical as one might expect, and there's a lounge with entertainment named the After Deck (for after dinner . . .). The Landing is open for lunch and dinner daily, and has many familiar dishes available: steaks, baked stuffed lobster, and the other varieties of local seafood. Entrees are in the range of $8.75 to $14.

Of course, the cheapest way to have a lobster dinner is to wander down to the lobster pound. Although many restaurants have appropriated the name "Lobster Pound," a real pound is simply the place where the live lobsters are kept in saltwater vats until a customer comes and buys them. Most lobster pounds these days have a few simple cooking facilities, and will boil up the lobsters for you if you wish, provide butter and salt and a paper plate, and charge just a little above the price of a live lobster. There are several such lobster pounds in Kennebunkport, where a cooked lobster will cost about $5, depending on season. Bring a homemade salad or a few raw vegetables and you can turn it into an inexpensive lobster picnic.

WHAT TO DO: Shops and galleries around Dock Square draw lots of shoppers and window shoppers at all times, and one can spend some time browsing very pleasantly.

Gooch's Beach is right at the southern end of Beach Street, on the western shore of the Kennebunk River; Kennebunk Beach is west of Gooch's, along the coast. These fine, gradual beaches are good for swimming, especially on very hot days (the water tends to the chilly), for sunning on any sunny day, for walking, thinking, or jogging on almost any day.

Be sure to take a drive or a walk along **Maine Street** for a look at Kennebunkport's fine old mansions. For a look at the rocky coast, go south on Ocean Avenue to **Spouting Rock** to hear the crash of the surf.

A Trip to Cape Porpoise

Three miles northeast of Kennebunkport along Route 9, on the shore, is the village of **Cape Porpoise.** This charming little bit of Maine coastal life is a vacation haven for a small, knowledgeable few. Not fancy, not crowded, it has only a few craft shops, a few eateries, a few guest houses, and a lot of Maine atmosphere. Drive out and head for the Pier, with its pretty views of the sea. A brass plaque on a rock atop the sand hill there bears this legend: "August 8, 1782, a British ship of 18 guns attacked a small force of inhabitants gathered on Goat Island and was driven away by severe musket fire, losing 17 men. James Burnham of this town was killed. This tablet erected by the Maine State Council, Daughters of the American Revolution, August 8, 1921."

Well, not an awful lot exciting has happened in Cape Porpoise since that signal victory, and it's just as well, for the quiet is what makes it nice.

Should you decide to stay here, Mrs. Lyman P. Huff will rent you a room in her guest house, the **Old Garrison House,** Pier Road, Cape Porpoise, ME 04014 (tel. 207/967-3522), for $28.35 double (shared bath) or $30.45 double (private bath). You'll see the big yellow house on the left-hand side of the road as you head for the Pier.

As for sustenance, there's **Tilly's Shanty** (tel. 967-5015), right on the Pier. It looks like a fisherman's snack shack should look, and you can have a lobsterman's lunch of two one-pound lobsters, steamers, and corn-on-the-cob for a mere $13. Not that hungry? There's lobster stew, clam rolls, and other light fare.

The alternative is **Spicer's Galley** (tel. 967-2745), next to the Pier, a dinner establishment open 5 to 9:30 p.m. only, serving fancier fare in fancier surroundings.

To work up an appetite, rent a canoe or boat from **Cape Porpoise Canoes** (tel. 967-5863), on the Pier Road in Cape Porpoise. Drop your canoe in the water right at the shop and take off for your own mini-exploration of the Maine coast. Rates, including all the necessary paraphernalia, are $21 per day.

3. Portland

Cities in Maine have never had a reputation for chic or avant-garde ambience because Maine is a rural state, and it's the farmlands, woodlands, and coastal industries such as lobstering that count. But Portland, the state's largest city and its transportation hub and business center, may be changing all that. **Civic Center** draws sports events, conventions, and big-name entertainers, and its revitalized waterfront area, known as the **Old Port Exchange,** is now even more attractive than it was in its Victorian heyday when the railroads, the huge sailing fleet, and the trade in lumber and fish made Portland what it is.

You can spend a day profitably in Portland, visiting the city's colonial, early American, and Victorian landmarks, the **Portland Museum of Art,** or in taking a cruise in Portland Harbor or Casco Bay. Portland is also the American end of the Prince of Fundy Cruises, which will take you and your car to Yarmouth, Nova Scotia, on a ten-hour, overnight cruise or on any one of a number of other cruises and tours (details below).

INFORMATION: The **Maine Publicity Bureau** and the **Greater Portland Chamber of Commerce**, 142 Free St., Portland, ME 04101 (tel. 207/772-2811), next to the Civic Center, can fill you in on Portland life.

WHERE TO STAY: The newest hostelries in Portland are almost all out at the Maine Turnpike's Exit 8, a short drive from downtown on Route 25. I'll mention these first, then go on to the several downtown.

Holiday Inn has a downtown hotel in Portland, but out on the highway it's the **Portland-West Holiday Inn** (tel. 207/774-5601), 81 Riverside St. (Exit 8 from the Turnpike), Portland, ME 04104. The 200 rooms here are all modern, with color TV, and are priced at $50.40 to $75.60 double in July and August, a few dollars less per room just on the other side of high season. There's live entertainment in the lounge most evenings in summer. These rates, as you'll notice, are just about the same as the Holiday Inn downtown.

Howard Johnson's Motor Lodge (tel. 207/774-5861, or toll free 800/654-2000) is nearby at 155 Riverside St., Portland, ME 04103, and here the facilities include an indoor heated swimming pool and a sauna, a restaurant and lounge, and rooms with color TV and—in some rooms—waterbeds! Special weekend mini-vacation packages are available, but normally the doubles rent for $50.40 to $56.70 in high season. If you're flying, a limo will bring you here from the airport, but you should call in advance.

The bargain place to stay, as ever, is the dependable **Susse Chalet Motor Lodge** (tel. 207/774-6101, or toll free 800/258-1980), on Brighton Avenue (Portland, ME 04103), near the other motels mentioned. At the Susse Chalet, rooms are modern, heated, and air-conditioned, with bright new bathrooms and TV, plus all the other facilities you'd normally find in a modern motel, but the price is only $24.90 for one person, $29.10 for two, $32.25 for three, or $35.40 for four in a room with two double beds. You can't do any better than this!

Hotels Downtown

The **Portland-Downtown Holiday Inn**, 88 Spring St., Portland, ME 04111 (tel. 207/775-2311), is very near the Civic Center, and was meant to handle parties of conventioneers and those coming to the center for large meetings. An indoor pool awaits you, if you have time for a swim. Room prices are $55.65 to $77.70 in high summer (July and August).

Portland's **Best Western Executive Inn, City Center** (tel 207/773-8181), is right downtown at 645 Congress St., Portland, ME 04101, only four blocks from the International Ferry Terminal. The 120 rooms are all newly fitted out with color TV, AM/FM radios, and coffee-makers in each room; and the inn (actually, more a luxurious downtown motel) has an outdoor pool and ample free parking for guests. In the summer season, rates are $54.60 single, up to $75.60 double. You can even call toll free for reservations: 800/528-1234.

WHERE TO DINE: The renaissance of Portland's waterfront district has given rise to numerous restaurants in recent years, and a short walk through the tidy and picturesque restored blocks of Fore, Exchange, Middle, and Moulton Streets will reveal interesting and moderately priced places for a snack, a meal, or a relaxing drink.

The **Baker's Table** (tel. 775-0303), 434 Fore St., is just that: the restaurant attached to the little Port Bakehouse at street level. For the restaurant, descend a flight of steps to the bright stuccoed walls and wooden beams in the dining rooms. An elegant cafeteria with bar adjoining, the system here is to pass through the line at lunchtime for, say, soup and salad, and after you're seated everything else you may need—more wine, coffee, or dessert—can be brought by a waiter or waitress. The salads ($1.35 to $4) are almost meals in themselves, but with a big bowl of fish chowder ($2.85) it'll fill you for sure. Such a lunch will cost about $4.50 with fresh bread and beverage—that's a daily special. Lunch is from 11:30 a.m. to 5:30 p.m.; after that the heartier and more expensive dinner menu comes into play until 10 p.m. (10:30 on Friday and Saturday). For dinner, have bouillabaisse ($12), tournedos, or something like chicken provençale. It's nice here for either meal: soft background music, paintings by local artists on the walls, an interesting crowd, well-stocked bar, and espresso machine.

The young and hip head for **Horsefeathers** (tel. 773-3501), 193 Middle St. near Temple Street. Set up in what was once a bank, the restaurant decor has a little bit of everything, but not too much. The menu, very hip-talk and funky, has something for everyone: sandwiches, seafood, stir-fried Szechuan dishes, even prime rib. Meals range from a lowly $6 to a lofty $22 (if you go all-out). It's open for lunch and dinner daily; booze is served; there's entertainment on weekends.

Portland's choice for Chinese cuisine is **Hu Shang** (tel. 774-0800), 7-13 Brown St., right downtown near the Civic Center. The cooking is drawn from Hunan, Szechuan, Shanghai, and Mandarin (Peking/Beijing) traditions: spring rolls, pan-fried dumplings, fried wonton, hot-and-sour or bean-curd soup are among the appetizers. Then lamb with ginger and scallions, chicken with cashews, moo shu beef, fresh scallops with peanuts and scallions—it's difficult not to order half a dozen entrees. But appetizer, entree, and lichee nut dessert will cost about $13, tea, tax, and tip included. Several people sharing just a few main-course plates can dine very well for much less. This is one of the city's best restaurants, open every day for lunch and dinner.

For Meeting People

The **Seamen's Club**, 375 Fore St., is a good place to meet Portlanders who work in or near the waterfront, particularly at lunchtime when the sandwiches (about $3) and the low-price table d'hôte ($5.50) draw a crowd. Sunday brunch is good too. At dinner the menu is filled with the popular classics, tried and proven: baked stuffed shrimp, roast duckling with orange sauce, filet mignon—solid and satisfying. Prices per main course may be anywhere from $6 to $13 (the higher end for the steaks, of course). A liter of the house wine is a reasonable $5.50.

The **Old Port Tavern**, right across the street and down a short distance at 11 Moulton, is another popular watering spot where the people and the drink are as good, or better, than the food.

Outside of Town

If you have a car, you can drive out of town a ways to dine at **Smith Farm** (tel. 793-3034), on Route 26/100, a mile north of Maine Turnpike Exit 10, and about five or six miles from downtown Portland at 226 Gray Rd., Falmouth.

Smith Farm's restaurant started decades ago as a simple roadside stand, but the business kept expanding until it got to the point where Mrs. Marguerite H. Smith was serving full dinners to neighbors and passersby. Mrs. Smith has now retired, having sold her restaurant to Portland restaurateur F. Parker Reidy, but the attractive restaurant in the farm's refurbished barn has remained a Portland area landmark. As for the food, it's home-style, and the prices are the best around: a roast Maine turkey dinner, with lots of herb stuffing plus appetizer, salad, vegetables, potatoes, relish tray, bread, butter, dessert, and coffee is only $9; similarly lavish dinners featuring things like broiled sirloin ($11) are always available. The boiled lobster is priced according to market, and comes with french fries, coleslaw, and coffee. Sandwiches, burgers, large luncheon salads, and omelets are also served. How can you go wrong at such prices? Smith Farm is open noon to 9 p.m. every day.

WHAT TO SEE AND DO: First thing to do is to ask at your hotel for a copy of the Greater Portland Chamber of Commerce's brochure called *The Portland History Trail,* which sets forth details and a walking tour (with map) of all the notable sights in the city. Here are some highlights:

Wadsworth Longfellow House

Henry Wadsworth Longfellow's grandfather built this brick house at 485 Congress St. in 1785—the first brick house in the city. The poet lived here as a child, before moving off to Cambridge, Mass., and although he left, the house is still filled with Longfellow family possessions. The Longfellow House has been called the most historic in Maine, and it's open for your inspection Tuesday through Saturday only from 10 a.m. to 4 p.m., at $2 for adults, $1 for children under 12, or $5 for a family. The fee includes a 30-minute guided tour.

Tate House

The Maine forest was for a long time the prime source of masts for the British navy, and the man who managed the whole trade was one George Tate, who had this house built in 1755. The house is shown by guided tour from June 15 to September 15, Tuesday through Saturday from 11 a.m. to 5 p.m.; on Sunday 1:30 to 5 p.m. To get to the house, at 1270 Westbrook St. in the Stroudwater section of Portland, go southwest on Congress Street for two miles, cross the stream, and turn left onto Westbrook Street, very near the Portland Jetport. The fee to get in is $1.50 for adults, 50¢ for kids under 12.

Victoria Mansion (Morse-Libbey House)

Built between 1859 and 1863, the Victoria Mansion has fascinating Victorian decorations, all of which are on view Tuesday through Saturday from 10 a.m. to 4 p.m., closed Sunday and Monday, from mid-June through Labor Day. It's at 109 Danforth St., and costs $1.50 per adult, 50¢ per child under 12, to see.

Portland Museum of Art

Portland has a fine museum with a fine collection at 111 High St. (tel. 775-6148). Particularly strong are the collections of 19th- and 20th-century American art relating to Portland and to Maine, with paintings by Andrew Wyeth, Winslow Homer, and Edward Hopper. A gift of 17 Winslow Homer paintings is featured in the new wing (done by I. M. Pei). The new wing expands the space already available in the historic McLellan-Sweat House (1800) and the L. D. M. Sweat Memorial Galleries (1911). Hours are 10 a.m. to 5 p.m. Tuesday through Saturday, 2 to 5 p.m. on Sunday; closed Monday.

Boats and Cruises

Portland is the prime dock for Casco Bay and indeed northern New England, and you can climb aboard a boat with your car or without, for a few hours or overnight. Here are the major lines:

Casco Bay Lines (tel. 207/774-7871), Custom House Wharf, will take you (but *not* your car) over to Bailey's Island in summer. While on the four-hour cruise, you'll be told all about the island's history and its geologic features, plus lots of Portland and Casco Bay lore. On a sunny day, this is a very fine way to "take the air." The price for this cruise is $9.75 for adults, $6.25 for children. Other cruises are a bit shorter and a bit cheaper, and leave all year: there's a sunset cruise to the islands (three hours), a cruise around Casco Bay (2½ hours), and the cruise on the U.S. Mail boat which goes to each of the Calendar Islands (three hours). The M.V. Longfellow (tel. 774-3578), 1 Long Wharf, has a similar program.

Lazy Day Deep-Sea Fishing

During the summer, you can sail on the *Lazy Day* (tel. 774-0122) for a seven-hour fishing cruise at a price of only $20 per person, tackle included. The cruise leaves from Central Wharf, next to Harris Co., Monday through Saturday, at 9 a.m. to return at 4 p.m. If business warrants it, they'll go out on trips off-season as well, at special rates. Call for details.

Prince of Fundy Cruises to Nova Scotia

May through October on most days, the M/S *Scotia Prince* leaves Portland in the evening for Yarmouth, Nova Scotia, on an 11-hour overnight cruise. Return sailings from Yarmouth are in mid- or late morning. You can take your car with you, and duty-free shops are aboard. Current high-season prices for the cruise are $50 (U.S. dollars) per adult, $25 for children 5 to 14, accompanied by an adult; children under 5 go free. The fare for a car is normally $70. A cabin for two costs in the range of $32 to $50. But there are several special fares which might suit your needs and which will save you money. Be sure to call Prince of Fundy Cruises for full particulars, latest fares, and schedules. In Portland, call 207/775-5616; elsewhere in Maine, call toll free 800/482-0955; in New England, New York, New Jersey, Pennsylvania, Delaware, Washington, D.C., Maryland, and northern Ohio, call toll free 800/341-7540; in Canada, call 902/742-5164; and in Yarmouth, Nova Scotia, call 902/742-3411.

EXCURSIONS NORTH: Most people head east from Portland, aiming at Camden, Boothbay, Bar Harbor, or the Canadian border. But an excursion deep into Maine's forested hinterland will bring you right up against North Woods life.

Sebago Lake

Of Maine's hundreds of beautiful, clear lakes, **Sebago Lake,** is one of the largest and most accessible. The eastern shore of the lake is somewhat developed with small villages, highway establishments, and the like; at the southern tip, the town of Sebago Lake is hardly more than a few dozen houses, two stores, and a gas station. But along the western shore in the area of the settlement called East Sebago there are a number of places which rent rooms and cabins, mingled among the larger private summer cabins and houses.

Although the roads which skirt the lake do have collections of cabins and houses here and there, it's hardly what you'd call thickly settled. One place where people gather is at **Simpson's,** on Route 11/114 in East Sebago, where a nice lake beach and picnic facilities are to be had for $2 per carload ($3 on Sunday and holidays). The other place to go is **Sebago Lake State Park,** at the northern tip of the island, where there's also a fine beach, picnic facilities, and a camping area. Although very busy in summer, the park is yours to enjoy with only a handful of others in early June or after Labor Day.

Bethel

Tucked away in the mountains on the western edge of Maine is the village of Bethel. Although the village is on U.S. 2, the highway which heads west to skirt the border of the White Mountains National Forest, there is little else which would bring travelers to the place were it not for two attractions: a well-known preparatory school called **Gould Academy** (founded 1836); and an excellent inn.

Where to Stay and Dine: The inn referred to above is the **Bethel Inn** (tel. 207/824-2175), on the town common, Bethel, ME 04217. A feeling of tastefulness and elegance is what you get as you drive to the inn's entrance through the greenswards in the center of the village. The main inn has a famous dining room, a large lounge with a fireplace to match, French doors leading out onto a terrace overlooking the mountains and the inn's manicured grounds. Special services include a swimming pool, tennis courts, a music room complete with Steinway, a library, a golf course, a boathouse (for boating and fishing) on a nearby pond, and entertainment and dancing in the evenings. The rooms are done with colonial accents (although the inn itself dates from 1913), and are priced to include breakfast and dinner at $85 to $150 double. The inn has rooms in the main building, and also in a number of old Bethel houses surrounding the common, and so the selection of accommodations is very good.

Even less expensive is **Conrad's Tourist Home** (tel. 207/824-2505), Main Street, Bethel, ME 04217, the large gray house right across the street from the post office in the middle of the village. Drop over and see one of the simple but attractive rooms priced at $15 double ($5 for an extra person).

The town's inexpensive place to dine is the **R.F.D. #1 ("Real Friendly Dining"),** near the post office on Main Street, where a Northburger (a cheeseburger with lettuce and tomato) is only $1.05, other sandwiches cost up to $2, and full lunches and dinners can be had for $4 to $7. Local newspapers wait in a rack for regular customers' leisure hours, a jukebox terminal graces every table, and the service is hometown friendly. Cocktails are served, and all soups and pies are made on the premises.

What to See: Should you have an hour to spend in Bethel, drop in at the **Moses Mason House,** 15 Broad St. (tel. 824-2908), on the common, open in July and August, Tuesday through Sunday from 1 to 4 p.m. and by appointment (call during business hours) the rest of the year. Moses Mason was a congressman during the Jackson administration, and had this Federal house built in 1813. Today it's furnished in antiques of the period and also holds several murals attributed to Rufus Porter. Admission is $1, or 50¢ for children.

4. Freeport, Brunswick, and Bath

North of Portland, the next major tourist destination is Boothbay Harbor. But you'll pass several interesting towns along the way, each with an attraction peculiar to Maine.

FREEPORT: This small Maine town, nothing special though nice enough, is known all over the country and throughout the world as the headquarters of L. L. Bean, the company that sells equipment, clothing, and supplies for outdoor activities. L. L. Bean has been in Freeport for decades, but in recent years the store's popularity has burgeoned to epic proportions. A half dozen parking lots, administered by Bean employees, fill up quickly every day with cars bearing license plates from all over America and Canada. The large, attractive store is always mobbed during the day, and busy even at night, for Bean's is open all the time. It *never* closes.

Bean's reputation was built by selling sturdy, good-quality items at reasonable prices. The returns policy is absolute: if you find a Bean item unsatisfactory at any time, return it for a refund. Should you stop at Bean's, keep in mind that prices in the store are slightly lower than in Bean's famous mail-order catalog, as store items need not be shipped and insured.

The boom at Bean's has brought prosperity to Freeport, and a dozen other shops, including many factory outlets, have opened in order to profit from the press of Bean buyers. In effect it's becoming Maine's town-size shopping mall.

BRUNSWICK: Surrounded by coastal resort towns, Brunswick is the cultural center of this part of Maine, for **Bowdoin College** is in Brunswick along with Maine's only professional music theater. The **Brunswick Music Theater** (tel. 207/725-8769) is on the Bowdoin campus, and presents musical productions from mid-June through Labor Day each summer.

Bowdoin's fame comes not from its theater, although that is certainly famous enough among summer visitors and residents, but rather from the distinguished alumni who have spent their time in Brunswick and then moved on to fame and glory: Longfellow, Hawthorne, and Pres. Franklin Pierce were all Bowdoin graduates. The college is at Pine and College Streets, and free tours are available year round. While you're here visit Bowdoin's **art museum** to see its collection of colonial works.

Where to Stay in Brunswick

Brunswick's downtown section is right out of a picturebook of old New England towns, and one of its finest streets, Federal Street, is lined with lovely houses out of the era which gave the street its name. One of the finest of these is now a hotel and restaurant, and will do very well for a stopover in Brunswick. It's the **Stowe House** (tel. 207/725-5543), 63 Federal St., a registered National Historic Landmark. Stowe House gets its name from Harriet Beecher Stowe, who wrote her famous *Uncle Tom's Cabin* while living here. Longfellow and Hawthorne put up here while they were college students, and thus the house has a virtual monopoly of the great-and-famous-slept-here department. Guest rooms are in a well-disguised addition of 54 modern motel-style rooms with all the conveniences, including private baths and color TV. Prices are $41 single, $47.25 double, $56.70 for a room with two double beds. The restaurant is modern as well, although decorated with early American-style furniture. Breakfast, lunch, and dinner are served, and prices tend to the expensive side of the moderate range.

BATH: A ten-mile drive along U.S. 1 north from Brunswick brings you to Bath, another fine town of colonial and Federal houses built when Bath was a wealthy seaport and shipbuilding center. Take a drive along Washington Street to see what I mean. While on Washington Street, stop at no. 963, **Sewall House,** headquarters for Bath's famous **Maine Maritime Museum.** One ticket allows you to visit all four of the museum's exhibit areas: Sewall House; Winter Street Center, 880 Washington St.; the **Apprenticeshop** at 375 Front St.; and **Percy and Small Shipyard,** 263 Washington St., where *Seguin,* the oldest steam tug on the U.S. Registry is under restoration. Admission to all four museum sites during spring and fall is $4.50 for adults and $1.75 for children 6 through 16, or $12.50 total for a family. In the summer season a boat trip along the river between sites is included in your admission, $5.50 for adults and $2.25 for children, $15.50 total for a family. Just about everything you'd associate with the sea is represented at the museum: diver's gear, ship models (and real boats being made by students in the apprentice shop), nautical instruments, and memorabilia; there's even a room for children in which they get to touch and play with all of the exhibits. You may need more than a day to see all there is in the museum, and for this purpose the museum staff will validate your ticket for an extra day at no extra charge. (During the winter months, two sites of the museum are open: call or write to the Maine Maritime Museum, 963 Washington St., Bath, ME 04530; tel. 207/443-6311.)

WISCASSET: Billing itself "the prettiest town in Maine," Wiscasset might live up to its boast if Maine did not have such an abundance of pretty towns. It is pretty, though, and as you pass through the center on U.S. 1 you can confirm this. As you cross the Sheepscot River toward Damariscotta, look right (south) and note the two enormous hulks derelict in the water. The proud four-masted schooners *Hesperus* and *Luther Little* once carried cargoes along the Atlantic coast. But the many-masted schooners (a few were even built with six masts!) were the last of a proud breed, replaced by the more reliable steamboats. These two sad relics of a proud and romantic age sit forlorn in the mud, awaiting restoration or final destruction.

5. Boothbay Harbor

North and east of Portland, the Maine coastline is a choppy succession of peninsulas, sea inlets, islands, and river outlets. The country here is beautiful, and vacation communities abound. Reaching many of these communities means driving down a peninsular road for quite a number of miles to the tip, and upon leaving one drives back up to U.S. 1—few bridges or causeways span the inlets or rivers.

Boothbay Harbor is the principal town in a region of vacation settlements which include Boothbay, Boothbay Harbor, East Boothbay, Southport, and Ocean Point. I could write a book on this region alone, and so I've simplified by limiting my recommendations to Boothbay Harbor itself, which is the center of the action.

INFORMATION: As you drive down Route 27 from U.S. 1, several miles from town you'll come to an **information bureau,** on the right. If it's closed, don't worry for there's another one a bit farther along, right at the edge of town, and this one has longer hours. Both bureaus are open seasonally only, from late spring to early fall. Or get in touch with the **Boothbay Harbor Region Chamber of Commerce** (tel. 207/633-2353), P.O. Box 356, Boothbay Harbor, ME 04538.

WHERE TO STAY: As mentioned, Boothbay Harbor and the surrounding region have a plethora of vacation accommodations, hundreds of places in all. I've concentrated on the congenial places, like cozy guest houses on a hilltop with a splendid view.

Captain Sawyer's Place, 87 Commercial St., Boothbay Harbor, ME 04538 (tel. 207/633-2474), is at the bottom of McKown Hill in town, looking out over the harbor. The "Yellow House" is a classic Boothbay residence with guest rooms, all of which have private bath and rates of $42 to $47.25 double. Nearby, the "Admiral's Quarters" is a bit more like a motel, but still very homey. Rooms here have private baths as well, and prices of $47.25 to $52.50 double, in season. Morning coffee is on the house. The location couldn't be better.

Hilltop House, c/o The Mahrs, Boothbay Harbor, ME 04538 (tel. 207/633-2941), is just that, right at the top of McKown Hill in town, next to Topside (see below). Mrs. Mahr, a real Maine native, will rent you a homey room in her house for $36.75 double with private bath, $25.20 with shared bath. The porch, and its marvelous view, are yours to enjoy anytime you like.

Topside says it all about this charming hilltop house just two blocks from the center of Boothbay Harbor atop McKown Hill, Boothbay Harbor, ME 04538 (tel. 207/633-5404). A nice big old vacation house has been meticulously restored down to its marble fireplaces (in the living rooms) and has been stocked with antiques and newly landscaped. All rooms have refrigerators. Several new motel additions have been added, but in keeping with the architectural style of the house. And what a view! Many rooms have this view, and for variety you can sit in a lawn chair in the midst of Topside's lush green grass to take it all in as the cool breezes waft up from the harbor. Although there are other places on McKown Hill, Topside is smack at the top. Rates are $47.25 to $63, depending on the size of the room, its degree of comfort, and its exposure. As the number of rooms is limited, be sure to write or call well in advance for reservations.

Welch House (tel. 207/633-3431) shares the crest of McKown Hill with the aforementioned Topside, and it also shares the view, although perhaps a slightly smaller portion of it. The official address is 36 McKown Street, Boothbay Harbor, ME 04538, and signs in the center of town point the way to it. Here, every room has some sort of a sea view, and there's a nice little sundeck with the view along the side of the main house. Rooms in the main house all share the bathrooms, and cost $32 single, $33 to $38 double in season. In addition, a small building next door called the Sail Loft has a few units with private baths which are rented for slightly more. The rooms are all done very nicely, some in traditional styles, others with modern wood paneling and furniture. This could be one of the best places in Boothbay Harbor to stay, considering the price.

While it does not have the advantage of a waterfront location, the **Thistle Inn,** Oak and Union Streets, Boothbay Harbor, ME 04538 (tel. 207/633-3541), has to be the most convivial budget hostelry in all the Boothbay region. It's actually a number of blocks from the center of town on Route 27 as you come into Boothbay Harbor (the highway is one way along this street, and so as you go out it's a block from the northbound part of Route 27). The house is over a century old, but bears lots of fresh paint both on its white clapboards and on its black shutters. A big old porch with sunning chairs gives you a view over—well, some other houses. A room with private bath here goes for $44.10 double; rooms in which you share a bath are $36.75 double, $29.40 to $36.75 single. Reductions of about 15% to 20% are granted off-season, in the winter. Rooms are furnished in a sort of old-fashioned manner, but the style fits the house, after all. The restaurant and tavern, mentioned below, are among the town's prime gathering places.

For something closer to a motel, check out the **Tugboat Inn,** 100 Commercial St., Boothbay Harbor, ME 04538 (tel. 207/633-4434), a few steps from the center of town, at the lower edge of McKown Hill. The inn has four lodging buildings and a good variety of accommodations, from simple but tidy inn rooms through efficiencies and motel-style rooms to luxury rooms and suites. Prices in high season range from $33.60 to $69.30 double; all but the very cheapest rooms have private bath. You're right on the harbor here, with good views, handy to town, in an attractive and congenial establishment.

Outside of Town

Though it's somewhat pricey, the **Ocean Point Motel** (tel. 207/633-4200), East Boothbay, ME 04544, couldn't have a better location. Way down at Ocean Point by the lighthouse, on the southern tip of a peninsula overlooking the harbor mouth, Ocean Point is all by itself except for a few houses. It's quiet here, and very serene. You stay in the motel, the inn, the lodge, or one of the cottages, and rates depend on which, though all rooms have private bath, electric heat, and color television. Least expensive rooms are in the inn ($38.85 to $46.20 double), but the other lodgings are not much more expensive ($42 to $55.60), though a few suites and cottages are higher in price. The Ocean Point has its own restaurant, as there's no other place to dine without driving into Boothbay Harbor.

The **Lawnmeer Inn and Motel,** Route 27, Southport, ME 04569 (tel. 207/633-2544), is a short drive from Boothbay Harbor, across the drawbridge in Southport. In a quiet country setting, the Lawnmeer offers motel-style rooms with private bath, television, and the other modern conveniences for $31.50 to $42 double. This is the place to go if you need to get away from it all.

Bed and Breakfast

I've chosen mostly establishments in town or in special locations outside. The Boothbay region does have a number of bed-and-breakfast houses, most off the beaten track. For information, check (or call) the information booth.

WHERE TO DINE: While Boothbay is no culinary Mecca swarming with gourmet Muhammeds, there are still a few places where you can find things besides fried foods or the infamous surf-and-turf.

At Gilchrist's East (tel. 633-5692), on Commercial Street just south of Fishermen's Wharf, the boiled Maine lobster goes for $10 (whole dinner) or $7.50 (lobster only), which is reasonable; haddock, halibut, and scallops go for a bit less. But the most interesting item on the menu is the Candlelight Dinner, a succession of salads, vegetables, and fish dishes served on miniature china, for $10. The point is to give you various tastes without overfilling you. Otherwise, they serve coquilles St-Jacques, the scallops and mushrooms in shells. Liquor is served. You'll like it here. Open for lunch and dinner daily in season.

The place for lobster is obviously the **Lobstermen's Co-op** (tel. 633-4900), on Atlantic Avenue along the east side of the harbor. Open 8 a.m. to 8 p.m., the Co-op sells lobsters wholesale and retail, and will cook up a live lobster while you wait, at the retail price. Select a few side dishes, a beverage (wine, beer, soft drinks, coffee, or tea), a hamburger for the one who can't stand seafood, and you're all set to munch lunch at one of their tables. Cheap, fresh, good, authentic.

For finer dining, find your way to the **Coburn House** (tel. 633-2120), Route 27 in Boothbay, where you'll see such things as shrimp amaretto, veal aux pommes, and sole primavera (served with spinach and tomatoes) on the menu. Start with marinated herring or French onion soup, finish with a tasty dessert, and the evening will set you back about $20 to $24 per person, all in.

The **Thistle Inn** (tel. 633-3541) is known more for its restaurant and bar than its rooms, actually, and it's easy to see why. The "thistle" here is the incarnation of the Scottish spirit, and so the dining rooms have very low and white stucco ceilings, with crooked beam supports, Scottish clan coats-of-arms, bottles with candles stuck in them, and rustic booths made of dark wood. Start your meal with a cup of lobster stew or fish-clam chowder, and then for dinner have lobster prepared any one of a half dozen ways for $10 to $13, or something like baked haddie (haddock) with Swiss cheese and bread crumbs, cooked in celery soup ($8), or steak and onions ($9.50). On weekends (Friday and Saturday) there's roast beef, "verra verra rare." At lunchtime smaller portions of many of the seafood dishes are available for several dollars less than at dinner, and the sandwich selection includes a Maine lobster roll, a good hot Reuben, or the house club sandwich. For dessert, if you've never had a real Scottish sherry trifle, have it here. Beers, brandies, whiskies, and wines are all on order from the bar. The crowd is youngish, the spirit very congenial.

WHAT TO DO: In Boothbay Harbor, the sea comes first, as it always has. As the rocky, rugged coastline made travel overland virtually impossible until the day of the automobile and the modern highway, Boothbay Harbor was for centuries served from the sea.

Cruises

In the mornings, the *Argo* takes off from the Fishermen's Wharf Motel on nature cruises to see the local seals, water birds, and marine creatures. The tour takes 2¼ hours and costs $7. In the afternoons the cruises take in sea life and also a lot of famous coastal locations and sights in three hours or a little more, for $9. Evening cruises take 2½ hours and you can just cruise (for $5), or can partake of a "chicken bake afloat," a full-course dinner for $10.50, and that price includes the boat ride fare (lower prices for children's dinners). On Sunday a special schedule prevails, prices are the same or slightly lower, and trips are a bit shorter. When the moon is near full, special moonlight cruises are arranged—call 207/633-4925 or 633-5090, or go down to the docks at Fisherman's Wharf for full details. Children under 12 pay half fare on all cruises. Get reservations for your chosen cruise.

The M/V *Goodtime's* cruises are similar in style, content, and price to those run by the *Argo*, with a comfortable boat, congenial captain, and a good selection of varied cruises to just about all the places there are to see in the region—each day offering slightly different itineraries. As is usual, coffee and snacks are available on board, and children under 12 ride for half fare. For details call 207/633-3244 or 633-2626.

There are numerous other boats as well.

To Monhegan Island

The *Balmy Days* is a sail-assisted motor craft which makes the run 16 miles out to sea to Monhegan Island, Maine's famous windswept and spare resort-at-sea. One trip out, leaving in the morning, and one trip back from the island, leaving in midafternoon, are made daily, and you cannot stay overnight on the island without previous hotel reservations, but the *Balmy Days*'s schedule allows you to have between three and four hours on the island if you go out and back in one day. Monhegan is noted for its interesting paths and walks, and that's mostly what there is to do. A one-way ticket to Monhegan Island is $14; a round-trip is $18; children under 10 pay $14 round trip. While it's out at Monhegan, the *Balmy Days* makes one run around the island so you can see the rugged cliffs, and this costs $1 extra. By the way, you can easily hike all there is to hike (pretty much) in one four-hour stay on Monhegan. For detailed information call 207/633-3244 or 633-2626.

Other Activities

Should your spirit be nautically inclined but your stomach a landlubber, you can get in the sailing mood without putting to sea by a visit to the **Grand Banks Schooner Museum,** aboard the 142-foot dory schooner *Sherman Zwicker,* moored at 100 Commercial St. at Boothbay Harbor, and open from 9 a.m. to 5 p.m. daily, mid-June through September.

Also rich in maritime lore is the small-but-growing **Boothbay Museum** on McKown Street, located in one of the town's fine old white clapboard houses. Artifacts from the town and region have been collected and displayed here, and the admission fee is only 50¢.

The **Carousel Music Theater,** on Todd Street a half block from Fisherman's Wharf, is open from the first week in July through Labor Day with summer stock musical productions. Tickets and programs are available right at the theater.

The Brick House, on Oak Street very near the central Town Square, is the present home of the **Boothbay Region Art Gallery** (tel. 633-2703), which arranges three shows of local artists each season. Paintings are on view daily from 11 a.m. to 5 p.m., on Sunday from 2 to 5 p.m. The handsome old house was built in 1807 of bricks brought from England as ballast in ships which came to carry away Maine lumber—in such a forest-rich region, a brick house is a curiosity, as most houses would naturally be made from wood.

6. Camden

Picture a small Maine coastal town wedged between the salt waters of Penobscot Bay and a range of rocky hills, and that's Camden. With a population of barely 4000 souls it's small, picturesque, and manageable. Edna St. Vincent Millay came from these parts, but today Camden's chief claim to fame is that it is the home port for several two-masted schooners which take eager landlubbers for cruises along the Maine coast. The hills behind the town are included in the **Camden Hills State Park,** with campgrounds and picnic spots, and an auto road to the top of Mt. Battie, the highest hill of the range.

TOURIST INFORMATION: The **Rockport-Camden-Lincolnville Chamber of Commerce,** P.O. Box 246, Camden, ME 04843 (tel. 207/236-4404), maintains an information booth on the public landing in Camden where you can get a schematic map of the area and also a brochure describing the walking and bike tours of Camden and Rockport outlined by the Camden Historical Society. The tours point up all of the most historic places, and tell you much about the town, as well.

WHERE TO STAY: Camden is not packed with places to stay, and that's part of its charm. Many people stay at the motels which are scattered along both sides of U.S. 1, north and south of town. Here, I'll mention the best inns and guest houses right in town, within walking distance of everything.

On U.S. 1 a few blocks south of the center of Camden is **Blue Harbor,** 67 Elm St., Camden, ME 04843 (tel. 207/236-4385), a nice bed-and-breakfast guest house run by the charming Clayton family. The five guest rooms all share baths and cost $44.10, $47.25, or $49.35 double, breakfast included. Have breakfast on the sun porch if you like. Look for Blue Harbor right across the street from the Towne Motel. You're only a few minutes' walk from the center here.

Goodspeed's Guest House, 60 Mountain St., Camden, ME 04843 (tel. 207/236-8077), is on Route 52, a half mile up the hill west of the center. The house has been beautifully redone and furnished with antiques by its owners, who provide a warm welcome and rooms with shared bath for $44.62 double. A tiny deck, set with umbrella-shaded tables and chairs, allows you to enjoy the quiet of this location.

Boswell's Bight, 49 Mountain St., Camden, ME 04843 (tel. 207/236-8275), is almost across the street from the aforementioned Goodspeed's, charging comparable rates for bed and breakfast.

The Maine Stay, 22 High St., Camden, ME 04843 (tel. 207/236-9636), is a big white house built in 1813 with very charming rooms, all of which share baths and cost $36.75 single, $47.25 double, breakfast included. A pretty living room and a deck overlooking the backyard are for guests' use. The Maine Stay is north of the center on U.S. 1, about a ten-minute walk to the commercial district.

Of the new, restored inns in Camden, the most pristine is without doubt the **Hawthorn Inn,** 9 High St., Camden, ME 04843 (tel. 207/236-8842), just a few minutes' walk north of the commercial district on U.S. 1. The big Victorian house with a view of Camden Harbor has been carefully and lovingly restored, and the large, airy rooms furnished with antiques. Rooms come with shared bath ($52.50), semiprivate bath (an extra-large room, $57.75), or private bath with a fine harbor view ($68.25). Rates include fresh muffins, fruit, and coffee in the morning; a full breakfast is served for a few dollars more.

The **Camden Harbour Inn** (tel. 207/236-4200), atop the hill at the far end of Bay View Street (no. 83), Camden, ME 04843, stays open all year round. A nice big old inn with white clapboards and, from some guest rooms and from the dining room, beautiful views of Penobscot Bay, the Camden Harbour could be a model for the typical coastal Maine inn. The rooms are rented in season with breakfast for $29.40 single without private bath, $44.10 to $72.45 double, the more expensive rooms generally being the ones which have private baths and the best views. The inn has a few family rooms as well.

The **Owl and the Turtle Bookmotel** (tel. 207/236-4769) is, perhaps, the strangest name for a motel, but it is explained when one realizes that the building which houses the Owl and the Turtle Bookshop at 8 Bay View St., Camden, ME 04843, also houses a tearoom and a few very nice motel-type rooms, each with a marvelous view of the bay. Prices for the rooms—while they last—are $47.25 for two, continental breakfast included, in summer. Believe me when I say the Owl's rooms are nice: Maine-made furniture, color TVs, and private baths; but there are so few of them you *must* reserve in advance by phone or mail.

WHERE TO DINE: Restaurants tend to open and close in Camden. Here are some that have managed to please customers well, and prosper.

The **Waterfront** (tel. 236-3747), Harborside Square off Bay View Street, is true to its name. It caters to the yachting bunch and those who sit longingly gazing at the tall ships, and because of its beautiful location and deckside tables, does a booming business. The restaurant is open from 11:30 a.m. to 10 p.m. every day of the week, with the full luncheon menu being served from opening to 2:30 p.m., a light menu from 2:30 to 5 p.m., and dinner thereafter. While the dinner menu does carry always at least one steak and one chicken selection, seafood is what you'll want to eat if you dine here. The seafood brochette (scallops, Gulf shrimp, sole filet, peppers, and mushrooms are skewered and broiled; $10.25) is a favorite, but not everything is that expensive. The mussels creole, served in a spicy tomato and pepper sauce, is only $6.25, for example. Most main-course dishes are priced between $7 and $10, in fact.

Cappy's Chowder House (tel. 236-2254), right in the center of Camden at the intersection of Main, Bayview, and Commercial Streets, has a rich nautical decor and an eclectic menu. The seafood—clam, fish, and lobster chowders, plates, salads—is excellent and moderately priced, there are burgers, baked brie, barbecued back ribs. A bar provides a social center and quick-lunch place; tables and booths are for serious diners. Liquor is served, and is cheapest during the happy hour from 4 to 6 p.m. Cappy's is open from 7:30 a.m. to midnight daily, so you can get breakfast here as well.

The **Round Top Ice Cream Parlor,** 44 Bayview St., Harbor Square, has delicious ice cream made on its own farm, plus the least expensive light fare in town. Go around to the "Galley" in back for $2.25 hamburgers, $5 lobster rolls, and similar treats. Take your purchases to the picnic tables overlooking the harbor (exclusively for Round Top customers), and you'll have some of the best restaurant seating in Camden at the lowest price.

READER'S RESTAURANT SELECTION: "At the suggestion of one of the local inhabitants we ate at the **Spinnaker Restaurant** (tel. 596-6804), about a mile north of Rockport, Maine. The food and service were excellent. We had shrimp, scallops, fresh salmon, salad bar, potatoes, bread and butter, and wine, for a total bill of $25! It was one of the better meals on our trip" (Mrs. Irma Jean Fallon, Manhattan, Kans.).

WHAT TO SEE AND DO: If you have a car, drive north from town along U.S. 1 and follow the signs to the entrance to **Camden Hills State Park** and the auto road to the top of Mt. Battie. Besides the town itself, the drive up will afford you a view of the rocky hills themselves, the countryside beyond, and of blue, sparkling Penobscot Bay.

Camden's **Windjammer fleet** of schooners provides the adventurous with a very different vacation: dipping in and out of the myriad of small harbors and inlets along the Maine coast. Cruises usually leave on Monday and last a week, cost about $360 to $400 per person, and space must be reserved in advance. The thing to do is to write to the chamber of commerce for current lists of who's sailing, and what the cost will be. You might also try calling some of the telephone numbers listed for the ships: 207/236-2750; 236-2938; 236-8873; 236-4449.

Go southeast along Bay View Street a ways and you'll come to **Laite Memorial Park and Beach,** with picnic areas and rest rooms as well as a nice, chilly Maine beach.

For the rest of your time in Camden, latch onto a copy of the walking tour brochure (mentioned above) put out by the Camden Historical Society, and stroll through the town to get the flavor of it.

From Rockland Ferry Terminal (tel. 207/594-5543), you can take a car ferry to **Vinalhaven Island**, in Penobscot Bay, for a taste of island vacation life, cooled by sea breezes. The *Governor Curtis* (State Ferry Service, P.O. Box 645, Rockland, ME 04841) makes the 1½-hour run to Vinalhaven three times a day, and the return trip is the same number of times. On Sunday there are two sailings in each direction.

7. Castine

This little village, set apart on a peninsula in the Penobscot Bay, is a gem. Turn right onto Route 175 at Orland, east of Bucksport, and continue on Route 166 and 166A to Castine. With only a few places to stay and to dine, Castine draws a steady crowd of summer regulars who come for the beauty, the seclusion, the quiet, the easy summer life.

No small part of Castine's charm is in its history. In the winter of 1613, Sieur Claude de Turgis de la Tour founded a small trading post here among the Tarrantine Indians, but it was not to remain in French hands for long. The struggle for North America's forest, natural, and maritime wealth was already beginning, and the Fort Pentagoet founded by Turgis de la Tour would be conquered by the English in 1628. Treaty returned Pentagoet to France in 1635, and during the tumultuous period until 1676, the place changed hands many times. The British took it and called it Penobscot Fort; the French retook it and built the formidable Fort Saint Peter. At one time the village was the capital of all French Acadia (the lands in what is now Atlantic Canada). Even the Dutch coveted the fort, and ruled here from 1674 to 1676. In the latter year, Baron de Saint Castin recaptured the town for France, and opened a trading station. Fortifications were strengthened, and despite raids by the British, the family of Baron de Saint Castin ruled over the town (now called Bagaduce) even after the baron himself returned to France, a wealthy man, in 1703. By 1760, however, the fate of French North America was sealed, and Castin's Fort, or Bagaduce, was to be held by the British after that year.

English settlers brought new life to Bagaduce during the 1760s, and the dissatisfaction which boiled in the English colonies at this period didn't leave the town untouched. Some of the townspeople were loyal to the king, others sympathized—actively and passively—with the American revolutionaries. But in 1779 a British naval force came from Nova Scotia, intent on making the town safe for British Loyalists (and thereby influencing the negotiations which would determine the fledgling United States' northern border). The British built Fort George to defend the town.

The challenge to American sovereignty was taken up by the General Court (legislature) of Massachusetts, which governed the territory at the time, and the ill-fated Penobscot Expedition was outfitted and launched at an ultimate cost of $8 million (in those days!). Bad luck and bad commanding resulted in the destruction of most of the American force, almost bankrupting the Commonwealth of Massachusetts. Fort George was enlarged and strengthened over the years, and the town thrived until the border between the U.S. and Canada was determined. Unhappily for residents of Bagaduce, the boundary was to be the St. Stephen River (the present boundary), and not the Penobscot. Those loyal to the British crown put their houses on boats and *sailed* them to sites along the coast of what is today New Brunswick, at St. Andrews, mainly. Some of the houses moved thus still stand in St. Andrews.

In 1796 the name of Bagaduce was changed to Castine, and although it was occupied by British forces during the War of 1812, there was never again to be much military action. But in the 350 years of Castine's history its forts—Fort Pentagoet, Fort George, and the American Fort Madison—saw a surprising amount of attack and defense.

You can visit Fort George and the sites of the other forts in Castine, but first, get a place to stay the night.

WHERE TO STAY AND EAT: As I mentioned, Castine has only a few places to put up for the night. Have advance reservations to be sure of a bed.

The **Pentagoet Inn** (tel. 207/326-8616), P.O. Box 4, Castine, ME 04421, a beautiful old gabled and turretted pale-yellow house with dark-green trim, is right in the center of the village. Interior decoration harkens back to Castine's fascinating Revolutionary period, although the inn building dates from Victoria's time, 1894. The comforts are modern, though, and a double with bath ranges from $42 to $47.25; a double with half bath costs $36.75; and a double without bath is $31.50. Drinks are served on the porch daily in the summer. For an extra $2, guests at the Pentagoet can have afternoon "tea," which is actually tea and snacks. Dinner is served at the inn. The menu and the price (about $10, not including wine or dessert) are posted in the morning, and those who would like dinner sign up for it then. This is a charming place, and I recommend it for those who want a quiet getaway to a beautiful town.

Just across the street and up a short distance is the **Castine Inn** (tel. 207/326-4365), which flies the four flags—French, British, Dutch, and American—of the peoples who have ruled Pentagoet-Bagaduce-Castine. The inn is an elegant old home stuffed with antiques, fireplaces, and shades of a gracious past, and run by a friendly woman, Virginia Wetmore. Room rates run from $36.75 to $57.75 double, including a continental breakfast. Dinner every night but Tuesday, with a Pub.

Other than at the two inns, one can dine at **Lafferty's Restaurant** (tel. 326-4776), down by the dock in the basement of the big brick building. Hours for breakfast are 7:30 a.m. to 10 a.m. and lunch from 11:30 a.m. to 2:30 p.m. Soup ($1 to $1.50), burgers ($2 to $3), sandwiches, and treats like quiche, omelets, and shrimp cocktail fill the lunch menu. Dinnertime is devoted to seafood: haddock stuffed with crabmeat is a specialty ($8), and lobster is sold at a very reasonable price. Dinner is served from 5:30 to 9:30 p.m. Lafferty's draws the crowd from the boats in the harbor, and from the marine academy.

For a quick snack anytime, drop by the lunch counter of the **Castine Variety Store**, at the corner of Main and Water Streets. It's a fine old drugstore in the traditional sense, with the old pharmacy shelves and drawers behind the counter, and a stamped-metal ceiling, plus the regulation soda fountain/lunch counter.

WHAT TO DO: Visit the sites for the forts: **Fort Pentagoet,** near the Wilson Museum on Perkins Road; **Fort George,** near the entrance to town, and **Fort Madison.** Fort George is now a State Memorial, kept up by the Bureau of Parks and Recreation.

Historical signboards placed around the village outline Castine's fascinating history. For a closer look, visit the **Wilson Museum,** on Perkins Road, three blocks from Main Street to the southwest. It's open daily from 2 to 5 p.m. from late May to October, with displays of china, guns, Indian relics—the artifacts of Castine's storied past.

Downeast Chamber Music Concerts (tel. 207/326-4311), Castine, ME 04421, sponsors chamber music concerts every summer in July and August in the Federated Church on Main Street, or in the gym at the Maritime Academy. Write or call for times, dates, programs, and ticket prices. What a marvelous thing to have in a peaceful town!

8. Bar Harbor

When a Yankee talks about a "Downeaster," he's talking about somebody from Maine, but when somebody from Maine talks about a Downeaster, he means somebody from the region of Bar Harbor or even farther east. Most of the rest of us think of the Maine coastline as running its ragged way north, but a quick look at the map will show that Bar Harbor is at about the same longitude as San Juan, Puerto Rico, and that indeed the Maine coastline heads more directly east than it does north at this point. These are the wilder shores of Maine and the settlements are fewer, the vegetation not so lush, and the climate a bit harsher than in other parts of the state, but at the same time the scenery is more dramatic, the air is charged with life, and a sense of wild nature surrounds one.

The French influence was for a long time paramount in these parts, and many Downeasters today speak French as a second language—the French of Québec, the French brought to these shores by the great Champlain. In fact it was Samuel de Champlain who gave Mount Desert Island its name, in the form of "L'Île des Monts-Deserts," and even today the local pronunciation is *dez-ZERT* (like what you have after dinner, not like what's in Arabia), following the French style.

When steamships and railroads were opening up in America in the 1800s, they also opened up Downeast Maine, and by the end of the century Bar Harbor, a small town on rocky Mount Desert Island, boasted almost as many palatial summer homes as Newport, although the ones here were perhaps not quite so lavish—but pretty close. In any case, only a small number of the original dozens of mansions are still standing, for a great number were wiped out in the Great Fire of 1947.

Today, Bar Harbor is a nice town with a fantastically large number of motels and other lodging establishments, most (luckily for the town) lining the roads into town from Ellsworth. The big attractions in the area, for which so much housing must be provided, are the town itself, the cruise boats to Yarmouth, Nova Scotia, and of course Acadia National Park. The park takes up something like half of the land of Mount Desert Island and much of that on the smaller surrounding islands, and is one of the few national parks in the eastern United States. It draws tremendous numbers of visitors every year.

INFORMATION: Bar Harbor's livelihood has been tourism for 100 years now, and so the townspeople know how to treat a guest. The chamber of commerce maintains an information booth on the municipal pier in town (tel. 207/288-3393; in winter, call the business office on Cottage Street at 207/288-5103, mornings). They'll help you out with information and with any questions you may have.

WHERE TO STAY: While the area draws thousands of visitors each year, there are plenty of rooms to handle the crowds. The problem is to get the room you want rather than one you're forced to take. Reservations are advisable in all recommended places, and as these are some of the choicer spots, I'd recommend that you reserve early.

Motels

Prime among Bar Harbor's elite places to stay is the **Bar Harbor Motor Inn** (tel. 207/288-3351), set amid its own lush grounds on a point overlooking Frenchman's Bay, Bar Harbor, ME 04609. Once a large old private club, it has been converted and expanded to take in summer visitors (mid-May to late October), and the feeling is that of a very plush country club or a posh resort in the glittering 1920s. One dresses for dinner in the semicircular dining room overlooking the bay; white pillars frame the front porch; attendants pad quietly here and there. The inn's large heated swimming pool is next to a little copse of trees and only a few yards from the waters of the Atlantic, and here, as everywhere else at the inn, the views are magnificent. The rooms are not all old-fashioned, however, and all have private baths, color TV, and lots of windows looking either onto the bay or the inn's lush grounds. The poolside rooms are cheaper, of course, at $75.60 for two from mid-July to mid-September; in the same period, a room with a bay view will cost $86.10. The atmosphere is formal but friendly.

If the Bar Harbor Motor Inn is full, the desk clerk directs disappointed visitors to the **Golden Anchor Inn** (tel. 207/288-5033), out on Granite Point off West Street near the Municipal Wharf, Bar Harbor, ME 04609. The Golden Anchor is not at all like the Bar Harbor Motor Inn, but is, rather, a new and luxurious motel right over the water with many sea-view rooms, all with little balconies over the water. The decor is a modern adaptation of early American, and the luxury extras include a pool, direct-dial phones, color TV (the motel even has its own closed-circuit station), and docking facilities for your boat. The motel is open year round, and the highest prices are charged in July and August, to Labor Day: $78.75 to $89.25. The Golden Anchor is easily within walking distance of everything downtown.

On the other side of town from those choices is the **Villager Motel** (tel. 207/288-3211), 207 Main St. (Route 3 heading south out of town), Bar Harbor, Me 04609. The Villager is a very neat two-story motel of moderate size (63 units) and the usual comforts: a heated outdoor pool, modern rooms with private bath and TV, and a convenient location which still leaves you within walking distance of the sights, shops, and restaurants in town. All of these advantages, plus the moderate rates, assure that the Villager is often full, so it's good to make reservations in advance. From July 1 through Labor Day the rates are $37.80 to $54.60 double; from after Labor Day through April the rooms cost $33.60 to $40, and in May and June they're $29.40 to $40.

The **Rockhurst Motel** (tel. 207/288-3140), right next to the grand Ledgelawn Inn on Mount Desert Street, Bar Harbor, ME 04609, has 14 clean and modern rooms, quiet and shady, for $46.20 double in season. The small pool is shared with the guests at the Ledgelawn. The Rockhurst has the prettiest situation, and one of the best locations, of any motel in Bar Harbor. Off-season, rooms cost a mere $29.40 double.

Inns

In 1900 a retired Boston publisher named Lewis Roberts built himself a "cottage" in Bar Harbor. The sumptuous result of his efforts has gone through several hands since then, lately having been owned by a former dean of Harvard Medical School. Today, however, it is owned by Alonzo and Elinor Geel, who have turned it into what I would term Bar Harbor's most desirable place to stay. It's called **Thornhedge,** 47 Mount Desert St., Bar Harbor, ME 04609 (tel. 207/288-5398), and the aim of its owners is to "recapture the spirit of Bar Harbor at the turn of the century." This they have done by arranging to purchase many of the house's original furnishings, and so today the large, sunny, gracious master bedroom on the second floor is done in the turn-of-the-century style which suits it; adjoining is the original bathroom, which is a good deal larger than the standard motel *room* today. The bathroom is equipped with its own 1900s scale and chaise lounge. Rooms on the second floor have private baths; rooms on the third floor, which were originally meant for children and servants, share bathrooms in the hall. Many rooms have working fireplaces, in which fire laws allow artificial logs to be burned. The fireplaces in the elegant and ornate public rooms—the parlor and dining room—are allowed to burn real logs, and will bear fires on a chilly day. You can tell that I like Thornhedge, and when you stay there, you'll know why. The season is mid-March through mid-November. In high summer, rooms range from $47.25 to $68.25; off-season rates are lower. Morning coffee, juice, fruit, and muffins are included in these rates, as well as wine, cheese, and crackers at 5 p.m. As you're driving or walking along Mount Desert Street, you can't miss Thornhedge, for it's painted a bright, cheery yellow.

The **Manor House Inn,** 106 West St., Bar Harbor, ME 04609 (tel. 207/288-3759), is another huge Victorian "cottage" which has been carefully restored by new owners, Frank and Jan Matter. Period furnishings fill the guest rooms, each of which has its own bathroom. Breakfast (included in the rates) is served in the sitting room downstairs. The Manor House is right across the street from the prestigious Bar Harbor Club, and Manor House guests can use club facilities for swimming and tennis, plus the reading room, lounge, and grounds. What does it cost to stay in a charming house, now listed in the National Register of Historic Places? Prices are $58.80 to $84, tax included, from July through late September; the inn is open mid-May through mid-November.

The **Ledgelawn Inn,** 66 Mount Desert St., Bar Harbor, ME 04609 (tel. 207/288-4596), is a palatial mansion just being fully converted now to a luxurious and elegant inn. Having escaped destruction in the Great Fire of 1947, the "cottage" built for Boston shoe magnate John Brigham now lives on. The public rooms are positively grand in scale, the lawns and trees elaborate, the guest rooms elegant. Many have working fireplaces and private baths, and prices are $40 to $89.25 per night double, depending on size, bath, view, fireplace, etc. Children under 12 staying with their parents pay $5 extra per night; over that age, an extra person must pay $10. The Ledgelawn has a widow's walk on top, open for the view or the warm rays of the sun until 6 p.m. There's a swimming pool, a laundry, and access to the clay tennis courts and Olympic-size pool at the Bar Harbor Club for inn guests. By the way, a buffet breakfast is included in the price of your room here.

The **Hearthstone Inn,** 7 High St., Bar Harbor, ME 04609 (tel. 207/288-4533), is on a quiet street not far from the center of town. The living room of the inn has a fireplace, the music room houses a grand piano, and other touches of past Bar Harbor elegance (recreated here) abound. Most rooms have private baths, some have fireplaces or balconies; all come with continental breakfast baked at the inn, and cost from $46.20 to $63 double. To find High Street, stay on Route 3 as it becomes Mount Desert Street and take the third left (High Street), a one-way street just before the Episcopal church.

Farther from the center of town, 500 yards from the *Bluenose* dock, up on a cliff, is the **Cleftstone Manor** (tel. 207/288-4951), Route 3 (Eden Street),

Bar Harbor, ME 04609. What was it like to spend the summer in a 30-room cottage? You can get a taste of it here for about $31.50 to $54.60 (shared bath) or $63 to $89.25 (private bath), double. Breakfast of home-baked breads and pastries is included in the fee, as is afternoon tea, evening refreshments, and car service between the Cleftstone and Bar Harbor Airport.

Guest Houses

Ron and Terry Baker bought the **Rocky Coast Manor,** P.O. Box 634, Bar Harbor, ME 04609 (tel. 207/288-3243), a large guest house at 74 Mount Desert St., several years ago, and have worked hard to fix up the big, sunny rooms in a simple but attractive way. Although a few rooms have private facilities, most of the rooms share baths, and thus constitute an unusual bargain: $25.20 to $31.50 pays for a double room that's clean and well kept, and the jovial assistance of the hosts comes at no extra charge. You'll like the rocky coast, you'll like the Bakers. If you have a large family, you can save on accommodations by taking a family room at a cost of $33.60 to $42. Here you're only a five-minute stroll from downtown.

At 69 Mount Desert St., Bar Harbor, ME 04609, is the **Sign of the Gull** (tel. 207/288-4210 or 288-5403), a guest house owned by Elsie and Bernie Dowd. The big Bar Harbor house is homey and comfortable, and the pool at the big National Park Motel nearby is open to guests at the Gull. Room prices include a continental breakfast. There are ten rooms in all, at $29.40 to $33.60 double without bath, $36.75 to $41 with bath or shower, also double. Nice place.

WHERE TO DINE: Bar Harbor is well provided with restaurants to satisfy all appetites, but rather than beginning with the most deluxe, let's start with the one that's the most traditional and also the most fun.

Lobster Pounds

As you drive toward Bar Harbor from Ellsworth, the road is lined with little shacks and stores bearing the magic word LOBSTERS. Outside of each is a strange arrangement of backyard barbecues in a row, with large pots or drums on them and stovepipes (in some cases very rickety ones) shooting up. These contraptions are used to prepare a traditional lobster clambake. The drums or kettles are filled with lobsters, clams, corn-on-the-cob, and seaweed, and then salt water is poured in, the fire is started, and the whole business is cooked up and served to the droves of motorists who have been dreaming of such a feast, perhaps for days and for hundreds of miles. Some places have tables where you can sit to consume your feast, at others you take the goodies home with you, but in any case this is the way to get the most seafood for your dollar, and the eating couldn't be better! This is the real Maine experience, and shouldn't be missed.

How does one pick the right place to stop? Every single one seems to have a signboard out front giving the price-per-pound of lobster, and you can go by this to some degree. But the price and poundage depend on how the lobster is stored: the best places will store the live lobsters on ice, and *not* in seawater, as the seawater can add a great deal of weight to the lobster as it's put on the scale. Make sure the lobster is alive, in any case, not dead and limp.

If you'd rather have your lobster clambake in beautiful, genteel surroundings, head south into the wilds of Mount Desert Island and look for **Abel's,** on Route 198 south of the intersection with Route 233. Abel's is beautiful: right down by the water in a grove of pines, with a little shingled hut where the lobsters and clams are kept fresh and alive in constantly circulating seawater (very good for the clams), and then cooked in seawater in the same shack. Dining is at outside tables in good weather, or in the sunporch of the restaurant, which is glassed in and has a marvelous view. Prices at Abel's depend on the base price at the market for lobsters, but last time I visited Abel's, lobster plates were priced from $10 to $20. For $16 one could get steamed clams, a lobster weighing over a pound, rolls, french fries, and coffee. Cocktails, wine, and beer are served here, with Michelob on tap.

Restaurants

The dining room at the **Bar Harbor Motor Inn** (tel. 288-3351) is certainly one of Bar Harbor's choice places to dine. The plush semicircular room is filled with brocade chairs and white-clothed tables, all of which share in the view of the bay. Open for dinner from 6 to 10 p.m. daily, the Bar Harbor is a place where you must "dress for dinner," and so men must have jacket and tie, women something of similar formality. The full-course shore dinner is a splurge at $24, but is a feast in itself, although a Maine seafood platter ($16.50) will do if you're not up to the extras such as appetizer, soup, and dessert. A shrimp kebab is a good selection for the relatively light eater, whereas a hearty eater may want to tuck into one of the many kinds of steak offered. Besides the rich atmosphere and good service which comes with a meal here, dinner guests have the pleasure of an evening's stroll around the inn's grounds, and then perhaps through the small town park with fountain which is right next to the inn.

Very near the Bar Harbor Motor Inn in terms of both location and price is the **Quarterdeck Restaurant** (tel. 288-5292), at the corner of Main and West Streets near the town pier. While the items on the Quarterdeck's menu are almost as expensive as those at the inn, they are very different items, tending to be more adventurous. For instance, you can start with champignons aioli (raw mushrooms in a cream garlic sauce) and then go on to boiled or broiled Maine lobster or lobster diablo (lobster stuffed with Maine shrimps, in a tomato sauce), and the price will be about $15 to $20. There are a good number of other, cheaper selections as well, such as various spaghetti plates and omelets. The Quarterdeck is modern in decor, and the lights are kept fairly low in the evening so diners can take advantage of the views from the restaurant's many windows. Both lunch and dinner are served.

The **Town Farm Restaurant** (tel. 288-5359) is for those devoted to healthful, vegetarian food, and also for those devoted to healthful, delicious, not-necessarily-vegetarian food. The attractive, modern-rustic restaurant is near the Bar Harbor Fire Station, behind the park, right next to the Greyhound bus stop on Kennebec Place. In good weather you can sit on the deck in front to dine. Breakfast (with buckwheat pancakes; $2.25) starts the Town Farm day, then lunch with over 12 different salads. If you don't favor a sandwich or hamburger, order the quiche of the day, with rice and soup or salad, for $6.85. Hours at the Town Farm are from 7 a.m. every day, closing at 11:30 p.m. Sunday through Wednesday, at 2:30 a.m. Thursday through Saturday in summer. No liquor served, but they'll provide set-ups if you BYO. There's a liquor store right in the rear of the fire station.

The **Brick Oven Restaurant** (tel. 288-3708), 21 Cottage St., is almost as proud of its decor as it is of its cuisine. Downstairs, the lights are low, lots of stained glass shines, and a turn-of-the-century atmosphere prevails. Upstairs is a Victorian Dining Car room, done up with real fixtures for authenticity. Another room has a cathedral ceiling hung with all sorts of flotsam and jetsam, including an ancient "Whizzer" motorbike. In fact, it will take you a few minutes to explore all the dining rooms before sitting down to dinner. My meal of Maine clam chowder, a plate of spaghetti and meatballs, and a salad came to only $11, tax and tip included. Prices are moderate, but if you have chicken or fish or steak, you may end paying a bit more. The special dinner of the day is only $6, however. The Brick Oven is among the few places to serve lobster at a reasonable price—depending on the season, one may cost only $7 to $8 here. Liquor served.

Especially for Breakfast and Brunch

Many of the restaurants on Main Street, recommended in the expensive-minded travel guides, do a booming business all summer long with bus tours and groups. The food is good perhaps, but must suffer somewhat from the incredible press of diner-traffic. Not so at the **Harbor View Restaurant**, on Main Street next to the little harborside park and near the driveway to Bar Harbor Motor Inn. Breakfast, brunch, and lunch are the specialties here, and all the chef's powers of imagination are concentrated in those meals. Where else, for example, can you get blueberry pancakes, topped with vanilla ice cream and blueberry compote, for $3.25? Or french toast, Danish ham, and eggs in a cheddar cheese sauce (called the "French Connection") for $3.85? Other pancake dishes, omelets, sandwiches, and salads, fill out the list of things to eat. Some of the little tables and booths do indeed have a view of the water. Hours for the Harbor View are from 7 a.m. to 2 p.m., making breakfast the prime meal.

For Meeting People

Bubba's, at 30 Cottage St., is a favorite sandwich-and-drinks place for many of the more interesting people in Bar Harbor on vacation. Soups, salads, and sandwiches ($2.25 to $6.95) make up the bill of fare all day, but sipping and socializing are what it's all about. The big bar and the bentwood make it all upbeat and enjoyable.

For a Bit of Nightlife

At **Geddy's,** on Main Street near the corner of West Street, every night in summer is witness to some sort of live performance. Jazz, dixieland, pop, and rock all issue forth from its sidewalk windows. Check the playbill out front, and then walk in. There's no cover or minimum, and beer is only $1.50 (Miller's, for example) or $2 (for Heineken and the like). Happy hour, from 3 to 7 p.m., sees all drinks reduced to about half price.

READERS' RESTAURANT SELECTIONS: "I had a delicious stuffed lobster for $12 at the **Acadian Restaurant** (tel. 288-5493), on Route 3 in Hulls Cove, which is on the road into Bar Harbor but not far from town. It's not difficult to get to, and they have the best homemade pies in the whole region. There is a view of the sea" (Desiree Desden, Salem, Ore.) . . . "We liked the **Sea View Restaurant** (tel. 288-3726) at 100 Eden St., because of their lobster and clam pound (which our girls enjoyed just as much as we did) and they had 'family specials' on the menu which brought down the price of seafood dinners for us, dramatically" (Bob and Sue Macfarlane, El Paso, Tex.).

WHAT TO DO: As I mentioned above, Bar Harbor has been a resort for many years and the town fathers, along with the chamber of commerce, throw themselves into organizing activities and making sure there's lots to do.

Special Events

Special events are scheduled throughout the summer, and you should drop down to the information bureau on the town pier for a list of the latest ones. The **Bar Harbor Festival,** with concerts and similar goings-on, is held in July and August, and during the summer months free **band concerts** take place each Monday and Thursday evening on the Village Green.

Bicycling

Should you want to rent a bike for trips around town or into the national park, check with **Bar Harbor Bicycle Rentals** at 141 Cottage St., corner of Eden Street, Route 3 (Cottage Street is parallel to West Street but one block south of it, away from the water). Rates are $7.50 per day, plus deposit.

Cruises

The **Frenchman's Bay Boating Company** (tel. 288-5741) organizes sightseeing and fishing trips out into Frenchman's Bay, and you can take your choice of either one-hour trips for $4.75 (kids 5 to 12, $2.75), or two-hour trips ($5.75 for adults, $3.50 for kids 5 to 12). A half-day's fishing costs $14, this includes rod, reel, and bait. Cruises are offered from mid-May to October, and all trips leave from the boat company's pier right next to the municipal (town) pier.

A Harbor View Walk

If you're willing to walk for 30 to 45 minutes, you can enjoy one of Bar Harbor's nicest little hikes. Follow Main Street (Route 3) south out of town, past the park on the right, and about a mile down the road (15 to 25 minues' walk) is a pull-off spot for cars (capacity: four vehicles). If you reach the Ocean Drive Motor Inn, you've gone too far. Walk down the dirt road, closed by a chain, near the little metal sign marking the boundary of U.S. government land, posted on a tree. It's less than a ten-minute walk to Rocky Harbor along the dirt road through the fragrant forests. When you come to a fork, bear left with the road (a path goes off straight). When you reach the viewing-point, you'll find a grassy clearing furnished with litter barrels for picnickers (no tables). If you've brought a picnic, you can share it with the gulls and ducks. It's secluded, beautiful, quiet, and in walking distance from town—a fine place.

A Visit to Acadia National Park

The rugged terrain of Mount Desert Island has attracted lovers of natural beauty for over a century, and soon after summer visitors began to arrive here in numbers, preservation efforts were begun. By the end of World War II, Acadia National Park was well along to its present size of over 30,000 acres, or something like half the land on the island (the other half is still in private hands). Focal point of park activities is **Cadillac Mountain,** at 1530 feet the highest point on America's Atlantic coast. The thing to do with Cadillac Mountain is to hike (or drive) to the top of it for the views. In fact local people have recognized that those who see the sun break forth on the horizon from Cadillac Mountain are the first people in the United States to greet the new day, and so there's a "Sunrise From Mount Cadillac Club" which you can join by picking up a blank from the Bar Harbor Information Bureau, and filling it out with the help of your hotel manager the night *before* you plan to see the sunrise. Then, if you follow through, you get to be a member of this exclusive club.

Besides Cadillac Mountain, the first thing to do in the park is drive the Loop Road, a one-way scenic ocean drive which takes you past many of the most interesting scenic, topographic, and geologic features of the island. Stop at **Thunder Hole** when the surf's up to feel the bashing and pushing of the waves, or at **Sand Beach** for a chilly ocean swim. There's national park camping at **Black Woods** (follow the signs).

On the island's western peninsula, **Echo Lake** is the park's freshwater swimming area, there's a lookout tower atop **Beech Mountain,** and a park campground is down near the peninsula's southern tip at **Seawall.** And throughout the park are 100 miles of hiking trails (maps sold at park headquarters), and lots of "carriage roads" good for bike trips or horseback riding (horses can be rented in the park).

Not far from the town of Bar Harbor, in the park at Sieur des Monts Spring, is the **Abbe Museum of Stone Age Antiquities,** a wildflower garden, and a nature center. There's no admission charge to the park proper, but there are fees for various activities such as the campgrounds.

The beach at **Seal Harbor** is very fine, and open to the public for free. Park in the lot across the street. Seal Harbor, by the way, is one of Mount Desert Island's poshest summer resorts, with all sorts of famous and wealthy people inhabiting the big houses secluded along the forested streets of the village.

Tours

National Park Tours (tel. 207/288-3327) runs two tours daily from Bar Harbor (only one on Sunday), beginning from Testa's Hotel, 53 Main St. The cost is $5 per adult, $2.50 per child under 12. The tour takes you through the town of Bar Harbor and past many of the mansions left from its heyday, and also past Cadillac Mountain, Sieur des Monts Spring, and Thunder Hole. Traditionally the tours have left at 10 a.m. and 2 p.m., but call in advance to check the times, and to make a reservation.

If you have a car, you can rent a cassette tape recorder with a prerecorded tour narration from **Sightseeing Tapes, Inc.** You put a deposit on the machine, and pay the $8 rental fee for the tape, and start out to follow the description of many interesting points in the national park. The advantage here is that this tour is cheaper overall if you have several people in your car, and you can turn off the tape at any time should you want to spend a while at some point. Tapes and machines are for rent at the National Park Visitor Center at Hulls Cove, the first park entrance you come to when approaching Bar Harbor from the north on Route 3.

A Ferry to Nova Scotia

The CN Marine ship M/V *Bluenose* sails from Bar Harbor to Yarmouth, Nova Scotia, and back again daily in summer between mid-June and late September. It's a car-ferry with room for 700 passengers and 150 cars, a sundeck, cafeteria, bar, casino, and duty-free shop. The *Bluenose* leaves Bar Harbor every morning in summer and returns from Yarmouth in late afternoon, arriving back in Bar Harbor at night. The trip takes about six hours each way, and costs $22 per adult, $11 per child 5 to 13 years; cars cost $52.50; trailers and campers cost $5.30 per foot, with a summertime minimum charge of the normal car's fare. You can rent a day-use cabin for an extra $19. Off-season schedules are such that the ferry leaves Bar Harbor one day and returns the next; fares are about 40% lower. The vehicle fees do not include the driver's ticket, so a car-and-driver crossing in summer would pay a total of $74.50. Note that *you must make reservations in advance.* Write to the Marine Reservations Bureau, P.O. Box 250, North Sydney, NS B2A 3M3, Canada; or call these toll-free numbers: in Maine, 800/432-7344; in the continental U.S., 800/341-7981. The number in Bar Harbor is 207/288-3395. In Yarmouth, write to the terminal supervisor there or call 902/742-3513.

ON TO CANADA: The coastal highway, U.S. 1, winds east and north from Ellsworth. You might want to wander south along Route 186 for views of the scenic **Schoodic Peninsula.** If not, head ever northeastward, toward the Canadian frontier.

When you get to Cobscook Bay, you will have reached the easternmost limits of the United States. Cobscook Bay can boast two state parks, **Cobscook Bay State Park** and **Quoddy Head State Park.** Another park is even more interesting, however.

Roosevelt Campobello International Park

A Canadian island with an Italian-sounding name on which an American president spent his summers? These little mysteries are not at all as difficult to solve as one might suppose. Campobello Island is officially part of Canada, even though the major access road comes from Lubec, Maine. And the "Italian" name is nothing more than the name of a former Nova Scotian governor, William Campbell, with two "o's" added for exotic flavor. When the island was granted to Capt. William Owen by Governor Campbell in 1767, it was still part of the Canadian province of Nova Scotia. (The province of New Brunswick was not formed until 1784, when large numbers of United Empire Loyalists fled New England to live in King George III's still-loyal dominions to the north.)

Franklin Delano Roosevelt's father, James, bought some land on the island in 1883, at a time when lots of important city people were building vast "summer cottages" at Bar Harbor, Passamaquoddy Bay, and other northern coastal locations. Young Franklin—to solve that last little mystery—came here long before he was president of the United States, and spent many a teenaged summer rowing, paddling, and sailing on the waters, and hiking through the woods.

In 1920 FDR ran for the vice-presidency—and lost. Taking on a banking job instead, he looked forward to a relaxing summer at Campobello in 1921. On August 10 of that year the first signs of illness showed, and two weeks later the doctors diagnosed the crippling disease as polio. When he left the island in September, he had no way of knowing that the few more times he would see the summer cottage and his Campobello friends would be brief weekend visits —as president of the United States.

The day-to-day lives of the great and powerful are fascinating to explore in detail, and a visit to the Roosevelt house on Campobello Island gives one a peek at the early years of this incredibly courageous man who went on to become governor of New York and president of the United States after having been crippled by polio. It is no less intriguing to see how a well-to-do family spent its summers at the turn of the century, with long and leisurely days filled by sports, games, and family fun. Servants saw to the chores, and even they must have enjoyed getting away from the city to such a beautiful spot.

The Roosevelt Cottage is now part of **Roosevelt Campobello International Park,** a joint American-Canadian effort open to everyone from late May to mid-October, 9 a.m. to 5 p.m. Guides at the reception center will point out the path to the Roosevelt Cottage, show you movies about the island, and map out the various walks and drives in the 2600-acre nature preserve.

Calais–St. Stephen

Residents of Maine and New Brunswick, while the best of friends, cling to memories of their ancestors' fervent support for, respectively, George Washington and George III. With the success of the American Revolution, United Empire Loyalists flocked across the frontier into Canada so as not to be disloyal to the monarch. The "Loyalist" and "Revolutionary" towns preserve this good-natured rivalry.

But things are different in Calais, Me. (pronounced like "callous"), and its sister city, St. Stephen, N.B. Folks in these two towns, cheek-by-jowl on the St. Croix River, make a point of telling visitors how they ignored the affinities of *both* sides during the War of 1812, and St. Stephen even supplied powder-poor Calais with gunpowder for its Fourth of July celebrations! In fact by the time the war came families in the twin towns were so closely intermarried that no one wanted to take the time to sort out who should be loyal to whom.

These days residents celebrate this unique plague-on-both-their-houses philosophy with an International Festival in the first week of August. The two bridges over the river between the towns are thronged with merrymakers moving back and forth—through the watchful but benevolent eye of Customs, of course—and Canadian and American flags fly everywhere.

Despite its interesting history, there's little to detain you in Calais, and soon you'll be heading onward, into Canada (see Frommer's *Dollarwise Guide to Canada*), or back down U.S. 1 to points south and west. When you return home, however, you'll know what the maritime forecasters mean when they predict weather for the coastline "from Eastport (on Cobscook Bay) to Block Island (Rhode Island)." And you'll be able to say that you've been at the easternmost point in the United States.

Chapter XIII

VERMONT

1. Brattleboro
2. Marlboro, Newfane, and Grafton
3. Bennington
4. Mount Snow
5. Manchester and Dorset
6. Woodstock and Plymouth
7. Killington
8. Middlebury
9. Sugarbush
10. Stowe
11. Burlington

THE GREEN MOUNTAIN STATE is one of the nation's most rural, with lots of trees and very few people—only about half a million (people, not trees) in the whole state. But the greenery is Vermont's glory, and green has even become the color of the state's auto license plates. To protect the sylvan beauty of their state, and to keep the roads from becoming cluttered with "off-site advertising," the state government has devised a plan whereby participating stores, restaurants, lodging places, and attractions put information on their establishments in a little book called the *Vermont Visitors' Handbook*, yours for free by writing to the Vermont Development Agency, Montpelier, VT 05602. The establishments in the handbook have numbers, and an attractive green sign out on the highway nearby will direct you to the store, restaurant, or motel, and will also bear its number.

Skiing is another of Vermont's glories, and resorts in this state are usually more winter than summer oriented. Heavy precipitation gives many ski areas a good, long season, and the mountain scenery and imported "alpine" architecture help get one into the spirit of winter fun. No Vermont lodge would think of opening without its fireplace stocked with logs to give the glow to an après-ski cocktail and conversation.

Although winter is its prime season, Vermont is very much open in summer. Room rates are lower, many ski resorts run their chair and gondola lifts for sightseers, and the state parks do a booming business with campers, hikers, and picnickers. And, winter or summer, most places in Vermont have the distinct advantage of being quite accessible, whether you plan to come by car, bus, train, or air.

The tax on rooms is 5%, and the telephone area code for the entire state is 802.

INFORMATION: Vermont rates tourism as its second most important industry, and it's therefore out to tell you what you want to know. In New York City, ask them at the **New England Vacation Center**, 630 Fifth Ave., between 50th and 51st Streets, Rockefeller Center Concourse Shop No. 2 (tel. 212/307-5780). State information booths are maintained on the major access roads to the state; stop at one for a map and for the *Vermont Visitors' Handbook* mentioned above.

GETTING THERE: For being so rural, resorts and towns in Vermont are surprisingly accessible.

By Car

The fastest way to get anywhere by car is to take the Interstates: I-91 from New York City and Connecticut, I-93 to I-89 from Boston and Canada, 10 to 133 to I-89 if you're driving from Montréal. But the heart of Vermont is on and off Vermont's Route 100 which winds through the center of the state from north to south, linking most of the resort areas. By the way, Vermont has a law which prohibits skis from sticking out beyond the normal width of the car. Roads are very well maintained in Vermont in winter, but remember that the roads into the mountains are gradients, so it's best to have snowtires. Dry gas, to prevent your fuel lines from freezing, isn't a bad idea either.

By Air

Two large airlines, **Delta** and **USAir** run services to Burlington from the Eastern Seaboard and the Midwest, and also from Boston. Here's a summary of regional air service:

Air North, 1150 Airport Dr. (P.O. Box 2326), Burlington, VT 05401 (tel. toll free 800/451-3432), connects Vermont and northern New York state with Boston and Washington (National). The route between Boston and Burlington (Vt.) is the most popular. They also serve White Plains (N.Y.).

Air Vermont, 1795 South Williston Rd., South Burlington, VT 05401 (tel. 802/863-1110, or toll free 800/322-9300 in Vermont, 800/343-8828 outside Vermont). Air Vermont cities are New York (JFK), Hartford/Springfield, Albany, Burlington, Newport (Vt.), Berlin (N.H.), Portland (Me.), Boston, Worcester, and Nantucket, plus Long Island.

Precision Airlines, Springfield-Harkness State Airport, North Springfield, VT 05150 (tel. toll free 800/451-4221 in New York and New England), connects Vermont with Boston, New York City (La Guardia) and other points, flying among these cities: Rutland, Montpelier and Springfield (Vt.); Pittsfield (Mass.); Manchester, Keene, Lebanon (White River Junction), and Laconia (N.H.).

By Rail

Two Amtrak trains serve Vermont; both running between New York City and Montréal. The *Montrealer* runs daily between Washington, D.C., via New York City to Montréal, stopping in Brattleboro (for Mt. Snow), Bellows Falls, White River Junction (for Woodstock and Killington), Montpelier, Waterbury (for Stowe), Essex Junction (for Burlington), and St. Albans. Unfortunately, the *Montrealer* is the New York-Montréal night train.

The *Adirondack* runs daily between New York City and Montréal, skirting Vermont as it runs up the Hudson. Stops at Whitehall (for Rutland), Port Henry, and Port Kent (for Burlington) are the most convenient for reaching points in Vermont, although there are lots of other stops. The *Adirondack* is a day train.

By Bus

Luckily for visitors, Vermont has its own large bus line, **Vermont Transit Lines,** which operates from New York (in conjunction with Greyhound), Montréal (in conjunction with Voyageur), and Boston to virtually all points of interest in Vermont. Other services run from Portsmouth, N.H., Portland, Me., and Concord, N.H., to points in Vermont. The only important exception to Vermont Transit's all-state operations is the route between Keene (N.H.)— Brattleboro—Bennington, which is operated by **People's Bus Lines, Inc.**

1. Brattleboro

The first town you are likely to encounter if you come from New York or Boston is Brattleboro, and in a way this is as it should be, for Brattleboro was the site of Vermont's first colonial settlement. In 1724 a small fortress was built at the spot now marked by a granite commemoration stone, and named Fort Dummer. There had been white settlers in the area before that, but the fort became the focal point of a community as well as its principal defense against the Indians.

Today Brattleboro is one of the state's larger cities, with a population around 13,000, and industries that range from printing and book manufacture to furniture making and the manufacture of optical products. As for famous sons, the great Mormon leader Brigham Young was born (1801) nearby in Windham County, and Rudyard Kipling married a Brattleboro girl in 1892, and they lived near the town for some time.

Brattleboro has some attractive residential sections and a decent collection of lodging places and dining places. The largest collection of motels is on U.S. 5 north of Brattleboro on the way to Putney (Exit 3N from I-95); another collection of places to stay and to dine is on Route 9 west of Brattleboro (I-95 Exit 2).

If you have an hour to spend in town before you rush off to the music festival at Marlboro, or the hiking and skiing at surrounding resorts, check out the **Brattleboro Museum and Art Center,** in the town's old Union Station down near the intersection of Routes 119, 142, and U.S. 5, only a few steps from the center of town. Established in 1972, the fledgling museum is the center of art appreciation in a town filled with creative people. It's open Tuesday through Sunday from 1 to 4 p.m.

INFORMATION: The chamber of commerce information office is at 180 Main St., right in the center of town (tel. 802/254-4565), open during business hours.

WHERE TO STAY: Here's a look at the motels which line U.S. 5 (Putney Road) north of Brattleboro.

Try the **Lamplighter Motel** (tel. 802/254-2357), near the Holiday Inn on U.S. 5, Brattleboro, VT 05301. The Lamplighter has an older wing of rooms with double beds, and a newer building with larger and slightly more modern rooms equipped with queen-size beds. Although the rooms in the newer section are a bit more comfortable, those in the older section have the advantage of looking onto a small fenced patch of lawn with some nice evergreens. The lower prices are for the older section: $27.30 to $33.60 double; and in the newer section, it's $35.70 to $50.40 double. Rooms are air-conditioned, equipped with TVs, and the motel has a pool. The room buildings are positioned perpendicular to the highway (as are most hotels on this stretch of U.S. 5), and so road noise is not really much of a problem. Whether you stay at the Lamplighter or not, you can stop in to try their little Steak House restaurant, where a steak for supper will cost $7 to $11 depending on size and cut.

The best motel buy in town is, as always, the **Susse Chalet Motor Lodge** (tel. 802/254-6007, or toll free 800/258-1980), near the Holiday Inn and the Lamplighter, Brattleboro, VT 05301. At the Susse Chalet you get a modern, air-conditioned motel room with shiny private bath, TV, and comfortable modern furnishings for the low prices of $24.90 for one, $29.10 for two, $32.25 for three, or $35.40 for four in a room. Prices stay the same year round. The motel even has a small outdoor pool. Most people read the name "Susse" and think it should be "Suisse," but there's no connection between these motels and Switzerland, except that they are both clean, pretty, and efficient. The big difference these days is that Switzerland is expensive and rooms at Susse Chalets are not!

WHERE TO DINE: Brattleboro's restaurants are found out in the countryside as well as downtown.

On Route 9 a few miles west of town, two of Brattleboro's favorite dining places await you. Foremost is the famous **Country Kitchen** (tel. 257-0338), always busy with local patrons and others from farther away, but the interesting new building must have half a dozen dining rooms, and so can accommodate large crowds. All the rooms are different, some are low-ceilinged and old-fashioned, one has an A-frame cathedral ceiling, others have skylights, fireplaces, and large and somewhat disturbing modern paintings; some have cozy dark-wood booths and others have dressy tables and chairs. The main building materials are dark wood and white stucco or plaster. The dinner menu features seafood, poultry, and steaks, besides many other popular choices. At lunch, try the New England turkey pot pie ($5.75) if it's offered, or have one of the money-saving daily specials such as chopped sirloin with mushroom gravy ($4, or $6 for the full lunch). When most Brattleboro people want to celebrate an anniversary, a birthday, or the like, the Country Kitchen is where they come. It's open for lunch Monday through Saturday from 11:30 a.m. to 4 p.m.; for dinner the same days 4 to 10 p.m.; on Sunday to 9 p.m.

Located on Route 9 in West Brattleboro is **The Jolly Butcher's Tavern** (tel. 254-6043), open for lunch (June through October only) from 11:30 a.m. to 2:30 p.m., and all year for dinner each evening 5 to 10 p.m., on Sunday noon to 9 p.m. The restaurant is ten years old but built to look like a barn, with an oxen yoke over one door as you enter, replicas of Tiffany lamps here and there, and the popular bentwood furniture. The Jolly Butcher's is a seafood and beef place: seven beef and seven seafood entrees are served ($8.50 to $10), but there's also chicken. A trip to the salad bar, potato, and hot bread are included. For dessert, there's Häagen-Dazs ice cream.

Common Ground (tel. 257-0855) is downtown Brattleboro's natural-foods restaurant, and also its foremost coffeehouse (live music on weekends) and gallery for local artists. It's at 25 Elliot St. (upstairs), and its second-floor location allows it to utilize a nice upper-level outdoor terrace set with café tables and umbrellas in the warm months. As you enter from the street, you'll notice that the entryway and stairwell serves as Brattleboro's "alternative" bulletin board. The menu is interesting and international, with dishes from Greece, Italy, China, France, Spain, Austria, Japan, and the U.S.A., to name but a few. The prices are certainly reasonable (about $8 for dinner), the food delicious, and the staff friendly. At lunch, the menu is scratched on a blackboard at the top of the stairway. Common Ground is open for lunch Monday through Saturday from 11:30 a.m. to 2:30 p.m., for Sunday brunch from 10:30 a.m. to 1:30 p.m. Dinner service is provided Wednesday through Sunday only, 5:30 to 9 p.m.

Near Common Ground is Brattleboro's Italian restaurant, the **Via Condotti** (tel. 257-0094), 69 Elliot St., just a block off Main in the center of town. Stucco walls give the place an old country air, and copper kitchen utensils hung here and there add to the effect. Although it's much more pleasant to have a waiter or waitress serve you, it's useful to know that all orders can be put up to take out, from the grinders (the large sandwiches at $2.50 to $3) to the calamari alla marinara (squid). Pasta dishes start at $3.75; baked manicotti is $4.35; the price range ascends slowly to a high of $7.95 for the veal parmigiana. In the restaurant's La Grotta lounge, wines are sold by the glass, half liter, or liter, beers by the mug or the pitcher, and all sorts of cocktails are available. The Via Condotti is open seven days a week, Monday through Saturday for lunch and dinner, Sunday for dinner from 4 p.m.; the lounge is open from 4 p.m. to 1 a.m. daily, with food service until 11 p.m. on weekdays, to midnight on weekends.

Although Brattleboro is a nice city, it's the surrounding villages and resorts which draw the crowds. One of the most popular of these is Marlboro, home of the famous annual Marlboro Music Festival.

2. Marlboro, Newfane, and Grafton

West and north of Brattleboro are some of Vermont's—and all New England's—loveliest unspoiled villages, worthy of a few days' stay, or at least a meal or a rest stop. Newfane is north of Brattleboro on Route 30, and Grafton is even farther north on Route 35 between Townshend and Chester. Visit them on your way north to Woodstock or Killington. Marlboro is on Route 9, west of Brattleboro, in the direction of Bennington.

MARLBORO: The town's name brings to mind immediately the **Marlboro Music Festival,** directed by Rudolf Serkin each summer. The festival brings together dozens of the most talented musicians in the country, some famous and some soon to be famous, for two months' practice, consultation, and tutorial. On weekends, the school is opened to concert audiences, most of whom have ordered their tickets weeks or months in advance and have also made early lodging reservations. The auditorium at Marlboro College seats fewer than 700 people, and to keep the spirit of the chamber music, demands for a larger hall are resisted by the directors and performers. If you're interested in attending weekend festival concerts, write early to: Marlboro Festival, Marlboro, VT 05344; or phone the box office at 802/254-8163 or 254-2394, and ask for schedules, prices, and purchase forms. Then, when you've got your tickets, make a reservation either in Marlboro, or nearby Brattleboro, or even in Bennington—that city is only a 45-minute drive away through the forests of southern Vermont.

Where to Stay and Eat

Marlboro is a location more than a town, although when you drive to the dot on the map you will find a church, a small town office building, and several houses. But that's about all, and so for many products and services you must drive to Brattleboro. Several inns and restaurants in the area, however, provide well for year-round travelers as well as festival visitors.

The only lodging house right in Marlboro proper is the fine old **Whetstone Inn** (tel. 802/254-2500), Marlboro, VT 05344. Many establishments call themselves "country inns," even though they may have motel-style rooms, color TVs, and all the other paraphernalia of 20th-century travel, but the Whetstone Inn is a country inn in the true sense: a gracious old house filled with period furniture and run by a friendly and engaging couple, Harry and Jean Boardman. In fact, the Whetstone Inn has been an inn for close to two centuries: the upstairs was once a "ballroom" where the local gentry could stage their get-togethers; the downstairs was a tavern along the stagecoach route between Brattleboro and Bennington. In winter, cross-country ski trails start at the inn's back door. The inn's pond (the reservoir in case of fire) is right out back, bordered by rushes and cattails, and in a nearby copse of white birches are tables and chairs for an afternoon's reading or an evening's conversation. As there's no great activity in the town, nothing will disturb you unless you take to your feet or your bicycle to go to the music festival, two miles away. Many rooms at the Whetstone Inn have private bathrooms, others have lavatories; rates are $21 single, $31.50 to $52.50 double, the higher rates being for apartments with kitchenette. Rates are a bit higher during the Marlboro Music Festival. Meals are not included, but you can get breakfast each morning (waffles, pancakes, popovers, and home-baked muffins and biscuits), dinners on concert nights during the summer and on weekends and certain weekdays at other times in the year.

On Route 9, a half mile from the center of Marlboro village, is the **Silver Skates Inn** (tel. 802/254-2894), Marlboro, VT 05344, a modern place known as much for its food as for its rooms. Part of the ground floor and the second floor of the inn is given over to modern guest rooms with private baths, priced at $35.70 to $46.20 double. The restaurant is continental, with prices on the higher side of the moderate range, but with food worthy of the prices: onion soup gratiné, a seafood aspic, viande des grisons (air-dried beef, a Swiss specialty) are priced from $3 to $4. Main courses ($10.50 to $14) include coq au vin, European pepper steak, wienerschnitzel, and for those with an urge to splurge, chateaubriand frascati made with liver pâté and mushrooms in a madeira sauce. The dining room is pleasant but simple, the emphasis being on the food. Owner-chef Hans Imboden has run the Silver Skates for years and has built a solid reputation for gracious and very friendly service, excellent food, and fair prices.

The **Skyline Restaurant** (tel. 464-5535) is just across Route 9 from a hilltop lookout. The restaurant is open daily in summer from 8 a.m. to 8:30 p.m.; from November 1 until July 1 the hours are 8 a.m. to 8 p.m. Wednesday through Sunday, and 8 a.m. to 3 p.m. Monday and Tuesday. Thus you can start the day here with a breakfast of griddle cakes and maple syrup for about $4.50. Luncheon special plates cost $3.50 to $7.50; entrees à la carte cost about $6 to $9. For dinner, pan-fried trout with almond butter is a good choice, or have cured ham steak in apricot brandy. Saturday night is prime rib of beef night, when this specialty comes with vegetable and potato for $11. The emphasis at the Skyline is obviously not on the expensive or exotic, but rather on traditional dishes made with care and with the best local ingredients. Rough wood furniture and accents make the decor, and fresh flowers cheer up every table in season. During the cold weather, the cheer is provided by a fireplace, and as always, by the friendliness of the staff and management.

READER'S INN SELECTION: "Our inn at Marlboro turned out to be the high point of our trip. The **Longwood Inn** (tel. 802/257-1545) is run by Tom and Janet Durkin. Our lovely room was $42 double, and included a huge breakfast served by a picture window overlooking the terrace and pond. The chef at the Longwood is superb, and we thought our dinner there to be on a par with some of the best restaurants in the Washington, D.C., area: excellent braised rabbit and poached salmon, with wine, for $42" (Mrs. Robert Perry, Falls Church, Va.).

HOGBACK SKIING: The Hogback area (tel. 802/464-5494) is small but pleasant, with four T-bars taking skiiers to the top of a 500-foot vertical drop. It's a favorite with local people and with families, and has a cafeteria, equipment rental shop, and plans for ski touring.

NEWFANE: A small New England town right out of a picturebook, Newfane has churches and town hall and old inns clustered around the Town Green, pretty as can be. Although it is beautiful and well preserved, visitors flock to Newfane not so much for the town itself as for its gastronomic reputation. Several old inns have been bought up by chefs and operated as lodging places, certainly, but more important, as restaurants.

The thing to do in Newfane is walk around and admire the town, its rows of sugar maples along the main streets (tapped by the town's youngsters in spring), drop in at the little municipal library, or peek into a church, and then go for lunch or dinner at Jacques and Sandra Allembert's **Four Columns Inn** (tel. 365-7713). Lunch is served from noon to 2 p.m., dinner from 6 to 9 p.m. every day but Tuesday in summer (end of May through October). In winter, dinner only is served. The inn and restaurant are closed every Tuesday and the entire months of April and November (until Thanksgiving).

The Four Columns' dining room, in the red barn behind the inn proper, makes one think immediately of a hunting lodge in Europe: stuffed deer heads, rough-hewn beams, a big fireplace, spindle-back chairs. But the cuisine is elegant and French inspired. For example, one starts with pheasant pâté or oysters, passing on to sole, salmon, duck, or steaks, with fancy pastries and continental concoctions for dessert. Dinner can cost $60 to $75 for two, with wine, tax, and tip included. Wines are priced from $10 to $50 a bottle. Have reservations.

Should you want to stay overnight at the Four Columns, double rooms cost $52.50 to $84, with private bath and air conditioning. It's a good idea to look at the room before you sign in.

GRAFTON: Like Newfane, Grafton is a piece of old New England, but there is a nobility about this town—something like Woodstock—that makes it special. Carefully preserved houses and public buildings from a century or two ago are joined unobtrusively by more modern structures on the outskirts. Summer or winter, Grafton is a place bewitching in its beauty. Stop for a cup of coffee, a drink or a meal, or even for overnight. Be careful though—one overnight easily leads to week-long stays here.

Grafton's hostelry, the **Old Tavern** (tel. 802/843-2231), Grafton, VT 05146, is also a town landmark. It's been the center of Grafton's social life since it was built in 1801 as a way-station on the stagecoach road. In its long history as a place to stay the night, the Old Tavern has played host to General Grant, Woodrow Wilson, Rudyard Kipling, and even woodsman-philosopher Henry David Thoreau. With its annexes, the inn can lodge about 100 people. Its rooms have private baths and modern conveniences, but the ambience is still old New England. Rates vary with the exact situation, size, and facilities, but range from $35 to $80, plus the 5% Vermont tax. The Old Tavern is an authentic landmark, but it is not what one would call "quaint." Charming, hospitable, very comfortable—it is all these, though.

To dine here, you have a choice of dining rooms. The jacket rule is in force each evening. For a drink before dinner, make you way to the Barn, with its own separate bar, several fireplaces, and a TV room. Lunch is served at the Old Tavern from noon to 2 p.m., dinner from 6:30 to 9 p.m., by reservation. At dinner, main courses range from the raisin-stuffed veal steak ($11.50) to broiled filet mignon ($16.50), and these prices include soup, relish tray, potato, and vegetable.

What to Do

Grafton is perfect just for relaxing walks and sitting by the fireplace, but there are lots of other things to do as well. Start with a horse-and-carriage ride (in summer) around town. You'll see the driver, her steed, and her buggy at the stand in front of the Old Tavern daily except Sunday between mid-June and the end of October. The ride is not just for fun—you'll get a complete narrative tour of Grafton as you trot along.

Grafton harbors a number of antique shops, artists' galleries, a village store, and the **Grafton Village Cheese Company** (tel. 843-2221). The Cheese Company makes its own brand, Covered Bridge Cheddar, and you can see it being made and buy samples or supplies by following the Townshend Road about a half mile south of the village. Hours are 8:30 a.m. to 4 p.m. weekdays all year; 10 a.m. to 4:30 p.m. on Saturday from June through October; closed Sunday all year.

By now no doubt you are completely enchanted with the town. To delve into its history, pay a visit to the **Grafton Historical Society Museum** (tel. 843-2388), on Main Street just down from the post office. The exhibits of Grafton memorabilia, old photographs, history, and genealogical books are open from 2:30 to 4:30 p.m. on Saturday from June through mid-October, on Sunday in July and August, and on holiday weekends and holiday Mondays.

3. Bennington

"Vermont's most historic area" is how the citizens of Bennington tout their town. The reason for this civic pride is that the Revolutionary War's Battle of Bennington was fought near here (the actual site is now in neighboring Walloomsac, N.Y.) in 1777. The battle is looked upon as a turning point in the war, since the British troops expected to encounter little resistance at Bennington, and instead were forced to retreat after having lost a good number of casualties and prisoners to the Revolutionaries. Soon afterward, at the Battle of Saratoga, the British soldiers thus weakened were forced to surrender, giving the Americans their first great victory of the war.

Although the Battle of Bennington was certainly influential in the winning of the war, it is doubtless remembered so well today because of a 300-foot-high obelisk which was built in 1891 to commemorate it. Both the monument (which has an observation platform) and the well-known Bennington Museum's collection of Americana are open to visitors.

INFORMATION: The **Greater Bennington Chamber of Commerce** is at Veterans' Memorial Drive (Route 7 North; tel. 442-5900 or 442-4545), about a mile from the intersection of Main and North/South Streets. Open during business hours, the chamber can give you a good, detailed map of the town and lots of information on both the town and the surrounding region.

WHERE TO STAY: Bennington has dozens of motels on the highways which approach it, but as is my custom I will concentrate most heavily on the establishments right in town. Several are within only a few blocks of the monument, the museum, and Old Bennington.

Whether or not it bears any resemblance to the celestial place of the same name, the **Paradise Motor Inn** (tel. 802/442-5418 or 442-8351) is certainly plush. Three different modern buildings contain lodging units, and the price and degree of luxury varies a bit from one to another. All are quite modern and comfortable, many have extra-large beds, and each room has some view of the Vermont greenery which abounds in these parts; some look right out onto the swimming pool. Prices for the rooms in summer are $50.40 to $68.25, all double, depending on building and view, and the room's size. Besides its many rooms, the Paradise has its own fancy restaurant with a fine indoor dining room and an outdoor shaded terrace for warm-weather lunches and suppers, a heated swimming pool, and several new tennis courts which guests can use free of charge. The center of town is only a ten-minute walk away, the museum and monument are just around the corner: from the town's main crossroads, go west on Main Street toward these attractions, and the motel will be several blocks down on your left. The mail address is 141 Main St., Bennington, VT 05201.

An exception to the in-town rule is the particularly nice **Best Western New Englander Motor Inn** (tel. 802/442-6311, or toll free 800/528-1234), 220 Northside Dr., Bennington, VT 05201. (Northside Drive is Route Business 7 between Bennington and North Bennington.) The New Englander is a fairly large motel of over 50 rooms arranged around a central court with a swimming pool and the motel's Heritage House restaurant, which helps block noise from the busy street. Trees and garden patches dot the inner court, and the layout is such that very few rooms are directly exposed to street noise. As this is Bennington, the rooms have been done with early American inspiration, although all furnishings are modern. In the clutter and strip development of Northside Drive, the New Englander is a very pleasant oasis, complete unto itself, and rooms are moderately priced at $46.20 for a double-bedded room for two, $50.40 for a similar room equipped with a steambath, $38.85 for a room with one double and one twin bed (a slightly larger room), and $4 for an extra person. These summer prices are about $9 or so less per room during the winter months. Note that the New Englander's rooms have cable color TV, coffeemakers, and air conditioning. It's a comfortable, pleasant place.

The **Kirkside Motor Lodge** is just that: right beside the handsome Gothic church, at 250 W. Main St., Bennington, VT 05201 (tel. 802/447-7596). Recently the hotel came under new owner/management, and all the rooms have been modernized and refurbished. Rates are $36.75 for a double bed, $42 for a queen-size bed, $46.20 for a king-size bed, all rooms for two people. Off-season, prices will be about one-third less. The rooms come with cable color TV and the usual motel comforts, only here they're shiny and new. There's little problem with street noise because of the motel's position and location. If you stay here, you'll be about equidistant from the center of town and the museum or monument.

The **Bennington Motel** (tel. 802/442-5479), has the same location as the expensive Paradise, but at much reduced prices. At 143 W. Main St., the Bennington is smack up against the Paradise, its 16 little units right at the base of the hill holding the museum and monument. The little extras here include coffee-makers in the rooms, color TV on the cable (which also pipes in FM radio), individual thermostats, air conditioners, and direct-dial telephones. Some of the larger rooms, designated "family units," can sleep up to six people, and these rooms also have little refrigerators for baby's bottle—or for papa's. In one double bed, two people pay $29.40 to $31.50, for two beds they pay $33.60 to $37.80, and an extra person pays $4; an extra bed is $4. These are the higher summer-season rates, and if you come during the colder months (the Bennington Motel's open all year) you'll find the rates lower.

An Authentic Inn

Your first glance at the **Walloomsac Inn** will leave you cold, even though it is located at 67 Monument Ave. in Old Bennington, VT 05201 (tel. 802/442-4865). This is Bennington's most beautiful street, and the inn looks as though little has been done to its exterior since it was built a century ago. But go inside and you'll find a charming, clean, and comfy inn operated by the Berry family, descendants of the people who have run the inn since the 1890s. The entire interior of the Walloomsac is a period piece, from the grilled cashier's desk to the rooms themselves. Huge, replete with the original furnishings which are now antiques, and complete with large bathrooms, the Walloomsac's rooms are the biggest bargains in Bennington at only $25.20 for two, with bath. At these prices, they go fast, so you should have ironclad reservations for any busy period.

Guest Houses

Luckily for our budget readers, Bennington is particularly well endowed with fine guest houses, those establishments which give you more warmth and home comfort than any other type of lodging place. One of the nicest and best located is in the grand old house at 226 W. Main St., Bennington, VT 05201, not far from the Bennington Museum. It's the **Mount Anthony House** (tel. 802/447-7396), a fine aristocratic dwelling with a large, almost wrap-around sunporch and cozy rooms which rent for $14.70 single, $16.80 double with shared baths, $20 with private baths. People paying three times that much for a place to sleep are almost across the street in the Paradise. The house accepts guests all year round.

The **Colonial Guest House** (tel. 802/442-2263) seems more like an inn than a tourist home, with seven bedrooms (six with running water), a dining room with fireplace, two parlors, and a nice outdoor patio and picnic area. Doubles with a shared bath are $15.75 to $18.90, in either twin beds or a double bed. One room has a private bath and costs $28 double, another has four single beds and a cable TV all for $28. Some rooms are air-conditioned. If you let Mr. and Mrs. Reis know in advance, they'll fix you a fine family-style breakfast or dinner. The Colonial Guest House is at Historic Route 7A North and Orchard Road, on Harwood Hill, Bennington, VT 05201.

READER'S SUGGESTION: "We made a wonderful stop at the **Hill Farm Inn** (tel. 802/375-2269), R.R. No. 2, Box 2015, Arlington VT 05250. It's a short distance north of Bennington off Route 7A. It's been an inn since 1905; George and JoAnne Hardy keep up the tradition well, and are so friendly. They have seven guest rooms in the inn, plus some cabins in the summer months. For a room with shared bath, double, we paid $58.80, and that included full breakfast, dinner, and tax. Rooms with private bath were only a few dollars more" (Arthur and Leonore Johnson, Toledo, Ohio).

WHERE TO EAT: A few restaurants in Bennington (besides those in the motels) provide plain and fancy cuisine for travelers and local folks. I'll start with the fancy places.

In Bennington there is a place called the Potters' Yard, a complex of shops and galleries in which local works of art and craft are displayed and sold, and in this same complex at School and County Streets is the **Brasserie in Potters' Yard** (tel. 447-7922). As the name might suggest, the Brasserie is fashioned on a French tavern restaurant, with beer and wine and delicious dishes such as the pâté maison with french bread or southern-style pickled shrimp. For lunch, have the Yard Special, a platter with Danish pâté, french bread, butter, and a Boston lettuce salad, for $4.50. A chef's salad or Greek salad, and a variety of sandwiches and omelets are about the same. The patio is the choice place to dine in good weather: it's paved in marble, and the little café tables all have marble or granite tops. Note that the Brasserie is open for lunch from noon to 4:30 p.m., cocktails from 4:30 to 6 p.m., and dinner from 6 to 9 p.m., closed Tuesday and Wednesday in winter only. To get to the Brasserie and Potters' Yard, turn off Main Street by the Dunkin' Donuts (which is at 460 Main), and go straight down the street until it ends right at the Yard.

Dependable, convenient, and inexpensive, that's **Geanelli's** (tel. 442-9778), 520 Main St. right downtown in Bennington. This modern lunch counter/restaurant is open seven days a week from 7 a.m. to 8 p.m., serving hamburgers for only $1.50, "maxi-cheeseburgers" for $2.50. The specialties, however, are plates called "epicurios," which come with a choice of two vegetable or salad items, rolls, and butter, and might be based on chopped sirloin smothered in onions ($4.85), or perhaps a fried haddock filet for a similar price, up to $7 for the grilled club steak "epicurio." Seating is at your choice of colorful booths or a convenient lunch counter.

Reader Nancy Roudebush of Chevy Chase, Md., tipped me off to **Schwinn's** (tel. 442-2000), 101 W. Main St., just down the hill from the Bennington Museum. No, this is not a bicycle-rental shop, but an attractive Swiss-chalet-style stucco restaurant, complete with geranium-filled window boxes. Schwinn's is open from 11 a.m. to 8 p.m. every day except Tuesday, serving sandwiches for around $2, and salads, cheeseburgers, knockwursts, weiss-würsts, and bratwürsts for the same. After 5 p.m. dinner is served, and the most expensive main course, including vegetable and potato, is sauerbraten or pot roast for $5.25. How can you beat it? They even serve wine and beer.

WHAT TO SEE: The historic sights of the town are mostly grouped along West Main Street, in the section called Old Bennington.

The Bennington Museum

The museum has a collection dominated by that for which the town was famous: its Revolutionary and early American history. Paintings, glass items both blown and pressed, American-made furniture and carvings, arms, toys, and costumes are all included, and there are considerable numbers of very attractive treasures. The Bennington pottery, for instance, is more like china with its gold or colored trim; it was made here for wealthy customers for over 100 years. Of the paintings, the most fascinating are the ones in the Grandma Moses collection. Anna Mary Moses (1860–1961) was a farm girl in nearby New York state, and later as a farmer's wife she did all the heavy, hard work that life on a farm demands. But after she was 70 years old and could no longer keep up with heavy work, she taught herself to paint in a charming and primitive way which had such spirit to it that one of her paintings now hangs in the Metropolitan in New York, and many others are here in the Bennington Museum. At the age of 100 she was still at work, and she died at 101. You can look back into what life was like for her in the exhibit called the Grandma Moses Schoolhouse Museum, also in the Bennington Museum.

The Bennington Museum is open daily, 9 a.m. to 5 p.m., and is closed during the months of December, January, and February. Admission is $2.50 for adults, $1.50 for young people 12 to 17, free for children under 12 when accompanied by an adult.

The Bennington Battle Monument

You will want to know, first of all, that there is indeed an elevator in this 300-foot-high structure so that you needn't climb granite stairs to get to the observation deck. The stirring tale of the Battle of Bennington is outlined in a little leaflet which you can pick up as you pay the admission fee for the ride to the top. First, you will learn that the battle didn't take place here, but several miles west in what is today New York; but the storehouse of American arms which attracted Gentleman Johnny Burgoyne to divert his troops from their march to Saratoga was right where the monument now stands, and so the spot is, after all, a suitable place for a commemorative monument. Should you want to visit the battlefield, go west on Route 67 from Bennington and just before Walloomsac, N.Y., is the Bennington Battlefield State Historic Site, open daily from 9 a.m. to 7 p.m. between Memorial Day weekend and Labor Day.

Park-McCullough House

Of Bennington's outstanding Victorian mansions, one is exceptionally well kept. The Park-McCullough House (tel. 442-2747), corner of West and Park Streets in North Bennington, is open for guided tours through the house daily from noon to 4 p.m. (last tour leaves at 4 p.m.) Monday through Thursday between mid-June and Mid-October. Adults pay $2; students 12 to 18, $1; under 12, free if accompanied by an adult; and there are special group rates. Besides the house, still stuffed with period furnishings and personal effects, there's a pint-size "manor" for a children's play house and a cupola-topped carriage house complete with century-old carriages.

While you're here in North Bennington, drive or walk through the campus of **Bennington College,** the unique loosely structured four-year college which stresses artistic creation and an acquaintance with nature. The situation of the college is particularly beautiful, and thus particularly well adapted for the creative efforts of the students.

4. Mount Snow

Because of its southern Vermont location, fairly near the metropolitan centers of Boston, Hartford, and New York, Mount Snow is one of the state's largest ski resorts. As of this writing, the resort, on Route 100 nine miles north of Wilmington, has been taken over by the firm which owns and operates the Killington area, and so skiers can expect to see the strong points of Killington appearing at Mount Snow: extensive snowmaking, careful attention to trail grooming, reorganization of the trail system, and an aggressive marketing strategy to give more skiers more of what they want. No doubt Mount Snow's summer programs will benefit from the experience of the Killington hands who will be brought in as advisors.

In the past, the Mount Snow lodges and hotels have aimed mostly at the motor coach trade in summer, and many places wouldn't even accept transient visitors. But with the new ownership a new outlook on summer travel will no doubt change this, and more emphasis will be given to the staples of summer resort vacations: golf, tennis, hiking, and swimming. For the latest information on doings at Mount Snow, call 802/464-3333; for snow conditions, the number is 802/464-2151; for lodging information, it's 802/464-8501.

WHERE TO STAY: Close to 100 lodges, inns, and motels are clustered near the ski area or out on the approach roads, and more lodgings are available in the nearby towns of Brattleboro and Marlboro.

The centerpiece of the ski area's accommodations is the **Snow Lake Lodge** (tel. 802/464-3331, or toll free 800/451-4211), Mount Snow, VT 05356, a mammoth hotel which looks out across the man-made lake to the ski slopes. All 105 rooms have some view, but of course one pays a little more for the view of the slopes: in summer the standard room with bath, air conditioning, and a mountain view is $50.40 for two people. Color cable TV is standard in most rooms, and some rooms have waterbeds which you can get on a first-come, first-served basis. Summer golf-week and winter ski-week packages are always offered.

The **Ironstone** (tel. 802/464-3796), Mount Snow, VT 05356, is very near the Snow Lake Lodge, and, like the lodge, has a good number of rooms overlooking the lake and the slopes. All rooms here are quite modern, and have either two double beds or three beds, and all have private bath with tub and shower. A restaurant, lounge, and pool (heated) complete the services. Weekday rates *per person* include two meals in winter, and run $50.40 in a double with color TV and a mountain view, $63.60 on weekends, $69.60 on holidays; slightly less luxurious rooms with black-and-white TV and no mountain view are $45.60, $60, and $66. Extra persons pay $24.60 to $48. The food at the Ironstone is particularly good, with the standard MAP entrees (which you've already paid for) including such things as prime beef, fowl, or fish prepared differently each day (some gourmet sauces). Even if you're not staying here you can drop in for a meal. The above entrees are priced around $10 for a full-course meal.

Of the motels along Route 100 near Mount Snow, I think **Abroad Motor Inn**, West Dover, VT 05356 (tel. 802/464-3911), has the friendliest and most polite staff, the best rooms, and the most handsome design. Whereas most of the lodges right at the slopes cater only to bus tours in summer, Abroad welcomes all comers, summer and winter, with an indoor pool and whirlpool, and a charmingly rustic dining room. Summer rates are $26.25 to $44.10 per room.

Kitzhof (tel. 802/464-8310), on Route 100 in West Dover, VT 05356, is a particularly nice alpine-style lodge set back from the highway. No two rooms are alike except in their comfort, sparkling cleanliness, and the presence of private baths. Knotty-pine boards and logs add rustic emphasis, a Finnish-style sauna and a whirlpool bath are added luxuries open to all guests. There's a BYOB bar with set-ups. *Per person* rates daily in ski season are $45.15 double, $46.20 twin, $36.75 for four in a room, $35.70 for six in a room. Reductions are in order for lots of things, such as two- to four-day weekday stays, 5½-day economy ski weeks, paying in cash (5%), coming early or late in the ski season. The Kitzhof takes bus tours in summer and can provide lodging for transient guests only if there's room.

And now for a special place. **Trail's End Lodge** (tel. 802/464-9396) is about two miles from Mount Snow, four miles north of Wilmington, VT 05363, off Route 100 on a side road (watch for small signs). Despite its woodland location, Trail's End is now backwoods establishment, for it has its own swimming pool and clay tennis court, and a dining room in which remarkably delicious meals are the rule. The rates both summer and winter are usually based on room-and-two-meals: $32.20 *per person* for a small room with twin beds and shower; a larger room with a double bed and a cot costs $37.95 *per person;* a suite with two bedrooms (bunk beds) and a shower, plus a living room with a fireplace, hideaway bed, and kitchenette is $42.55 *per person;* and then $20.70 for each additional person up to six. Five- and seven-day rates are offered at a savings. Service charge of 10% and a tax of 5% are included in these prices. Trail's End is certainly one of Mount Snow's most attractive, architecturally interesting, congenial places to stay.

READER'S RESTAURANT SELECTION: "We tried a place called the **Roadhouse** (tel. 464-5017 or 464-5694), on Route 100 at Old Ark Road in Wilmington, Vt. It turned out to be good value. For $9 each we were served an above-average full dinner (except dessert), including good homemade bread. Lack of linen and a rough appearance might discourage a stranger, but the meal was really very nice. We ordered in preference to the house wines" (Mrs. Robert Perry, Falls Church, Va.).

SKIING MOUNT SNOW: The ski area is immense, with three different faces of the mountain covered with trails and lifts—13 lifts in all, including two enclosed, skis-on gondolas. The highest vertical drop is almost 2000 feet, and you could take the same lift a dozen times and never come down the same trail or slope. It's crowded, yes, because it's close to the cities, and is a good mountain for beginners and intermediate skiers, but it's also got a lot of variety, and certainly a lot of activity. A resort this big has all the facilities: a "Pumpkin Patch" nursery for small children, a bar named Reuben's, a cafeteria named Reuben's Cuzzin, and equipment rentals, a ski school, and 40 miles of cross-country trails.

In the past, Mount Snow's great size and sleeping capacity has earned it the reputation of being the "Disneyland of the North," with something for everyone in a blinding array of people, attractions, and special programs. But as it is now under the management of the Killington staff (Sherburne Corporation), programs will undoubtedly be changed and streamlined.

5. Manchester and Dorset

MANCHESTER: The town of Manchester was once a summer resort on the order of the Berkshire towns. Settled before the Revolution, its wide main street and handsome houses retain the charm of the early Federal period.

As the county seat of Bennington County, Manchester was an important place long before Mount Equinox (3800 feet), to the west, drew crowds of hikers and skiers. The sprawling Equinox resort hotel right in the center of town is undergoing a $3.4 million renovation. Its golf course, swimming pool, and other outdoor facilities are currently in use.

In the modern town of Manchester Center, just a few miles north along U.S. 7, all is bustle and activity, with traffic lights, filling stations, shopping centers, supermarkets, restaurants, motels.

On U.S. 7 is Manchester's modern claim to fame: a beautifully restored house which holds the editorial offices of *Country Journal,* the magazine which has successfully combined city polish with country concerns.

Manchester is busy with locals in the summer, busier with skiers in the winter. Several inns and restaurants serve travelers year round.

Information

The **Manchester Chamber of Commerce** (tel. 802/362-2100) maintains an information office on U.S. 7 in Manchester Center for your convenience.

Where to Stay

One can't find a bed at the Equinox yet, but by following U.S. 7 north from the center of Manchester, you'll come to several good hostelries.

The **Worthy Inn** (tel. 802/362-1792), P.O. Box 408, Manchester, VT 05254, is a huge old rambling white clapboard inn surrounded by shady lawns. A big old veranda is perfect for sitting on a warm summer day. Tennis and swimming (June through September) are free to inn guests; two 18-hole golf courses are nearby. As with many such inns, the Worthy Inn has an assortment of rooms. Some are large, with two double beds, cable color TV, and private bath ($43.20 double; $76.80 double with breakfast and dinner); others are on the second floor and share a bath ($33.60 double; $74.40 with breakfast and dinner). Yet other rooms, with and without private bath, are priced in between these two. After three days, seniors receive a 5% discount. These rates are for summer, and they include the inn's 15% service charge and the 5% Vermont tax. In winter, ski-week packages and dormitory accommodations bring down the cost of lodging and meals.

Close by is the **Inn at Manchester** (tel. 802/362-1793), P.O. Box 356, Manchester, VT 05254, a restored Vermont house with plenty of room for guests in ten bedrooms, several family rooms, and ski dorms. There's a swimming pool for summer cooling, and cheery fireplaces for après-ski. Depending on your accommodation, from simple dorm to large room with private bath, you'll pay $39.50 to $54 for a double room in summer with breakfast, or just under twice those amounts for double room with two meals in winter, tax included.

READER'S SELECTION: "We like the **Inn at Weston** (tel. 802/824-5804), on Route 100 in Weston VT 05161, mostly because of the Douglases (Sue and Stu) who run it. The food is fresh and good (you get breakfast and dinner with your room), the location is great for side trips in central Vermont. We paid $84 double per night, and that includes the two meals, and tax" (Judy Kaliontzis, Cambridge, Mass.).

What to Do

In winter, this question is easy to answer: you ski. Big Bromley, Snow Valley, Magic Mountain, Stratton Mountain, and numerous ski touring centers are located within a few miles of Manchester Center. Right in Manchester is the ski touring center at Hildene, more about which below.

In summer, you can play golf, swim, hike, or ride a bike. Rent a bike from **Battenkill Sports** (tel. 362-2734), in the stone house 1.2 miles east of U.S. 7 along Route 11/30, Manchester Center; or from the **Bicycle Shop** in Manchester Hardware (tel. 362-1625), on Route 11/30 in Manchester Center. Three-speed, ten-speed, men's, women's, and children's bikes are available.

At the Bromley ski area, an **Alpine Slide** (tel. 824-5522) draws downhill racers in summer. You pay the several dollars, take the lift to the top, and then hurtle along a twisty concrete trough on a small cart. The slide is open from late May through October from 9:30 a.m. on, if the weather's good. Bromley is eight miles east of Manchester along Route 11. By the way, the slide is fun, but the chairlift ride which takes you up over the verdant hills is equally enjoyable.

Take in a play at the **Dorset Playhouse** in nearby Dorset—see the next section in this chapter for details.

Hildene

Abraham Lincoln had four sons, but only one of them lived to adulthood. When President Lincoln was assassinated in 1865, Robert Todd Lincoln was an officer serving under General Grant in the Union Army. Later a successful lawyer and businessman, Lincoln came to Manchester in 1902, bought 412 acres of land, and began construction of Hildene. The mansion was completed in 1904, and Lincoln spent the summers there until his death in 1926. The estate was inherited by his wife, and then his granddaughter, who left it to the Church of Christ, Scientist, in 1975. It's now owned and maintained by a nonprofit group, the Friends of Hildene (tel. 362-1788).

Robert Todd Lincoln built more than a house here. In all, Hildene includes 22 buildings: a dairy barn, horse barn, sugar house, greenhouse, even a small observatory. You can roam the grounds, tour the 22-room Georgian Revival mansion, inspect Lincoln family heirlooms, any day of the week from late May through October, 10 a.m. to 4 p.m. Admission costs $3 for adults, $1.50 for children. In winter, Hildene is the site of a ski touring center. To find it, go two miles south along U.S. 7 from the intersection with Route 11/30—the intersection is the main crossroads in Manchester Center.

DORSET: Settled in 1768, Dorset is one of the many villages in New England which is older than the American Republic. It's a gem of a village, having kept its rural spirit and fine buildings intact over the centuries, and any new structures were required to add to the harmony of the village and its setting.

For a number of years Dorset was an artists' and writers' summer resort, but these days it is usually only the successful in those fields who can afford to stay in one of Dorset's few charming old inns; rather, the village now caters to those who have become successful in the city, and who need to get away to the peace of the countryside for a few days or weeks.

In Dorset the sidewalks are marble, and so is a nice church with Gothic touches not far from the town green. There's a marble quarry about a mile south of town, and besides supplying the soft, easily cut stone for a myriad of uses in Dorset, the quarry supplied most of the marble for the New York Public Library building.

For recreation, Dorset has the Dorset Playhouse (tel. 802/867-5777), down past the church just past the end of the town green on Cheney Road. Plays are performed June through October. Also, the J.K. Adams Company Factory Store, on Route 30 a mile south of town, makes fine wood products—carving boards, butcher blocks. Kitchen work tables, even kitchen organizers like a spice block which holds 16 glass jars and revolves on a lazy susan. All the items are available at a reduced price, and the "seconds" are sold at prices up to 40% off the norm.

Where to Stay and Dine

The Dorset Inn (tel. 802/867-5500 or 867-9392), right on the town green, Dorset, VT 05251, claims to be Vermont's oldest continuously operated inn. The inn has several older rooms in the original building, and a larger number of rooms in an artfully disguised modern addition which blends in well with the older part. Room prices include breakfast and dinner, and are $50.40 to $60 single, $84 to $86.40 double in one bed, $86.40 to $93.60 double in twin beds. Winter rates are similar to these summer ones. Tax and 15% service are included in these figures. Dorset Inn guests enjoy privileges at the Field Club, which is virtually next door.

On the menu at the Dorset Inn, steak appears just about every night (on nights it's not featured, though, there's an extra charge of $2 to $3), and there's also usually a seafood and a fowl entree; salad and relishes, a vegetable, and potato come with the meal, as does dessert. Dinner prices (should you just be dropping in for the meal) are $11 to $16, 15% service and 5% tax included. Cocktails, wine, and beer are served.

6. Woodstock and Plymouth

Woodstock was chartered in 1761, and within five years it had been designated the shire town (county seat) of Windsor County. The particular significance of these little facts is that they explain why the town is so beautiful today, and why so many lovely buildings survive, and why the town escaped the ravages (and riches) brought by 19th-century industry. The industry here was government, the only pollutant from which is hot air, and this rises out of sight at once.

Besides its fine buildings, Woodstock boasts no fewer than four church bells made by Paul Revere. Three are still in service, but one cracked after two centuries of use and is now on display on the south porch of the Congregational Church.

Woodstock is particularly well situated, in a beautiful valley of the Ottaquechee River with mountains all around. In winter, skiers can put up in the town while they spend the day on the slopes of Mount Tom or Suicide Six.

INFORMATION: From late June through the foliage season, there is a town information booth in service on the village green. Go here for a free village map and list of town businesses.

WHERE TO STAY: I must admit that its particular beauty and its popularity with the wealthy have made Woodstock room prices a good deal higher (for what you get) than the norm. Still, it is a beautiful town, and the lodging places are certainly nice.

Woodstock has a good variety of accommodations, grouped together here according to type:

Inns

The **Village Inn of Woodstock,** 41 Pleasant St., at the eastern end of the village, Woodstock, VT 05091 (tel. 802/457-1255), is a large old Victorian house converted to a warm and friendly inn. Many of the downstairs rooms have been turned into dining rooms for the inn's noted restaurant, and another is a cocktail lounge. The guest rooms have been restored and furnished with pieces in congruence with the house's age: one room has a very fine marble washbasin. Rates are $36.75 to $42, the higher price being for a double room with bath. In the restaurant, the food is finely prepared, and will cost from $8 to $17 for a full dinner. The inn is open all year, and is a popular place, so it's wise to reserve a room in advance. The restaurant serves breakfast, dinner, and Sunday brunch.

Guest Houses

Several private homes are set up to receive guests. In fact, these are simple inns which provide only lodging, no meals or beverages.

If the Village Inn is full, or if you find the prices a bit high for your budget, just go right next door to **Cambria House,** 43 Pleasant St., (Route 4), Woodstock, VT 05091 (tel. 802/457-3077). Here the accommodations are fairly similar to those at the New England Inn, and although there is no restaurant, a TV lounge serves as an evening focal point. The Cambria House charges $18.90 to $27.25 for two in summer, a few dollars less off-season, and it's open all year.

If the Cambria is full, check with the guest house across the street at 52 Pleasant St. Similar place, similar prices.

Motels

As for motels, my first choice would be the **Woodstock Motel,** a mile or so east of the village on Route 4, Woodstock, VT 05091 (tel. 802/457-2500). The building is up on a bank a short distance away from the road, very neat and new in appearance, and with 15 rooms of modern comfort. A shower, TV, and wall-to-wall carpets are in each room, all rooms have air conditioning, and the motel's swimming pool is at your disposal. Rates are $31.50 to $35.70 single, $35.70 to $42 double in season (which continues, as in most Woodstock establishments, through foliage season). You should have a car or bicycle to get to the center of Woodstock from here.

The **Shire Motel** (tel. 802/457-2211) is very near the Village Inn of Woodstock and Cambria House, east of the center of town along Route 4, at 46 Pleasant St., Woodstock, VT 05091. Newer than the Woodstock Motel, it is equally well kept and has the advantage of being within walking distance of the Green. A room with bath, TV, and air conditioning, and with one double bed, costs $37.80 for two persons; a larger room with two double beds costs $46.20. I've found the proprietors at the Shire Motel to be particularly helpful and friendly.

East of town on Route 4, in the neighborhood of the aforementioned Woodstock Motel, is the attractive **Braeside Motel** (tel. 802/457-1366), P.O. Box 411, Woodstock, VT 05091, set up on the hillside away from road noise. You get the view from here, and also 12 modern wood-paneled rooms with wall-to-wall carpet, cable color TV, and Scottish touches. The thistles on the motel's handsome carved wood sign are no idle boast, for owners Charlie and Jean Dawson are both Scottish natives: he's from Inverness, she's from Glasgow. Prices at the Braeside are $39.90 to $47.25 double.

If you continue past the Braeside for several miles, you'll soon come to scenic Quechee Gorge, and also to the **Quechee Gorge Motel** (tel. 802/295-7600), U.S. 4 (P.O. Box Q, Quechee, VT 05089). Open all year, the Quechee Gorge Motel is nice, modern, two-story'd, and just a few minutes' stroll from the gorge. Room rates are very reasonable: $30.45 to $36.75 double, $38.85 for a room with two double beds which can sleep four persons, $52.50 for a two-room suite which can house up to six. Some rooms even have kitchenettes. You may be 20 minutes' drive from Woodstock here—but you're right near Quechee Gorge.

West of Woodstock on U.S. 4, heading toward Killington, you'll pass the small, well-kept **Pond Ridge Motel** (tel. 802/457-1667), on the left, Woodstock, VT 05091. The 13 rooms here are clean, tidy, simple, but comfortable, with decent pricetags. A room with double bed and shower goes for $26.25 single or double; one with two beds, more space, and a tub-and-shower combination, costs $31.50. The motel has a tennis court for guests' use.

Resort Hotels

Woodstock's top of the line is the **Woodstock Inn and Resort** (tel. 802/457-1100), No. 14 on the Green, Woodstock, VT 05091, a very large and plush place which reminds me of a similar style hostelry found in college towns. The guest rooms are all quite new and modern, with color TV, air conditioning, and private baths, but the decorator has tried to keep to the early American style by using beds, chairs, and papers for a 1700s effect.

Other facilities at the inn include ten tennis courts, two paddle tennis courts, putting green (the Robert Trent Jones golf course is nearby), and a wading pool. As for food, the Woodstock Inn's "coffeeshop" is like many other restaurants, with full-course dinners centering on entrees in a price range of $7 to $11. The restaurant, then, is super-elegant, and prices there for entrees go from $11 to $17, and you must have a reservation.

As for the rooms, prices are the same year round, and the ones quoted here include tax. Doubles cost $78.75 to $110.25; singles are just a few dollars less. No meals are included. You do much better if you avail yourself of a sports package plan—call for details.

WHERE TO DINE: Bentley's Restaurant (tel. 457-3232), is at 3 Elm St., just a few steps and around the corner from the village green. Bentley's has captured the spirit of a Victorian tavern but without the heaviness: a pillared bar with potted palms, bentwood chairs, and lots of verdure. The crowd is often young and spirited, the prices are moderate, and the food is good and simple or good and fancy. Lunch is burgers and sandwiches, light lunch plates, and omelets in the $4 to $6 area; for dinner, these same dishes are on order, or you can indulge in chicken Alexandra ($13) or veal Milanaise ($13). For lunch, Bentley's is open from 11:30 a.m. till about 3 p.m.; for dinner, the hours are 5:30 to 9 or 10 p.m.

Very near Bentley's, and right beside the Woodstock Historical Society at 24 Elm St., is **The Prince and the Pauper** (tel. 457-1818), actually down an alley named Dana Lane which runs alongside the society's building. Low beamed ceilings, candle lanterns casting a golden aura onto the small tables, a worldly clientele, and good conversation are what make the mood here, but the exotic array of dishes and delicacies add to it: where else would you find smoked trout as an appetizer, or main courses like entrecôte au sauce whisky? Roast duckling is on the menu too. The menu changes frequently, of course, but the intimate atmosphere and the international flair remain. Expect to pay $30 to $36 per person for dinner, wine, tax, and tip included. The Prince and the Pauper is open daily noon to 2 p.m. and 6 to 9:30 p.m.; on Sunday, it's brunch from noon to 2 p.m. Reservations are a good idea.

Outside of town on the way to Plymouth and Killington, the **Weaving Room Restaurant** is in Bridgewater Mill Mall (described below), on Route 4. From 11:30 a.m. to 3 p.m. weekdays and noon to 4 p.m. on Sunday you can get sandwiches or a "Meal in a Bowl," a thick soup with bread and salad, for $3. The dinner menu changes daily, and prices for full-course dinners are about $5.25 to $11. Dinner is on from 6 to 9 p.m. on Thursday, Friday, and Saturday nights.

For Breakfast and Brunch

The inexpensive breakfast or light lunch survives in attractive surroundings. Seek out the **Downtown Deli-Café** (tel. 457-3286), on Central Street in Woodstock, right next to the Kedron Brook. Set breakfasts run about $3 here, luncheon sandwiches and quiches about the same. Sit out front à la sidewalk café, or inside viewing the brook through large windows, or out back on the small deck perched right over the bubbling water. The Deli-Café is open daily from 7 a.m. to 3 p.m., Sunday from 9 a.m. to 3 p.m.

WHAT TO SEE: Two fine houses, both built in 1807, are open to visits. One is the Woodstock Historical Society's **Dana House** (tel. 457-1822), on Elm Street, just around the corner from the green, open daily from 10 a.m. to 5 p.m., on Sunday 2 to 5:30 p.m.; admission costs $1.50 for an adult, $1 for a senior citizen, 50¢ for a child. The collections here are of furniture and paintings, farm implements, and personal effects, and often the displays are as interestingly made as the objects which they exhibit. The other house is also a museum, that administered by the DAR Historical Society on the village green. The building was put up in 1807 to house the state legislature, and now contains exhibits of the museum's collection of Revolutionary era furnishings. It's open Monday to Saturday from 2 to 4 p.m. in summer, for $1 admission.

In your walks around town, you might want to look for the three **covered bridges** across the Ottaquechee, including one built in 1969 and rebuilt five years later—Middle Bridge, just off the green in the middle of town.

On the far side of the Ottaquechee from the town green is a cemetery, and at the east edge of the cemetery is the beginning of a walking trail. The **Billings Park Trails** are maintained by the town, and are yours to enjoy for free.

Quechee Gorge

While in Woodstock, take a spin over to Quechee Gorge, eight miles to the east. The highway bridge carries U.S. 4 right across the picturesque gorge; below, the Ottaquechee River slips swiftly between boulders and jagged rock walls. The Grand Canyon it's not, but pretty? Definitely.

For the best view, follow the signs to the viewpoint north of the highway. Or enter Quechee State Park, on the east side of the gorge, and take the short hiking trail down to the edge of the gorge. The walk will take 15 minutes, one way. By the way, there's camping and picnicking at Quechee State Park.

SKIING AT WOODSTOCK: Woodstock was the site of the first ski tow in the United States—a rope on a pulley which pulled skiers up the slopes in a farmer's field. Today a well-known ski area is close by, called **Suicide Six.** In addition, the Woodstock Ski Touring Center (tel. 802/457-2114) at the Woodstock Country Club, Route 106, Woodstock, VT 05091, has over 40 miles of marked trails, plus equipment rental, cross-country ski shop, lessons, and picnic lunch ski tours. Trail-use fee is only a few dollars per day.

Suicide Six (despite the terrifying name) is a fine, small, family ski area with two double-chair lifts, and a free J-bar on the beginners' slope. Located on Route 12 three miles north of Woodstock, it is under the management of the Woodstock Inn's parent company. Package plans are available through the inn; there is 60% snowmaking capability, and lessons and equipment can be had on the spot in a new base lodge which also houses a ski rental shop, restaurant and lounge (tel. 802/457-1666).

You can stay in Woodstock and ski elsewhere, of course, and the Killington and Pico ski areas present all the challenge and facilities a skier could want. They're just a short drive away.

PLYMOUTH: Calvin Coolidge was born in this tiny Vermont hamlet not far from the intersection of Routes 100 and 100A, and you can visit the **Coolidge Homestead** and the **Calvin Coolidge Birthplace.** The former president's early history is interesting, but the story of his "inauguration" is full of fascination. While he was vice-president, Mr. Coolidge came to Plymouth for a vacation in August 1923. Before he could even unwind, news came that President Harding was dead, and that he, Calvin Coolidge, was the thirtieth president of the United States. But he had to take the oath of office! The local notary public in the tiny town was none other than the new president's own father, Col. John Coolidge, and it was Colonel John who—as the only judicial official handy—administered the oath to his son by the light of a kerosene lamp at 2:47 a.m., August 3, 1923.

You can visit the Homestead, the Birthplace, the **Wilder Barn** (a farmers' museum), the village church, the cemetery where President Coolidge is buried, and **Wilder House,** which was once Coolidge's mother's house. Wilder House today holds a small restaurant and lunch counter.

But don't miss Plymouth's outstanding attraction, the **Plymouth Cheese Company,** P.O. Box 1, Plymouth, VT 05056 (tel. 802/672-3650). The company's president, Mr. John Coolidge, is a scion of the famous village clan. Come to see the delicious Vermont cheddar being made on weekdays from 11:30 a.m. to 1 p.m., or come to sample and purchase the cheese Monday through Saturday from 8 a.m. to 5:30 p.m., on Sunday from 9 a.m. to 5:30 p.m. Since the first time I tasted it, I've been hooked on Plymouth cheese. It comes cut to order by the ounce or the pound, or in three- and five-pound wheels, and it is aged 3, 6, or 12 months to produce mild, medium, or sharp cheddar. By the way, watching the cheese-making costs nothing; the cheese, last time I bought, was about $17.50 for the five-pound wheel (I get as much as I can carry).

7. Killington

With many skiers, Killington is the only word they have to hear before they begin thinking snow. The resort is one of Vermont's prime ski areas, and is especially noted for its progressive approach to development of its facilities (for instance, the addition of "gladed" ski trails which give one the feeling of skiing right in the forest) and its snowmaking and grooming capabilities. But in recent years Killington has expanded its breadth of activities so that now you can go there for skiing in winter, organized backpacking and camping trips in summer, tennis practice and lessons, or for the summer Playhouse. The resort is booming, but it is laid out so well on the side of the mountain that there is plenty of room for all the activities and the visitors.

INFORMATION: The whole Killington area, which is part of the town of Sherburne, is organized with the **Killington Lodge Bureau** in charge of making room reservations for you. You can call or write to a lodge or motel directly, or you can call the Lodging Bureau to see what's available at 802/422-3711. **The Killington–Pico Area Association,** Killington, VT 05751, also maintains an information booth at the junction of U.S. 4 and Route 100 in Sherburne, just at the base of the Killington access road; the booth is open during business hours.

WHERE TO STAY AND EAT: Killington is a well-organized resort community, and so virtually all activities here are organized around various package plans which are designed to save visitors money over the normal daily rates. A package would usually include lodging, meals, and the price of the activity: lift tickets, tennis lessons, horseback riding, backpacking trips. In ski season most inns operate on the Modified American Plan (MAP), in which you are required to take breakfast and dinner with your room. I've given the daily room rates below for comparison purposes, but do call the Lodging Bureau at 802/422-3711 to ask about the package plans, or to make reservations; or send a card to Killington Ski Area, Killington, VT 05751, asking for information on ski, hiking, or tennis package plans. Also, I'd never have room to describe the four-score-and-seven lodging facilities in the Killington area in these pages, so I've chosen a few favorites for mention here.

Starting right at the base of the slopes, the first place you should know about is the **Villager at Killington** (tel. 802/242-0762, 422-3101, or 422-3613), 512 Killington Rd., Killington, VT 05751. The Villager is where the action is, winter and summer; it's in walking distance to the lifts and is right next door to the Playhouse, tennis courts, swimming pool, golf course, and seven-acre pond for boating and fishing. The Villager has 96 rooms, most with a double bed and a single bed, some with two twin beds, and several rooms (the higher price ones, of course) have fireplaces. Rates in winter are $91.35 to $138.60 for each person on a two-day weekend, with breakfasts and a dinner costing $23 per person extra; $183.75 to $286.65 per person for a five-day ski week, with four dinners and five breakfasts costing $95.55 per person extra.

The **Chalet Killington** (tel. 802/422-3451), P.O. Box 144, Killington, VT 05751, is one of the closest inns to the lifts and the Chalet provides free transportation to the base station for skiers; they'll also have someone run down to Rutland to pick you up from the airport or bus station for a nominal fee if you make reservations in advance. The Chalet has 30 modern rooms in an alpine-inspired building; rooms have tiled baths, TV, individually controlled electric heat, and wall-to-wall carpeting. A very nice living room with fireplace, a sauna, a game room, dining room, and bar/lounge are all in the same building. Rooms in winter here are rented with breakfast and dinner included for $60.90 *per person* double occupancy, or $42 *per person* in the dormitory (you must be 12 years or older). As at all Killington establishments, special two-, five-, and seven-day rates are available. Also as at all Killington establishments, these rates do not apply on holidays.

The **Killington Village Inn** (tel. 802/422-3301), P.O. Box 153, Killington, VT 05751, should not be confused with the Villager at Killington mentioned above. This is a separate inn about a mile from the slopes, with free transportation to the lifts and back provided by the inn. It's an older, more traditional building with modern rooms, some large and very good for families. The lounge, dining room, and bar are kept rustic and woody while the rooms have colonial touches and modern facilities, including color TVs. A room here costs from $54 to $66 *per person* in ski season, breakfast and dinner included. As at many other Killington places, you don't tip here, but a 15% service charge has been added to these rates.

Skol Haus Motor Lodge, Killington Road, Killington, VT (tel. 802/422-3305), is an attractive, modern motel-style inn right on Killington Road, and I hasten to say that it is tastefully done so as not to bring any hint of strip development to the area. Rooms are on two levels entered by outside doors in the motel fashion, and include full tile baths, TV, and either two queen-size beds or twin beds. Although there is no restaurant, a continental breakfast is served, and there's also a BYOB bar which can provide set-ups for drinks. The lounge has a fireplace, of course. Winter rates are $47.52 double daily, breakfast included. In summer, children under 10 stay free with their parents, and babysitting service is offered. Closed June and July.

The **Mountain Meadows Lodge,** 20 Thundering Brook Rd., Killington, VT 05751 (tel. 802/775-1010), is not far from the intersection of Killington Road and its intersection with U.S. 4 and Route 100—actually, it's off on a side road just a few hundred yards east of this intersection, on Kent Lake. The lodge consists of a fine old barn and farmhouse which have been converted to accommodate 90 people in winter, half that number in summer. One can stay in a very comfortable room with bath which is capable of sleeping from two to six people, or in a room without private bath. Whatever your choice, the rate you pay includes breakfast, dinner, and service, and is listed here *per person:* in a double room with bath, $41.40 ($186.30 per person for a five-day ski week); without private bath, $35.65 ($161 for five days). In summer, rates also include two meals and are $34.50 per person; for weekly stays you pay for six days, and the seventh day is free. Mountain Meadows has a pretty dining room and BYOB bar in the barn with a wall of windows looking out over Kent Lake, which is good for sailing, canoeing, and fishing in summer; there's also a swimming pool. In winter, the lodge has its own ski touring center with marked trails, ski rentals, and lessons, right at the lodge itself. The setting is private and quiet—a good choice, and it's only about four miles from the Killington ski lifts.

The **Val Roc Motel** (tel. 802/422-3881), U.S. 4 and Route 100 very near the Killington Gondola base station, Killington, VT 05751, is a nice-looking modern motel some distance from the ski lifts at Killington Village, but very near the gondola, which is on the other side of the mountain from the village. In summer, Val Roc is a convenient highway stopping place. The Val Roc has the comforts in its modern rooms, with combination tubs and showers, TV, coffeemakers in the rooms, electric heat, and many rooms with air conditioning; some rooms have cooking facilities as well. Next door are the motel's own pool and tennis courts. Winter rates are quoted *per person* and continental breakfast is included: $24.15 and up per person, $105 a week, all these rates applying to a room with one double bed for two people. Summer rates are quite a bit lower.

CONDOMINIUM RENTALS: Certainly the most comfortable and luxurious way of all to take a ski or summer vacation at Killington is to rent a fully furnished apartment unit complete with a full kitchen, all linens, a fireplace, perhaps even a dishwasher. A good number of these units, within a half mile or less of the Killington lifts, are up for rental both winter and summer. Rates vary by what sort of unit you want (a one-bedroom can sleep four, maximum; a two-bedroom does for up to six, a three-bedroom for eight), and also the exact week or weekend you want to rent: a normal Sunday to Friday ski-week rate in the middle of ski season would be $210 per person for a four-person one-bedroom unit. For full information and very-necessary reservations, call the **Village Center Condominiums,** 218 Killington Rd., Killington, VT 05751 (tel. 802/422-3101 or 422-3613; or toll free 800/343-0762).

STAYING AT PICO: The **Pico Peak Lodge** (tel. 802/773-6331), on U.S. 4 west of the intersection with Route 100 and Killington Road, is a motel-style place with a lofty two-story lobby and a fireplace equally as high. It's convenient to the Pico slopes, not far from Killington, and a good place to put up on a summer trip. Rooms are of the standard, very comfortable motel variety with both indoor and outdoor entrances, color TV, and tubs and showers. In summer, rooms cost $31.50 to $36.75 double, $23.10 single, $6 for an extra person. Of course, the lodge has its own full restaurant and cocktail lounge, a game room for children, ice skating, and ski movies on Thursday.

READER'S SELECTION: "I stopped at **Hemingway's Restaurant** (tel. 802/422-3886), Route 4 in Killington VT 05751. They have classic cuisine, using all fresh local ingredients, served in a restored farmhouse. The pheasant with red cabbage was delicious; I almost ordered the trout with black beans and scallions. It's not cheap, but it's a find out here in the center of Vermont" (Boyd Osler, Shunk, Pa.).

SKIING AT KILLINGTON AND PICO: Well, here you have it: one of the best managed ski areas in the United States, with a good snowmaking capability, a variety of trails, a well-organized ski school, a very accessible location, lots of parking, three lounges, quick food service or a nice restaurant, several bars, and a long skiing season—what more can I say? The vertical drop is over 3000 feet, there are six chair lifts, a gondola said to be the longest in the world, and four Poma lifts, all with a total capacity of 10,000 skiers per hour. If that sounds like a mob scene, I must admit that it does get crowded, but also that it's a big mountain, and there does seem to be room for everyone. The first thing to do when considering a weekend or week at Killington is to send for information on the package plans, for they will undoubtedly save you money. Even if you don't choose a package plan which includes room, meals, and lift tickets, Killington Resort has various packages just for the slopes, including special rates on lifts for two to seven days, or plans with which you get lifts and lessons for two to seven days at reduced rates, or all three—lifts, lessons, and equipment rentals—all for one price.

At Pico (pronounced pie-coh) Peak near Killington there are five chair lifts, two T-bars, a vertical drop of 2000 feet, and plenty of easy parking. It's a good, challenging area in its own right, although today it is too often thought of as Killington's elder sister.

Vermont has two central ski report phones, 802/223-2957 and 223-2352. Call either one for weather and conditions reports at any Vermont ski resort.

SUMMER AT KILLINGTON: Everyone coming to the Killington area will want to take the **Killington Gondola,** on Route 4/100 north of West Bridgewater. The gondola is the longest such ski lift in North America traveling 3½ miles up to the 4241-foot summit. They say that this was the point from which the territory of "Verd-mont" ("green mountain") was christened in 1763. At the top you'll find the Killington Peak Restaurant and a self-guiding nature trail. In winter the gondola carries skiers; in summer it operates from early June to mid-October, Wednesday through Sunday from 10 a.m. to 4 p.m. Tickets are $6.50 round trip for adults, $4.50 for children 6 to 12.

Killington Playhouse (tel. 802/422-3333) is at the Snowshed Vacation Center, Killington, VT 05751 and has performances of Broadway musicals from the beginning of June through Labor Day, Tuesday through Saturday at 8 p.m. Tickets are $7 to $8 for adults; under 12 and over 65, $5.50 to $6. You can buy tickets at the door.

Killington's School for Tennis (tel. 422-3613) is in operation from late May through mid-September, offering two- and five-day tennis clinic package plans which include lodging, all meals, tennis lessons, a social program, use of videotape pictures in instruction, and tips. Prices for the two-day stay are about $223 to $246 per person, in all; for the five-day program, about $545 to $599 per person, in all. Send for details.

8. Middlebury

Like its more famous counterpart of Hanover, N.H., the town of Middlebury is replete with beautiful old Georgian and 19th-century buildings, a small college of high quality, and a pretty town green. Hanover has Dartmouth, and Middlebury has Middlebury College, but only Middlebury has the Vermont State Craft Center at Frog Hollow and the University of Vermont's Morgan Horse Farm—but more of that later.

INFORMATION: The local chamber of commerce has an information office just outside the center of town, on the right-hand side as you come into Middlebury from the south (on U.S. 7) or the east (Route 125). The office is open during business hours.

WHERE TO STAY AND EAT: You can't miss the **Middlebury Inn and Motel** (tel. 802/388-4961, or toll free 800/842-4666), 20 Court House Square, Middlebury, VT 05753, as you enter the heart of town. The great old inn dominates the square even more than the red-brick courthouse just up the hill from it. The rooms, though, are all quite modern with early American decoration; most have private baths, TV sets, and telephones, and rent for $33.60 to $69.30 single, $52.50 to $73.50 double; an additional person pays $5 a night. Price is determined by the size and location (and thus the views) of the room. The modern motel rooms right next to the older inn are among the largest, and thus the most expensive. The inn has its own dining room, which serves breakfast, lunch, and dinner.

For an inexpensive motel on the edge of town, try the **Blue Spruce Motel,** on U.S. 7 south of town exactly three miles from the town green, Middlebury, VT 05753 (tel. 802/388-7512). Set back from the road behind a swath of green lawn, the Blue Spruce rents nice rooms with color TV, FM radio, two double beds, and tub and shower, for $31.50. The real bargain, however, is the little cabins behind the motel. Quaint and very quiet, the cabins are in fact guest rooms, smaller than the motel rooms and with shower only rather than shower-and-tub. But the price is very good: $25.20 for two.

The **Addison County Chamber of Commerce,** 35 Court St., Middlebury, VT 05753 (tel. 802/388-7579), maintains a list of homeowners who rent rooms to visitors. When crowds of parents swell the town for graduation, or alums return for homecoming, the town's lodging places are always filled. The "Homeowners Listing" is a very useful service. Drop by the chamber's Information Office at the same address, or call.

For light meals, the **Rosebud Café,** 66 Main St. at the corner of Frog Hollow Lane, serves light meals and drinks in an atmosphere of stained glass, dark wood, low lights, Oriental rugs, and live plants. A long list of daily special plates (each is a full meal), might include perhaps turkey tetrazzini for $4.40, or crêpes for less, or pizza, tacos, and many styles of sandwiches. Hours at the Rosebud are 11:30 a.m. to 1 a.m. Monday through Saturday; on Sunday, 5 p.m. to midnight. Downstairs (enter from Frog Hollow Lane) is the Rosebud Saloon, a drinkin', dancin', and listenin' place.

Out of Town

The town of East Middlebury is east of Middlebury along Route 125, and it's here you'll find the **Waybury Inn** (tel. 802/388-4015), East Middlebury, VT 05740. Rooms in the cozy, quaint (1810) inn are homey, useful, and pretty—Martha Washington bedspreads, etc. Most have private baths, although some share baths with adjoining rooms, which makes them just right for families. Rooms are $26.25 per person in summertime, with a full country breakfast. The Waybury's dining room serves breakfast, lunch, and dinner at moderate prices. At dinnertime, a full-course meal of juice, main course, two vegetables, potato, and bread made right in the inn, and fruit compote, will cost between $8.50 and $15. Service is family style. By the way, if you need a hard bed, be sure to specify this when you make your reservation. Folk music is featured in the tavern on Friday and Saturday nights from 9 p.m. to midnight.

WHAT TO DO: Once you've settled in and taken a stroll around this pretty town, wander over to **Middlebury College** for a look at its exceptionally pretty campus and old granite buildings. Those in need of information about the college can get it by dropping in at the admissions office in Emma Willard House on Main Street (Route 30). Middlebury was founded by local people in the 19th century and went on to become a high-quality school. Robert Frost's participation in the Breadloaf Writers' Conference (held in Middlebury's mountain campus close to nearby Ripton) spread the college's reputation even farther.

Robert Frost wasn't the only person of renown to tramp the streets of Middlebury. A man named John Deere was an apprentice here from 1821 to 1825, after which he moved to Illinois and invented the world's first steel moldboard plow and his name became a household word in farms across the nation.

Deere's apprenticeship took place at **Frog Hollow,** which is down the hill from Court House Square, across the river bridge, and down Frog Hollow Lane on the right. The Vermont State Craft Center at Frog Hollow has fascinating craft exhibitions all year, not to mention craft classes and a gallery of Vermont crafts. Gallery hours are 10 a.m. to 5 p.m. Monday through Saturday in May through December; Tuesday through Saturday in February through April; closed in January.

To see the magnificent steeds at the University of Vermont's **Morgan Horse Farm** (tel. 388-2011), head west on Route 125 from Middlebury, turn right onto Route 23 (Weybridge Street), and follow signs to the farm for about 2½ miles. Admission to the farm is $2 per adult, 75¢ for teens (kids under 12 get in for free), 9 a.m. to 4 p.m. daily, May through October. Once into the farm, you'll get a guided tour of the stables, an audio-visual presentation about the farm and the Morgan horse, and the chance to roam the farm's spacious grounds and perhaps have a picnic at the picnic area.

9. Sugarbush

The area centered on Warren, Vt., along Route 100, can boast three well-known ski resorts: Sugarbush Valley, Mad River Glen, and Sugarbush North. Although much of the crowd here comes to stay in its own condominiums, a number of inns, motels, and guest houses amply provide for the rest.

INFORMATION: The **Valley Area Association** (VAA) will help you out with information if you write to P.O. Box 173, Waitsfield, VT 05673, or if you call 802/496-3409. For lodging and information, call Sugarbush at 802/583-2381.

WHERE TO STAY: The **Sugarbush Inn** (tel. 802/583-2301) is the area's posh resort inn. Its own pools (indoor and outdoor), batteries of tennis courts, golf course, and nature paths through the woods are all part of this complex on the Sugarbush Access Road, two miles west of Route 100. Rooms are tasteful and very comfy, and the inn gives off that quiet *something* that denotes class. Prices are European plan and begin at $78.20 for two in a standard room.

The **Valley Inn** (tel. 802/496-3450, or toll free 800/451-4590), P.O. Box 8, Waitsfield, VT 05673, on Route 100 just north of the intersection of Route 17, is woody and nice, with lots of knotty pine in the public rooms and guest rooms, a "rathskeller," and a large comfy living room with fireplace. In winter, rooms are rented with two meals, and cost $40 to $49 *per person* on weekdays; on weekends there is a special rate, *per person,* which covers lodging Friday and Saturday nights, plus two breakfasts and one dinner: it's $74.20 to $91 *per person* in a double room, with a slight discount early in the season, and a surcharge on the holidays. Tax and service are included in these rates. In summer the rates are considerably less.

Birch Wood (tel. 802/583-2100) is a small, modern chalet which can take only six people. The Horsts, who own Birch Wood, are in effect sharing their home with you, which makes for a very congenial and personal atmosphere. During ski season one person pays $31.50, two sharing a bathless room pay $42; a full breakfast and a snack at cocktail time is included in the price. Five-day ski-week rates at a discount of 20% are also available. Summer rates are much lower. It's imperative to write ahead or call for reservations as space is so limited: write Mr. Jack Horst, Birch Wood . . . by the mountain, Warren, VT 05674. Birch Wood is located on German Flats Road, which runs parallel to Route 100 between the Sugarbush Ski Area and Route 17.

WHERE TO DINE: Right at Sugarbush Village are four eating places which can very easily fill all your alimentary needs:

The **Phoenix** (tel. 583-2777) is in the same building as the Hotel Sugarbush and has a very fine, second-floor view of the Green Mountains through its large plate-glass windows. The rustic wood and heavy beams of the room contrast with the silver and linen on the tables, and a very impressive antique espresso coffee-maker stands glittering to one side. The food is international, from fettucine Alfredo to slices of veal cooked with chestnuts and cream. Highest price items on the menu are the tournedos of beef and the filet mignon ($15 to $17). There's also a bar at the Phoenix, fashioned from—of all things!—a communion rail, and stained-glass windows above finish off the ecclesiastical effect. The Phoenix is closed Wednesday, but any other day you can have dinner from 6 to 10 p.m. (6 to 11 p.m. on Saturday and holidays), and reservations are good to have.

Make-it-yourself meals are up for grabs at **Ron's Delicatessen,** in the Sugarbush Village complex. Sandwishes costing $3 or $4 can be made for you on the spot to be eaten in the deli-restaurant, or you can buy cheese, bread, salami, pickles, and so forth and make you own.

A good old down-home traditional Vermont Cantonese restaurant? Yes, the **China Barn** (tel. 496-3579), on Route 17 one mile from Waitsfield, is a Chinese restaurant in an old Vermont barn, and in addition to the Cantonese specialties there are Szechuan and Mandarin dishes too. Moo goo gai pan (sliced chicken cooked with water chestnuts, mushrooms, and vegetables) or Szechuan spiced beef (watch the red pepper!) is $7. Duck, seafood, and vegetarian entrees are on the menu every night. China Barn is open for dinner daily except Tuesday, 5:30 to 10 p.m. Liquor is served, and any of their dishes can be made to take out.

SUGARBUSH SKIING: Sugarbush has lots of opportunities for good skiing,

and although the resort is not so highly ramified as those at Mt. Snow, Killington, or Stowe, well, perhaps that's part of the charm here—an absence of big-time crowds. That doesn't mean you'll have no wait for the lift lines, though. Short lift lines these days are only at places with reserved-seat lift tickets, or at places which aren't worth skiing, and Sugarbush, Sugarbush North, and Mad River Glen are not among these.

Sugarbush Valley

At Sugarbush proper, the slopes and trails come down almost 2500 feet from top to bottom, and they're laid out so that close to half of them are rated as suitable for expert skiers. Lifts include a gondola almost two miles long, four chair lifts, and a Poma. Rentals, instruction, and cross-country ski trails are all part of the establishment. The ski school offers a ski-week "saturation skiing workshop" which claims to instruct students in centeredness and energy awareness as well as techniques on the slopes. Lots of package plans are up for grabs—call the information numbers given at the beginning of this section.

Mad River Glen

Mad River Glen is near Waitsfield, on Route 17, an easy drive from the hotels I've named above. It's a smaller area than Sugarbush, but still a good size, with four chair lifts all radiating out from one base station. The vertical drop is 2000 feet, and the preponderance of trails (four-fifths of them) are for moderately well-trained or expert skiers. Lift rates on weekdays are $18; on weekends, $22; juniors and senior citizens pay $15 and $18 respectively. Mad River Glen has a rental shop, a ski school, and a nursery, besides lots of package plans: for information, write Mad River Glen, Waitsfield, VT 05673; or call 802/496-3551.

Sugarbush North

Sugarbush North's trails and slopes descend 2600 feet from top to bottom, and about half of the runs are classed as good for the median-level skier. But a look at the mountain trail plan will show you that taking the no. 4 chair lift to the top of Mount Ellen will start you on some very long and pretty tricky runs. Sugarbush North has 36 trails and slopes in all, and usually a good amount of cover for a long season; there's not a lot in the way of snowmaking equipment. Lift rates are $24 per adult, $18 per child. Ski weeks, two- and three-day lift tickets, and package plans with lodging are all offered. For lodging information, call toll free 800/451-5030 or 802/583-2381. Equipment and lessons are yours at the base station for the appropriate fees.

SUMMER SOARING: The air currents around Sugarbush make it good for soaring or gliding, and the **Sugarbush Soaring Association,** P.O. Box 123, Warren, VT 05674 (tel. 802/496-2290), can fill you in on getting airborne. In fact, soaring is not the only aeronautical sport to be pursued here. Ballooning and powered flight are featured as well. Call or write for details. Just so you'll know: you can qualify for solo glider flight in less than two weeks of good, full daily lessons and flights.

A SIDE TRIP TO MONTPELIER AND BARRE: The reason to take a detour and visit the state capital of Vermont is to take a look at the capitol building, a comely classical structure modeled on the Grecian Temple of Theseus. It's made of granite from nearby Barre, of course, but the dome is of wood covered in copper and then gilded. The State House will surprise you: it's so small, but then you'll notice that the capital city, Montpelier, is pretty small too; and thus it is brought home to the visitor that he or she is in the midst of the most rural state in the Union, 48th in population (only about a half million Vermonters in all, spread through almost 10,000 square miles). It comes home to you that, as a Vermont schoolchild once wrote, in Vermont "the trees are close together and the people are far apart."

The first thing you must know about Barre is that its name is pronounced like the masculine name "Barry," and not like a drinking place. The next thing to know is that Barre is the granite capital of the world, having the world's largest quarry for the stone, and also a good number of the world's finest craftspeople to work it. Guided tours of the quarries and the workshops are offered daily, and prove a fascinating way to spend a few hours; but even more fascinating is a visit to the **Hope Cemetery,** eight-tenths of a mile north of the U.S. 302/Vt. 14 intersection, on Vermont Route 14. The cemetery has two gates, and is open until sunset. We speak of making "monuments to survive ourselves," and we usually mean something like a corporation, a law, a charitable institution, or a poem. In Barre the phrase is literal! Stonecutters here create the monument of their dreams for their own resting places. You'll see a balanced granite cube resting precariously on one corner, self-portraits and statues, a ponderous granite armchair (empty, of course!), even a relief of a man and his wife sitting up in bed, hands joined in eternal friendship. Hope Cemetery is more like a sculpture garden, a touching memorial to artisans and artists who came here from many parts of the world.

Details: The Rock of Ages quarry is open from the beginning of May through October, with tours every day from 8:30 a.m. to 5 p.m., free. You can take a quarry train ride from 10 a.m. to 3 p.m., Monday through Friday, June through September, for $2 per adult, half price for children.

READER'S INN SELECTION: "My family and I spent a wonderful day at the **Old Cutter Inn** (tel. 802/626-5152), East Burke, VT 05832, about 12 miles north of St. Johnsbury. The Old Cutter is owned and operated by Fritz Walther, a delightful native of Bern, Switzerland. He cooks the most superb, moderately priced cuisine I've ever tasted. The inn is convenient to the Burke Mountain Ski Academy and Ski Area" (Rev. Phillip Ayers, North Haven, Conn.).

READER'S SUGGESTION: "There's a good, reasonably priced bed and breakfast inn called the **Old Homestead Inn** (tel. 802/633-4100) on Route 5 in Barnet VT 05821, operated by Robert and Mary Gordon. Your readers should know about this place. Barnet is a few miles south of St. Johnsbury, at Exit 18 from I-91, and the Old Homestead is a good spot to stop for the night" (Harriet Heyer, Stowe, Vt.).

10. Stowe

The lodges and inns around Stowe adopt alpine or Central European names, and although the terrain here is hardly "alpine," somehow the names make sense. The village is dominated by Vermont's highest mountain, Mt. Mansfield (4393 feet), certainly no Matterhorn; but there is definitely a European feeling in Stowe, the feeling one has in some tiny Austrian village amid emerald green rolling hills, winding roads, and steep slopes. Perhaps it is the lushness (in summer) of the lawns, forests, and wildflowers, or perhaps it is the rain and mists—Lamoille County is said to have the greatest amount of precipitation in the state—which make everything so lush. Whatever, there is certainly an especially attractive air about Stowe.

The frequent rain is not a liability, either, for local people learn to plan on it, and the earth scents after the rain are part of the pleasure of Stowe. And besides, it's all this precipitation which makes Stowe one of the best skiing areas in the East, with plenty of deep cover and a long season.

Winter or summer, the narrow rocky mountain defile known as **Smuggler's Notch** is a dramatic place for a hike or a drive, and is just another one of those things which make Stowe special.

INFORMATION: Businesses in the area are organized in the Stowe Area Association, P.O. Box 1230, Stowe, VT 05672 (tel. 802/253-7321). During ski season the information office, in the center of Stowe very near the intersection of Routes 100 and 108 (the Mountain Road), is open from 8 a.m. to 9 p.m., to 10 p.m. on Friday, Saturday, and on holidays. If you don't have a reservation when you arrive in Stowe, drop in here and they'll help you out.

For information on snow conditions in the area, call 802/253-8521 anytime; or during business hours, call 514/845-9840 in Canada, or 212/757-4455 in New York City.

WHERE TO STAY: Stowe has a good variety of lodging places. Posh or modest, dauntingly expensive or surprisingly cheap, it's here. In summer there is no problem finding exactly the room you want at the price you want to pay. But on busy winter weekends you'd be well advised to reserve in advance. Just give the Stowe Area Association a ring and they'll make the reservation for you. In winter a toll-free number is in operation; in summer, call on the regular line.

Most hostelries in Stowe require winter visitors to have breakfast and dinner; in the jargon this is called the Modified American Plan. Smaller places generally have BYOB bars or lounges, which helps greatly in reducing the expense of an after-ski glow. For supplies, trundle down to the Vermont State Liquor Store on Route 100 south of town, open 9:15 a.m. to 6 p.m., till 8 p.m. on Friday, closed Sunday.

What follows is a selection of my favorite places to stay in Stowe, summer or winter. Bus service along Route 100 (the Mountain Road) connects the ski slopes to Stowe Village during the busy winter season.

When I wrote of Stowe's having a European air about it, I must have been thinking particularly of the **Trapp Family Lodge** (tel. 802/253-8511), two miles along a side road up the mountain slope of Mountain Road, Stowe, VT 05672. The singing Trapp family of *Sound of Music* fame left the mountains of their native Austria before World War II and settled here in Stowe, later using this as home-base for their worldwide concert tours. Members of the family still are involved in operating the resort, and in planning a new Main Lodge to replace the huge old alpine house which was totally destroyed by fire in 1980.

The Lower Lodge, with 25 rooms, is open as usual, and a double room with private bath and balcony (what a view!) costs $92.40, tax included. Breakfast and dinner come with the room. By the time you arrive, the new Main Lodge and time-sharing condos may be in service.

To get to the Trapp Family Lodge, start up Route 108, Mountain Road, from the center of Stowe, and go two miles to a fork by a white church; Route 108 bears right, but you bear left and follow this side road up the mountain slope, following the signs to the lodge, for another two miles until you arrive.

The **Andersen Lodge** (tel. 802/253-7336), R.R. 1, Box 1450, Stowe, VT 05672, is a small, friendly Tyrolian inn which has an authentic European ambience lent by its Austrian proprietors, Trude and Dietmar Heiss. Mr. Heiss is an Austrian-trained chef as well, and so the meals (which come with your room in ski season) are particularly hearty and "alpine." You can play the piano, or bumper pool, or just sit in front of the fire. Each room is equipped with color TV and air conditioner. Winter rates with meals, *per person,* are $27.30 to $38.85. Summer rates are $10.50 to $18.90 without meals, $27.30 to $36.75 with meals, *per person.* The Andersen is on Mountain Road, on the right-hand side as you're coming from Stowe.

The **Scandinavia Inn** (tel. 802/253-8555), Stowe, VT 05672, keeps close to the spirit of its name. It's a dark-wood building with peaked gables and white trim, decked with Scandinavian flags, right on Mountain Road. In summer, flower boxes provide splashes of color, and in winter neat stacks of wood on the porch are a ready source of fuel for the living room fireplace. This inn has a surprising range of services, including a sauna, whirlpool bath, game room, library, BYOB bar, and even heat lamps. In summer, inn rooms without bath are $31.50 for two, inn rooms with bath are $36.75 for two, the motel rooms with bath are $39.90; these rates go up $4 a room in foliage season, and note that these summer prices are for the *room,* not per person. A delightful place with a very good range of accommodations, and Swedish pancakes in the morning!

The **Ski Inn** (tel. 802/253-4050), "on the lower slopes of Mt. Mansfield," on Mountain Road (Route 108), Stowe, VT 05672, specializes in good food and good conversation. Very near the ski areas, the Ski Inn is a large white country inn with a big living room/BYOB lounge with a fireplace, a pine-paneled game room in the basement, and simple but bright and pleasing rooms rented with breakfast and dinner during ski season for $22.05 to $23.10 *per person* without bath, $29.92 with bath. Mr. and Mrs. Heyer, who operate the Ski Inn, share their conversation, helpful hints, and friendly atmosphere with all their guests, and particularly lucky ones may even get some of Mrs. Heyer's wild berry preserves. In summer, the rooms rent without meals for $8.92 to $10.50 per person.

Of the inns right in Stowe village, I feel you can't beat **The Yodler** (tel. 802/253-4836), "first on Mountain Road," Stowe, VT 05672, for price, facilities, comfort, service, or food. Besides the lovely old house which serves as the main part of the inn, there are a number of motel units next door, all done up in the white paint and black shutters which is a New England hallmark. Rooms are comfortable and traditional in the main lodge, but all have showers or baths and telephones; some are more modern in the addition to the lodge, and the motel-style rooms have combination tub/shower and two double beds, the traveling family's boon. Winter ski-season rates include breakfast and dinner, and can range anywhere from $28 *per person* in a tiny "roomette" without private bath in the main lodge, to $42 *per person* for a motel room; a normal lodge room with double or twin beds and either a bath or shower is $37 *per person.* You can save several dollars per room if you stay five, six, or seven days, except during the holiday weeks, of course. Besides breakfast and dinner in the Yodler's well-known dining room, the rates include tea, cocoa, cookies, and canapés every afternoon and also set-ups for the BYOB bar. Although it's not absolutely required, the Yodler recommends that you submit to a 10% service charge rather than bother with tips. In summer, the Yodler's rates are for room only. Summertime prices are $22 to $40 single, $28 to $46 double, and some of these are housekeeping units; all these summer rates are without meals, and represent the *total* tax-included price for the room, not per person. The swimming pool's open in the summer only, and there's a clay tennis court.

The Yodler's attractive dining room has bright wood floors, large windows, soft waltzes in the air, and famous hot buffet dinners every night from 5:30 to 9 p.m., with all you can eat for a very moderate price. Drinks and wine are available, and reservations are requested. Also served is a traditional New England breakfast, 8 to 10:30 a.m.

READERS' INN SELECTION: "We got a wrong number and lucked out at **The Gables Inn** (tel. 802/253-7730), on the Mountain Road. Our double with private bath was only $35. It's a large house and we felt we were at home, really part of the family. Breakfast comes with the room" (Nancy and Gary Meeker, Bedford, Texas).

Motels

I've concentrated on ski lodges and inns as these places provide the most atmosphere and convenience for the money, but those who prefer a modern, well-run hotel will be happy to know that there are several good choices on the Mountain Road.

First of these is the **Alpine Motor Lodge,** on Mountain Road, Stowe, VT 05672 (tel. 802/253-7700), a luxury "resort" motel with a heated swimming pool in summer, a badminton court, restaurant, lounge, game room, and a Pine Room lounge and BYOB bar for skiers. Besides these features, the motel is set well back from the road and nicely landscaped, with ivy even climbing its large chimney. Rooms are in several wings. In summer, the rates are $36.75 to $57.75 and that's for two people, no meals. During foliage season, there's a few dollars' surcharge on each room.

Another attractive motel is the **Innsbruck Inn** on Mountain Road, Stowe, VT 05672 (tel. 802/253-8582), a modern place with quite large rooms, each with a full bath plus an extra wash basin outside the bathroom, a color TV, two double beds, outside and inside entrances, and with its own restaurant and bar downstairs. As the name implies, the Innsbruck's flavor is Austrian, with an alpine dark-wood-and-white-stucco half-timbered effect, Austrian coats-of-arms and flags, even though the owners are from Québec. The inn has an outdoor, heated pool. Winter rates are for the room only: $48.50 to $52.50 for two, $52.75 for three, $63 for four during the week. In summer, the rooms are about $2 cheaper, in foliage season only about $1 cheaper than the winter rates.

Budget Rooms

A number of places offer rooms—or at least beds—at rock-bottom prices. The state park at Mount Mansfield has a **State Ski Dorm** (tel. 802/253-4010) for those interested just in basic sleeping space with none of the frills that drive prices up. The dorm is on Mountain Road, walking (or skiing) distance from the slopes. Rates and regulations are similar to those of a youth hostel (no alcohol, lights out by 11 p.m., etc.), and indeed you must be young to stay at the dorm: high school freshmen to college seniors are accepted. Bring your own sheets, blankets, and pillows, or sleeping bags (no linen available), then pay $6 per person for a bed, $3 for breakfast, $5 for dinner, plus tax for a total of $15 *per person*—you *must* take the whole deal. Reservations are accepted.

In the summer, the State Ski Dorm operates as a youth hostel with the usual rules and regulations. It's open to those of all ages who come by bicycle or on foot (not in cars or on motorcycles). No reservations accepted.

Also on Mountain Road is a basic but congenial hostelry called the **Round Hearth** (tel. 802/253-7223), exactly three miles from the village, at the intersection with Edson Hill Road (P.O. Box 2240, Stowe, VT 05672). A large circular fireplace gives the place its name and typifies its friendly, informal atmosphere. The dorms here can hold 130 people. In winter, a bed and three meals cost only $20 per person; in summer you can pay the same price for the same deal, or rent the bed only for $10. Note that groups sometimes rent the entire lodge in summer. Call and check to be sure there will be space.

Finally, **Mile Away** (tel. 802/253-7569) is a private home on Mountain Road fairly near the ski areas with room for ten people in four rooms, all sharing the bath. The price here, per person per night, is $15.

WHERE TO DINE: During ski season, of course, most people will want to eat at their inn, or will be obliged to do so. But for summer, or the odd day out, here are some other dining places to think about.

Look first at the recommendations (above) on the Yodler, for this is one of the preferred dining places in the valley. Almost every other inn serves meals as well.

An interesting, bright, well-run restaurant right in Stowe is the **Restaurant Swisspot** (tel. 253-4622), right on Main Street just north of the intersection with Mountain Road. The accent is on rusticity of course, with copper buckets hanging from the rough ceiling beams, butcher-block tables, a bar of very rough wood, and the flags of the cantons in the Swiss confederation decked on the walls; for summer supping, tables with umbrellas are set outside with a view of the road. I was not surprised to find on the Swisspot's menu a luncheon hamburger called the burger Verbier ($3.75), which weighs a half pound and is covered in Swiss cheese and curry sauce; you can get one with tomatoes and horseradish sauce for the same price, or you can pick from a dozen other burgers and just as many sandwiches. But there are appetizers, salads, fondues ($6 to $12 per person), quiches, and main courses such as grilled veal sausages ($6.95), a char-broiled sirloin ($9.95), or manicotti ($6.95), each entree coming with salad and rice or potato.

The Shed (tel. 253-4364), on Mountain Road a mile and a half from the village of Stowe on the way to the ski areas, is a dependable family-type place for lunch or dinner: the food is always good, and except for two ten-day stretches in spring and autumn it's open every day from 11:30 a.m. to midnight. For lunch, my favorite is the Shedburger, served on an English muffin ($4.50), but you can choose from other hearty sandwiches and luncheon plates costing up to $7. The dinner menu is short but extremely sweet: steak Tivoli, a cut of sirloin flavored with pepper and smothered in mushrooms for $11.75, is the most expensive offering. Duck, chicken breast stuffed with Vermont cheddar, shrimp, and fish all cost less. There's even a vegetarian plate. If you're in luck, they'll have fresh marzipan-and-raspberry strudel for dessert. Wine and beer are served, and the rustic Shed pub room adjoining the restaurant is one of Stowe's most congenial taverns. In summer, an outdoor patio gives you the chance to dine without having to hide yourself from Vermont's fantastic scenery.

The **Green Door,** which you'll pass just before coming to the Shed, is a bit less expensive and very popular with Stowe's young people. Burgers, pizza, a salad bar, and lively atmosphere are the big attractions, but fancier dinners are served as well. Like the Shed, the Green Door is open during the off-season periods; service starts at 5 p.m.

READER'S RESTAURANT SELECTION: "In the Stowe area, try the **Ten Acres Lodge** (tel. 253-7638), Luce Hill Road, for excellent food and reasonably priced good wine. We did not stay here, but we dined. It's near the Trapp Family Lodge, a half mile from the turn off Mountain Road" (Mrs. Robert Perry, Falls Church, Va.).

WHAT TO SEE AND DO: Much of the territory around Stowe is part of Vermont's **Mt. Mansfield State Forest and Park,** and for summer visitors that means hiking trails (especially the Long Trail from Massachusetts to Canada), camping areas, and picnicking. Winter visitors will want to note the state ski area, and Spruce Peak ski area.

Skiing Stowe

The trails are down both Mt. Mansfield and Spruce Peak, the mountains on either side of the Smuggler's Notch defile, and the variety of trails is such that there's plenty of adventure for everyone, no matter what your ability. In fact, the mountains, the staff in charge of trail maintenance, and especially the Sepp Ruschp Ski School have all worked hard over many years to earn for Stowe the high regard it has among skiers. The vertical drop is over 2000 feet, and the lifts include five chairs, three T-bars, and a gondola with four-passenger cars. Beginners will want to start off at the Toll House Slopes, near the base of the Toll Road up Mt. Mansfield; the next logical step is to Spruce Peak; and after you've mastered that, go on to the more difficult among the Mt. Mansfield trails and slopes. Lessons and rentals are available, and there are restaurants at **Cliff House** (top of the Mansfield gondola) and **Octagon** (top of the Toll Road), as well as at the base camps.

A big event of the winter season at Stowe is the annual Winter Carnival, held during the second week in January, when special races, church suppers, square dances, hockey and skating matches, a snow sculpture contest, and even a Queen's Ball are held—hotel rates are not raised for this event. Check with the Stowe Area Association for a carnival schedule.

Summer at Stowe

Some of Stowe's pleasures are best appreciated during warm weather. The breathtaking ride to the top of Vermont's highest mountain in a gondola costs $6 round trip for adults, $3 for children. Or you can drive to the top of Mt. Mansfield on the toll road, climbing ever higher into the mist, past bunches of exotic wildflowers, feeling the air get cooler. The toll road base station is near the ski areas just south of Smuggler's Notch; you pay $7 for your car and then proceed up the road which is only paved for a quarter of a mile—the rest is stabilized dirt. (But the quarter of a mile at the bottom is so perfect for skateboarding that the management has had to erect a sign prohibiting the fast and fancy rollers from monopolizing this stretch of its land!) Both the gondola and the toll road are open daily from mid-June through mid-October, weather permitting.

It's hardly less exciting just to make the drive through Smuggler's Notch. You approach the mountains and the defile, and start turning the sharp bends in the road as you meet a sign saying, "Shift to Low Gear Now"—and it *means* it. The road begins to twist among tremendous boulders fallen from the steep sides of the defile over the eons; the foliage gets very thick, the trees block much of the sun's light, and as you grind along up the switchback slope, a sense of wildness and excitement takes over. Just over the pass is a stopping place (you dare not stop unless you can pull off the road) with benches, toilets, and a snack stand, and several impromptu trails which invite one to clamber—at least for a few hundred feet—into the rocks.

Cinema and Theater

Stowe now has a movie house, in the complex called **Stowe Center** which is exactly a mile north of Stowe Village along Mountain Road. Call 253-4678 to see what's playing. When you get there, you can choose a regular theater seat or a comfy corner of the Projection Room—a cocktail lounge—from which to see the film. What a good idea!

The **Green Mountain Guild of White River Junction** brings summer theater to Stowe during July and August, every week from Tuesday through Saturday. Performances are at Stowe High School on Barrows Road. Contact the Stowe Area Association for current schedules, reservations, and prices.

Other Activities

It's no exaggeration to say that something's always happening here in June, July, and August. Antique car rallies, horse and dog shows, a craft fair, even a fiddlers' meeting, and a surprisingly authentic Oktoberfest (in October, natch) crowd into the schedule. English Leather hosts a tennis tournament at Topnotch at Stowe in August: the purse is a whopping $75,000, so it's no minor event. Speaking of **Topnotch,** that posh resort on Mountain Road near Mt. Mansfield, this is the place to rent horses by the hour or for a trail ride: call 253-8585 and ask for the stables. The going rate is $12 per hour.

Stowe now has an **Alpine Slide,** operated by the Mount Mansfield Company (tel. 253-7311). You start by taking a cool and scenic ride up a ski lift. At the top, you mount a small slidecar, and begin your descent along a concrete runway which weaves and turns like a bobsled run all the way to the bottom of the mountain slope. It's fun! The idea (and the Alpine Slide design) came from West Germany. The slide is open from early July to mid-October, although it closes on days of rain. Rides cost $3.25 per adult, $2 per child, and you get one ride for free when you buy a book of five tickets. Take your slide-ride any day, 9 a.m. to 5 p.m., weather permitting. The Alpine Slide is six miles north of Stowe Village on Route 108 at Spruce Peak.

The more familiar summer pastimes are well covered too. **Stowe Country Club** has an 18-hole golf course; tennis courts abound, many hotels and lodges having their own; hiking, bicycling, fishing, and photographing can fill whole weeks.

11. Burlington

The largest city in Vermont is a town of only about 40,000 population, but in this state small is beautiful. Burlington's situation on the shores of Lake Champlain brings it extra attractiveness and aquatic sports opportunities as well. The town is the seat of the University of Vermont, and student activities and cultural events add an extra dimension to Burlington's daily life. Of the city's native sons, the educator and philosopher John Dewey is the most famous, and Ethan Allen, while not born here, chose Burlington as his home in his later years. Today part of his farm is encompassed by Ethan Allen Park.

Besides being a college town, Burlington is industrial: weapons, data processing equipment, textiles, and consumer products are all made here, and Burlington's medical facilities serve the northern part of the state. Burlington is one of two termini for Lake Champlain ferryboat crossings, the other being Port Kent, N.Y.

INFORMATION: The **Lake Champlain Regional Chamber of Commerce** (tel. 802/863-3489) operates two information booths in Burlington, at the Burlington International Airport, and at Main and South Willard Streets, on U.S. 2 as it enters the downtown section of the city from I-89. The chamber's office is at 209 Battery St., Burlington, VT 05401.

WHERE TO STAY: Most of Burlington's acceptable lodgings are a short way from the center of town, but there is one hotel right downtown.

Out at the intersection of U.S. 2 and I-89 is a 150-year-old **Sheraton-Burlington Inn** (tel. 802/862-6576, or toll free 800/325-3535). No, that's not a printer's error, there actually is a modern Sheraton Inn built around an old farm's barns and carriage shed. As much of the old structure as possible has been used for effect, but of course all the motel rooms are quite modern. The official address is 870 Williston Rd., Burlington, VT 05401, and there are 170 rooms, a restaurant, lounge with live entertainment, a new health spa, and indoor and outdoor swimming pool. Room prices in summer (July through October) are $36.04 single, $46.64 twin. Higher prices are for the new additional wing rooms, connected to the main building by an authentic old Vermont covered bridge. At this location, you're only a mile from the airport.

Howard Johnson's Motor Lodge (tel. 802/863-5541, or toll free 800/654-2000) is also here at the intersection of U.S. 2 and I-89 (mail address: P.O. Box 993, Burlington, VT 05402). Prices are on the order of the other chain hotels, but there are several advantages to staying at Hojo's, including indoor-outdoor pool, cable color TV, and a courtesy car which makes runs to the airport and downtown. Lots of rooms are equipped with two double beds, and the family plan allows kids under 18 to stay free with their parents. In the months from May to October singles are $37.80 to $57.75; doubles are $38.85 to $57.75.

Going down the price scale somewhat, **Econo Lodge** (tel. 802/863-1125, or toll free 800/446-6900) has an installation at the intersection of U.S. 2 and I-89, a quarter mile from Exit 14E, at 1076 Williston Rd., Burlington, VT

05401. At the Econo Lodge, you get the usual, expected motel comforts—rooms with one or two double beds, color TV, full baths, even an outdoor swimming pool—but prices are very reasonable and set the same year round: $25.73 for one, $31.50 for two, $34.13 for three or four (usually a family, but nothing says two couples can't share a room).

Right downtown is the shiny new **Radisson Burlington Hotel** (tel. 802/658-6500, or toll free 800/228-9822), at Burlington Square, Burlington, VT 05401. Many of the 200 rooms have gorgeous views of Lake Champlain, others open onto the indoor swimming pool. The Radisson, part of a fast-growing national hotel group, bills itself as "Vermont's most luxurious hotel," and although many other hotels may dispute the claim, there's no disputing the Radisson's luxury quality. Tropical plants bring freshness to an enclosed Garden Court next to the pool and whirlpool bath. The price is $57.75 to $68.25; doubles, $70.35 to $80.85; the more expensive rooms are those with a lake-and-mountain view. An extra person or bed is $12, but children under 18 stay with their folks for free. Parking is free too.

Of the many motels on U.S. 7 south of town, the **Colonial Motor Inn** (tel. 802/862-5754), 462 Shelburne St., Burlington, VT 05401, is among the best. A substantial establishment, it boasts 40 modern rooms with air conditioning, color TV, telephones; an outdoor swimming pool is open in good weather. A shopping center with services and restaurants is a short walk away. For one double bed (single or double occupancy) the price is $31.50 to $33.60; for two double beds it's $35.70 to $44.10. From I-89 take Exit 13 to I-189; take I-189 to U.S. 7 and go north to the Colonial.

WHERE TO DINE: Two of my favorite restaurants in all Vermont are located in Burlington, near City Hall Park. First of these is the **Rathskeller** (tel. 863-4429), and it's a bit hard to find so follow these directions carefully: from City Hall Park, walk north away from Main Street (left if you're coming out of the hotel), and then left down a little alley which looks as though it goes nowhere but actually leads to the front door of the restaurant; enter this door and then take the door to the right (there is a door there, but it may be darkish and hard to see), and descend to the Rathskeller. After all this you no doubt think you'll have found your way into some medieval dungeon, and there are indeed some resemblances: low ceilings, brick and stone walls and pillars, heavy wood beams overhead, orange and green lanterns with candles burning in them. It's a favorite with businesspeople and young people for lunch (11:30 a.m. to 2 p.m. daily except Sunday), when you can have a daily special platter such as meatloaf with salad and french fries for $5 to $8, or a luncheon steak and salad for the same, or something from the selection of burgers and sandwiches for even less. Then comes happy hour, from 4 to 6 each afternoon (except Sunday), when drinks are lower in price and free hors d'oeuvres such as peeled shrimp might be passed around. At dinnertime the menu goes classy and somewhat French, with suprême de poulet flambée Monsieur for $12, boeuf bourguignon for the same price, steaks for several dollars more. Dinnertime has its daily specials as well, and these are even more reasonably priced than the entrees above. Liquor, wine, and beer are served, and dinner is on every night 5:30 to 9:30 p.m., except Sunday.

My other choice on City Hall Park is **Carbur's** (tel. 862-4106), at 117 St. Paul St. facing the park. Carbur's is done in heavy mod-Victoriana, and tends to the quietly outrageous: a sign in the window says "Famous Since 1974." The dining room has a tremendously high ceiling equipped with ceiling fans which spin slowly even on cool days, just for atmosphere. Soup and a large sandwich cost about $5 at lunch, and salad plates for only slightly more. The menu is a book 25 pages long, filled with sandwiches, soups, salad plates, almost all—with a few exceptions like the monster five-decker sandwich—for $5 or less. You can easily dine at Carbur's for $5, or with drinks, soup, tax, and tip, for about $10. The menu, by the way, is laden with enough drawings and amusing patter to keep you entertained all through your meal.

WHAT TO DO: Much of Burlington's cultural life centers on the **University of Vermont** campus, and on the campuses of the other three colleges in the area: **St. Michael's, Trinity,** and **Champlain.** The university, of course, has a good museum on Colchester Avenue, called the **Fleming Museum,** open every day of the year and free to all visitors. Exhibits run the gamut: a Kang Hsi vase, Wei terracotta, a Cole painting, 17th-century Persian miniatures, early Roman glass, Coptic carvings, and a bona fide Egyptian mummy.

The University of Vermont also stages an annual summer **Champlain Shakespeare Festival,** held at the Royall Tyler Theatre (tel. 802/656-2094), on the Main Street side of the campus. A **Mozart Festival** is held in summer as well.

Much of the lakefront land in Burlington is encompassed by parks, including **Oak Ledge Park** and **Red Rocks Park** in South Burlington, **Battery Park** near Burlington's center and only five blocks from the ferries, and **Burlington Municipal Beach** on Institute Road north of the ferry dock along the lake shore. **Ethan Allen Park** is north of the center of town; take North Avenue (Route 127) starting at Battery Park.

Shelburne Museum

From mid-May to mid-October, visitors to Burlington must make a detour to the town of Shelburne, seven miles south of the city along U.S. 7, to see the Shelburne Museum, a gala festival of Americana collected into 35 historic buildings—a smoke house, a sawmill, an inn, a toy house, apothecary shop, and many historic houses—spread over 45 acres. The entrance to the museum is through a real double-lane covered bridge, brought here from a nearby town. Having entered, you find yourself surrounded by the sights of a New England town of a century or more ago: the church complete with prayerbooks and wood-burning stoves, the schoolhouse, the livery stable. Each building is filled with the artifacts of earlier American life, and the museum is said to have about the best and fullest collection of Americana ever assembled. Among the artifacts are "Old 220," a ten-wheeled steam locomotive, and even the huge 220-foot sidewheeler steamboat S.S. *Ticonderoga,* pulled up on shore here after its last run on the lake. Three art galleries feature paintings and sculpture by European and American artists, and handicrafts both charming and authentic: quilts for instance, and decoys, and glassware, and furniture, plus the tools used to make these items.

The Shelburne Museum (tel. 985-3344) is open daily from mid-May to mid-October; admission is $7.75 for adults, $3.75 for children 6 through 17, and free for under-6s. If you arrive late in the day, a small extra charge will allow you to return for a full day's visit the following day (you should allow at least several hours to tour the exhibit). Off-season, four buildings are open Sundays only, 11 a.m. to 4 p.m. The museum boasts a cafeteria, a museum shop, and free parking.

Lake Champlain Ferries

One of the favorite things to do in Burlington is to take the ferry over to Port Kent, N.Y., whether you're actually interested in getting to Port Kent or not. Ferries, leaving from the King Street Dock in Burlington, operate in spring, summer, and fall, leaving each terminus at about one-hour intervals from 8 or 9:20 a.m. to 7 or 8 p.m., a bit more frequently in summer, with 12 trips a day in each direction. You can take your car across if you're going somewhere: price for car and driver, one way, is $9.50; each extra adult pays $2.50 one way; children 6 through 12 pay $1. The trip, a marvelous way to get to know Lake Champlain, takes about an hour each way. This ferry doesn't run in winter, but ferries between Grand Isle, Vt., and Plattsburgh, N.Y., operate year round. You'll also find a ferry chugging between Charlotte, VT., and Essex, N.Y., from early April through early December.

NOW, SAVE MONEY ON ALL YOUR TRAVELS!
Join Arthur Frommer's $25-A-Day Travel Club

Saving money while traveling is never a simple matter, which is why, over 21 years ago, the **$25-A-Day Travel Club** was formed. Actually, the idea came from readers of the Arthur Frommer Publications who felt that such an organization could bring financial benefits, continuing travel information, and a sense of community to economy-minded travelers all over the world.

In keeping with the money-saving concept, the membership fee is low—$14 (U.S. residents) or $16 (Canadian, Mexican, and foreign residents)—and is immediately exceeded by the value of your benefits which include:

(1) An annual subscription to an 8-page quarterly tabloid newspaper *The Wonderful World of Budget Travel* which keeps you up-to-date on fastbreaking developments in low-cost travel in all parts of the world—bringing you the kind of information you'd have to pay over $25 a year to obtain elsewhere. This consumer-conscious publication also provides special services to readers:

Travelers' Directory—a list of members all over the world who are willing to provide hospitality to other members as they pass through their home cities.

Share-a-Trip—requests from members for travel companions who can share costs and help avoid the burdensome single supplement.

Readers Ask . . . Readers Reply—travel questions from members to which other members reply with authentic firsthand information.

(2) The latest edition of any TWO of the books listed on the following page (except for *The Adventure Book*, which is available at only $7.50 to members).

(3) A copy of *Arthur Frommer's Guide to New York.*

(4) Your personal membership card which entitles you to purchase through the Club all Arthur Frommer Publications for a third to a half off their regular retail prices during the term of your membership.

So why not join this hardy band of international budgeteers NOW and participate in its exchange of information and hospitality? Simply send $14 (U.S. residents) or $16 U.S. (Canadian, Mexican, and other foreign residents) along with your name and address to: $25-A-Day Travel Club, Inc., 1230 Avenue of the Americas, New York, NY 10020. Remember to specify which *two* of the books in section (2) above you wish to receive in your initial package of members' benefits. Or tear out this page, check off any two books on the opposite side and send it to us with your membership fee.

FROMMER/PASMANTIER PUBLISHERS \Date_____
1230 AVE. OF THE AMERICAS, NEW YORK, NY 10020

Friends, please send me the books checked below:

$-A-DAY GUIDES
(In-depth guides to low-cost tourist accommodations and facilities.)

☐ Europe on $25 a Day	$10.95
☐ Australia on $25 a Day	$9.95
☐ England and Scotland on $25 a Day	$9.95
☐ Greece on $25 a Day	$9.95
☐ Hawaii on $35 a Day	$9.95
☐ Ireland on $25 a Day	$7.95
☐ Israel on $30 & $35 a Day	$9.95
☐ Mexico on $20 a Day	$8.95
☐ New Zealand on $20 & $25 a Day	$9.95
☐ New York on $35 a Day	$8.95
☐ Scandinavia on $25 a Day	$7.95
☐ South America on $25 a Day	$8.95
☐ Spain and Morocco (plus the Canary Is.) on $25 a Day	$8.95
☐ Washington, D.C. on $35 a Day	$8.95

DOLLARWISE GUIDES
(Guides to tourist accommodations and facilities from budget to deluxe, with emphasis on the medium-priced.)

☐ Egypt	$9.95	☐ Canada	$10.95
☐ England & Scotland	$7.95	☐ Caribbean (incl. Bermuda & the	
☐ France	$8.95	Bahamas)	$10.95
☐ Germany	$9.95	☐ California & Las Vegas	$7.95
☐ Italy	$7.95	☐ Florida	$9.95
☐ Portugal (incl. Madeira & the Azores)	$9.95	☐ New England	$9.95
☐ Switzerland	$9.95	☐ Southeast & New Orleans	$9.95

THE ARTHUR FROMMER GUIDES
(Pocket-size guides to tourist accommodations and facilities in all price ranges.)

☐ Amsterdam/Holland	$3.95	☐ Montreal/Quebec City	$3.95
☐ Athens	$3.95	☐ New Orleans	$3.95
☐ Boston	$3.95	☐ New York	$3.95
☐ Hawaii	$3.95	☐ Orlando/Disney World/EPCOT	$3.95
☐ Dublin/Ireland	$3.95	☐ Paris	$3.95
☐ Las Vegas	$3.95	☐ Philadelphia/Atlantic City	$3.95
☐ Lisbon/Madrid/Costa del Sol	$3.95	☐ Rome	$3.95
☐ London	$3.95	☐ San Francisco	$3.95
☐ Los Angeles	$3.95	☐ Washington, D.C.	$3.95
☐ Mexico City/Acapulco	$3.95		

SPECIAL EDITIONS

☐ How to Beat the High Cost of Travel	$4.95	☐ Memorable Weekends	$10.95
☐ New York Urban Athlete (NYC sports		(NY, Conn, Mass, RI, Vt, NJ, Pa)	
guide for jocks & novices)	$9.95	☐ The Adventure Book: 237 Adventure	
☐ Where to Stay USA (Accommodations		Trips World-wide (8½ × 11 with 115	
from $3 to $25 a night)	$8.95	color photos)	$14.95
☐ Fast 'n' Easy Phrase Book		☐ Museums in New York (Incl. historic	
(Fr/Sp/Ger/Ital. in one vol.)	$6.95	houses, gardens, & zoos)	$8.95
		☐ Travel Guide for the Disabled	$10.95

In U.S. include $1 post. & hdlg. for 1st book; 25¢ any add'l. book. Outside U.S. $2 and 50¢ respectively.

Enclosed is my check or money order for $_____

NAME_____

ADDRESS_____

CITY_____ STATE_____ ZIP_____